THE PERSISTENT OBJECTOR RULE IN INTERNATIONAL LAW

The Persistent Objector Rule in International Law

JAMES A. GREEN

OXFORD
UNIVERSITY PRESS

OXFORD
UNIVERSITY PRESS

Great Clarendon Street, Oxford, OX2 6DP,
United Kingdom

Oxford University Press is a department of the University of Oxford.
It furthers the University's objective of excellence in research, scholarship,
and education by publishing worldwide. Oxford is a registered trade mark of
Oxford University Press in the UK and in certain other countries

First Edition published in 2016

Published in the United States of America by Oxford University Press
198 Madison Avenue, New York, NY 10016, United States of America

British Library Cataloguing in Publication Data
Data available

Library of Congress Control Number: 2016932198

ISBN 978–0–19–870421–8

This book is for Robert.

When I was about sixteen, while sat in the coffee shop inside the large Debenhams in Exeter (which is no longer there), I took from you the entirely erroneous impression that being an academic meant that one had loads of free time and got paid for sitting around reading, thinking about interesting things, and occasionally writing some of them down. While I suspect that this fundamental misunderstanding of the job was entirely down to me, I still blame you.

This is all your fault.

I wish I saw you far more often than I do. But it turns out that academics are actually quite busy. I promise I'll try to make more of an effort …

Much love.

Foreword by Sir Michael Wood

The persistent objector rule—whereby a state which objects to a rule of customary international law while it is emerging, and which persistently maintains its objection, is not bound by the rule—is an important aspect of the theory and practice of international law. While quite controversial, the rule is not infrequently relied upon by states, and is regarded by them as a safety valve within the customary international law process.

Professor Green's monograph is thorough, thoughtful, timely, and above all moderate. While recognizing the theoretical difficulties with the rule, the author pays particular attention to its application in the practice of states.

The book contains much that will be of interest to practitioners and academics alike. The relatively recent origins of the rule, not least in key decisions of the International Court of Justice, are examined with care, as is its application since 1945. The detailed analysis of the requirements—'core elements', 'criteria'—for the rule's operation (objection, persistence, consistency, and timeliness) are at the heart of the book. Of particular interest is the author's emphasis on consistency as a separate element, something that has often been overlooked and which is usually considered to be implicit in the persistence requirement.

The relationship between the persistent objector rule and peremptory norms of general international law (*jus cogens*) is examined at length. The conclusion that there can be no persistent objector to a peremptory norm may seem obvious, but in fact requires a careful and clear-headed consideration. The author's treatment of the interface between *jus cogens* and persistent objection is a major contribution to both topics.

What, then, of the role and value of the persistent objector rule? For challenging and original thoughts one cannot do better than turn to Chapter 9. Neither 'voluntarism' (often regarded as *the* basis for the rule), nor 'communitarianism' (thought to be opposed to it) offers real answers to the theoretical mysteries behind the rule. In fact, 'states use the rule, and they must do so for a reason'. As Professor Green explains, there are many reasons why the rule has value, both real value and, which may be as important, perceived value: 'the rule has value not just in terms of what it actually does, but also in terms of the perception of autonomy that it engenders'. In a word, the persistent objector rule is beneficial not only to the objecting state but to states generally and to workings of the international legal system.

It is a happy coincidence that the International Law Commission took up the persistent objector rule at precisely the time when Professor Green's study was nearing completion. It did so at its sixty-seventh session (2015), under the topic *Identification of customary international law*. It is encouraging to see that Commission and author seem to tend towards similar conclusions—though the Commission's work has some way to go before a definitive position is reached.

In July 2015, the Commission's Drafting Committee provisionally adopted a full set of *Draft conclusions on the identification of customary international law*, including one on the persistent objector rule. Draft conclusion 15, together with an accompanying commentary (still to be prepared), is expected to be considered by the Commission at its 2016 session. The matter was not without controversy within the Commission in 2015. Some questioned the inclusion of the draft conclusion, either on the ground that it did not really have a place in a topic that was concerned with the identification of rules of customary international law, or—more radically—because they were not convinced that the persistent objector rule formed part of international law. Still others seem to have felt that the rule was too rarely invoked and too exceptional to justify inclusion in the draft conclusions. Others, however, agreed with my view, as Special Rapporteur, that draft conclusion 15 did have a place in the text, that the rule was well established in international law, that it arose in practice rather more frequently than is commonly supposed (including before a wide range of international and domestic courts and tribunals), and that it was therefore important to spell out the stringent requirements for its application. It was also pointed out that the Commission had acknowledged the existence of the rule as recently as 2011 in its *Guide to practice on reservations to treaties*.

This book will undoubtedly be of great service to members of the International Law Commission as they proceed with the topic *Identification of customary international law*, and to the representatives of states and others as they consider the Commission's product. It will be a primary resource for all those—state officials, judges, practitioners, academics—who may be called upon to consider and apply the persistent objector rule. It will quickly establish itself as the leading work on the subject, and is likely so to remain for many years.

Sir Michael Wood, KCMG

London
August 2015

Preface

Somewhat terrifyingly, this book is the culmination of a research project that I have been working on for around six years. I began my initial investigations into the academic writing on the persistent objector rule in the autumn/winter of 2009. While I have certainly not spent all of my time since then working on this—various other smaller projects and publications have been both started and completed in the same period, and I have of course gone through six cycles of the teaching–marking–admin merry-go-round that all academics endure—this work has represented a huge chunk of my life. I am both ecstatic and saddened to see it reach its end.

Mostly ecstatic.

I'd like to highlight an early point on this project's timeline, during the formative stages of this book: on 15 April 2010 I gave a paper presenting my tentative initial thoughts on the persistent objector rule at Oxford Brookes University, at the Annual Conference of the British Branch of the International Law Association. I also gave a version of the same paper a couple of months later (16 June 2010) at the University of Reading, as part of the School of Law's internal staff seminar series. For anyone who was at either presentation—particularly the first of these at Brookes—I have to provide a disclaimer here. Or perhaps it is better described as a 'retraction'. I'm not quite sure.

My view in early 2010, after a mere few months of sporadic work on the topic, was that the persistent objector rule was essentially an academic fiction: I had found little state practice to support it, and felt that it was built on some very shaky conceptual foundations. I was certainly not the first to take this general position, but I felt that I could highlight the non-existence of the rule in a manner not before done. In other words, this project began life based on the assumption that the persistent objector rule was a complete nonsense: the intention of the project was to demonstrate this. However, the more I read and the more deeply I delved into state practice, the more support for the rule I found. A project that was initially supposed to be a simple comment piece arguing that there was no persistent objector rule slowly morphed into what you are about to read: an attempt to set out the most detailed understanding of the rule (and way in which it operates) to date in the literature.

Anyone who sat through either of my 2010 presentations, where I was arguing—admittedly with some heavy disclaimers about 'work-in-progress' and 'tentative conclusions'—that *there is no persistent objector rule at all* might be somewhat surprised to come across this book, the entire basis of which being that the rule *does* exist and is, moreover, well worth examining. The evidence ultimately led me down a different path, and I am pleased with myself that I wasn't too proud to follow it. I can only own up to 'jumping the gun' somewhat in 2010, and hope that those who heard me do so can forgive such blatant inconsistency. I suspect that you will be willing: after all, one can only be bound post-crystallization, and I was some way away from having any crystallized views on the topic at that time. Yes, that was a persistent objector rule 'joke'.

There are numerous people that I would like to thank. I would particularly like to express my deepest gratitude to Sir Michael Wood, who—as well as being kind enough to write the foreword for this book—has significantly supported the project throughout (providing advice, comments on work-in-progress and general encouragement). I am indebted to him. Dr David Leary also deserves a special thank you for his invaluable research assistance and insightful suggestions during the final stages of preparing the book. Another important person whom I wish to thank may well not even realize that he contributed to this project: Professor Maurice Mendelson's tough but largely correct critique of my 2010 Brookes paper (during the Q&A session) got me thinking and digging deeper at that formative stage. I thank him so much for this, even though we have not discussed the project since. I felt rather chastized at the time, but Professor Mendelson was undoubtedly the person who set me on the right path.

There are, of course, also many other people who provided crucial encouragement, comments on drafts, advice, direction, and other support (both general and specific) in relation to this project: my thanks go to Dr Amos O. Enabulele, Dr Robert P. Barnidge, Jr, Dr Théo Boutruche, Professor Susan Breau, Professor Sandy Ghandhi, Professor Christian Henderson, Dr Lawrence Hill-Cawthorne, Dr Reuven (Ruvi) Ziegler, Professor Daniel Joyner, Stephen Samuel, Omri Sender, and Professor Christopher Waters. I'm sure I have missed out other people, but hopefully you know who you are.

I would also like to express my thanks to everyone at OUP: I could not have asked for a more supportive publishing team. My parents, as always, deserve more thanks than I can ever give them for their love and support, and my brother Adam—the artist in the family—deserves a special mention for his wonderful cover design for this book. Saving the most important person for last, I want to thank my wife, Dr Lia Emanuel. She has consistently put up with my (persistent) objections about this project (I have somehow regularly forgotten over the years that it's not as if anyone forced me to take it on), and the other myriad trials and tribulations associated with me writing this book. She even proofread the final chapter and the conclusion for me, poor woman. Without her endless support and (at times wholly incongruous) sunny disposition I would have had a breakdown long ago. I love her more than I can say.

The dogs and the cat have, if anything, made work on this book harder: torn-up journal articles, muddy footprints on my notes, and clambering over the laptop while I was trying to write. As such, no thanks at all go to them.

All errors in this book are mine, and mine alone. Please do your best not to spot them.

James A. Green

Pewsey, Wiltshire
August 2015

Table of Contents

Table of Cases

INTERNATIONAL COURT OF JUSTICE/PERMANENT COURT OF INTERNATIONAL JUSTICE

INTERNATIONAL CRIMINAL TRIBUNAL FOR THE FORMER YUGOSLAVIA

INTERNATIONAL CRIMINAL TRIBUNAL FOR RWANDA

SPECIAL TRIBUNAL FOR LEBANON

WORLD TRADE ORGANIZATION APPELLATE BODY

EUROPEAN COURT OF HUMAN RIGHTS

INTER-AMERICAN COURT OF HUMAN RIGHTS

INTER-AMERICAN COMMISSION ON HUMAN RIGHTS

GERMANY-VENEZUELA MIXED CLAIMS COMMISSION

ERITREA-ETHIOPIA CLAIMS COMMISSION

AD HOC ARBITRATIONS

DOMESTIC COURTS

Federal Republic of Germany

Hong Kong

South Africa

United Kingdom

United States

Table of Treaties

Introduction

This book examines the persistent objector rule in international law. A core aspect of mainstream international law doctrine, the rule ostensibly holds that if a state persistently and consistently objects to a newly emerging norm of customary international law during the period of the 'formation' of that norm (i.e. prior to its crystallization as a binding rule of customary international law), then the objecting state is exempt from the customary norm in question once it has crystallized and for so long as the objection is maintained. The 'majority (but far from unanimous) view'[1] of the persistent objector rule thus presents it as a mechanism for states to pre-emptively exempt themselves from newly emerging norms of customary international law.

The classic articulation of the sources of international law is to be found in Article 38(1) of the Statute of the International Court of Justice (ICJ),[2] which lists 'international custom, as evidence of a general practice accepted as law' as one of those sources.[3] Customary international law is, of course, one of the formal 'primary' sources of international law.[4] Along with treaties, custom acts as one of the two most important sources for norm creation within the international legal system. Custom—which is generally viewed as being manifested through state practice and *opinio juris*[5]—is a source of binding law. Moreover, unlike obligations derived from treaties (which apply only to states for which the treaty in question

[1] T. Treves, 'Customary International Law' in R. Wolfrum (ed.), *Max Planck Encyclopaedia of Public International Law, vol. II* (Oxford, Oxford University Press, 2012), 937, 945, para. 39.

[2] Statute of the International Court of Justice, 26 June 1945, 59 Stat. 1055, 33 UNTS 93.

[3] Ibid., Article 38(1)(b).

[4] See H. Charlesworth, 'Law-Making and Sources' in J. Crawford and M. Koskenniemi (eds), *The Cambridge Companion to International Law* (Cambridge, Cambridge University Press, 2012), 187, particularly at 189–95; and A.T. Guzman, 'Saving Customary International Law' (2005–6) 27 *Michigan Journal of International Law* 115, 116.

[5] See *North Sea Continental Shelf* cases (*Federal Republic of Germany v Netherlands, Federal Republic of Germany v Denmark*), merits, 1969 ICJ Rep. 3, para. 77; *Continental Shelf* (*Libyan Arab Jamahiriya/Malta*), merits, 1985 ICJ Rep. 13, para. 27; *Military and Paramilitary Activities in and against Nicaragua* (*Nicaragua v United States of America*), merits, 1986 ICJ Rep. 14, para. 207. The meanings of both 'state practice' and '*opinio juris*' remain highly contentious among scholars. See, for example, J. Kammerhofer, 'Uncertainty in the Formal Sources of International Law: Customary International Law and Some of Its Problems' (2004) 15 *European Journal of International Law* 523, 525–36. However, these concepts are at least broadly accepted, and their content has been developed in the ICJ's jurisprudence to the extent that in 2012, the Court noted that it needed to apply 'the criteria which it [the Court] *has repeatedly laid down* for identifying a rule of customary international law': *Jurisdictional Immunities of the State* (*Germany v Italy: Greece intervening*), merits, 2012 ICJ Rep. 99, para. 55, emphasis added.

is in force), norms of customary international law bind all states prima facie.[6] The persistent objector rule is therefore generally seen as forming an optional 'escape hatch'[7] to this universal binding force of custom. At least in theory, the rule allows states to elude the otherwise inescapable reach of customary international law. It is important to stress that this means that persistent objection is necessarily a relatively solitary exercise: if there were a notable number of states objecting to the evolution of a new customary international law norm, then this would likely mean that the emerging norm will fail to crystallize at all, as there would be insufficient state practice and *opinio juris* for its creation.[8] Persistent objector states are thus legally justified pariahs.[9] The very nature of persistent objection means that 'objectors' are swimming against the tide of the vast majority of the international community of states and are essentially doing so alone (or, at least, in very small numbers). In this sense—while it is actually both conceptually and substantively something quite different—the persistent objector rule can broadly be conceived of as the customary international law equivalent to reservations to treaties, in that both constitute procedural legal mechanisms for state exceptionalism when it comes to the binding force of norms of international law.[10]

[6] See, for example, *North Sea Continental Shelf* cases, merits, n. 5, para. 63 ('customary law rules ... by their very nature, must have equal force for all members of the international community, and cannot therefore be the subject of any right of unilateral exclusion exercisable at will by any one of them in its own favour'); and *Committee on Formation of Customary (General) International Law*, Final Report of the Committee, 'Statement of Principles Applicable to the Formation of General Customary International Law', International Law Association, London Conference (2000), http:// www.ila-hq.org/en/committees/index.cfm/cid/30, section 1. The exception to the universal binding force of customary international law (other than persistent objection) is what is variously called 'particular', 'special', 'regional' or 'local' customary international law, which by its nature binds some states but not all. On particular customary international law, see, generally, M. Akehurst, 'Custom as a Source of International Law' (1974–5) 47 *British Yearbook of International Law* 1, 28–31; A. D'Amato, 'The Concept of Special Custom in International Law' (1969) 63 *American Journal of International Law* 211; Third Report on Identification of Customary International Law (M. Wood, Special Rapporteur), International Law Commission, Sixty-seventh session, 27 March 2015, UN Doc. A/CN.4/682, paras 80–4; and *Right of Passage over Indian Territory* (*Portugal v India*), merits, 1960 ICJ Rep. 4, particularly at 39.

[7] D.A. Colson, 'How Persistent Must the Persistent Objector Be?' (1986) 61 *Washington Law Review* 957, 957; and T.L. Stein, 'The Approach of the Different Drummer: The Principle of the Persistent Objector in International Law' (1985) 26 *Harvard International Law Journal* 457, 472.

[8] See C.G. Guldahl, 'The Role of Persistent Objection in International Humanitarian Law' (2008) 77 *Nordic Journal of International Law* 51, 54; A. Kaczorowska, *Public International Law* (Abingdon, Routledge, 4th edn, 2010), 41; H. Thirlway, *International Customary Law and Codification* (Leiden, A.W. Sijthoff, 1972), 116; and M.E. Villiger, *Customary International Law and Treaties: A Manual on the Theory and Practice of the Interrelation of Sources* (The Hague, Kluwer, 2nd edn, 1997), 36.

[9] See *Legality of the Threat or Use of Nuclear Weapons*, advisory opinion, 1996 ICJ Rep. 226, dissenting opinion of Vice-President Schwebel, 312.

[10] See E. David, 'L'objecteur persistent, une règle persistent?' *in* P. Tavernier and J-M. Henckaerts (eds), *Droit international humanitaire coutumier: enjeux et défis contemporains* (Brussels, Bruylant, 2008), 89, 90; M.A. Hansen, 'Preventing the Emasculation of Warfare: Halting the Expansion of Human Rights Law into Armed Conflict' (2007) 194 *Military Law Review* 1, 17; B.B. Jia, 'The Relations between Treaties and Custom' (2010) 9 *Chinese Journal of International Law* 81, 89, 97 and 101–2; H. Lau, 'Rethinking the Persistent Objector Doctrine in International Human Rights Law' (2005–6) 6 *Chicago Journal of International Law* 496, 509; and F.F. Martin, *The Constitution as Treaty: The International Legal Constructionalist Approach to the U.S. Constitution* (Cambridge, Cambridge University Press, 2007), 74–5.

All of this means that the persistent objector rule is a purported 'secondary rule'[11] of the international legal system.[12] It is not a substantive rule, but a rule about substantive rules. Having said this, it is worth being clear that the persistent objector rule is not, strictly speaking, a 'secondary rule *of recognition*',[13] in that it does not contribute to the *creation* or *determination of content* of substantive primary rules as such (as do, say, the dual requirements of state practice and *opinio juris*). Instead, the persistent objector rule 'concerns the scope of application of a customary international law rule or its "opposability" '.[14] The rule does not create law, but contributes to establishing its correct application. It is in this sense that the persistent objector rule is a secondary rule of the system.

It is worth noting that this means that the subject matter to which the persistent objector rule could relate is prima facie unlimited within international law. The rule could potentially be a means of exemption from an emerging norm of custom relating to any of international law's plethora of substantive areas of influence, from investment law or the laws of war to civil aviation and telecommunications. In a discipline in which there is ever increasing concern over 'fragmentation',[15] both practically and academically, the persistent objector rule is a norm that transcends substance and looks instead to process. As such, it is crucial for every international legal actor that we understand the rule and how it works.

I. The Persistent Objector Rule in Doctrine: Ubiquity and Critique

The persistent objector rule is ubiquitous within mainstream international law scholarship. It makes at least a cameo appearance in most modern textbooks on

[11] To use Hart's famous term. See H.L.A. Hart, *The Concept of Law* (Oxford, Oxford University Press, 2nd edn, 1994), particularly at 79–99. In the international law context, see S. Besson, 'Theorizing the Sources of International Law' in S. Besson and J. Tasioulas (eds), *The Philosophy of International Law* (Oxford, Oxford University Press, 2010), 164, 178–9; and J.I. Charney, 'Universal International Law' (1993) 87 *American Journal of International Law* 529, 533–4.

[12] Stein, n. 7, 458.

[13] Hart, n. 11, particularly at 94–9. For discussion specifically in the international law context, see Besson, n. 11, 180–4.

[14] S. Yee, 'Report on the ILC Project on "Identification of Customary International Law"' (Report by the Special Rapporteur of the Asian-African Legal Consultative Organisation (AALCO) Informal Expert Group on Customary International Law) (2015) 14 *Chinese Journal of International Law* 375, 381, para. 25. See also 'Identification of Customary International Law', Statement of the Chairman of the Drafting Committee, Mr Mathias Forteau, 29 July 2015, International Law Commission, Sixty-seventh session, Geneva, 4 May–5 June and 6 July–7 August 2015, 18 (discussing the views of members of the ILC Drafting Committee to this effect); and D. Kritsiotis, 'On the Possibilities of and For Persistent Objection' (2010) 21 *Duke Journal of Comparative and International Law* 121, 122 (noting that the persistent objector rule relates to 'the *basis* of obligation in public international law', emphasis in original).

[15] See, for example, *Study Group of the International Law Commission*, Report finalised by M. Koskenniemi, 'Fragmentation of International Law: Difficulties Arising from the Diversification and Expansion of International Law' (2006), UN Doc. A/CN.4/L.682. See, generally, J. Pauwelyn, 'Fragmentation of International Law' in R. Wolfrum (ed.), *Max Planck Encyclopaedia of Public International Law, vol. IV* (Oxford, Oxford University Press, 2012), 211.

international law.[16] Similarly, the rule is an inevitable feature of more specialized works focusing on customary international law.[17] It is usually seen as having been endorsed by two merits decisions of the ICJ,[18] and also has appeared in various individual opinions of ICJ judges.[19] The persistent objector rule additionally has been invoked or referenced in the jurisprudence of a number of other courts and tribunals (both international[20] and domestic[21]). Similarly, it has been endorsed by the International Law Association (ILA)[22] and within the International Law Commission (ILC), most notably in its recent draft conclusions on the 'identification of customary international law'[23] (as well as by the ILC's special rapporteur on that subject, Sir Michael Wood, in his third report).[24] The persistent objector rule is therefore undeniably part of the *language* of modern international law. It is uncontroversial to say that, for most international lawyers at least, the persistent

[16] See, for example, A. Abass, *Complete International Law: Text, Cases, and Materials* (Oxford, Oxford University Press, 2nd edn, 2014), 46–9; J. Crawford, *Brownlie's Principles of Public International Law* (Oxford, Oxford University Press, 8th edn, 2012), 28; M. Dixon, *Textbook on International Law* (Oxford, Oxford University Press, 7th edn, 2013), 34–5; J. Dugard, *International Law: A South African Perspective* (Cape Town, Juta, 3rd edn, 2008), 32; D. Harris, *Cases and Materials on International Law* (London, Sweet and Maxwell, 7th edn, 2010), 31–3; T. Hillier, *Sourcebook on Public International Law* (London, Cavendish Publishing, 1998), 74; R. Jennings and A. Watts, *Oppenheim's International Law, vol. I: Peace* (New York, Longman, 9th edn, 1996), 29; Kaczorowska, n. 8, 41–2; J. Klabbers, *International Law* (Cambridge, Cambridge University Press, 2013), 30–1; A.V. Lowe, *International Law* (Oxford, Oxford University Press, 2007), 55–8; P. Malanczuk, *Akehurst's Modern Introduction to International Law* (New York Routledge, 7th edn, 1997), 48; and M.N. Shaw, *International Law* (Cambridge, Cambridge University Press, 7th edn, 2014), 63–5.

[17] See, for example, M. Akehurst, 'Custom as a Source of International Law' (1974–5) 47 *British Yearbook of International Law* 1, 23–7; R.B. Baker, 'Customary International Law in the 21st Century: Old Challenges and New Debates' 21 *European Journal of International Law* 173, 176; M. Byers, *Custom, Power and the Power of Rules: International Relations and Customary International Law* (Cambridge, Cambridge University Press, 1999), particularly at 102–5 and 180–3; B.D. Lepard, *Customary International Law: A New Theory with Practical Applications* (Cambridge, Cambridge University Press, 2010), 36–7, 229–42, 250–2, 333–6 and 364–5; M.H. Mendelson, 'The Formation of Customary International Law' (1998) 272 *Recueil des cours* 155, 227–44; G.J. Postema, 'Custom in International Law: A Normative Practice Account' in A. Perreau-Saussine and J.B. Murphy (eds), *The Nature of Customary Law: Legal, Historical and Philosophical Perspectives* (Cambridge, Cambridge University Press, 2007), 279, 282–3; Villiger, n. 8, 33–6; and K. Wolfke, *Custom in Present International Law* (Dordrecht, Martinus Nijhoff, 1993), 66–7.

[18] See *Asylum* (*Columbia v Peru*), merits, 1950 ICJ Rep. 266, 277–8; and *Fisheries* (*United Kingdom v Norway*), merits, 1951 ICJ Rep. 116, 131. For discussion, see Chapter 2, sections I.*i* and I.*ii*.

[19] See Chapter 2, section I.*iii*, n. 67–n. 80 and accompanying text.

[20] See ibid., section I.*iii*, n. 84–n. 104 and accompanying text.

[21] See ibid., section I.*iii*, n. 105–n. 109 and accompanying text.

[22] ILA Final Report, n. 6.

[23] 'Identification of Customary International Law: Text of the Draft Conclusions Provisionally Adopted by the Drafting Committee', International Law Commission, Sixty-seventh session, Geneva, 4 May–5 June and 6 July–7 August 2015, UN Doc. A/CN.4/L.869. See also Guide to Practice on Reservations to Treaties with commentaries, 2011, International Law Commission, UN Doc. A/66/10/Add.1, commentary (7) to guideline 3.1.5.3, 371. This was confirmed by Formation and Evidence of Customary International Law: Elements of the Previous Work of the International Law Commission that Could be Particularly Relevant to the Topic, 2013, Memorandum by the Secretariat, UN A/CN.4/659, 28, footnote 97 (a document setting out and reviewing the previous views of the ILC in relation to customary international law).

[24] Third Report on Identification of Customary International Law, ILC, n. 6, paras. 85–95.

objector rule is 'firmly established in the orthodox doctrine of the sources of international law'.[25]

Yet, while it is true that, for the most part, the persistent objector rule 'has been treated by jurists and scholars as practically axiomatic',[26] there has also been a significant minority critique of the rule in the literature. Plenty of writers doubt whether the persistent objector rule exists *at all* and see it as a mere academic fiction,[27] while others—although accepting the rule's existence per se—argue that it both is theoretically incoherent and has extremely limited utility within the modern international legal system.[28] This book engages with these critiques, and others, throughout.

D'Aspremont therefore puts it rather mildly when he says that the persistent objector rule is a 'much discussed theory'.[29] However, it is equally the case that neither supporters nor critics of the rule have examined it in significant detail. To an extent, for all of the targeted discussion of the rule that has occurred in the literature in the past thirty years,[30] the leading works examining persistent

[25] Stein, n. 7, 463.

[26] M.P. Scharf, *Customary International Law in Times of Fundamental Change: Recognizing Grotian Moments* (Cambridge, Cambridge University Press, reissue, 2013), 41. See also Mendelson, n. 17, 227.

[27] See, for example, L. Condorelli, 'Custom', in M. Bedjaoui (ed.), *International Law: Achievements and Prospects* (Paris, UNESCO, 1991), 179, particularly at 205; P. Dumberry, 'Incoherent and Ineffective: The Concept of Persistent Objector Revisited' (2010) 59 *International and Comparative Law Quarterly* 779, particularly at 780 and 794; P-M. Dupuy, 'A propos de l'opposabilité de la coutume générale: enquête brève sur "l'objecteur persistant" ', in *Le droit international au service de la paix, de la justice et du développement: Mélanges offerts à Michel Virally* (Paris, Pédone, 1991), 257; R. Higgins, *Problems and Process: International Law and How We Use It* (Oxford, Clarendon Press, 1994), 34; J.P. Kelly, 'The Twilight of Customary International Law' (1999–2000) 40 *Virginia Journal of International Law* 449, 508–16; I.M. Lobo de Souza, 'The Role of Consent in the Customary Process' (1995) 44 *International and Comparative Law Quarterly* 521, 533 (arguing that the existence of the rule is 'disputable'); J.P. Paust, 'The Complex Nature, Sources and Evidences of Customary Human Rights' (1995–6) 25 *Georgia Journal of International and Comparative Law* 147, 152; and C. Tomuschat, 'Obligations Arising for States Without or Against Their Will' (1993) 241 *Recueil des cours* 195, 284–90 and 308. See also Report of the International Law Commission, Sixty-seventh session, 4 May–5 June and 6 July–7 August 2015, UN Doc. A/70/10, advance unedited version, 24 August 2015, 40, para. 93 (noting that, during the consideration of the 'Identification of customary international law' topic at the ILC's Sixty-seventh session, at least some members of the ILC 'considered that [the persistent objector rule] was a controversial theory not supported by sufficient State practice and jurisprudence').

[28] See, for example, O. Barsalou, 'La doctrine de l'objecteur persistant en droit international public' (2006) 19 *Revue québécoise de droit international* 1; J.I. Charney, 'The Persistent Objector Rule and the Development of Customary International Law' (1985) 56 *British Yearbook of International Law* 1; B. Conforti, 'Cours général de droit international public' (1988-V) 212 *Recueil des cours* 13, 74–7; J.H.H. Weiler, 'Editorial' (2013) 24 *European Journal of International Law* 1, 3; and P-H. Verdier and E. Voeten, 'Precedent, Compliance, and Change in Customary International Law: An Explanatory Theory' (2014) 108 *American Journal of International Law* 389, particularly at 429.

[29] J. d'Aspremont, *Formalism and the Sources of International Law: A Theory of the Ascertainment of Legal Rules* (Oxford, Oxford University Press, 2011, paperback edn, 2013), 166.

[30] The list of works that have sought to engage *specifically* with the persistent objector rule over the past thirty years is a long one, but some key examples include: Barsalou, n. 28; Colson, n. 7; David, n. 10; P. Dumberry, 'The Last Citadel! Can a State Claim the Status of Persistent Objector to Prevent the Application of a Rule of Customary International Law in Investor-State Arbitration?' (2010) 23 *Leiden Journal of International Law* 379; Dumberry, n. 27; Dupuy, n. 27; O. Elias, 'Some Remarks on the Persistent Objector Rule in Customary International Law' (1991) 6 *Denning Law Journal* 37; O. Elias, 'Persistent Objector' in R. Wolfrum (ed.), *Max Planck Encyclopaedia of Public International Law, vol. VIII*

objection remain two relatively short articles, both published in 1985, by Ted Stein[31] and Jonathan Charney.[32] Prior to the publication of the book you are currently reading, there existed only one monograph in print[33] that was (at least apparently) focused on the rule: Charles Quince's *The Persistent Objector and Customary International Law* from 2010.[34] However, despite its title, Quince's book actually only devotes thirty-three of its 131 pages to the rule itself, with the rest of the book considering customary international law more generally. With all due respect to Quince's book (which, to avoid any doubt, is excellent on its own terms), its engagement with persistent objection is comparatively limited. The present work thus aims to be the most comprehensive examination of the rule to date.[35]

II. The Commonly Accepted Elements of the Persistent Objector Rule

While there is little clarity as to the exact nature of the persistent objector rule in the literature, the rule does have a few commonly accepted core elements that are apparent in virtually all of the numerous references to it in scholarship. As Guldahl has noted, the 'theoretical underpinnings of [the persistent objector rule] doctrine have been the subject of much debate, but the basic characteristics of the rule are generally accepted'.[36] There is at least a degree of common understanding as to what the rule *is*.

(Oxford, Oxford University Press, 2012), 280; J.A. Green, 'India and a Customary Comprehensive Nuclear Test-Ban: Persistent Objection, Peremptory Norms and the 123 Agreement' (2011) 51 *Indian Journal of International Law* 3; J.A. Green, 'Persistent Objector Teflon? Customary International Human Rights Law and the United States in International Adjudicative Proceedings' in J.A. Green and C.P.M. Waters (eds), *Adjudicating International Human Rights: Essays in Honour of Sandy Ghandhi* (Leiden, Brill Nijhoff, 2015), 167; Guldahl, n. 8; Kritsiotis, n. 14; Lau, n. 10; L. Loschin, 'The Persistent Objector Rule and Customary Human Rights Law: A Proposed Analytical Framework' (1996) 2 *University of California Davis Journal of International Law and Policy* 147; J.B. McClane, 'How Late in the Emergence of a Norm of Customary International Law May a Persistent Objector Object?' (1989) 13 *International Law Students Association Journal of International Law* 1; and A. Steinfeld, 'Nuclear Objections: The Persistent Objector and the Legality of the Use of Nuclear Weapons' (1996) 62 *Brooklyn Law Review* 1635.

[31] Stein, n. 7. [32] Charney, n. 28.

[33] It is important to also note G. Pentassuglia, *La rilevanza dell'obiezione persitente nel diritto internazionale* (Bari, Laterza, 1996). This book appears to be out of print: as such, it has not been possible for this author to review it. According to Oellers-Frahm's review of Pentassuglia's book, it is an extensive investigation of the persistent objector rule (meaning that it is the only monograph truly dedicated to the rule that existed prior to the present one). However, Oellers-Frahm also notes that Pentassuglia ultimately concludes that the persistent objector rule *does not exist*. See K. Oellers-Frahm, 'Buchrezension: Pentassuglia, Gaetano, *La rilevanza dell'obiezione persitente nel diritto internazionale*' (1997) 57 *Zeitschrift für ausländisches öffentliches Recht und Völkerrecht* 1180.

[34] C. Quince, *The Persistent Objector and Customary International Law* (Denver, Outskirts Press, 2010).

[35] Although, having said this, one must also note the earlier publication of Pentassuglia, n. 33. See text in n. 33.

[36] Guldahl, n. 8, 53. See also Yee, n. 14, 391, para. 57 ('The general contour of the persistent objector rule is well known').

For example, it is worth considering the understanding of the persistent objector rule provisionally adopted in July 2015 by the Draft Committee of the ILC—tasked by the UN General Assembly to contribute to the progressive development and codification of international law—as part of the Commission's ongoing work on the identification of customary international law:

1. Where a State has objected to a rule of customary international law while that rule was in the process of formation, the rule is not opposable to the State concerned for so long as it maintains its objection.
2. The objection must be clearly expressed, made known to other States, and maintained persistently.[37]

Similarly, the ILA—an organization currently composed of around 3,500 international law experts throughout the world—adopted a definition of the persistent objector rule in 2000, based on its committee report on the *Formation of Customary (General) International Law*.[38] The ILA's definition, as drafted by its committee, set out the rule thus: '[i]f whilst a practice is developing into a rule of general law [that is, customary international law], a State persistently and openly dissents from the rule, it will not be bound by it.'[39]

These definitions—from the ILC and ILA respectively—are representative of the usual articulation of the rule in the wider literature. The persistent objector rule is therefore almost always viewed as being composed of a number of core aspects. Some of these elements are more explicitly advanced than others, but they are present, at least to some extent, in the vast majority of existing representations of the rule.

The first of these core elements, which is not always made explicit, perhaps because it is seen as being self-evident, is a requirement of *objection*.[40] Silence is not seen as enough. Secondly, objection must be *persistent*.[41] Single or isolated objections will not suffice. Thirdly, objections must be *consistent*.[42] This consistency criterion is often only implicitly referenced in the literature or is conflated with the persistence requirement, but in fact most accounts of the rule seemingly accept that however *persistent* objection may be, it also needs a degree of internal coherence: persistent but inconsistent objection is likely to be insufficient. Fourthly, the objection must be *timely*,[43] in that it must occur prior to the norm being objected to 'crystallizing' as a binding norm of customary international law. 'Subsequent objection' after the customary norm in question has formed will not avail the objector.

These criteria for the rule's operation are all relatively easily stated, but there remains very little understanding of what they entail in practice and how they are to be applied: '[t]he modalities of the establishment of persistent objection have not been the subject of systematic examination.'[44] Improving our understanding

[37] ILC, Text of the Draft Conclusions, n. 23, 5, Draft Conclusion 15: Persistent Objector.

[38] ILA Final Report, n. 6. [39] Ibid., section 15. [40] See Chapter 3.

[41] See Chapter 4.

[42] See Chapter 5. [43] See Chapter 6.

[44] Elias, 'Persistent Objector', n. 30, 284, para. 15. See also O. Elias and C.L. Lim, *The Paradox of Consensualism in International Law* (The Hague, Kluwer Law International, 1998), 72–3; D.W. Greig,

of the requirements for, and mechanics of, persistent objection is crucial, because 'the right to dissent under the persistent objector rule is seriously weakened if no-one knows *how* to dissent'.[45] As such, much of this book is devoted to examining the criteria for the rule's operation.

III. Voluntarism: The Commonly Advanced Rationale for the Rule

Flowing from a conception of international relations as a system of sovereign equality and supremacy, from the early nineteenth century onwards, international law was seen in predominant positivist understandings as being premised on state *consent*.[46] This undoubtedly flawed,[47] but still often advanced,[48] 'voluntarist' account of the root of international legal obligation holds that the horizontal structure of the international legal system means that states are only bound by law that they have consented to be bound by.[49] In relation to treaty law, just as with contracts in domestic legal systems, the identification of consent is at least comparatively straightforward: the question is whether the state has expressed its consent to be bound by the treaty or not.[50] However, for customary international law—the other main formal source of legal obligation in the system—finding state 'consent' is, to put it mildly, rather more difficult.[51]

'Reflections on the Role of Consent' (1988–9) 12 *Australian Yearbook of International Law* 125, 145–6; Lau, n. 10, 498; and Steinfeld, n. 30, 1651. *Contra* T. Christiano, 'The Legitimacy of International Institutions' in A. Marmor (ed.), *The Routledge Companion to the Philosophy of Law* (Abingdon, Routledge, 2012), 380, 387 ('states understand the persistent objector rule').

[45] Elias and Lim, n. 44, 73. See also UN Doc. A/70/10, n. 27, 36, para. 73 and 42, para. 106 (views of the Special Rapporteur for the ILC's ongoing work on the 'Identification of customary international law', Sir Michael Wood, during the consideration of the topic at the ILC's Sixty-seventh session: '[t]he Special Rapporteur ... pointed out that the persistent objector rule could be and not infrequently is raised before judges asked to identify customary international law and that *it was therefore important to provide practitioners with guidelines on the matter, and especially to clarify the requirements for a State to become a persistent objector*'; emphasis added, quoted at para. 106).

[46] The most famous expression of the 'voluntarist' consent-theory remains the statement of the Permanent Court of International Justice (PCIJ) to the effect that '[t]he rules of law binding upon states ... emanate from their own free will as expressed in conventions or by usages generally accepted as expressing principles of law.' *Lotus* (*France v Turkey*) 1927 PCIJ Series A, No. 9, 18.

[47] See Chapter 9, section I.*iii*.

[48] See, for example, J-A. Carrillo-Salcedo, 'Droit international et souveraineté des États—Cours général de droit international public' (1996) 257 *Recueil des cours* 35, 92 ('[p]our ce qui de la coutume internationale, le rôle du consentement de l'Etats est indéniable'); and L. Henkin, 'International Law: Politics, Values and Functions' (1989-IV) 216 *Recueil des cours* 11, 46 ('[s]tate consent is the foundation of international law').

[49] This is often still seen as a fundamental aspect of the system, and is well expressed by A. Cassese, *International Law in a Divided World* (Oxford, Clarendon Press, 1986), 169.

[50] See A. Aust, *Modern Treaty Law and Practice* (Cambridge, Cambridge University Press, 3rd edn, 2013), 87–113.

[51] See H.C.M. Charlesworth, 'Customary International Law and the *Nicaragua* Case' (1984–5) 11 *Australian Yearbook of International Law* 1, 3 (comparing the relative ease of identifying state

In the context of custom, the orthodox voluntarist 'consent-theory' of international law formation is usually premised on silence as constituting tacit state consent.[52] It is here where the persistent objector rule is most often seen as fulfilling a crucial role. At least theoretically, the rule preserves state autonomy—not to mention the voluntarist conception of a consent-based system in the context of custom—by providing states with a means to exercise 'consent' in the law-making process (albeit purely through the option of *withholding* consent). The traditional understanding is therefore that '[t]he Persistent Objector Rule is a logical product of the consent theory'.[53] Indeed, the rule's importance to the voluntarist conception of the international legal system in part helps to explain its ubiquity within mainstream international law scholarship.[54]

The underpinning voluntarist rationale for the persistent objector rule will be critiqued throughout this book, and particularly in Chapter 9.[55] However, it is important to note from the outset that this author rejects the claim that only the will of individual states has any constituting effect when it comes to international law-making. The notion that international law can only be created by state consent is, at least in its pure form, patently incorrect. The plurality of modern international legal norm creation[56] means that classic 'voluntarist positivism' ultimately fails to comply with positivism's own basic tenet of identifying law 'as it is'.[57] Of course, this rejection of voluntarism means that the rationale for the persistent objector rule must itself be rejected, at least as it is most commonly presented. This issue will therefore be returned to in due course.[58]

IV. A Socio-Legal Positivist Approach

This book takes a broadly positivist approach to international law. 'Legal positivism', of course, means many things to many people.[59] The various positivist

consent in treaty law with the problems inherent in so doing for custom). For further discussion, see Chapter 9, section I.*iii*, n. 64–n. 82 and accompanying text.

[52] See, for example, J.L. Dunoff, S.R. Ratner and D. Wippman, *International Law: Norms, Actors, Process: A Problem-Orientated Approach* (New York, Aspen, 2nd edn, 2006), 78–9; and Treves, n. 1, 945, para. 35.

[53] Steinfeld, n. 30, 1655.

[54] Green, 'Persistent Objector Teflon?', n. 30, 170.

[55] See, in particular, Chapter 9, sections I and IV.

[56] See Chapter 9, sections I.*iii*, II and III.

[57] See J. Kammerhofer and J. d'Aspremont, 'Introduction' in J. Kammerhofer and J. d'Aspremont (eds), *International Legal Positivism in a Post-Modern World* (Cambridge, Cambridge University Press, 2014), 1, 5.

[58] See, in particular, Chapter 9.

[59] See, for example, H.L.A. Hart, 'Positivism and the Separation of Law and Morals' (1958) 71 *Harvard Law Review* 593, 601–2, footnote 25 (famously setting out five different meanings of legal positivism, as well as explicitly noting that there may be more). With regard to international law specifically, see U. Fastenrath, 'Relative Normativity in International Law' (1993) 4 *European Journal of International Law* 305, particularly at 306–24.

understandings of international law are unsettled,[60] and this is not the place to attempt to untangle them (or even to explore the version(s) of positivism applied in this book in any great detail). Equally, given that this project examines whether or not the persistent objector rule exists and—following the conclusion that it does—the rule's content and the criteria governing its application, it is necessary to at least briefly (and admittedly very simplistically) set out the basic assumptions made in undertaking that inquiry. In so doing, it is again worth emphasizing that this book is 'positivist', but at the same time—in places, at least—represents a critique of purely voluntarist positivism.

This author rejects the 'classic' voluntarist international legal positivism that was particularly prominent in the nineteenth and early twentieth centuries, which took as its core premise the notion that only the expressed will of states had any constituting effect when it came to international law creation.[61] However, 'one need not necessarily associate positivism with state voluntarism'.[62] This book uses the label 'positivism' more broadly, to indicate that rules of international law must be identified (at least predominantly) by way of an *inductive* methodology, focused on the accepted law-making processes of the system (and, thus, in practice, on the actions of states and other actors within the international community).[63] This is as opposed to a purely *deductive* methodology, based on conceptual desirability or the aspirational pull of policy or value-based goals.

It has already been noted that the persistent objector rule is a secondary rule of the international legal system. The secondary rules of international law are 'notoriously vague',[64] and it is clear that they cannot themselves be traced back to the modern 'sources' of the international legal system, as commonly set out in Article 38(1) of the Statute of the ICJ.[65] For example, the notion of *pacta sunt servanda*—which was established long before its appearance in Article 26

[60] For an excellent recent examination, see, generally, J. Kammerhofer and J. d'Aspremont (eds), *International Legal Positivism in a Post-Modern World* (Cambridge, Cambridge University Press, 2014).

[61] See, generally, R. Collins, 'Classical Legal Positivism in International Law Revisited' in J. Kammerhofer and J. d'Aspremont (eds), *International Legal Positivism in a Post-Modern World* (Cambridge, Cambridge University Press, 2014), 23.

[62] B. Simma and A.L. Paulus, 'The Responsibility of Individuals for Human Rights Abuses in Internal Conflicts: A Positivist View' (1999) 93 *American Journal of International Law* 302, 304.

[63] See ILA Final Report, n. 6, 4; S. Breau, 'State Practice, Customary Humanitarian Law and Civilian Casualties of Armed Conflict' (2014) 1 *State Practice and International Law Journal* 45, 49 and 52–3; Condorelli, n. 27, 180; Guldahl, n. 8, 61; R. Kolb, 'Selected Problems in the Theory of Customary International Law' (2003) 50 *Netherlands International Law Review* 119, 130–3; Mendelson, n. 17, 239; Quince, n. 34, 35–6; A. Roberts, 'Traditional and Modern Approaches to Customary International Law: A Reconciliation' (2001) 95 *American Journal of International Law* 757, particularly at 757–8 and 762; and Tomuschat, n. 27, 303.

[64] J. Pauwelyn, 'Is It International Law or Not, and Does It Even Matter?' in J. Pauwelyn, R.A. Wessel, and J. Wouters (eds), *Informal International Lawmaking* (Oxford, Oxford University Press, 2012), 125, 131.

[65] *Contra* M. Virally, 'The Sources of International Law' in M. Sørensen (ed.), *Manual of Public International Law* (London, Macmillan, 1968), 116, 122 (arguing that all secondary rules of international law can be derived from Article 38(1) of the ICJ's Statute).

of the 1969 Vienna Convention on the Law of Treaties[66]—was almost certainly not 'created' through, say, a process of consistent and general state practice combined with *opinio juris*.[67] It is also not the case that the secondary rules of international law owe their existence to some kind of immemorial historical legitimacy.[68] A number of the secondary rules of the modern international legal system can be traced back to a relatively recent genesis point. Take, for example, the notion of *opinio juris*: although it is possible to identify something that looks somewhat akin to *opinio juris* in classical writings from the seventeenth century onwards,[69] and even—in a more general sense—in Roman law,[70] it is fairly clear that the concept as understood today (even as *broadly* understood) only emerged in the late nineteenth century.[71] It cannot be said that the secondary rules of international law are what they are 'because always has it ever been'.

How, then, does one identify the existence and content of secondary rules of international law, especially given its largely non-hierarchical nature? To hugely over-simplify, like both Hart and Kelsen, the present author takes the view that secondary rules of international law are rooted in social practice. However, going beyond their formalized approaches, this book adopts a comparatively deformalized[72] account of law-ascertainment at the 'secondary rule' level, based on *social acceptance*.[73] It thus draws on various understandings of international

[66] Vienna Convention on the Law of Treaties (VCLT), 23 May 1969, 1155 UNTS 331.

[67] See Kolb, n. 63, 127; H. Lauterpacht, *The Function of Law in the International Community* (Oxford, Oxford University Press, 1933), 428–31 (discussing *pacta sunt servanda* from a voluntarist perspective, but accepting that the principle cannot have a positivist nature in this sense); Lobo de Souza, n. 27, 535; A.V. Lowe, 'Do General Rules of International Law Exist?' (1983) 9 *Review of International Studies* 207, 211; and Stein, n. 7, 480 (arguing that *pacta sunt servanda* is 'inherent' in the international legal system). See also Virally, n. 65, 127 (noting the different understandings of the source of *pacta sunt servanda*: i.e., natural law, general principles and custom). *Contra* Jia, n. 10, 87.

[68] Kelsen, for example, formulated his '*grundnorm*' for the international legal system thus: '[s]tates ought to behave as they have customarily behaved'. See H. Kelsen, *Principles of International Law* (R.W. Tucker (ed. and revns.), New York, Holt, Rinehart and Winston, 2nd edn, 1966), 564; and H. Kelsen, *General Theory of Law and State* (A. Wedberg (trans.), New York, Russell and Russell, 1945), 369. See also R. Ago, 'Positive Law and International Law' (1957) 51 *American Journal of International Law* 691, 706 (arguing that secondary rules of international law 'are only explicable historically'). This seems unlikely, given that a number of accepted secondary norms do not have any notable historical pedigree. See C.A. Bradley and M. Gulati, 'Customary International Law and Withdrawal Rights in an Age of Treaties' (2010) 21 *Duke Journal of International and Comparative Law* 1, 14.

[69] See O. Elias, 'The Nature of the Subjective Element in Customary International Law' (1995) 44 *International and Comparative Law Quarterly* 501, 505.

[70] Virally, n. 65, 133.

[71] See ibid.; Elias, 'Some Remarks on the Persistent Objector Rule', n. 30, 504–6; and B. Stern, 'Custom at the Heart of International Law' (2001) 11 *Duke Journal of Comparative and International Law* 89 (M. Byers and A. Denise (trans.), originally published as 'La coutume au cœur du droit international: Quelques réflexions' *in Le droit international: unité et diversité: Mélanges offerts à Paul Reuter* (Paris, Pedone, 1981), 479), 95–7.

[72] See, generally, Pauwelyn, Wessel, and Wouters (eds), n. 64.

[73] See Postema, n. 17, 292 ('[c]ustomary norms are established and mature in a community not by repetition [at least, not *necessarily* by repetition], but by *integration*'; emphasis added).

law-ascertainment that are premised on sociological analysis,[74] and, particularly, on the understanding advanced by a number of Italian international lawyers writing in the twentieth century.[75] The 'Italian doctrine' sought to distinguish 'custom as a *basis* of international law' (*consuetudine-fondamento*) from 'custom as a *source* of international law' (*consuetudine-fonte*), arguing that the former was characterized by non-formalized socio-historical evolution, whereas the latter is a process based on the usual (and more formal) state practice/*opinio juris* approach.[76]

To avoid disappearing down the rabbit-hole of detailed analysis of such sociological perspectives, suffice it to say here that the underpinning theoretical claim made in this book is that secondary rules of international law develop in social practice in a non-formalized manner, and must be ascertained based on whether they have been *accepted as secondary rules* by the key actors in the international community.[77] Put simply, the secondary rules of international law (including those that govern the creation or alteration of customary international law) *must themselves be seen as being 'customary'*,[78] albeit that this term as used here should be taken to broadly mean 'customary social acceptance and usage' rather than an application of the state practice/*opinio juris* test with which international lawyers are so familiar.

It is necessary to slightly qualify this approach, as adopted in this book. Firstly, in response to a possible charge that many sociological approaches to law-ascertainment veer uncomfortably close to 'legal realist' claims that international law is only valid to the extent that states comply with it,[79] it must be stressed that the 'social acceptance' understanding adopted in this book is advanced only in relation to the *secondary rules* of international law. It is argued that once the system's secondary rules are accepted and used as social fact these rules then, themselves, in a much more formalized 'Hartian' manner, govern the determination of the primary rules.[80]

[74] For some prominent sociological accounts of international law (from which this book variously borrows certain aspects and abandons others) see, for example, J. Brunnée and S.J. Toope, *Legitimacy and Legality in International Law: An Interactional Account* (Cambridge, Cambridge University Press, 2010); and B. Kingsbury, 'The Concept of "Law" in Global Administrative Law' (2009) 20 *European Journal of International Law* 23.

[75] For a recent summary of this scholarship, see E. Cannizarro, 'Il mutamento dei paradigmi della scienza giuridica internazionalista e la dottrina Italiana' (2014) 1/14 *Annuario di diritto comparator e di studi legislative* 77. For an analysis of this approach in the influential writings of Dionisio Anzilotti, see G. Gaja, 'Positivism and Dualism in Dionisio Anzilotti' (1992) 2 *European Journal of International Law* 123. For the classic English-language example of the 'Italian doctrine', see Ago, n. 68.

[76] See Kolb, n. 63, 123–4 (neatly setting out this core aspect of the 'Italian doctrine').

[77] Another way of viewing the approach taken in this book is perhaps to orient it in Hart's understanding of 'pre-legal' societies: see Hart, n. 11, particularly at 91–2.

[78] Elias and Lim, n. 44, 78 (stating that 'the rules on the application of customary law, including the persistent objector rule, are themselves rules of customary law'; however, Elias and Lim adopt this view based on a more overtly voluntarist understanding than the present author); V. Fon and F. Parisi, 'Stability and Change in International Customary Law' (2004) 21 *American Law and Economics Association Annual Meetings* 1, 1; Guldahl, n. 8, 55; G. Norman and J.P. Trachtman, 'The Customary International Law Game' (2005) 99 *American Journal of International Law* 541, 544; and Tomuschat, n. 27, 279 ('The basic layer is constituted by general practice', see also at 290–1).

[79] For this critique see d'Aspremont, n. 29, 122–7, particularly at 126.

[80] See Cannizarro, n. 75, particularly 82–4; and Kolb, n. 63, 124. Again, as an example, take the norm of *pacta sunt servanda*, which—having been established as a secondary rule through social acceptance—now acts as a 'qualifier' for primary rules. See n. 66–n. 67 and accompanying text.

The approach taken herein does not open the door to legal realism at the substantive, primary-rule level.

Secondly, it is not the case that the only relevant 'acceptance' of secondary rules is *state acceptance*.[81] The adoption of a 'social acceptance' understanding is not a return to the pure voluntarist theory already rejected. Other important actors, particularly courts and tribunals, clearly contribute to the creation and development of secondary rules of international law.[82] Having said this, for good or ill, states remain the most important actors in the international legal system, and thus their acceptance and usage (or lack of acceptance and usage) of purported secondary norms undoubtedly carries the most weight.[83]

Thirdly, it is not the case that this book adopts any natural law underpinnings in its investigation of the persistent objector rule.[84] The present author self-consciously 'shears' the influence of natural law from (certain) sociological accounts of international law,[85] to root the inquiry in empiricism.[86] This approach is adopted in part for pragmatic reasons, because it is argued that without some degree of 'tethering' of legal norms to social acceptance and usage, the actors in the international legal system (most pertinently, states) will simply not view purported norms as being prescriptive.[87]

It is ultimately through the observation of social acceptability and usage, as part of the inherently messy to-and-fro of international relations, that we must consider the emergence and nature of the persistent objector rule.[88] In practice, this means that this book looks to assess the existence and content of the rule in the writings of scholars, the judgments of courts/tribunals, and the actions of states. As such, while we must not allow ourselves to be 'caught in the positivistic cage of Article 38(1) of [the ICJ's] Statute',[89] when it comes to searching for the existence or content of secondary rules of international law, the process of inquiry

[81] See, for example, Brunnée and Toope, n. 74, 8 and 77–86.

[82] d'Aspremont, n. 29, 203–13 (although it should be noted that d'Aspremont's social theory of law-ascertainment is firmly rooted in formalism).

[83] See section V.

[84] Certain deformalized sociological approaches have been criticized on this basis by more 'formal' positivist scholars. See, for example, P. Capps, 'International Legal Positivism and Modern Natural Law' in J. Kammerhofer and J. d'Aspremont (eds), *International Legal Positivism in a Post-Modern World* (Cambridge, Cambridge University Press, 2014), 213, 225–7.

[85] Thus, this book adopts the position of the 'Italian doctrine' in this regard: see Gaja, n. 75, 123–6 (specifically examining Anzilotti's rejection of natural law). In contrast, see, for example, Brunnée and Toope, n. 74 (from whom this author borrows aspects of their 'interactional', 'effects-based' theory, while rejecting their use of the work of Fuller to 'populate' that understanding).

[86] See Gaja, n. 75, 129 (identifying the core empirical basis of the 'Italian doctrine', upon which this book draws). *Contra* Kolb, n. 63, 124 (asserting that the 'Italian doctrine' is not based on empirical method).

[87] See Simma and Paulus, n. 62, 303.

[88] It is worth noting that a sociological approach to law does not merely result in 'mundane' descriptivism; it can also 'open up a more fruitful way of thinking about problems in jurisprudence and ethics', because it roots such inquiries in reality, rather than in grand theory. See B.Z. Tamanaha, 'A Socio-Legal Methodology for the Internal/External Distinction: Jurisprudential Implications' (2006) 75 *Fordham Law Review* 1255, quoted at 1258.

[89] Tomuschat, n. 27, 304. See also Besson, n. 11, 164–5.

is, in effect, perhaps not as much of a departure from Article 38(1) as one might expect given the foregoing discussion in this section. The focus, ultimately, still must be on the actions of the relevant legal actors in the system, including courts, writers, and—most crucially—states.

V. A Focus on State Practice

The most convenient and authoritative place where the social acceptability/usage of a norm of international law can be identified is, of course, in treaty law. However, the persistent objector rule is neither a product of, nor codified in, any international treaty.[90] Neither is the rule set out in any other 'authoritative' hard or soft law instrument, such as, for example, a resolution of a UN organ. This fact itself is neutral in terms of what it tells us of the existence or content of the rule, but it means that it is necessary to search for the legal source of the persistent objector rule elsewhere. Based on the discussion in the previous section, the primary (albeit certainly not sole) reference point for the persistent objector rule must be the practice of *states*.[91] International law remains deeply rooted in the actions of states, and it is there—in the real-world cut-and-thrust of international relations—that the contours of the persistent objector rule can be identified. One must be careful not to throw the baby of the primacy of states in international law out with the bathwater of absolute state voluntarism. Significant weight is also placed in this book on jurisprudential engagement with the rule, and on the extensive (if often rather cursory) treatment of the rule in the literature: both, especially the former (because of the law-applying authority vested in courts and tribunals),[92] are crucial touchstones. However, this book seeks to root much of its analysis in the practice of states, to the extent possible: 'the elements of persistent objection must be set out and developed through state practice.'[93]

This focus on actual state usage of the persistent objector rule, which forms the core methodology of this book, is relatively unusual in the context of the academic

[90] *Contra* E.L. Chalecki, 'Science before the Law: American Exceptionalism in the Kyoto Protocol and the Development of a Global Norm of Environmental Compliance' (2007) *Selected Works*, http://works.bepress.com/cgi/viewcontent.cgi?article=1000&context=elizabeth_chalecki, 19, footnote 45. Chalecki argues that the persistent objector rule can be identified in '*a number* ... of international conventions' (emphasis added) and, as an example, cites the Convention on Consular Agents: Duties, Rights, Prerogatives, and Immunities (Inter-American) (Havana Convention), 25 February 1928, 155 LNTS 291. However, she does not point to a particular provision in the Havana Convention to support her assertion in this regard, and a review of the treaty confirms that nothing even vaguely approaching the persistent objector rule can be identified anywhere in it.

[91] Greig, n. 44, 166.

[92] Having said this, in the international legal system, states rarely submit their disputes to review by adjudicative mechanisms. The jurisprudence in the international legal system is, therefore, necessarily comparatively limited. This means that an analysis of the persistent objector rule in state practice is particularly crucial. See Colson, n. 7, 958.

[93] Guldahl, n. 8, 55. See also See ILA Final Report, n. 6, 4; Kelly, n. 27, 512 ('[i]f the persistent objector rule [is to be considered] part of [customary international law] theory, it must be demonstrated that the principle has generally been accepted by states', although Kelly ultimately takes the

engagement with the rule. To the extent that writers have examined persistent objection, this has generally been from quite an abstract perspective. A key reason for this is the common perception that states rarely, if ever, persistently object to the formation of new customary international law, and the few states that do cannot maintain any such exemption.[94] This claim will be returned to throughout the book, particularly in Part I (with regard to the view that there is no, or extremely limited, state usage of the rule)[95] and Chapter 8 (with regard to the view that states are never, or almost never, able to maintain their exempt status having gained it by virtue of the rule).[96] For present purposes, though, it is enough to note that this book takes the position that states certainly do use the rule, and can gain exemption from norms of customary international law through that use. Equally, it is also undoubtedly the case that usage of the rule is rare; *gaining* exemption by way of persistent objection is particularly difficult for states (because the criteria for the rule's operation are so onerous), as is *maintaining* exempt status after the crystallization of the norm being objected (because extra-legal factors, such as political pressure, often make continued persistent objection untenable).

In response to the critique that there is little or no state usage of the rule, Maurice Mendelson asserted in his 1998 Hague Academy course that there is, in fact, 'quite a wealth of state practice in support of the persistent objector rule' and that scholars have simply not 'looked hard enough' to find this.[97] While the claim that there is 'quite a wealth of state practice' is a significant over-exaggeration, there are certainly a number of instances of persistent objection in state practice. The rule has been used rather more often than its critics indicate. A key goal of this book is therefore to take up Mendelson's challenge and 'look hard enough' for (and at) that practice,[98] as well as coupling this, as already noted, with reference to judicial decisions and the writings of scholars.

VI. The Structure of This Book

This book is split into three parts. Following this Introduction, Part I (Chapters 1 and 2) begins this book's analysis of the persistent objector rule by examining the rule's origin and legal validity. In particular, Part I tackles a fundamental

view that the rule has not been sufficiently accepted by states in this way); and H. Thirlway, *The Sources of International Law* (Oxford, Oxford University Press, 2014), 87.

[94] See scholars cited in Chapter 2, n. 117, n. 118 and n. 119.

[95] See, particularly, Chapter 1, section III; and Chapter 2, section II.

[96] See, particularly, Chapter 8, section II.

[97] Mendelson, n. 17, 238.

[98] It is worth noting that analysis of the persistent objector rule *sensu stricto* always occurs in retrospect: the rule only comes into play after the customary norm being objected to has crystallized into a binding obligation, as the exemption that the rule provides is only relevant after this point. Equally, objection must occur prior to the point of crystallization. See Chapter 6, section IV on the 'timeline' of the persistent objector rule; and Chapter 6, in general, regarding the requirement for objection before the norm being objected to has crystallized. Therefore, it is necessary to consider instances where states express objection even if not yet clear that the emerging norm to which the state is objecting has formed. See Colson, n. 7, 958.

question, which is whether the persistent objector rule *exists at all* as a norm of public international law. Chapter 1 examines the 'history' of the persistent objector rule: its emergence in academic doctrine and its basis in pre-1945 state practice and case law. Chapter 2 then assesses the modern legal status of the rule by considering relevant case law and state practice since the Second World War.

Having concluded in Part I that there is a persistent objector rule in international law, Part II (Chapters 3–6) examines the criteria for the rule's operation. Chapter 3 assesses what is required for 'objection'. It is axiomatic to say that states must 'object' to qualify as 'persistent objectors', but what does 'objection' *mean* in this context? The chapter particularly focuses on the question of whether a state must object to the *applicability* of the norm in question to that state, or whether it is sufficient for the state to object to the binding force of the norm per se. Chapter 3 also considers the 'form' that objection must take, and assesses the extent to which objection must be communicated.

Chapter 4 then turns to the 'persistence' criterion. It first references state practice to argue that the persistence requirement is, indeed, a feature of the rule. It then turns to the theoretical rationale for that requirement, ultimately arguing that there are practical and policy reasons underpinning the persistence criterion (rather than it necessarily being based on sound theoretical foundations). Chapter 4 also assesses the troublesome question of how 'persistent' persistent objection must be, taking a context-specific approach (which explicitly links the required degree of persistence to other factors).

The 'consistency' criterion is considered in Chapter 5. The need for consistent objection is actually identified regularly in the literature on the persistent objector rule, but this is often implicit or amalgamated/confused with the persistence standard. Chapter 5 argues that objection must be *both* persistent *and* consistent. Indeed, it is worth noting that the 'persistent objector rule' should perhaps more accurately be termed the 'persistent and consistent objector rule'. As that is something of a mouthful, and so as to stick with the familiar nomenclature (for the purposes of 'brand recognition' on the topic, if for no other reason), this book has chosen to retain the name 'persistent objector rule'. In any event, Chapter 5 explores the meaning of 'consistency' in the context of persistent objection, including whether 'absolute consistency' is required, as some claim (and, indeed, what 'absolute consistency' itself might mean). It also explores whether objections have to be substantively consistent.

Chapter 6 considers the criterion of 'timeliness': the requirement that a state must object to the emerging norm of customary international law prior to its crystallization. The chapter examines state practice to assess whether timely objection is required as is commonly supposed, and considers how late in the formation of the customary norm the objection can occur. Chapter 6 further discusses the problematic nature of any attempt to determine when, in fact, a new custom has emerged. It also considers in detail the possible phenomenon of 'subsequent objectors' (including new states), and questions whether a state must maintain objection even *after* crystallization.

Part III of the book (Chapters 7–9) analyses the limitations and role of the persistent objector rule. Chapter 7 engages with the often asserted claim that persistent objection is unavailing in the context of *jus cogens* (or 'peremptory') norms of international law. It uses state practice to test the majority view that it is impossible, as a matter of law, to be exempt as a persistent objector from a *jus cogens* norm. In so doing, the chapter considers the conceptual incompatibility of the universality and normative superiority of *jus cogens* norms with the inherent exceptionalism of persistent objection. It is ultimately argued that the majority view—that persistent objection does not allow a state to remain exempt from a customary international law norm that acquires peremptory status—is correct. However, this conclusion is far from being as self-evident as many indicate.

Chapter 8 examines issues—other than peremptory status—that may affect whether a state *maintains* its persistent objector stance. First, it considers the debate as to whether 'fundamental' (but nonetheless non-peremptory) norms of customary international law—such as human rights norms or rules of international humanitarian law or international environmental law—are beyond the reach of the persistent objector rule by virtue of their particularly 'important' nature. It is concluded that this is not the case de jure, but that maintaining exemption to norms of this sort will be particularly difficult for dissenting states de facto. The chapter then further argues that a range of extra-legal factors make maintaining persistent objection per se extremely difficult, irrespective of the nature of the norm being objected to. It is thus argued that the utility of the persistent objector rule is perhaps more limited than one might expect.

Finally, Chapter 9 engages with the 'value' or 'role' of the persistent objector rule. In the first instance, this involves analysis of—and rejection of—the 'voluntarist' conception of international law-making that the rule purportedly serves. However, the chapter also argues that, while one must dismiss the claim that all international law is made by the consent of states, this does not mean that state will is irrelevant in the context of customary international law: far from it. Drawing on a (carefully qualified) rational choice theory approach, Chapter 9 then argues that the persistent objector rule serves, and can serve, various important functions within the international legal system.

PART I

THE ORIGIN AND LEGAL SOURCE OF THE PERSISTENT OBJECTOR RULE

1

The History and Emergence of the Persistent Objector Rule

This first part of the book, composed of two chapters, examines the emergence and legal basis of the persistent objector rule: its origin and validity. In particular, it tackles a fundamental question, which is whether the rule *exists at all* as a norm of public international law. While the vast majority of scholars see the rule as an aspect of the system, a notable minority of commentators have argued that it is an academic fiction with no basis in law, and that it was simply designed by scholars to try to plug a theoretical hole in the shaky positivist understanding of international legal obligation based on state consent.[1] It is undeniable that supporters of the rule have generally not provided much in the way of evidence for its existence.[2] A number of writers simply have evidenced the rule by pointing to its acceptance elsewhere in the literature.[3] The overwhelming support for the persistent objector rule in modern academic doctrine[4] is, of course, important as part of a pattern of 'social acceptance' within the international legal system.[5] Reference to the literature alone, however, hardly helps to rebut the charge that the rule is an 'academic

[1] See writers referenced in Introduction, n. 27.

[2] See J. Charney, 'The Persistent Objector Rule and the Development of Customary International Law' (1985) 56 *British Yearbook of International Law* 1, 6 (correctly noting that most writers 'report the existence of the persistent objector rule but with little explanation and few supporting authorities'). See also O. Elias, 'Some Remarks on the Persistent Objector Rule in Customary International Law' (1991) 6 *Denning Law Journal* 37, 42; and P. Weil, 'Le droit international en quête de son identité—Cours général de droit international public' (1992-VI) 237 *Recueil des cours* 9, 189.

[3] See, for example, O. Elias and C.L. Lim, *The Paradox of Consensualism in International Law* (The Hague, Kluwer Law International, 1998), 30 (evidencing the rule by citing five other academic works, but nothing else); and L. Tabassi, 'The Nuclear Test Ban: *Lex Lata* or *de Lege Ferenda*?' (2009) 14 *Journal of Conflict and Security Law* 309, 333 (unequivocally supporting the existence of the persistent objector rule, but, in support of this, referencing only the Committee on Formation of Customary (General) International Law, Final Report of the Committee, 'Statement of Principles Applicable to the Formation of General Customary International Law', International Law Association, London Conference (2000), http://www.ila-hq.org/en/committees/index.cfm/cid/30).

[4] See Introduction, section I, n. 16–n. 25 and accompanying text.

[5] See A. Steinfeld, 'Nuclear Objections: The Persistent Objector and the Legality of the Use of Nuclear Weapons' (1996) 62 *Brooklyn Law Review* 1635, 1653 (arguing that the strongest support for rule is to be found in the writings of scholars).

fiction'. Similarly, perhaps the most commonly advanced support for the existence of the persistent objector rule are two decisions of the International Court of Justice (ICJ) from the early 1950s,[6] but, as will be discussed in Chapter 2, the value of these cases as foundational authorities for the rule's existence is somewhat debatable.[7]

As such, one may well wonder whether the minority view is correct. Perhaps there is no persistent objector rule after all. It will probably come as no surprise to readers, given that this is the first of nine chapters examining the persistent objector rule in this book, that it is ultimately concluded herein that the rule does exist. However, this conclusion is far from as self-evident as some claim: for example, Fry's recent uncritical assertion that there is 'certainly' a persistent objector rule[8] needs to be tested. Before beginning any analysis of how the persistent objector rule might operate, it is necessary to explore the origins and legal basis of the rule more generally, and—as part of this—engage with some of the fundamental critiques of the rule from the outset.

This chapter begins the assessment of the legal basis of the persistent objector rule by assessing the rule's 'history'. A notable critique of the persistent objector rule, advanced by the minority of (persistent) objectors to its existence, has been that it is a recent creation without historical legitimacy: the 'history of the doctrine is rather thin'.[9] Section I of this chapter assesses the emergence of the persistent objector rule in the scholarly literature. Section II then examines whether the rule can be identified in jurisprudence prior to the inception of the UN in 1945. Finally, section III considers the crucial question of whether one can identify examples of the use of the rule *by states* in pre-1945 practice. The chapter as a whole therefore assesses the competing claims that (1) the rule has no historical basis or legitimacy at all, and (2) that it in fact emerged as a secondary rule of international law well before the Second World War (as a matter of academic doctrine, in case law and in state practice). Chapter 2 then goes on to examine the rule's basis in post-1945 case law and state practice.

[6] *Asylum* (*Columbia v Peru*), merits, 1950 ICJ Rep. 266; and *Fisheries* (*United Kingdom v Norway*), merits, 1951 ICJ Rep. 116. In relation to the ubiquity of these cases in the scholarship on the persistent objector rule, see Chapter 2, section I.*i*, n. 7–n. 8 and accompanying text.

[7] See, in particular, ibid., section I.*ii*.

[8] J.D. Fry, 'Pluralism, Religion, and the Moral Fairness of International Law' (2014) 3 *Oxford Journal of Law and Religion* 393, 413.

[9] H. Lau, 'Rethinking the Persistent Objector Doctrine in International Human Rights Law' (2005–2006) 6 *Chicago Journal of International Law* 496, 499. See also, for example, C.A. Bradley and M. Gulati, 'Customary International Law and Withdrawal Rights in an Age of Treaties' (2010) 21 *Duke Journal of International and Comparative Law* 1, 2, and 14; J.P. Kelly, 'The Twilight of Customary International Law' (1999–2000) 40 *Virginia Journal of International Law* 449, 508; and C. Tomuschat, 'Obligations Arising for States Without or Against Their Will' (1993) 241 *Recueil des cours* 195, particularly at 286.

I. The Emergence of the Persistent Objector Rule in Academic Writing

The late Ian Brownlie has been commonly credited[10] with coining the phrase 'persistent objector' in the first edition of his seminal *Principles of Public International Law*,[11] which was published as recently as 1966. It is quite possible that the now familiar *term* 'persistent objector' did indeed make its first appearance in Brownlie's 1966 masterpiece. This cannot be said with certainty, of course, but the present author has not found an earlier usage of the recognizable nomenclature that Brownlie employed. This might lead one to date the 'emergence' of the rule in academic commentary to a point less than fifty years ago. However, it would be unwise to draw any implications in this regard based on the (apparent) coining of the term in 1966. After all, what's in a name? Legal terminology can and does change, and the question being considered in this chapter is when the rule may have begun to emerge (in scholarship, jurisprudence, and practice), not when the name that we now know it by was first adopted.

Some commentators have dated the emergence of the persistent objector rule in academic doctrine—at least its *meaningful* emergence—to a point even later than its appearance in Brownlie's book in the 1960s. It has been said that the acceptance of the rule in mainstream scholarship is only thirty to forty years old. Bradley and Gulati, for example, have argued that while some limited academic discussion of the rule occurred (for the first time) in the late 1950s, '[t]he doctrine did not become a canonical part of [customary international law] doctrine until sometime later, perhaps not until the 1970s or 1980s'.[12] Writing in 2010, Dumberry similarly claimed that '[a]lthough the concept of persistent objector can be traced back to more than 50 years ago, it only *truly emerged* as a coherent theory some 20 years ago when it was embraced by the United States'.[13]

Scholars making such claims have made much of the first appearance of the persistent objector rule in the third edition of the American Law Institute (ALI)'s *Restatement of the Law, Foreign Relations Law of the United States* in 1987,[14] considering it to be significant that the rule did not appear in earlier versions of the

[10] See, for example, C.A. Bradley and M. Gulati, 'Withdrawing from International Custom' (2010) 120 *Yale Law Journal* 202, 236–7; P-M. Dupuy, 'A propos de l'opposabilité de la coutume générale: enquête brève sur "l'objecteur persistant"' in *Le droit international au service de la paix, de la justice et du développement: Mélanges offerts à Michel Virally* (Paris, Pédone, 1991), 257, 258; Elias, n. 2, 37; and M. Ragazzi, *The Concept of International Obligations* Erga Omnes (Oxford, Oxford University Press, 1997), 60.

[11] I. Brownlie, *Principles of Public International Law* (Oxford, Oxford University Press, 1st edn, 1966), 8.

[12] Bradley and Gulati, n. 10, 233–4.

[13] P. Dumberry, 'Incoherent and Ineffective: The Concept of Persistent Objector Revisited' (2010) 59 *International and Comparative Law Quarterly* 779, 779, emphasis added.

[14] *Restatement of the Law, Third, Foreign Relations Law of the United States*, American Law Institute, 1987, Section 102, Comment (d).

Restatement.[15] Others point out that while the rule was endorsed in the ninth edition of Oppenheim's hugely influential modern treatise on international law,[16] published in 1992 (around a century after the first edition was published and some seventy years after Oppenheim's death), it was not present in earlier editions.[17] These assertions are, again, correct, but do not mean all that much in themselves.

Indeed, claims that the persistent objector rule only took hold in scholarly doctrine in the 1980s can be dismissed relatively easily. Even critics of the rule tend to accept that it was examined by a number of scholars in the immediate post-Second World War period.[18] For example, the rule was notably discussed in two key contributions by Fitzmaurice[19] and Waldock,[20] in 1953 and 1962 respectively. Both of these writers identified the persistent objector rule in terms that mirror its commonly accepted contours today. Moreover, these accounts of the rule from that period were highly influential at the time.[21] The 'late' appearance of the persistent objector rule in such influential material sources of international law as Oppenheim's treatise or the ALI's *Restatement* should not be dismissed: this could indeed be indicative of the relatively recent emergence of the rule per se. However, while it has gained significant further traction since,[22] the modern conception of the persistent objector rule can undoubtedly be identified as having been a widely accepted aspect of international law scholarship in the 1950s and 1960s.[23]

In contrast to many of its critics, some supporters of the persistent objector rule trace its emergence in scholarship back much further, to the eighteenth century. Perhaps most notably, the International Law Association (ILA)'s *Committee on Formation of Customary (General) International Law* referenced Cornelius van Bynkershoek's 1721 work *De Foro Legatorum Liber Singularis* as an 'early example' of the acceptance in doctrine of the rule.[24] In 1721 Bynkershoek wrote:

[15] See, for example, Charney, n. 2, 4; P. Dumberry, 'The Last Citadel! Can a State Claim the Status of Persistent Objector to Prevent the Application of a Rule of Customary International Law in Investor-State Arbitration?' (2010) 23 *Leiden Journal of International Law* 379, 391; Kelly, n. 9, 513–15; and Tomuschat, n. 9, 288–9.

[16] R. Jennings and A. Watts, *Oppenheim's International Law, vol. I: Peace* (New York, Longman, 9th edn, 1996), 29.

[17] Kelly, n. 9, 508, footnote 242, and 514.

[18] See, for example, O. Barsalou, 'La doctrine de l'objecteur persistant en droit international public' (2006) 19 *Revue québécoise de droit international* 1, 7; Bradley and Gulati, n. 10, 236–7; and Charney, n. 2, 6, footnote 8.

[19] G. Fitzmaurice, 'The Law and Procedure of the International Court of Justice, 1951–54: General Principles and Sources of Law' (1953) 30 *British Yearbook of International Law* 1, 24–6.

[20] H. Waldock, 'General Course on Public International Law' (1962) 106 *Recueil des cours* 1, 49–53.

[21] See H. Thirlway, *The Sources of International Law* (Oxford, Oxford University Press, 2014), 86 (arguing that Fitzmaurice's article in particular was 'very influential' and, indeed, that the wider acceptance of the persistent objector rule in scholarship was 'the result' of this publication).

[22] See Kelly, n. 9, 513–15.

[23] See, for example, Brownlie, n. 11, 8; Fitzmaurice, n. 19, 24–6; E. Lauterpacht (ed.), *International Law, Being the Collected Papers of Hersch Lauterpacht, vol. I: The General Works* (Cambridge, Cambridge University Press, 1970), 66; J.H.W. Verzijl, *International Law in Historical Perspective, vol. I: General Subjects* (Utrecht, A.W. Sijthoff, 1968), 37–8; and Waldock, n. 20, 49–53.

[24] ILA Final Report, n. 3, 27, footnote 68.

Can a nation abolish the immunities of ambassadors, which they are enjoying in accordance with the common law of the nations? ... [I]t can if it makes a public announcement in regard to them, because these immunities owe such validity as they have not to any law but only to a tacit presumption. One nation does not bind another, and not even a consensus of all nations except one binds that one, isolated though it be, if it is independent and has decreed to use other laws ... The law of nations is nothing but a presumption based on custom, nor has this presumption any validity in the face of *a definitely expressed wish on the part of him who is concerned*.[25]

This notion—that a dissenting state can gain exemption through expressing its will not to be bound by customary international law—certainly looks rather like a description of the persistent objector rule. Having said this, the usual elements of the rule (persistence, consistency, timeliness) are not present in Bynkershoek's formulation: there is no evidence that he felt that the dissenting state's 'public announcement' needed to be repeated or made before the norm became binding on that state. It is quite possible, therefore, that Bynkershoek was in fact endorsing unilateral exit by a state to *established* customary international law norms (i.e. what would today be termed 'subsequent objection').[26]

Although the ILA Committee did not reference his work, one might similarly point to[27] Emmerich de Vattel's endorsement of something at least akin to the persistent objector rule in 1758:

When a custom or usage is generally established ... between all the civilized nations in the world ... it becomes obligatory on all the nations in question, who are considered as having giving their consent to it, and are bound to observe it towards each other, *as long as they have not expressly* declared their resolution of not observing it in future.[28]

Like Bynkershoek, Vattel included the notion of an 'express declaration' in his version of the mechanism for withdrawal from customary international law. Again like Bynkershoek, however, Vattel made no reference to the criteria of persistence, consistency, or timeliness.

It is also worth noting Georg Friedrich von Martens' contention, from 1788, that:

As to rights founded on simple custom, each power may discontinue them whenever it makes a timely declaration, either express or tacit of its intention so to do. Such rights may also cease by giving place to others, established by the mutual will of the nations

[25] C. van Bynkershoek, *De Foro Legatorum Liber Singularis: A Monograph on the Jurisdiction over Ambassadors in both Civil and Criminal Cases* (G.J. Laing (trans.), Oxford, Clarendon Press, 1946 (1721/2nd edn, 1744)), chapter XIX, 106–7, emphasis added.

[26] This is the interpretation of Bynkershoek's position that is taken by Bradley and Gulati, n. 10, 217, footnote 57 and 239, footnote 161.

[27] See F.F. Martin, *The Constitution as Treaty: The International Legal Constructionalist Approach to the U.S. Constitution* (Cambridge, Cambridge University Press, 2007), 76 (viewing this passage from Vattel's work as a clear eighteenth-century endorsement of the persistent objector rule).

[28] E. de Vattel, *The Law of Nations, or Principles of the Law of Nature Applied to the Conduct and Affairs of Nations and Sovereigns* (J. Chitty (ed.), Philadelphia, T & J.W. Johnson, 6th American edn, 1844 (1758)), preliminaries, lxv, para. 26, emphasis in original.

concerned: but this change made by some powers cannot oblige other powers to change their conduct.[29]

As with those of Bynkershoek and Vattel, Martens' formulation looks somewhat like a description of persistent objection, albeit that any reference to 'persistence' or 'consistency' is again absent. Yet Martens did include the need for 'a timely declaration',[30] which could be seen as an endorsement of the need for objection prior to crystallization. Again, however, this could just as easily be read as indicating that the state must provide a reasonable notice period for withdrawal from already established custom,[31] especially given Martens' use of the word 'whenever'.[32]

It is ultimately something of a stretch to identify the persistent objector rule per se in the eighteenth-century writings of scholars such as Bynkershoek, Vattel, or Martens; these theorists did not endorse the rule as we know it. To an extent, then, it may be said that 'classic consensualists, while referring to consent, ma[de] no reference to the persistent objector rule',[33] at least as we understand it today. Equally, the writings of such scholars show that a broad concept of state exit from the binding force of customary international law in a manner *akin* to persistent objection actually has significant historical pedigree in scholarly doctrine.

Rather more recently, the same general notion of exemption by an individual state to binding customary international law can be identified in various writings from the early twentieth century.[34] Indeed, in some cases, one can undoubtedly identify rudimentary expressions of the modern persistent objector rule from this period: François, for example, wrote in 1938 that '[l]a règle coutumière ne devra pas être invoquée à l'égard d'un Etat qui, d'une manière permanente et expresse, s'est toujours opposé formellement à son acceptation'.[35] Nonetheless, as with their eighteenth-century counterparts, most of the early twentieth-century writings do not seem to identify the persistent objector rule *as such*, but rather a nebulous conceptual precursor to it. Strupp, for example, identified in 1934 a 'rebuttable presumption' that states would be bound by customary international law irrespective of their specific consent, but then did not go on to set out the required nature and form that such a rebuttal would (or must) take, other than that 'l'Etat défendeur ne puisse prouver qu'il ne l'a jamais accepté [the norm in question]'.[36]

[29] G.F. von Martens, *A Compendium of the Law of Nations, Founded on the Treaties and Customs of the Modern Nations of Europe* (W. Cobbett (trans.), London, Cobbett and Morgan, 1802 (1788)), 356.

[30] Ibid.

[31] Again, this is the interpretation of Martens' position that is taken by Bradley and Gulati, n. 10, 217, footnote 57.

[32] Martens, n. 29, 356.

[33] Elias and Lim, n. 3, 33.

[34] Although others at this time took the view that customary international law formation did not require universal consent, and that there *was no* right of opt-out for dissenters. See, for example, J. Basdevant, 'Règles générales du droit de la paix' (1936-IV) 58 *Recueil des cours* 471, 512, including footnote 3.

[35] J-P-A. François, 'Règles générales du droit de la paix' (1938) 66 *Recueil des cours* 1, 175. See also C. de Visscher, 'La codification du droit international' (1925) 6 *Recueil des cours* 328, 363.

[36] K. Strupp, 'Les règles générales du droit de la paix' (1934) 47 *Recueil des cours* 258, 310–11.

Overall, one would be hard pressed to argue that the 'modern' persistent objector rule existed as an accepted element of international law theory in the writings of scholars much before 1945, or even the early 1950s.[37] Equally, one should keep in mind the fact that the seeds of the rule's emergence stretch back significantly further in international legal theory, to at least the eighteenth century, and that a more general notion of state exemption from customary international law through protest is well embedded in historical doctrine.

II. The Persistent Objector Rule in Pre-1945 Case Law

Moving beyond academic scholarship, a number of judicial and arbitral decisions of the nineteenth and (very) early twentieth centuries have been cited by supporters of the persistent objector rule as providing evidence of the existence of the rule during that period.

For example, the 1817 case of *The Louis*[38] has been seen as a judicial endorsement of the persistent objector rule.[39] In that decision, Sir William Scott, as senior judge in the High Court of Admiralty, considered inter alia whether France was bound under international law by a prohibition of the slave trade. He concluded that, while many states had indeed abolished the practice, there was no prohibition of the slave trade that was opposable to France, because France had rejected any such prohibition.[40] To an extent, therefore, it is possible to identify something that looks reminiscent of the modern persistent objector rule within *The Louis* decision: a state was considered able to remain 'exempt' from a prohibition that the majority of states had accepted.

Equally, the link between *The Louis* case and the modern concept of persistent objection is tenuous. There is nothing in the decision to suggest that Scott accepted the general customary status of the prohibition of the slave trade in the first instance (indeed, one can more easily infer that he did not).[41] His reasoning concerning the non-opposability of the increased abolition of the slave trade against France was actually primarily based on the general right of the French crew to enjoy the freedom of the high seas,[42] which would only have been restricted if France had accepted a limitation of this right by way of treaty.[43] In other words, the approach in *The Louis* ultimately looks rather more like an extreme version of the voluntarist theory (i.e. states must *explicitly consent* to an international legal

[37] See M.P. Scharf, *Customary International Law in Times of Fundamental Change: Recognizing Grotian Moments* (Cambridge, Cambridge University Press, reissue, 2013), 41; and E.T. Swaine, 'Bespoke Custom' (2010) 21 *Duke Journal of Comparative and International Law* 207, 213.

[38] A Report of the Case of *The Louis, Forest, Master*, 1817, appealed from the Vice Admiralty Court at Sierra Leone, and determined in the High Court of Admiralty (J. Dodson, London, Butterworths, 1817).

[39] M.H. Mendelson, 'The Formation of Customary International Law' (1998) 272 *Recueil des cours* 155, 233.

[40] *The Louis*, n. 38, 48–52.

[41] See, for example, ibid., 49.

[42] Ibid., particularly at 9 and 49.

[43] Ibid., 50–6.

norm before they can be considered bound by it), rather than 'persistent objection' as we would understand it today.

A similar story emerges when one considers the 1825 decision of the United States Supreme Court in *The Antelope* case,[44] which, again, some writers have cited as an endorsement of the persistent objector rule.[45] *The Antelope* concerned the question of whether the arrest by United States officials of a Spanish slaving vessel was lawful.[46] As with *The Louis*, the case turned on whether the slave trade itself was a violation of international law (on the basis that if it was not, then the seizure would, in turn, be unlawful).[47] In his decision Marshall CJ took the view that, while a majority of states had prohibited the practice of slaving, those states that had *not* accepted the prohibition were not in violation of international law by trading in slaves.[48] Thus, once more, there are perhaps elements of something akin to the persistent objector rule that can be broadly discerned from the decision. However, while Marshall CJ seemed to imply that there may be a customary international law prohibition of the slave trade (unlike Sir William Scott in *The Louis*), he ultimately still focused on the minority group's lack of explicit *acceptance* of the prohibition: '[t]hat which has received *the assent* of all must be the law of all.'[49]

Even more of a stretch is the claim that persistent objector rule was endorsed in the 1900 *Paquete Habana* judgment of the United States Supreme Court.[50] The *Paquete Habana* decision,[51] of course, is famous for the Supreme Court's pronouncements on the relationship between international law and American domestic law.[52] In the more specific context of persistent objection, though, one might point to the fact that the Court concluded that customary international law was binding based on the '*general consent* of the civilized nations of the world'[53] and, then, that customary international law was *only* binding on the United States 'where there is no treaty, and no controlling executive or legislative act or judicial decision' contrary to it.[54] By combining these two pronouncements—general consent as the basis for customary international law binding on all, *unless* contrary domestic law exists—it could, perhaps, be argued that the Court envisaged that the United States could exempt itself from custom that would be otherwise binding on it without its explicit consent, through specific contrary actions (which

[44] *The Antelope*, 1825, 23 U.S. 10 Wheat. 66, appeal from the Circuit Court of Georgia, per Marshall CJ.

[45] W.W. Bishop, 'General Course on Public International Law' (1965-II) 115 *Recueil des cours* 151, 226–7 (at least implicitly); Martin, n. 27, 76; and Mendelson, n. 39, 232–3.

[46] *The Antelope*, n. 44, 66–7. [47] Ibid., 122. [48] Ibid., particularly at 121–2.

[49] Ibid., 121, emphasis added. It is perhaps telling that Marshall CJ significantly relied on the *The Louis* judgment to reach his decision in *The Antelope*; ibid., 18–20.

[50] See E.L. Chalecki, 'Science before the Law: American Exceptionalism in the Kyoto Protocol and the Development of a Global Norm of Environmental Compliance' (2007) *Selected Works*, http://works.bepress.com/cgi/viewcontent.cgi?article=1000&context=elizabeth_chalecki, 19, footnote 45 (making this claim without pointing out specifically how the Court endorsed it or where in its judgement it did so).

[51] *Paquete Habana*, 1900, 175 U.S. 677. [52] Ibid., particularly at 700.

[53] Ibid., 667, emphasis added. [54] Ibid., 700.

might look a bit like the persistent objector rule).[55] The intention of the Court in relation to its apparent conclusion that contrary domestic law trumped customary international law is far from clear, however,[56] and it is just as likely that the Court was simply further considering the implications of the incorporation of customary international law into American domestic law. Overall, the claim that the persistent objector rule was endorsed in *Paquete Habana* simply cannot be supported.

Finally, another potential 'early' instance of the jurisprudential recognition of the persistent objector rule[57] is the 1903 *Fischbach and Friedricy* cases decided by the Germany-Venezuela Mixed Claims Commission.[58] The cases concerned two German nationals who were taken prisoner, assaulted, and had their property stolen by revolutionaries in 1902, during one of the Venezuelan civil wars of the late 1800s/early 1900s.[59] At issue, inter alia, was whether Venezuela was legally responsible not only for property seized by government forces, but also for seizures by revolutionaries. In relation to Venezuela's contention that international law did not prescribe state responsibility for seizure by revolutionary forces in this way, Umpire Duffield stated that 'Obedience to [international law] is voluntary only and can not be enforced by a common sovereign power. *Any nation has the power and the right to dissent from a rule or principle of international law, even though it is accepted by all the other nations*'.[60]

This could arguably be seen as an invocation of the persistent objector rule. However, as Dumberry points out,[61] Umpire Duffield nonetheless concluded that 'substantially all the authorities on international law agree that a nation *is responsible* for acts of revolutionists under certain conditions … [and, as such] [*t*]*here is* a rule of international law under which Venezuela would be held liable in certain cases for acts of revolutionists'.[62]

In other words, Venezuela's 'right to dissent' did not avail it in exempting itself from the reach of the customary international law obligation identified.[63] It is worth noting that the Umpire had already concluded that Venezuela had accepted responsibility for the actions of the revolutionaries by way of the 1903 Protocol that it had signed with Germany,[64] and that this was sufficient to uphold Germany's claim in

[55] Bradley and Gulati, n. 10, 223–5 (arguing something along these lines, at least as a possible reading of these combined pronouncements, although actually identifying this as the Court advocating a general right of withdrawal, including post-crystallization, rather than an invocation of the persistent objector rule).

[56] See, for example, M.J. Glennon, 'Raising *The Paquete Habana*: Is Violation of Customary International Law by the Executive Unconstitutional?' (1985–6) 80 *Northwestern University Law Review* 321.

[57] Cited as such by both O. Elias, 'Persistent Objector' in R. Wolfrum (ed.), *Max Planck Encyclopaedia of Public International Law, vol. VIII* (Oxford, Oxford University Press, 2012), 280, 283, para. 14; and Mendelson, n. 39, 232.

[58] *Fischbach and Friedricy* cases, Germany-Venezuela Mixed Claims Commission, 1903, 10 RIAA 357.

[59] Ibid., 388–9. [60] Ibid., 397, emphasis added. [61] Dumberry, n. 13, 787.

[62] *Fischbach and Friedricy* cases, n. 58, 397–8, emphasis in original.

[63] Dumberry, n. 13, 787.

[64] Protocol between Germany and Venezuela for the Reference of Certain Questions to the Permanent Court of Arbitration at The Hague, 1903, English-language version of the text reproduced in (1908) 2 *American Journal of International Law* 905.

any event.[65] For Dumberry, the fact that the Umpire read the Protocol as evidencing Venezuela's acceptance of responsibility is further confirmation of the view that the persistent objector rule was not in fact invoked in the decision, on the basis that he otherwise would have interpreted it differently.[66] This is certainly a possible reading, although one could equally interpret the Umpire's determination as an indication of *inconsistent* objection[67] on the part of Venezuela, or simply a revocation of persistent objector status, which would mean that its persistent objections (if, indeed, they were truly persistent, which is also unclear) were no longer relevant.

Either way, it is again evident that the decision provides, at most, limited support for the persistent objector rule. Umpire Duffield only identified a broad right of exemption through dissent, without referencing the various contours—persistence, consistency, timeliness—of the modern rule.[68] Even then, he endorsed this right in something of an abstract manner, given that he ultimately nonetheless found Venezuela to be in breach of the norm in question.

As with the persistent objector rule's pedigree in the literature, then, when one tries to identify the rule in jurisprudence prior to the Second World War, the picture that emerges is a mixed one. It is, in the view of this writer, not possible to find judicial endorsement of the rule as such before 1945. Equally, there are a number of decisions that point to an emerging acceptance in the nineteenth and early twentieth centuries of the general concept of a state's exit from the binding force of a norm of customary international law by way of its expressed dissent.

III. The Persistent Objector Rule in Pre-1945 State Practice

It is similarly difficult to identify the persistent objector rule as understood today, or even something that looks all that much like it, in the actual *practice* of states prior to the Second World War. This fact, beyond the rule's pre-1945 emergence in case law and scholarship (to the extent that this can be identified either), is obviously crucial given that there ultimately must have been some degree of state acceptance/usage of the rule to conclude that it 'existed' or 'emerged' in this period. This is not to say that the relationship between state 'protest' and 'acquiescence' was anything other than an important element in determining the opposability of international law to states in the nineteenth and early twentieth centuries.[69] The importance of protest was deeply rooted in state practice at that time, as can clearly be seen, for example, in the context of disputes over territorial acquisition by prescription.[70] Here, again, lie the roots of the persistent objector rule, not just in theory but in practice.

[65] *Fischbach and Friedricy* cases, n. 58, 397.

[66] Dumberry, n. 13, 787.

[67] See Chapter 5 regarding the requirement of consistent objection.

[68] Dumberry, n. 13, 786–7.

[69] See, generally, I. MacGibbon, 'Some Observations on the Part of Protest in International Law' (1953) 30 *British Yearbook of International Law* 293 (providing a number of examples).

[70] See, generally, D.H.N. Johnson 'Acquisitive Prescription in International Law' (1950) 22 *British Yearbook of International Law* 332.

There are, however, almost no instances of pre-1945 state protest that can be considered 'persistent objection' proper. One potential early example of state usage of the persistent objector rule[71] may perhaps be the rejection by the United Kingdom of the immunity of neutral vessels from search under right of convoy.[72] The norm that Britain protested against was enshrined in Article 61 of the 1909 London Declaration Concerning the Laws of Naval War,[73] which famously never entered into force. The United Kingdom continued to exercise its belligerent right of visit irrespective of the purported customary international law norm—reflecting Article 61 of the Declaration—which insulated merchant vessels under convoy from this practice, and Britain's right to do so seemingly went uncontested by other states.[74] This can probably be considered an instance of 'persistent objection' in the modern sense. The British protests occurred before any 'crystallization' of the norm being objected to,[75] were notably repeated (particularly by way of deed, in that the United Kingdom actually *practised* the right of visit in this way),[76] and were maintained well into the second half of the twentieth century.[77]

Yet if the British exemption in relation to naval convoy is accepted as a true pre-1945 state usage of the persistent objector rule in practice, it is a pretty lonely one. One might perhaps also consider the fact that Scandinavian states effectively maintained a 4-mile exclusive fishing zone throughout the early twentieth century, contrary to the increasingly accepted 3-mile limit, as an instance of pre-1945 persistent objection.[78] Whether the 3-mile limit actually crystallized as customary international law in the relevant period is doubtful, however,[79] and it is also possible that any 'exemption' for these states was rooted in prescriptive title rather than persistent objection.[80] It would be something of a stretch to view this as another pre-1945 instance of persistent objection. Moreover, even if such examples are taken as 'early' persistent objection, they fall some way short of providing enough evidence for one to be able to assert that persistent objection was an 'accepted' secondary rule of international law based on state practice (notwithstanding the fact that the usage of related principles, such as 'protest' to

[71] As argued by Verzijl, n. 23, 37–8.

[72] A. Gioia and N. Ronzitti, 'The Law of Neutrality: Third States' Commercial Rights and Duties' in I.F. Dekker and H.H.G. Post (eds), *The Gulf War of 1980–1988: The Iran–Iraq War in International Perspective* (Dordrecht, Martinus Nijhoff, 1992), 221, 237.

[73] Declaration Concerning the Laws of Naval War, 1909, 208 Consol. T.S. 338 (not in force).

[74] Verzijl, n. 23, 37–8.

[75] See R.W. Tucker, *The Law of War and Neutrality at Sea* (Washington, US Government Print Office, 1955), 401–2, footnote 10.

[76] Verzijl, n. 23, 37–8.

[77] Gioia and Ronzitti, n. 72, 237.

[78] See *Third Restatement*, n. 14, 'Reporter's Note' commentary to Section 102, Comment (d) (arguing that the maintenance of a 4-mile jurisdiction by Scandinavian states constitutes an example of persistent objection in practice).

[79] For example, given that no agreement could be reached by states—which were asserting various contrary limits—at the Hague Conference for the Codification of International Law in 1930. See L.S. Parson, *Management of Marine Fisheries in Canada* (Ottawa, National Research Council of Canada, 1993), 223–4. See also Charney, n. 2, 15.

[80] Ibid., 15–16; and I. MacGibbon, 'Customary International Law and Acquiescence' (1957) 33 *British Yearbook of International Law* 115, 122.

assert and maintain rights—especially territorial rights, and rights of navigation and passage—was commonplace).

IV. Conclusion

This chapter has indicated that the critics of the persistent objector rule are broadly correct in asserting that there is comparatively little evidence that the persistent objector rule, as ubiquitously presented today, existed prior to 1945 (be it as a matter of scholarly doctrine, jurisprudence, or—particularly and crucially—in state practice). To argue that the rule 'existed' in its modern incarnation as an accepted secondary norm of the international legal system prior to 1945 would, in the view of the present author, be incorrect.

However, the critique of the 'historical legitimacy' of persistent objection has also been overstated. Supporters of the rule who have tried to root it in the nineteenth century may not have been able to make a convincing case that the modern rule existed in this period, but this is not to say that it has no historical basis: claims that the rule suddenly 'sprang up' in the mid-twentieth century, as a new academic construct, are just as difficult to support as claims that the rule has existed for centuries. Elements underpinning the persistent objector rule—notions such as the role of protest in determining legal obligation and the general possibility of withdrawal from, or non-consent to, customary international law norms—can be identified in pre-1945 case law, scholarship, and even, to some limited degree, state practice. Thus, while the persistent objector rule did not exist in international law in the nineteenth century, the *seeds* of persistent objection (conceptual and practical) as we now understand it certainly did.

As we have seen, some critics of the persistent objector rule have made much of its (comparative) lack of historical pedigree. However, ultimately one might ask why 'historical pedigree' should be viewed as being in any way determinative as to the rule's existence today. Just because a secondary rule is not 'old' does not mean that it is not *valid*. It has already been noted, in the Introduction, that the secondary rules of international law have emerged at various points in the system's development.[81] Social practice changes, as does the social acceptance of law-making procedures: one need only consider the late nineteenth-century emergence of the concept of *opinio juris* to see this in the international legal context.[82] Nonetheless, as argued previously, the modern persistent objector rule cannot be seen as having existed prior to 1945, albeit that the seeds of it can. The key question, then, is whether the rule has been accepted in the social practice of the international legal system *since*: did those nineteenth-century seeds grow into a secondary rule of international law? Chapter 2 will focus on this question.

[81] See, in particular, Introduction, section IV, n. 64–n. 71 and accompanying text.
[82] As discussed in ibid., section IV, n. 69–n. 71 and accompanying text.

2

The Persistent Objector Rule in Case Law and State Practice Post-1945

In Chapter 1, it was argued that while the 'roots' of the persistent objector rule can be traced back well before 1945, there is insufficient evidence to assert that the rule in its modern incarnation had emerged prior to the Second World War. As such, if the rule exists, it has to be viewed as a 'modern' normative development. This chapter continues the assessment of the legal status of the rule by examining its basis in post-1945 case law and post-1945 state practice and *opinio juris*. The overwhelming support for the existence of the persistent objector rule in modern academic doctrine[1]—while being relevant to, and indicative of, the emergence of the rule—cannot be viewed as enough to constitute the rule as a matter of international law in itself.

Moreover, one of the most common justifications advanced for the existence of the persistent objector rule can be quickly dismissed at the outset of this chapter, based on the inductive 'social acceptance' positivist approach taken in this book.[2] To the extent that supporters of the rule seek to justify its existence at all, a number have essentially argued that the rule exists because it plays a crucial role in preserving the voluntarist conception of international law creation and obligation.[3] This is on the basis that the rule provides a means for states to withhold consent to the formation of customary international law norms, which would otherwise be binding on the state (on the understanding that 'silence' is considered tacit consent). Leaving aside the fact that this author rejects the voluntarist understanding of international law in any event, at least in its absolute form, it is important to note that those who justify the persistent objector rule's existence in this way are merely asserting that the persistent objector rule exists because it is *desirable* for it to exist (in that it purportedly plugs a notable hole in the voluntarist understanding of the international legal system). The desirability of the persistent objector rule is, of course, crucial, and the role(s) that it does, or might, fulfil will be considered throughout this book and will be particularly examined in Chapter 9. However, the rule's possible role(s) ultimately have no

[1] See Introduction, section I, n. 16–n. 25 and accompanying text.

[2] See ibid., sections IV and V.

[3] See writers cited in Chapter 9, n. 24 and n. 25.

bearing on whether it exists as a rule of the international legal system, only on whether it *should* exist.[4]

To exist, the persistent objector rule must have a basis in practice and jurisprudence, and, given that limited evidence can be found to underpin the rule pre-1945, it must have a basis in *recent* practice and jurisprudence. Section I of this chapter therefore examines the persistent objector rule in post-1945 case law: i.e. the reference to and use of the rule in courts and tribunals (both international and domestic). In particular, it focuses on the two oft-cited authorities for persistent objection, the International Court of Justice (ICJ) judgments in the *Asylum* case (*Columbia v Peru*)[5] and the *Fisheries* case (*United Kingdom v Norway*),[6] both of which were decided in the 1950s. Section I engages with critiques of the 'value' of these cases in terms of underpinning the rule. It also goes beyond these two decisions, however, to explore other relevant judicial and arbitral authorities. Section II then considers the crucial question of whether there exists support for the rule in post-1945 state practice. The section sets out some examples of state invocation and usage of the rule to establish its modern existence, although it should be noted that more (and more detailed) practice will be examined throughout subsequent chapters.

I. The Persistent Objector Rule in the Decisions of Courts and Tribunals After 1945

i. The *Asylum* and *Fisheries* cases as leading authorities

The obvious starting point from which to begin to assess the legal basis of the persistent objector rule post-1945 are two contentious merits decisions of the ICJ: *Asylum* and *Fisheries*. The reason that these cases are—almost by necessity—our first port of call is because, to the extent that commentators make any attempt to support or justify the existence of the persistent objector rule, they most commonly do so by reference to these decisions. Indeed, scholarly discussion of persistent objection almost inevitably uses the *Asylum* and *Fisheries* cases as touchstones. In his seminal 1985 article on the persistent objector rule, Stein correctly noted that '[m]ost of the [scholarly] authorities ... content ... themselves with citing these two decisions as proof of the existence of the persistent objector principle',[7]

[4] See *Committee on Formation of Customary (General) International Law*, Final Report of the Committee, 'Statement of Principles Applicable to the Formation of General Customary International Law', International Law Association, London Conference (2000), http://www.ila-hq.org/en/committees/index.cfm/cid/30, 4 (adopting an inductive method, as does this book, and thus arguing that 'the question of whether there is a "persistent objector" rule is to be determined by reference to the practice of States, not to an a priori method of reasoning'; references omitted).

[5] *Asylum* (*Columbia v Peru*), merits, 1950 ICJ Rep. 266.

[6] *Fisheries* (*United Kingdom v Norway*), merits, 1951 ICJ Rep. 116.

[7] T.L. Stein, 'The Approach of the Different Drummer: The Principle of the Persistent Objector in International Law' (1985) 26 *Harvard International Law Journal* 457, 460. See also C.A. Bradley and M. Gulati, 'Withdrawing from International Custom' (2010) 120 *Yale Law Journal* 202, 234; and H. Meijers, 'How is International Law Made?—The Stages of Growth of International Law and the Use of Customary Rules' (1978) 9 *Netherlands Yearbook of International Law* 3, 22.

while Kelly—a notable critic of the rule—has more bluntly asserted that '[s]upporters of the principle [of persistent objection] cite the *Fisheries* and *Asylum* cases *as their lone evidence*'.[8] Kelly's claim here is unquestionably an overstatement but it is nonetheless undeniable that the two ICJ cases are continually referenced to underpin the persistent objector rule, almost by rote. Equally, critics of the rule, while being notably fewer in number, have also spilt significant ink attempting to rebut the presumed 'value' of these two decisions in underpinning the notion of persistent objection.[9] As such, the cases need to be considered rather carefully.

The *Asylum* case concerned Colombia's decision to grant diplomatic asylum, on 3 January 1949, to Víctor Raúl Haya de la Torre, who was the head of a political party (the American People's Revolutionary Alliance) in Peru.[10] It was claimed by Peru that Haya de la Torre had committed the crime of 'military rebellion',[11] and Colombia asserted that it was entitled to grant asylum to Haya de la Torre, on the basis that he constituted a political offender.[12] Moreover, Colombia argued before the ICJ that, based on various treaties[13] and—importantly for present purposes—under a 'regional or local custom peculiar to Latin-American States',[14] it was entitled to qualify the nature of Haya de la Torre's offence (as being political) for the purposes of granting asylum. By contrast, Peru took the view that Haya de la Torre had committed common crimes and was thus not entitled to enjoy the benefits of asylum,[15] and, further, that it was not bound under international law to defer to Colombia's determination as to his status as a political offender.[16]

[8] J.P. Kelly, 'The Twilight of Customary International Law' (1999–2000) 40 *Virginia Journal of International Law* 449, 512, emphasis added.

[9] See, generally, for example, Bradley and Gulati, n. 7, 234–5; J.I. Charney, 'The Persistent Objector Rule and the Development of Customary International Law' (1985) 56 *British Yearbook of International Law* 1, 9–11; J.I. Charney, 'Universal International Law' (1993) 87 *American Journal of International Law* 529, 539–40; B. Conforti, 'Cours général de droit international public' (1988-V) 212 *Recueil des cours* 13, 75; A. D'Amato, *The Concept of Custom in International Law* (New York, Cornell University Press, 1971), particularly at 233–63; P. Dumberry, 'Incoherent and Ineffective: The Concept of Persistent Objector Revisited' (2010) 59 *International and Comparative Law Quarterly* 779, 785–90; Kelly, n. 8, 512–13; C. Tomuschat, 'Obligations Arising for States Without or Against Their Will' (1993) 241 *Recueil des cours* 195, 284–7; and P. Weil, 'Le droit international en quête de son identité—Cours général de droit international public' (1992-VI) 237 *Recueil des cours* 9, 192.

[10] See *Asylum*, merits, n. 5, 272–3.

[11] *Asylum* (*Columbia v Peru*), counter-memorial submitted by the Government of the Republic of Peru, 1950 ICJ Plead., 116.

[12] See, for example, *Asylum* (*Columbia v Peru*), memorial submitted by the Government of the Republic of Colombia, 1950 ICJ Plead., 45 (reproducing the letter sent by the Colombian Ambassador in Lima: 'Víctor Raúl Haya de la Torre comme réfugié politique').

[13] Specifically the Bolivarian Agreement on Extradition, 18 July 1911, Law 26 of 1913; the Convention on Asylum, Havana, 20 February 1928, OAS Official Records, OEA/Ser.X/I. TS 34; and the Convention on Political Asylum, Montevideo, 26 December 1933, Seventh International *Conference of American States*, 6 Hudson 597. See *Asylum*, memorial submitted by Colombia, n. 12, 17.

[14] *Asylum*, merits, n. 5, 276. Colombia repeatedly argued that there existed 'd'une façon générale, du droit international américain' to this effect. See *Asylum*, memorial submitted by Colombia, n. 12, 17, 19, 32, 37, and 43.

[15] See, for example, *Asylum*, counter-memorial submitted by Perun. 11, 154.

[16] See, for example, ibid., 118.

The ICJ determined, in its merits decision of 20 November 1950, that Colombia had not established the existence of a right, opposable to Peru, to determine that the offence in question qualified for asylum, either in conventional[17] or—again, importantly in our context—customary international law.[18] However, the Court then went on to say:

[E]ven if it could be supposed that such a custom existed between certain Latin-American States only, it could not be invoked against Peru which, far from having by its attitude adhered to it, has, on the contrary, repudiated it by refraining from ratifying the Montevideo Conventions of 1933 and 1939, which were the first to include a rule concerning the qualification of the offence in matters of diplomatic asylum.[19]

This unquestionably vague statement is commonly referenced as the first invocation by the ICJ of the persistent objector rule.

The second oft-cited decision of the Court in the context of persistent objection is the *Fisheries* case, which concerned whether Norway's system for delimitating the baselines of its territorial sea—which restricted the ability for British trawlers to fish off the Norwegian coast[20]—was in violation of international law. The United Kingdom, as applicant, argued that Norwegian baselines were inconsistent with customary international law, inter alia, because there was 'a general [customary] rule for the defining of inlets which may be claimed as national waters' restricting the length of straight lines across bays to 10 nautical miles (the so-called '10-mile rule').[21]

The ICJ concluded, in its judgment of 18 December 1951, that the 10-mile rule advocated by the United Kingdom had not acquired the status of a binding customary international law norm, as there was insufficient state practice and *opinio juris* to support its crystallization.[22] However, the Court then appeared to take the view that Norway was nonetheless an exempt persistent objector state:

[A]lthough the ten-mile rule has been adopted by certain States both in their national law and in their treaties and conventions, and although certain arbitral decisions have applied it as between these States, other States have adopted a different limit. Consequently, the ten-mile rule has not acquired the authority of a general rule of international law.

In any event the ten-mile rule would appear to be inapplicable as against Norway *inasmuch as she has always opposed any attempt to apply it to the Norwegian coast.*[23]

This passage of the ICJ's *Fisheries* merits decision 'is widely regarded as the *leading* authority for the persistent objector principle'.[24]

[17] *Asylum*, merits, n. 5, 274–6. For a dissection of the Court's reasoning in rejecting Colombia's contention that various treaties provided it with the right to qualify the nature of Haya de la Torre's offence, see C. Quince, *The Persistent Objector and Customary International Law* (Denver, Outskirts Press, 2010), 53–6.

[18] *Asylum*, merits, n. 5, 276–7.

[19] Ibid., 277–8.

[20] *Fisheries*, merits, n. 5, 124–6.

[21] See, generally, *Fisheries* (*United Kingdom v Norway*), memorial submitted by the Government of the United Kingdom of Great Britain and Northern Ireland, 1950 ICJ Plead., vol. I, quoted at 25.

[22] *Fisheries*, merits, n. 5, particularly at 130–1.

[23] Ibid., 131, emphasis added.

[24] O. Elias, 'Persistent Objector' in R. Wolfrum (ed.), *Max Planck Encyclopaedia of Public International Law, vol. VIII* (Oxford, Oxford University Press, 2012), 280, 283, para. 12, emphasis

ii. Critiques of the authority provided by the *Asylum* and *Fisheries* cases

While the majority of writers on persistent objection have regularly cited the *Fisheries* and *Asylum* cases over the last sixty-plus years to evidence the rule, as was noted above, a (vocal) minority of scholars have questioned the extent to which these cases provide any genuine support for it. For example, much has been made of the fact that the apparently relevant pronouncements of the ICJ were not ultimately determinative as to the decision in question in either case. The argument here is that the Court had, in both judgments, already found that the purported norm of customary international law being objected to did not exist. In other words, it has been argued that judicial support for the persistent objector rule by the ICJ has been *obiter dicta*, at best, and that this therefore 'undermines the value' of the decisions as 'solid judicial precedent[s] in support of the concept of persistent objector'.[25]

In response to this critique, Mendelson has argued that it is far from self-evident that the pronouncements of the ICJ (that both Peru and Norway were exempt individually from the norms in question) were necessarily 'secondary' *dicta* when compared to the other conclusion that was reached in both cases (that no binding norm—on asylum and the 10-mile rule, respectively—had emerged in custom at all).[26] Mendelson's point is that the fact that the Court made the 'no rule at all' finding before the 'persistent objector' finding in each case can be viewed as a coincidence of ordering: the Court could just as easily have said that (a) Peru/Norway was a persistent objector state; and (b) there was no customary norm anyway.

It is difficult to support Mendelson's argument here, because the timeline of the persistent objector rule's operation is that it takes effect only once the customary international law norm in question has crystallized, albeit that the objection itself must occur prior to this.[27] As such, it would have been less logical (if, admittedly, not exactly irrational) for the Court to have addressed the issues in the

added. See also M. Ragazzi, *The Concept of International Obligations* Erga Omnes (Oxford, Oxford University Press, 1997), 60.

[25] Dumberry, n. 9, 785 (discussing only *Fisheries*). See also M. Bos, *A Methodology of International Law* (Amsterdam, TMC Asser, 1984), 251–2; Bradley and Gulati, n. 7, 235; Charney, 'The Persistent Objector Rule', n. 9, 9; Charney, 'Universal International Law', n. 9, 540; Conforti, n. 9, 75; F. Ingman, 'Persistent Objector—The Demise of a Hero?' (2008), unpublished Masters thesis, Lund University, http://lup.lub.lu.se/luur/download?func=downloadFile&recordOId=1558532&fileOId=1564685, 48 (discussing only *Fisheries*); Kelly, n. 8, 512; Stein, n. 7, 460, footnote 7; A. Steinfeld, 'Nuclear Objections: The Persistent Objector and the Legality of the Use of Nuclear Weapons' (1996) 62 *Brooklyn Law Review* 1635, 1653; Tomuschat, n. 9, 286–7; P-H. Verdier and E. Voeten, 'Precedent, Compliance, and Change in Customary International Law: An Explanatory Theory' (2014) 108 *American Journal of International Law* 389, 428; and Weil, n. 9, 192.

[26] M.H. Mendelson, 'The Formation of Customary International Law' (1998) 272 *Recueil des cours* 155, 230.

[27] See Chapter 6, section IV on the 'timeline' of the persistent objector rule, and Chapter 6 in general regarding the requirement for objection before the norm being objected to has crystallized.

manner proposed by Mendelson in either case. Perhaps more tellingly, a quick glance at the language used in the relevant pronouncements of the Court in each of the cases makes it pretty clear that they were secondary, buttressing conclusions (*Asylum*: '*even if it could be supposed* that such a custom existed...'/*Fisheries*: '[*i*]*n any event* the ten-mile rule would appear to be inapplicable as against Norway...').[28]

However, while it is fairly clear that neither the *Fisheries* case nor the *Asylum* case were decided on the basis of the persistent objector rule, it is unclear what *difference* this fact makes in terms of assessing the value of the cases as authorities for the rule. A (much more convincing) additional argument made by Mendelson,[29] as well as by Elias,[30] is that the concept of '*obiter dicta*' has little meaning in the international legal system, which does not—of course—recognize a doctrine of binding judicial precedent. Moreover, even in domestic common law jurisdictions, where a distinction between *obiter dicta* and *ratio decidendi* is much more pertinent, making that distinction is often problematic.[31] The pronouncements of the ICJ in the two cases in question are ultimately of the same subsequent authority whether or not they were determinative for the decision made at the time.[32] At least in terms of their '*obiter dicta*' nature, then, 'the legal significance of these passages should not so easily be dismissed'.[33]

Another critique that has been levelled at the general view that the two ICJ cases support the existence of the persistent objector rule relates to what is variously termed 'particular', 'special', 'local', or 'regional' customary international law: that is, custom that applies to a specific group of states, as opposed to 'general' customary international law, which is binding on all.[34] In the *Asylum* case, for example, Colombia invoked a purported customary international law rule applicable to Latin American states only (not a rule of general customary international law).[35] Noting this, some writers have questioned the relevance of the

[28] See *Asylum*, merits, n. 5, 277–8; and *Fisheries*, merits, n. 5, 131 respectively, emphasis added to both quotations.

[29] Mendelson, n. 26, 230.

[30] Elias, n. 24, 283, para. 13.

[31] Mendelson, n. 26, 230–1.

[32] See, generally on the importance of international judicial pronouncements that do not directly relate to the outcome of the case in which they are made, and the distinction between such pronouncements and '*obiter dicta*' in the common law sense, S. Rosenne, *Provisional Measures in International Law: The International Court of Justice and the International Tribunal for the Law of the Sea* (Oxford, Oxford University Press, 2004), 213, including at footnote 63; and K. Wellens, *Negotiations in the Case Law of the International Court of Justice: A Functional Analysis* (Farnham, Ashgate, 2014), 65–8.

[33] C.G. Guldahl, 'The Role of Persistent Objection in International Humanitarian Law' (2008) 77 *Nordic Journal of International Law* 51, 56. See also O. Elias and C.L. Lim, *The Paradox of Consensualism in International Law* (The Hague, Kluwer Law International, 1998), 59–61.

[34] On particular (or 'special', 'regional', or 'local') customary international law, see, generally, M. Akehurst, 'Custom as a Source of International Law' (1974–5) 47 *British Yearbook of International Law* 1, 28–31; A. D'Amato, 'The Concept of Special Custom in International Law' (1969) 63 *American Journal of International Law* 211; Third Report on Identification of Customary International Law (M. Wood, Special Rapporteur), International Law Commission, Sixty-seventh session, 27 March 2015, UN Doc. A/CN.4/682, paras 80–4; and *Right of Passage over Indian Territory* (*Portugal v India*), merits, 1960 ICJ Rep. 4, particularly at 39.

[35] See *Asylum*, merits, n. 5, 276; and *Asylum*, memorial submitted by Colombia, n. 12, 17, 19, 32, 37 and 43.

Asylum decision to the existence of the persistent objector rule on the basis that particular custom, by its nature, reverses the usual presumption for general custom that silence on the part of states to emerging customary law constitutes tacit consent to its creation.[36] Particular custom, it is said, requires states to *expressly* consent to it: i.e. silence is equal to rejection, meaning that regional custom is inapplicable to a state that has not expressly accepted it.[37] As the ICJ stated elsewhere in the *Asylum* merits judgment, '[t]he Party which relies on a custom of this kind [i.e. a particular custom] must prove that this custom is established in such a manner that it has become binding on the other Party'.[38] It has therefore been argued that the ICJ's recognition that the asserted customary norm on asylum was not individually binding on Peru was not an invocation of the persistent objector rule, but simply a recognition that—had the particular customary norm existed—its reach had not extended to Peru in the first instance because Peru had not expressly accepted it (just as was also the case with the majority of other states, including all of those outside of Latin America).[39]

The ICJ was undeniably examining a purported local Latin American custom in the *Asylum* merits judgment: indeed, the case is often considered the paradigmatic decision on particular custom.[40] This undermines the Court's apparent endorsement of the persistent objector rule in the case to some extent.[41] It is perhaps notable, however, that the ICJ saw Peru's *opposition* to the purported asylum norm in the decision as being determinative, and not merely the fact that it did not *consent* to it (which would surely have been enough, if the question was simply whether Peru had explicitly accepted the particular rule).[42] Even if the Court was making the above point in relation to the opposability of particular custom—it is possible that it simply saw opposition as an especially 'clear' indication of non-acceptance[43]—there is nothing to suggest that the ICJ saw the objections of a

[36] The most famous expression of this argument is D'Amato, n. 9, 233–63. See also, for example, Bradley and Gulati, n. 7, 235; Conforti, n. 9, 75; P-M. Dupuy, 'A propos de l'opposabilité de la coutume générale: enquête brève sur "l'objecteur persistant"', *in Le droit international au service de la paix, de la justice et du développement: Mélanges offerts à Michel Virally* (Paris, Pédone, 1991), 257, 265; and Ragazzi, n. 24, 62, footnote 79.

[37] D.J. Bederman, 'Acquiescence, Objection and the Death of Customary International Law' (2010) 21 *Duke Journal of Comparative and International Law* 31, 32–3; and I. MacGibbon, 'Customary International Law and Acquiescence' (1957) 33 *British Yearbook of International Law* 115, 123.

[38] *Asylum*, merits, n. 5, 276.

[39] Bradley and Gulati, n. 7, 235; Conforti, n. 9, 75; D'Amato, n. 9, 233–63; and Ragazzi, n. 24, 62, footnote 79.

[40] Charney, 'The Persistent Objector Rule', n. 9, 7; and Guldahl, n. 33, 56.

[41] S. Yee, 'Report on the ILC Project on "Identification of Customary International Law"' (Report by the Special Rapporteur of the Asian-African Legal Consultative Organisation (AALCO) Informal Expert Group on Customary International Law) (2015) 14 *Chinese Journal of International Law* 375, 391–2, para. 59; Elias, n. 24, 282, para. 9; Guldahl, n. 33, 56; and Ingman, n. 25, 23 and 49.

[42] *Asylum*, merits, n. 5, 277–8.

[43] A. D'Amato, 'International Soft Law, Hard Law, and Coherence' Northwestern Public Law and Legal Theory Series, No. 08-01, 1 March 2008, available on the *Social Science Research Network*, http://papers.ssrn.com/sol3/papers.cfm?abstract_id=1103915, 18 (actually making this

state as *only* being relevant in the context of particular custom.[44] There is no reason 'why regional and universal law should lack any common ground' in relation to the implications of persistent objection,[45] nor is there any indication that the Court took the view that there was any difference in this regard.

Moreover, whatever interpretation one takes of the *Asylum* case in relation to its focus on particular custom, this has little bearing on the way that the ICJ's pronouncement on Peru's exemption has developed in the subsequent consciousness of international legal actors. The *Asylum* decision also famously required 'a constant and uniform usage practised by the States in question'[46] for new norms of customary international law to emerge. Despite its obvious invocation by the Court in the context of particular custom,[47] the need for 'constant and uniform usage' is today widely accepted as a standard that is also relevant to *general* customary international law: the decision is regularly invoked as authority for this.[48] The fact that particular custom was at the centre of the *Asylum* case may lessen the decision's impact as 'authority' for the persistent objector rule in itself, but it neither precludes it entirely from acting as authority nor lessens its subsequent impact on the acceptance of the rule.

Stretching this critique of the *Asylum* case, D'Amato has further argued that the ICJ's relevant pronouncement in *Fisheries* was similarly made in relation to particular customary international law.[49] D'Amato's argument here is that the Court rejected the existence of binding general customary international law and then also rejected any possible particular customary rule as between the United Kingdom and Norway because Norway had not *explicitly* consented to this. He has dismissively stated that 'speed readers' have missed that the ICJ made a distinction between general and particular custom when noting that Norway had 'always opposed' the 10-mile rule, and argued that the wider context of the decision supports this.[50]

D'Amato's reading of *Fisheries* in this regard must be rejected and, notably, *has been*, even by some fellow critics of the persistent objector rule.[51] In the passages immediately prior to its pronouncement seemingly endorsing the persistent objector rule, the Court made it clear that the United Kingdom had 'not abandoned its contention that the ten-mile rule is to be regarded as a rule of international law', and that 'the ten-mile rule has not acquired the authority of a *general* rule of international law'.[52] In other words, it firmly situated its finding that the 10-mile

point in relation to *Fisheries*, which is unconvincing in the context of that case but is a possible reading of *Asylum*).

44 Mendelson, n. 26, 229.

45 Tomuschat, n. 9, 286.

46 *Asylum*, merits, n. 5, 276.

47 See ibid. for context; and D'Amato, n. 9, 253–4.

48 See, for example, M.N. Shaw, *International Law* (Cambridge, Cambridge University Press, 7th edn, 2014), 54 (setting out the 'textbook' position in this context: '[t]he basic rule as regards continuity and repetition [of state practice for customary international law formation] was laid down in the *Asylum* case').

49 D'Amato, n. 9, 260–2.

50 D'Amato, n. 43, 18.

51 See, for example, Charney, 'The Persistent Objector Rule', n. 9, 7–9.

52 *Fisheries*, merits, n. 5, 131, emphasis added.

rule was nonetheless inapplicable to Norway due to Norway's opposition in a wider examination of general custom.[53] There is nothing to suggest that the Court 'switched' from one sentence to the next—without signalling this—to a consideration of particular custom (especially as neither of the parties raised particular custom at all in their pleadings).[54] Thus, while the reference to persistent objection in the *Asylum* case related to particular custom, the equivalent passage in *Fisheries* did not.

The final critique of the two cases with regard to their value as authorities for the persistent objector rule is perhaps the most persuasive; somewhat ironically, however, it is the least commonly advanced by the rule's critics.[55] It is not entirely clear that the ICJ, in either decision, was articulating the rule as we know it in doctrine today, as opposed to something broadly akin to it. Leaving aside the fact that in neither judgment did the Court actually explicitly use the term 'persistent objector rule'—a fact which essentially means nothing: as was noted in Chapter 1,[56] what's in a name?[57]—the key elements of the rule as routinely presented in doctrine (persistent, consistent objection prior to the formation of the norm being objected to) are rather difficult to distil from the decisions.

For example, while the 'consistency' element can be identified in the passage from *Fisheries*, in that the ICJ noted that Norway had '*always opposed any attempt to apply*' the purported customary norm in question to it,[58] there is nothing in the decision to indicate that the Court felt it necessary that this opposition was persistent or that it occurred prior to the crystallization of the norm.[59] Of course, perhaps because the ICJ decided that the norm had not yet crystallized, the fact that objection had occurred prior to the (potential, future) point of crystallization was considered to be self-evident. In the *Asylum* decision, though, the Court mentioned *none of* the persistence, consistency, or timeliness criteria in relation to Peru's objection.[60] Indeed, it specifically referenced only the fact that Peru had refrained from ratifying the Montevideo Conventions of 1933 and 1939 as

[53] Elias, n. 24, 283, para. 13.

[54] Akehurst, n. 34, 25, emphasis added. It is worth noting that D'Amato argues that a later passage from the judgment contextualizes the Court's apparent endorsement of the persistent objector rule by showing that it moved from analysing general to analysing particular custom: D'Amato, n. 9, 262. The passage in question is as follows: 'The notoriety of the facts, the general toleration of the international community, Great Britain's position in the North Sea, her own interest in the question, and her prolonged abstention would in any case warrant Norway's enforcement of her system against the United Kingdom.' *Fisheries*, merits, n. 5, 139. However, this passage does not in fact establish that the Court was considering particular custom at all: it is too vague to even be seen as broadly suggesting this (indeed, it specifically references 'the general toleration of the international community').

[55] Although see, for example, Bradley and Gulati, n. 7, 235.

[56] See Chapter 1, n. 11–n. 12 and accompanying text.

[57] See I. Brownlie, 'International Law at the Fiftieth Anniversary of the United Nations—General Course on Public International Law' (1995) 255 *Recueil des cours* 11, 42 (arguing that the *Fisheries* case 'provides the source, if not the phraseology of the principle of the "persistent objector"').

[58] *Fisheries*, merits, n. 5, 131, emphasis added.

[59] Bradley and Gulati, n. 7, 235; and Elias and Lim, n. 33, 61.

[60] Bradley and Gulati, n. 7, 235; and Elias and Lim, n. 33, 58.

providing a basis for the inapplicability of the norm to it, which does not sound like especially 'persistent' objection at all.

This means that even if one takes the view that the cases do act as authority for the persistent objector rule per se, it is extremely difficult to see them as providing support for the generally accepted *elements* of the rule, which ultimately define it. At most, the decisions only offer a tentative sketch of the persistent objector rule. The present author would reject the claim that they provide *no* authority for the rule, but it is hard to argue with the view that they provide relatively weak authority for it.

Given that those who identify the persistent objector of the rule so heavily rely on these decisions, it is important to note that the critique of that reliance is broadly correct (if overstated). The *Asylum* and *Fisheries* cases certainly do not establish the existence of the modern persistent objector rule in themselves, and their value in determining its existence has to be approached with caution.[61] Equally, they cannot be dismissed either: none of the critiques of the cases in relation to persistent objection are convincing enough to displace the fact that the World Court set out the right of a state to remain exempt from a customary international law norm by way of explicit objection.[62] The cases are authorities for the persistent objector rule, just not especially good authorities.[63]

iii. The persistent objector rule in jurisprudence beyond the *Asylum* and *Fisheries* cases

On top of the critique of the *Asylum* and *Fisheries* cases in relation to the persistent objector rule, some commentators have made much of the fact that they are the *only* ICJ decisions that have invoked it (assuming that one accepts that they *did* invoke it).[64] In this context it is worth noting the 1974 *Fisheries Jurisdiction* case,[65] where the United Kingdom had persistently rejected the extension by Iceland of its fisheries jurisdiction from 12 to 50 nautical miles.[66] The ICJ held that the extension of the jurisdiction was 'not opposable to the United Kingdom', but did

[61] Ibid., 62–3.

[62] See Yee, n. 41, 391, para. 57 (nicely summing this up: *Fisheries* 'recognized in essence if not in express terms' the persistent objector rule).

[63] Bradley and Gulati, n. 7, 239; and E.T. Swaine, 'Bespoke Custom' (2010) 21 *Duke Journal of Comparative and International Law* 207, 212.

[64] B. Chigara, *Legitimacy Deficit in Custom: A Deconstructionist Critique* (Aldershot, Ashgate, 2001), 237 (arguing that the ICJ has therefore treated 'the persistent objector theory as a fair-weather friend'); H. Lau, 'Rethinking the Persistent Objector Doctrine in International Human Rights Law' (2005–6) 6 *Chicago Journal of International Law* 496, 499–500; and A. Roberts, 'Traditional and Modern Approaches to Customary International Law: A Reconciliation' (2001) 95 *American Journal of International Law* 757, 765, footnote 90.

[65] *Fisheries Jurisdiction* (*United Kingdom of Great Britain and Northern Ireland v Iceland*), merits, 1974 ICJ Rep. 3.

[66] *Fisheries Jurisdiction* (*United Kingdom of Great Britain and Northern Ireland v Iceland*), memorial on the merits of the dispute submitted by the Government of the United Kingdom of Great Britain and Northern Ireland, 1973 ICJ Plead., particularly at paras 18–29.

not formally base this determination on the persistent objector rule.[67] This has been seen by some as a notable avoidance of the persistent objector rule by the ICJ in a judgment where—if the rule truly existed or mattered—one could reasonably have expected the Court to employ it.[68]

Yet the reasoning underpinning the Court's conclusion that Iceland's jurisdictional extension was 'not opposable to the United Kingdom' was not made clear in the judgment.[69] While it is likely that the decision was reached based on an Exchange of Notes agreement between the United Kingdom and Iceland in 1961,[70] it may in fact have been premised on persistent objection.[71] Even if it were the case that the ICJ entirely ignored the persistent objector rule in *Fisheries Jurisdiction*, though, this would mean very little. The Court reaching a finding on other grounds in a dispute that *might* have been resolved with reference to persistent objection tells us nothing about the rule's validity.[72] Indeed, it is important to keep in mind that the United Kingdom did not claim to be a persistent objector state in its pleadings[73] (and Iceland did not submit any pleadings on the merits at all); under the *non ultra petita* rule the ICJ is required not to adjudicate beyond the claims that the states themselves advance.[74]

The fact that the ICJ has only (arguably) endorsed the persistent objector rule twice cannot be seen as indicating anything with regard to the rule's existence or usefulness either. In the international legal system, states rarely submit their disputes to review by adjudicative mechanisms, and so it is no surprise that the corresponding jurisprudential reference to the persistent objector rule is also relatively infrequent.[75] Other than *Asylum* and *Fisheries*, there have been extremely few instances where the ICJ might, even *potentially*, have applied the persistent objector rule. The absence of repeated endorsement is not rejection, and while the extent to which the ICJ has endorsed the rule can be debated, it has certainly not rejected it. Every case where the ICJ might have employed the rule but did not do so is, of course, *also* a case where it might have taken the opportunity to confirm that there was no such rule but did not.

Moreover, while there are only two merits decisions of the Court that have (arguably) invoked the persistent objector rule, a number of individual opinions of the judges of the ICJ have referenced and accepted it. Individual opinions are

[67] *Fisheries Jurisdiction*, merits, n. 65, para. 67.

[68] Charney, 'The Persistent Objector Rule', n. 9, 10–11; Chigara, n. 64, 237; Dumberry, n. 9, 785–6; and Tomuschat, n. 9, 287–8.

[69] Mendelson, n. 26, 231.

[70] This can be inferred (but no more than that) from *Fisheries Jurisdiction*, merits, n. 65, para. 67.

[71] Mendelson, n. 26, 231.

[72] Guldahl, n. 33, 57; and Mendelson, n. 26, 231.

[73] See, generally, *Fisheries Jurisdiction*, memorial submitted by the United Kingdom, n. 66.

[74] See *Case Concerning Certain German Interests in Polish Silesia* (*Germany v Polish Republic*) merits, 1926 PCIJ Rep., Series A 7, 35; *Asylum*, merits, n. 5, 402; and *Military and Paramilitary Activities in and against Nicaragua* (*Nicaragua v United States of America*), merits, 1986 ICJ Rep. 14, para. 207. See also I.F.I. Shihata, *The Power of the International Court to Determine its Own Jurisdiction* (The Hague, Martinus Nijhoff, 1965), 219–21.

[75] D.A. Colson, 'How Persistent Must the Persistent Objector Be?' (1986) 61 *Washington Law Review* 957, 958.

undoubtedly less legally significant than majority ICJ decisions,[76] but these opinions still represent judicial endorsements of the rule by members of the World Court.[77] To provide an example, Judge Lachs took the view in his dissenting opinion to the *North Sea Continental Shelf* cases that the existence of a rule of general customary international law cannot

> prevent some States from adopting an attitude apart. They may have opposed the rule from its inception and may, unilaterally, or in agreement with others, decide upon different solutions of the problem involved ... Thus the fact that some States ... have enacted special legislation or concluded agreements at variance with the equidistance rule and the practice confirming it represents a mere permitted derogation and cannot be held to have disturbed the formation of a general rule of law on delimitation.[78]

To give another example: while the majority refrained from referencing the persistent objector rule in *Fisheries Jurisdiction*, Judge Waldock endorsed it in his separate opinion (albeit relatively tentatively).[79]

One can also find references to the rule made in a number of other individual opinions, with varying amounts of clarity and precision.[80] These individual

[76] Guldahl, n. 33, 57. [77] Ibid.

[78] *North Sea Continental Shelf* cases (*Federal Republic of Germany v Netherlands, Federal Republic of Germany v Denmark*), merits, 1969 ICJ Rep. 3, dissenting opinion of Judge Lachs, 229. Judge Lachs also later stated, at 232, that once a rule has attained customary legal status, '[t]his may be contested in a particular case by a State denying its opposability to itself'.

[79] *Fisheries Jurisdiction*, merits, n. 65, separate opinion of Judge Waldock, para. 36 ('In the present instance, Iceland's unilateral extension of her exclusive fishery limits from 12 to 50 miles as from 1 September 1972 was at once objected to by the United Kingdom. Consequently ... I would consider the Court justified in holding that Iceland's extension of her fishery jurisdiction beyond the 12-mile limit agreed to in the 1961 Exchange of Notes is also not opposable to the United Kingdom under general international law').

[80] See *Asylum*, merits, n. 5, dissenting opinion of Judge Azevedo, 337 ('To destroy such a custom, a clear, coherent, unilinear attitude would be required, such as that of the United States for instance, which, while refusing to become in any way involved in the institution of asylum adopted by their sister-republics, have in practice shown toleration in some extreme cases, although with restricted effects'); *South West Africa* cases (*Ethiopia v South Africa, Liberia v South Africa*), second phase, 1966 ICJ Rep. 6, separate opinion of Judge van Wyk, para. 55 ('since acquiescence is a prerequisite to the creation of a new [customary international law] norm, it is the Respondent's acquiescence that is required [which was absent because of repeated dissent]'); *North Sea Continental Shelf* cases, merits, n. 78, separate opinion of Judge Fouad Ammoun, para. 31 ('a general rule of customary law does not require the consent of all States ... but at least the consent of those who were aware of this general practice and, being in a position to oppose it, have not done so'); *North Sea Continental Shelf* cases, merits, n. 78, dissenting opinion of Judge Sørensen, 247 ('the Convention on the Continental Shelf would be inapplicable as against the Federal Republic [of Germany], if she had consistently refused to recognize it as an expression of generally accepted rules of international law and had objected to its applicability as against her'); and (arguably) *Nuclear Tests* case (*Australia v France*), questions of jurisdiction and admissibility, 1974, ICJ Rep. 253, separate opinion of Judge Gros, para. 18 ('[t]he conduct of the Original Parties which laid down the rules of the present nuclear statute by mutual agreement shows that those nuclear States which have refused to accede to this statute cannot be considered as subjected thereto by virtue of a doctrinal construction contrary to the formally expressed intentions of the sponsors and guardians of the Statute. The French Government, for its part, has always refused to recognize the existence of a rule opposable to it, as many statements made by it show').

opinions certainly add buttressing support to the admittedly somewhat shaky foundations of *Asylum* and *Fisheries*.

Although the ICJ is undoubtedly the premier court of the international legal system, one must be very careful not to over-fetishize its place within international adjudication. Claims that there is *no* judicial support for the persistent objector rule[81] are demonstrably false, even if one rejects all of *Asylum*, *Fisheries*, and the various individual opinions of ICJ judges as authorities.[82] At the international and regional levels, there have been various decisions in judicial and arbitral forums other than the ICJ that reference the rule.

For example, the Inter-American Commission on Human Rights (IACmHR) has explicitly endorsed the persistent objector rule twice, both times in relation to the juvenile death penalty, in *Roach and Pinkerton v United States* (1987)[83] and *Domingues v United States* (2002).[84] In *Roach and Pinkerton* the IACmHR held that customary international law 'does not bind States which protest the norm'[85] and identified the United States as a prima facie persistent objector state in relation to the juvenile death penalty.[86] In *Domingues*, the Commission made it clear that

> a [customary international law] norm which has been accepted by the majority of States has no binding effect upon a State which has persistently rejected the practice upon which the norm is based ... as customary international law rests on the consent of nations, a state that persistently objects to a norm of customary international law is not bound by that norm.[87]

Roach and Pinkerton and *Domingues* both represent explicit endorsements of the persistent objector rule in an international adjudicative context. It is worth stressing in this regard that while the IACmHR's decisions are not binding,[88] this does not affect the value of these decisions as general jurisprudential endorsements of persistent objection.[89] After all, the decisions of the ICJ are non-binding other than in relation to the parties and dispute before it,[90] and yet the legal 'value' of these decisions extends well beyond this.[91]

[81] A. Cassese, *International Law* (Oxford, Oxford University Press, 2nd edn, 2005), 163; and H. Thirlway, 'The Sources of International Law' in M.D. Evans (ed.), *International Law* (Oxford, Oxford University Press, 4th edn, 2014), 91, 103.

[82] See Chigara, n. 64, 236 (seeing *Asylum*, *Fisheries*, and the various ICJ individual opinions as at least possible authorities for the persistent objector rule, but then arguing that '[a]side from [these ICJ authorities] ... there does not seem to be other judicial support [for the rule]').

[83] *Roach and Pinkerton v United States*, 1987 IACmHR, Resolution No. 3/87, Case 9647.

[84] *Domingues v United States*, merits, 2002 IACmHR, Report No. 62/02, Case 12.285.

[85] *Roach and Pinkerton*, merits, n. 83, para. 52.

[86] Ibid., para. 54.

[87] *Domingues*, merits, n. 84, paras 48–9.

[88] Statute of the Inter-American Commission on Human Rights, 1 October 1979, OAS Resolution 447 (IX-0/79), OAS Official Records, OEA/Ser.P/IX.0.2/80, Article 19.

[89] *Contra* Dumberry, n. 9, 790.

[90] Statute of the International Court of Justice, 26 June 1945, 59 Stat. 1055, 33 UNTS 93, Article 59.

[91] See, in general, H. Lauterpacht, *The Development of International Law by the International Court* (London, Stevens & Sons, revised edn, 1958).

Also at the regional level, but this time in a binding context, the Grand Chamber of the European Court of Human Rights (ECtHR) endorsed persistent objection in 2011 in *Sabah El Leil v France*.[92] The ECtHR was considering the customary international law status of a norm equivalent to that set out in Article 11 of the (not yet in force) 2004 UN Convention on Jurisdictional Immunities of States and Their Property (relating to state immunity and contracts of employment).[93] In this context, the Court noted in the abstract that a treaty provision may be binding on a non-party state under customary international law 'provided it has not opposed it',[94] clearly in reference to persistent objection.[95] It then went on to apply this, holding that France was bound by the customary international law in question because it had not sufficiently 'opposed' it, on the basis that France's objections had not been *consistent*.[96] In *Cudak v Lithuania* the ECtHR Grand Chamber engaged with the possible persistent objector status of Lithuania in a similar context—the erosion in customary international law of 'absolute' state immunity—and, again, found that Lithuania's objections had been inconsistent, meaning that it was not exempt.[97]

The persistent objector rule has also been endorsed by other international adjudicative bodies. In the 2007 investment arbitration case of *BG Group v Argentina*,[98] for example, Argentina was asserting that the wrongfulness of its (contested) breach of the terms of a 1990 bilateral investment treaty between it and the United Kingdom[99] was in any event precluded by the defence of 'necessity', given the overwhelming financial context in which the alleged breach took place.[100] The applicants' response to this claim was to argue that the defence of necessity was not opposable to the United Kingdom because it was a persistent objector state to that defence.[101] The tribunal dismissed the possibility of the United Kingdom being a persistent objector in that regard, but it accepted the existence of the rule per se.[102] Another example is the endorsement of the

[92] *Sabah El Leil v France*, application no. 34869/05, judgment, 2011, ECtHR (Grand Chamber).

[93] United Nations Convention on Jurisdictional Immunities of States and Their Property, 2 December 2004, Doc. A/59/508 (adopted by General Assembly Resolution 59/38, 2 December 2004, UN Doc. A/RES/59/38, not in force).

[94] *Sabah El Leil*, n. 92, para. 54.

[95] See Third Report on Identification of Customary International Law, ILC, n. 34, para. 87, footnote 211 (interpreting the Court's statement in this way).

[96] *Sabah El Leil*, n. 92, para. 54 (albeit that the Court did not phrase this in terms of 'consistency'). See Chapter 5 in relation to the consistency criterion.

[97] *Cudak v Lithuania* application no. 15869/02, judgment, 2010, ECtHR (Grand Chamber), paras 66–8. The ECtHR was not especially explicit as to the fact that it was applying the persistent objector rule in *Cudak*, but it is evident when one reviews the decision that the Court was in fact applying the rule, and dismissing its application because its requirements had not been met.

[98] *BG Group Plc v Republic of Argentina*, final award, 2007, http://ita.law.uvic.ca/documents/BG-award_000.pdf.

[99] Agreement between the Government of the United Kingdom of Great Britain and Northern Ireland and the Government of the Republic of Argentina for the Promotion and Protection of Investments, 11 December 1990, 1765 UNTS 30682.

[100] *BG Group v Argentina*, n. 98, particularly paras 84–6 and 88.

[101] Ibid., para. 400.

[102] Ibid., para. 410, footnote 328. For discussion, see Chapter 4, n. 54–n. 62 and accompanying text.

persistent objector rule by the Special Tribunal for Lebanon in 2011, in relation to an examination of the definition of terrorism.[103] Admittedly, the tribunal was rather vague as to the application of the rule in that context,[104] but it nonetheless explicitly noted the rule's existence.

Beyond these various international adjudicative decisions, and perhaps of more note than them, are the various *domestic* judgments since 1945 that have accepted the persistent objector rule. Domestic judgments, of course, can constitute examples of state practice for the purposes of identifying the formation of customary international law per se,[105] but, more generally, they are further formal, judicial endorsements of persistent objection as a secondary rule of the international legal system. For example, since the late 1970s, the rule has been endorsed in United States case law;[106] by the German Federal Constitutional Court;[107] in two judgments of the South African courts (albeit that the rule is referenced rather obliquely in one of these);[108] and in two cases from the autonomous region of Hong Kong.[109] There are very likely other instances of domestic

[103] *Interlocutory Decision on the Applicable Law: Terrorism, Conspiracy, Homicide, Perpetration, Cumulative Charging*, case no. STL-II-01/I, 2011, Special Tribunal for Lebanon (Appeals Chamber), 3 and 73.

[104] Ibid., 73 ('[t]he very few States still insisting on an exception for "freedom fighters" and therefore objecting to the coalescing international definition of terrorism could, at most, be considered persistent objectors thereof').

[105] See, for example, *Arrest Warrant (Democratic Republic of the Congo v Belgium)*, merits, 2002, ICJ Rep. 3, para. 58 (where the ICJ considered domestic judgments in terms of identifying state practice). See also Second Report on Identification of Customary International Law (M. Wood, Special Rapporteur), International Law Commission, Sixty-sixth session, 22 May 2014, UN Doc. A/CN.4/672, para. 41(e).

[106] *Siderman de Blake v Republic of Argentina*, 1992, United States Court of Appeals for the Ninth Circuit 965 F.2d 699 (9th Cir. 1992), per Fletcher J., 715 ('[a] state that *persistently* objects to a norm of customary international law that other states accept is not bound by that norm').

[107] *Philippine Embassy* case, 1977, BVerfGE (German Federal Constitutional Court) 46, 342 2 BvM 1/76 (English translation: http://www.utexas.edu/law/academics/centers/transnational/work_new/german/case.php?id=584), para. 6 ('a State can successfully uphold from the outset against application of an existing general rule of international law by way of perseverant protestation of rights').

[108] *Inter-Science Research and Development Services (Pty) Ltd v Republica Popular Moçambique*, per Margo J., 1980 2 SA 111 T, 125 ('if a custom becomes established as a general rule of international law, it binds all States which have not opposed it'); and *S v Petane*, 1988 (3) SA 51 (C), per Conradie J., 64A-B ('customary international law rests on a foundation of consensuality' and so will not be applied by a court against a dissenting state).

[109] *C* et al. *v Director of Immigration and Secretary for Security*, 2011, Hong Kong Special Administrative Region, Court of Appeal, CACV 132-137/2008, particularly at para. 68 ('The concept of "persistent objector" is a principle in public international law where "a State ... in the process of formation of a new customary rule of international law, disassociate[s] itself from that process, declare[s] itself not to be bound, and maintain[s] that attitude" ... Evidence of objection must be clear', references omitted); *Democratic Republic of the Congo v FG Hemisphere Associates LLC (No 1)* 2011, 14 HKCFAR, Final Appeal Nos. 5, 6 and 7 of 2010 (civil), para. 121, per Bokhary PJ ('Since I am not speaking of—and cannot speak of—the position in the Mainland, it is unnecessary for me to say whether I consider restrictive immunity to be a rule of customary international law. Nor is it necessary for me to decide whether persistent objection works. If it were necessary to do so, I would accept that China has been a persistent objector to restrictive immunity'). See also previous decisions in both sets of proceedings: *C* et al. *v Director of Immigration*, 2008, 2 HKC 167, particularly at paras 69–72; and *FG Hemisphere Associates LLC and Democratic Republic of the Congo*, 2010,

judicial endorsement: the present author does not claim that these examples represent an exhaustive list. In any event, it is clear that there is a notable degree of acceptance of the persistent objector rule in domestic case law.

Most of the decisions noted in this subsection will be considered in more detail in later chapters, in relation to the way in which the persistent objector rule has been applied or defined. As such, they will not be examined further here. For present purposes it is sufficient to take note of the fact that there are (at least) a dozen judicial decisions—international, regional, and domestic—where the persistent objector rule can be seen as having been endorsed, with the majority of those endorsements being in indisputable, unequivocal terms. Perhaps just as importantly, as far as the present author has been able to ascertain, there are *no judicial decisions* (international, regional, or domestic) that have rejected the persistent objector rule.[110] It must be borne in mind that the instances where the rule would potentially be at issue at all before any adjudicative body are likely to be few. As such, the number of decisions that have accepted it, seen in the light of the fact that apparently none have rejected it, has to be viewed as significant support for the rule's existence within the modern international legal system.

While the *Asylum* and *Fisheries* cases do not conclusively establish the existence of the persistent objector rule by any means, they can certainly be interpreted as endorsing it. Crucially, critics of the authority that these cases provide overlook the fact that *this is the way in which they have been interpreted* in subsequent adjudicative practice,[111] irrespective of the extent to which one might be able to critique their individual 'value' in this regard. There now exists much stronger jurisprudential support for the rule from elsewhere in any event, but, for all their equivocalness, *Asylum* and *Fisheries* remain the key touchstones for the rule in case law precisely because they are still viewed in this light. This should not, however, obscure the fact that since the 1950s judicial endorsement of the persistent objector rule has continued (and, over the past twenty years in particular, notably increased). There is now a body of jurisprudential support for the rule. One should not get carried away with regard to this fact: the judicial reference to the rule is perhaps not overwhelming.[112] Nonetheless, it is now difficult to dispute

COA, Civil Appeals Nos. 373 of 2008 and 43 of 2009 HKLR&D, paras 93–115 (per Stock V-P) 258 and 266 (per Yuen JA).

[110] This point is also made by ILA Final Report, n. 4, 27; and Third Report on Identification of Customary International Law, ILC, n. 34, para. 86.

[111] Elias and Lim, n. 33, 60–1. For example, both *Domingues*, merits, n. 84, para. 48 and *Philippine Embassy*, n. 107, para. 6 cite *Fisheries* as authority for the rule.

[112] See, making the argument that judicial support for the rule is limited: O. Barsalou, 'La doctrine de l'objecteur persistant en droit international public' (2006) 19 *Revue québécoise de droit international* 1, 13; Charney, 'The Persistent Objector Rule', n. 9, 5; Chigara, n. 64, 236–7; Dumberry, n. 9, 780 and 785; M. Koskenniemi, *From Apology to Utopia: The Structure of International Legal Argument* (Cambridge, Cambridge University Press, reissue, 2005), 443; T. Treves, 'Customary International Law' in R. Wolfrum (ed.), *Max Planck Encyclopaedia of Public International Law, vol. II* (Oxford, Oxford University Press, 2012), 937, 945, para. 39; and Verdier and Voeten, n. 25, 428.

the assertion that the persistent objector rule has been accepted in international, regional, and domestic case law as a feature of contemporary international law.[113]

II. The Persistent Objector Rule in State Practice After 1945

While the increasingly significant support for the persistent objector rule in case law is very important in terms of identifying its 'social acceptance' within the modern international legal system, it is nonetheless essential to further identify the existence and content of the rule in its usage by states.[114] For good or ill, state 'acceptance' is the acceptance that matters most.[115] We have seen that there was little, if any, usage of the rule (at least as conceived today) in pre-1945 state practice.[116] Perhaps the most fundamental of all the (many) critiques of the persistent objector rule is that it has *never* been used by states, including post-1945, or, at least, that where states have invoked it this has not led to any de jure exemption from the customary international law norm being objected to.[117] A 'softer', and more credible, version of this critique is that states very rarely use the rule,[118] and that when they do they often find that they are unable to maintain their exempt status post-crystallization.[119] Either way, 'commentators have *invariably* noted the

[113] See Report of the International Law Commission, Sixty-seventh session, 4 May–5 June and 6 July–7 August 2015, UN Doc. A/70/10, advance unedited version, 24 August 2015, 36, para. 73 and 42, para. 106 (views of the Special Rapporteur for the ILC's ongoing work on the 'Identification of customary international law', Sir Michael Wood, during the consideration of the topic at the ILC's Sixty-seventh session: '[t]he Special Rapporteur ... pointed out that the persistent objector rule could be and not infrequently is raised before judges asked to identify customary international law', quoted at para. 106); ILA Final Report, n. 4, 27; and Brownlie, n. 57, 42.

[114] See Introduction, section V.

[115] See Kelly, n. 8, 513 (arguing that acceptance of the rule in case law does not tell us whether it has been accepted by *states*, which is the crucial factor).

[116] See Chapter 1, section III.

[117] See, for example, Cassese, n. 81, 163; D'Amato, n. 43, 20; A. D'Amato, 'Groundwork for International Law' (2014) 108 *American Journal of International Law* 650, 668; P. Dumberry, 'The Last Citadel! Can a State Claim the Status of Persistent Objector to Prevent the Application of a Rule of Customary International Law in Investor-State Arbitration?' (2010) 23 *Leiden Journal of International Law* 379, 380–1, 388, and 399–400; Dumberry, n. 9, particularly at 780 and 794; Dupuy, n. 36, particularly at 259 and 266; and Kelly, n. 8, particularly at 512.

[118] See, for example, Barsalou, n. 112, particularly at 13; Bradley and Gulati, n. 7, 211, 239–40 and 245; C.A. Bradley and M. Gulati, 'Customary International Law and Withdrawal Rights in an Age of Treaties' (2010) 21 *Duke Journal of International and Comparative Law* 1, 14 and 23–5; Charney, 'The Persistent Objector Rule', n. 9, particularly at 5 and 9; Charney, 'Universal International Law', n. 9, 538 and 540; J.L. Dunoff, S.R. Ratner and D. Wippman, *International Law: Norms, Actors, Process: A Problem-Orientated Approach* (New York, Aspen, 2nd edn, 2006), 78; D.P. Fidler, 'Challenging the Classical Concept of Custom: Perspectives on the Future of Customary International Law' (1996) 39 *German Yearbook of International Law* 198, 209; A.V. Lowe, *International Law* (Oxford, Oxford University Press, 2007), 56; A. Roberts, 'Who Killed Article 38(1)(b)? A Reply to Bradley & Gulati' (2010) 21 *Duke Journal of Comparative and International Law* 173, 176 and 189; Stein, n. 7, in general, but particularly at 459–63; H. Thirlway, *The Sources of International Law* (Oxford, Oxford University Press, 2014), 87; Treves, n. 112, 945, para. 39; and Weil, n. 9, 191.

[119] See, for example, O. Abasheikh, 'The Validity of the Persistent Offender Rule in International Law' (2004) 9 *Coventry Law Journal* 40, 46; Bederman, n. 37, 36; Charney, 'The Persistent Objector

paucity of examples of practice ... supporting the persistent objector rule',[120] and this includes many of its exponents.[121]

Equally, some scholars have argued that there is in fact a notable amount of state usage of the rule.[122] As was noted in the Introduction,[123] for example, Mendelson asserted in his 1998 Hague Academy course that there is actually 'quite a wealth of state practice in support of the persistent objector rule' and that scholars have simply not 'looked hard enough' to find this.[124] Admittedly, Mendelson perhaps failed to then pick up his own thrown gauntlet in this regard, as Barsalou notes:

> Il est ironique de constater que [d]eux ans plus tard, alors qu'il était Chairman du Committee on Formation of Customary (General) International Law de la Conférence de 2000 de l'International Law Association, Mendelson n'a pas tard en mesure d'identifier les nouvelles pratiques ainsi que les nouvelles décisions promises [on the persistent objector rule].[125]

In any event, it is clear that many commentators have taken the view that there is little or no state usage of the rule, while others argue that there is a substantial amount. The reality falls somewhere in between these positions. It is undeniable—when one does 'look hard enough' at practice—that states do not commonly use the rule. A 'wealth of practice' there is not. It is also correct to say that maintaining a de jure exemption obtained through persistent objection is extremely difficult de facto.[126] Equally, D'Amato's 2014 assertion that '[t]he persistent objector rule has never been invoked in state practice'[127] is utterly incorrect. It has.

This can be demonstrated most simply by referring to state pleadings before courts and tribunals, given that states necessarily present formal legal positions in

Rule', n. 9, 11–16; M.E. Villiger, *Customary International Law and Treaties: A Manual on the Theory and Practice of the Interrelation of Sources* (The Hague, Kluwer, 2nd edn, 1997), 34; Weil, n. 9, 191; and K. Wolfke, *Custom in Present International Law* (Dordrecht, Martinus Nijhoff, 2nd edn, 1993), 66–7.

[120] C.L. Lim and O. Elias, 'Withdrawing from Custom and the Paradox of Consensualism in International Law' (2010) 21 *Duke Journal of Comparative and International Law* 143, 147, emphasis added.

[121] See, for example, *Restatement of the Law, Third, Foreign Relations Law of the United States*, American Law Institute, 1987, Section 102, Comment (d); J. Klabbers, *International Law* (Cambridge, Cambridge University Press, 2013), 31, footnote 31; Lau, n. 64, 496; B.D. Lepard, *Customary International Law: A New Theory with Practical Applications* (Cambridge, Cambridge University Press, 2010), 37 and 229; L. Loschin, 'The Persistent Objector Rule and Customary Human Rights Law: A Proposed Analytical Framework' (1996) 2 *University of California Davis Journal of International Law and Policy* 147, 151 and 171; Quince, n. 17, 80; M.P. Scharf, *Customary International Law in Times of Fundamental Change: Recognizing Grotian Moments* (Cambridge, Cambridge University Press, reissue, 2013), 42; and Steinfeld, n. 25, 1654–5.

[122] See, for example, ILA Final Report, n. 4, 27–8; Colson, n. 75, 969 ('[t]he principle of persistent objector *is often applied by States*', emphasis added); Brownlie, n. 57, 42; and J. Crawford, *Brownlie's Principles of Public International Law* (Oxford, Oxford University Press, 8th edn, 2012), 28.

[123] See Introduction, n. 97–n. 98 and accompanying text.

[124] Mendelson, n. 26, 238.

[125] Barsalou, n. 112, 13, footnote 84.

[126] See Chapter 8, section II.

[127] D'Amato, n. 117, 668. See also D'Amato, n. 43, 20 (making the same point).

that context. Going back to the influential *Fisheries* case, for example, it is clear that both Norway and the United Kingdom acknowledged the existence of the persistent objector rule in their respective pleadings before the ICJ (albeit that they did not use the *term* 'persistent objector'). Norway explicitly took the view that '[u]ne règle coutumière ne peut lier un État qui a manifesté d'une manière constante et non équivoque son refus de l'accepter'.[128] Indeed, Norway argued at some length in its written submissions that the 10-mile rule propounded as customary international law by the United Kingdom did not apply to it, given that it had consistently maintained its own system of delimitating its territorial sea and fisheries zone.[129] The United Kingdom also endorsed the persistent objector rule in its written pleadings, or at least accepted something that looked very much like it,[130] by arguing that 'a State may acquire an exceptional position with regard to some general rule of customary law by some process which is analogous to that of acquiring an historic title'.[131] Of course, unsurprisingly, the United Kingdom also took the view that the Norway had not attained an exemption in this way in the particular circumstances of the case.[132]

Stein[133] and Dumberry[134] have made note of the fact that neither Norway nor the United Kingdom referred to any state practice in support of their acceptance of the rule in their respective *Fisheries* pleadings, and have implied that because neither state referred to previous invocations of the rule, there was no (or little) usage of the rule to which the parties could refer. Yet just because the states in question did not advance any state practice does not confirm that no such practice existed; at most it might be said to be indicative of this being the case (and, if so, of course, it is indicative of this being the case *in 1950*). Far more importantly, Stein and Dumberry seem to miss the fact that the pleadings of both parties in the *Fisheries* themselves constitute state invocations of the rule.

The persistent objector rule has been accepted and invoked by states on numerous occasions since the *Fisheries* case in the context of adjudicative pleadings, both international and domestic.[135] There is little value in setting all of these out

[128] *Fisheries (United Kingdom v Norway)*, rejoinder submitted by the Government of the Kingdom of Norway, 1951 ICJ Plead., vol. III, 291.

[129] See *Fisheries (United Kingdom v Norway)*, counter-memorial submitted by the Government of the Kingdom of Norway, 1950 ICJ Plead., vol. I, 381–4; and *Fisheries*, rejoinder submitted by Norway, n. 128, 291–6.

[130] See Bradley and Gulati, n. 7, 235.

[131] *Fisheries (United Kingdom v Norway)*, reply submitted by the Government of the United Kingdom of Great Britain and Northern Ireland, 1950 ICJ Plead., vol. II, 428–9, quoted at 429. See also ibid., 303 (arguing that Norway was required to show that other states had acquiesced in its historic claim).

[132] See, for example, ibid., 429.

[133] Stein, n. 7, 460.

[134] Dumberry, n. 9, 785, footnote 39.

[135] See, for example, *Right of Passage over Indian Territory (Portugal v India)*, preliminary objection of the Government of India, 1957 ICJ Plead., vol. I, 97, 178, para. 184 (India: 'even where a general custom can be proved, a State which has persistently adopted a different attitude in its own practice is not bound by the general custom'); *South West Africa* cases (*Ethiopia v South Africa, Liberia v South Africa*), Rejoinder of Dr VerLoren van Themaat (South Africa), 1966 ICJ Plead., vol. X, 9–10 (South Africa); *North Sea Continental Shelf* cases (*Federal Republic of Germany v Netherlands, Federal Republic of Germany v Denmark*), common rejoinder submitted by the

in the main text in this chapter; again, as with the various judicial and arbitral decisions where the rule has been accepted, many of the instances where states have invoked the rule before adjudicative bodies will be referred to in later chapters. To provide a recent representative example, however, both Mauritius and the United Kingdom accepted the persistent objector rule in the context of the 2015 *Chagos Marine Protected Area* UN Convention on the Law of the Sea (UNCLOS) arbitral proceedings.[136] The dispute concerned the creation of a marine protected area (MPA) in the Chagos Archipelago by the United Kingdom, which claimed that it was entitled to declare the MPA, inter alia, on the basis that it had formally 'detached' the archipelago from Mauritius in 1965.[137] It was further argued by the United Kingdom that this 'detachment' was not in violation of the right of self-determination because—at the time of Mauritian independence in 1968—the United Kingdom was a persistent objector to that right: '[t]he United Kingdom persistently objected to any such rule'.[138] In response, Mauritius also explicitly accepted the persistent objector rule, albeit that it argued that the United Kingdom's objections were insufficiently communicated and too inconsistent for the asserted exemption to have been constituted by those objections.[139]

Pleadings before courts and tribunals of this sort provide a notable amount of cumulative evidence that states accept the persistent objector rule. It has

Governments of the Kingdom of Denmark and the Kingdom of the Netherlands, 1968 ICJ Plead., vol. I, 509–10 (Netherlands and Denmark, acknowledging the existence of the rule but arguing its inapplicability in the dispute at issue); *Domingues v United States*, Response of the Government of the United States to May 1, 2000 Petition, Case No. 12.185 (Michael Domingues), http://www.state.gov/documents/organization/16525.pdf, 10–11 (United States); *Case Concerning the Audit of Accounts between the Netherlands and France in Application of the Protocol of 25 September 1991 additional to the Convention for the Protection of the Rhine from Pollution by Chlorides of 3 December 1976*, PCA, counter-memorial of France, 2001, particularly at para. 6 (France); *In Re 'Agent Orange' Product Liability Litigation*, 2005, statement of interest of the United States, http://www.state.gov/documents/organization/87322.pdf, 31–2 (United States: arguing that its 'persistent and consistent public pronouncements ... qualify it as a persistent objector under international law'); *Grand River*, counter-memorial of the respondent, merits phase, 2008, UNCITRAL/NAFTA, http://www.naftaclaims.com/disputes/usa/GrandRiver/GRE-USA-Merits-Counter-Memorial-R.pdf, 128–9, particularly at footnote 466 (United States).

[136] *In the Matter of the Chagos Marine Protected Area Arbitration (The Republic of Mauritius v The United Kingdom of Great Britain and Northern Ireland)*, 2015, award, Arbitral Tribunal Constituted under Annex VII of the United Nations Convention on the Law of the Sea, http://www.pca-cpa.org/MU-UK%2020150318%20Awardd4b1.pdf?fil_id=2899. See generally I. Papanicolopulu, '*Mauritius v. United Kingdom*: Submission of the Dispute on the Marine Protected Area around the Chagos Archipelago to Arbitration', *EJIL:Talk!*, 11 February 2011, http://www.ejiltalk.org/mauritius-v-united-kingdom-submission-of-the-dispute-on-the-marine-protected-area-around-the-chagos-archipelago-to-arbitration/; and M. Waibel, '*Mauritius v. UK*: Chagos Marine Protected Area Unlawful', *EJIL:Talk!*, 17 April 2015, http://www.ejiltalk.org/mauritius-v-uk-chagos-marine-protected-area-unlawful/.

[137] *Chagos Marine Protected Area Arbitration (The Republic of Mauritius v The United Kingdom of Great Britain and Northern Ireland)*, counter-memorial submitted by the United Kingdom, 2013, http://www.pca-cpa.org/4.%20Counter%20Memoriale29c.pdf?fil_id=2586, particularly at 8–47.

[138] Ibid., 183–90, quoted at 184.

[139] *Chagos Marine Protected Area Arbitration (The Republic of Mauritius v The United Kingdom of Great Britain and Northern Ireland)*, reply of the Republic of Mauritius, 2013, http://www.pca-cpa.org/5.%20Replya480.pdf?fil_id=2587, 123-127.

increasingly formed a common aspect of their legal claims in such settings in the late twentieth and early twenty-first centuries. However, it is important to note that the rule is also used outside of the courtroom. There are a number of such examples from practice here too, although equally, again, not a huge number. To provide just one illustrative example at this juncture, Turkey is a persistent objector to the extension to a 12-nautical-mile limit for territorial waters.[140] During discussions concerning the issue of the 'breadth of territorial waters' as part of the lengthy negotiations towards UNCLOS[141] at the Third Conference in 1982, Turkey explicitly claimed persistent objector status with regard to any customary extension—reflected in Article 3 of UNCLOS—to a 12-mile limit, as it was keen to avoid the emerging extension from being used against it by Greece in the Aegean.[142] Turkey asserted that it was 'a persistent objector to the 12-nautical mile limit [because of its] consistent and manifest refusal to accept' the customary status of the extension to territorial sea limits.[143] Turkey had been objecting to the rule since the early twentieth century, but was particularly vociferous in objecting in the twenty-five years immediately prior to the adoption of UNCLOS. There is little question, outside of Greece and Cyprus at least, that Turkey is an exempt persistent objector state to the 12-mile limit.[144]

While Turkey explicitly invoked the persistent objector rule in relation to the 12-mile limit, however, it is important to note that—unlike in the context of adjudicative proceedings, where states are necessarily required to present formal legal arguments and, thus, are more likely to explicitly invoke the persistent objector rule—in general international practice states in most instances use the persistent objector rule (i.e. by persistently objecting to an emerging norm) without necessarily explicitly *invoking* the rule itself: at least, not unless or until they absolutely have to. This issue will be examined in Chapter 3 in relation to the examination of what constitutes 'objection' for the purposes of the rule.[145] It is clear that states often prefer to argue that the custom in question has not crystallized, even when this is patently not the case, rather than claiming persistent objector status. No more will be said on this point here (other than to note that this makes identifying examples of persistent objection in practice all the more difficult, which helps to explain why commentators so often claim that the rule is never, or hardly ever, used), but it is important to keep in mind.

[140] See, generally, Y. Acer, *The Aegean Maritime Disputes and International Law* (Aldershot, Ashgate, 2003); D. Anderson, *Modern Law of the Sea: Selected Essays* (Leiden, Martinus Nijhoff, 2008), 91, particularly at footnote 14; and D. Bölükbaşı, *Turkey and Greece: The Aegean Disputes—A Unique Case in International Law* (London, Cavendish, 2004).

[141] United Nations Convention on the Law of the Sea (UNCLOS), 10 December 1982, 1833 UNTS 3.

[142] See, for example, Official Records of the Third United Nations Conference on the Law of the Sea, Volume XVII (Plenary Meetings, Summary Records and Verbatim Records, as well as Documents of the Conference, Resumed Eleventh Session and Final Part Eleventh Session and Conclusion), 1982, UN Doc. A/CONF.62/SR.189, 76, para. 150.

[143] Ibid.

[144] See, for example, E.A. Georgiades, 'The Imia Islets: A Beginning to the Maritime Delimitation of the Aegean Sea Dispute' (2011) 17 *Ocean and Coastal Law Journal* 103, 103, footnote 3.

[145] See, in particular, Chapter 3, section II.

Examples of state persistent objection outside of the context of pleadings before international courts and tribunals will again be referenced and examined throughout subsequent chapters of this book to highlight the operation of the rule, so to avoid repetition they will not all be detailed here. Moreover, this author does not claim to have identified every single example of state usage or invocation of the rule by any means. A number of examples have been identified over the course of this project, however, and these will be considered throughout this book. It is clearly the case that there is, today, a degree of 'social acceptance' of the persistent objector rule in international law by states.

There are a few points to note with regard to the state practice in relation to the persistent objector rule. Firstly, it is important to distinguish the *existence* of the rule in state practice from its *efficacy*. A more subtle critique of the rule than (incorrectly) holding that it is never invoked is that it is extremely difficult for states to maintain exemption acquired through persistent objection after the norm being objected to has crystallized.[146] This is undeniably true, but this does not speak to the existence of the rule as such, only to how effective it is in relation to its commonly asserted *raison d'etre* (being the preservation of the voluntarist theory of state consent).[147] This question—the issue of maintaining exemption—will be examined in Chapter 8.[148] What is crucial to note at this stage is that states do use the rule, and that this has in a number of instances led to them maintaining an exemption from the binding force of the norm to which they have objected. This is true irrespective of the fact that it is often extremely difficult for the state to maintain this exemption for long.

Secondly, it is worth noting that the invocation and usage of the rule by states has been increasing since the late 1990s.[149] It was argued by Stein in 1985 that there would likely be 'increasingly frequent and effective resort to the principle of the persistent objector in the future'.[150] In 1992, Weil suggested that this prediction may already have been realized and that, in state practice, 'la Belle au bois dormant [of the persistent objector rule] s'est réveillée'.[151] In fact, Weil was incorrect: Stein's prediction was not borne out in the decade or so immediately following it. As Steinfeld rightly noted in 1996, just over ten years after the publication of Stein's article, no significant increase in practice had yet occurred, although admittedly, Steinfeld then went on to make the same prediction that it soon *would*.[152] Today, it can be said that Stein was correct in 1985 to suggest that the usage of the rule by states would increase: it is simply that it has taken rather longer than he perhaps thought for this increase in usage to occur. A decade and a half into the

146 See sources cited at n. 119.

147 See ILA Final Report, n. 4, 28; A. Abass, *Complete International Law: Text, Cases, and Materials* (Oxford, Oxford University Press, 2nd edn, 2014), 48; G.M. Danilenko, *Law-Making in the International Community* (Dordrecht, Martinus Nijhoff, 1993), 112; Dumberry, n. 9, 793–4; O. Elias, 'Some Remarks on the Persistent Objector Rule in Customary International Law' (1991) 6 *Denning Law Journal* 37, 47; Guldahl, n. 33, 58; Mendelson, n. 26, 237; and Wolfke, n. 119, 66–7.

148 See, in particular, Chapter 8, section II.

149 C.A. Bradley, 'The Juvenile Death Penalty' (2002–3) 52 *Duke Law Journal* 485, 517.

150 Stein, n. 7, 463.

151 Weil, n. 9, 193.

152 Steinfeld, n. 5, 1646.

twenty-first century, the rule is being used with increasing regularity by states,[153] solidifying its place as a secondary rule of the international legal system.

Finally, it is important not to lose sight of the fact that, as already noted and in spite of all of the foregoing, state usage of the rule remains limited. There are examples of states explicitly invoking the rule or using it without explicitly referencing it and (in either case) gaining de jure exemption by virtue of that usage. However, the increase in the number of examples that can be identified in recent years does not belie the fact that they remain few in number.

III. Conclusion

It is probably correct to say that persistent objection's emergence as a secondary rule of the international legal system has been due, more than any other factor, to its ever-increasing endorsement in scholarship.[154] As was discussed in Chapter 1, at least its broad conceptual basis can be traced to the theorists of the eighteenth century, albeit that one has to skip forward to the mid-twentieth century to find its modern form articulated in the literature. Yet the fact that the doctrine most notably has its roots in scholarship, and *recent* scholarship at that (at least when it comes to the modern conceptualization of the rule), does not ultimately affect the question of its existence today. International law, rather more so than most legal systems, owes much of its content to scholarly endeavour.[155] The persistent objector rule has now generally been accepted by the wider international community, including in case law and, pertinently, in state practice. This social 'acceptance' has been somewhat tentative: it has not been as extensive as one may perhaps have expected given the ubiquity of the rule in scholarly doctrine.

However, the present author submits that there is nonetheless more than enough evidence to support the existence of the persistent objector rule today. The state acceptance and usage of the rule, especially when taken alongside the increasingly notable judicial endorsement of it and its ubiquity in scholarship, confirms that the rule is indeed a secondary rule of the international legal system. It is a new and comparatively underused rule, to be sure: Mendelson's assertion in 1998 that 'the existence of the persistent objector rule is well established in State practice, case law and the literature'[156] is probably still an overstatement of the matter. Lepard's rather more tentative perspective is a better reflection of the legal reality:

> despite the paucity of practice of invocation [of the persistent objector rule,] it has become generally accepted as one of the secondary rules of customary law formation. That is,

[153] See Crawford, n. 122, 28.
[154] Bradley and Gulati, n. 118, 14.
[155] See G. Triggs, 'The Public International Lawyer and the Practice of International Law' (2005) 24 *Australian Yearbook of International Law* 201, particularly at 202; and M. Wood, 'Teachings of the Most Highly Qualified Publicists (Art. 38(1) ICJ Statute)' in R. Wolfrum (ed.), *Max Planck Encyclopaedia of Public International Law, vol. IX* (Oxford, Oxford University Press, 2012), 783, particularly at 783, para. 3 and 786, para. 19.
[156] Mendelson, n. 26, 240. See also UN Doc. A/70/10, n.113, 36, para. 73 (views of the Special Rapporteur for the ILC's ongoing work on the 'Identification of customary international law',

states generally believe that the doctrine should be maintained in some form, and this is a good reason to recognise it.[157]

Investigation reveals a relatively small but cumulatively convincing degree of support for the persistent objector rule. *Further* investigation into this body of practice allows us to analyse the mechanics of the rule: it is one thing to conclude that it exists, but how does it function? The next chapter begins Part II of this book, and the analysis of this question.

Sir Michael Wood, during the consideration of the topic at the ILC's Sixty-seventh session: '[t]he Special Rapporteur emphasized that the [persistent objector] rule was *well established* in jurisprudence, in the previous work of the Commission, and in the literature'; emphasis added).

[157] Lepard, n. 121, 229. See also Third Report on Identification of Customary International Law, ILC, n. 34, para. 90 (noting the assertion in the literature that 'States themselves have come to recognize [the persistent objector rule] as forceful'); Koskenniemi, n. 112, 443, footnote 203 ('[m]ost lawyers (*and States*) … adhere to [the persistent objector rule] in one way or another'; emphasis added). Based on his own analysis of practice, the present author concurs with such statements.

PART II

THE CRITERIA FOR THE OPERATION OF THE PERSISTENT OBJECTOR RULE

3

The Objection Criterion

Having considered the origins and general legal basis of the persistent objector rule in Part I, Part II now examines the way in which the rule functions, and the various criteria for its operation. Subsequent chapters in Part II will consider the persistence, consistency, and timeliness criteria respectively, but this chapter begins the analysis by exploring what actually constitutes 'objection' for the purposes of the rule. It is perhaps rather inane to say that a state must object for it to be considered a persistent objector. However, the *meaning* of 'objection' requires some clarification in relation to the operation of the rule.

This chapter begins by noting briefly, in section I, that only *states* can be persistent objectors. It then goes on to consider to what exactly an objector state must be objecting, in section II. In particular, section II highlights the usual strategy of states in objecting not to the individual applicability of the emerging norm *to them* but to the very existence of the emerging norm itself. The chapter then turns, in section III, to the need for objection to be communicated and openly expressed. Finally, section IV assesses the necessary form of objection: it first considers whether objection by either words or deeds (or both) is required for a state to gain persistent objector status, and then examines rather more specifically the question of what form objection can take, by looking at the various possible 'types' of persistent objection.

I. The Objector Must Be a State

An initial, but rather straightforward, point that must be made at the start of this chapter concerns the *identity* of the objector. It may seem axiomatic to say that the objector must be a state—the state-as-objector position has essentially been thus far assumed in this book—but this may not be quite as self-evident as one might think, given that customary international law is increasingly seen as being binding upon non-state actors in certain circumstances.[1] One might therefore ask

[1] This is perhaps most starkly the case in the context of the law of non-international armed conflict: see D. Murray, 'How International Humanitarian Law Treaties Bind Non-State Armed Groups' (2015) 20 *Journal of Conflict and Security Law* 101; and A. Roberts and S. Sivakumaran, 'Lawmaking by Nonstate Actors: Engaging Armed Groups in the Creation of International Humanitarian Law' (2012) 37 *Yale Journal of International Law* 107.

whether de facto 'states', autonomous (or semi-autonomous) regions, and an array of other 'state-like' entities might be able to gain exemption through persistent objection.

There is very little to guide us in answering such questions: few academics have explored the possibility of anyone other than states persistently objecting[2] and, more importantly, non-state actors do not generally attempt to employ the persistent objector rule. One attempt—perhaps the *only* notable attempt—is the argument made by counsel for Hong Kong's Director of Immigration in *C* et al. in 2008.[3] Hong Kong asserted that it was a persistent objector to the customary international law norm of *non-refoulement*.[4] However, even in making this argument, Hong Kong was clear that it did not have the capacity in itself to 'object' for the purposes of the rule, given that it was a non-state actor.[5] Instead, it claimed that the objections of both the United Kingdom and China—in particular by way of treaty reservations—constituted objections 'on its behalf' and thus established its exempt status.[6]

At first instance, Hartmann J accepted this argument, and determined that Hong Kong was indeed a persistent objector to the *non-refoulement* rule.[7] Yuen JA disagreed on appeal, determining that Hong Kong did not have any exempt status to the customary norm.[8] She categorically concluded that 'it is important to remember that *only States can be persistent objectors*'.[9] However, when this pronouncement is read in context, it is clear that Yuen JA was referring to the *process* of persistent objection, not necessarily the resulting *status*. She actually took no position on whether Hong Kong could gain exemption, as a matter of principle, based on the objections of the sovereign states in which it was respectively incorporated. Yuen JA instead took the view that the 'objections' of the United Kingdom and China in respect of the *non-refoulement* rule were not sufficient to lead to exempt status for those states (or Hong Kong as a region of them). This was because the objections were almost entirely manifested as treaty reservations, and thus did not constitute enough evidence of a rejection of a wider corresponding customary norm.[10]

One may therefore point to a distinction here between two understandings of being 'a persistent objector', leading to two different (tentative) conclusions regarding non-state actors. First, the *C* et al. first instance decision indicates that certain non-state actors—autonomous regions, at least—may be able to gain

[2] Although see F. Ingman, 'Persistent Objector—The Demise of a Hero?' (2008), unpublished Masters thesis, Lund University, http://lup.lub.lu.se/luur/download?func=downloadFile&recordOId=1558532&fileOId=1564685, 54–5; and O. Jones, 'Customary *Non-Refoulement* of Refugees and Automatic Incorporation into the Common Law: A Hong Kong Perspective' (2009) 58 *International and Comparative Law Quarterly* 443, 454–5.

[3] *C* et al. *v Director of Immigration*, 2008, 2 HKC 167; and *C* et al. *v Director of Immigration and Secretary for Security*, 2011, Hong Kong Special Administrative Region, Court of Appeal, CACV 132-137/2008.

[4] Ibid., para. 37. [5] Ibid., paras. 71–2. [6] Ibid., para. 72.

[7] *C* et al., first instance, n. 3, para. 194.

[8] *C* et al., Court of Appeal, n. 3, paras 70–2. [9] Ibid., para. 70, emphasis added.

[10] Ibid., para. 72. For further discussion, see n. 164–n. 178 and accompanying text.

exempt status by virtue of the objections made by a state (be it on behalf of the region or generally). The *C* et al. appeal decision does nothing to alter that determination. This link between the exempt status of the region and the state of which it is part is further supported by the appeal decision in *Democratic Republic of the Congo v FG Hemisphere Associates LLC*, where Bokhary PJ in the Hong Kong Court of Final Appeal noted that China was a persistent objector to the concept of restricted immunity, although this was not determinative for the Court's decision.[11] The Court further held that Hong Kong was *required* to apply the absolute immunity principle in its courts, because that was the position of China.[12] Although the Court did not make the link between this finding and persistent objection explicit, it essentially took the view that because China was a persistent objector, Hong Kong was too, even if it did not wish to be: it was estopped by China's exempt status.[13]

It is entirely logical that if a state persistently objects to a particular emerging norm and gains an exemption to it, then that exemption would be prima facie valid for all of the state's regions and territories. A *state's* status as an objector may therefore have implications for a non-state actor's equivalent status, albeit that this will only likely be relevant in the limited circumstances where the non-state actor is a region of a state, or an entity for which the state is responsible under international law.

Secondly, however, all the evidence (accepting, admittedly, that there is very little evidence) suggests that non-state actors do not have the capacity in themselves to 'object' for the purposes of the persistent objector rule. Hong Kong conceded this point in *C* et al., and Yuen JA confirmed it in her decision on appeal in that case. More broadly, this would seem to be a correct reflection of practice, in that this author has not been able to find any examples of a non-state actor gaining exemption by way of *its own* objections to an emerging customary norm. Almost all of the various academic,[14] judicial,[15] and state[16] expressed definitions of the

[11] *Democratic Republic of the Congo v FG Hemisphere Associates LLC (No 1)* 2011, 14 HKCFAR, Final Appeal Nos. 5, 6, and 7 of 2010 (civil), para. 121, per Bokhary PJ.

[12] Ibid., paras 181–416. Joint judgment of the majority.

[13] M. Ramsden, 'Using International Law in Hong Kong Courts: An Examination of Non-Refoulement Litigation' (2013) 42 *Common Law World Review* 351, 363. For discussion of the background and first instance decision in this case, see O. Jones, 'Let the Mainland Speak: A Positivist Take on the Congo Case' (2011) 41 *Hong Kong Law Journal* 177.

[14] A classic academic definition of the rule is that set out in *Committee on Formation of Customary (General) International Law*, Final Report of the Committee, 'Statement of Principles Applicable to the Formation of General Customary International Law', International Law Association, London Conference (2000), http://www.ila-hq.org/en/committees/index.cfm/cid/30, 27, section 15 ('[i]f whilst a practice is developing into a rule of general law [that is, customary international law], *a State* persistently and openly dissents from the rule, it will not be bound by it'; emphasis added).

[15] A representative example from case law is *Siderman de Blake v Republic of Argentina*, 1992, United States Court of Appeals for the Ninth Circuit 965 F.2d 699 (9th Cir. 1992), per Fletcher J., 715, para. 54 ('[a] *state* that persistently objects to a norm of customary international law that other states accept is not bound by that norm'; emphasis added).

[16] For a representative example of the way in which states have defined the rule, see *Right of Passage over Indian Territory (Portugal v India)*, preliminary objection of the Government of India, 1957 ICJ Plead., vol. I, 97, 178, para. 184 ('even where a general custom can be proved, *a State* which

persistent objector rule, of course, identify the objector as being 'a state', and there is no reason to doubt this understanding (especially given that it has been expressed by states themselves). Ultimately, it would seem that 'only states can make the objections needed to become persistent objectors'.[17]

It is worth noting two further points that relate to this conclusion. Firstly, there is no necessary correlation between the fact that a non-state actor may be bound by customary international law and its ability to exempt itself from it, just as there is not necessarily any correlation between the binding nature of custom on a non-state actor and that actor's (in)ability to contribute directly to the formation of the custom in question.[18] Secondly, for a non-state actor that objects during the formation of a customary norm and then later acquires statehood, it would seemingly only be objections that it makes *after* its acquisition of statehood that would 'count' in terms of assessing whether it had gained an exemption. If the customary norm in question crystallized prior to the state gaining statehood, then it would be bound just like any other 'new' state,[19] because it did not persistently object—*as a state*—in time.[20]

II. Objection to What?

Having concluded that objectors must be states, the next and most important issue to be considered in this chapter is the question of what a state must object to. A state seeking to evade the binding force of a new norm of customary international law has two options: 'it may concede that there is a rule, but maintain that that rule is not binding on it ... [or] it may deny the *existence* of the rule itself, rather than its *applicability*.'[21] The former approach means that the dissenting state explicitly objects by arguing that the newly emerging customary norm is inapplicable to it specifically (objecting to applicability). In the latter case, the dissenting state objects to the norm's obligatory nature per se, by arguing that the customary rule has not yet formed at all (objecting to existence). For the purposes

has persistently adopted a different attitude in its own practice is not bound by the general custom'; emphasis added).

[17] Ingman, n. 2, 55. See also I. MacGibbon, 'Some Observations on the Part of Protest in International Law' (1953) 30 *British Yearbook of International Law* 293, 294 (discussing the concept of 'protest' in international law more generally). *Contra* Jones, n. 2, 454–5 (arguing that Hong Kong has the capacity, in itself, to persistently object).

[18] See, for example, Roberts and Sivakumaran, n. 1 (arguing that there should be a greater correlation between the binding force of customary international law upon non-state actors and the influence of those actors on the formation of the relevant rules of custom, but, even from this perspective, asserting that this is not and should not be a 'direct' correlation).

[19] See Chapter 6, section VIII regarding the position of new states in relation to the persistent objector rule.

[20] Ingman, n. 2, 55; and Murray, n. 1, 117.

[21] O. Elias and C.L. Lim, *The Paradox of Consensualism in International Law* (The Hague, Kluwer Law International, 1998), 106, emphasis in original. See also P. Weil, 'Le droit international en quête de son identité—Cours général de droit international public' (1992-VI) 237 *Recueil des cours* 9, 191.

of the persistent objector rule, which understanding of objection must the dissenting state adopt?

The intuitive understanding of 'objection' in the context of the persistent objector rule is that the dissenting state repeatedly articulates that an emerging norm is inapplicable to it. That is, those scholars who have written on the rule commonly assume that State X will explicitly assert that 'State X is not bound by a norm requiring Y' or 'a norm requiring Y is inapplicable to State X'. Moreover, once norm Y is considered to have crystallized, there is a further assumption that persistent objection requires that State X goes on to invoke the persistent objector rule explicitly: for example, 'State X is not bound by norm Y, because it persistently objected to norm Y during norm Y's formation'. The majority of writers implicitly adopt this understanding of the process of persistent objection, assuming that a state must 'announce that it does not view itself as bound'.[22]

It was noted in Chapter 2 that a relatively common critique of the persistent objector rule is that it is rarely used by states,[23] but that, while this claim is correct to an extent, the rule has been used far more often than its critics indicate.[24] One of the reasons that it is regularly asserted that the persistent objector rule is so rarely used is because scholars have, in general, only considered instances where a state has objected to the applicability of the emerging norm and then explicitly invoked the persistent objector rule.[25] This is an overly narrow understanding of what is meant by 'objection'. States almost never claim that the embryonic customary norm in question does not apply to them. They instead simply argue that the customary norm has not yet crystallized and is thus inapplicable to all.[26] Indeed, they commonly maintain this stance even when it is generally accepted that the norm in question has crystallized (rather than explicitly claiming to be a persistent objector state).

This can be seen, for example, in the United States' response to the 2005 International Committee of the Red Cross (ICRC) Study on *Customary International Humanitarian Law*.[27] The ICRC accepted in the Study that the

[22] R.B. Baker, 'Customary International Law in the 21st Century: Old Challenges and New Debates' (2010) 21 *European Journal of International Law* 173, 176.

[23] See Chapter 2, particularly at n. 117–n. 121 and accompanying text.

[24] See ibid., section II.

[25] See, for example, T.L. Stein, 'The Approach of the Different Drummer: The Principle of the Persistent Objector in International Law' (1985) 26 *Harvard International Law Journal* 457, 462 (stating, with regard to the possible persistent objector status of the United States in the context of deep seabed mining, that he was 'unable to find evidence that the principle of the persistent objector has been invoked by those asserting that deep seabed mining is lawful', and seemingly assuming that this fact was determinative as to a lack of persistent objection on the part of the United States).

[26] T. Meron, 'International Law in the Age of Human Rights' (2013) 301 *Recueil des cours* 13, 394; M. Ragazzi, *The Concept of International Obligations* Erga Omnes (Oxford, Clarendon Press, 1997), 65; and A. Roberts, 'Who Killed Article 38(1)(b)? A Reply to Bradley & Gulati' (2010) 21 *Duke Journal of Comparative and International Law* 173, 187.

[27] J.B. Bellinger III and W.J. Haynes II, 'A US Government Response to the International Committee of the Red Cross Study on Customary International Humanitarian Law', reproduced in 'Reports and Documents' (2007) 89 *International Review of the Red Cross* 433.

United States, United Kingdom, and France were all persistent objectors in relation to a customary international law prohibition on the 'the use of methods or means of warfare that are intended, or may be expected, to cause widespread, long-term and severe damage to the natural environment',[28] at least so far as this rule applied 'to the use of nuclear weapons'.[29] In spite of the fact that the ICRC therefore explicitly took the view—presumably rather grudgingly, given the humanitarian mandate of that organization—that the three states in question were exempt persistent objectors and, thus, were not bound by the customary prohibition that the Study identified in the nuclear weapons context, the United States made a point in its response of arguing that there *was no such prohibition in custom at all*.[30] In other words, even having been recognized as an exempt persistent objector, the United States' preference was to continue to assert that there had been insufficient state practice and *opinio juris* for the norm to emerge per se and that it was therefore not bound because there was no such rule to bind it.

Persistent objectors rarely *say* that they are persistent objectors. Instances where states have objected to the emergence/existence of the norm in question nonetheless constitute 'objection' to that norm, albeit that it is perhaps not the sort of objection that one may intuitively look for when examining state practice for usage of the persistent objector rule.[31] Thus, if a state finds that it has absolutely no choice but to plead persistent objector status, it can rely on previous objections regarding the existence of the rule.

There are a number of reasons why it is unsurprising that the persistent objector rule is explicitly invoked only rarely by states and that a version of objection based on the existence of the norm per se is far more commonplace in practice. First, and probably most importantly, for a state to invoke the persistent objector

[28] J-M. Henckaerts and L. Doswald-Beck (eds), *Customary International Humanitarian Law, vol. I*, International Committee of the Red Cross (ICRC) Study (Cambridge, Cambridge University Press, 2005), 151. As an aside, it is worth noting that both Bethlehem and Dumberry have criticized the ICRC IHL Study because it explicitly refrained from taking a view on whether it was legally possible for a state to exempt itself from a customary international law norm by way of persistent objection. See D. Bethlehem, 'The Methodological Framework of the Study' in E. Wilmshurst and S. Breau (eds), *Perspectives on the ICRC Study on Customary International Humanitarian Law* (Cambridge University Press, Cambridge, 2007), 3, 10; and P. Dumberry, 'Incoherent and Ineffective: The Concept of Persistent Objector Revisited' (2010) 59 *International and Comparative Law Quarterly* 779, 792–3. However, while the Study made its fence-sitting stance on the persistent objector rule pretty evident (ICRC IHL Study, *vol. I*, n. 28, xlv), it is hard to dispute that it ultimately accepted that France, the United Kingdom, and the United States were persistent objectors (however qualified its language may have been in so doing). In practice, then, despite the critique of Bethlehem and Dumberry, the Study did accept the persistent objector rule's existence and, indeed, its applicability to this particular norm of IHL. See D. Kritsiotis, 'On the Possibilities of and For Persistent Objection' (2010) 21 *Duke Journal of Comparative and International Law* 121, 139, footnote 75.

[29] ICRC IHL Study, *vol. I*, n. 28, 151.

[30] Bellinger and Haynes, n. 27, 457.

[31] See Third Report on Identification of Customary International Law (M. Wood, Special Rapporteur), International Law Commission, Sixty-seventh session, 27 March 2015, UN Doc. A/CN.4/682, para. 92 (arguing that either 'approach' qualifies as 'objection' for the purposes of the persistent objector rule: '[i]n practice, a State may deny that an emerging rule has become a rule of customary international law, object to the applicability of the rule to itself, or do both').

rule is for it to immediately brand itself as an outsider. It was notable that in his dissenting opinion to the *Legality of the Threat or Use of Nuclear Weapons* advisory opinion, Judge Schwebel referred to a persistent objector state, *in abstracto*, as 'a pariah Government crying out in the wilderness of otherwise adverse international opinion'.[32] Such graphic language highlights the political undesirability for states of the legal self-ostracization that comes with a resort to the rule. After all, a state that explicitly claims persistent objector status is essentially making two assertions: (a) we accept that a customary rule of international law exists, and it binds all states; (b) except us. The negative political implications for the objector of such a stance are obvious.[33]

In addition to the undesirability for a state of opting to label itself a dissenting trouble-maker—the 'odd State out'[34]—the timeliness requirement for persistent objection[35] means that the rule is inapplicable at the point at which the state is objecting. It is commonly agreed that objection must occur during the rule's formation, but that the exemption that the persistent objector rule creates is only triggered *after* an emerging customary norm has in fact emerged.[36] As such, states are very unlikely to refer explicitly to the persistent objector rule whilst objecting. For a state to say 'we object because *if* this emerging customary norm becomes binding in the future, we will want to remain exempt from it' would be both politically unwise and legally unnecessary, given that the emerging norm may never crystallize at all.

Another point to note here is that objection to the *existence* of an emerging norm can potentially 'snowball', with other states joining the dissenter's position (ultimately leading to a 'weight' of state practice sufficient to stop the norm emerging at all).[37] In contrast, objection to the *applicability* of the emerging norm to the dissenting state alone is more likely to lead to other states distancing themselves from its position, rather than garnering support; it draws attention to the standard

[32] *Legality of the Threat or Use of Nuclear Weapons*, advisory opinion, 1996 ICJ Rep. 226, dissenting opinion of Vice-President Schwebel, 312.

[33] O. Barsalou, 'La doctrine de l'objecteur persistant en droit international public' (2006) 19 *Revue québécoise de droit international* 1, 15; C.A. Bradley and M. Gulati, 'Customary International Law and Withdrawal Rights in an Age of Treaties' (2010) 21 *Duke Journal of International and Comparative Law* 1, 24; D.A. Colson, 'How Persistent Must the Persistent Objector Be?' (1986) 61 *Washington Law Review* 957, 962 ('legal objections, so fundamental to the persistent objector, inadvertently take on political character'); Dumberry, n. 28, 791; C.L. Lim and O. Elias, 'Withdrawing from Custom and the Paradox of Consensualism in International Law' (2010) 21 *Duke Journal of Comparative and International Law* 143, 151–2; C.G. Guldahl, 'The Role of Persistent Objection in International Humanitarian Law' (2008) 77 *Nordic Journal of International Law* 51, 59; M.H. Mendelson, 'The Formation of Customary International Law' (1998) 272 *Recueil des cours* 155, 234; and Ragazzi, n. 26, 65.

[34] Guldahl, n. 33, 59.

[35] See Chapter 6.

[36] During the emergence of a new norm, there is no difference in legal status between an objecting state and a non-objecting state: neither is bound because an emerging norm is, *ipso facto*, not yet a binding norm of customary international law. See Kritsiotis, n. 28, 131–2. For further discussion, see Chapter 6, section IV, n. 131–n. 140 and accompanying text.

[37] For further discussion, see Chapter 9, section VII.*i*, particularly at n. 206–n. 210 and accompanying text.

and the dissenter's exceptionalist stance, which may in fact make the crystallization of the norm more likely than it might otherwise have been.[38]

One might intuitively think that it will be easier for a state to demonstrate that it has persistently objected to a norm (which requires the state to provide evidence of positive actions or statements, and its *own* actions/statements at that) than to demonstrate that the norm being objected to does not exist (which requires the state to provide evidence of other states' actions or statements, or, perhaps, the *absence* of their actions/statements).[39] However, such an assumption would ignore the reversal of the burden of proof that persistent objection involves. Explicit reliance on persistent objector status means that a dissenting state must take upon itself the burden of proof.[40] The nature of the persistent objector rule, as providing an exception to a binding legal norm, necessarily means that a state seeking to avail itself of the rule must establish that the rule's requirements are met: there is a rebuttable presumption that a state accepts the emerging rule and it must therefore *demonstrate* that it does not.[41] Such a demonstration is far from easy because the requirements for the operation of the persistent objector rule are not well defined, and are notably onerous.[42] In contrast, the 'burden' of establishing the existence of a new customary international law norm falls, at least initially, on the state(s) asserting that the norm exists.[43] Therefore, it is to be expected that a dissenter will usually opt to take the evidentially less onerous stance of maintaining that the norm is not yet binding custom until it has been unquestionably established that the new norm exists as customary international law.

Indeed, the uncertainty over the point at which a new norm of customary international law crystallizes[44] means that states are often able to maintain a

[38] Barsalou, n. 33, 15–16; A. D'Amato, *The Concept of Custom in International Law* (New York, Cornell University Press, 1971), 70; R-J. Dupuy, 'Coutume sage et coutume sauvage' in C. Rousseau and S. Bastid (eds), *Mélanges offerts à Charles Rousseau: la communauté international* (Paris, Pedone, 1974), 75, 85; and Ragazzi, n. 26, 65.

[39] See Stein, n. 25, 459.

[40] Third Report on Identification of Customary International Law, ILC, n. 31, para. 94; T. Hillier, *Sourcebook on Public International Law* (London, Cavendish Publishing, 1998), 74; and A. Kaczorowska, *Public International Law* (Abingdon, Routledge, 4th edn, 2010), 41.

[41] O. Elias, 'Some Remarks on the Persistent Objector Rule in Customary International Law' (1991) 6 *Denning Law Journal* 37, 38; Elias and Lim, n. 21, 32; H. Lau, 'Rethinking the Persistent Objector Doctrine in International Human Rights Law' (2005–6) 6 *Chicago Journal of International Law* 496, 498; L. Loschin, 'The Persistent Objector Rule and Customary Human Rights Law: A Proposed Analytical Framework' (1996) 2 *University of California Davis Journal of International Law and Policy* 147, 150; A.V. Lowe, 'Do General Rules of International Law Exist?' (1983) 9 *Review of International Studies* 207, 209; Mendelson, n. 33, 234; R. Price, 'Emerging Customary Norms and Anti-Personnel Landmines' in C. Reus-Smit (ed.), *The Politics of International Law* (Cambridge, Cambridge University Press, 2004), 106, 123; Ragazzi, n. 26, 60; M.E. Villiger, *Customary International Law and Treaties: A Manual on the Theory and Practice of the Interrelation of Sources* (The Hague, Kluwer, 2nd edn, 1997), 34; and P. Weil, 'Towards Relative Normativity in International Law' (1983) 77 *American Journal of International Law* 413, 437.

[42] See Conclusion, n. 44–n. 49 and accompanying text for discussion of the onerousness of being a persistent objector. See also Chapters 4, 5, and 6 for discussion of the problems associated with the application of the requirements of persistence, consistency, and timeliness.

[43] Elias and Lim, n. 21, 32.

[44] Quantifying the exact point at which new customary international law crystallizes is notoriously difficult. See, for example, ILA Final Report, n. 14, generally, but particularly at 2; A. Boyle

credible argument that a norm they dislike has not yet emerged (and is therefore not binding per se) even after a majority of states have accepted that the new norm has crystallized.[45] The position of Egypt with regard to antipersonnel landmines (APLMs) usefully highlights this fact. It has been argued by an increasing number of commentators that a customary international law prohibition of the use, production, and stockpiling of APLMs now exists under international humanitarian law,[46] but whether the norm is emerged or emerging is debatable based on the supporting state practice/*opinio juris*.[47] A small number of states have objected to this avowed norm and, among these, Egypt's objections to any possible customary APLM ban have been the most vociferous.[48] However, Egypt has never explicitly

and C. Chinkin, *The Making of International Law* (Oxford, Oxford University Press, 2007), 21; A.T. Guzman and T.L. Meyer, 'Customary International Law in the 21st Century' in R.A. Miller and R.M. Bratspies (eds), *Progress in International Law* (Leiden, Martinus Nijhoff, 2008), 197, 197–200; J. Kammerhofer, 'Uncertainty in the Formal Sources of International Law: Customary International Law and Some of its Problems' (2004) 15 *European Journal of International Law* 523 (discussing numerous uncertainties surrounding the formation and content of customary international law); J.O. McGinnis, 'The Comparative Disadvantage of Customary International Law' (2006) 30 *Harvard Journal of Law and Public Policy* 7, 10; and J.P. Trachtman, 'The Obsolescence of Customary International Law' (21 November 2014), *Social Science Research Network*, http://papers.ssrn.com/sol3/papers.cfm?abstract_id=2512757, 20 and 31. For more discussion, see Chapter 6, section IV.

45 Koskenniemi goes as far as to say that the inherent uncertainty at the heart of customary international law means that objection 'can *always* be formulated in such a manner': M. Koskenniemi, *From Apology to Utopia: The Structure of International Legal Argument* (Cambridge, Cambridge University Press, reissue, 2005), 444, emphasis in original. See also J.B. McClane, 'How Late in the Emergence of a Norm of Customary International Law May a Persistent Objector Object?' (1989) 13 *International Law Students Association Journal of International Law* 1, 6, footnote 14.

46 See J.M. Beier, 'Siting Indiscriminacy: India and the Global Movement to Ban Landmines' (2002) 8 *Global Governance* 305, 307–8; S. Benesch, G. McGrory, C. Rodriguez, and R. Sloane, 'International Customary Law and Antipersonnel Landmines: Emergence of a New Customary Norm' (1999), Allard K. Lowenstein International Human Rights Clinic, Yale Law School, Landmine Monitor, http://lm.icbl.org/index.php/publications/display?url=lm/1999/appendices/custom_law.html; and Price, n. 41, 106–7. Moreover, the use of APLMs almost certainly contravenes the wider customary international humanitarian law requirements banning indiscriminate weaponry and restricting unnecessary suffering during conflicts in any event, as noted by Price, n. 41, 111–12.

47 See, for example, International Campaign to Ban Landmines, http://www.icbl.org/index.php/icbl/Universal/MBT/Making-the-MBT-Universal (referring to 'the *emerging* international norm of a total ban on anti-personnel landmines'; emphasis added); *The Federal Democratic Republic of Ethiopia v The State of Eritrea*, partial award, 2004, central front, Ethiopia's Claim 2, Eritrea-Ethiopia Claims Commission, para. 18 (taking the view that there was no separate customary international humanitarian law ban on APLMs because the state practice in that regard was 'varied and episodic'); and ICRC IHL Study, *vol. I*, n. 28, 282 ('[contrary] practice means that it cannot be said at this stage that the use of anti-personnel landmines is prohibited under customary international law'). If such a prohibition does exist, it is relatively new and would presumably stem from the obligations contained in the Convention on the Prohibition of the Use, Stockpiling, Production and Transfer of Anti-Personnel Mines and on their Destruction (Ottawa Convention), 18 September 1997, 2056 UNTS 35597. See Benesch, McGrory, Rodriguez, and Sloane, n. 46 (suggesting that those states that have not signed the Ottawa Convention may be exempt from any customary equivalent norm by virtue of persistent objection, although then ultimately concluding that states are not able to persistently object to the emerging customary norm on the basis that it is a 'fundamental' rule of international law: see Chapter 8, section I for a discussion of this possibility).

48 Mary Wareham of Human Rights Watch, quoted in 'Egypt, Others Urged to Sign Mine Ban Treaty' (2000) International Campaign to Ban Landmines, Africa Policy Information Center,

argued that it is a persistent objector state, nor that it rejects the emerging norm's applicability to it. It has, instead, objected by denying the existence of the prohibition in custom per se.[49]

The doubt as to whether the customary prohibition being objected to by Egypt has in fact crystallized means that Egypt can continue to object to the binding force of the norm rather than branding itself as a lone objector. Objection to the existence of the norm therefore presents the dissenting state with a cake that can be both had and eaten: while consistently objecting to the APLM ban, Egypt has been able to at least imply that it might accept the binding nature of the prohibition were it ever to evolve into a legal requirement.[50] The emphasis of the stance presented by Egypt is thus on *conforming* to customary international law, not diverging from it. Yet, if it became undeniable that a customary APLM ban had crystallized, Egypt has a record of sustained and forceful objection to fall back on to establish its exempt status as a persistent objector.

Overall, then, it is totally understandable that states only explicitly lay claim to being a persistent objector as a last resort.[51] Comparatively ambiguous objection, made in relation to the existence of the norm being objected to rather than its applicability, is the political reality of the operation of the persistent objector rule. States will almost always favour such an approach, because it means they can avoid impliedly recognizing the existence of a norm by which they do not wish to be bound.[52]

However, this does not mean that this form of objection is any less valid in terms of establishing exemption under the rule:

> [I]t does not matter whether objecting States express their objection or lack of consent in relation to the formation or the existence of the rule, or whether they express their rejection to the applicability of the rule in question to themselves only ... either means of expressing their objection would appear to suffice [for the operation of the persistent objector rule].[53]

https://www.essex.ac.uk/armedcon/story_id/Egypt%20and%20others%20urged%20to%20sign%20Mine%20Ban%20treaty.pdf ('Egypt increasingly seems to be emerging as a leading opponent of a comprehensive ban on antipersonnel mines').

[49] See, for example, General Assembly, Official Records, Sixty-seventh session, First committee 20th meeting, 5 November 2012, UN Doc. A/C.1/67/PV.20, 18.

[50] Ibid.

[51] Elias and Lim, n. 21, 106–7.

[52] P. Dumberry, 'The Last Citadel! Can a State Claim the Status of Persistent Objector to Prevent the Application of a Rule of Customary International Law in Investor-State Arbitration?' (2010) 23 *Leiden Journal of International Law* 379, 388; Dumberry, n. 28, 781; Guldahl, n. 33, 82; C. Quince, *The Persistent Objector and Customary International Law* (Denver, Outskirts Press, 2010), 77 (with particular reference to the position of Mauritania in relation to the practice of female genital mutilation); Stein, n. 25, 468; S. Estreicher, 'A Post-Formation Withdrawal from Customary International Law? Some Cautionary Notes' (2010) 21 *Duke Journal of Comparative and International Law* 57, 62; A. Steinfeld, 'Nuclear Objections: The Persistent Objector and the Legality of the Use of Nuclear Weapons' (1996) 62 *Brooklyn Law Review* 1635, 1669; and E.T. Swaine, 'Bespoke Custom' (2010) 21 *Duke Journal of Comparative and International Law* 207, 217.

[53] O. Elias, 'Persistent Objector' in R. Wolfrum (ed.), *Max Planck Encyclopaedia of Public International Law, vol. VIII* (Oxford, Oxford University Press, 2012), 280, 284, para. 17. See also

The practice of Turkey in objecting to the extension to a 12-nautical-mile limit for territorial waters[54] acts as a useful example. During discussions concerning the issue of the 'breadth of territorial waters' as part of the negotiations towards the UN Convention on the Law of the Sea (UNCLOS)[55] in 1982, Turkey argued that the '12-nautical miles limit for territorial waters has not acquired the character of [a] rule of customary international law' and that any application of this avowed extension was thus unlawful.[56] In other words, Turkey took the position that no customary international law norm had formed. It had moreover maintained that stance for a number of years before the adoption of UNCLOS in 1982. However, as will be recalled from Chapter 2,[57] Turkey then went on to argue that—even if the new limit was now binding in custom—it was not opposable to Turkey because it was 'a persistent objector to the 12-nautical mile limit' through its 'consistent and manifest refusal to accept' the customary status of the extension to territorial sea limits.[58] Turkey therefore argued that its sustained objections as to the very existence of a customary 12-nautical-mile limit *in themselves* constituted persistent objection for the purposes of the persistent objector rule.[59]

Another, rather more recent, example of the way in which objection to the existence of an emerging norm operates in practice is the 2008 claim by the United States in the context of the *Grand River v United States* arbitration under Chapter 11 of the North American Free Trade Agreement (which was decided in 2011).[60] The *Grand River* dispute related to the attempt by various federal states within the United States to reach a settlement with tobacco manufacturers for health-care costs stemming from smoking. The salient aspect of the dispute in this context related to the claimants' contention that the practice of the United States was in breach of certain customary rights of indigenous investors, given the fact that many of the shareholders and employees of Grand River were Native American. This contention included what the claimants saw as an 'obligation to

F.F. Martin, *The Constitution as Treaty: The International Legal Constructionalist Approach to the U.S. Constitution* (Cambridge, Cambridge University Press, 2007), 74–5.

[54] See, generally, Y. Acer, *The Aegean Maritime Disputes and International Law* (Aldershot, Ashgate, 2003); D. Anderson, *Modern Law of the Sea: Selected Essays* (Leiden, Martinus Nijhoff, 2008), 91, particularly at footnote 14; and D. Bölükbaşı, *Turkey and Greece: The Aegean Disputes—A Unique Case in International Law* (London, Cavendish, 2004).

[55] United Nations Convention on the Law of the Sea (UNCLOS), 10 December 1982, 1833 UNTS 3.

[56] Official Records of the Third United Nations Conference on the Law of the Sea, Volume XVII (Plenary Meetings, Summary Records and Verbatim Records, as well as Documents of the Conference, Resumed Eleventh Session and Final Part Eleventh Session and Conclusion), 1982, UN Doc. A/CONF.62/SR.189, 76, para. 148.

[57] See Chapter 2, n. 140–n. 144 and accompanying text.

[58] UN Doc. A/CONF.62/SR.189, n. 56, 76, para. 150.

[59] There is little question, outside of Greece and Cyprus at least, that Turkey is an exempt persistent objector state to the 12-mile limit. See, for example, E.A. Georgiades, 'The Imia Islets: A Beginning to the Maritime Delimitation of the Aegean Sea Dispute' (2011) 17 *Ocean and Coastal Law Journal* 103, 103, footnote 3.

[60] *Grand River Enterprises Six Nations Ltd*, et al. *v Government of the United States of America*, final award, 2011, UNCITRAL/NAFTA, http://www.naftaclaims.com/disputes/usa/GrandRiver/GRE-USA-Award-Merits.pdf.

pro-actively consult with [indigenous persons] prior to taking legislative action that will have a substantial impact upon them'.[61] In response, the United States argued (a) that the norm in question did not exist because the custom had not yet formed and (b) that, if the norm *did* exist, the United States was exempt from the norm under the persistent objector rule because it had repeatedly objected to the existence of such a rule.[62]

The two-stage argumentation employed by the United States in the *Grand River* pleadings is illustrative. Its primary argument was that there was insufficient state practice and *opinio juris* to find that there was a customary international law obligation to consult indigenous peoples in relation to investment.[63] As a secondary argument, however, the United States also took the view that, because it had 'clearly and consistently' maintained the stance that no such norm had formed, the persistent objector rule applied even if the Tribunal found that the norm did now exist.[64]

Like Turkey, the United States was therefore clear that its previous and repeated non-acceptance of the crystallization of the 'indigenous consultation norm' amounted to persistent objection for the purposes of the application of the rule if the norm was considered to have crystallized:

> Even if Claimants had established the existence of such an 'emerging' norm, the United States clearly and consistently has articulated its view that ... [the requirement of] consultation prior to the adoption of legislation does not reflect customary international law ... [therefore] the United States cannot be bound by any consultation requirements.[65]

The examples above highlight the endemic approach in state practice of objecting to a newly emerging norm through rejecting the very formation of the norm at all, but also show that such objection is considered by states as later constituting

[61] *Grand River*, claimants' memorial, merits phase, 2008, UNCITRAL/NAFTA, http://www.naftaclaims.com/disputes/usa/GrandRiver/GRE-USA-Merits-Memorial-R.pdf, particularly paras 184–92 and 213–17, quoted at para. 192. Having said this, the claimants were less than definite about their assertion that the United States was under an obligation to consult indigenous people in this way, arguing that 'customary international law *arguably* requires' such consultation: see para. 188, emphasis added. Any possible customary obligation of this kind—if it exists—would likely have its roots in Articles 19 and 38 of United Nations Declaration on the Rights of Indigenous Peoples, 2007, annexed to General Assembly Resolution 61/296, 13 September 2007, UN Doc. A/RES/61/296.

[62] *Grand River*, counter-memorial of the respondent, merits phase, 2008, UNCITRAL/NAFTA, http://www.naftaclaims.com/disputes/usa/GrandRiver/GRE-USA-Merits-Counter-Memorial-R.pdf, 128–9, particularly at footnote 466.

[63] Ibid., 127–9.

[64] Ibid., 129, particularly at footnote 466. It is of note that the claimants did not contest the assertion of exempt persistent objector status in this regard by the United States. However, it is also the case that in the 2011 final award, the Tribunal did not pronounce on the (secondary and alternative) claim of the United States that it was a persistent objector. The matter was ultimately immaterial, as the Tribunal determined that even if there was a customary rule of consultation, it did not apply to individual investors and so was irrelevant to the decision, see *Grand River*, final award, n. 60, particularly para. 213.

[65] *Grand River*, counter-memorial of the respondent, n. 62, 128–9, references omitted.

'objection' for the purposes of the application of the persistent objector rule, should resort to the rule become necessary.

This 'subtle manner'[66] in which objections are usually advanced does, of course, make 'clear examples of persistent objection harder to find'.[67] Explicit invocations of 'the persistent objector rule' are preferable for commentators and non-objecting states because they are simpler to identify.[68] Indeed, as Koskenniemi has noted, the manner in which states object is a key issue of concern with regard to the persistent objector rule, because it makes 'delimitating the category of persistent objectors' extremely difficult.[69] Nonetheless, this is the reality of the rule.

It is argued here that a required distinction over what a state is objecting *to* during a norm's formation—the binding nature of the emerging norm or the inapplicability of the emerging norm to the objector in particular—would be an impractical feature of the persistent objector rule. It also does not fit with the commonly understood, if somewhat contested in this book,[70] theoretical basis of the rule: that is, the voluntarist notion of state consent. Either form of objection equally represents a withholding of consent:

> A State denying the existence/applicability of a custom has not consented to that custom ... In other words, if there is a difference between a State's claim that there is no rule of customary law on the matter, on the one hand, and a claim that the rule exists but is not binding on the State, on the other, it may well be no more than a difference of taste ... [a] question of argumentative strategy.[71]

States rarely style themselves as persistent objectors unless they have no other option. Objection is commonly oblique because of unwillingness on the part of the objector to label itself as a political and legal pariah, but such dissent is persistent objection nonetheless.

III. The Communication of Objection

It was argued in the previous section that objection does not necessarily need to explicitly reference the persistent objector rule to qualify as usage of the rule. However, while reference to the persistent objector rule itself need not be explicit, it is important to note that the objections required for the rule to operate do need to be. In other words, objection must be *communicated*.

Were a state to dissent internally—let us say through private communications between government officials—it could conceivably later attempt to rely on these communications as evidence of persistent objection.[72] However, it is commonly

[66] Guldahl, n. 33, 59. [67] Ibid.

[68] K. Wolfke, *Custom in Present International Law* (Dordrecht, Martinus Nijhoff, 2nd edn, 1993), 67.

[69] Koskenniemi, n. 45, 444. [70] See, particularly, Chapter 9, section I.*iii*.

[71] Elias and Lim, n. 21, 106. See also Colson, n. 33, 969; and Elias, n. 53, 284, para. 17.

[72] It is worth noting that the Second Report on Identification of Customary International Law (M. Wood, Special Rapporteur), International Law Commission, Sixty-sixth session, 22 May 2014,

asserted in the literature that persistent objection 'must be expressed, not entertained purely privately within the internal counsel of the State'.[73] The predominant academic view is, therefore, that any instance of persistent objection—whether by way of objection to the norm's binding force per se or to its specific applicability—has to be communicated in some way to other states.

More importantly, this is also seemingly the view of states. This can be seen in the classic example of persistent objection in the *Fisheries* case, where Norway argued at some length in its written pleadings submitted to the International Court of Justice (ICJ) in 1950 and 1951 that it was a persistent objector state with regard to the delimitation of territorial sea and fishery zones, having consistently maintained its own system in contrast to the '10-mile rule' propounded as custom by the United Kingdom.[74] However, the United Kingdom claimed that the objections of Norway were insufficiently expressed and that, as a result, it was unaware of them: on this basis, the United Kingdom argued that Norway's objections were not opposable to it.[75] The ICJ dismissed this assertion, holding

UN Doc. A/CN.4/672 took the view that 'internal memoranda by State officials' could constitute 'state practice' for the purposes of customary international law creation (at para. 41(g)), but then went on to say that it would be difficult to see how such 'confidential practice' could contribute to the formation of custom 'unless and until it has been disclosed publicly' (at para. 47).

[73] ILA Final Report, n. 14, 28. See also 'Identification of Customary International Law: Text of the Draft Conclusions Provisionally Adopted by the Drafting Committee', International Law Commission, Sixty-seventh session, Geneva, 4 May–5 June and 6 July–7 August 2015, UN Doc. A/CN.4/L.869, 5, Draft Conclusion 15: Persistent Objector ('[t]he objection must be clearly expressed [and] made known to other States'); Third Report on Identification of Customary International Law, ILC, n. 31, para. 92; Elias and Lim, n. 21, 30; Elias, n. 53, 284, para. 16; G. Fitzmaurice, 'The Law and Procedure of the International Court of Justice, 1951-54: General Principles and Sources of Law' (1953) 30 *British Yearbook of International Law* 1, 25; Guldahl, n. 33, 53; A.T. Guzman, *How International Law Works: A Rational Choice Theory* (Oxford, Oxford University Press, 2008), 188 and 197; J.F. Hartmann, '"Unusual" Punishment: The Domestic Effect of International Norms Restricting the Application of the Death Penalty' (1983) 52 *University of Cincinnati Law Review* 655, 684 (arguing that 'outer-directed action' is required); L.R. Helfer, 'Exiting Custom: Analogies to Treaty Withdrawals' (2010) 21 *Duke Journal of Comparative and International Law* 65, 69; Kaczorowska, n. 40, 41; E. Kontorovich, 'Inefficient Customs in International Law' (2006–7) 48 *William and Mary Law Review* 859, 875 and 910; P. Malanczuk, *Akehurst's Modern Introduction to International Law* (New York, Routledge, 7th edn, 1997), 48; Martin, n. 53, 73–5; H. Meijers, 'How is International Law Made?—The Stages of Growth of International Law and the Use of Customary Rules' (1978) 9 *Netherlands Yearbook of International Law* 3, 18; Mendelson, n. 33, 241; V.M. Padmanabhan, 'The Human Rights Justification for Consent' (2013) 35 *University of Pennsylvania Journal of International Law* 1, 17; N. Petersen, 'The Role of Consent and Uncertainty in the Formation of Customary International Law' (2011) *Reprints of the Max Planck Institute for Research on Collective Goods*, http://www.coll.mpg.de/pdf_dat/2011_04online.pdf, 1; Price, n. 41, 123; Ragazzi, n. 26, 63; Stein, n. 25, 458; J. Tasioulas, 'Customary International Law and the Quest for Global Justice' in A. Perreau-Saussine and J.B. Murphy (eds), *The Nature of Customary Law: Legal, Historical and Philosophical Perspectives* (Cambridge, Cambridge University Press, 2007), 307, 312; and H. Thirlway, *International Customary Law and Codification* (Leiden, A.W. Sijthoff, 1972), 110 and 116.

[74] See *Fisheries* (*United Kingdom v Norway*), counter-memorial submitted by the Government of the Kingdom of Norway, 1950 ICJ Plead., vol. I, 381–4; and *Fisheries* (*United Kingdom v Norway*), rejoinder submitted by the Government of the Kingdom of Norway, 1951 ICJ Plead., vol. III, 291–6.

[75] *Fisheries* (*United Kingdom v Norway*), reply submitted by the Government of the United Kingdom of Great Britain and Northern Ireland, 1950 ICJ Plead., vol. II, 291, particularly at paras 58 and 71.

that Norway's objections were appropriately communicated, and that 'the United Kingdom could not have been ignorant [of the Norwegian position]'.[76] The Court ultimately accepted, of course, that Norway was an exempt persistent objector state, if rather equivocally.[77] Nonetheless, it would seem that both parties, and the ICJ itself, were of the view that open communication was essential.

A much more recent example supporting the need for open and communicated objection is the position taken by Mauritius in 2013, in the context of the *Chagos Marine Protected Area* UNCLOS arbitral dispute (which was decided in 2015).[78] In response to the United Kingdom's claim in its pleadings that it was, in 1965, a persistent objector to the right of self-determination,[79] Mauritius argued that:

> The persistent objector rule requires a State to display persistent objection during the formation of the norm in question. The objection must be expressed: it is not sufficient for government officials to voice objections to themselves, but not communicate them outside the confines of their home working environment. The UK cites an internal document which, it claims, shows its objection to the right. Whatever may have been the view expressed in the internal workings of government, the UK has provided little evidence that it voiced any objection *externally*.[80]

The assertion of Mauritius that 'objection must be expressed' is surely correct.[81] As a simple matter of legal practicality, some degree of external expression of objection must be necessary, because the predominant view is that silence equates to 'consent' for the purposes of calculating the formation of new rules of customary international law.[82] 'Private' objection within a state during the formation of a customary norm, however persistent it may be, cannot be seen as constituting

[76] *Fisheries* (*United Kingdom v Norway*), merits, 1951 ICJ Rep. 116, 139.

[77] See Chapter 2, sections II.*i* and II.*ii* for discussion.

[78] *In the Matter of the Chagos Marine Protected Area Arbitration* (*The Republic of Mauritius v The United Kingdom of Great Britain and Northern Ireland*), 2015, award, Arbitral Tribunal Constituted under Annex VII of the United Nations Convention on the Law of the Sea, http://www.pca-cpa.org/MU-UK%2020150318%20Awardd4b1.pdf?fil_id=2899.

[79] *Chagos Marine Protected Area Arbitration* (*The Republic of Mauritius v The United Kingdom of Great Britain and Northern Ireland*), counter-memorial submitted by the United Kingdom, 2013, http://www.pca-cpa.org/4.%20Counter%20Memoriale29c.pdf?fil_id=2586.

[80] *Chagos Marine Protected Area Arbitration* (*The Republic of Mauritius v The United Kingdom of Great Britain and Northern Ireland*), reply of the Republic of Mauritius, 2013, http://www.pca-cpa.org/5.%20Replya480.pdf?fil_id=2587, 124, emphasis in original, references omitted.

[81] It should be noted that the UNCLOS tribunal did not ultimately examine the question of the United Kingdom's asserted persistent objector status, as it did not find that it had jurisdiction to consider the first two submissions made by Mauritius, to which this aspect of the pleadings related. See *Chagos Marine Protected Area*, award, n. 78, paras 163–230.

[82] For an excellent discussion of the implications of silence during the formation of customary international law, see Villiger, n. 41, 37–40. See also ILA Final Report, n. 14, 23–5; M. Byers, *Custom, Power and the Power of Rules: International Relations and Customary International Law* (Cambridge, Cambridge University Press, 1999), 149; and Quince, n. 52, 48. More specifically with regard to persistent objection, see Loschin, n. 41, 150–1; and J.P. Trachtman, 'Persistent Objectors, Cooperation, and the Utility of Customary International Law' (2010) 21 *Duke Journal of Comparative and International Law* 221, 230. *Contra* J.I. Charney, 'The Persistent Objector Rule and the Development of Customary International Law' (1985) 56 *British Yearbook of International Law* 1, 16. See Chapter 9, particularly at section I, for a discussion of the persistent objector's place within the voluntarist theory of international law.

objection for the purposes of the persistent objector rule. If a state does not express its objection to a newly emerging norm openly then other states would be unaware of the objection, and this would create uncertainties in terms of reliance and legitimate expectations: 'it is [therefore] important that other States are aware of the dissenting State's position, it is vital that the objection is communicated.'[83]

The persistent objector rule's timeliness requirement is another reason why other states must be made aware of the objections of the dissenter. For persistent objection to operate there is a common acceptance that objections must occur during the gestation of the norm; once it has crystallized, the 'book is closed' on persistent objection.[84] To accept that 'unexpressed objection' can later lead to exemption would obviously circumvent this requirement and allow for abuse of the persistent objector rule, with subsequent objectors retrospectively being able to claim that they had in fact been 'private persistent objectors' all along.

Perhaps more interesting, then, is the question of whether objection can be private as between states—that is, communicated between states but only to a limited audience—or whether objections must be made to the world at large. Disagreements as to the requirements of international law are often a purely diplomatic matter, involving exchanges of non-public communiqués between the states concerned.[85] To take an example, Walker claims that numerous objections involving emerging norms of the customary international law of the sea—an area of international law where persistent objection has been comparatively common—have been filed by states,[86] but that a majority of these objections have been 'filed in the chancelleries and are not in public records'.[87] If Walker is correct on this point, this means that while communication of objection on law of the sea norms has occurred on many occasions *between states*, only the tip of the protestation iceberg on the customary law of the sea is visible publicly. The question is, therefore, whether such interstate communication constitutes 'objection' in the 'persistent objector' sense. Walker, at least, appears to take the view that it does.[88]

[83] Guldahl, n. 33, 54. See also V. Fon and F. Parisi, 'Stability and Change in International Customary Law' (2004) 21 *American Law and Economics Association Annual Meetings* 1, 5; Martin, n. 53, 74; Petersen, n. 73, 10; E.F. Sherman, Jr., 'The U.S. Death Penalty Reservation to the International Covenant on Civil and Political Rights: Exposing the Limitations of the Flexible System Governing Treaty Formation' (1994) 29 *Texas International Law Journal* 69; N. Stürchler, *The Threat of Force in International Law* (Cambridge, Cambridge University Press, 2007), 100; Steinfeld, n. 52, 1639, footnote 14 and 1652; and D. Weissbrodt, 'Execution of Juvenile Offenders by the United States Violates International Human Rights Law' (1988) 3 *American University Journal of International Law and Policy* 339, 367–8.

[84] See, generally, Chapter 6.

[85] Mendelson, n. 33, 234.

[86] G.K. Walker, 'Professionals' Definitions and States' Interpretative Declarations (Understandings, Statements, or Declarations) for the 1982 Law of the Sea Convention' (2007) 21 *Emory International Law Review* 461, 523 (in the main text and in more detail in footnote 330). See also J.A. Roach and R.W. Smith, *Excessive Maritime Claims* (Leiden, Martinus Nijhoff, 3rd edn, 2012), 8 (noting, in 2012, that since 1948 the United States filed more than 140 formal notes of protest in relation to issues concerning the law of the sea, as well as objecting through various other means).

[87] Walker, n. 86, 523.

[88] Ibid., 523 footnote 330.

One could perhaps argue that such instances of interstate 'private' dissent should be considered as 'objection' for the purposes of the rule.[89] This would be on the basis that communication between states (even if only between two or a handful of states) means that such states have been put on notice, significantly reducing the risk of fraudulent claims of objection at a later date. However, at least with regard to general customary international law, the exemption provided by persistent objection is potentially opposable to *all* other states: communications between 'some' states will therefore not suffice. Even if dissent was expressed to all states that had an 'interest' in the emerging norm in question without being made overtly public, communication of objection to the world at large is crucial for any wider objective legal assessment of whether a state has in fact exempted itself from a new customary norm. More generally, requirements of predictability and certainty, inherent in the rule of law[90] (requirements that are already, at times, somewhat lacking in relation to customary international law formation generally, and the persistent objector rule specifically), mean that objection must be expressed beyond the walls of foreign offices.

The present author has been unable to find a single example of a state claiming persistent objector status, or being regarded by others as having attained such status, by virtue of unpublished dissent to an emerging norm (either within or between states), including in the context of the law of the sea. It is perhaps unsurprising, then, that the few writers who have touched on this question have argued that '[t]he position of the objecting State must be made known *internationally*'.[91] Loschin goes as far as to say that objection should be as open and widely disseminated as possible, and that 'louder' forms of objection may be acceptable while less fully expressed objections may not suffice.[92] To an extent this is correct: other states are less likely to accept ambiguous or partially 'hidden' indications of dissent as constituting persistent objection. Yet while the *openness* of the objection is certainly a requirement for the rule, there is nothing in state practice to indicate that persistent objection must be *bombastic* in nature: such a requirement may be overly onerous.[93] Similarly, while '[a]t least some statements or conduct should be made to

[89] For example, 'objection' or 'protest' in the international legal context generally was classically defined simply as 'a formal communication from one state to another', without reference to a wider audience: R. Jennings and A. Watts, *Oppenheim's International Law, vol. I: Peace* (New York, Longman, 9th edn, 1996), 1193.

[90] Indeed, many considerations of the rule of law refer to a requirement of 'openness' as to legal norms and positions. Perhaps the most famous example of this is the work of Fuller: see, particularly, L.L. Fuller, *The Morality of Law* (Fredericksburg, Yale University Press, revised edition, 1969), 38 (listing the need for law to be 'publicized' as the second of his eight requirements that must govern the law-making process).

[91] Elias, n. 53, 284, para. 16, emphasis added. See also H. Charlesworth, 'Law-Making and Sources' in J. Crawford and M. Koskenniemi (eds), *The Cambridge Companion to International Law* (Cambridge, Cambridge University Press, 2012), 187, 195; and Loschin, n. 41, 165 and 168.

[92] Loschin, n. 41, 165. See also D.J. Bederman, *Custom as a Source of Law* (Cambridge, Cambridge University Press, 2010), 154 ('[s]tates are obliged to protest *loud* and often'; emphasis added).

[93] A fact that Loschin admittedly goes on to note: see Loschin, n. 41, 165, footnote 93. See also B.D. Lepard, *Customary International Law: A New Theory with Practical Applications* (Cambridge, Cambridge University Press, 2010), 238 (albeit specifically making this point with regard to a 'case where persistent objection should be relatively easy').

an international audience ... domestic political or legal announcements *that have been published or broadcast in some way*, including electronically, are also relevant'.[94]

IV. The Form of Objection

i. Words or deeds?

While it can be said that objection must constitute some form of positive, open action, it is not apparent from the literature what types of 'external-facing' action will actually constitute objection. This issue was notably raised by Stein in his seminal 1985 article on the persistent objector rule: '[i]t is ... far from clear ... by what means [the] objection must be made known.'[95] Stein did not go on to consider this issue further, but more recent exploration of the necessary form of objection in the literature has identified four possibilities in this context: (a) objection must, at least inter alia, take the form of actual deeds (i.e. the state must in fact *practise* the right that it is seeking to retain); (b) objection must take the form of an explicit statement (meaning that deeds will not suffice, or, at least, that deeds *alone* will not suffice); (c) the state must object by way of *both* deeds and statements of objection; and (d) either mode of objection—word *or* deed—is enough.

In considering these options, Colson has argued that, within state foreign offices, there is 'a perceived need to take action beyond a verbal or written statement of position'[96] and that 'one often hears "we're going to lose our rights if we don't use them"'.[97] This would suggest that states tend to adopt the view that deeds are needed to maintain a stance of persistent objection. A number of writers have argued that deeds are a necessary element of any process of persistent objection: that is, for a state to qualify as a persistent objector it must exercise the right that it claims.[98] The rationale underpinning this position is that a requirement for physical acts of objection will limit the use of the persistent objector rule to exceptional circumstances only, by demonstrating that the state in question is genuinely committed to its position.[99] Linked to this is a wider perception that states *say* many things, but only *do* what they truly mean.[100] As such, 'a physical act certainly provides the most easily understood example of a state's legal position'.[101]

[94] Jones, n. 2, 455, emphasis added.

[95] Stein, n. 25, 478.

[96] Colson, n. 33, 962.

[97] Ibid., 963.

[98] See, for example, MacGibbon, n. 17, 317; D.P. O'Connell, *The International Law of the Sea, vol. I* (Oxford, Clarendon Press, 1982), 40–4; and Price, n. 41, 123. This possibility has also been noted by Colson, n. 33, 963; Guldahl, n. 33, 55; and Steinfeld, n. 52, 1650, though these writers do not ultimately subscribe to this position.

[99] Guldahl, n. 33, 55.

[100] See D'Amato, n. 38, 87–98; and W.H. Parks, 'The ICRC Customary Law Study: A Preliminary Assessment' (2005) 99 *American Society of International Law Proceedings* 208, 210. It should be noted that both D'Amato and Parks were making this point with regard to state practice for the purposes of customary international law formation, and not specifically with regard to persistent objection: however, it can be reasonably inferred that this view additionally applies to the form of objection for the purposes of the rule. See also Steinfeld, n. 52, 1650.

[101] Ibid., 1650. See also Guldahl, n. 33, 55; and A.V. Lowe, *International Law* (Oxford, Oxford University Press, 2007), 56.

However, insistence that a state's objections include some form of positive physical action would be problematic for a number of reasons. Firstly, it is entirely possible that a state may not be presented with the opportunity to exercise the right that an emerging norm will ultimately restrict during the formation of that norm.[102] The state may nonetheless wish to reserve the right to exercise the yet-to-be-prohibited practice in the future, in spite of the fact that it has simply had no chance to act against the emerging norm until it is too late. Secondly, 'acting' will usually be rather more costly (financially and administratively) for a state than simply stating its position.[103] This would in some cases be unnecessarily onerous on any possible persistent objector,[104] and it would have particularly notable implications for smaller or weaker states, which may not necessarily have the resources to exercise rights through deeds during the formation of the norm in question.[105]

It is also worth considering the fact that acts, more so than statements, have the potential to provoke other states, leading to confrontation and 'tit-for-tat' escalation.[106] Indeed, the exercise of certain rights may lead to significant adverse consequences,[107] to the point that a requirement for deeds of objection could be 'subversive to world peace'.[108] Steinfeld points to the extreme hypothetical example of states using nuclear weapons as a means of asserting an objection to a possible emerging norm prohibiting the use of such armaments.[109] The notion of a state detonating a nuclear device purely as a means of establishing a legal position—indeed, presumably detonating a number of such devices *persistently*—demonstrates the absurdity of an absolute requirement that 'objections' must include deeds for the purposes of the persistent objector rule.

To require physical action purely in the service of maintaining a legal position therefore seems unnecessarily onerous, when persistent statements of objection can, one might reasonably assume, sufficiently highlight the dissenter's stance.[110] Other writers have therefore taken an opposing view: indeed, some have suggested not only that communication by 'word' is sufficient (without the need for physical action to demonstrate a state's objection), but also that express, verbal communication of the dissenting state's position is *required*. For example, Bradley and Gulati have argued that the traditional understanding of the rule is that '[p]ersistent objection *must* involve affirmative international communications, not [just] ... adherence to contrary laws or practices.'[111] In other

102 See Colson, n. 33, 964, footnote 19. 103 Ibid., 964.

104 Steinfeld, n. 52, 1651.

105 Colson, n. 33, 964, footnote 19; and Mendelson, n. 33, 241.

106 Colson, n. 33, 964. 107 Ibid. 108 Mendelson, n. 33, 241.

109 Steinfeld, n. 52, 1651. See also Guldahl, n. 33, 55 (similarly giving the prohibition of nuclear weapons as an example in this context, as well as pointing to objections to a possible customary prohibition on belligerent reprisals against civilians—and the inherent undesirability of states actually acting against the prohibition purely to ensure exemption—as another example).

110 Colson, n. 33, 963–4.

111 C.A. Bradley and M. Gulati, 'Withdrawing from International Custom' (2010) 120 *Yale Law Journal* 202, 211, emphasis added.

words, they indicate that the majority understanding is that persistent objection requires some formal statement of objection, with physical actions by themselves being insufficient.[112]

One might note, as an example of this view, the *C* et al. decision of the Hong Kong Court of Appeal. When presented with the claim that Hong Kong was a persistent objector to a customary international law norm of *non-refoulement*, Yuen JA stated: 'I do not think we have been referred to any *clear statements* where there has been a disassociation from the process of the development of the concept of non-refoulement of refugees into a CIL.'[113] Yuen JA thus saw 'deeds of objection' as being insufficient for the operation of the persistent objector rule, at least in themselves. Other commentators have gone further still, and argued that physical actions can *never* constitute instances of objection, even if combined with written or verbal statements.[114]

It is evident—when one considers state practice—that in the majority of instances, the objector adopts *both* deeds and statements to indicate its dissent. The classic example of persistent objection in *Fisheries* is again illustrative here. In the context of that dispute, Norway had not only repeatedly objected through formal statements, but was also *applying* its own delimitation rule, most obviously through the repeated arrest of United Kingdom trawlers.[115] The ICJ, of course, accepted that Norway was an exempt persistent objector state (albeit in a rather vague manner).[116]

One might also consider the practice of United States in relation to the use of herbicides in armed conflict. In the *Agent Orange* case in 2005,[117] the Vietnamese Association for Victims of Agent Orange/Dioxin and a number of Vietnamese nationals filed a class action suit against various American chemical manufacturers for harm allegedly caused by the United States' use of 'Agent Orange' and other herbicides during the Vietnam war.[118] In a 'statement of interest' issued during the *Agent Orange* proceedings, the United States argued that it was a persistent objector state,[119] and set out in significant detail its repeated and consistent practice—by way of deed, voting practice, *and* statement—in rejecting any prohibition of the use of herbicides in warfare (both generally and specifically in relation to crop destruction).[120] There has also been consistent reiteration of this view in various American military manuals and handbooks.[121] As we will see in

112 Ibid. (noting this position without necessarily subscribing to it).

113 *C* et al., Court of Appeal, n. 3, para. 72, emphasis added.

114 Martin, n. 53, 74.

115 See *Fisheries*, merits, n. 76, 125.

116 Ibid., 131.

117 *In Re 'Agent Orange' Product Liability Litigation*, 2005, memorandum, order and judgment, United States District Court Eastern District of New York, 373 F. Supp. 2d 7 (E.D.N.Y).

118 *In Re 'Agent Orange' Product Liability Litigation*, 2005, Brief *Amici Curiae* of the Center for Constitutional Rights, Earthrights International and the International Human Rights Law Clinic at the University of Virginia School of Law, 04 CV 0400 (JBW).

119 *In Re 'Agent Orange' Product Liability Litigation*, 2005, statement of interest of the United States, http://www.state.gov/documents/organization/87322.pdf, 31–2.

120 Ibid., 4–13.

121 See ICRC IHL Study, *vol. II*, n. 28, 1764–5; and ICRC, 'United States of America: Practice Relating to Rule 76: Herbicides', http://www.icrc.org/customary-ihl/eng/docs/v2_cou_us_rule76.

Chapter 5, it is fairly clear that the United States has gained persistent objector status through this combination of words and deeds.[122]

This author has elsewhere argued[123] that India is a persistent objector state to a customary nuclear test-ban norm deriving from Article I of the 1996 Comprehensive Nuclear Test-Ban Treaty (CTBT).[124] Persistent objection in this context again took the form of both words and deeds. India's Pokhran-I nuclear tests of 1974 and, more notably, its 1998 Pokhran-II tests were obviously acts that constituted the 'rejection by deed' of any customary test-ban norm. India has also repeatedly rejected the obligations of the international legal nuclear non-proliferation regime (and its differentiated framework) through repeated pronouncements.[125] More specifically, India has objected—by a succession of explicit statements—to the possibility of a test-ban binding it.[126]

These examples of objection through both word and deed are representative, and it is perhaps unsurprising that states tend to object in both 'forms'. Combining these methods of objection provides the clearest indication that the state in question does not view itself as bound by the emerging norm. By exercising a right and (re)asserting that right through official statements, a state increases the effectiveness of the *communication* of its objections, something that was noted in section III as being crucial to exemption. As a practical matter, it is also commonly the case that the reason why the objector is objecting in the first place is because it in fact practises behaviour that is under threat from the emerging norm, meaning that statements are issued to underpin already occurring acts.

[122] See Chapter 5, n. 84–n. 98 and accompanying text.

[123] J.A. Green, 'India and a Customary Comprehensive Nuclear Test-Ban: Persistent Objection, Peremptory Norms and the 123 Agreement' (2011) 51 *Indian Journal of International Law* 3, generally, but particularly at 18–41.

[124] Comprehensive Nuclear Test-Ban Treaty, 10 September 1996, UN Doc. A/50/1027 (adopted by General Assembly Resolution 50/245, 10 September 1996, UN Doc. A/RES/50/245, not in force).

[125] A classic example is a speech made by Prime Minister Indira Gandhi to the Indian Parliament in 1968, in which she was explicit in rejecting the entire nuclear law framework, based on a policy of 'enlightened self-interest and the considerations of national security'. Debate on Foreign Affairs with Indira Gandhi, Lok Sabha, New Delhi, 5 April 1968, quoted in A. Ghose, 'Negotiating the CTBT: India's Security Concerns and Nuclear Disarmament' (1997) 51 *Journal of International Affairs* 239, 242. See, generally, K. Frey, *India's Nuclear Bomb and National Security* (New York, Routledge, 2006), 19 (arguing that India's discourse on nuclear weapons has always 'vehemently dismissed' the legal status quo as 'discriminatory and imperialist'); A.K. Rai, *India's Nuclear Policy after Pokhran II* (New Delhi, Dorling Kindersley, 2009), 208 (noting that India has always been 'against [the international legal regime relating to nuclear weapons] and its philosophy because of its discriminatory character'); and W. Walker, 'International Nuclear Relations after the Indian and Pakistani Test Explosions' (1998) 74 *International Affairs* 505, 511 (noting that India has famously promulgated the term 'nuclear apartheid' to describe international law's approach to nuclear non-proliferation).

[126] For example, India's chief negotiator at the 1996 Conference on Disarmament in Geneva, Arundhati Ghose, unequivocally stated that 'India will never sign this unequal treaty—not now, not ever'. Quoted in M. Goozner, 'Holdouts Endanger Nuclear Treaty', *Chicago Tribune*, 11 September 1996, http://articles.chicagotribune.com/1996-09-11/news/9609110214_1_test-ban-treaty-five-declared-nuclear-powers-nuclear-weapons. See also General Assembly, Official Records, Fiftieth session, 125th plenary meeting, 10 September 1996, UN Doc. A/50/PV.125, 3–4 (where India claimed that the CTBT 'betrayed' the goal of enhancing peace and security).

There are, however, certainly examples of persistent objection where no physical 'acts' of objection (or very few acts) have occurred. For example, objections by the United Kingdom to a possible customary international law prohibition on belligerent reprisals against civilians have almost exclusively taken the form of statements and not physical practice.[127] It is debatable whether such a prohibition is in fact binding in custom[128] but, if it is, it would seem that the United Kingdom is a persistent objector state, essentially by virtue of its statements alone.[129]

Similarly, in his separate opinion in the *North Sea Continental Shelf* cases, Judge Ammoun was of the view that the Federal Republic of Germany qualified as a persistent objector to any possible customary international law equivalent to the principle of equidistance as defined in Article 6 of the 1958 Geneva Convention on the Continental Shelf,[130] which The Netherlands and Denmark argued was applicable to the dispute. This was on the basis that West Germany had 'expressly recorded its opposition to the rule in question' by way of a *note verbale* and a formal proclamation.[131] The majority of the ICJ determined that no such customary norm had come into being in any event,[132] so the possible persistent objector status of West Germany was moot. Indeed, whether two instances of objection could be considered a sufficiently 'persistent' amount is open to debate.[133] Nonetheless, it is clear that, for Judge Ammoun, objection by words alone was acceptable.

It would therefore appear that while states commonly object through both words and deeds, there is no requirement that they exercise the right to which they are objecting. Words alone are sufficient. This is a desirable position, given the fact that in some instances a *requirement* of objection by deed would be unnecessarily onerous for various reasons, as previously discussed.

In contrast, the present author has not been able to identify any instances from state practice where *deeds* alone have been sufficient to provide a state with exemption through persistent objection. Admittedly, this does not necessarily mean that there are not any. It would nonetheless at least appear that persistent objection does require at least some form of 'objection by statement'. This is not

[127] See, for example, United Kingdom, *The Law of Armed Conflict*, D/DAT/13/35/66. Army Code 71130 (revised 1981), Ministry of Defence, prepared under the direction of the Chief of General Staff (1981), Section 4, 17 ('[t]he United Kingdom reserves the right to take proportionate reprisals against an enemy's civilian population or civilian objects where the enemy has attacked our own civilians or civilian objects').

[128] The ICRC Study appeared to identify this prohibition as being binding under customary international law, though its conclusions on the matter were far from unequivocal. See ICRC IHL Study, *vol. I*, n. 28, 520–3. However, others have expressed doubt as to the binding status of the norm in custom. See, for example, E. Kwakwa, 'Belligerent Reprisals in the Law of Armed Conflict' (1990–1) 27 *Stanford Journal of International Law* 49, 71–2.

[129] See Guldahl, n. 33, 76–7.

[130] Convention on the Continental Shelf, 29 April 1958, 499 UNTS 311.

[131] *North Sea Continental Shelf* cases (*Federal Republic of Germany v Netherlands, Federal Republic of Germany v Denmark*), merits, 1969 ICJ Rep. 3, separate opinion of Judge Ammoun, para. 31.

[132] *North Sea Continental Shelf* cases, merits, n. 131, para. 81.

[133] See, generally, Chapter 4 in relation to the criterion of persistence.

to say that there are not instances where the exercise of the right at issue has been the *main* form of persistent objection. One might, for example, consider the United Kingdom's continued exercise of its belligerent right of visit in relation to neutral vessel convoys in the early twentieth century, as discussed in Chapter 1.[134] The United Kingdom primarily expressed its objections to the purported customary rule on the immunity of neutral vessels (reflected most notably in Article 61 of the 1909 London Declaration Concerning the Laws of Naval War[135]) simply by *continuing to act in a manner that was contrary to it*.[136] The United Kingdom also issued statements of objection,[137] but these were clearly 'secondary' in nature to the practice itself. Britain's right to continue its policy of inspection of neutral vessels went uncontested by other states,[138] and the practice has rightly been considered an early example of successful persistent objection.[139]

However, even instances such as this—where deeds have acted as the *primary* form of objection—are notably rare. As a practical matter, this is not a surprise: it costs states very little to issue statements asserting the lawfulness of their actions, and they will be likely to do so when the lawfulness of the actions in question is challenged by the contrary state practice of others. In addition, the need for some form of explicit statement is further supported by the fact that this will strengthen the clarity and communication of the objection.

Overall, while a combination of both words and deeds is commonly preferred by objecting states, practice appears to indicate that there is not necessarily a requirement that a state objects through physical actions. As we have seen, there are various policy reasons for not insisting on 'acts of objection' in every case. Many writers have thus taken the view that *either* acts or statements of objection will suffice.[140] However, while deeds are not necessarily required, statements of objection would appear to be (even if only to a limited extent). Although it cannot be said with absolute certainty that deeds alone are insufficient, any want-to-be exempt state would be unwise to rely solely on its physical acts of objection, and in many cases it will be best served by expressly objecting through statements while *also* practising the right that it wishes to preserve.

[134] See Chapter 1, n. 72–n. 77 and accompanying text.

[135] Declaration Concerning the Laws of Naval War, 1909, 208 Consol. T.S. 338 (not in force).

[136] See J.H.W. Verzijl, *International Law in Historical Perspective, vol. I: General Subjects* (Utrecht, A.W. Sijthoff, 1968), 37–8.

[137] See, for example, Letter of 25 April 1918 by the Secretary of State for Foreign Affairs, cited by Lord Beresford, HL Deb 16 July 1918, vol. 30, cc 898-915.

[138] Verzijl, n. 136, 37–8.

[139] Ibid.

[140] See, for example, Third Report on Identification of Customary International Law, ILC, n. 31, para. 92; ILA Final Report, n. 14, 28; Bölükbaşı, n. 54, 217; Byers, n. 82, 103; Colson, n. 33, 955; Elias, n. 53, 248, para. 16; Lepard, n. 93, 239; McClane, n. 45, 6 (implicitly accepting that either word or deed will suffice); Steinfeld, n. 52, 1645, 1647, and 1673; and Villiger, n. 41, 33. Indeed, the present author has elsewhere made this claim: see J.A. Green, 'India's Status as a Nuclear Weapons Power under Customary International Law' (2012) 24 *National Law School of India Review* 125, 140; and Green, n. 123, 20. However, after further investigation, he is now of the view that 'deeds alone' are likely insufficient.

ii. What 'types' of activities can constitute objection?

Having considered whether 'objection' for the purposes of the operation of the persistent objector rule must take the form of word, deed, or both, this subsection considers the question of the form of objection rather more specifically. That is, it looks at the 'types' of act or statement that can be considered as instances of persistent objection.

Given the discussion in the previous subsection, it is relatively straightforward to conclude that the physical actions of the dissenting state can be a source of objection. A state that is *exercising* the right it is seeking to protect is, by definition, 'objecting'. 'Deeds' may not be required for persistent objection, but they can be a potent manifestation of it.[141] As noted, however, it is unlikely that physical action can constitute the *only* form of persistent objection in any given instance. Acts are a possible but not sufficient form of persistent objection.

Perhaps the next most obvious 'type' of objection is the pleadings of states before international courts and tribunals.[142] The courtroom provides a structured forum for objection, where states are necessarily required to present unambiguous legal positions. It is clear that, in practice, pleadings can be seen as constituting objection for the purposes of the operation of the rule.[143] Indeed, it is also true that the pleadings of a state at the domestic level, in the context of internal adjudication, can act as instances of persistent objection, where these are publicly available.[144]

Take, for example, the 1999 pleadings of the United States submitted to its own Supreme Court in *Michael Domingues v State of Nevada*.[145] The case concerned, inter alia, the question of whether the United States had violated a customary international law prohibition of the execution of juveniles; a question that the Supreme Court of Nevada had answered in the negative.[146] As part of its pleadings at the United States Supreme Court level, the United States argued that it was a persistent objector state to the avowed customary norm (if such a norm indeed existed).[147] The case went to the Inter-American Commission on Human Rights in 2002 after the United States Supreme Court declined to hear it without discussion.[148] Of note here is that the Commission's report strongly implied that it saw the American claim of persistent objector status (made as part of internal judicial proceedings) as *itself* constituting an instance of 'objection',[149] albeit that the Commission ultimately determined that the

[141] Roach and Smith, n. 86, 8, footnote 16. [142] Colson, n. 33, 958.

[143] Ibid.; Dumberry, n. 28, 781; and Guldahl, n. 33, 54–55. [144] Jones, n. 2, 455.

[145] *Michael Domingues v State of Nevada*, in the Supreme Court of the United States, on petition for a writ of *certiorari* to the Supreme Court of Nevada, brief for the United States as *amicus curiae*, 1999, No. 98-8327, http://www.justice.gov/osg/briefs/1999/2pet/6invit/98-8327.pet.ami.inv.pdf.

[146] See *Domingues v State*, 1998, 961 P.2d 1279, Sup. Ct. Nev., particularly at 1279–81 in relation to Mr Domingues' claim that his sentencing violated customary international law.

[147] *Domingues, amicus curiae* brief, n. 145, 15–18.

[148] *Domingues v United States*, merits, 2002 IACmHR, Report No. 62/02, Case 12.285.

[149] Ibid., particularly at paras 14, 48–9, and 85.

United States was not in fact an exempt persistent objector to the prohibition on juvenile executions.[150]

However, it is worth noting that instances of both persistent objection[151] and international adjudication[152] are rare, making occasions of their convergence even rarer still. Although the pleadings of states in the domestic law context, where adjudication is much more common, can also constitute persistent objection, dissenting states are similarly rarely called upon to advance positions of dissent in relation to international law norms internally.

In addition to physical acts and judicial pleadings, one might question whether oral forms of protest can constitute objection. Writing in the early 1950s, MacGibbon colourfully warned that '[t]he impertinence of the spoken word renders oral protests liable to the twin dangers of distortion and oblivion'.[153] Entirely 'oral' statements of objection must certainly be treated with care for these reasons. Having said that, oral statements made in the context of international law are commonly recorded in writing in any event (for example in summary or verbatim records, through press releases or on official websites), which lessens such concerns somewhat. Indeed, even if they have not been recorded in writing in this way, as long as oral statements are formal and 'external-facing' or 'open' (which, as has already been noted in section III, is required for all forms of persistent objection), then they would seem an acceptable method of expressing dissent. A majority of writers therefore hold that positions taken during formal negotiations and debates can constitute persistent objection.[154] Internal or closed debates will not suffice, but there is little doubt that dissent expressed during formal debates in, for example, the UN General Assembly or Security Council can qualify, as these forums offer obvious instances where explicit statements of legal position can be expressed. For the same reason, voting practices within such organs may also be relevant.[155]

It has been argued that positions advanced during debates that relate directly to the norm being objected to—for example, discussions as part of a drafting conference for a treaty that covers the relevant subject matter—should be seen as having particular weight.[156] However, there is little evidence in practice

[150] Ibid., para. 85. This was on the dual basis that the United States had not objected consistently to the emerging norm and that the norm in question—in the view of the Commission—had achieved peremptory status. For discussion, see, respectively, Chapter 5, n. 6–n. 23 and accompanying text; and Chapter 7, n. 51–n. 71 and accompanying text.

[151] See Chapter 2, section II.

[152] Colson, n. 33, 958.

[153] MacGibbon, n. 17, 295.

[154] Colson, n. 33, 958; Dumberry, n. 28, 781; Guldahl, n. 33, 55: Quince, n. 52, 42 (specifically with regard to debates in, and documents submitted to, the UN General Assembly); and Steinfeld, n. 52, 1649. It is notable, by way of analogy, that the ICJ took the view in the *Rights of Nationals in Morocco* case that negotiations and diplomatic correspondence could be evidence of state practice in relation to the formation of customary international law more generally (although the Court did not find that the correspondence between France and the United States was sufficient to establish a 'particular' customary norm on the facts). See *Case Concerning Rights of Nationals of the United States of America in Morocco* (*France v United States of America*), judgment, 1952 ICJ Rep. 176, 200.

[155] Dumberry, n. 28, 781; Guldahl, n. 33, 55; Quince, n. 52, 61; Stein, n. 25, 467; and Villiger, n. 41, 33.

[156] Guldahl, n. 33, 55; and Steinfeld, n. 52, 1648.

to indicate that objections made in the context of a debate specifically relating to the subject matter of the emerging norm being rejected actually carry any additional legal significance. It is probably simply the case that states are—unsurprisingly—more likely to advance their protests in the context of debates that have a key bearing on the emergence of the norm in question. It is therefore worth noting that *any* explicit official pronouncement of a state can be viewed as an instance of objection, even if this is not tied to a particular type of forum, negotiation, or debate.[157]

Thus, in relation to Turkey's objections to an extension of the territorial waters limit to 12 nautical miles, discussed in section II,[158] its 'stand-alone' official pronouncements setting out its position regarding territorial jurisdiction in the Aegean,[159] objections lodged in the context of both the General Assembly[160] and the Security Council,[161] and its repeated dissent during the drafting of UNCLOS[162] all appear to have been given equal weight as cumulatively constituting persistent objection.[163]

A number of writers have argued that treaty reservations can be viewed as constituting objection on the part of a state, with regard to any customary international law norm that may subsequently flow from the provisions of a treaty.[164] The International Law Commission (ILC) has similarly taken the view that a treaty reservation can at least form part of a pattern of persistent objection.[165] In addition to the general acceptance of the relevance of treaty reservations to persistent objection in the literature and by the ILC, this was also recognized in the 2008 first instance decision of *C* et al.[166] Hartmann J relied in that decision, inter alia, on treaty reservations of the United Kingdom and China as evidence of persistent objection on behalf of Hong Kong in relation to the customary international law norm of *non-refoulement*.[167] Specifically, he cited a reservation by the United Kingdom to Article 13 of the International Covenant on Civil and Political Rights[168] (which he saw as allowing Hong Kong to derogate from aspects of that article concerning the expulsion of immigrants),[169] and China's reservation

157 Colson, n. 33, 958.

158 See also Chapter 2, n. 140–n. 144 and accompanying text.

159 'The Outstanding Aegean Issues', policy document of the Republic of Turkey Ministry of Foreign Affairs (2008), http://www.mfa.gov.tr/maritime-issues---aegean-sea---the-outstanding-aegean-issues.en.mfa.

160 See, for example, General Assembly, Official Records, Fiftieth session, 29th plenary meeting, 11 October 1995, UN Doc. A/50/PV.29, 29–30.

161 See, for example, Letter dated 21 June 1995 from the Permanent Representative of Turkey to the United Nations addressed to the Secretary-General, 23 June 1995, UN Doc. A/50/256 – S/1995/505.

162 See, for example, UN Doc. A/CONF.62/SR.189, n. 56, 76, para. 150.

163 Bölükbaşı, n. 54, 206.

164 See Dumberry, n. 28, 781; Lau, n. 41, 509; Quince, n. 52, 78; Steinfeld, n. 52, 1648; and Villiger, n. 41, 33.

165 Guide to Practice on Reservations to Treaties with commentaries, 2011, International Law Commission, UN Doc. A/66/10/Add.1, commentary (7) to guideline 3.1.5.3, 371.

166 *C* et al., first instance, n. 3.

167 For discussion, see Jones, n. 2, 451.

168 International Covenant on Civil and Political Rights, 16 December 1966, 999 UNTS 171.

169 *C* et al., first instance, n. 3, para. 89.

to Article 22(1) of the Convention on the Rights of the Child[170] (which he felt afforded Hong Kong scope to derogate from the rights of asylum seekers or refugee minors contained therein).[171]

Conceptually, it is logical that states can object by way of their treaty reservations, given that persistent objection is in some respects the customary international law equivalent to reservations to treaties.[172] If a state lodges a reservation with regard to a provision of a treaty, it is not unreasonable for this to 'double up' as an instance of objection on the basis that the state in question has clearly expressed its dissent in relation to the norm articulated therein. Just as in the context of objections expressed during negotiations and debates, however, it has further been argued that particular 'weight' should be attached to dissent expressed through treaty reservations because such practice relates directly to the subject matter of the state's objection.[173] This observation is again rather inane: states are, somewhat obviously, most likely to raise their objections to an emerging norm when acting or speaking in relation to the relevant subject matter. This fact does not necessarily indicate that reservations to treaties are considered by states to be 'better' instances of persistent objection than, say, official statements of dissent provided in other contexts.

Moreover, while it is fairly clear that reservations to treaties can act as examples of objection for the purposes of the operation of the persistent objector rule, they will be unlikely to suffice in themselves. It will be recalled from section I of this chapter that—while Hartmann J took the view at first instance in *C* et al. that Hong Kong was a persistent objector to the norm of *non-refoulement* based largely on the treaty reservations of the United Kingdom and China[174]—on appeal, Yuen JA concluded that Hong Kong was not a persistent objector, partly because it was not enough for the respondents to point to 'objection' by way of treaty reservations alone.[175] This was on the basis that such reservations related to the conventional provisions in question, and could not necessarily in themselves be seen as a sufficiently clear objection to a related customary international law rule.[176] It is also worth recalling that the general consensus is that objection needs to be persistent.[177] A treaty reservation *in itself* will almost certainly not suffice,[178] but it can be seen as contributing to a 'pattern' of persistent objection.

[170] Convention on the Rights of the Child, 20 November 1989, 1577 UNTS 3.

[171] *C* et al., first instance, n. 3, paras. 144–6.

[172] See E. David, 'L'objecteur persistent, une règle persistent?' in P. Tavernier and J-M. Henckaerts (eds), *Droit international humanitaire coutumier: enjeux et défis contemporains* (Brussels, Bruylant, 2008), 89, 90; M.A. Hansen, 'Preventing the Emasculation of Warfare: Halting the Expansion of Human Rights Law into Armed Conflict' (2007) 194 *Military Law Review* 1, 17; B.B. Jia, 'The Relations between Treaties and Custom' (2010) 9 *Chinese Journal of International Law* 81, 89, 97, and 101–2; Lau, n. 41, 509; Martin, n. 53, 74–5.

[173] Steinfeld, n. 52, 1648.

[174] *C* et al., first instance, n. 3, particularly at paras 85–163.

[175] *C* et al., Court of Appeal, n. 3, paras. 70–2.

[176] Ibid., para. 72.

[177] See, generally, Chapter 4.

[178] W. Czapliński, 'Sources of International Law in the *Nicaragua* Case' (1989) 38 *International and Comparative Law Quarterly* 151, 160.

A related issue with regard to state practice and treaties is whether the mere act (or, rather, omission) of not signing or ratifying a treaty can constitute objection. 'Contracting out' of an emerging norm through *signing* a treaty that includes contrary obligations is almost certainly a 'positive act' of persistent objection,[179] but the implication of merely *omitting* to sign or ratify a treaty that contains obligations that correspond to the emerging norm is less clear. In this context it has been argued that:

> Mere failure to ratify treaties incorporating a rule that might be a customary rule should not qualify as explicit objection because a state's decision not to ratify a treaty may be based on many grounds that have no bearing on the state's attitude to the rule in question.[180]

This position is correct to an extent. A decision not to ratify a treaty may relate to any number of its provisions, and the state in question may—despite its general non-acceptance of the treaty—actually be very willing to conform to a particular norm therein, were that norm to later take on customary status. To derive 'objection' from a failure to ratify a treaty therefore runs the risk of ascribing a desire on the part of the state to remain exempt where no such desire exists. Moreover, a decision not to ratify a treaty can, again, hardly be said to be *persistent* in itself, as it constitutes a single act (or, rather, act of omission). That is unless one takes the view that every day that goes by where the state continues not to ratify the treaty constitutes a further—increasingly persistent—instance of objection through omission, which seems something of a stretch.

A failure to ratify a treaty is therefore in itself surely not sufficient to constitute persistent objection, because it is an action that is both vague and, notably, not persistent.[181] However, the present writer sees no reason why a failure to ratify a treaty could not be considered to be a contributory instance of persistent objection, so long as this is then combined with other objections (which would make the objection to the norm in question persistent, and also less ambiguous).

Indeed, where a state does not ratify a treaty that has a very specific object and purpose there will, in any event, be relatively little ambiguity as to what the state is objecting to by not ratifying it. The present author has thus argued elsewhere that the very fact that India is not a signatory to the CTBT is an act of objection to any customary norm equivalent to Article I of that treaty,[182] which comprehensively prohibits the testing of nuclear weapons. Given that the CTBT, by its very nature, puts virtually all its normative eggs into the basket of Article I, it is fairly clear what India was objecting to by not signing and ratifying the CTBT. However, the fact that India has not signed or ratified the CTBT is only legally

[179] Guldahl, n. 33, 54–5; Lepard, n. 93, 230; Quince, n. 52, 52.

[180] Lepard, n. 93, 238. See also Villiger, n. 41, 33.

[181] J. Crawford, 'Chance, Order, Change: The Course of International Law—General Course on Public International Law' (2013) 365 *Recueil des cours* 9, 247 ('[p]ersistent objection ... must be consistent and clear, and is not manifested by a *simple* failure to ratify a treaty'; emphasis added).

[182] Green, n. 123, 22. See also M. E. Carranza, *South Asian Security and International Nuclear Order: Creating a Robust Indo-Pakistani Nuclear Arms Control Regime* (Farnham, Ashgate, 2009), 130.

relevant to the operation of the persistent objector rule because India had *also* objected through physical acts and numerous explicit statements.[183]

In both of the cases where the ICJ has applied the persistent objector rule, the Court has made reference to the failure of the state concerned to sign a relevant treaty as evidence of that state's dissent to the norm in question. Thus, Norway's failure to sign the North Sea Fisheries (Police) Convention of 1882[184] was seen by the Court as a key indication of the Norwegian position in relation to the delimitation of territorial sea and fishery zones in the *Fisheries* case.[185] Admittedly, the Court was unclear as to the relationship between Norway's rejection of this treaty and the persistent objector rule, but this is nonetheless of note, given that Norway was considered by the ICJ to be a persistent objector state.[186]

It will be recalled from Chapter 2 that the *Asylum* case[187] concerned the right of a state to determine whether a crime was political or 'ordinary' in the context of granting asylum.[188] Here, the ICJ was more explicit about the fact that one of the key reasons why it did not see Peru as being bound by the regional customary obligation asserted by Colombia was that 'Peru ... , far from having by its attitude adhered to it, has, on the contrary, repudiated it *by refraining from ratifying the Montevideo Conventions of 1933 and 1939*'.[189] The ICJ has thus seemingly viewed a failure to ratify a treaty as being an acceptable instance of objection. A number of scholars have also taken this view.[190]

Domestic law-making is another possible source of persistent objection;[191] that is, objection can be found where a state enacts law that is contrary (or its judiciary interprets law in a way that is contrary) to an emerging norm, or where the state fails to enact law that is required by an emerging norm. An example is the position of Mauritania with regard to the practice of female genital mutilation (FGM). It is arguable whether a prohibition on FGM has yet emerged in customary international law,[192] but it can be said with a high degree of certainty that it is *emerging*, particularly given the unanimous adoption by the General Assembly of a resolution condemning the practice in December 2012.[193] At least up until 2005, Mauritania was generally regarded as having met the criteria for persistent objection in relation to the emerging norm,[194] and was thus seen as being exempt from it (or, probably

[183] Green, n. 123, 20–3.

[184] International Convention for Regulating the Police of the North Sea Fisheries outside Territorial Waters, 6 May 1882 (1882) 73 *British and Foreign State Papers* 39.

[185] *Fisheries*, merits, n. 76, 139.

[186] Ibid., 131.

[187] *Asylum (Columbia v Peru)*, merits, 1950 ICJ Rep. 266.

[188] See Chapter 2, n. 10–n. 18 and accompanying text.

[189] *Asylum*, merits, n. 187, 277–8, emphasis added.

[190] See Green, n. 140, 141 (by implication); Green, n. 123, 22 (by implication); Guldahl, n. 33, 55; Lau, n. 41, 508, footnote 53 (by implication); and Stein, n. 25, 467.

[191] Colson, n. 33, 958; Dumberry, n. 28, 781; Guldahl, n. 33, 55; Lau, n. 41, 508 (by implication); and Steinfeld, n. 52, 1649–50.

[192] For example, Gillia argued in 1997 that there was not sufficient state practice to make this assertion, which was certainly correct at the time: B.A. Gillia, 'Female Genital Mutilation: A Form of Persecution' (1997) 27 *New Mexico Law Review* 579, 589. See also Quince, n. 52, 77 (who similarly took the view, in 2010, that no FGM prohibition had yet crystallized in custom).

[193] General Assembly Resolution 67/146, 20 December 2012, UN Doc. A/RES/67/146.

[194] See Lau, n. 41, 507–8; and Quince, n. 52, 77.

more accurately, as being in a position that it *would be* exempt from the norm once it crystallized).[195] A key method of objection for Mauritania was that, for a significant period, it refused to pass a law proscribing FGM: this in itself was viewed as forming part of its pattern of persistent objection.[196] Equally, in 2005, Mauritania finally reversed its stance by adopting Ordonnance n°2005-015,[197] Article 12 of which criminalizes FGM. This act of domestic law-making has been considered enough to undermine any possible persistent objector status.[198] Thus, domestic law-making can be 'objection' but it can, depending on the circumstances, *also* constitute inconsistent behaviour (or the reversal of an objector's stance): in either sense, domestic law can be legally relevant to the operation of the persistent objector rule.

It therefore appears that any of the following actions can amount to instances of 'objection' for the purposes of the persistent objector rule: physical actions; pleadings before international courts and tribunals; official statements (including, but not limited to, statements made in formal debates of international organizations or other similar fora); treaty reservations and the failure to ratify a treaty; and domestic law-making and judicial decisions. This is not necessarily an exhaustive list. However, whether any particular pattern of state objection identified from one or more of these 'types' of dissent in relation to an emerging customary norm will be considered *sufficient* objection to gain exemption is another matter, and will depend on a range of additional factors to be discussed in subsequent chapters. What is important here is to note that an objection expressed in any of these ways will have the capacity to act as part of a pattern of persistent objection.

V. Conclusion

It is relatively clear that persistent objectors must be states. More importantly, this chapter has argued that objection by a state for the purposes of the persistent objector rule can take a variety of forms and can be formulated in a variety of ways.

[195] Lau, n. 41, 507–8.

[196] See ibid. 508, footnote 53. Mauritania long objected to the regulation of certain Islamic practices, including FGM. For example, it lodged reservations when it signed both the Convention on the Elimination of All Forms of Discrimination against Women, 18 December 1979, 1249 UNTS 13 and the Convention on the Rights of the Child, n. 170. It also refused to sign the African Charter on the Rights and Welfare of the Child, 11 July 1990, OAU Doc. CAB/LEG/24.9/49. Up until 2005, Mauritania had no laws proscribing FGM, and the practice was widespread in the state.

[197] Ordonnance n°2005-015 portant protection pénale de l'enfant, 2005, Présidence du Conseil Militaire pour la Justice et la Démocratie, Republique Islamique de Mauritanie, http://legislationmauritanienne.files.wordpress.com/2011/06/ordonnance-nc2b02005-015-portant-protection-pc3a9nale-de-l_enfant.pdf.

[198] See 'Legislative Reform to Support the Abandonment of Female Genital Mutilation/Cutting', (2010) UNICEF Report, http://www.unicef.org/policyanalysis/files/UNICEF_-_LRI_Legislative_Reform_to_support_the_Abandonment_of_FGMC_August_2010.pdf, 7, 21 and 46. For discussion of the abandonment of persistent objector status post-crystallization, see Chapter 6, section X.

There is an endemic approach in state practice of objecting to a newly emerging norm by rejecting the very formation of the norm per se, rather than claiming persistent objector status from the outset of the new norm's development. This approach of objecting to the existence (rather than particular applicability) of the norm in question undoubtedly makes it more difficult for states, commentators, and other actors to identify instances of persistent objection than would be the case if the dissenter were simply to invoke the persistent objector rule from the outset and while it was objecting. However, a rejection of the binding nature of the developing norm is the way in which states generally object, and understandably so given that they are necessarily objecting while a norm is forming (and, thus, necessarily before it is binding). It should be of little surprise that objectors refrain from singling themselves out as a trouble-maker before they need to. Importantly, it is clear that objection to the existence of an emerging norm can, in the right circumstances, be considered by other states as later constituting 'objection' for the purposes of the application of the persistent objector rule.

It is also evident that, as with the types of state (in)action for the formation of customary international law more generally,[199] there are a variety of methods through which persistent objection can be expressed: 'the action necessary to constitute an objection to a customary rule can take a variety of forms'.[200] Objection by words alone will be acceptable, as will objecting through a combination of both words and deeds (even where physical actions form the main method of the objection). However, it is unlikely that deeds *alone* will be sufficient.

The key question is whether the objection is sufficiently clear and demonstrates an intention not to be bound. As the ICJ stated in the *Nuclear Tests* cases, when considering the estopping legal effect of official statements made by the French President and other members of the French Government, 'whatever form these

[199] For the view that there are many possible material sources of the 'state practice' element of customary international law formation, see Interim Report: Draft Conclusions on the 'Identification of Customary International Law', Statement of the Chairmen of the Drafting Committee, Mr. Gilberto Saboia, 7 August 2014, International Law Commission, Sixty-sixth session, Geneva, 5 May–6 June and 7 July–8 August 2014, Draft Conclusion 6, 19 (commentary at 11–14); ILA Final Report, n. 14, 14; M. Akehurst, 'Custom as a Source of International Law' (1974–5) 47 *British Yearbook of International Law* 1, 1–11; J. Crawford, *Brownlie's Principles of Public International Law* (Oxford, Oxford University Press, 8th edn, 2012), 24; R. Müllerson, 'On the Nature and Scope of Customary International Law' (1997) 2 *Austrian Review of International and European Law* 341, 342–4; and M. Wood and O. Sender, 'State Practice' in R. Wolfrum (ed.), *Max Planck Encyclopaedia of Public International Law*, online edition (Oxford University Press), 2014 update, http://opil.ouplaw.com/view/10.1093/law:epil/9780199231690/law-9780199231690-e1107?rskey=N2neCH&result=3&prd=EPIL. However, it is worth noting that there remains some debate on this issue: see Kammerhofer, n. 44, 525–30 (setting out the debate); and D'Amato, n. 38, particularly at 88 (being the most famous articulation of the minority view that state practice can be found only in the physical acts of states).

[200] Steinfeld, n. 52, 1673, emphasis removed from original. See also 'Identification of Customary International Law', Statement of the Chairman of the Drafting Committee, Mr. Mathias Forteau, 29 July 2015, International Law Commission, Sixty-seventh session, Geneva, 4 May–5 June and 6 July–7 August 2015, 20 (reflecting the agreement in the ILC Drafting Committee that there exists a 'certain flexibility as to the manner in which the statement of position of the objector is communicated to the States concerned'); and Fon and Parisi, n. 83, 5.

statements were expressed [in], they must be held to constitute an engagement of the State, *having regard to their intention and to the circumstances in which they were made*'.[201] The same may be said of persistent objection: '[t]he question of the objection's form is not decisive; what matters is the intention of the State.'[202]

Irrespective of the form or source of the objection, if a state formally and openly expresses dissent to an emerging norm, with clear intention to remain unbound by that norm, then such an expression of dissent constitutes 'objection' for the purposes of the persistent objector rule.

201 *Nuclear Tests* case (*Australia v France*), questions of jurisdiction and admissibility, 1974, ICJ Rep. 253, para. 49, emphasis added.

202 Dumberry, n. 28, 781.

4

The Persistence Criterion

This chapter examines the persistent objector rule's 'persistence' requirement. As one might expect, given the usual name for the rule, a requirement of *persistent* objection is referenced across the literature as being a key criterion for the rule's operation. More importantly, it can also be identified in state practice. This chapter first confirms, in section I, that a single objection, or a small number of objections, will not be sufficient to gain exemption to an emerging norm of customary international law. Section II then considers the underlying rationale for the persistence requirement. The voluntarist understanding of international law cannot, in itself, provide an adequate explanation for the need for persistence. It is argued instead that there are practical and policy reasons underpinning the criterion (rather than it necessarily being entirely based on sound theoretical foundations). Finally, section III engages with the tricky question of *how persistent* objection must be before a state can gain exempt status. The view is taken herein that there is no exact answer to this question; the necessary degree of persistence will be context-specific, based on a range of factors (including extra-legal ones).

I. Objection Must Be Repeated

Fairly obviously, the word 'persistence' indicates the need for a degree of *repetition* to a state's objection. Given its common name, it would perhaps seem self-evident that a degree of repetition of objection is a key element of the 'persistent' objector rule. However, in 1985, Charney stated that there 'exists a difference of opinion as to whether the objection must be persistent'.[1] Even at the time, this statement was probably something of an exaggeration. There have, admittedly, been occasional expressions of the persistent objector rule in the literature that could at least be interpreted as indicating that the objection need not in fact be repeated. For example, the American Law Institute's *Restatement of the Law, Third, Foreign Relations Law of the United States* from 1987 holds that 'a state that indicates its dissent from a practice while the law is still in the process

[1] J.I. Charney, 'The Persistent Objector Rule and the Development of Customary International Law' (1985) 56 *British Yearbook of International Law* 1, 3, footnote 8.

of development is not bound by that rule even after it matures'.[2] This could be read as dispensing with the requirement of persistence, and viewing a single indication of dissent as being sufficient.[3] More recently, in his 2004 article on the subject, Abasheikh seems to overlook any need for the objection to be persistent: '[a] state that clearly declares its rejection of a norm of international law [prior to that norm's crystallization] ... is not bound by it.'[4] However, there are extremely few instances where the rule has been discussed in the literature without any reference being made to a 'persistence' requirement, and—even where possible examples of this sort can be identified, such as in the *Third Restatement* or Abasheikh's article—this element of the rule has not been explicitly *rejected*: it simply has not been noted.

Today, there is no longer any debate in doctrine (if, indeed, there ever was) as to whether objection must be persistent.[5] That is, of course, aside from the caveat that some writers do not accept the existence or effective operation of the persistent objector rule at all.[6] Thus, for the most part, the literature is clear that it is not enough for a state to merely object once to a newly emerging norm of customary international law.[7] Nor are a 'small' number of objections usually viewed as being

[2] *Restatement of the Law, Third, Foreign Relations Law of the United States*, American Law Institute, 1987, Section 102, Comment (d).

[3] As Charney noted in reference to the initial draft of the *Third Restatement*: Charney, n. 1, 3.

[4] O. Abasheikh, 'The Validity of the Persistent Offender Rule in International Law' (2004) 9 *Coventry Law Journal* 40, 41.

[5] Notably, seven years after arguing that there was a lack of agreement in the literature as to whether persistence is required, Charney seemed to have resolved this in his mind, simply stating that '[t]he objection must be persistent'. J.I. Charney, 'Universal International Law' (1993) 87 *American Journal of International Law* 529, 539.

[6] See writers referenced in Introduction, n. 27.

[7] See, for example, Identification of Customary International Law: Text of the Draft Conclusions Provisionally Adopted by the Drafting Committee', International Law Commission, Sixty-seventh session, Geneva, 4 May–5 June and 6 July–7 August 2015, UN Doc. A/CN.4/L.869, 5, Draft Conclusion 15: Persistent Objector (objection must be 'maintained persistently'); Third Report on Identification of Customary International Law (M. Wood, Special Rapporteur), International Law Commission, Sixty-seventh session, 27 March 2015, UN Doc. A/CN.4/682, particularly at para. 93; *Committee on Formation of Customary (General) International Law*, Final Report of the Committee, 'Statement of Principles Applicable to the Formation of General Customary International Law', International Law Association, London Conference (2000), http://www.ila-hq.org/en/committees/index.cfm/cid/30, 27; C.G. Guldahl, 'The Role of Persistent Objection in International Humanitarian Law' (2008) 77 *Nordic Journal of International Law* 51, 59; J.A. Green, 'India and a Customary Comprehensive Nuclear Test-Ban: Persistent Objection, Peremptory Norms and the 123 Agreement' (2011) 51 *Indian Journal of International Law* 3, 18; J.A. Green, 'India's Status as a Nuclear Weapons Power under Customary International Law' (2012) 24 *National Law School of India Review* 125, 139; J.A. Green, 'Persistent Objector Teflon? Customary International Human Rights Law and the United States in International Adjudicative Proceedings' in J.A. Green and C.P.M. Waters (eds), *Adjudicating International Human Rights: Essays in Honour of Sandy Ghandhi* (Leiden, Brill Nijhoff, 2015), 167, 170; E. Kontorovich, 'Inefficient Customs in International Law' (2006–7) 48 *William and Mary Law Review* 859, 875; I.M. Lobo de Souza, 'The Role of Consent in the Customary Process' (1995) 44 *International and Comparative Law Quarterly* 521, 533; F.F. Martin, *The Constitution as Treaty: The International Legal Constructionalist Approach to the U.S. Constitution* (Cambridge, Cambridge University Press, 2007), 73–5; and E.T. Swaine, 'Bespoke Custom' (2010) 21 *Duke Journal of Comparative and International Law* 207, 212.

sufficient.[8] Put simply, the vast majority of writers agree that 'sporadic or isolated objections will not do'.[9]

The persistence requirement can similarly be identified in case law. In *Siderman de Blake v Republic of Argentina*,[10] for example, Fletcher J reiterated the common understanding of the rule in the United States Court of Appeals for the Ninth Circuit: '[a] state that *persistently* objects to a norm of customary international law that other states accept is not bound by that norm'.[11] Most famously, of course, the ICJ stated in the *Fisheries* case that, with respect to the '10-mile rule' for the delimitation of the territorial sea and fishery zones, the rule 'would appear to be inapplicable as against Norway inasmuch as she *always opposed* any attempt to apply it to the Norwegian coast'.[12] Vague as this pronouncement may be, it is certainly indicative of the need for some degree of repetition of objection. More specifically, writing in 1953, MacGibbon pointed to a single German protest of 1935 in relation to Norway's Decree of the same year setting out its stance on fishery limits.[13] Essentially, this amounted to an objection on the part of Germany to what later was viewed by the ICJ as Norway's persistent objector stance, but which—in 1935—could potentially have become the mainstream customary norm. Yet this German protest was 'not followed by further action',[14] and the fact that it ultimately amounted to a single objection 'deprived [the state's] initial protest of all significance'.[15] In its pleadings to the ICJ in the *Fisheries* case Norway took the same view as MacGibbon, in that it argued that the single protest on the part of Germany was entirely ineffectual:

> Le ministre d'Allemagne à Oslo a bien adressé, le 23 octobre 1935, une communication verbale au ministre des Affaires étrangères, dans laquelle il déclarait que son Gouvernement ne pouvait pas reconnaitre la limite de pêche de 1935. Mais cette communication est restée sans effet et *elle n'a été suivie d'aucune autre démarche. Apres avoir fait ce geste, le Gouvernement allemand s'est abstenu d'en tirer la moindre conséquence.*[16]

On the merits, the ICJ in its examination of the enforceability of the 1935 Decree took no note of the single German protest at all throughout its decision.[17]

Considering a more recent example from state practice, the fact that a single objection (or very small number of objections) will be ignored by other states can usefully be highlighted by the position of Venezuela in relation to the Universal Periodic Review mechanism (UPR), created by the UN General Assembly alongside

[8] I. MacGibbon, 'Some Observations on the Part of Protest in International Law' (1953) 30 *British Yearbook of International Law* 293, 310–11 (arguing, more generally, that for 'protest' to have any effect in international law, a small number of objections will be insufficient).

[9] D. Kritsiotis, 'On the Possibilities Of and For Persistent Objection' (2010) 21 *Duke Journal of Comparative and International Law* 121, 130.

[10] *Siderman de Blake v Republic of Argentina*, 1992, United States Court of Appeals for the Ninth Circuit 965 F.2d 699 (9th Cir. 1992).

[11] Ibid., per Fletcher J., 715, para. 54, emphasis added.

[12] *Fisheries (United Kingdom v Norway)*, merits, 1951 ICJ Rep. 116, 131, emphasis added.

[13] MacGibbon, n. 8, 310–11. [14] Ibid., 311. [15] Ibid.

[16] *Fisheries (United Kingdom v Norway)*, oral proceedings, 1951 ICJ Plead., vol. IV, 234, emphasis added.

[17] *Fisheries*, merits, n. 12.

the Human Rights Council (HRC) in 2006.[18] The UPR started its operation in 2008, and purportedly requires all UN members to be monitored, with the reviews occurring every four years.[19] There is no obligation requiring states to submit to the operation of the UPR in treaty law,[20] but it can be argued that a norm of customary international law has quickly emerged to this effect (particularly given the fact that there has ultimately been 100 per cent state compliance with the procedure during its first cycle).[21]

However, in discussions over the creation of the HRC (and, as part of this, the UPR), Venezuela initially expressed explicit dissent in a statement to the General Assembly,[22] as well as abstaining from the vote on the draft resolution creating the HRC and UPR.[23] It has been postulated that Venezuela was, at the time, positioning itself to later deploy a persistent objector claim in relation to the UPR (although Venezuela itself never came close to making this claim, even implicitly).[24] Whether this is correct or not, what is important to note here is that Venezuela made no further expressions of dissent, and there is no suggestion that it ever achieved anything approaching exempt status by virtue of its initial limited dissent.[25] Indeed, it ultimately took active part in the first cycle of the UPR process.[26]

In the context of international environmental law, there remains some debate as to whether the so-called 'precautionary principle' has crystallized into binding customary international law. There is a significant amount of state practice now supporting the conclusion that it has,[27] although the uncertainty as to how the principle is to be applied in concrete cases and its undeniable soft-law roots mean that the binding status of the principle in customary international law remains contested.[28]

[18] See General Assembly Resolution 60/251, 3 April 2006, UN Doc. A/RES/60/251.

[19] See, generally, C. Tomuschat, 'Universal Periodic Review: a New System of International Law with Specific Ground Rules?' in U. Fastenrath, R. Geiger, D-E. Khan, A. Paulus, S. von Schorlemer, and C. Vedder (eds), *From Bilateralism to Community Interest: Essays in Honour of Judge Bruno Simma* (Oxford, Oxford University Press, 2011), 609.

[20] M. Szappanyos, 'Obligatory or Voluntary?—Participation in the UPR' (2012) 150 *Studia Iuridica Auctoritate Universitatis Pecs Publicata* 273, 277–9.

[21] See E. Dominguez-Redondo, 'The Universal Periodic Review—Is There Life Beyond Naming and Shaming in Human Rights Implementation?' (2012) 24 *New Zealand Law Review* 673, 705–6; and Szappanyos, n. 20, 280–1.

[22] General Assembly, Official Records, Sixtieth session, 72nd plenary meeting, 15 March 2006, UN Doc. A/60/PV.72, 5.

[23] Ibid., 6. [24] Szappanyos, n. 20, 284.

[25] To the point that Tomuschat argues that '[n]o State has raised any objections against the procedure': Tomuschat, n. 19, 612. This is not quite accurate, but can be considered as correct to the extent it can be read as no '*meaningful* objections'.

[26] See 'Universal Periodic Review of Venezuela', Human Right's Watch's Submission to the Human Rights Council, 21 March 2011, http://www.hrw.org/news/2011/03/21/universal-periodic-review-venezuela.

[27] See W. Gullett, 'Environmental Protection and the "Precautionary Principle": A Response to Scientific Uncertainty in Environmental Management' (1997) 14 *Environmental and Planning Law Journal* 52, 57; and P. Sands and J. Peel, *Principles of International Environmental Law* (Cambridge, Cambridge University Press, 3rd edn, 2012), 228. See also *Request for an Examination of the Situation in Accordance with Paragraph 63 of the Court's Judgment of 20 December 1974 in the Nuclear Tests (New Zealand v France)* case, order, 1995, ICJ Rep. 288, dissenting opinion of Judge Weeramantry, 342–4 (seemingly accepting the customary status of the principle, albeit not stating this explicitly).

[28] See B. Sage-Fuller, *The Precautionary Principle in Marine Environment Law: with Special Reference to High Risk Vessels* (Abingdon, Routledge, 2013), 112–35; and P. Ørebech and M. Chanock, 'Towards

What may be said with a degree of certainty is that there is at least an *emerging* rule of customary international law requiring active environmental precautionary measures.[29] In the *Meat and Meat Products* (*Hormones*) WTO arbitration,[30] decided in 1998, Canada objected to the customary status of the precautionary principle. It accepted that the principle was emerging as a binding custom, but was clear that it felt that the custom had not yet crystallized.[31]

However, Canada's position in *Meat and Meat Products* (*Hormones*) seemingly represents its *only* objection to the possible binding force of the precautionary principle.[32] While Canada was probably correct in 1998 that no binding norm of this sort had yet crystallized (meaning that it was objecting during the acceptable timeframe for persistent objection),[33] its objection was clearly not *persistent*. For those who hold that a customary precautionary principle has since crystallized, there is no possibility that this single objection could be construed as being sufficient for Canada to have gained a later exemption from the norm.[34] More tellingly, there was no recognition of any such exemption by other states, and Canada itself has since seemingly accepted the binding status of the principle, both in general and as applicable to itself.[35]

Overall, it seems clear that there must be at least some degree of repetition for the persistent objector rule to take effect. Single objections are, quite simply, not

Sustainability: The Basis in International Law' in P. Ørebech, F. Bosselman, J. Bjarup, D. Callies, M. Chanock, and H. Petersen (eds), *The Role of Customary Law in Sustainable Development* (Cambridge, Cambridge University Press, 2005), 384, 388–90.

[29] See R. Andorno, 'The Precautionary Principle: A New Legal Standard for a Technological Age' (2004) 1 *Journal of International Biotechnology Law* 11, generally, but particularly at 19; and A. Sirinskiene, 'The Status of Precautionary Principle: Moving towards a Rule of Customary Law' (2009) 4 *Jurisprudence* 349.

[30] *EC Measures Concerning Meat and Meat Products* (*Hormones*), Doc. WT/DS26/AB/RWT/DS48/AB/R, AB-1997-4, 16 January 1998 (Report of the WTO Appellate Body).

[31] *Meat and Meat Products* (*Hormones*), Complaint by Canada, 1998, WT/DS48/R, para. 34. It is worth recalling that it was argued in Chapter 3, section II that an assertion that a customary rule has not yet formed should, in itself, be viewed as an 'objection' for the purposes of the persistent objector rule.

[32] The single Canadian objection is in contrast to the practice of the United States, which has persistently and consistently objected to the emergence of the principle: see Chapter 6, n. 173–n. 184 and accompanying text.

[33] The WTO Appellate Body itself expressed uncertainty as to the customary status of the principle in 1998: see *Meat and Meat Products* (*Hormones*), report, n. 30, para. 123.

[34] See, for example, U. Thiratangsathira, 'The Precautionary Principle in International Environmental Law (with a Special Focus on the Marine Environment of Thailand)' (2010), unpublished PhD thesis, Queen Mary, University of London, 2010, https://qmro.qmul.ac.uk/jspui/handle/123456789/405, 112.

[35] See, for example, 'Planning for a Sustainable Future: A Federal Sustainable Development Strategy for Canada', Government of Canada, Sustainable Development Office, 'Environment Canada', October 2010, https://www.ec.gc.ca/dd-sd/default.asp?lang=En&n=06E31414-1. Indeed, Canada's support for the precautionary principle can clearly be identified *prior* to its submissions in *Meat and Meat Products* (*Hormones*) as well. For a summary of the Canadian state practice, see J. Cameron and J. Abouchar, 'The Precautionary Principle: A Fundamental Principle of Law and Policy for the Protection of the Global Environment' (1991) 14 *Boston College International and Comparative Law Review* 1, 10–11.

enough. Indeed, as Chalecki has stated, it is arguable that 'the *hallmark* of [persistent objector] status is the persistence [of the objection]'.[36]

II. The Rationale for the Persistence Criterion

Overall, it is fairly clear that repetition is, at least to some extent, a necessary element of the persistent objector rule. One objection will not suffice, and nor will a small number of objections. However, on a theoretical level, one might ask *why* repetition is required. If the overall rationale for the persistent objector rule itself is to preserve state voluntarism in the context of customary international law formation, as is often claimed,[37] then even a single expression of objection (if sufficiently communicated and unequivocal) would presumably suffice in notifying other states of the objector's position and act as a clear expression of sovereign will not to be bound. In other words, if the binding effect of customary international law is indeed premised on consent (including tacit consent), then one expression of the state's desire to withhold that consent should be enough.[38]

It is true that a single expression of dissent constitutes an expression of sovereign will, and so from an entirely voluntarist perspective any requirement for a state's objection to be repeated would seem unnecessary. However, the voluntarist foundation of the persistent objector rule is—at least in the sense of absolute voluntarism in all circumstances—full of conceptual holes and, thus, something of a fiction.[39] As noted in the Introduction, appraisal of the persistent objector rule cannot be deductive, based on a consent-based understanding of customary international law formation, but instead must be inductive, by reference to the way in which the rule is actually used.[40] Leaving aside for the present the fact that the persistent objector rule is built on somewhat shaky theoretical foundations, it is enough at this stage to note that its operation is, in reality, premised rather more on pragmatic and political concerns than purely on a voluntarist conceptual framework.

The persistent objector rule necessarily represents an exception to the universal binding force of customary international law, and exceptions should—and generally will—be interpreted narrowly.[41] Exceptionalism in connection with the binding nature of international law is potentially problematic in terms of the

[36] E.L. Chalecki, 'Science before the Law: American Exceptionalism in the Kyoto Protocol and the Development of a Global Norm of Environmental Compliance' (2007) *Selected Works*, http://works.bepress.com/cgi/viewcontent.cgi?article=1000&context=elizabeth_chalecki, 19, emphasis added.

[37] See, particularly, Chapter 9, section I.*i*.

[38] P. Dumberry, 'Incoherent and Ineffective: The Concept of Persistent Objector Revisited' (2010) 59 *International and Comparative Law Quarterly* 779, 795; Guldahl, n. 7, 59; A.T. Guzman, 'Saving Customary International Law' (2005–6) 27 *Michigan Journal of International Law* 115, 166; and M.H. Mendelson, 'The Formation of Customary International Law' (1998) 272 *Recueil des cours* 155, 239 (noting but not subscribing to this argument).

[39] See, particularly, Chapter 9, section I.*iii*.

[40] See Introduction, section IV.

[41] G. Boas, *Public International Law: Contemporary Principles and Perspectives* (Cheltenham, Edward Elgar, 2012), 94–5.

effectiveness and coherent development of international legal norms.[42] It is therefore desirable from a policy perspective to curtail the 'frivolous' use of the persistent objector rule: the operation of the rule represents a pragmatic balancing act between the notions of sovereign supremacy and legal universalism.[43] Requiring *persistent* objection helps to tip that balance towards universalism, other than in instances where the state concerned has a significant interest in remaining exempt and, thus, the will to reiterate that interest.

If a single objection were sufficient, a state may well be willing to object once—an action that will likely only have relatively limited negative political consequences—and then stay silent for the remainder of the new norm's emergence, simply to have that single objection 'in its back pocket' for later use, in case it were to subsequently decide that it wished to claim exempt objector status. Indeed, one could envisage a situation where *all states* objected at least once to any potentially emerging customary norm, merely as an insurance policy.[44] Such a scenario would be farcical, and would obviously impede effective customary international law development. Thus, a requirement of persistence ensures that the dissenting state is truly willing to accept the political implications of taking an isolationist position, in that 'it makes the role of persistent objector more costly and, therefore, discourages opportunistic objections by states that can be deterred'.[45] The need for persistence is therefore intended to ensure that objectors really 'mean it'. In this context, it is perhaps worth noting that, along with the key element of repetition, the word 'persistence' also denotes an element of *resolve* or *perseverance* to the objection; therefore, perhaps there is a reason that the scholarship refers to 'persistence' as being the required standard, and not just 'repetition'.

A related explanation for the existence of the persistence criterion is that repeated objection is easier to spot and so helps to promote clarity in the operation of the persistent objector rule. States are prima facie bound by new norms of customary international law, and the persistent objector rule represents a rebuttal

[42] See, generally, Charney, n. 5; and A. Mills, *The Confluence of Public and Private International Law: Justice, Pluralism, and Subsidiarity in the International Constitutional Ordering of Private Law* (Cambridge, Cambridge University Press, 2009), 98.

[43] See Chapter 9, particularly at section V.*ii*.

[44] A rational choice analysis is useful to highlight this: it is clear that the 'cost' of objection (as applied in any game theory calculation) would be *extremely* low for a state if objection did not need to be persistent to be effective. The benefits would significantly outweigh any (very minimal) cost for states, and so one might reasonably expect them to object ad nauseam. A number of scholars have considered the persistent objector rule from a rational choice perspective, see, for example, Guzman, n. 38, 166–71; A.T. Guzman, *How International Law Works: A Rational Choice Theory* (Oxford, Oxford University Press, 2008), 187–8 and 197–9; V. Fon and F. Parisi, 'Stability and Change in International Customary Law' (2004) 21 *American Law and Economics Association Annual Meetings* 1, 7–11; Kontorovich, n. 7, 874–5 and 910–11; G. Norman and J.P. Trachtman, 'The Customary International Law Game' (2005) 99 *American Journal of International Law* 541, 569; and N. Petersen, 'The Role of Consent and Uncertainty in the Formation of Customary International Law' (2011) *Reprints of the Max Planck Institute for Research on Collective Goods*, http://www.coll.mpg.de/pdf_dat/2011_04online.pdf, 5–10. See Chapter 9, particularly at section V.*i*, for further discussion.

[45] Guzman, n. 38, 169.

of that general presumption. Quite simply, repeated objection will constitute clearer evidence of that rebuttal than an isolated objection: a number of expressions of dissent will inevitably be less equivocal than a single objection, and will be easier to identify.[46] It may be that a single objection would go unnoticed by the wider international community. The need for objection to be persistent thus aims to ensure that other states (as well as other entities, such as international organizations, commentators, or courts) will be on notice that a dissenting state is indeed 'objecting'.[47] Sustained objection can be seen as an unambiguous statement of legal purpose, whereas a single objection might be less clearly an example of a state seeking to exempt itself from an emerging norm of customary international law.

Finally, as a practical matter, it is clear that other states are not likely to pay much heed to a single objection. So if the objector is truly serious about objecting, it will need to object a number of times: 'it seems clear that scant regard will be paid to the isolated protest of a State which takes no further action.'[48] This practical reality—that other states will likely ignore a single protest—has been reflected in the actual way in which the rule has been used. We saw this in relation to the 1935 German protest to Norway's Decree on fishing limits and the isolated Venezuelan dissent with regard to the UPR mechanism, discussed in section I. The theoretical basis for the requirement of persistence is therefore both to limit exceptionalism to only 'genuine' instances where the state has a significant interest in remaining exempt, and to ensure that objection to an emerging norm is unambiguous. However, it is worth keeping in mind that, while these underpinning justifications that can be advanced to support the persistence criterion feed in to the way in which states will react to the protests of other states, persistence has solidified as an element of the rule not as a direct consequence of coherent theory or policy concerns as such, but simply because objectors are aware that the international community is inclined to ignore isolated protests.

III. How Persistent is 'Persistent'?

Academic commentary and state practice both point towards the need for objection to be persistent, and there are good policy reasons for supporting this view (if not, perhaps, an entirely sound theoretical rationale underpinning it). This is all very well, but—while it is usually agreed that neither one objection nor a handful will suffice—it is entirely unclear how many separate instances of objection are enough to qualify: exactly how persistent is 'persistent'?

[46] H. Lau, 'Rethinking the Persistent Objector Doctrine in International Human Rights Law' (2005–6) 6 *Chicago Journal of International Law* 496, 498.

[47] A. Steinfeld, 'Nuclear Objections: The Persistent Objector and the Legality of the Use of Nuclear Weapons' (1996) 62 *Brooklyn Law Review* 1635, 1639, footnote 14 and 1652.

[48] MacGibbon, n. 8, 310. See also D. Bölükbaşı, *Turkey and Greece: The Aegean Disputes—A Unique Case in International Law* (London, Cavendish, 2004), 217; and Guldahl, n. 7, 54.

There is very little indication in scholarship as to the necessary level of persistence.[49] The problem of identifying the required number of repetitions of objection before a state can rely upon the persistent objector rule is something that a number of scholars have identified[50] but few have engaged with. However, a notable attempt to assess this question was made by Colson, in an important article from 1986.[51] Colson took a context-specific approach to understanding the required level of persistence. In particular, he argued that the more *isolated* a state becomes (in terms of the breadth of acceptance amongst other states of the norm to which the state is objecting, and the resultant 'solidity' of the emerging or emerged norm), the more often the objector will need to reassert (or will need to have previously reasserted) its position.[52] Thus, Colson argued that if an emerging norm of customary international law enjoys widespread support and a high degree of consensus on its development is quickly reached, then the isolated state 'needs to be especially vigilant in protecting its legal position'.[53]

Colson's context-specific approach to persistence appears to be borne out by state practice. A useful example to highlight the need for a higher degree of persistence in instances where the norm being objected to is well-established and the objector's position is notably isolated is the 2007 investment arbitration case of *BG Group v Argentina*.[54] The dispute involved a British company, BG Group Plc (BG), which commenced arbitration proceedings against Argentina. BG claimed that Argentina had breached the terms of a 1990 bilateral investment treaty between the United Kingdom and Argentina.[55] This was on the basis that a number of actions taken by Argentina during its financial crisis (in particular between 1999 and 2003) contravened provisions of that treaty in relation to BG's investment in the privatized gas industry in Argentina.[56] In response, Argentina argued that—as the action complained of by BG had occurred in the context of an overwhelming financial crisis—it was precluded

49 See, as a representative example, D.J. Bederman, 'Acquiescence, Objection and the Death of Customary International Law' (2010) 21 *Duke Journal of Comparative and International Law* 31, 35 (simply arguing that states must object 'often', without further qualification).

50 See O. Elias, 'Persistent Objector' in R. Wolfrum (ed.), *Max Planck Encyclopaedia of Public International Law, vol. VIII* (Oxford, Oxford University Press, 2012), 280, 284, para. 15; Guldahl, n. 7, 54; C.L. Lim and O. Elias, 'Withdrawing from Custom and the Paradox of Consensualism in International Law' (2010) 21 *Duke Journal of Comparative and International Law* 143, 148; T.L. Stein, 'The Approach of the Different Drummer: The Principle of the Persistent Objector in International Law' (1985) 26 *Harvard International Law Journal* 457, 478; and Steinfeld, n. 47, 1646.

51 D.A. Colson, 'How Persistent Must the Persistent Objector Be?' (1986) 61 *Washington Law Review* 957.

52 Ibid., particularly at 965–9. See also F. Ingman, 'Persistent Objector—The Demise of a Hero?' (2008), unpublished Masters thesis, Lund University, http://lup.lub.lu.se/luur/download?func=downloadFile&recordOId=1558532&fileOId=1564685, 28.

53 Colson, n. 51, 967.

54 *BG Group Plc v Republic of Argentina*, final award, 2007, http://ita.law.uvic.ca/documents/BG-award_000.pdf.

55 Agreement between the Government of the United Kingdom of Great Britain and Northern Ireland and the Government of the Republic of Argentina for the Promotion and Protection of Investments, 11 December 1990, 1765 UNTS 30682.

56 *BG Group v Argentina*, n. 54, particularly paras 84–6.

from wrongfulness by virtue of the notion of 'necessity' as provided for by customary international law and as codified in Article 25 of the (in themselves non-binding) International Law Commission (ILC)'s Draft Articles on State Responsibility.[57] This, in turn, led BG to argue that the United Kingdom had persistently objected to the defence of necessity and that, as such, Argentina could not rely on this defence.[58]

However, while there has been some repetition of objection to the notion of a defence of necessity in the practice of the United Kingdom, this has only occurred on a comparatively small number of occasions.[59] The ad hoc arbitral tribunal in *BG Group v Argentina* dismissed the assertion that the United Kingdom was a persistent objector out of hand.[60] Against the background of the ILC having codified the necessity defence in its Draft Articles on State Responsibility, and the majority of states having accepted that necessity exists as a condition precluding wrongfulness (something that is particularly evident in the context of investment obligations),[61] the British objections to the customary defence of necessity—constituting, as they did, a relatively small number of equivocal expressions of dissent—were insufficiently persistent.[62]

[57] Ibid., para. 88. See Draft Articles on the *Responsibility of States for Internationally Wrongful Acts, with commentaries*, adopted by the International Law Commission at its fifty-third session, November 2001, http://legal.un.org/ilc/texts/instruments/english/commentaries/9_6_2001.pdf.

[58] *BG Group v Argentina*, n. 54, para. 400.

[59] For example, the United Kingdom expressed the view that the necessity defence should not be included in the ILC's Draft Articles ('State Responsibility: comments and observations received from Governments', International Law Commission, Fifty-third session Geneva, 23 April–1 June and 2 July–10 August 2001, 19 March 2001, UN Doc. A/CN.4/515, 32–3). Indeed, this was an instance of objection that was cited by BG in the proceedings: *BG Group v Argentina*, n. 54, para. 400. Another instance where the United Kingdom can be seen as rejecting necessity as a condition precluding wrongfulness in international law is William Pitt the younger's famous statement in 1783 that '[n]ecessity is the plea for every infringement of human freedom. It is the argument of tyrants; it is the creed of slaves' (Speech to Parliament, quoted in S.F. Hill, 'Necessity Defense and the Emerging Arbitral Conflict in Its Application to the US-Argentina Bilateral Investment Treaty' (2007) 13 *Law and Business Review of the Americas* 547, 566). For the most part, though, the United Kingdom has been relatively silent on the issue, or may in fact be seen to have affirmed the necessity defence. Indeed, the ILC itself has suggested that a customary international law defence of necessity was invoked by the United Kingdom as far back as 1837, with regard to the famous *Caroline* incident (Draft Articles on State Responsibility, n. 57, commentary on Article 25, 81, para. 5). It is not entirely clear whether the United Kingdom invoked the defence of necessity with regard to the *Caroline* incident, although this is certainly one possible reading of the argument made by the United Kingdom at the time: see J.A. Green, 'Docking the *Caroline*: Understanding the Relevance of the Formula in Contemporary Customary International Law Concerning Self-Defence' (2006) 14 *Cardozo Journal of International and Comparative Law* 429, particularly at 438–9. A much more recent example would be the United Kingdom's apparent invocation of the necessity defence with regard to the NATO bombings in Kosovo in 1999: see Security Council, Official Records, Fifty-fourth year, 3988th plenary meeting, 24 March 1999, UN Doc. S/PV.3988, 12.

[60] This rejection could perhaps be seen as a matter of *obiter dicta*: see *BG Group v Argentina*, n. 54, para. 410, footnote 328. Having said this, see Chapter 2, n. 29–n. 33 and accompanying text in relation to the 'value' of the concept of '*obiter dicta*' in the international legal system.

[61] M.C. Hoelck Thjoernelund, 'State of Necessity as an Exemption from State Responsibility for Investments' (2009) 13 *Max Planck Yearbook of United Nations Law* 423, particularly at 443–9.

[62] Admittedly, the tribunal did not explicitly set out its reasons for rejecting the assertion by BG that the United Kingdom had attained persistent objector status, so this is not a conclusive reading of its reasoning in this regard. See *BG Group v Argentina*, n. 54, para. 410, footnote 328.

In asserting his view that the required level of persistence will be different in each instance of persistent objection, Colson points to the fact that, by the 1980s, virtually all coastline states accepted and claimed exclusive coastal state jurisdiction over tuna fishing within 200 nautical miles.[63] The United States, however, did not accept this rule, at least during the 1970s and 1980s, and objected to it on a significant number of occasions.[64] While some writers have made much of the fact that the United States' position in relation to coastal state exclusivity over migratory tuna fishing had started to waver somewhat by the late 1980s (potentially to the point of it reversing its persistent objector position),[65] at least during the 1970s and 1980s the United States' high degree of persistence of objection was seemingly sufficient to maintain its exempt status. One can, for example, point to the 1987 treaty signed between the United States and twelve Pacific Island states, whereby the island states recognized a special right of the United States to fish for tuna within parts of the South Pacific.[66] It has been argued on this basis that the United States 'triumphed' in maintaining its persistent objection.[67] Whether this remains true is perhaps debatable, but the United States was undoubtedly an exempt persistent objector for decades in relation to tuna fishing. However, given the significant weight of acceptance of the norm by other states, the United States was extremely careful to sustain its status by way of a large number of reiterations; less 'persistent' objection may well not have been sufficient.[68]

While these illustrative examples can be read in other ways, in that it cannot be said with certainty that the 'isolation' of the state concerned directly affected the necessary number of repetitions of objection in the examples considered, they are at least indicative of a context-specific approach to the persistence criterion where the rule has been employed by states. Certainly it can be said that reference to state practice shows that one cannot put a numerical figure on the required number of objections for a state to gain exemption in any given circumstance. There is evidently fluctuation across the usage of the rule, and it would appear that Colson is correct that the more isolated the state is and the better established the norm being objected to is, the more times the objector will need to object (or *have objected*).

[63] Colson, n. 51, 966–7.

[64] See Charney, n. 1, 13, particularly at footnote 56 (quoting the relevant section of a Presidential Statement on this point from 1983). See also C.R. Kelly, 'Law of the Sea: The Jurisdictional Dispute over Highly Migratory Species of Tuna' (1987–8) 26 *Columbia Journal of Transnational Law* 475, 494–504 (setting out the United States' objections in some detail); and J.A. Roach and R.W. Smith, *Excessive Maritime Claims* (Leiden, Martinus Nijhoff, 3rd edn, 2012), 169–70.

[65] See, for example, C. Tomuschat, 'Obligations Arising for States Without or Against Their Will' (1993) 241 *Recueil des cours* 195, 289.

[66] Treaty on Fisheries between the Governments of Certain Pacific Island States and the Government of the United States of America (South Pacific Tuna Treaty), 2 April 1987, 2176 UNTS 38287.

[67] O. Elias, 'Some Remarks on the Persistent Objector Rule in Customary International Law' (1991) 6 *Denning Law Journal* 37, 44. See also Kelly, n. 64, 506–7.

[68] Colson, n. 51, 966–7.

Further investigation suggests that it is not simply the extent of the objector state's isolation that will affect the required level of persistence, however. Building on Colson's 'context-specific' analysis, other writers have argued, for example, that if an emerging norm is viewed as particularly 'fundamental' (in the sense of it being inherently value-based, such as a civil or political human rights norm),[69] or as having particularly important consequences if breached (such as norms affecting international peace and security),[70] then it is similarly likely that more repetitions of objection will be required. As will be discussed in Chapter 8, it is evident that it is extremely difficult, at least de facto, for states to gain and maintain exemption from what might be perceived as 'fundamental' customary international law standards (even if the 'fundamental' norm in question is non-peremptory).[71] We know that there are relatively few examples of 'successful' persistent objection in general,[72] but even with that in mind there are particularly few examples of states gaining such an exempt status with regard to, say, rules of customary human rights law. It is worth noting that in the rare instances in which states have been able to maintain objection to emerging human rights norms or other 'fundamental' rules, this has been based on a *significant* pattern of objection. In other words, to stand any chance of securing exempt status with regard to customary international human rights law, the objecting state must have objected especially persistently.

As an example, one might consider the United States' position on the customary international law 'right to food' (or, as it is termed by some, the 'right to adequate food'). There is a large amount of evidence to support the view that the right to food crystallized as a binding rule of customary human rights law somewhere in the 2000s, if not before.[73] However, the United States has objected to the binding

[69] See, for example, L. Loschin, 'The Persistent Objector Rule and Customary Human Rights Law: A Proposed Analytical Framework' (1996) 2 *University of California Davis Journal of International Law and Policy* 147, 164–6.

[70] See, for example, Steinfeld, n. 47, 1652.

[71] See, particularly, Chapter 8, section II.

[72] See Chapter 2, section II.

[73] The customary international law right to adequate food has its roots in a combination of the Universal Declaration of Human Rights, General Assembly Resolution 217 (III), 10 December 1948, UN Doc. A/RES/3/217 A, Article 25; the International Covenant on Economic, Social and Cultural Rights, 16 December 1966, 993 UNTS 3, Article 11; and the *Voluntary Guidelines to Support the Progressive Realization of the Right to Adequate Food in the Context of National Food Security*, adopted by the hundred and twenty-seventh session of the FAO Council, November 2004, Food and Agriculture Organization of the United Nations, Rome, 2005, http://www.fao.org/docrep/009/y7937e/y7937e00.htm. The right has also been identified in a number of recent UN General Assembly Resolutions, all of which were adopted by a significant number of votes: see, for example, General Assembly Resolution 63/187, 18 December 2008, UN Doc. A/RES/63/187; General Assembly Resolution 63/235, 22 December 2008, UN Doc. A/RES/63/235; and General Assembly, Sixty-eighth session, Third committee agenda item 69(b), revised draft resolution: The right to food, 20 November 2013, UN Doc. A/C.3/68/L.60/Rev.1. On the customary status of the right, see 'The Right to Adequate Food', Office of the United Nations High Commissioner for Human Rights, 2010, Fact Sheet No. 34, http://www.ohchr.org/Documents/Publications/FactSheet34en.pdf, 9; S. Narula, 'The Right to Food: Holding Global Actors Accountable under International Law' (2005–6) 44 *Columbia Journal of Transnational Law* 691, particularly at 780–91; and S. Söllner, 'The "Breakthrough" of the Right to Food: The Meaning of General Comment No. 12 and the Voluntary Guidelines for the Interpretation of the Human Right to Food' (2007) 11 *Max Planck Yearbook of United Nations Law* 391, 408–9.

nature of this norm on a large number of occasions, going back many years.[74] On this basis, in a 2005 report to the UN General Assembly, transmitted by the Secretary General, the Special Rapporteur of the Commission on Human Rights on the Right to Food identified the United States as an exempt persistent objector state.[75] This assertion then went unremarked upon by UN member states, suggesting a general acceptance of the United States' exempt status, irrespective of the norm in question being one of international human rights law. This may be explained by the fact that, despite the ethical credentials of the right to food, the United States' objections have been overwhelmingly persistent.

The context of the objection in terms of the degree of isolation and the perceived 'importance' and 'ethical value' of the norm therefore seemingly play their part, but it would also be naïve to ignore the role that power plays in establishing the required degree of persistence. It is perhaps unsurprising that it is the United States, as the most powerful state in the world, that has been able to assert exempt persistent objector status in relation to the right to food (a norm of customary international human rights law) and—for a significant period at least—with regard to coastal state exclusivity in tuna fishing (even in the face of near-universal opposition). The political reality is that less powerful states will likely have to object more often than a powerful state would have to, even in circumstances where the norm in question is not especially 'fundamental' or particularly well accepted. Having said this, regarding both the right to food and tuna fishing rights, it is notable that, even for the United States, maintaining its exemption required significant, almost rote, repetitions of dissent.

Ultimately, it is the *acceptability* of the objection to other states that determines the required level of persistence in any given instance. The operation of the persistent objector rule is highly political, and the acceptability of the objector's claim to other states will contribute to the rule's (in)ability to shield particular objectors. Put simply: the less 'acceptable' the state's objections are seen as being by other

[74] There are numerous examples of objection by the United States to the emerging right to food. See, generally, E. Messer and M.J. Cohen, 'US Approaches to Food and Nutrition Rights, 1976–2008' (2009) *Hunger Notes*, http://www.worldhunger.org/articles/08/hrf/messer.htm. Some specific examples include: 'Interpretative Statements for the Record by the Government of the United States of America', reproduced in *Report of the World Food Summit*, Food and Agriculture Organization of the United Nations, 1996, Annex II, http://www.fao.org/docrep/003/w3548e/w3548e00.htm#Annexii (in relation to the Declaration on World Food Security, 1996, Rome, World Food Summit, 13–17 November 1996); 'U.S. Mission to the UN Agencies for Food and Agriculture, Rome, Reservation', 2002, http://www.fao.org/docrep/MEETING/005/Y7106e/y7106e03.htm#P192_62571 (in relation to 'International Alliance against Hunger', Declaration of the World Food Summit: *five years later*, 2002, Rome, 10–13 June 2002); 'Explanation of Position by Craig Kuehl, United States Advisor, on Resolution L.30, Rev. 1 – The Right to Food, in the Third Committee of the Sixty-fourth Session of the United Nations General Assembly', 19 November 2009, http://usun.state.gov/remarks/4560. In addition, in 2008 the United States was the only state to vote against UN Doc. A/RES/63/187, n. 73, on the right to food, a resolution that 184 states voted in favour of (see General Assembly, Official Records, Sixty-third session, 70th plenary meeting, 18 December 2008, UN Doc. A/63/PV.70, 24).

[75] *The Right to Food*, note by the Secretary-General, transmitting the interim report of the Special Rapporteur of the Commission on Human Rights on the Right to Food in accordance with General Assembly Resolution 59/202, 12 September 2005, UN Doc. A/60/350, 23, footnote 44.

states, the more the objector will need to object in order to defend its position. A range of extra-legal factors—such as the breadth of approval for the norm being objected to and the consequent degree of isolation of the objector, the 'importance' attached to the norm by other states, and the relative political power of the objector—will all contribute to the acceptability of the objection and, thus, the required level of persistence. On this basis, Lepard argues that:

> [I]t is not possible to assert that objection … must manifest a certain level of intensity in every case. *Depending on the beliefs of the generality of states* an objection may not even need to be 'persistent,' so that the very term 'persistent objector exception' itself might be a misnomer.[76]

In the view of the present author, Lepard goes too far in claiming that the persistence requirement might, on occasion, be dispensed with entirely. There is no evidence to support this claim: at least some repetition is necessary, as was argued in section I. Where Lepard is entirely correct, however, is in stating that the acceptability of the objection to other states will influence how persistent that objection must be.

This is not, perhaps, an entirely desirable conclusion. The lack of certainty as to the required number of objections potentially undermines the effective operation of the persistent objector rule by lessening the scope for states to rely upon it (either as objectors, or as others seeking to interact with objectors). The necessary level of persistence is a 'how long is a piece of string' question, and that hardly sits well with concepts of predictability and certainty that are at the heart of the rule of law.[77] Lawyers may also be rather uncomfortable with the effect that entirely non-legal factors can have on the persistence criterion (particularly, perhaps, the influence of power on the process).

However, these same issues of uncertainty and the influence of extra-legal factors plague the formation of customary international law more generally.[78] It is well known that there is no set 'amount' or 'quality' of state practice necessary for a new norm to form: the question of whether there has been sufficient state practice for a new customary international law norm to crystallize will depend on context and on the acceptability of the new norm to the international community.[79] It should therefore come as no surprise that, for good or ill, this is also true of the persistence criterion in relation to the persistent objector exception to the binding

[76] B.D. Lepard, *Customary International Law: A New Theory with Practical Applications* (Cambridge, Cambridge University Press, 2010), 235–8, emphasis added.

[77] See, generally, L.B. Tremblay, *The Rule of Law, Justice and Interpretation* (Bakerville, McGill-Queen's University Press, 1997), particularly at 149–65.

[78] See, generally, ILA Final Report, n. 7, particularly at 2; A. Boyle and C. Chinkin, *The Making of International Law* (Oxford, Oxford University Press, 2007), 21; A.T. Guzman and T.L. Meyer, 'Customary International Law in the 21st Century' in R.A. Miller and R.M. Bratspies (eds), *Progress in International Law* (Leiden, Martinus Nijhoff, 2008), 197, 197–200; and J. Kammerhofer, 'Uncertainty in the Formal Sources of International Law: Customary International Law and Some of its Problems' (2004) 15 *European Journal of International Law* 523 (discussing numerous uncertainties surrounding the formation and content of customary international law).

[79] See, for example, Charney, n. 5, 545–6.

force of customary international law. Indeed, it cannot be otherwise: an arbitrary threshold of any set number of objections would be just as objectionable (as it were) as is the context-specific approach. And who would set such a threshold, anyway? Moreover, even if a set number of repetitions could be agreed upon in doctrine, this kind of clear threshold is certainly not evident in practice.

To be safe, then—or, at least, as safe as possible—a dissenting state is best advised to object *often*. By objecting a significant number of times, a state inherently strengthens its claim to exempt status, by demonstrating its political will to remain apart. However, objector states will be looking to strike a balance here. The exemption that can be gained through persistent objection comes linked, of course, to the undesirable political implications of being viewed as a legal pariah by other states.[80] The more often a state objects, the more often it self-identifies as a trouble-maker, further heaping the political fallout from that stance upon itself. Therefore, an objecting state will look to walk the fine (and, indeed, largely unknowable) line between keeping silent where possible so as to avoid unnecessary political backlash, and objecting on a sufficient number of occasions to maintain its position. Unfortunately, it is impossible to provide even a useful set of guidelines as to how 'persistent' objection must be to help the dissenting state tread this path. What at least may be said, however, is that the following factors will likely influence the required number of objections:

1. The norm in question has quickly gained significant support from the majority of states (and, perhaps, commentators, NGOs, and other influential entities).
2. Related to point 1, the objector is the sole persistent objector, or one of a very small number of persistent objectors.
3. The norm being objected to is of particular significance to issues of international peace and security.
4. The norm being objected to has a value-based nature (such as a human rights norm).
5. The objector is not a particularly powerful state.

The International Law Association's *Committee on Formation of Customary (General) International Law* neatly summed up the position with regard to the persistence requirement thus: 'objection … must be repeated *as often as circumstances require* (otherwise it will not be "persistent").'[81] This conclusion is vague and frustratingly uncertain, but it is the reality of the operation of the persistence criterion.

[80] See O. Barsalou, 'La doctrine de l'objecteur persistant en droit international public' (2006) 19 *Revue québécoise de droit international* 1, 15; Colson, n. 51, 962 ('legal objections, so fundamental to the persistent objector, inadvertently take on political character'); Dumberry, n. 38, 791; Lim and Elias, n. 50, 151–2; Guldahl, n. 7, 59; and Mendelson, n. 38, 234.

[81] ILA Final Report, n. 7, 28.

IV. Conclusion

There is little question that if a state wishes to later rely on the persistent objector rule, it must have objected *persistently*. Single or isolated objections will not suffice: this is very clear in doctrine, but it is also an obvious element of the state usage of the rule. The theoretical rationale for this is, however, less clear. Voluntarist theory—so often said to underpin the persistent objector rule—cannot explain the need for persistence: a single withholding of consent is still a withholding of consent. Persistence instead has its roots in more pragmatic and practical concerns. A need for repetition tests the will of the objector to ensure that the persistent objector rule is not used frivolously and, at least to some degree, promotes clarity and certainty in the operation of the rule.

However, the degree of clarity and certainty gained by requiring objectors to object persistently is significantly undermined when one attempts to assess precisely *how* persistent the objector must be. There is no exact answer to this question: the necessary level of persistence will depend on the circumstances at hand, and—particularly—on the acceptability of the state's dissent to the wider international community. Various factors (including extra-legal factors) will be likely to influence that acceptability and thus influence the degree of repetition required. Ultimately, objector states will need to be vigilant in repeating their dissent and keeping other states on notice as to their position, especially as they become more isolated.

Persistence is, of course, the first of the two commonly identified requirements for the rule's operation, with the second being timeliness: it is generally argued that the persistent objections must occur before the norm being objected to has crystallized into binding custom. However, persistence is not the end of the story with regard to the necessary 'quality' of objection required to gain exemption. Before turning to the 'timeliness' element in Chapter 6—i.e. when a state must object—Chapter 5 first considers a criterion that has many similarities with, and is just as important as, persistence, but is often overlooked: the *consistency* of the state's objection.

5

The Consistency Criterion

Chapter 4 examined the commonly expressed requirement that objection must be persistent. This chapter considers a crucial but largely overlooked related criterion: the consistency of objection. The need for consistency is actually identified regularly in the literature on the persistent objector rule, but this is often implicit or amalgamated/confused with the persistence criterion.

This chapter confirms, in section I, the need for *consistent* objection—a requirement related to, but distinct from, persistence—as identified in both doctrine and state practice. It then briefly assesses, in section II, the rationale for the consistency criterion, before turning to the important question of what 'consistent objection' in fact entails. Section III considers whether a state's objections must be 'absolutely consistent' (in the sense of any contrary practice being terminal for its exemption from the relevant norm), or whether a generally consistent pattern of objection will suffice. Section IV then asks whether the silence of a state—in circumstances where it might reasonably be *expected* to object—can be interpreted as inconsistent practice. Finally, section V considers the notion of 'substantive consistency', meaning the consistency of a state's position as between related norms: does a persistent objector need to have a principled stance of objection across comparable rules?

I. Objection Must Be Consistent

A survey of the literature concerning persistent objection indicates that many scholars refer not (or not merely) to a requirement of *persistence*, but to a criterion of *consistency*.[1] Indeed, while the rule is commonly labelled the 'persistent objector'

[1] See, for example, M. Akehurst, 'Custom as a Source of International Law' (1974–5) 47 *British Yearbook of International Law* 1, 24; R.B. Baker, 'Customary International Law in the 21st Century: Old Challenges and New Debates' (2010) 21 *European Journal of International Law* 173, 176; D. Bölükbaşı, *Turkey and Greece: The Aegean Disputes—A Unique Case in International Law* (London, Cavendish, 2004), 207; M. Byers, *Custom, Power and the Power of Rules: International Relations and Customary International Law* (Cambridge, Cambridge University Press, 1999), 149 and 180; A. Cassese, *International Law in a Divided World* (Oxford, Clarendon Press, 1986), 178; A. Cassese, *International Law* (Oxford, Oxford University Press, 2nd edn, 2005), 163; J. Crawford, 'Chance, Order, Change: The Course of International Law—General Course on Public International Law' (2013) 365 *Recueil des cours* 9, 247; D.P. Fidler, 'Challenging the Classical Concept of Custom: Perspectives on the Future of Customary International Law'

rule, more of the writers who have discussed its operation have actually referred to a 'consistency' criterion to describe the required quality of objection (either explicitly or by using the term 'persistence' but then discussing something that actually looks rather more like consistency) than have referred to a true persistence criterion.[2] While this recognition of a need for consistency has been largely implicit in doctrine, it is in fact extremely widespread in the literature. We saw in Chapter 4 that a (largely unspecified) degree of persistence is necessary,[3] but we

(1996) 39 *German Yearbook of International Law* 198, 209; G. Fitzmaurice, 'The Law and Procedure of the International Court of Justice, 1951–54: General Principles and Sources of Law' (1953) 30 *British Yearbook of International Law* 1, 25; V. Fon and F. Parisi, 'Stability and Change in International Customary Law' (2004) 21 *American Law and Economics Association Annual Meetings* 1, 5–6; A.T. Guzman, *How International Law Works: A Rational Choice Theory* (Oxford, Oxford University Press, 2008), 188; M.A. Hansen, 'Preventing the Emasculation of Warfare: Halting the Expansion of Human Rights Law into Armed Conflict' (2007) 194 *Military Law Review* 1, 17; T. Hillier, *Sourcebook on Public International Law* (London, Cavendish Publishing, 1998), 74; A. Kaczorowska, *Public International Law* (Abingdon, Routledge, 4th edn, 2010), 41; E. Kontorovich, 'Inefficient Customs in International Law' (2006-2007) 48 *William and Mary Law Review* 859, 910; H. Lau, 'Rethinking the Persistent Objector Doctrine in International Human Rights Law' (2005–6) 6 *Chicago Journal of International Law* 496, 498; B.D. Lepard, *Customary International Law: A New Theory with Practical Applications* (Cambridge, Cambridge University Press, 2010), 239, 238–9; C.L. Lim and O. Elias, 'Withdrawing from Custom and the Paradox of Consensualism in International Law' (2010) 21 *Duke Journal of Comparative and International Law* 143, 146, and 148; L. Loschin, 'The Persistent Objector Rule and Customary Human Rights Law: A Proposed Analytical Framework' (1996) 2 *University of California Davis Journal of International Law and Policy* 147, 151, and 168; P. Malanczuk, *Akehurst's Modern Introduction to International Law* (New York, Routledge, 7th edn, 1997), 48; F.F. Martin, *The Constitution as Treaty: The International Legal Constructionalist Approach to the U.S. Constitution* (Cambridge, Cambridge University Press, 2007), 73–5; J.B. McClane, 'How Late in the Emergence of a Norm of Customary International Law May a Persistent Objector Object?' (1989) 13 *International Law Students Association Journal of International Law* 1, 2, and 20–1; H. Meijers, 'How is International Law Made?—The Stages of Growth of International Law and the Use of Customary Rules' (1978) 9 *Netherlands Yearbook of International Law* 3, 23; T. Meron, 'International Law in the Age of Human Rights' (2013) 301 *Recueil des cours* 13, 394; C. Quince, *The Persistent Objector and Customary International Law* (Denver, Outskirts Press, 2010), 60–1; C. Rousseau, *Droit international public, vol. I: introduction et sources* (Paris, Sirey, 1970), 320; A. Steinfeld, 'Nuclear Objections: The Persistent Objector and the Legality of the Use of Nuclear Weapons' (1996) 62 *Brooklyn Law Review* 1635, 1639, footnote 14, 1647 and 1652; J. Tasioulas, 'Customary International Law and the Quest for Global Justice' in A. Perreau-Saussine and J.B. Murphy (eds), *The Nature of Customary Law: Legal, Historical and Philosophical Perspectives* (Cambridge, Cambridge University Press, 2007), 307, 312; H. Thirlway, *International Customary Law and Codification* (Leiden, A.W. Sijthoff, 1972), 110 and 116; H. Thirlway, *The Sources of International Law* (Oxford, Oxford University Press, 2014), 86 and 159; M.E. Villiger, *Customary International Law and Treaties: A Manual on the Theory and Practice of the Interrelation of Sources* (The Hague, Kluwer, 2nd edn, 1997), 34–5; M. Virally, 'The Sources of International Law' in M. Sørensen (ed.), *Manual of Public International Law* (London, Macmillan, 1968), 116, 136; D. Weissbrodt, 'Execution of Juvenile Offenders by the United States Violates International Humanitarian Law' (1988) 3 *American University Journal of International Law and Policy* 339, 367–8; and K. Wolfke, *Custom in Present International Law* (Dordrecht, Martinus Nijhoff, 2nd edn, 1993), 66.

[2] Interestingly, in a break from the normal terminology, Greig terms the rule the 'consistent objector' rule: D.W. Greig, 'Reflections on the Role of Consent' (1988–9) 12 *Australian Yearbook of International Law* 125, 145, and 173. It would, in fact, be most accurate to refer to the rule as the 'persistent *and* consistent objector rule'.

[3] See, in particular, Chapter 4, section III.

might further ask whether persistence alone is enough, or whether objection must be both persistent and consistent.

Consistency is, of course, not the same thing as persistence. As was noted in the previous chapter, the term 'persistence' denotes repetition,[4] as well as a degree of steadfastness.[5] Consistency, on the other hand, requires a level of *uniformity* of objection, or what might be termed 'non-derogation' by the state from its dissenting stance. A state could 'persistently' object to a newly forming law (by regularly and repeatedly rejecting it), but in fact do so inconsistently (by accepting or affirming the norm on a minority of occasions, in the midst of its general policy of objecting persistently).

The distinction between persistence and consistency can be usefully illustrated by the United States' objector stance in relation to the customary international law prohibition of the juvenile death penalty. The United States claimed to be a persistent objector to this prohibition twice before the Inter-American Commission on Human Rights (IACmHR), in *Roach and Pinkerton v United States* (1987)[6] and *Domingues v United States* (2002).[7] The latter of these decisions, the *Domingues* proceedings in 2002, concerned a death sentence imposed by the State of Nevada on an individual who was sixteen years old at the time that he had committed two homicides.[8] From the early 1990s onwards, there had been increasing claims made that a norm prohibiting the execution of persons under the age of eighteen had crystallized into customary international law.[9] There exists a good deal of evidence indicating that this was the case,[10] and the IACmHR certainly took this view in *Domingues*.[11] However, the United States argued, as it had previously done in *Roach and Pinkerton*,[12] that it was exempt from the prohibition on juvenile executions in relation to Mr Domingues—or, at least, was exempt from a rule that took eighteen rather than sixteen as the threshold for minority executions—on the basis that it was a persistent objector.[13]

[4] See ibid., text prior to n. 1. [5] See ibid., text following n. 45.

[6] *Roach and Pinkerton v United States of America*, merits, 1987, IACmHR, Resolution No. 3/87, Case 9647.

[7] *Domingues v United States*, merits, 2002, IACmHR, Report No. 62/02, Case No. 12.285.

[8] Ibid., 1–2.

[9] See, for example, Amnesty International, 'United States of America: Open Letter to the President on the Death Penalty', 1994, https://www.amnesty.org/en/documents/amr51/001/1994/en/, particularly the state practice referenced at 8.

[10] The state practice supporting the establishment, in the early 1990s, of a customary norm prohibiting juvenile executions is set out in detail in E.F. Sherman, Jr, 'The U.S. Death Penalty Reservation to the International Covenant on Civil and Political Rights: Exposing the Limitations of the Flexible System Governing Treaty Formation' (1994) 29 *Texas International Law Journal* 69, 88–90.

[11] *Domingues*, merits, n. 7, para. 83.

[12] *Roach and Pinkerton v United States*, memorandum of the United States to the Inter-American Commission on Human Rights in Case 9647, IACmHR 147, OEA/ser.L/V./II.71, doc. 9 rev. 1, 15.

[13] See *Domingues v United States*, response of the government of the United States to May 1, 2000 Petition, Case No. 12.185 (Michael Domingues), http://www.state.gov/documents/organization/16525.pdf, 10–11; and *Domingues*, merits, n. 7, para. 14.

One issue for the Commission in assessing the United States' persistent objector claim in *Domingues* was the *consistency* of the United States' objection. Prior to 2002, there had certainly been a pattern of objection on the part of the United States. Indeed, its dissent was repeated to an extent that it would be difficult to argue that the objections of the United States were anything other than *persistent.* Bradley, for example, provides detailed evidence of the United States' repeated objection—by both action and statement—to any emerging customary international law norm on juvenile executions, going back to the first recorded juvenile execution in the United States in 1642 (meaning also that the United States' dissent started *well before* any possible norm could have crystallized).[14] Other examples evidencing the United States' repeated objection include the decision in *Gregg v Georgia* in 1976 (allowing for the juvenile death penalty in certain restricted instances)[15] and the famous opinion authored by Justice Scalia in *Stanford v Kentucky* in 1989 (holding that the Eighth Amendment did not prohibit the execution of an individual who was sixteen or seventeen years of age at the time of the commission of the offence).[16]

However, while the objections of the United States were persistent—and were repeated over a significant period of time—a number of writers have concluded that its objections were insufficiently *consistent* for it to gain exemption from the prohibition on executing juveniles.[17] One might, for example, point to the domestic case law of the United States as evidence of inconsistent practice in relation to the application of the juvenile death penalty in a number of instances.[18] In addition, the State Department explicitly denied that the United States intended to reserve a right to execute juvenile offenders on more than one occasion.[19] It is also clear that the United States' wider international engagement with the prohibition somewhat belied its dissenting stance:

> [T]he United States ratified the Fourth Geneva Convention without objecting to the norm. It signed the American Convention on Human Rights without objecting to the norm. It signed the Convention on the Rights of the Child without objecting to the norm. It participated in the framing of the ICCPR and signed it without objecting to the norm; indeed, it even jointly sponsored a United Nations General Assembly resolution [UN

[14] See C.A. Bradley, 'The Juvenile Death Penalty' (2002–3) 52 *Duke Law Journal* 485, particularly at 492–500.

[15] *Gregg v Georgia*, 1976, 428 US 153, 206–7.

[16] *Stanford v Kentucky*, 1989, 492 US 361.

[17] See P. Dumberry, 'Incoherent and Ineffective: The Concept of Persistent Objector Revisited' (2010) 59 *International and Comparative Law Quarterly* 779, 789; J.F. Hartmann, '"Unusual" Punishment: The Domestic Effect of International Norms Restricting the Application of the Death Penalty' (1983) 52 *University of Cincinnati Law Review* 655, 682–6; Lepard, n. 1, 239; Loschin, n. 1, 171; D. Shelton, 'Application of Death Penalty on Juveniles in the US' (1987) 8 Human Rights Law Journal 355, 359; and Weissbrodt, n. 1, 368. Indeed, even some who have argued that the United States should be exempt from the customary international law prohibition on juvenile executions have accepted that its practice had not always been entirely consistent in this regard: see Bradley, n. 14, 493.

[18] For discussion, and examples of domestic cases that seemingly contradict the United States' general stance of objection, see ibid., 493; and Quince, n. 1, 66–9.

[19] For details, see Loschin, n. 1, 171; and Weissbrodt, n. 1, 368, particularly at footnote 158.

Doc. A/35/48] that [asserted that] Article 6 of the ICCPR, which embodies the norm, establishes a 'minimum standard' for all member states, whether or not they had adopted [the ICCPR].[20]

On the basis of all this, the IACmHR in *Domingues* concluded that the United States had not been a sufficiently consistent objector to the prohibition of the juvenile death penalty (for those aged below eighteen years at the time of the offence) for the persistent objector exemption to apply to it:

[T]he United States . . . rather than persistently objecting to the standard, has in several significant respects recognized the propriety of this norm by, for example, prescribing the age of 18 as the federal standard for the application of capital punishment and by ratifying the Fourth Geneva Convention without reservation to this standard.[21]

Interestingly, the language used here by IACmHR would suggest that it took the view that the inconsistent practice of the United States meant that its objections had not been sufficiently *persistent*. This is incorrect: it has already been noted that objection on the part of the United States almost certainly *was* persistent. When one considers the substance of the Commission's statement, however, it is evident that it actually took the view that the United States had not been *consistent* enough in its objections.

It is important to note that the IACmHR saw the consistency issue as something of an aside, as it had already determined that the United States could not be viewed as a persistent objector on other grounds.[22] Nonetheless, it is evident that the Commission viewed the objections of the United States as insufficiently consistent, in spite of these objections being repeated a significant number of times.[23] *Domingues* therefore both highlights that consistency is required for the persistent objector rule to take effect and provides evidence of the pervasive confusion between the persistence and consistency criteria in doctrine.

Another useful example on the question of consistent objection is the 2015 *Chagos Marine Protected Area* UN Convention on the Law of the Sea (UNCLOS) arbitral dispute,[24] which related to the creation by the United Kingdom of a

[20] *Commonwealth of Pennsylvania v Hector Huertas*, motion to preclude the Commonwealth from seeking the death penalty against a juvenile and consolidated memorandum of law, 2002, CP 0009-0941, CTD, 25–6.

[21] *Domingues*, merits, n. 7, para. 85.

[22] Specifically, the Commission concluded that the juvenile death penalty prohibition was a *jus cogens* norm, and that its peremptory status overrode the persistent objections of the United States. *Domingues*, merits, n. 7, para. 85. See Chapter 7, n. 51–n. 71 and accompanying text for discussion.

[23] It is worth noting that the United States Supreme Court subsequently ruled—in *Roper v Simmons*, 2005, 543 US 551—that the juvenile death penalty was cruel and unusual punishment and was therefore unlawful under the American Constitution. Thus, the United States did not maintain its persistent objector stance on the issue for long following *Domingues*.

[24] *In the Matter of the Chagos Marine Protected Area Arbitration (The Republic of Mauritius v The United Kingdom of Great Britain and Northern Ireland)*, 2015, award, Arbitral Tribunal Constituted under Annex VII of the United Nations Convention on the Law of the Sea, http://www.pca-cpa.org/MU-UK%2020150318%20Awardd4b1.pdf?fil_id=2899.

marine protected area (MPA) up to the outer limit of the exclusive economic zone of the Chagos Archipelago, purportedly to help preserve the marine environment. In December 2010, Mauritius initiated proceedings against the United Kingdom under the dispute settlement provisions of UNCLOS (Article 287 and Annex VII, Article 1), asking an arbitral tribunal to declare that the establishment of the MPA violated UNCLOS and other rules of international law.[25] The United Kingdom argued in response that it was entitled to declare the MPA, in part on the basis that, in 1965, it had formally 'detached' the Chagos Archipelago from Mauritius (which was then its colony) and retained the archipelago as part of a wider 'British Indian Ocean Territory' following Mauritian independence in 1968.[26] Of relevance here is the fact that Mauritius argued, inter alia, that the detachment and retention of the Chagos Archipelago in 1965 and 1968 respectively were 'contrary to the right of the people of Mauritius to self-determination'.[27]

The United Kingdom's response to this assertion was to argue that even if the right of self-determination was applicable in the circumstances and prima facie precluded the detachment and retention of the archipelago in the mid-1960s, *at that time* the United Kingdom had the status of an exempt persistent objector to the right of self-determination.[28] Based on the intertemporal law rule, the United Kingdom asserted that the title to the territory was validly retained in 1968, and thus could form a basis for its creation of the MPA in 2010. In particular, it stressed that 'The United Kingdom had *consistently*, throughout the 1950s and 1960s, objected to references to a "right" of self-determination in United Nations instruments, including in the drafts of the International Covenants of 1966'.[29]

There was certainly a pattern of objection by the United Kingdom prior to the mid-1960s,[30] which—as with the United States' dissent in relation to the juvenile death penalty—it would be difficult to argue was not persistent. Nonetheless, Mauritius, in its Reply, argued that '[t]he UK did not ... *consistently* object to the development of the right.'[31] This claim was set out in some detail.[32] Indeed,

[25] *Dispute Concerning the 'Marine Protected Area' related to the Chagos Archipelago* (*Mauritius v United Kingdom*), notification under Article 287 and Annex VII, Article 1 of UNCLOS and the statement of the claim and grounds on which it is based, 2010, 1982 UNCLOS—Annex VII Arbitration, http://www.pca-cpa.org/1.%20Notice%20of%20Arbitration.pdfdc8e.PDF?fil_id=2583.

[26] *Chagos Marine Protected Area Arbitration* (*The Republic of Mauritius v The United Kingdom of Great Britain and Northern Ireland*), counter-memorial submitted by the United Kingdom, 2013, http://www.pca-cpa.org/4.%20Counter%20Memoriale29c.pdf?fil_id=2586, particularly at 8–47.

[27] *Chagos Marine Protected Area Arbitration* (*The Republic of Mauritius v The United Kingdom of Great Britain and Northern Ireland*), memorial of the Republic of Mauritius, 2012, http://www.pca-cpa.org/2.%20Memorial%20on%20Merits1142.pdf?fil_id=2584, 104.

[28] *Chagos Marine Protected Area*, counter-memorial submitted by the United Kingdom, n. 26, 183–90.

[29] Ibid., 184, emphasis added.

[30] As set out by the United Kingdom itself in its pleadings in *Mauritius v United Kingdom*: see ibid., 183–90.

[31] *Chagos Marine Protected Area Arbitration* (*The Republic of Mauritius v The United Kingdom of Great Britain and Northern Ireland*), reply of the Republic of Mauritius, 2013, http://www.pca-cpa.org/5.%20Replya480.pdf?fil_id=2587, 124, emphasis added.

[32] Ibid., 124–7.

in its Reply, Mauritius presented significant evidence indicating that the United Kingdom's objections to the right of self-determination prior to 1965 had been inconsistent, including statements made by the United Kingdom in relation to the right of self-determination in the context of General Assembly Resolution 421 (V) in 1950, the position it took in the discussion of Gibraltar before the Committee of 24 in 1964–5, and the fact that the United Kingdom voted to adopt General Assembly resolution 1723 (XVI) in 1961 (which specifically affirms the right of self-determination), with no statement of reservation.[33]

Ultimately, at the award stage, the UNCLOS tribunal did not examine the question of the United Kingdom's asserted persistent objector status, as it concluded that it did not have jurisdiction to consider Mauritius' first two submissions, to which this aspect of the pleadings related.[34] As such, the dispute tells us relatively little about the required *degree* of consistency necessary for a state to gain exemption by way of persistent objection: an issue that will be examined in sections III–V of this chapter. What is of note, though, is that both the United Kingdom and Mauritius were very clear in their written submissions that the operation of the persistent objector rule requires objection to be *consistent*. They disputed whether the objections of the United Kingdom in the context at hand met this criterion, but were in agreement that consistent objection was necessary.

The argumentation of both states in *Chagos Marine Protected Area* as regards the consistency of objection echoes the assertions of both of the parties in the 1951 *Fisheries* case. The United Kingdom argued that Norway had not achieved exempt status because 'the Norwegian Government had not *consistently* followed the principles of Delimitation'.[35] Norway, in contrast, asserted that '[i]l n'est pas douteux en effet, que la Norvège a, d'une manière *constante et non équivoque*, refusé d'accepter, en ce qui la concerne, les règles en question'.[36] Again, then, while Norway and the United Kingdom disagreed as to whether Norway's objections had been sufficiently consistent, they agreed that a criterion of consistency existed.

In the 2008 first instance decision of *C* et al. *v Director of Immigration*,[37] Hartmann J took the view that Hong Kong was an exempt persistent objector in relation to the customary international law norm of *non-refoulement* (inter alia, based upon repeated treaty reservations of the United Kingdom and China).[38] Specifically, he held that 'by *consistent* and longstanding objection, Hong Kong has refused to accede to the rule'.[39] Hartmann J's conclusion that Hong Kong was a

[33] Ibid., Appendix III to Chapter 5, 143–8.

[34] See *Chagos Marine Protected Area Arbitration*, award, n. 24, paras 163–230.

[35] *Fisheries* (*United Kingdom v Norway*), merits, 1951 ICJ Rep. 116, 137, emphasis added. The actual British argument in this regard can be found at *Fisheries* (*United Kingdom v Norway*), memorial submitted by the Government of the United Kingdom of Great Britain and Northern Ireland, 1950 ICJ Plead., vol. I, paras 123–40.

[36] *Fisheries* (*United Kingdom v Norway*), counter-memorial submitted by the Government of the Kingdom of Norway, 1950 ICJ Plead., vol. I, 383, emphasis added.

[37] *C* et al. *v Director of Immigration*, 2008, 2 HKC 167.

[38] Ibid., paras 89, 144–6 and 194.

[39] Ibid., 194, emphasis added.

persistent objector was overruled, and this was partly on the basis that Yuen JA in the Hong Kong Court of Appeal was of the view that any relevant objections were neither sufficiently expressed nor consistent.[40] This would seem correct: the objections of the United Kingdom and China in relation to *non-refoulement*—while persistent—had been notably inconsistent, as had Hong Kong's own practice.[41] For example, Hong Kong has regularly refrained from repatriating people to face prosecution in circumstances that would entail the application of the rule; a pattern of 'acceptance by deed' that can be seen as rather undermining the Director of Immigration's claim that Hong Kong was exempt.[42] In any event, again, while there has been disagreement as to whether Hong Kong's objections (that is, the objections of the United Kingdom and China as 'proxy objectors') were sufficiently consistent, both the first instance and appeal decisions in *C* et al. indicate that consistency is necessary.

In another example from Hong Kong case law, in the Court of Appeal, Stock V-P asserted in 2010, in *FG Hemisphere Associates LLC and Democratic Republic of the Congo*,[43] that consistency is required for persistent objection.[44] Judges of the International Court of Justice (ICJ) have seemingly taken the same view in individual opinions,[45] and the consistency requirement can also be inferred from two judgments of the Grand Chamber of the European Court of Human Rights (ECtHR): *Cudak v Lithuania*[46] and *Sabah El Leil v France*.[47] Admittedly, the requirement is not explicitly referred to in either ECtHR decision, but a contextual reading of them certainly suggests that the persistent objector rule was viewed by the Court as being inapplicable on the basis that dissent, from Lithuania and

[40] *C* et al. *v Director of Immigration and Secretary for Security*, 2011, Hong Kong Special Administrative Region, Court of Appeal, CACV 132-137/2008, paras 71–2.

[41] See, for example, O. Jones, 'Customary *Non-Refoulement* of Refugees and Automatic Incorporation into the Common Law: A Hong Kong Perspective' (2009) 58 *International and Comparative Law Quarterly* 443, 450–7.

[42] Ibid., particularly at 451.

[43] *FG Hemisphere Associates LLC and Democratic Republic of the Congo*, 2010, COA, Civil Appeals Nos. 373 of 2008 and 43 of 2009 HKLR&D.

[44] Ibid., paras 99–100.

[45] See *North Sea Continental Shelf* cases (*Federal Republic of Germany v Netherlands, Federal Republic of Germany v Denmark*), merits, 1969 ICJ Rep. 3, dissenting opinion of Judge ad hoc Sørensen, 247 ('it might be argued in the present cases that the Convention on the Continental Shelf would be inapplicable as against the Federal Republic, if she had *consistently refused* to recognize it as an expression of generally accepted rules of international law and had objected to its applicability as against her'; emphasis added). Some support for a need for consistency can also perhaps be identified in Judge Azevedo's dissenting opinion in the *Asylum* case, where he noted that it is necessary to identify 'une attitude nette, cohérente, unilinéaire'. This must be read with some care, however, as Judge Azevedo was referring to dissenting positions that may undermine the establishment of the new customary norm per se, and not specifically to the operation of the persistent objector rule itself. It can nonetheless reasonably be analogized to the need for consistency of persistent objection. See *Asylum Case* (*Columbia v Peru*), merits, 1950 ICJ Rep. 266, dissenting opinion of Judge Azevedo, 337.

[46] *Cudak v Lithuania*, application no. 15869/02, judgment, 2010, ECtHR (Grand Chamber), paras 66–8.

[47] *Sabah El Leil v France*, application no. 34869/05, judgment, 2011, ECtHR (Grand Chamber), para. 54.

France respectively, had been inconsistent during the formative stages of the customary rule in question (which, in both instances, was the change in customary international law away from 'absolute' state immunity).

These various decisions and pleadings all demonstrate that not only is repetition required for the operation of the rule, but also that a degree of consistent repetition is necessary in order for a state to gain exemption from an emerging customary norm. In fact, then, there are two criteria (persistence and consistency) at times masquerading in doctrine as a single requirement for the rule's operation. Szappanyos correctly notes, when considering the general view that the persistent objector rule is premised upon two requirements—persistence and timeliness—that '[t]he first condition [persistence] also expresses another implicit criterion: the objection should also be consistent'.[48] As noted previously, most writers who have referred to a need for 'consistency' have not been this explicit and have used 'consistency' as a synonym for 'persistence', employing the two terms interchangeably.[49] With a few exceptions,[50] those that argue that the rule requires *consistent* objection generally do not explicitly note that this differs in any way from *persistent* objection. This amalgamation of these similar but different criteria in the literature—as also reflected in judicial and arbitral decisions, such as in *Domingues*—unhelpfully clouds the operation of the persistent objector rule. In most cases, there does not appear to be any awareness among commentators that persistence and consistency are conceptually different things. In any event, irrespective of this unhelpful blending of the concepts in the literature, it is clear that both persistence and consistency are necessary.

II. The Rationale for the Consistency Criterion

The rationale for consistent objection is rather similar to that for persistence, as examined in Chapter 4,[51] and so it need not be discussed in detail here. As with persistence, the consistency requirement cannot be justified in relation to the voluntarist account of international law, at least not entirely. If the state has clearly expressed the view that it does not wish to be bound, then it seems a stretch to

[48] M. Szappanyos, 'Obligatory or Voluntary?—Participation in the UPR' (2012) 150 *Studia Iuridica Auctoritate Universitatis Pecs Publicata* 273, 286–7.

[49] See, for example, C.G. Guldahl, 'The Role of Persistent Objection in International Humanitarian Law' (2008) 77 *Nordic Journal of International Law* 51, 54; A.T. Guzman, 'Saving Customary International Law' (2005–6) 27 *Michigan Journal of International Law* 115, 164, 164–9; Lepard, n. 1, 239; and M. Ragazzi, *The Concept of International Obligations* Erga Omnes (Oxford, Clarendon Press, 1997), 63.

[50] See, for example, Third Report on Identification of Customary International Law (M. Wood, Special Rapporteur), International Law Commission, Sixty-seventh session, 27 March 2015, UN Doc. A/CN.4/682, para. 93; Bölükbaşı, n.1, 184–5; Lim and Elias, n. 1, 148; Steinfeld, n. 1, 1639, footnote 14 and 1647; and Szappanyos, n. 48, 286–7.

[51] See Chapter 4, section II.

argue that a number of contrary actions undermine that expression of sovereign will (certainly, at least, if the amount of contrary practice is small).[52]

Again like persistence criterion, then, the consistency requirement's rationale is to be found by reference to more pragmatic concerns. The consistency criterion places notable political pressure on objecting states, and so helps to guard against frivolous uses of the rule.[53] It also leads to increased clarity in the process of customary international law formation, and provides greater certainty in identifying the objector state's stance by putting other states on notice.[54] However, consistency 'ups the ante' on all of these underlying reasons for the persistence criterion. A need not just for repeated objection but for *consistently* repeated objection obviously further increases the ability of others to identify any given pattern of objection, and thus the certainty that the objector state is, indeed, just that.[55]

Instead of merely preventing a state from benefiting from a single objection (or small number of objections), consistency more onerously prevents the state from benefiting from *ambiguity* in its objections.[56] As with the persistence requirement, the existence of the consistency requirement in practice has its roots in the fact that the persistent objector rule—as an exception—will be treated restrictively by other states; inconsistent practice is a sign that the objector is not fully committed to its stance, such that any exemption will not be tolerated by other states.

III. 'Absolute' vs. 'General' Consistency

It was noted in Chapter 4 that the statement of the ICJ in the *Fisheries* case to the effect that the avowed customary norm at issue in the case 'would appear to be inapplicable as against Norway inasmuch as she *always opposed* any attempt to apply it to the Norwegian coast'[57] can be viewed as an endorsement of the persistence requirement.[58] This passage can, however, also be read as additionally requiring consistent objection—the Court did not merely refer to the repeated opposition of Norway, but instead noted that it had 'always' objected to the applicability of the norm in question, suggesting that a level of constant or consistent objection may be necessary in addition to persistence.[59] However, as a number of writers have noted, it is not clear 'what the phrase "always opposed" signifies'.[60]

[52] Dumberry, n. 17, 795. [53] Guzman, n. 49, 169.

[54] Steinfeld, n. 1, 1639, footnote 14.

[55] Guldahl, n. 49, 54 ('it is important that an objecting State is consistent in its position so that other States know what law is applicable'); and Villiger, n. 1, 34.

[56] Fon and Parisi, n. 1, 6; and Villiger, n. 1, 34.

[57] *Fisheries*, merits, n. 35, 131, emphasis added.

[58] See Chapter 4, n. 12 and accompanying text.

[59] G. Gaja, 'The Protection of General Interests in the International Community—General Course on Public International Law' (2012) 364 *Recueil des cours* 13, 43.

[60] O. Elias, 'Persistent Objector' in R. Wolfrum (ed.), *Max Planck Encyclopaedia of Public International Law, vol. VIII* (Oxford, Oxford University Press, 2012), 280, 283, para. 12. See also Akehurst, n. 1, 24; and D. Kritsiotis, 'On the Possibilities of and For Persistent Objection' (2010) 21 *Duke Journal of Comparative and International Law* 121, 129.

In other words, having concluded that objection needs to be not only repeated but *consistently* repeated, one might ask: what will be considered to be sufficiently 'consistent' objection?

One possibility is that for the persistent objector rule to take effect there must be what might be termed 'absolute consistency' in the state's expressions of dissent.[61] Under this approach, a state wishing to avail itself of the persistent objector rule must not, *at any point* during the new law's formation, affirm or accept that new norm. Any inconsistent practice at all will void a later persistent objector claim. For example, in *Commonwealth of Pennsylvania v Hector Huertas*, the petitioners argued that contrary behaviour of any sort meant that the objection was insufficiently consistent: 'if an objecting state even has simply signed a treaty that covers the issue to which it then objects, it is not a "persistent objector".'[62] In a similar vein, Jones takes the view that a single divergent act (or a small number of inconsistencies) cannot 'simply be discounted as exceptional, as all international conduct must be relevant to persistent objection'.[63]

A slightly less onerous understanding of the 'consistency' criterion would be that the state must object with 'general consistency', meaning that in *most* instances it has maintained its objector stance, but that one isolated occasion (or perhaps a small number of occasions) of affirmation will not necessarily be enough to undermine its overall persistent objector status. This version of consistency would not require—to borrow a famous phrase used by the ICJ on the separate issue of customary international law formation—that the state's actions 'be in absolutely rigorous conformity'[64] with its objector stance. For example, to the extent that Dumberry accepts the persistent objector rule, he takes the view that while consistency is required, this does not necessitate permanent adherence.[65] Similarly, Loschin argues that if there are either domestic court decisions or legislation that are consistent with the objection, this will 'strengthen the objector's position',[66] but that indications that the state has changed position on the issue '*weaken*' its claim to be exempt.[67] For Loschin, then, consistency is important but not necessarily determinative: consistent behaviour strengthens a persistent objector claim, while (some, limited) inconsistent behaviour weakens, rather than entirely derails, it.

When one turns to state practice, it appears that the former standard—of absolute, unadulterated consistency—reflects the way in which states have engaged with the rule. One example of this is the position of Turkey in relation to anti-personnel landmines (APLMs) up until 2003. An increasing number of commentators take the view that a customary international law prohibition of the use,

[61] See, for example, Akehurst, n. 1, 24 (implicitly adopting this understanding); McClane, n. 1, 2, 20–1; Steinfeld, n. 1, 1652 (arguing that states must 'adhere' to the position adopted, implying an inclination towards this understanding of consistency); and Villiger, n. 1, 34.

[62] *Hector Huertas*, motion, n. 20, 25.

[63] Jones, n. 41, 456–7.

[64] *Military and Paramilitary Activities in and against Nicaragua (Nicaragua v United States of America)*, merits, 1986 ICJ Rep. 14, para. 186.

[65] Dumberry, n. 17, 781.

[66] Loschin, n. 1, 165.

[67] Ibid., 166, emphasis added.

production, and stockpiling of APLMs now exists under international humanitarian law.[68] It is not entirely clear whether this norm has 'emerged' or has been merely 'emerging' since the late 1990s,[69] but what is clear is that a handful of states have resolutely rejected the potential applicability to them of this new/emerging norm. Up until 2003, Turkey was one such state: throughout the 1990s and early 2000s, Turkey repeatedly (i.e. *persistently*) objected to the binding force of a customary APLM prohibition, by way of both word and deed. Turkey was in the minority of states that did not sign the Ottawa Convention when it was drafted in 1997,[70] and argued at the time that 'we have to protect our borders. Although we respect the reasons for that treaty, in order to keep our borders secure, we have to take measures'.[71] Turkey's deputy permanent representative at the UN, Tuluy Tanc, was similarly clear in 1997 that most of the obligations contained in the Ottawa Convention were necessarily inapplicable to Turkey, citing security concerns.[72]

From the mid-1990s to 2003, Turkey generally maintained this stance of objection. It rejected the final declaration of the Brussels conference on the total ban of APLMs, which took place after the adoption of the Ottawa Convention in the summer of 1997, and was signed by ninety-seven states.[73] Turkey was also one of only ten nations that abstained in 1996 from voting on General Assembly Resolution 51/45 [S], which called for a binding international agreement to solidify the general prohibition on the use, sale, and stockpiling of APLMs (a resolution supported by 156 states).[74] It similarly abstained regarding Resolution 52/38 [A] in 1997, which called on states to sign and ratify the Ottawa Convention.[75] Perhaps most pertinently, Turkey used mines quite extensively throughout the 1990s and early 2000s, particularly in its southeast region (along its borders with Syria, Iran, and Iraq).[76]

As such, there is little question that Turkey presented its objections to any possible customary APLM ban repeatedly and clearly (including during the early 1990s, when the customary ban had unquestionably not crystallized). It may also

[68] See writers cited in Chapter 3, n. 46. [69] See evidence referenced in ibid., n. 47.

[70] Convention on the Prohibition of the Use, Stockpiling, Production and Transfer of Anti-Personnel Mines and on their Destruction (Ottawa Convention), 18 September 1997, 2056 UNTS 35597.

[71] 'Turkey: Citing Security Concerns, Ankara Opposes the Ban', *Turkish Daily News*, 4 December 1997.

[72] 'Official Explains why Turkey Won't Sign Landmines Agreement', *Anatolia News Agency*, 16 October 1998.

[73] Declaration agreed at the Conference for a Global Ban on Anti-Personnel Mines, Brussels, 24–7 June 1997, transmitted to the Conference on Disarmament by a letter dated 9 July 1997 by the Office of the Permanent Representative of Belgium to the Conference on Disarmament, CD/1467.

[74] General Assembly Resolution 51/54, 10 December 1996, UN Doc. A/RES/51/45, 33.

[75] General Assembly Resolution 52/38, 9 December 1997, UN Doc. A/RES/52/38, 1.

[76] Landmine and Cluster Munitions Monitor, International Campaign to Ban Landmines, 'Turkey', http://www.the-monitor.org/index.php/publications/display?url=lm/1999/turkey.html. Indeed, it was estimated in 2013 that over a million landmines still remain buried in Turkish territory: 'One Million Landmines "Still Buried in Turkey"', *Global Post*, 29 November 2013, http://www.globalpost.com/dispatch/news/afp/131129/one-million-landmines-still-buried-turkey.

be said that Turkey's position was 'generally' consistent during this period. Up until 2003, in most instances where it referred to the Ottawa Convention or the possible wider customary international law prohibition, Turkey was clear that the ban was not applicable to it; indeed, it was generally willing to give its reasons for taking this stance in some detail.

While it may be said that Turkey acted with 'general consistency' in its rejection of the APLM ban, however, it did not object with 'absolute consistency'. In among its general pattern of persistent objection, Turkey occasionally presented a contrary position on APLMs. For example, it signed a bilateral agreement with Bulgaria in 1999 committing both states not to mine their common border and to remove the existing mines from the area.[77] In a joint statement by the two states' foreign ministers it was said that:

> According to the Agreement, the two countries undertake not to use under any circumstances antipersonnel mines and to destroy or remove all stocked or emplaced antipersonnel mines from the area of application as defined in the Agreement ... [B]y signing this Agreement the two countries *have proved their determination to contribute to the ongoing efforts of the international community aimed at the total elimination of this inhumane weapon*.[78]

Turkey's voting practice in 1998 in relation to General Assembly Resolution 53/77 [N][79] also seems anomalous when compared to the vast majority of its actions relating to APLMs from 1990 to 2003. Resolution 53/77 [N] uses language similar to Resolution 52/38 [A] in calling on states to sign and ratify the Ottawa Convention, yet Turkey voted in favour of the resolution, placing a degree of political pressure *upon itself* to move towards conforming its practice on APLMs to that of the majority.

On the basis of these few, but perhaps significant, 'lapses' in objection, Price argued that:

> Turkey has not consistently maintained practices that establish a contrary rule that permits the unquestioned use of AP landmines. Such behaviour [of occasional inconsistency] would seem to fall short of the kind of opposition ... necessary to establish persistent objector status.[80]

This analysis seems to be correct. Unlike, for example, Egypt, which arguably has an entirely consistent record of objection to the possible APLM ban even up to the present,[81] by the early 2000s, states began to express the view that Turkey

[77] See UN Department for Disarmament Affairs, *The United Nations Disarmament Yearbook* (1999) 24, 105.

[78] Joint Statement of the Minister of Foreign Affairs of the Republic of Turkey, H.E. Ismail Cem and the Minister of Foreign Affairs of the Republic of Bulgaria, H.E. Ms Nadezhda Mihhailova, on the 'Agreement between the Republic of Turkey and the Republic of Bulgaria on Non-Use of Anti-Personnel Mines and their Removal from or Destruction in the Areas Adjacent to their Common Borders', Sofia, 22 March 1999, emphasis added.

[79] General Assembly Resolution 53/77 [N], 12 January 1999, UN Doc. A/RES/53/77, 20-21.

[80] R. Price, 'Emerging Customary Norms and Anti-Personnel Landmines' in C. Reus-Smit (ed.), *The Politics of International Law* (Cambridge, Cambridge University Press, 2004), 106, 124.

[81] See Chapter 3, n. 46–n. 50 and accompanying text.

was already obliged to remove APLMs from its territory.[82] Of course, Turkey signed and ratified the Ottawa Convention in 2003, effectively ending its potential status as a persistent objector to any parallel customary norms by accepting conventional obligations of the same sort.[83] Moreover, it is impossible to say for sure whether Turkey's inconsistent objection 'voided' its persistent objector status prior to 2003, because it is not certain that the prohibition has become binding customary international law at all, and the persistent objector rule only 'kicks in' once the norm in question has crystallized. Nonetheless, it certainly appears that one or two inconsistent acts were enough to notably undermine Turkey's otherwise uniform and decade-long stance of opposition in the eyes of other states. Even prior to Turkey formally conceding its position by signing the Ottawa Convention in 2003, it was considered to have acted too inconsistently to be a true persistent objector—irrespective of its widespread and 'generally consistent' pattern of objection.

It will be recalled[84] that the United States argued in the 2005 *Agent Orange* case[85] that it was a persistent objector to a possible customary international law prohibiting the use of herbicides in the context of warfare,[86] and set out extensive evidence of its objections by way of deed, voting practice, and statement.[87] The United States' claim in this regard also acts as another useful example in relation to the notion of 'absolute consistency' of objection.

The commentary to Rule 76 of the International Committee of the Red Cross (ICRC) Study on *Customary International Humanitarian Law* holds that '[s]tate practice establishes this rule [i.e. a general prohibition on the use of herbicides in armed conflict] as a norm of customary international law applicable in both international and non-international armed conflicts'.[88] While the United States District Court in *Agent Orange* determined that no such customary norm had formed,[89] there is a good deal of state practice and *opinio juris* supporting the ICRC's view that there is a prohibition on the use of herbicides in armed conflict under customary international law (at least to the extent that this is indiscriminate

[82] See, for example, the expressed position of Greece on this matter in 2002, in K. Tzilivakis, 'Greece Ratifies Ottawa Treaty', *Athens News*, 30 March 2002.

[83] Having said this, it is worth noting that in March 2013 Turkey applied for an eight-year extension period in relation to its obligations under the Ottawa Convention; n. 70, Article 5. 'Extension Report: Turkey', Permanent Mission of Turkey to the United Nations, Geneva', 29 March 2013, 2013/62441669/73841, http://www.apminebanconvention.org/fileadmin/APMBC/clearing-mined-areas/art5_extensions/countries/Turkey-ExtRequest-Received-29Mar2013.pdf. This was ahead of the Third Review Conference of states parties in Maputo in June 2014, http://www.maputoreviewconference.org/.

[84] See Chapter 3, n. 117–n. 121 and accompanying text.

[85] *In Re 'Agent Orange' Product Liability Litigation*, 2005, memorandum, order and judgment, United States District Court Eastern District of New York, 373 F. Supp. 2d 7 (E.D.N.Y).

[86] *In Re 'Agent Orange' Product Liability Litigation*, 2005, statement of interest of the United States, http://www.state.gov/documents/organization/87322.pdf, 31–2.

[87] Ibid., 4–13.

[88] J-M. Henckaerts and L. Doswald-Beck (eds), *Customary International Humanitarian Law, vol. I*, International Committee of the Red Cross (ICRC) Study (Cambridge, Cambridge University Press, 2005), 266.

[89] *Agent Orange*, memorandum, order and judgment, n. 85, 191.

or analogous to other prohibited chemical and biological weapon use).[90] In light of this, in a 'statement of interest' issued during the *Agent Orange* proceedings, the United States argued that:

> [E]ven if the Court determined that a norm of international law prohibiting the use of chemical herbicides existed at the time in question, such a norm would not be binding upon the United States as a matter of international law ... Here, the United States' *persistent* and *consistent* public pronouncements that customary international law did not prohibit the use of chemical herbicides qualify it as a persistent objector under international law, and thus not bound by any rule that might have developed.[91]

It would indeed appear that the United States has been both a persistent and *consistent* objector to any customary prohibition on the use of herbicides in the context of warfare.[92] Having said this, one might point to the fact that Executive Order No. 11850, issued by the United States President in 1975, states that '[t]he United States renounces, as a matter of national policy, first use of herbicides in war except use, under regulations applicable to their domestic use, for control of vegetation within U.S. bases and installations or around their immediate defensive Perimeters'.[93] This may be read as an instance of inconsistent practice on the part of the United States, and thus—if we take absolute consistency as the required standard—as potentially undermining its persistent objector status. Reference was made to Executive Order No. 11850 in the ICRC IHL Study, perhaps for this very reason (although the implications of the Order in relation to any possible persistent objector claim were not made explicit in the Study).[94] However, it is important to note that Executive Order No. 11850 goes on to add the catch-all caveat that such use of 'chemical herbicides in war is prohibited *unless such use has Presidential approval, in advance*'.[95] As such, it is perhaps not the revocation that it first appears.

This one highly debatable deviation aside, then, the United States may be said to have objected with 'absolute' consistency to the binding force of any such norm: there are, at least, no indisputable examples of contrary practice. In the *Agent Orange* case, the United States' exempt status was not even questioned by Judge Weinstein (although, given that he had already concluded that there was no customary prohibition on the use of herbicides in armed conflict, this is perhaps unsurprising).[96] The dismissal of the plaintiffs' claim in *Agent Orange* was

90 See ICRC IHL Study, *vol. II*, n. 88, 1762–70; and ICRC, 'Rule 76: Herbicides', http://www.icrc.org/customary-ihl/eng/docs/v1_rul_rule76.

91 *Agent Orange*, United States statement of interest, n. 86, 31–2, emphasis added.

92 In addition to the evidence presented by the United States in ibid., 4–13, there has also been consistent reiteration of this view in various American military manuals and handbooks: see ICRC IHL Study, *vol. II*, n. 88, 1764–5; and ICRC, 'United States of America: Practice Relating to Rule 76: Herbicides', http://www.icrc.org/customary-ihl/eng/docs/v2_cou_us_rule76.

93 Executive Order 11850 of Apr. 8, 1975, 40 FR 16187, 3 CFR, 1971-1975 Comp., 980, http://www.archives.gov/federal-register/codification/executive-order/11850.html.

94 ICRC IHL Study, *vol. II*, n. 88, 1768.

95 Executive Order 11850, n. 93, Section 1, emphasis added.

96 See, generally, *Agent Orange*, memorandum, order and judgment, n. 85.

reaffirmed on appeal in 2008, without further reference being made by the Court of Appeals for the Second Circuit to the United States' assertion of persistent objector status.[97] There has been no formal rejection by any state of the United States' exempt position in this regard, and even the ICRC seems to have at least tacitly accepted it.[98] In this instance, it appears that consistent objection on the part of the United States—meaning objection with 'absolute consistency'—has led to exemption.

The Turkish objections to the APLM prohibition prior to 2003 and the continuing exemption of the United States from the customary prohibition on the use of herbicides in warfare both suggest that any inconsistency in a state's objection will be terminal for a later attempt to gain exemption by way of the persistent objector rule. This may seem rather onerous: it was noted above that the rationale for the consistency requirement is to demonstrate the state's willingness to remain exempt, and to ensure that the political cost is high so that exemption is not frivolously sought. A requirement of generally consistent behaviour could reasonably be seen as sufficiently putting other states on notice of the objector's stance, as well as demonstrating the state's position and placing political pressure on it to conform—irrespective of a 'slip up' or two. Again, though, it is important to remember that the persistent objector rule is an exception, and therefore should, and seemingly will, be narrowly construed. It appears evident that states will not tolerate an objector that allows even a few chinks of the light of conformity to shine on its position.

IV. Silence as Inconsistency

Even if we conclude that a state must object with absolute consistency to an emerging norm to gain exemption from it post-crystallization, it is still necessary to further investigate what constitutes inconsistent behaviour. In particular, it is unclear whether *silence* on the part of the objecting state can, in the right circumstances, be considered to be an action that is inconsistent with the state's general position of dissent.

On one understanding of 'consistency', the persistent objector rule would require that whenever the objecting state *refers to or acts upon* the emerging norm, it must formally and openly object to that norm's binding effect upon it. If every time that the state engages with the subject-matter of the norm in question, either by way of word or deed, it expresses objection (and never expresses any form of acceptance), this could be viewed as being a pattern of objection that is 'absolutely consistent'. This standard was, for example, met in the context of the United States' approach to the use of herbicides in warfare discussed in section III: whenever the United States made reference to the question, it

[97] *In Re 'Agent Orange' Product Liability Litigation*, 2008, judgment, United States Court of Appeals for the Second Circuit, 517 F.3d 76 (2d Cir.).

[98] 'United States of America: Practice Relating to Rule 76: Herbicides', n. 92.

asserted that any possible prohibition on herbicide use in armed conflict was inapplicable to it.

However, it could be argued that the need for consistency is rather more onerous than this. 'Absolute consistency' could be interpreted to mean that the dissenting state is required to object not only when it takes action (through word or deed) in relation to an emerging customary norm, but also in all instances that might be reasonably seen as an 'opportunity' for it to object.[99] To put this differently, on this understanding, a state must object in situations that one might view as being an 'appropriate occasion' for it to express dissent, or, perhaps, in all instances where its interests in relation to its purported exemption from the rule are notably threatened. A state may have a perfect record of consistent objection when acting but, in *omitting* to act at an appropriate juncture, its silence could be interpreted as 'inconsistent' behaviour.

A still stricter approach would be to require, on the basis of the criterion of *persistence*,[100] that the state objects regularly even if its interests are not at issue and there are no appropriate opportunities or forums for it to express its dissent. On this understanding, silence for any length of time during the norm's formation would be considered 'inconsistent practice' irrespective of circumstance. Fon and Parisi, for example, suggest that consistency of objection is required not merely when a state is 'called upon' to express its dissent, but at regular intervals during the formation of the norm.[101] A number of other writers have taken a similar view, at least implicitly.[102] If this is correct, 'consistency' would require not just an absence of explicit inconsistent behaviour, or even of silence when objection might reasonably be expected, but that the state actively reiterate its objector stance on a periodic basis. Under this approach, the objecting state would have to regularly reaffirm its objection, *if necessary apropos of nothing*, to keep its subsequent exempt status from falling into unacceptable dormancy.

The approach of Turkey in objecting to an extension to a 12-nautical-mile limit on territorial waters[103] is potentially illustrative in this context. As was noted in previous chapters,[104] during discussions concerning the issue of the 'breadth of

[99] See Bölükbaşı, n. 1, 208; Guldahl, n. 49, 54; Hartmann, n. 17, 686 (arguing that '[m]ere failure to conform to the norm' at appropriate occasions where other states might reasonably expect explicit objection is insufficiently consistent); Jones, n. 41, 457 (by implication); A. McBeth, *International Economic Actors and Human Rights* (Abingdon, Routledge, 2010), 20; M.H. Mendelson, 'The Formation of Customary International Law' (1998) 272 *Recueil des cours* 155, 241; D.P. O'Connell, *The International Law of the Sea, vol. I* (Oxford, Clarendon Press, 1982), 40–4; and Steinfeld, n. 1, 1652.

[100] See, generally, Chapter 4.

[101] Fon and Parisi, n. 1, 11.

[102] A. Abass, *Complete International Law: Text, Cases, and Materials* (Oxford, Oxford University Press, 2nd edn, 2014), 46 (arguing that objection must be 'constant'); J.I. Charney, 'Universal International Law' (1993) 87 *American Journal of International Law* 529, 539; M. Dixon, *Textbook on International Law* (Oxford, Oxford University Press, 7th edn, 2013), 34; and Price, n. 80, 115 and 123.

[103] See, generally, Y. Acer, *The Aegean Maritime Disputes and International Law* (Aldershot, Ashgate, 2003); D. Anderson, *Modern Law of the Sea: Selected Essays* (Leiden, Martinus Nijhoff, 2008), 91, particularly at footnote 14; and Bölükbaşı, n. 1.

[104] See Chapter 2, n. 140–n. 144 and accompanying text; and Chapter 3, n. 54–n. 59 and accompanying text.

territorial waters' as part of the lengthy negotiations towards the UNCLOS[105] at the Third Conference in 1982, Turkey explicitly claimed persistent objector status with regard to any customary extension—reflected in Article 3 of UNCLOS—to a 12-mile limit.[106] Indeed, Turkey was very clear that it was 'a persistent objector to the 12-nautical mile limit' by virtue of its '*consistent* and manifest refusal to accept' the customary status of the extension to territorial sea limits.[107]

Turkey therefore made much of that fact that it had consistently objected to the 12-mile limit. In particular, Turkey had been careful to lodge objections whenever the subject of a 12-mile limit (especially in relation to the Aegean) was raised or of relevance. As Bölükbaşı has noted, Turkey formally protested 'in all fora where the subject has come up',[108] including at UN Conferences,[109] at the General Assembly,[110] and at the Security Council.[111]

Equally, even in this context, Turkey's objections were undeniably 'intermittent'.[112] Turkey objected persistently over a seventy-year period, particularly in the twenty-five years immediately prior to the adoption of UNCLOS, and did so consistently (in the sense that it neither explicitly accepted the 12-mile limit at any point *nor* failed to object to this emerging norm at the various instances where one might have expected it to have done so). However, there were periods where Turkey remained relatively silent on the question of the 12-mile limit, either because there was not a clear opportunity to object or because the norm was not at issue. One could perhaps, therefore, argue that Turkey did not object 'consistently' in the sense of periodically objecting, whatever the circumstances. However, there is little question that Turkey is an exempt persistent objector state.[113] This example from practice would thus suggest that there is a general expectation that a state will object when presented with the opportunity to do so, and that silence in such circumstances may undermine its exempt status, but that repeated objection apropos of nothing is not required.

Another useful example concerns the generally accepted position[114] that the respective norms of international human rights law and international

[105] United Nations Convention on the Law of the Sea (UNCLOS), 10 December 1982, 1833 UNTS 3.

[106] See, for example, Official Records of the Third United Nations Conference on the Law of the Sea, Volume XVII (Plenary Meetings, Summary Records and Verbatim Records, as well as Documents of the Conference, Resumed Eleventh Session and Final Part Eleventh Session and Conclusion), 1982, UN Doc. A/CONF.62/SR.189, 76, para. 150.

[107] Ibid., emphasis added.

[108] Bölükbaşı, n. 1, 206.

[109] See, for example, UN Doc. A/CONF.62/SR.189, n.106, 76, para. 150.

[110] See, for example, General Assembly, Official Records, Fiftieth session, 29th plenary meeting, 11 October 1995, UN Doc. A/50/PV.29, 29–30.

[111] See, for example, Letter dated 21 June 1995 from the Permanent Representative of Turkey to the United Nations addressed to the Secretary-General, 23 June 1995, UN Doc. A/50/256 – S/1995/505.

[112] Bölükbaşı, n. 1, 184.

[113] See, for example, E.A. Georgiades, 'The Imia Islets: A Beginning to the Maritime Delimitation of the Aegean Sea Dispute' (2011) 17 *Ocean and Coastal Law Journal* 103, 103, footnote 3.

[114] See, for example, *Bámaca-Velásquez v Guatemala*, merits, 2000, IACtHR (Ser. C) No. 70, para. 207; *Legal Consequences of the Construction of a Wall in the Occupied Palestinian Territory*, advisory opinion, 2004 ICJ Rep. 135, paras 106–13; *Armed Activities on the Territory of the*

humanitarian law (IHL) apply concurrently. Israel and the United States have traditionally contested this, and for a long period argued that if the law of armed conflict is applicable in any given situation, then this displaces the applicability of human rights law; in other words, these two states expressed the view on a number of occasions that the regimes are mutually exclusive.[115] In a 2005 working paper submitted to the now defunct UN Sub-Commission on the Promotion and Protection of Human Rights,[116] however, it was argued that neither of the states in question could be considered persistent objectors because their protestations had been insufficiently consistent. In particular, this was on the basis that:

> Neither Israel nor the United States made any reservation or declaration expressly excluding the applicability of HRsL where LOAC/IHL is applicable. *One would expect to find not only reservations at ratification but also objections to general comments which directly or indirectly deal with the issue.*[117]

The working paper therefore took the view that 'consistency' for the purposes of persistent objection requires the dissenting state to object whenever presented with a suitable opportunity to do so and in all appropriate circumstances where this might be expected. It is notable that, during discussions regarding the working paper in the Sub-Committee's sessional working group (which included representation of various NGOs and, importantly, active observers on behalf of states), this conclusion as to the insufficient consistency of Israeli and American objections was not questioned,[118] suggesting a degree of acceptance of this understanding of the consistency criterion. It is noteworthy that the United States, at least, accepted defeat in 2012, and abandoned its stance with regard to the purported 'displacement' of international human

Congo (*Democratic Republic of the Congo v Uganda*), merits, 2005 ICJ Rep. 168, para. 216; and UN Human Rights Committee, General Comment No. 31 [80], UN Doc. CCPR/C/21/Rev.1/Add.13, 2004, para. 11 ('both spheres of law are complementary, not mutually exclusive').

[115] See, for example, Consideration of reports submitted by states parties under article 40 of the covenant, Second Periodic Report, Israel, Human Rights Committee, 4 December 2001, UN Doc. CCPR/C/ISR/2001/2, para. 8 (Israel); and Letter dated 2 April 2003 from the Permanent Mission of the United States of America to the United Nations Office at Geneva addressed to the secretariat of the Commission on Human Rights, UN Doc. E/CN.4/2003/G/73 (United States). See, generally, F.J. Hampson, 'The Relationship between International Humanitarian Law and Human Rights Law from the Perspective of a Human Rights Treaty Body' (2008) 90 *International Review of the Red Cross* 549, 550–1.

[116] F. Hampson and I. Salama, 'Working Paper on the Relationship between Human Rights Law and International Humanitarian Law', Commission on Human Rights, Sub-Commission on the Promotion and Protection of Human Rights, Fifty-seventh session, Item 3 of the provisional agenda, Administration of Justice, Rule of Law and Democracy, 21 June 2005, UN Doc. E/CN.4/Sub.2/2005/14.

[117] Ibid., para. 70, emphasis added.

[118] Report of the Sessional Working Group on the Administration of Justice, Commission on Human Rights, Sub-Commission on the Promotion and Protection of Human Rights, Fifty-seventh session, Item 3 of the provisional agenda, Administration of Justice, Rule of Law and Democracy (Antoanella-Iulia Motoc, Chairperson-Rapporteur), 10 August 2005, UN Doc. E/CN.4/Sub.2/2005/11, paras 11–30.

rights law by IHL, to the point that it denied that it had ever persistently objected.[119]

These examples suggest that any state looking to retain its exempt status after crystallization would be wise to reiterate its position as and when the opportunity to do so arises. A failure to voice dissent in an appropriate forum or at an appropriate juncture may be viewed by other states as inconsistent practice. This can be seen in Turkey's fastidious policy of rejection in the context of the 12-mile limit: Turkey was careful to ensure that it objected on every occasion where the norm was at issue. The comparable failure of the United States and Israel to object to the simultaneous applicability of IHL and international human rights law in circumstances where they might have been expected to do so—and the apparent unacceptability of their exemption as a consequence—point towards the same conclusion from the opposite direction.

This understanding of 'consistency' is appropriate: as was noted previously, the consistency criterion helps to ensure clarity and certainty in the operation of the persistent objector rule, and such policy goals will obviously be enhanced if the objector expresses its dissent at instances where the rule is at issue, underlining its position not just when it chooses to speak but when other states might reasonably expect it to.

Indeed, another benefit of, or rationale for, the existence of the consistency requirement (other than those already discussed in section II) is that it encourages the objecting state to take an active role in the law-making process. To consistently object, a state must be an active participant in the process of the norm's formation, even if only to maintain consistently its objection to the norm's emergence or applicability.[120] If the norm being objected to is at issue in formal international debates, for example, to maintain consistency the objecting state will be required to involve itself in these discussions, potentially beneficially bringing its alternative perspective to the table. This is perhaps preferable to a state entirely withdrawing itself from the legal discourse: it may mean that it rethinks its objector stance as it engages with the rule, or, contrarily, might mean that it is able to influence other states to adopt its viewpoint and ultimately—if enough states take this position—to reframe the development of custom in its desired direction.[121] Either way, the consistency requirement forces the objector to remain at the table, at least in some capacity, and that is, it is suggested here, a better state of affairs.

Overall, then, there are good policy reasons for generally requiring that an objecting state raise its objection at appropriate points in the evolution of the new norm. It is worth recalling here that it was argued in Chapter 3 that, to be considered exempt, a state need not necessarily exercise a right that it seeks to protect by way of the persistent objector rule.[122] This was, in part, because it is unreasonable

[119] See Consideration of reports submitted by states parties under article 40 of the covenant, Fourth Periodic Report, United States of America, Human Rights Committee, 22 May 2012, UN Doc. CCPR/C/USA/4, paras 56–7.

[120] Steinfeld, n. 1, 1639, footnote 14.

[121] For discussion of this benefit of the persistent objector rule more generally, see Chapter 9, section VII.

[122] See Chapter 3, section IV.*i*, particularly at n. 96–n. 110 and accompanying text.

to expect a state to take physical action—outside of the appropriate context for such action—*simply to demonstrate objection*. However, this does not mean that if a state fails actively to engage with other states on the basis of the old norm that it is seeking to protest at instances where such engagement would be expected, this cannot be interpreted as inconsistent practice. While states do not necessarily need to exercise rights to retain them, if the state does not continue to engage with others on the basis of the old legal position when applicable and appropriate, 'it may effectively have abandoned its position of persistent objection'.[123]

While explicit and active inconsistency is relatively easy to identify, however, it may be overly onerous to require a state to object on *every single* occasion where one might expect it to, with any such failure costing the state its persistent objector exemption.[124] After all, there is no easy way of determining, or obvious arbiter of, which 'occasions' will require a reiteration to maintain consistent objection and which will not. For example, one might consider the position of Greece with regard to the so-called 'obligation to extradite or prosecute' (*aut dedere aut judicare*) individuals charged with serious international crimes. The status of this obligation as a binding rule of customary international law has been much debated in recent years.[125] There is a notable amount of state practice that is indicative of its existence in custom,[126] beyond numerous relevant treaty provisions,[127] but, equally, a small number of states have explicitly rejected the contention that it is customary international law.[128] In the 2012 *Questions Relating to the Obligation to Prosecute or Extradite* case, the ICJ determined that no dispute existed between the parties as to whether a customary *aut dedere aut judicare* obligation had been

[123] Byers, n. 1, 104.

[124] M.N. Shaw, *International Law* (Cambridge, Cambridge University Press, 7th edn, 2014), 64.

[125] See, for example, R. Cryer, *Prosecuting International Crimes: Selectivity and the International Criminal Law Regime* (Cambridge, Cambridge University Press, 2005), 101–17; A. Nollkaemper, 'Wither *Aut Dedere*? The Obligation to Extradite or Prosecute after the ICJ's Judgment in *Belgium v Senegal*' (2013) 4 *Journal of International Dispute Settlement* 501; R. van Steenberghe, 'The Obligation to Extradite or Prosecute' (2011) 9 *Journal of International Criminal Justice* 1089; M. Zgonec-Rožej and J. Foakes, 'International Criminals: Extradite or Prosecute?' (2013) *Chatham House*, Briefing Paper, IL BP 2013/01, particularly at 3–6; and International Law Commission: The Obligation to Extradite or Prosecute (*Aut Dedere Aut Judicare*), Amnesty International Report (London, Amnesty International Publications, 2009).

[126] See van Steenberghe, n. 125, particularly at 1091–102; and Amnesty Report, n. 125 (both of which set out this state practice, which takes a variety of forms, in considerable detail).

[127] See Survey of Multilateral Conventions which may be of Relevance for the Work of the International Law Commission on the Topic 'The Obligation to Extradite or Prosecute (*Aut Dedere Aut Judicare*)', International Law Commission, Study by the Secretariat, 2010, UN Doc. A/CN.4/630, particularly at para. 4 (identifying '61 multilateral instruments that contain provisions combining extradition and prosecution as alternative courses of action for the punishment of offenders').

[128] See, for example, General Assembly, Official Records, Sixty-second session, Sixth committee, Summary record of the 22nd meeting, 1 November 2007, UN Doc. A/C.6/62/SR.22, 11 (Austria); ibid., 16 (Germany); ibid., 18, and 'The Obligation to Extradite or Prosecute (*Aut Dedere Aut Judicare*)' [Agenda item 6]: comments and observations received from governments, International Law Commission, 2007, UN Doc. A/CN.4/579 and Add. 1–4, 85 (United States); General Assembly, Official Records, Sixty-second session, Sixth committee, Summary record of the 23rd meeting, 2 November 2007, UN Doc. A/C.6/62/SR.23, 3 (Malaysia); General Assembly, Official Records, Sixty-second session, Sixth committee, Summary record of the 24th meeting, 2 November 2007, UN Doc. A/C.6/62/SR.24, 7 (Greece); ibid., 18 (Israel).

breached at the date at which the Application was filed, meaning that the Court did not have jurisdiction to consider the issue of its customary status.[129] Similarly, in 2014, the International Law Commission (ILC)—having reviewed *aut dedere aut judicare* for a decade[130]—declined to reach a conclusion on the customary status of the obligation.[131] As such, it is difficult to say with any certainty whether the norm is *emerging* in custom, or whether it has *emerged.* In any event, Greece has been notably consistent in objecting to any possible customary obligation to extradite or prosecute, both by way of explicit statements to that effect[132] and through treaty reservation.[133]

However, when states were invited to provide written submissions to the ILC (by way of the Secretary General) in relation to the topic in 2006,[134] Greece did not make any submission at all (unlike fellow dissenters such as Austria[135] and, particularly, the United States,[136] which went out of its way to deny the customary status of the norm). Greece's lack of objection here when given an 'opportunity' to do so could be viewed as being terminal for any persistent objector claim in relation to *aut dedere aut judicare* (assuming that the norm has crystallized or does crystallize). However, the actual request of the ILC was specifically targeted at other issues related to the obligation: there was nothing in the request inviting states to comment on its customary status.[137] Therefore, one might question whether it can in fact be perceived as a 'missed opportunity' for Greece to object at all. Certainly there has been no suggestion from other states that Greece's position has changed,[138] and Greece is still viewed in the literature as at least a potential persistent objector state in relation to the obligation to extradite or prosecute.[139]

It would therefore seem that there is a *general* expectation that an objector will reiterate its position in appropriate fora and at suitable points in the norm's development where that norm is at issue, but this requirement is not absolute.

[129] *Questions relating to the Obligation to Prosecute or Extradite* (*Belgium v Senegal*), judgment, 2012 ICJ Rep. 422, paras 53–55.

[130] Report of the International Law Commission, Fifty-sixth session, 3 May–4 June and 5 July–6 August 2004, UN Doc. A/59/10, paras 362–3 and annex (proposing the topic as part of the ILC's programme of future work).

[131] 'The Obligation to Extradite or Prosecute (*Aut Dedere Aut Judicare*)', Final Report of the International Law Commission, 2014, adopted by the ILC at its sixty-sixth session, in 2014, and submitted to the General Assembly as a part of the Commission's report covering the work of that session, http://legal.un.org/ilc/texts/instruments/english/reports/7_6_2014.pdf, 16–17.

[132] See, for example, UN Doc. A/C.6/62/SR.24, n.127, 7.

[133] See Greece's reservation to Article 13 of the European Convention on the Suppression of Terrorism, 27 January 1977, CETS, N. 90, contained in a letter from the Permanent Representative of Greece, dated 5 September 1988, registered at the Secretariat General on 6 September 1988—Or Fr.

[134] Report of the International Law Commission, Fifty-eighth session, 1 May–9 June and 3 July–11 August 2006, UN Doc. A/61/10, 11.

[135] UN Doc. A/CN.4/579, n. 128, 86, 95, 105, and 107.

[136] Ibid., 85 (asserting that *aut dedere aut judicare* is not binding in custom), 94, 105, and 107.

[137] UN Doc. A/61/10, n. 134, 11.

[138] See, for example, UN Doc. A/C.6/62/SR.24, n.128 (Greece objecting in the Sixth Committee in 2007, with no states then giving any negative reaction to this in the subsequent debate).

[139] See, for example, van Steenberghe, n. 125, 1103, footnote 58.

The identification of a few instances where the state might have been expected to object but did not will not necessarily be terminal, depending on the context. Indeed, it is worth noting that—as with the related question of the required level of persistence[140]—the extent to which a state will be expected to object in circumstances where the norm being objected to is at issue will ultimately be context-specific. Depending on the circumstances, 'it may not be sufficient to object in only a minority of the instances that can be considered to constitute occasions for [a state] to have made its objections known'.[141] Equally, the expression of dissent in a minority of such instances may avail the objector in the right conditions. The geopolitical power of the state concerned and the 'importance' or 'ethical' credentials of the norm in question[142] are all likely to feed into the acceptability (or not) of silence in instances where one might expect further dissent. Perhaps most importantly of all—again, as with the necessary degree of persistence—the more isolated the state becomes, the more it will need to reiterate its protests at every available opportunity. This may further help to explain why Greece's failure to again raise its objections in response to the ILC's solicitation of views regarding the obligation to extradite or prosecute has seemingly not been detrimental to its overall objector status. There remains uncertainty as to the customary basis of the obligation[143] and, even if it has crystallized, Greece is not the only persistent objector state.[144] As Lepard argues:

> The required 'consistency' of protest may also depend on the state of development and recognition of a new customary rule. A rule that appears already to enjoy majority support among states will require more consistent protest for a state to be relieved of the obligation to follow it. Less consistency in protest in turn should suffice where support for a putative rule is still equivocal and diffuse.[145]

While there is at least a broad expectation that the dissenter will object when the opportunity arises, however, it seems clear that the notion that a state must object regularly even in circumstances where the norm being objected to is not at issue is not borne out by state practice, as can be seen from the fact that Turkey had intermittent periods of silence in relation to the 12-mile nautical limit and yet retained exempt status. Practically speaking, requiring repeated objections outside of their appropriate context would be asking too much of the objecting state. Adopting the stance of the persistent objector is, as we know, likely to be politically costly for the state concerned. Unsurprisingly, therefore, states 'are unlikely consistently to oppose the development or change of a rule unless they perceive that development or change to be significantly detrimental to their interests'.[146]

It is one thing to expect a state to speak up where its rights are at issue or where the norm that it is objecting to has been raised: at least in a general sense, this seems reasonable, if the objector truly wishes to stand apart. It is quite another

140 See Chapter 4, section III.
141 Elias, n. 60, 284, para. 16.
142 Lepard, n. 1, 23–9; and McClane, n. 1, 2, footnote 2.
143 See n. 125–n. 131 and accompanying text.
144 See n. 128.
145 Lepard, n. 1, 239. See also McClane, n. 1, 2, footnote 2.
146 Byers, n. 1, 180. For a contrary view, see Elias, n. 60, 284, para. 15.

thing to expect the state to stick its political neck out when there is no context for its objection, just to keep other states on notice.[147] In the same way that requiring a state to exercise a right that it is objecting to simply to manifest its dissent has the potential to undesirably escalate tensions,[148] requiring a state to object at all *in abstracto* would be unnecessarily antagonistic. It would force states to highlight their dissent and thus underline points of conflict with other states where such disagreement is not relevant. Perhaps more pertinently, states do not (and would not) take this step. It is therefore relatively clear that:

> [C]onsistency does not require that an objection (however lodged) be senselessly repeated. Rather, it appears that in most circumstances the objecting states simply must not act inconsistently with, contradict, or otherwise contravene the objection in order to maintain its position.[149]

Yet it is equally clear that the consistency 'required of the objector is quite substantial, and there is a tendency to aggressively construe a failure to raise objections at a particular moment as a waiver, despite previous and subsequent objections'.[150]

V. Substantive Consistency

In his seminal 1985 article on the persistent objector rule, Stein posed the following question: 'Should a requirement of substantive consistency be read into the principle [of persistent objection]'?[151] Stein was speculating as to whether a persistent objector state needs to be consistent in the sense of its dissent being in line with the stance that the same state has taken in relation to comparable international legal norms. In other words, Stein wondered whether it was appropriate to compare how a state had acted in relation to similar or related norms to ensure that its dissent was *principled* rather than merely opportunistic.

147 Third Report on Identification of Customary International Law, ILC, n. 50, para. 93 ('it may be unrealistic to demand total consistency [in relation to persistent objection]'); and 'Identification of Customary International Law', Statement of the Chairman of the Drafting Committee, Mr Mathias Forteau, 29 July 2015, International Law Commission, sixty-seventh session, Geneva, 4 May–5 June and 6 July–7 August 2015, 20 (reflecting the agreement in the ILC Drafting Committee that the objector state 'must maintain its objection both persistently and consistently, lest it be taken as having acquiesced ... nevertheless ... it may be unrealistic to demand total consistency').

148 It was argued in Chapter 3, section IV.*i*, particularly at n. 106–n. 110 and accompanying text, that requiring a state to object by taking action contrary to the norm in question may be overly onerous because taking action apropos of nothing may significantly escalate tensions in the international community (far more so than simply objecting by way of statement).

149 McClane, n. 1, 2, footnote 2. See also Thirlway, *International Customary Law and Codification*, n. 1, 116 (arguing that the persistent objector rule only requires that states object in relation to their interests, not in the abstract); and *Fisheries*, merits, n. 35, 138 ('[t]he Court considers that too much importance need not be attached to the few uncertainties or contradictions, real or apparent, which the United Kingdom Government claims to have discovered in Norwegian practice').

150 Kontorovich, n. 1, 875.

151 T.L. Stein, 'The Approach of the Different Drummer: The Principle of the Persistent Objector in International Law' (1985) 26 *Harvard International Law Journal* 457, 478.

To highlight this possible understanding of consistency, Stein referred to the persistent objector stance of the United States in relation to a generally agreed customary norm giving coastal states jurisdiction over tuna fishing, juxtaposing this with the fact that the United States was at the same time itself asserting jurisdiction over other migratory species of fish within 200 miles of the American coastline.[152] Somewhat understandably, Stein stated that '[i]t is hard to see why the need for international management of tuna is greater than it is for other highly migratory species; the United States position is in this sense substantively inconsistent'.[153]

A few other writers have taken note of Stein's comments on substantive consistency but, like Stein himself, those that have done so have generally not argued that such a requirement exists per se.[154] Stein saw advantages and disadvantages to a substantive consistency criterion. The main advantage that he envisaged was that this restrictive approach would allow for exemption only where states had a principled position of disagreement with the majority, resulting in the 'fuller consideration of the general international interest'[155] and discouraging '[w]holly self-interested objections'.[156] However, he also noted, on the flipside, that it would be difficult in any given case to determine whether a state had acted in a way that was substantively inconsistent, and such indeterminacy would undermine the effectiveness of the persistent objector rule.[157] Similarly, this restrictive reading would also diminish the 'safety valve' role of the persistent objector rule: it may perhaps be seen as preferable to have dissenting states operating within the system as recognized objectors than to have them simply abandoning all discourse (however substantively inconsistent and unprincipled their position may be viewed as being).[158]

While it is commendable to attempt to reframe the persistent objector rule so as to focus only on principled issues of legal contention rather than opportunistic exceptionalism, such an approach ultimately seems somewhat naïve. International law is, after all (at least largely), made by states for states, for good or ill. It seems unrealistic to expect states to be consistent in their objections in this broad, 'value-based' way. Weighing up the policy considerations raised by Stein, the present author would take the pragmatic position that a requirement of substantive consistency would be extremely difficult to implement and would, potentially, further alienate persistent objector states. A quest to ensure substantive consistency may, after all, encourage a state to object to *other* emerging norms so as to ensure substantive consistency of *objection* across norms, rather than encouraging it to accept the norm being objected to.

More importantly, it is perhaps of no surprise to find that state practice does not support any requirement of substantive consistency for persistent objectors. Taking Stein's own example, it is fairly clear—as we saw in Chapter 4[159]—that

[152] Ibid., 478–9. [153] Ibid.

[154] See Bölükbaşı, n. 1, 217; and Mendelson, n. 99, 241, footnote 230.

[155] Stein, n. 151, 479. [156] Ibid. [157] Ibid.

[158] Ibid. See also Mendelson, n. 99, 241, footnote 230.

[159] See Chapter 4, n. 63–n. 68 and accompanying text.

the United States remained an effective persistent objector to coastal state exclusivity over migratory tuna fishing for a significant period throughout the 1970s and 1980s (and, arguably, beyond).[160] This was the case irrespective of the undeniable substantive inconsistency that Stein identified in the state's objections in this context.

To take another example, in 2005, the ICRC accepted in its Customary IHL Study that the United States, United Kingdom, and France were all persistent objectors in relation to a customary prohibition on the 'the use of methods or means of warfare that are intended, or may be expected, to cause widespread, long-term and severe damage to the natural environment'.[161] The three states in question can all point to a persistent pattern of objection to the applicability of this customary norm, in that they have all consistently maintained that the prohibition on the use of weaponry that is severely damaging to the natural environment does not apply to nuclear weapons.[162] However, as the ICRC IHL Study notes, 'France, the United Kingdom and the United States ... have a certain amount of practice indicating their acceptance of the rule *provided that it applies to conventional weapons and not to nuclear weapons*'.[163] On this basis, the ICRC concluded that these states were exempt persistent objectors 'with regard to the application of the ... rule *to the use of nuclear weapons*',[164] but were not persistent objectors to the prohibition's applicability in other circumstances.[165]

Moreover, the ICRC Study went on to note that the objections of France, the United Kingdom and United States 'to the application of this specific rule [on using weaponry likely to cause severe damage to the environment] to such weapons [i.e. nuclear weapons] *has been consistent* since the adoption of the rule in treaty

160 See, for example, O. Elias, 'Some Remarks on the Persistent Objector Rule in Customary International Law' (1991) 6 *Denning Law Journal* 37, 44. The United States' exempt status is well illustrated by the Treaty on Fisheries between the Governments of Certain Pacific Island States and the Government of the United States of America (South Pacific Tuna Treaty), 2 April 1987, 2176 UNTS 38287.

161 ICRC IHL Study, *vol. I*, n. 88, 151.

162 Detailed evidence of this is provided in ICRC IHL Study, *vol. I*, n. 88, 153–5; and I ICRC IHL Study, *vol. II*, n. 88, 882–3, 894, and 896. See also Guldahl, n. 49, 82.

163 ICRC IHL Study, *vol. I*, n. 88, 154, emphasis added. For example, as referenced by the ICRC (ICRC IHL Study, *vol. II*, n. 88, 882–3), the United Kingdom, *The Law of Armed Conflict*, D/DAT/13/35/66. Army Code 71130 (revised 1981), Ministry of Defence, prepared under the direction of the Chief of General Staff (1981), Section 4, 14, section 5(h) holds that it is prohibited 'to use methods of warfare which are specifically intended to cause widespread, long-term and severe damage to the natural environment' but that 'this rule does not prohibit the use of nuclear weapons against military objectives.' Similar statements can be found in the United States' *Air Force Commander's Handbook* (1980), section 6-2(c) and the United States' *Operational Law Handbook* (1993), Q-182, section (i).

164 ICRC IHL Study, *vol. I*, n. 88, 151. See Guldahl, n. 49, 82 (arguing that, given the clear and repeated objections of these states, 'the conclusion reached in the ICRC study that these States are persistent objectors could be seen as accurate').

165 See S. Breau, 'Civilian Casualties and Nuclear Weapons: The Application of the Rule of Distinction' in J.L. Black-Branch and D. Fleck (eds), *Nuclear Non-Proliferation Law, vol. I* (The Hague, T.M.C. Asser Press, 2014), 105, 112 (noting that the nuclear weapons states were unsuccessful in claiming that none of the provisions in Additional Protocol I, or equivalent custom, were applicable to nuclear weapons, but accepting that some of these rules were inapplicable to nuclear weaponry).

form in 1977'.[166] Thus the fact that the three states in question had accepted the norm in relation to its restriction of the use of conventional weapons has had no bearing on their exempt status in the context of nuclear weapons.[167] Given that the substantive goal of the wider norm is the protection of the environment from damage by weapons, irrespective of the means used to cause such damage (indeed, the customary norm, in the ICRC Study at least, was deliberately framed in such terms), objection to its applicability to nuclear weapons while accepting its applicability to conventional armaments surely amounts to 'substantive inconsistency'. Nonetheless, the objections of these states have been viewed as being sufficiently consistent for the persistent objector rule to take effect.

Few writers have formally argued that a substantive consistency requirement exists (only that it may do, or that it may be desirable).[168] A rare exception is Lepard, who concludes that 'we should presume *in the absence of other evidence* that the community of states requires that a defecting state object ... on principled grounds'.[169] This view cannot be supported, because there is 'evidence' on this question, and it points us in the other direction: states' usage of the rule does not indicate that an objector must be 'substantively consistent' in its dissent, but instead suggests the contrary. It is perhaps also worth noting that no court or tribunal has referred to a requirement of substantive consistency either.

VI. Conclusion

It has been argued in this chapter that, to gain exemption by way of the persistent objector rule, a state's objections must be not only persistent, but also consistent. The consistency criterion is closely related to the need for persistence, in that both concern the necessary 'quality' of objection for a state to gain exemption. Both criteria are also premised on the need to ensure that the objector is truly willing to stand apart and take upon itself the political burden of its desire to remain exempt, as well as the desirability of making objection as unambiguous as possible. Unfortunately, the similarities between the two criteria have meant that they have often been unhelpfully amalgamated in doctrine, with few writers noting the distinction between the concepts, and many, instead, referring to them interchangeably.

Consistency of objection requires that a state objects with 'absolute consistency', meaning that it at no point explicitly contradicts its dissenting position. Moreover, states are generally expected to object at appropriate instances where the norm being objected to is at issue, or where the objector's interests in relation to that norm come into question. Silence in such circumstances will likely be

[166] ICRC IHL Study, *vol. I*, n. 88, 154–5, emphasis added.

[167] Elias, n. 60, 281, para. 4 (seemingly accepting the exempt status of these three states in this context).

[168] See Bölükbaşı, n. 1, 217; Mendelson, n. 99, 241, footnote 230; and Stein, n. 151, 478–9.

[169] Lepard, n. 1, 238, emphasis added.

interpreted as inconsistent behaviour, undermining the objector's use of the rule. However, the need to object 'when appropriate' is not absolute: some failure to object when one might reasonably have expected such an objection may be acceptable, so long as the dissenter has for the most part objected where the norm has been at issue. How consistent a state will need to be in breaking its silence in such circumstances will in large part depend on the wider acceptability of its position (something that will be influenced by various factors, much as with the required degree of persistence).

What is *not* required by the consistency criterion is for the objector to senselessly repeat its objections apropos of nothing. Silence will not, it seems, be interpreted as inconsistent behaviour where that silence has occurred entirely outside of the context of the norm being objected to. Finally, despite some tentative suggestions, there is no requirement of 'substantive consistency': states do not need to object consistently across the subject-matter of comparable norms and thereby establish a principled position in order to gain exemption.

The 'persistent objector rule' should perhaps more accurately be termed the 'persistent and consistent objector rule', given the importance of the consistency criterion to its operation. As that is something of a mouthful, and so as to stick with the familiar nomenclature, this book has chosen to retain the name 'persistent objector rule'. However, this is without prejudice to the consistency requirement. It must be kept in mind that consistency is just as important an element of the rule as persistence, and—despite the similarities between the two criteria—consistency should be considered as a distinct requirement: 'A State must maintain its objection *both* persistently *and* consistently, lest it be taken to have acquiesced.'[170]

[170] Third Report on Identification of Customary International Law, ILC, n. 50, para. 93, emphasis added.

6

The Timeliness Criterion

This chapter examines the final criterion for the operation of the persistent objector rule: timeliness. A common feature of all mainstream understandings of the rule is that a state's objections must occur during the period where the embryonic customary law being objected to is still 'emerging'. In other words, it is generally accepted that states must (persistently and consistently) object during the legal norm's gestation, prior to its crystallization as a binding norm of customary international law. Yet the exact requirements of the timeliness criterion are not necessarily clear; examination of its operation in practice is, therefore, crucial, as—at least to an extent—'the persistent objector rule is only meaningful if a State knows when to dissent'.[1]

In section I, this chapter identifies the timeliness criterion in the literature, and argues that state practice supports it in a broad sense. As a result, 'subsequent objectors'—states that object to a norm after it has crystallized—will be bound by that norm. Section II argues that the commonly advanced justifications for the timeliness criterion are unsatisfactory. Section III then examines more pragmatic rationales, as well as engaging with arguments that have been made by a minority of commentators in support of an *ex post facto* right of withdrawal from customary international law (that is, the 'subsequent objector rule').

The chapter then turns to the problems associated with actually applying the timeliness criterion. In section IV, the difficulties in determining both the points of initial gestation and crystallization of any given norm of customary international law are considered. Section V examines the problem of a state ensuring that it is aware of any 'emerging custom' that may later bind it, given that it must object before the norm crystallizes. The question of whether a state that has no interest in an emerging norm is still bound by it if that state later develops such an interest, post-crystallization, is examined in section VI. In section VII, the implications of the timeliness criterion in the context of 'instant' or 'accelerated' customary international law are considered. Section VIII explores the much-discussed problem that the timeliness criterion poses for new states. In section IX, the chapter turns to the question of whether there are further temporal restrictions *within* the period of emergence that may limit when a dissenting state can object. Finally, it

[1] O. Elias and C.L. Lim, *The Paradox of Consensualism in International Law* (The Hague, Kluwer Law International, 1998), 72.

is noted in section X that states must continue to object after the point of crystallization in order to maintain their exempt status.

I. Timeliness and the Subsequent Objector Rule

i. General support for the timeliness criterion

The 2015 draft conclusions provisionally adopted by the International Law Commission's (ILC) Drafting Committee on the 'Identification of customary international law' note that, for persistent objection to be effective, the state concerned must have 'objected to a rule of customary international law *while that rule was in the process of formation*...'[2] This requirement for persistent objection to occur in a timely manner—prior to the crystallization of the norm being objected to—is ubiquitous in doctrine.[3] Charney has gone so far as to state that '*virtually*

[2] Identification of Customary International Law: Text of the Draft Conclusions Provisionally Adopted by the Drafting Committee', International Law Commission, Sixty-seventh session, Geneva, 4 May–5 June and 6 July–7 August 2015, UN Doc. A/CN.4/L.869, 5, Draft Conclusion 15: Persistent Objector, emphasis added.

[3] See, for example, *Committee on Formation of Customary (General) International Law*, Final Report of the Committee, 'Statement of Principles Applicable to the Formation of General Customary International Law', International Law Association, London Conference (2000), http://www.ila-hq.org/en/committees/index.cfm/cid/30, 27; *Restatement of the Law, Third, Foreign Relations Law of the United States*, American Law Institute, 1987, Section 102, Comment (d); C.A. Bradley, 'The Juvenile Death Penalty' (2002–3) 52 *Duke Law Journal* 485, 518; A. Cassese, *International Law in a Divided World* (Oxford, Clarendon Press, 1986), 178; B. Chigara, 'European/Southern African Development Community (SADC) States' Bilateral Investment Agreements (BITS) for the Promotion of Foreign Investments vs Post-Apartheid SADC Economic and Social Reconstruction Policy' (2011) 10 *Journal of International Trade Law and Policy* 213, 216; P. Dumberry, 'Incoherent and Ineffective: The Concept of Persistent Objector Revisited' (2010) 59 *International and Comparative Law Quarterly* 779, 780–1; O. Elias, 'Persistent Objector' in R. Wolfrum (ed.), *Max Planck Encyclopaedia of Public International Law, vol. VIII* (Oxford, Oxford University Press, 2012), 280, 280, para. 1; G. Fitzmaurice, 'The Law and Procedure of the International Court of Justice, 1951–54: General Principles and Sources of Law' (1953) 30 *British Yearbook of International Law* 1, 24, and 26; V. Fon and F. Parisi, 'Stability and Change in International Customary Law' (2004) 21 *American Law and Economics Association Annual Meetings* 1, 5; J.A. Green, 'Persistent Objector Teflon? Customary International Human Rights Law and the United States in International Adjudicative Proceedings' in J.A. Green and C.P.M. Waters (eds), *Adjudicating International Human Rights: Essays in Honour of Sandy Ghandhi* (Leiden, Brill Nijhoff, 2015), 167, 170; A. Kaczorowska, *Public International Law* (Abingdon, Routledge, 4th edn, 2010), 41; E. Kontorovich, 'Inefficient Customs in International Law' (2006–7) 48 *William and Mary Law Review* 859, 875 and 910; M. Koskenniemi, *From Apology to Utopia: The Structure of International Legal Argument* (Cambridge, Cambridge University Press, reissue, 2005), 444; L. Loschin, 'The Persistent Objector Rule and Customary Human Rights Law: A Proposed Analytical Framework' (1996) 2 *University of California Davis Journal of International Law and Policy* 147, 166; F.F. Martin, *The Constitution as Treaty: The International Legal Constructionalist Approach to the U.S. Constitution* (Cambridge, Cambridge University Press, 2007), 73 and 75; R. Price, 'Emerging Customary Norms and Anti-Personnel Landmines' in C. Reus-Smit (ed.), *The Politics of International Law* (Cambridge, Cambridge University Press, 2004), 106, 115; M.P. Scharf, *Customary International Law in Times of Fundamental Change: Recognizing Grotian Moments* (Cambridge, Cambridge University Press, reissue, 2013), 42; T.L. Stein, 'The Approach of the Different Drummer: The Principle of the Persistent Objector in International Law' (1985) 26 *Harvard International Law*

all authorities maintain that [objection must be made in relation] to an evolving rule of general customary international law'.[4]

The corollary to this is, of course, that once the new norm has 'crystallized' into binding custom, objection will no longer avail a state wishing to exempt itself from the law in question. Objection to a formed—rather than forming—customary international law is often called 'subsequent objection',[5] and subsequent objectors are seen by most commentators as being bound in the same way as a state that has not objected at all.[6] Objections lodged after a norm has crystallized are therefore usually viewed as digressions[7] that have no legal effect in terms of the applicability of the crystallized norm to the objecting state.[8] Indeed, if the objections take the form of action that departs from the standard of conduct required by the new norm, they will constitute international legal wrongs.[9]

Journal 457, 458; A. Steinfeld, 'Nuclear Objections: The Persistent Objector and the Legality of the Use of Nuclear Weapons' (1996) 62 *Brooklyn Law Review* 1635, 1647 and 1652; E.T. Swaine, 'Bespoke Custom' (2010) 21 *Duke Journal of Comparative and International Law* 207, 211–12; H. Thirlway, *International Customary Law and Codification* (Leiden, A.W. Sijthoff, 1972), 110 and 116; M. Virally, 'The Sources of International Law' in M. Sørensen (ed.), *Manual of Public International Law* (London, Macmillan, 1968), 116, 137; and K. Wolfke, *Custom in Present International Law* (Dordrecht, Martinus Nijhoff, 2nd edn, 1993), 66.

[4] J.I. Charney, 'The Persistent Objector Rule and the Development of Customary International Law' (1985) 56 *British Yearbook of International Law* 1, 2, emphasis added to (and elsewhere removed from) the original.

[5] See, for example, C.G. Guldahl, 'The Role of Persistent Objection in International Humanitarian Law' (2008) 77 *Nordic Journal of International Law* 51, 53; C. Quince, *The Persistent Objector and Customary International Law* (Denver, Outskirts Press, 2010), 79–81; and M.E. Villiger, *Customary International Law and Treaties: A Manual on the Theory and Practice of the Interrelation of Sources* (The Hague, Kluwer, 2nd edn, 1997), 36–7.

[6] See, for example, ILA Final Report, n. 3, 27; O. Abasheikh, 'The Validity of the Persistent Offender Rule in International Law' (2004) 9 *Coventry Law Journal* 40, 46; M. Akehurst, 'Custom as a Source of International Law' (1974–5) 47 *British Yearbook of International Law* 1, 24; D.J. Bederman, 'Acquiescence, Objection and the Death of Customary International Law' (2010) 21 *Duke Journal of Comparative and International Law* 31, 31 and 35; M. Bos, *A Methodology of International Law* (Amsterdam, TMC Asser, 1984), 248; E.L. Chalecki, 'Science before the Law: American Exceptionalism in the Kyoto Protocol and the Development of a Global Norm of Environmental Compliance' (2007) *Selected Works*, http://works.bepress.com/cgi/viewcontent.cgi?article=1000&context=elizabeth_chalecki, 19; J.I. Charney, 'Universal International Law' (1993) 87 *American Journal of International Law* 529, 538; Charney, n. 4, 2; M. Dixon, *Textbook on International Law* (Oxford, Oxford University Press, 7th edn, 2013), 34–5; Elias and Lim, n. 1, 52; J.A. Green, 'India and a Customary Comprehensive Nuclear Test-Ban: Persistent Objection, Peremptory Norms and the 123 Agreement' (2011) 51 *Indian Journal of International Law* 3, 19; Guldahl, n. 5, 53; J.B. McClane, 'How Late in the Emergence of a Norm of Customary International Law May a Persistent Objector Object?' (1989) 13 *International Law Students Association Journal of International Law* 1, 7, 20–2; P. Malanczuk, *Akehurst's Modern Introduction to International Law* (New York Routledge, 7th edn, 1997), 48; M.H. Mendelson, 'The Formation of Customary International Law' (1998) 272 *Recueil des cours* 155, 244; H. Thirlway, *The Sources of International Law* (Oxford, Oxford University Press, 2014), 88; and J.P. Trachtman, 'Persistent Objectors, Cooperation, and the Utility of Customary International Law' (2010) 21 *Duke Journal of Comparative and International Law* 221, 221.

[7] Villiger, n. 5, 36.

[8] That is, unless the state has already been persistently objecting prior to crystallization: it should be noted that objection subsequent to crystallization plays a role in ensuring the *continuation* of the state's exempt persistent objector status. See section X.

[9] Stein, n. 3, 458; and Villiger, n. 5, 36.

Having said this, it is important to keep in mind that states do object to existing customary international law rules. Subsequent objection is far from being a legally irrelevant practice. In fact, quite the opposite: subsequent objection is a crucial element of customary international law formation and development.[10] This is because custom is necessarily altered by states adopting an attitude apart[11] and indeed, at least initially, by states violating the existing law.[12] If a sufficient number of other states adopt the position of a subsequent objector, rather than continuing with the status quo, then the custom changes.[13] This is not the same thing as a 'subsequent objector rule'.[14] Instead, it is better thought of as a 'revision rule'[15] and is simply the process by which customary international law develops. In such instances a subsequent objector becomes a trendsetter, and the development of the law itself centres upon the objection. If other states do not follow the lead of the subsequent objector, however, then its objections will be unavailing: it will not gain an exemption and, if it acts contrarily to the new norm, it will be in violation of it. To 'have its way', a dissenter must either convince other states to adopt its stance, or object prior to the crystallization of the norm in question.[16]

ii. The source of the timeliness criterion

It has been argued[17] that the timeliness criterion can be inferred from the two merits decisions of the International Court of Justice (ICJ) that have touched upon the persistent objector rule: the *Asylum*[18] and *Fisheries*[19] cases. However, it may be something of a stretch to claim that these judgments support the existence of the requirement. In reaching its determination in *Asylum* that Peru had objected sufficiently to remain exempt from a customary right of unilateral and definitive qualification of refugee status for asylum-granting states (had such a rule formed),[20] the ICJ actually made no reference to the *timing* of the Peruvian objections.[21] The ICJ did, of course, refer, in *Fisheries*, to the fact that that Norway had 'always opposed' the '10-mile rule' for the delimitation of territorial sea and

[10] S. Estreicher, 'A Post-Formation Withdrawal from Customary International Law?: Some Cautionary Notes' (2010) 21 *Duke Journal of Comparative and International Law* 57, 57, footnote 2.

[11] Dixon, n. 6, 35.

[12] C.A. Bradley and M. Gulati, 'Withdrawing from International Custom' (2010) 120 *Yale Law Journal* 202, 212; A. D'Amato, *The Concept of Custom in International Law* (New York, Cornell University Press, 1971), 97–8; and Quince, n. 5, 45.

[13] J. Crawford, *Brownlie's Principles of Public International Law* (Oxford, Oxford University Press, 8th edn, 2012), 29; and Villiger, n. 5, 36–7.

[14] Irrespective of the erroneous claim to this effect by some writers, who misunderstand to what subsequent objection rightly refers. See Crawford, n. 13, 29 and Fon and Parisi, n. 3, 12–14.

[15] Trachtman, n. 6, 223.

[16] O. Elias, 'Some Remarks on the Persistent Objector Rule in Customary International Law' (1991) 6 *Denning Law Journal* 37, 38.

[17] D. Kritsiotis, 'On the Possibilities Of and For Persistent Objection' (2010) 21 *Duke Journal of Comparative and International Law* 121, 129.

[18] *Asylum* (*Columbia v Peru*), merits, 1950 ICJ Rep. 266.

[19] *Fisheries* (*United Kingdom v Norway*), merits, 1951 ICJ Rep. 116.

[20] See *Asylum*, merits, n. 18, 277–8.

[21] Bradley and Gulati, n. 12, 235.

fishery zones.[22] This statement could perhaps be interpreted as indicating that the Court saw the fact that Norway's objections had occurred during the gestation of the norm as being determinative, but this is far from a conclusive reading of the passage.[23]

As was discussed in Chapter 2,[24] in both *Asylum* and *Fisheries*, the Court found that no customary norm—on the qualification of asylum status or the 10-mile fishery limit, respectively—had yet formed.[25] As such, its view must necessarily have been that both Peru and Norway objected prior to crystallization, and it identified both states as 'persistent-objectors-in-waiting' that would be exempt if the customary norms in question ever in fact reached crystallization point. This suggests that the Court saw prior persistent objection as *sufficient* to gain exemption; however, this is not quite the same thing as the Court holding that timeliness is a *necessary* element of the persistent objector rule. The decisions did not touch upon whether the objections of these two states would have been unavailing had they occurred later in the process of customary international law development.

While it thus takes a degree of interpretive sleight of hand to find support in the majority decisions of the ICJ for the timeliness criterion, the requirement has been endorsed in various individual opinions of judges of the Court.[26] For example, in the *North Sea Continental Shelf* cases, Judge ad hoc Sørensen contended that the Federal Republic of Germany (FRD) had failed to object '[a]t a decisive stage of th[e] formative process', and thus could not be seen as being exempt from a customary principle of equidistance in relation to the delimitation of the continental shelf.[27] The timeliness criterion has similarly been endorsed in adjudicative proceedings other than at the ICJ. For example, the Inter-American Commission on Human Rights stated in its 2002 *Domingues* decision that '[o]nce established, a norm of international customary law binds all states with the exception of only those states that have persistently rejected the practice *prior to its becoming law*'.[28]

The majority view in the literature and—at least to some extent—in the case law, therefore, is that for a state to gain exemption from the binding force of a new customary norm by way of the persistent objector rule, it must have (persistently and consistently) objected prior to the crystallization of that norm. Yet, despite the significant support for the timeliness criterion in doctrine, a small number of writers have rejected the orthodox temporal restriction on persistent objection,

[22] *Fisheries*, merits, n. 19, 131.

[23] Bradley and Gulati, n. 12, 235.

[24] See Chapter 2, section I.*i*.

[25] See *Asylum*, merits, n. 18, particularly at 276–8; and *Fisheries*, merits, n. 19, particularly at 131, respectively.

[26] See *North Sea Continental Shelf* cases (*Federal Republic of Germany v Netherlands, Federal Republic of Germany v Denmark*), merits, 1969 ICJ Rep. 3, dissenting opinion of Judge ad hoc Sørensen, 248; *North Sea Continental Shelf* cases, ibid., dissenting opinion of Judge Lachs, 232; and *Asylum*, merits, n. 18, dissenting opinion of Judge Azevedo, 336.

[27] *North Sea Continental Shelf* cases, merits, n. 26, dissenting opinion of Judge ad hoc Sørensen, 248.

[28] *Domingues v United States*, merits, 2002, IACmHR, Report No. 62/02, Case No. 12.285, para. 48, emphasis added. See also *C* et al. *v Director of Immigration and Secretary for Security*, 2011, Hong Kong Special Administrative Region, Court of Appeal, CACV 132-137/2008, para. 68.

arguing instead that states can also exempt themselves from customary international law by way of subsequent objection (or, in some versions of this argument, that they should be able to do so).[29] This chapter will engage with the arguments of this minority of writers who reject the timeliness criterion throughout, but at this point it is simply enough to note that the considerable majority of scholars reject the notion of subsequent objection and that it is extremely difficult to identify any basis for it in case law either.[30]

Irrespective of the view adopted in the literature and case law, the key question is whether the timeliness criterion can be identified in instances where the persistent objector rule has been used in state practice. It is certainly the case that states have *argued* that objection prior to crystallization is a requirement for the operation of the persistent objector rule.[31] However, a requirement of timely objection is difficult to establish with certainty based on actual state *usage* of the rule because, even in the context of the relatively small amount of state usage of the rule per se, there are *especially* few examples of states attempting to gain exemption by objecting after the crystallization of the customary international law in question.[32] One might postulate that this is because of a general recognition by states that subsequent objection will be unavailing: states know that persistent objection must be timely and so, if their objections come after crystallization, they do not attempt to argue that this entitles them to exempt status. This is a rather speculative assertion, however. In any event, when one considers the small number of examples of attempted subsequent objection, it is fairly clear that subsequent objectors have failed to gain exemption. The available state practice can at least be said to be highly indicative of a timeliness criterion as a key feature of the persistent objector rule's operation.

One useful example highlighting this may be found in the objections raised by various equatorial states—Brazil, Colombia, Congo, Ecuador, Indonesia, Kenya, Uganda, and Zaire—to the geostationary orbit of satellites around the equator,

[29] See, for example, Bradley and Gulati, n. 12; Quince, n. 5, 61–2 (specifically with regard to new states) and 79–81; A.T. Guzman, 'Saving Customary International Law' (2005–6) 27 *Michigan Journal of International Law* 115, 166–74; and L.R. Helfer, 'Exiting Custom: Analogies to Treaty Withdrawals' (2010) 21 *Duke Journal of Comparative and International Law* 65.

[30] See Abasheikh, n. 6, 46–7 ('neither jurists nor judicial decisions recognise the existence of a "subsequent objector rule"'); H. Charlesworth, 'Law-Making and Sources' in J. Crawford and M. Koskenniemi (eds), *The Cambridge Companion to International Law* (Cambridge, Cambridge University Press, 2012), 187, 195 (arguments in favour of the subsequent objector rule have had 'little impact'); and Elias, n. 16, 38 ('[n]one of the authoritative texts would permit a State to opt out of an existing rule of customary international law'). Admittedly, Bradley and Gulati point to some domestic case law from the United States, from the eighteenth and nineteenth centuries, which can be read as providing support for the subsequent objector rule. However, they provide no recent case law to indicate the continuation of this position (even if it is accepted that the subsequent objector rule had a degree of historical legitimacy in American case law). Plus, of course, one might question the weight that domestic case law from a single state has in the interpretation of international legal norms. See Bradley and Gulati, n. 12, 219–26.

[31] See, for example, United States, *Department of Defense Law of War Manual*, 12 June 2015, http://www.dod.mil/dodgc/images/law_war_manual15.pdf, 30, 33–4, and 37.

[32] Schachter incorrectly suggests that there are *no* examples of states ever attempting to gain exemption through subsequent objection: there are, in fact, a few. O. Schachter, 'International Law in Theory and Practice' (1982) 178 *Recueil des cours* 9, 38.

particularly by the United States. The equatorial states objected to the presence of these satellites on the basis that there was no customary right to launch them, and that the various segments of the satellites' orbit fell within their territorial jurisdiction; the objections manifested themselves in the mid-1970s, culminating in the Bogota Declaration of 1976, which formally rejected the practice of launching geostationary equatorial satellites.[33] Such satellites had, however, been deployed since the late 1950s, without any dissent on the part of the equatorial states.[34] Moreover, none of these states raised any objections in relation to Articles I and II of the Outer Space Treaty in 1967,[35] which designated 'outer space' as being beyond national appropriation; indeed, all but two of the states concerned (Congo and Kenya) had signed the treaty before the end of the 1960s.[36]

While some commentators have tentatively suggested that the customary status, in the mid-1970s, of the right to deploy geostationary equatorial satellites could be contested,[37] the majority view is that a binding customary international law had formed by this stage (based on a combination of repeated practice, acquiescence, and the Outer Space Treaty), and thus that the Bogota Declaration and the other objections of the equatorial states came too late.[38] The fifteen-year-plus period of silence during the formation of the custom was seemingly terminal for the states' claim to be exempt. The 'late' objections of the equatorial states hit a diplomatic 'brick wall',[39] with numerous other states holding that they had no legal effect.[40] The claim to territorial jurisdiction over an area 22,300 miles above the planet's surface was generally treated as a violation of provisions of the Outer Space Treaty (especially Article II) and/or of equivalent provisions of customary international law.[41] The equatorial states therefore abandoned their position (some

[33] Declaration of the First Meeting of Equatorial Countries, 3 December 1976 (Bogota Declaration), http://www.jaxa.jp/library/space_law/chapter_2/2-2-1-2_e.html.

[34] McClane, n. 6, 19.

[35] Treaty on Principles Governing the Activities of States in the Exploration and Use of Outer Space, Including the Moon and Other Celestial Bodies, 10 October 1967, 610 UNTS 205.

[36] For a list of the parties to the Outer Space Treaty, as of 15 August 2015, see: http://www.fas.org/nuke/control/ost/text/space5.htm.

[37] G. Oduntan, *Sovereignty and Jurisdiction in Airspace and Outer Space: Legal Criteria for Spatial Delimitation* (Abingdon, Routledge, 2012), 303–5.

[38] L. Martinez, *Communication Satellites: Power and Politics in Space* (Deadham, Artech House, 1985), 93–5; and D. St. John, 'The Bogotá Declaration and the Curious Case of Geostationary Orbit', *Denver Journal of International Law and Policy*, 'The View From Above' Blog, 31 January 2013, http://djilp.org/3494/the-bogota-declaration-and-the-curious-case-of-geostationary-orbit/.

[39] Oduntan, n. 37, 303.

[40] See, for example, General Assembly, Committee on the Peaceful Uses of Outer Space, Legal Sub-Committee, Seventeenth session, summary records, 5 April 1978, UN Doc. A/AC.105/C.2/SR.297, paras 1–2 (Poland); ibid., paras 10–11 (Czechoslovakia); ibid., paras. 12–14 (France); ibid., paras 19–23 (Italy); ibid., paras 24–7 (United Kingdom); ibid., paras. 28-29 (German Democratic Republic); ibid., paras 30–5 (Soviet Union); General Assembly, Committee on the Peaceful Uses of Outer Space, Scientific and Technical Sub-Committee, Sixteenth session, summary records, 26 February, 1979, UN Doc. A/AC.105/C.1/SR.219, paras 7–10 (United States); and General Assembly, Committee on the Peaceful Uses of Outer Space, Legal Sub-Committee, Eighteenth session, summary records, 9 April, 1979, UN Doc. A/AC.105/C.2/SR.314, paras 13–17 (Japan).

[41] G. Oduntan, 'The Never Ending Dispute: Legal Theories on the Spatial Demarcation Boundary Plane between Airspace and Outer Space' (2003) 1 *Hertfordshire Law Journal* 64, 78.

explicitly, and some by reverting back to the tacit acceptance of the customary norm through silence).[42]

A more recent example is France's position in the *Rhine Chlorides Arbitration* dispute with The Netherlands, decided by the Permanent Court of Arbitration (PCA) in 2004.[43] The dispute concerned the interpretation of the Additional Protocol to the Convention on the Protection of the Rhine against Pollution by Chlorides,[44] and particularly France's responsibility (most notably its financial responsibility) for the protection of the Rhine under that Protocol.[45]

Pertinently for the purposes of this chapter, France argued that, as it was not a party to the Vienna Convention on the Law of Treaties (VCLT)[46] and had demonstrated repeated rejection of some of that treaty's provisions, it was not bound to follow the methods of treaty interpretation set out in Articles 31–3 of the VCLT in relation to the application of the Additional Protocol.[47] France took the nuanced position that the rules contained in Articles 31–3 of the VCLT were *broadly* reflected in binding customary international law, but that the exact content of the customary rules on treaty interpretation applicable to it were rather different to those in the VCLT itself, as it had not fully accepted the approach of the VCLT.[48] The PCA concluded that the rules on treaty interpretation *as reflected in Articles 31–3 of the VCLT* had long since crystallized into customary international law (perhaps even having done so prior to the drafting of the VCLT itself), and thus that France's objections to the exact content of the custom came far too late.[49] As such, the Additional Protocol had to be interpreted based on the VCLT provisions (or, rather, on the parallel customary provisions that bound France). Although the PCA did not phrase this decision in exactly these terms, it viewed the subsequent objections of France to be unavailing.

Examples of states attempting to gain exemption through subsequent objection are admittedly extremely rare. The persistent objector rule is not often used and, when it is, this almost always involves prior persistent objection. When states do attempt to object post-crystallization, such objections prove unavailing. Indeed, examples of states *successfully* gaining exemption through subsequent objection are seemingly non-existent in modern international law: the present author has been unable to identify a single example since the mid-twentieth century, when the rule 'proper' emerged,[50] of a state gaining exemption from a customary norm

[42] St. John, n. 38.

[43] *Case Concerning the Audit of Accounts between the Netherlands and France in Application of the Protocol of 25 September 1991 Additional to the Convention for the Protection of the Rhine from Pollution by Chlorides of 3 December 1976*, 2004, PCA, 2005, 25 Rep. International Arbitral Awards 267.

[44] Additional Protocol to the Convention on the Protection of the Rhine against Pollution by Chlorides, 25 September 1991, 1840 UNTS 423.

[45] See, generally, ibid.

[46] Vienna Convention on the Law of Treaties (VCLT), 23 May 1969, 1155 UNTS 331.

[47] *Case Concerning the Audit of Accounts between the Netherlands and France in Application of the Protocol of 25 September 1991 Additional to the Convention for the Protection of the Rhine from Pollution by Chlorides of 3 December 1976*, counter-memorial of France, 2001, particularly at para. 6.

[48] Ibid.

[49] *Rhine Chlorides Arbitration*, n. 43, particularly at paras 57–9.

[50] See, generally, Chapter 1, in relation to the emergence of the persistent objector rule.

by objecting after it has been agreed that the customary rule in question has crystallized.[51]

Even supporters of the subsequent objector rule accept that there is 'relatively little concrete evidence of [successful subsequent objection in] state practice',[52] although they have, on occasion, suggested a few possible instances. For example, Bradley and Gulati[53] and Lepard[54] point to the 1945 'Truman Proclamation', by which the United States unilaterally asserted jurisdiction over the contiguous continental shelf, beyond its traditional territorial waters. The Truman Proclamation almost certainly contradicted the existing customary international law position in 1945 in relation to the freedom of the high seas.[55] Yet the United States was able to maintain this divergent position on the continental shelf and act upon it: as such, the Truman Proclamation could be—and has been—viewed as a successful example of subsequent objection. This would be a misunderstanding of what occurred, however. In fact, other states accepted the American objection to the customary status quo and, very quickly, began adopting the same stance themselves.[56] By the 1950s, the Truman Proclamation had become the legal orthodoxy,[57] and was enshrined in the Convention on the Continental Shelf in 1958 (particularly Article 2).[58] The United States was not, therefore, a subsequent objector that maintained an exemption to an otherwise binding rule. It was a trendsetter, of the sort discussed in the previous subsection.[59] The 'objections' of the United States were accepted by other states, leading to a change in the law.

Overall, then, there is strong evidence for the existence of the timeliness criterion. This aspect of the persistent objector rule can be identified in state practice, albeit that the criterion's existence must largely be based on the *absence* of practice (that is, the absence of successful subsequent objection).

[51] A. Roberts, 'Who Killed Article 38(1)(b)? A Reply to Bradley & Gulati' (2010) 21 *Duke Journal of Comparative and International Law* 173, 174 (noting that supporters of subsequent objection cite no examples from practice).

[52] C.A. Bradley and M. Gulati, 'Customary International Law and Withdrawal Rights in an Age of Treaties' (2010) 21 *Duke Journal of International and Comparative Law* 1, 28.

[53] C.A. Bradley and M. Gulati, 'Withdrawing from International Custom' (2010) *Social Science Research Network*, Working Paper, http://papers.ssrn.com/sol3/papers.cfm?abstract_id=1523906, 25. Interestingly, this example did not appear in the final published version of this article (Bradley and Gulati, n. 12).

[54] B.D. Lepard, *Customary International Law: A New Theory with Practical Applications* (Cambridge, Cambridge University Press, 2010), 231.

[55] See M. Byers, *Custom, Power and the Power of Rules: International Relations and Customary International Law* (Cambridge, Cambridge University Press, 1999), 91; and E.J. Cosford, 'The Continental Shelf: 1910–1945' (1958) 4 *McGill Law Journal* 245.

[56] J. Crawford, 'Chance, Order, Change: The Course of International Law—General Course on Public International Law' (2013) 365 *Recueil des cours* 9, 64–5; H. Lauterpacht, 'Sovereignty over Submarine Areas' (1950) 27 *British Yearbook of International Law* 377, 380–3.

[57] See H. Meijers, 'How is International Law Made?—The Stages of Growth of International Law and the Use of Customary Rules' (1978) 9 *Netherlands Yearbook of International Law* 3, 6; Scharf, n. 3, 114–22.

[58] Convention on the Continental Shelf, 29 April 1958, 499 UNTS 311.

[59] See n. 10–n. 16 and accompanying text.

II. The Commonly Advanced Justifications for the Timeliness Criterion Are Unsatisfactory

Despite the traditional understanding of the persistent objector rule as being a product of the consent-based nature of the international legal system,[60] the voluntarist account of the obligatory force of international law cannot explain why states should be bound after having formally objected, whenever that dissent might have been expressed.[61] As supporters of the subsequent objector rule have argued, if the persistent objector rule exists solely to preserve state autonomy in the context of customary international law formation, then it would seem irrelevant whether this expression of will was made before or after the crystallization of the norm in question.[62]

However, as will be discussed in more detail in Chapter 9, the voluntarist of customary international law formation—at least it its absolute form—is flawed, both with regard to the persistent objector rule[63] and more generally.[64] As such, this book has taken the view throughout that the operation and function of the persistent objector rule cannot be deduced by reference to voluntarism, but must be induced from the practice of states.[65] We saw in section I.*ii* that the timeliness criterion appears to be an element of the rule's operation in state practice: this is the case irrespective of the fact that voluntarism cannot explain why this requirement has been adopted by states in their usage of the rule. In contrast, supporters of the subsequent objector rule have struggled to find examples of states gaining an exemption by objecting after it has been agreed that the new norm has crystallized.

Given that the timeliness requirement can be seen in practice but cannot be rationalized by voluntarism, some writers have tried to explain the existence of the criterion on the basis that 'it is a *matter of principle* that states cannot avoid legal obligations once they have come into being'.[66] In other words, they argue that it is a core principle of the international legal system that custom—once formed—binds all states that have not previously objected, and that this in turn underpins

[60] See Introduction, section III; and Chapter 9, particularly at section I.*i*.

[61] See Bradley and Gulati, n. 52, 5; Charney, n. 4, 16; Dumberry, n. 3, 795; Guzman, n. 29, 166; and S. Hall, 'The Persistent Spectre: Natural Law, International Order and the Limits of Legal Positivism' (2001) 12 *European Journal of International Law* 269, 283.

[62] See, for example, Bradley and Gulati, n. 12, 205. Given that the timeliness requirement therefore runs counter to a purely voluntarist approach to customary international law, it is perhaps unsurprising, as Charlesworth, n. 30, 195 notes, to find that most of the (limited) literature supporting the subsequent objector rule has come from either the United States (in the long-standing tradition of American exceptionalism in relation to international law) and the developing world (because developing states may not have the same resources to be aware of an emerging norm or to articulate prior objections, or because new states have no opportunity to withhold their consent: on these two issues in relation to developing or new states, see, respectively, sections V and VIII).

[63] See Chapter 9, section I.*ii*.

[64] See ibid., section I.*iii*.

[65] See, particularly, Introduction, sections IV and V.

[66] Dixon, n. 6, 35, emphasis added.

the timeliness criterion. This claim is sometimes supported[67] by reference to a passage from the merits decision of the ICJ in the *North Sea Continental Shelf* cases, where the Court famously stated that:

> [C]ustomary law rules ... by their very nature, must have equal force for all members of the international community, and cannot therefore be the subject of any right of unilateral exclusion exercisable at will by any one of them in its own favour.[68]

Yet, while it almost certainly is 'a matter of principle' of international law that states cannot unilaterally opt out of established custom *ex post facto*, simply noting this fact (or pointing to the ICJ's *dicta* to this effect) seems insufficient in terms of identifying the basis for the timeliness criterion. The rationale here is rather circular: the timeliness criterion has emerged in practice because it is a principle of international law that subsequent objection is unavailing.[69] This is—it is argued herein—correct, but it does not explain *why* this principle of international law exists.

III. Pragmatic Justifications for the Timeliness Criterion and the Justifications Advanced for the Subsequent Objector Rule

i. The destabilizing implications of the subsequent objector rule

Given the unsatisfactory nature of the commonly advanced rationale(s) for the timeliness criterion, other commentators have sought to rationalize the principle of the universal binding force of established custom (and the corollary timeliness requirement) based upon pragmatic concerns, rather than on any unifying theoretical underpinning or self-justifying point of principle. In particular, it has been argued that if international law were to allow for subsequent objection—and states could therefore unilaterally exempt themselves from customary international law norms at any point—this would undermine any element of predictability in the binding force of customary international law.[70] On this basis, withdrawal from

[67] See, for example, Villiger, n. 5, 36. See, generally, Akehurst, n. 6, 25–6; P. Dumberry, 'The Last Citadel! Can a State Claim the Status of Persistent Objector to Prevent the Application of a Rule of Customary International Law in Investor-State Arbitration?' (2010) 23 *Leiden Journal of International Law* 379, 385; and Dumberry, n. 3, 780–1.

[68] *North Sea Continental Shelf* cases, merits, n. 26, para. 63. It is worth noting that this passage could potentially be read as a rejection of the persistent objector rule per se, as the ICJ did not explicitly exclude from its assertion 'unilateral exclusion' based on objection prior to the norm's crystallization. However, as Akehurst has pointed out, taken in the context of the relevant section of the judgment, it is fairly clear that the Court was referring to the universal binding force of *established* customary legal rules. The quoted passage from *North Sea Continental Shelf* acts as a further indication that subsequent objection is unacceptable; it says nothing either way on prior persistent objection. See Akehurst, n. 6, 25–6.

[69] Bradley and Gulati, n. 12, 258.

[70] See C.L. Lim and O. Elias, 'Withdrawing from Custom and the Paradox of Consensualism in International Law' (2010) 21 *Duke Journal of Comparative and International Law* 143, 148; Koskenniemi, n. 3, 444; and C. Ochoa, 'Disintegrating Customary International Law: Reactions to "Withdrawing from International Custom"' (2010) 21 *Duke Journal of Comparative and International Law* 157, 167.

customary international law obligations through subsequent objection can potentially be viewed as contrary to the rule of law, which requires a degree of certainty within any legal system.[71] Indeed, it could potentially even be argued that if states were able to 'drop' legal obligations whenever they felt like it then customary international law would, in effect, not be binding, and thus would not be *law* at all.[72]

To claim that subsequent objection would act as a death sentence for customary international law in this way would be hyperbolic, however. As has been pointed out by Bradley and Gulati, treaties allow, in many instances, for a right of withdrawal, and yet conventional international law is not viewed as being any less 'legal' because of this fact.[73] A right of withdrawal—if built into a legal system—clearly does not mean, in itself, that the legal rules that can be withdrawn from are no longer law: it is simply part of their legal fabric that they allow for withdrawal in certain circumstances.[74] Admittedly, Bradley and Gulati's analogy between subsequent objection and withdrawal provisions in treaties has its limitations.[75] So far as it goes, though, this analogy to treaty law shows that 'the law' can survive the possibility of *ex post facto* withdrawal.

Although a subsequent objector rule would not necessarily negate the entire legal content of customary international law, it is nonetheless fairly clear that subsequent objection would decrease the reliability of state compliance with customary norms: something that is, of course, already imperfect. States necessarily rely on the fact that other states will act in accordance with obligations that are binding upon them. If subsequent objection were permissible, this would undermine the reliability (such as it is) of the system of customary international law.[76] This unreliability inherent in subsequent objection would lead to co-ordination problems in the application of customary rules, which would have a destabilizing effect on international relations generally.[77]

On this basis, as a matter of policy, it is not unreasonable for states to expect others that have previously had the opportunity to object but not done so to conform to a norm once that norm has crystallized.[78] Here, states appear to view

[71] Ibid.

[72] See A.V. Lowe, *International Law* (Oxford, Oxford University Press, 2007), 55 (arguing on this basis that allowing for subsequent objection would 'make a nonsense of the international legal system'). See also F. Ingman, 'Persistent Objector—The Demise of a Hero?' (2008), unpublished Masters thesis, Lund University, http://lup.lub.lu.se/luur/download?func=downloadFile&recordOId=1558532&fileOId=1564685, 29 and 50; and Virally, n. 3, 137.

[73] Bradley and Gulati, n. 12, particularly at 258.

[74] Ibid.

[75] This is because the two sources of international law have differing functions and forms. See Roberts, n. 51, 173, 175–9, and 190. Treaty withdrawal clauses are built into individual treaties with clear rules on how and when states can withdraw from the obligations contained therein (see VCLT, n. 46, Articles 54 and 56). The direct equivalent to treaty withdrawal in the customary arena would therefore not be subsequent objection per se, but prior persistent objection by a state, where it carved out a right of withdrawal in advance. This would be a qualified persistent objection, not to the entire binding force of any given norm, but to the presumption that the norm does not allow for subsequent withdrawal.

[76] See Guzman, n. 29, 169; T. Hillier, *Sourcebook on Public International Law* (London, Cavendish Publishing, 1998), 74; Martin, n. 3, 75; Roberts, n. 51, 184; and Villiger, n. 5, 36.

[77] Roberts, n. 51, 181; and Trachtman, n. 6, 231.

[78] Mendelson, n. 6, 239.

notions of predictability and interreliance as outweighing any potential fear of majority law-making.[79] Of course, one might ask—if withdrawal from customary international law is so destabilizing in terms of the reliability of custom—why prior persistent objection is generally viewed as being acceptable.[80] The answer is that, in contrast to subsequent objection, prior persistent objection has the effect of putting other states on notice that the objector will not be bound, and this notice is necessarily provided before the norm becomes binding upon the dissenting state.[81] The notice of the withdrawal therefore occurs before other states can have developed any legitimate expectation of compliance upon which they might rely.[82]

Some writers have argued that subsequent objection might not have this destabilizing effect, because few states would actually *invoke* the subsequent objector rule; after all, few states currently make use of the (prior) persistent objector rule.[83] This is probably correct to an extent. It seems unlikely that there would be a multitude of subsequent objectors to any and all customary law norms if the option were available. Returning to Bradley and Gulati's analogy to treaty withdrawal,[84] it is rarely the case that treaties that provide for this option result in withdrawal *en masse*. Having said this, treaty withdrawal has been relatively commonplace in the UN era.[85] It has also steadily increased throughout that period,[86] which would suggest that states are increasingly willing to exercise *ex post facto* withdrawal rights.

The present author takes the view that the writers who argue that the subsequent objector rule would be rarely used underestimate the potential for withdrawal if such an *ex post facto* opt-out existed. In relation to prior persistent objection, states are faced with the political implications of self-ostracization in instances where the threat to their interests remains hypothetical; they are thus only likely to persistently object on the rare occasions when they are fundamentally opposed to the emerging norm.[87] In contrast, the cost/benefit analysis is rather different once a norm of customary international law has crystallized. Where a state is faced with a situation where that norm will, *now*, directly negatively affect its interests, it would seem much more likely that the state would be willing to take the political 'hit' of objecting if it knew that this would allow it

[79] On states' fear of majority law-making in international law, see Chapter 9, section V.*i*.

[80] Bradley and Gulati, n.12, 205.

[81] See Fitzmaurice, n. 3, 26 (framing this point in the context of the 'consent theory').

[82] Abasheikh, n. 6, 46.

[83] See, for example, Estreicher, n. 10, 58 and 61–3; and Quince, n. 5, 80.

[84] Bradley and Gulati, n. 12, 246.

[85] Based on his database of treaty withdrawals (compiled from various treaty offices of international organizations in 2005), Helfer identified a total of 1,547 withdrawals from treaties for the period 1945–2004: L.R. Helfer, 'Exiting Treaties' (2005) 91 *Virginia Law Review* 1579, 1602. Interestingly, Bradley and Gulati reference this figure to indicate the ubiquity of withdrawal within the international legal system: Bradley and Gulati, n. 12, 252. This reference to the ubiquitous nature of such withdrawals may be accurate, but that does not mean that this position is desirable.

[86] Helfer, n. 85, 1602–3.

[87] See Byers, n. 55, 180; Stein, n. 3, 468; and P. Weil, 'Le droit international en quête de son identité—Cours général de droit international public' (1992-VI) 237 *Recueil des cours* 9, 195.

to gain exemption and avoid the immediate concrete consequences of compliance.[88] The timeliness criterion ultimately helps to limit the use of the persistent objector rule, and restricts it to only instances where 'going with the flow' is simply not an option for the dissenter. This is a policy choice: it prioritizes the maximization of conformity and predictability within customary international law over absolute state voluntarism.

It was argued in Chapters 4[89] and 5[90] that a factor underpinning the requirements of persistence and consistency is that it is desirable from a policy perspective to curtail the 'frivolous' use of the persistent objector rule, because exceptions to the general binding force of customary international law can be problematic in terms of the effectiveness and coherent development of international legal norms.[91] In law, exceptions should—and generally will—be interpreted narrowly.[92] Just as with the persistence and consistency criteria, then, a requirement of timeliness helps to guard against the opportunistic or frivolous use of the persistent objector rule.[93] The political implications of any state seeking to exempt itself from otherwise universal obligations are likely to be high. A requirement of prior objection forces a dissenting state to weigh the negative political implications of its objections against the *potential* negative implications of a forming norm. This helps to ensure that the objector truly wishes to reject the emerging rule per se, rather than because its immediate interests are threatened.[94] Longstanding objection *in abstracto* prior to crystallization therefore increases the credibility of the state's desire to gain exempt status.[95]

ii. The implications of the subsequent objector rule for the development of legal norms

Allowing for exit through subsequent objection could decrease the likelihood of states engaging with the development of customary international law, and thus

[88] Fon and Parisi, n. 3, 11 and 27–8. Even Bradley and Gulati note that 'subsequent opt out rights will be used more often than the persistent objector doctrine'. See Bradley and Gulati, n. 52, 26.

[89] See Chapter 4, section II, particularly at n. 41–n. 45 and accompanying text.

[90] See Chapter 5, section II, particularly at n. 53–n. 56 and accompanying text.

[91] See, generally, Charney, n. 6; and A. Mills, *The Confluence of Public and Private International Law: Justice, Pluralism, and Subsidiarity in the International Constitutional Ordering of Private Law* (Cambridge, Cambridge University Press, 2009), 98.

[92] G. Boas, *Public International Law: Contemporary Principles and Perspectives* (Cheltenham, Edward Elgar, 2012), 94–5.

[93] A.T. Guzman, *How International Law Works: A Rational Choice Theory* (Oxford, Oxford University Press, 2008), 198–9; Guzman, n. 29, 169; Quince, n. 5, 80; and Roberts, n. 51, 174 and 185.

[94] Fon and Parisi, n. 3, 11 and 27–8; Guzman, n. 29, 169; and Quince, n. 5, 80.

[95] A. Abass, *Complete International Law: Text, Cases, and Materials* (Oxford, Oxford University Press, 2nd edn, 2014), 47; Kaczorowska, n. 3, 41; and Steinfeld, n. 3, 1647. It has been argued, in contrast, that this is a negative feature of the persistent objector rule, justifying a move to the subsequent objector rule, which would allow states to withdraw without such high political costs. See Bradley and Gulati, n. 52, 24. This ultimately comes down to a policy choice, in terms of the appropriate balance between autonomy and universalism.

lessen the possibility of new custom emerging.[96] This would be of particular concern in relation to the development of 'fundamental' value-based norms. Take, for example, a developing customary obligation to refrain from the use of, and to destroy stockpiles of, a particular weapon.[97] Subsequent objection would make the development of a customary norm of this type far less likely: why would a state commit to such reciprocal obligations when other states could later simply renege?[98]

It has been argued that this problem—of subsequent objection stalling the development of custom, especially in relation to 'fundamental' norms—might be overstated, in that key issues of mutual benefit, such as arms control or environmental protection, are commonly dealt with by treaty (for the very reason that the comparative uncertainty of custom makes it an unsuitable method for ensuring widespread compliance).[99] This is true to an extent, but custom still has a role to play in relation to the regulation of norms involving these sorts of universal issues. For example, we have already seen in previous chapters[100] that not all states are parties to the Ottawa Convention on antipersonnel landmines (APLMs),[101] but there are strong indications that an equivalent customary ban is evolving, if it has not already evolved.[102] This prohibition, of course, catches (or will catch) any remaining dissident states that have not already gained exemption through prior persistent objection, in relation to a matter of crucial and universal importance.[103]

Supporters of the subsequent objector rule have dismissed this concern, and have argued instead, in complete contrast, that allowing for subsequent objection would *facilitate* norm creation within customary international law. This is on the

[96] Roberts, n. 51, 174.

[97] For example, Bradley and Gulati envisage a customary international law rule that 'requires all nations to scuttle their biological weapons' to highlight this issue, although they ultimately go on to dismiss this concern. See Bradley and Gulati, n. 12, 255–6.

[98] Fon and Parisi, n. 3, 27 (although they further argue that subsequent objection, if tightly controlled, can also help to ensure a degree of reciprocity).

[99] Bradley and Gulati, n. 12, 255–6.

[100] See Chapter 3, n. 46–n. 50 and accompanying text; and Chapter 5, n. 68–n. 83 and accompanying text.

[101] Convention on the Prohibition of the Use, Stockpiling, Production and Transfer of Anti-Personnel Mines and on their Destruction (Ottawa Convention), 18 September 1997, 2056 UNTS 35597.

[102] See J.M. Beier, 'Siting Indiscriminacy: India and the Global Movement to Ban Landmines' (2002) 8 *Global Governance* 305, 307–8; S. Benesch, G. McGrory, C. Rodriguez, and R. Sloane, 'International Customary Law and Antipersonnel Landmines: Emergence of a New Customary Norm' (1999), Allard K. Lowenstein International Human Rights Clinic, Yale Law School, Landmine Monitor, http://lm.icbl.org/index.php/publications/display?url=lm/1999/appendices/custom_law.html; and Price, n. 3, 106–7.

[103] In critique of the argument that allowing for subsequent objection could lessen the possibility of new custom emerging in 'fundamental' areas, it has been noted that certain foundational law treaties, such as the Nuclear Non-Proliferation Treaty, provide for withdrawals. See Bradley and Gulati, n. 52, 11. However, just because there are treaties that allow for withdrawal in relation to such norms does not make subsequent withdrawal *desirable* in the context of inter-relational norms of mutual reliance: this fact in no way justifies the argument that the same option should be available in the context of custom. See D.A. Koplow, 'ASAT-isfaction: Customary International Law

basis that states would be more willing to engage in practice and provide *opinio juris* in support of emerging norms with which they may otherwise refrain from engaging, if they were safe in the knowledge that they could escape the norm's clutches if it later turned out that its application was contrary to the their interests.[104] The present author takes the opposite view, as outlined in the previous two paragraphs, although it must be admitted that either contention is speculative, given that the subsequent objector rule does not exist. In any event, even if it is correct that subsequent objection would in fact increase the likelihood of norms of customary international law developing, one might ask whether it would really benefit the system to have lots more customary rules, any and all of which states could abandon as it suited them. In this writer's view, having a smaller number of customary rules that truly bind is significantly preferable to having a larger number that do not.

iii. The implications of the subsequent objector rule for norm violation

Another argument made by the supporters of the subsequent objector rule relates to the fact that, at present, a state has no option but to either comply with a crystallized norm of customary international law or violate it (unless, that is, it has already gained persistent objector status). In this context, it has been argued, subsequent objection may act to lessen the number of violations of customary international law by providing states with the alternative of lawful opt-out.[105] Beyond the simple fact that minimizing the number of violations of the law sounds intuitively appealing,[106] it is clear that there are various systematic costs to norm violation, as well as reputational damage to the violator.[107] In particular, supporters of the subsequent objector rule have argued that subsequent objection would necessarily be transparent, whereas violation is often secretive or concealed.[108]

However, while allowing for subsequent objection would likely lessen the number of violations of the law by non-conformist states that will not be deterred, in the view of the present author, states are more likely to walk away from a customary law obligation if they are legally entitled to do so than they would be if such an action constituted a violation of the law. There are obviously political and reputational disadvantages to both subsequent objection and violation,[109] but a breach of *the law* is inevitably rather more disadvantageous in this regard (with, of course, added legal implications to boot).

and the Regulation of Anti-Satellite Weapons' (2008–9) 30 *Michigan Journal of International Law* 1187, 1267 (noting the importance of customary international law in protecting against unilateral withdrawals from arms control treaties).

[104] Estreicher, n. 10, 61–2; and Guzman, n. 29, 166.

[105] Bradley and Gulati, n. 52, 6.

[106] Guzman, n. 29, 167–8 and 170.

[107] See Chapter 9, section VI.*ii*.

[108] Bradley and Gulati, n. 52, 6.

[109] Bradley and Gulati, n. 12, 261.

The argument that violations are commonly 'secretive' hardly stands up to scrutiny either: states may try to conceal their breaches of the law, but in the modern age of global media and twenty-four-hour reporting, they are rarely likely to succeed in backing away from their international obligations unnoticed. Ultimately, despite the undeniable desirability of reducing norm violation, it is again preferable to have a system where the law is occasionally violated (even if 'secretly'), rather than a system with no violations, but lots of lawful, transparent withdrawals.

iv. Proposed safeguards for subsequent objection

It was argued in the previous subsection that the subsequent objector rule would reduce certainty within customary international law-making. Indeed, it is further worth noting that those writers who support the subsequent objector rule have generally not argued that subsequent objection needs to be either persistent[110] or consistent,[111] as would be the case with prior persistent objection.[112] This is, perhaps, because they support the existence of the subsequent objector rule on the basis that the timeliness requirement is unnecessary from a voluntarist starting point.[113] The persistence[114] and consistency[115] criteria similarly cannot be justified by reference to voluntarism, of course, meaning that these requirements are also dispensed with by those supporting subsequent objection. Yet, like timeliness, persistence and consistency have pragmatic systematic benefits, and can be justified by the need to impose a degree of stability and predictability to the process of persistent objection.[116] It would seem that if subsequent objection were permitted—at least in the way that its supporters tend to outline it—the objecting state would be free, not only from the timeliness requirement, but also from the other criteria for persistent objection (further adding to the destabilizing effects of the subsequent objector rule).

Having said this, while they generally do not see persistence or consistency as being necessary in the context of the subsequent objector rule, some supporters of subsequent objection have accepted that there may indeed be destabilizing risks associated with opportunistic objection *ex post facto*. With this in mind, it has been argued by some of those who oppose the timeliness requirement that there would need to be 'safeguards' built into any process of subsequent objection (although these are of a different form to the current persistence or consistency criteria).[117] For example, it has been suggested that it would be necessary to require a period of notice, from the point when the state first subsequently

[110] See, generally, Chapter 4. [111] See, generally, Chapter 5.
[112] See, for example, Bradley and Gulati, n. 12.
[113] Again, see ibid. as a good example of this.
[114] See Chapter 4, n. 37–n. 40 and accompanying text.
[115] See Chapter 5, n. 52 and accompanying text.
[116] See, respectively, Chapter 4, section II; and Chapter 5, section II.
[117] See, for example, Helfer, n. 29, 66.

objected, before it actually gained exemption.[118] Similarly, it has been suggested that a state could only subsequently object in the abstract: what has been called 'prospective withdrawal'.[119] In other words, the dissenting state would not be able to subsequently object when confronted with a particular set of circumstances where exemption would immediately benefit it. Instead, it would be limited to objecting when the norm in question was not at issue.

Such safeguards would admittedly provide a higher degree of certainty than a blanket right of subsequent objection and would allow other states to rely on the binding force of a crystallized custom at least in relation to any particular dispute: once the dispute was underway, the objector would be 'locked in'. However, the safeguards proposed by supporters of subsequent objection would be extremely difficult to define and apply in practice.[120] The chances of states agreeing upon an appropriate notice period for subsequent objection from customary international law, for example, would seem low (given the nebulous manner in which it evolves).[121] It is not the case that each customary rule is negotiated and agreed in the manner of a treaty, and therefore—at best—states might be able to agree a single arbitrary notice period applicable to all customary norms (an unlikely but possible scenario).[122] It would be impossible to try to agree such a notice-of-withdrawal period for individual customary norms, or even related groups of customary norms. The differing *nature* of different customary norms would mean that what might be an appropriate notice period for one rule would be entirely inappropriate for another.[123]

Similarly, it would also be extremely difficult to determine when a state was attempting to withdraw because of a particular immediate benefit—that is, when it was trying to avoid meeting its obligations in a specific instance—and when it was objecting in the abstract because of a general change in its attitude to the customary rule. What about periods where a dispute between states was 'on the horizon'? Would the savvy dissenter be able to pull out of a customary law obligation just before there was an 'actual' dispute? There is, of course, no such problem with prior persistent objection, because the state can necessarily *only* be objecting in the abstract.

v. Prioritizing pragmatism over voluntarism

The list of reasons for allowing subsequent objection—for those that support it[124]—is usually topped by the argument that the subsequent objector rule would

[118] Bradley and Gulati, n. 12, 258–9; Estreicher, n. 10, 62; Helfer, n. 29, 79; and Swaine, n. 3, 207.

[119] Bradley and Gulati, n. 12, 258; and Swaine, n. 3, 207.

[120] R. Brewster 'Withdrawing from Custom: Choosing between Default Rules' (2010) 21 *Duke Journal of Comparative and International Law* 47, 50–3. This is noted even by those who advocate such an approach: see Helfer, n. 29, 74.

[121] Estreicher, n. 10, 59.

[122] See, for example, Helfer, n. 29, 79 (arbitrarily setting the timeframe for the required notice period at 'at least one year notice to every other nation').

[123] Trachtman, n. 6, 231.

[124] See, for example, writers cited at n. 29.

protect state autonomy; indeed, given the fiction of 'tacit consent' in relation to customary international law-making,[125] it can be seen as the *only* way of truly protecting state sovereignty in this context.[126] This is essentially correct, but the operation of the persistent objector rule in fact represents a pragmatic balancing act between the notions of sovereign supremacy and legal universalism.[127] In practice, and in the majority of doctrine, the need for stability and consistency in customary international law takes precedence over absolute voluntarism.

There are credible policy arguments in favour of allowing for subsequent objection, including, of course, a desire to protect the role of state consent in relation to the binding force of customary international law.[128] The countervailing policy goals of predictability, certainty, and coherence ultimately outweigh the importance of absolute state autonomy, however. This is implicitly recognized in practice: as was noted in section I.*ii*, the timeliness requirement can be identified in the state usage of the persistent objector rule; a general right of subsequent objection cannot. There remain, however, significant issues in relation to actually *applying* the timeliness criterion. These issues will be considered in the following sections.

IV. The Timeline of a Customary Norm's Development

i. Conceptualizing the timeline for new norms of customary international law

The orthodox understanding that objection must occur prior to crystallization relates the process of persistent objection to 'a temporal arc of a given rule [of customary international law]'.[129] The timeliness requirement is therefore based on an assumption that all customary international law norms have a discernible timeline (or 'arc') of development.[130] Objection must occur during a certain 'window' along that timeline, between two points: the point of the norm's initial inception and the point of its crystallization into binding law.

Point *a* on *Figure 6.1* represents the point along the timeline at which a new custom begins to form, and point *b* is the point at which it becomes binding customary international law (i.e. the point of crystallization). The shaded area of *Figure 6.1* is, therefore, the 'window' during which a customary norm is in its nebulous, embryonic form.[131] It is in this window that dissenting states must persistently and consistently object.

[125] See Chapter 9, section I.*iii*, particularly at n. 64–n. 83 and accompanying text.

[126] For discussion of the limitations of the persistent objector rule itself in ensuring state autonomy in this regard, see ibid., section I.*ii*.

[127] See, particularly, Chapter 9, section V.*ii*.

[128] Guzman, n. 29, 166; Quince, n. 5, 80–1.

[129] Kritsiotis, n. 17, 130.

[130] As Swaine phrases this, the persistent objector rule assumes an inherent 'evolutionary capacity' on the part of customary international law formation. See Swaine, n. 3, 213, footnote 28.

[131] Meijers, n. 57, 13 (referring to this as 'the *first stage* of creation of customary law, the stage in which the rule takes shape, but in which it does not yet take on legal character'; emphasis added).

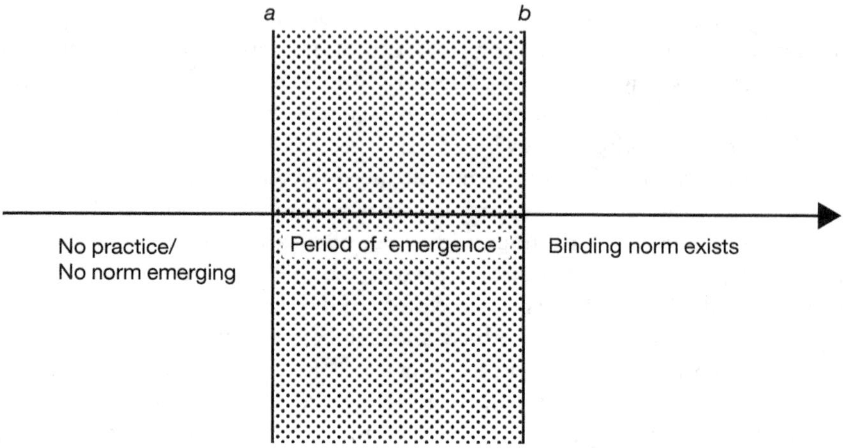

Figure 6.1 The timeline of a norm of customary international law

This shaded 'zone' represents a sort of strange normative limbo, where the emerging custom is neither one thing nor another.[132] The normative status of an emerging custom existing in this zone is difficult to quantify. As Kritsiotis notes, such an emerging norm cannot have the same status as a binding custom: it cannot directly bind states as a matter of law. Otherwise there would be no distinction between an emerging and a crystallized custom at all.[133] As such, during the period of 'emergence', customary practice is necessarily 'pre-legal'.[134] Its identification is 'a descriptive rather than a normative device'.[135] The status of 'emergence' does not have legal implications in itself for a state, other than to indicate that a process has begun (a process that may or may not ultimately be completed). Thus, 'emergence' is merely the indicator of *potential* normative change.[136]

This means, of course, that during the emergence of a new norm (that is, at any position between points *a* and *b* on *Figure 6.1*), there is no difference in legal status for an objecting state and a non-objecting state. Neither is bound, because an emerging norm is, *ipso facto*, not yet a binding norm of customary international law. The practice of the objector state during a norm's genesis is of legal

[132] See A. D'Amato, 'International Soft Law, Hard Law, and Coherence', Northwestern Public Law and Legal Theory Series, No. 08-01, 1 March 2008, *Social Science Research Network*, http://papers.ssrn.com/sol3/papers.cfm?abstract_id=1103915, 14 (noting that '[t]here is an Alice-in-Wonderland quality here of rules being in a state of suspended animation while awaiting news of their own birth or deletion', although then later arguing, at 17, that in fact 'there is no process of suspended animation, no lawless interval').

[133] Kritsiotis, n. 17, 131–2, including at footnote 44. See also T. Christiano, 'The Legitimacy of International Institutions' in A. Marmor (ed.), *The Routledge Companion to the Philosophy of Law* (Abingdon, Routledge, 2012), 380, 387.

[134] Elias, n. 16, 50.

[135] Kritsiotis, n. 17, 132, footnote 44.

[136] Ibid. (describing this status as '[a] harbinger of future normative change').

relevance only if and once the norm crystallizes.[137] However, the shaded zone of emergence nonetheless has legal *implications*: we know that the descriptive device of 'emergence' helps 'to demarcate when the possibilities of persistent objection must be realized, seized and acted upon'.[138] It does not have normative weight in and of itself,[139] but it delimitates a relevant period of a process leading to binding obligations.

The fact that a state's actions (or lack thereof) during a pre-legal stage will have direct legal implications once crystallization occurs seems somewhat counterintuitive on initial inspection.[140] However, the same is also true of the process of customary international law formation in general; the actions/silence of a state before it is bound are relevant to subsequent normative change (the creation, or not, of a new or amended customary international law), with direct legal implications for the state concerned. International law thus constantly derives legal implications from the pre-legal actions of states.

Another way at looking at the timeline for persistent objection, deriving from the application of rational choice theory,[141] is to view this as a two-stage decision-making process, with options at each stage (as represented by *Figure 6.2*).[142] The decision made at *Stage 1* dictates the available options for a state at *Stage 2*.[143]

ii. The problem of identifying the key points on the timeline

While the timeline of the persistent objector rule can be identified relatively easily in theory, a crucial issue for the operation of the rule in practice—given that objection must occur during the period of emergence—is determining exactly when 'emerging' status begins and when it ends: states must object 'dès le moment initial

[137] Ibid., 131–2; Elias, n. 16, 50.

[138] Kritsiotis, n. 17, 131.

[139] Having said this, Kritsiotis tentatively suggests that an embryonic norm may possess a status somewhat akin to 'soft law': ibid., 132, footnote 44. This is presumably on the basis that while an emerging custom does not bind the state, it may well *influence* state conduct, either in terms of objection or contribution to the norm's development (although Kritsiotis is not entirely explicit on this point). In any event, his analogy to soft law is useful, but it perhaps goes too far, in that soft law is more commonly seen as a guideline for conduct, *agreed* by states both in terms of its content and in terms of the fact that it is not binding. Emerging custom, in contrast, is defined by the fact that there has not yet been any agreement, and its non-binding nature is a *consequence* of that very lack of agreement.

[140] Elias, n. 16, 50 (seemingly somewhat disturbed by this reasoning, at least implicitly).

[141] A number of scholars have considered the persistent objector rule from a rational choice perspective, see, for example, Guzman, n. 29, 166–71; Guzman, n. 93, 187–8 and 197–9; Fon and Parisi, n. 3, 7–11; Kontorovich, n. 3, 874–5 and 910–11; G. Norman and J.P. Trachtman, 'The Customary International Law Game' (2005) 99 *American Journal of International Law* 541, 569; and N. Petersen, 'The Role of Consent and Uncertainty in the Formation of Customary International Law' (2011) *Reprints of the Max Planck Institute for Research on Collective Goods*, http://www.coll.mpg.de/pdf_dat/2011_04online.pdf, 5–10. See Chapter 9, particularly at section V.*i*, for further discussion.

[142] *Figure 6.2* is developed from the application of game theory to the process of persistent objection by Trachtman (although Trachtman himself does not use a visual representation of this concept): Trachtman, n. 6, particularly at 224.

[143] Ibid.

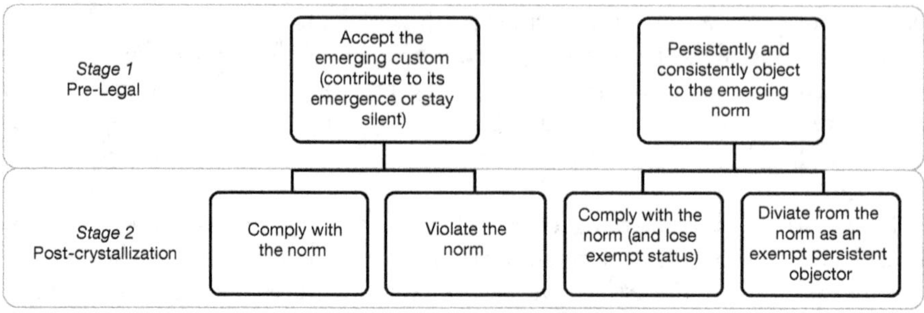

Figure 6.2 The decision-making stages of customary international law formation

de formation de la coutume (mais quand est-ce qu'on peut fixer ce moment?)'.[144] In relation to *Figure 6.2*, it may be said that there is significant difficulty in determining both when *Stage 1* begins and when *Stage 1* ends/*Stage 2* begins. Or, to frame this in reference to *Figure 6.1*, the issue is identifying points *a* and *b* along the norm's timeline. It is a simple enough matter to conclude that states must object between points *a* and *b*, but '[t]hese markings on [the rule's timeline]—at the points of conception and crystallization of the aforementioned rule—might appear problematic to say the least and ... provoke more questions than they are able to answer'.[145]

The point of crystallization for a norm of customary international law is extremely difficult to identify with any certainty.[146] There is no agreement in doctrine as to how much state practice is necessary for any given custom to crystallize.[147] Indeed, beyond the 'amount' of practice, it is also unclear what 'quality' of state practice is necessary for crystallization, in terms of the required duration of the practice, how widespread the practice needs to be within the international community, and how consistent states need to have been in following it.[148] This issue is not a problem that is specific to the operation of the

[144] B. Conforti, 'Cours général de droit international public' (1988-V) 212 *Recueil des cours* 13, 74. See also Kaczorowska, n. 3, 41; and M. Ragazzi, *The Concept of International Obligations* Erga Omnes (Oxford, Clarendon Press, 1997), 64.

[145] Kritsiotis, n. 17, 131. See also Helfer, n. 29, 70.

[146] See, for example, ILA Final Report, n. 3, generally, but particularly at 2; A. Boyle and C. Chinkin, *The Making of International Law* (Oxford, Oxford University Press, 2007), 21; A.T. Guzman and T.L. Meyer, 'Customary International Law in the 21st Century' in R.A. Miller and R.M. Bratspies (eds), *Progress in International Law* (Leiden, Martinus Nijhoff, 2008), 197, 197–200; J. Kammerhofer, 'Uncertainty in the Formal Sources of International Law: Customary International Law and Some of its Problems' (2004) 15 *European Journal of International Law* 523; J.O. McGinnis, 'The Comparative Disadvantage of Customary International Law' (2006) 30 *Harvard Journal of Law and Public Policy* 7, 10; and J.P. Trachtman, 'The Obsolescence of Customary International Law' (21 November 2014), *Social Science Research Network*, http://papers.ssrn.com/sol3/papers.cfm?abstract_id=2512757, 20 and 31.

[147] See Boas, n. 92, 79; and Lepard, n. 54, 35.

[148] See, for example, *North Sea Continental Shelf* cases, merits, n. 26, dissenting opinion of Judge Tanaka, 175 ('The repetition, the number of examples of State practice, the duration of time required for the generation of customary law cannot be mathematically and uniformly decided. Each fact requires to be evaluated relatively according to the different occasions and circumstances').

persistent objector rule, but relates to customary international law formation per se.[149] In any instance where a state seeks to rely on a binding customary norm, it faces the difficulty of establishing that the norm exists. The application of customary international law is, quite simply, an uncertain business. Yet it is worth remembering that this inherent indeterminacy is something that, in many respects, states *like*: because it allows scope for flexibility and context-appropriate norm application.[150]

Nonetheless, the difficulty in identifying when a custom crystallizes poses particular problems for the operation of the persistent objector rule, because it represents the 'deadline' for objection (point *b* on the *Figure 6.1* timeline).[151] If it is impossible to say for sure when this deadline is reached, how can we know that a state has objected in time? Indeed, one might even argue that it is inherently illogical to expect states to meet a deadline that cannot be ascertained.

The issue of identifying the point of crystallization in the context of the persistent objector rule can be illustrated by the *North Sea Continental Shelf* cases. The FRD had certainly objected with a degree of persistence to the any possible customary principle of equidistance in relation to the delimitation of the continental shelf. However, the majority of the ICJ did not engage with the question of whether the FRD was an exempt persistent objector to such a customary principle. This was on the basis, inter alia, that the Court determined that there was insufficient evidence of *opinio juris* supporting the existence of this principle in customary international law in the first place, meaning that the question of whether the FRD was a persistent objector was moot.[152] Some of the judges were also clear that no such custom had crystallized in their individual opinions.[153] However, both Judge Lachs and Judge ad hoc Sørensen argued, in contrast, that the custom had formed, and that the FRD was bound by this custom because it was a subsequent (rather than a persistent) objector.[154] For these judges, not only had the custom crystallized, but the state that had clearly objected to this did so *after* the point of crystallization. Even within the ICJ, then, the point of crystallization—and the consequent implications for an objecting state—could not be agreed upon.

[149] Steinfeld, n. 3, 1647, particularly at footnote 39.

[150] See, generally, D.J. Bederman, *Custom as a Source of Law* (Cambridge, Cambridge University Press, 2010), 162–3; and K.W. Abbott and D. Snidal, 'Hard and Soft Law in International Governance' (2000) 54 *International Organization* 421 (arguing in detail that states prefer flexibility and uncertainty in relation to 'soft law', rather than 'customary international law' per se, although explicitly noting, at 425, footnote 19, that their analysis applies equally to customary international law). *Cf.* Guzman, n. 93, 135–8.

[151] Elias, n. 3, 284.

[152] *North Sea Continental Shelf* cases, merits, n. 26, para. 78.

[153] Ibid., separate opinion of Judge Ammoun, para. 31; and separate opinion of Judge Padilla Nervo, paras. 97–8.

[154] See *North Sea Continental Shelf* cases, merits, n. 26, dissenting opinion of Judge Lachs, 232 (arguing that '[*s*]*ubsequent changes in its attitude … can have no legal effect* … [the FRD's] situation cannot be assimilated with that of a country which "has always opposed any attempt to apply" a rule [as per *Fisheries*]'; emphasis added); and dissenting opinion of Judge ad hoc Sørensen, 248 (contending that the FRD had failed to object '[a]t a decisive stage of th[e] *formative* process'; emphasis added).

The concern about identifying the point of crystallization has preoccupied much of the literature concerning the persistent objector rule.[155] For example, in his article rejecting the existence of the persistent objector rule, Barsalou argued that:

> Le processus de création des normes coutumières est un processus amorphe et atone. En d'autres termes, tant que la règle n'est pas formellement identifiée par les membres de la société internationale, nul ne peut identifier le moment de cristallization de la norme coutumière.[156]

Yet, despite this concern being raised regularly in the literature, there has been very little engagement with the problem in the context of persistent objection. A rare example, however, is a 1989 article by McClane, where the author attempted to shed some light on the exact time at which a persistent objector was required to persistently object.[157] As part of his analysis, McClane engaged with the question of when 'crystallization' took place.[158] Yet despite adopting a relatively unique approach of ascribing more importance to the *acquiescence* of other states to the norm during its formative period than most writers,[159] McClane ultimately concluded that 'the point after which an objection would be "subsequent" is necessarily defined by the potency of the elements comprising the norm'.[160] In other words, he essentially accepted the orthodox context-specific approach, where various factors—the generality, duration, and consistency of the practice, coupled with state support (and, particularly importantly in his model, acquiescence)—together determine the point of crystallization in a necessarily unquantifiable combination.

The fact remains that the exact point of crystallization of any given customary international law norm is going to be almost impossible to identify, and this inevitably makes the persistent objector rule more difficult to apply. It is worth remembering, however, that the inherent uncertainty of custom will often have its benefits for the dissenting state. For example, we saw in Chapter 3 that the uncertainty surrounding an arguable customary prohibition on APLMs has meant that Egypt has been able to maintain exempt status simply by arguing—quite credibly—that there is no such customary law ban at all.[161] This is a significantly less politically damaging stance to take for an objector than an explicit position of exemption, and one that can be maintained so long as any genuine doubt remains

[155] See Bradley and Gulati, n. 12, 210 and 243; Bradley and Gulati, n. 52, 24; Charney, n. 6, 537–8; D.A. Colson, 'How Persistent Must the Persistent Objector Be?' (1986) 61 *Washington Law Review* 957, 958; Elias, n. 16, 38, 40, and 50; Guldahl, n. 5, 60; Guzman, n. 29, 170–1, footnote 245; H. Lau, 'Rethinking the Persistent Objector Doctrine in International Human Rights Law' (2005–6) 6 *Chicago Journal of International Law* 496, 506; Lim and Elias, n. 70, 148; McClane, n. 6, in general, but particularly at 11–12; Quince, n. 5, 40, 62, and 75–6; and Steinfeld, n. 3, 1645–7 and 1652.

[156] O. Barsalou, 'La doctrine de l'objecteur persistant en droit international public' (2006) 19 *Revue québécoise de droit international* 1, 9.

[157] McClane, n. 6.

[158] Ibid., particularly at 12–16.

[159] Ibid., 12–15.

[160] Ibid., 16.

[161] See Chapter 3, n. 44–n. 50 and accompanying text.

as to the custom's crystallization. Moreover, if this rejection of the binding status of the norm per se is persistently and consistently maintained, it can in itself act as 'objection' if the point is reached where it is no longer possible to argue that the norm has failed to crystallize (meaning that the dissenter can then gain exemption).[162]

It is also important to note that the problem of identifying when a customary international law norm crystallizes might be somewhat exaggerated. Firstly, it has been argued that the rise of international adjudicative decisions has made it much easier to identify the 'birth' of a new custom by providing an authoritative statement to that effect.[163] This may perhaps go a little too far, in that it is not as though all avowed customary rules are reviewed by an adjudicative body, and one might well question how 'authoritative' any particular finding of crystallization by an adjudicative body is in any event. It also certainly cannot be said that a court decision crystallizes a new custom in itself.[164] However, recognition of a norm's crystallization by a court or tribunal provides a strong presumption that this has previously occurred.[165]

Secondly, it is worth recalling that the burden of establishing the applicability of customary international law lies with the state seeking to rely upon it.[166] Therefore, if it is unclear whether any given custom has crystallized, then the preponderance of evidence would suggest that it has not.[167] Of course, things are not quite this simple, in that there need not be universal agreement for a custom to have crystallized: but there does need to be *general* agreement.[168] If there remains any significant uncertainty as to whether the norm has formed, it is more likely than not that the objector will still have at least some time left to object.

In addition to identifying the point of crystallization, there exists the problem of determining when a custom *begins* to emerge (i.e. identifying point *a* on the *Figure 6.1* timeline). States will obviously be unlikely to object prior to this point, as there will be no practice to object to. It is, therefore, valuable to gain some sense of when the customary formation process begins. Interestingly, while writers have regularly noted the problem of identifying the crystallization point in relation to the persistent objector rule, very few have noted that the point at which a rule begins to emerge is similarly difficult to identify.[169] The picture in

162 See, generally, ibid., section II.

163 See Lau, n. 155, 506; and Quince, n. 5, 76.

164 N. Arajärvi, *The Changing Nature of Customary International Law: Methods of Interpreting the Concept of Custom in International Criminal Tribunals* (Abingdon, Routledge, 2014), 17.

165 See ibid.; and Lau, n. 155, 506.

166 See *Case Concerning Rights of Nationals of the United States of America in Morocco* (*France v United States*), merits, 1952 ICJ Rep. 176, 200; and *Asylum*, merits, n. 18, 276–7 (specifically in relation to regional custom).

167 See *Nahimana* et al. *v Prosecutor*, judgment, 2007, ICTR, Case No. ICTR-99-52-A, partly dissenting opinion of Judge Meron, para. 5 (if 'a consensus among states has not crystallized, *there is clearly no norm* under customary international law'; emphasis added).

168 See, for example, *North Sea Continental Shelf* cases, merits, n. 26, para. 74 ('State practice … should have been both extensive and *virtually* uniform'; emphasis added).

169 Although see ILA Final Report, n. 3, 30; McClane, n. 6, particularly at 11 and 20; and Quince, n. 5, 75–6.

relation to the latter threshold is perhaps even murkier than is the case in relation to the former.[170] In attempting to ascertain the point of crystallization there is at least a perceptible normative shift from the pre-legal to the legal (even if the exact moment of that shift is impossible to pin down); in the context of determining the point at which emergence begins there is simply a transition from one pre-legal state to another. International lawyers have developed at least some degree of intuitive sense as to when customary international law crystallizes, as this has direct legal implications. In contrast, the change from 'pre-emergence' to 'the period of emergence' is, as has been noted, merely descriptive of a transition into a period of *potential* normative change: understandably, international lawyers pay far less attention to that point of transition.

In an attempt to provide some degree of predictability to the point at which objection can begin, McClane suggested in his 1989 article that this should be pinpointed as being after the formative practice has become 'notorious for a period of time'.[171] By this, McClane means that the practice has been of a sufficient amount, and over a sufficient duration, to become particularly 'visible' to other states as being potentially norm-constituting. Unfortunately, McClane's analysis simply replaces one set of uncertainties with another: he does not define the required 'period of time' before a norm becomes 'notorious', nor does he define what the threshold of 'notoriety' is in any practical sense. Admittedly, his approach probably reflects the point at which states are, in most cases, *likely* to start objecting. The more practice that has occurred, the more likely they are to be aware of the possible custom, and thus realize that objection may be necessary.

However, in terms of defining the 'start date' for objection, McClane's approach overly complicates matters. There is, after all, no restriction on a persistent objector objecting *too early*. This probably explains why fewer writers have expressed concern about the starting point for objection than they have about its end date: the former may be harder to ascertain, but it is ultimately rather less crucial for the rule's operation. In contrast to McClane, therefore, the present author would suggest that the appropriate point at which to hold that norm-gestation begins for the purposes of persistent objection is simply when *any* practice occurs on the part of a state (or states) that could potentially constitute the beginning of the creation of a new norm in the future should other states follow the practitioner's lead. Savvy states can start objecting from the very first signs of change. Most will likely object rather later in the period of 'emergence', but there is no reason to limit the 'start line' to a later point at which the practice has become especially notorious.

Indeed, it may well be of benefit to the objector to start objecting as soon as possible. 'Early' objections might help to create a presumption in the eyes of other states, from the outset, that the dissenting state will become a persistent objector, solidifying this position if the objector feels that it needs to utilize the rule further down the road. Objecting from the earliest stages of the development of

[170] *Contra* ibid. (arguing the opposite: that it is more difficult to determine when a custom crystallizes than when it begins to gestate. This is surely incorrect, for the reasons given in the main text).

[171] McClane, n. 6, 20.

a customary norm also will give the objector the maximum amount of time for it to then continue to repeatedly object prior to crystallization, which increases the likelihood of it complying with the persistence criterion.[172]

One might note, as an example of particularly 'early' objection, the position taken by the United States right from the first international discussions concerning the 'precautionary principle' in international environmental law. As was discussed in Chapter 4, there exists a debate as to whether a binding customary 'precautionary principle' has yet crystallized in international environmental law, but there is undoubtedly evidence of at least an emerging norm of environmental precaution apparent in state practice.[173] It was argued in Chapter 4 that Canada's single objection to this possible customary principle in the *Meat and Meat Products* (*Hormones*)[174] WTO Appellate Body decision was insufficient for it to gain exemption, on the basis that this did not fulfil the persistence requirement.[175] In contrast to Canada, the United States *has* persistently and consistently rejected the existence of a precautionary principle under customary international environmental law. Of pertinence here is the fact that the United States began lodging objections right at the very beginning of the 'period of emergence' of the precautionary principle in the international context.

Despite some manifestations of limited versions of the precautionary principle in the late-1980s,[176] the 1990 Bergen Ministerial Declaration on Sustainable Development[177] was the first international instrument to treat the principle as one that might have general application in the international context.[178] By 1991 a few commentators had begun to cautiously talk of the beginnings of 'a rise to a developing consensus' in state practice,[179] but it was not until 1992 and Article 15 of the Rio Declaration[180] that there was any significant recognition of a trend towards the adoption of this principle at the international level.[181] The United States had already repeatedly objected to the precautionary principle well before this point, including in formal communications to fifteen different states in the run-up to

[172] See, generally, Chapter 4, in relation to the persistence criterion.

[173] See ibid., n. 27–n. 29 and accompanying text.

[174] *EC Measures Concerning Meat and Meat Products (Hormones)*, Doc. WT/DS26/AB/RWT/DS48/AB/R, AB-1997-4, 16 January 1998 (Report of the WTO Appellate Body).

[175] See Chapter 4, n. 30–n. 35 and accompanying text.

[176] See, for example, Second International Conference on the Protection of the North Sea, London, 24–5 November 1987, Ministerial Declaration, point VII, reproduced in D. Freestone and T. Ijlstra (eds), *The North Sea: Basic Legal Documents on Regional Environmental Cooperation* (Dordrecht, Martinus Nijhoff, 1991), 41-53.

[177] Ministerial Declaration on Sustainable Development in the ECE Region, 1990, Bergen, UN Doc. A/CONF.151/PC/10.

[178] See P. Sands and J. Peel, *Principles of International Environmental Law* (Cambridge, Cambridge University Press, 3rd edn, 2012), 219.

[179] J. Cameron and J. Abouchar, 'The Precautionary Principle: A Fundamental Principle of Law and Policy for the Protection of the Global Environment' (1991) 14 *Boston College International and Comparative Law Review* 1, 4.

[180] Rio Declaration on Environment and Development, 1992, annexed to the Report of the United Nations Conference on Environment and Development, UN Doc. A/CONF.151/26, vol. I.

[181] See A. Sirinskiene, 'The Status of Precautionary Principle: Moving Towards a Rule of Customary Law' (2009) 4 *Jurisprudence* 349, 351.

the Bergen conference in 1990.[182] Thus, while it is impossible to pinpoint an exact start date for the 'period of emergence' of the precautionary principle—as is the case with almost all customary norms—it can be broadly said that the United States started objecting right from the first embryonic signs of relevant state practice. It objected from the outset: there was clearly no need for it to 'wait' for the consensus to grow. Aside from a few suggestions to the contrary,[183] it is relatively clear that the United States is an exempt persistent objector to the precautionary principle, or—for those who argue that the customary principle has still not yet crystallized—that it will be.[184]

Ultimately, the indeterminacy in identifying both the start of a norm's emergence and the exact point of its crystallization is simply something that states seeking to gain exemption by way of persistent objection will have to put up with. As noted, such indeterminacy is a feature of all state engagement with customary international law and is, thus, the price that states pay for enjoying the flexibility of custom. However uncertain the exact points on a norm's timeline may be, though, there is a general agreement that custom must begin to form at some point and, more importantly, that there is a definite—albeit essentially unknowable—crystallization point too.[185] The key threshold positions on the norm's timeline therefore provide a 'rough and ready field guide' for the application of the timeliness requirement for persistent objection.[186] Such vagueness is, perhaps, far from ideal, but the problems that it causes are somewhat overstated and, to the extent that there is uncertainty, this is simply part and parcel of the uncertainty surrounding customary international law as a whole.

V. States That Are Unaware of the Norm's Gestation

There is no requirement that every state explicitly consents to a newly emerging norm of customary international law for that norm to crystallize.[187] It is, therefore, entirely possible that new customary international law can come into being

[182] Cameron and Abouchar, n. 179, 11–12 and 18, footnote 73.

[183] R.B. Deloso, 'The Precautionary Principle: Relevance in International Law and Climate Change' (2005), unpublished Masters thesis, Lund University, http://www.lumes.lu.se/database/alumni/04.05/theses/rabbi_deloso.pdf, 38–9.

[184] 'Precaution in International Sustainable Development Law', CISDL Legal Brief for the World Summit on Sustainable Development, Johannesburg, South Africa, 2002, http://cisdl.org/public/docs/news/brief_precaution2.pdf, 4; and A. Trouwborst, *Precautionary Rights and Duties of States* (Leiden, Martinus Nijhoff, 2006), 9, footnote 37.

[185] J.L. Goldsmith and E.A. Posner, *The Limits of International Law* (Oxford, Oxford University Press, 2005), 23. *Cf.*, Trachtman, n. 6, 222 (noting that one can view customary international law as 'always [being] in a zen-like process of becoming and unbecoming', with the result that the error of the persistent objector rule is to assume that there is any such thing as a crystallization point for customary norms).

[186] Kritsiotis, n. 17, 131.

[187] See, for example, *Military and Paramilitary Activities in and against Nicaragua* (*Nicaragua v United States of America*), merits, 1986 ICJ Rep. 14, para. 186; and Thirlway, n. 6, 54.

without every state of the world even being *aware* of the state practice and *opinio juris*—coming from other states—that has led to its crystallization.[188] Given that customary international law binds all,[189] a state can potentially find itself bound by a rule that it did not even know was emerging.[190] The timeliness criterion can thus be viewed as requiring states to keep track of all possible emerging norms of customary international law at all times, so as to be ready to object (if necessary) before it is too late. Such an expectation is both onerous and unrealistic.[191] As Bederman has phrased this, the timeliness criterion assumes 'that all countries in the world have minions of international lawyers in their employ who have nothing better to do than closely monitor what other states are "bidding" or "claiming" as new rules of custom, and then effectively protest them'.[192]

The two-stage decision-making process represented by *Figure 6.2* necessarily assumes that states are aware, at *Stage 1*, of the likelihood (or at least possibility) of the process reaching *Stage 2*.[193] If the state is not aware of this possibility then no 'choice' is made at *Stage 1*: the state will simply act in its immediate interests, oblivious to the implications of its action (or inaction) for its available choices at *Stage 2*. Without awareness, persistent objection becomes not a process of decision-making, but a lottery of circumstance. Put rather more simply, how can a state be expected to have objected if it did not even know that the norm was forming?[194]

While the majority view is that a subsequent objector state is bound irrespective of whether it was aware that the custom was forming until too late,[195] some commentators have argued that the timeliness criterion requires a dissenter to object immediately following it gaining an initial awareness of the norm's gestation (even if the state only becomes aware of the norm *after* it has emerged).[196] Taking this position in his separate opinion in the *North Sea Continental Shelf* cases, Judge Ammoun stated that 'while a general rule of customary law does not require the consent of all States … [it does] at least [require] the consent of those *who were aware of this general practice* and [thus] *being in a position to oppose it, have not done so*'.[197]

This claim represents a qualified version of the subsequent objector rule. Here, it is argued that states can subsequently object and gain exemption, but only if

[188] Kontorovich, n. 3, 874.

[189] Ibid., 54 and 56; J.A. Green, 'India's Status as a Nuclear Weapons Power under Customary International Law' (2012) 24 *National Law School of India Review* 125, 128; and J.P. Kelly, 'The Twilight of Customary International Law' (1999–2000) 40 *Virginia Journal of International Law* 449, 451.

[190] Byers, n. 55, 145–6; and A. Pellet, 'The Normative Dilemma: Will and Consent in International Law-Making' (1988–9) 12 *Australian Yearbook of International Law* 22, 37.

[191] Bradley and Gulati, n. 12, 253; Lim and Elias, n. 70, 149; and Quince, n. 5, 41.

[192] Bederman, n. 150, 154.

[193] Trachtman, n. 6, 224.

[194] Charney, n. 6, 537; Koskenniemi, n. 3, 444.

[195] McClane, n. 6, 13.

[196] See, for example, Fon and Parisi, n. 3, 5. See also, M.N. Shaw, *International Law* (Cambridge, Cambridge University Press, 7th edn, 2014), 58 (seemingly implicitly taking this view: 'acquiescence [to newly forming customary international law] must be based upon full knowledge of the rule invoked. Where a failure to take a course of action is in some way connected or influenced or accompanied by a lack of knowledge … then it cannot be interpreted as acquiescence').

[197] *North Sea Continental Shelf* cases, merits, n. 26, separate opinion of Judge Ammoun, para. 31.

they were not *aware* that practice was occurring, and thus that a new custom was forming, until too late. Supporters of this view further qualify it by holding that an 'unaware state' can only gain exemption through subsequent objection if it objects *immediately upon gaining awareness*.[198]

The claim that the timeliness requirement for persistent objection should not apply to a state that was unaware of the emergence of the new custom is based, in part, on a voluntarist understanding of international law formation: from a voluntarist perspective, a state cannot be seen as having truly consented, even tacitly, if it did not know that there was anything to consent to. Yet this qualified version of the subsequent objector rule also has its roots in practicality, in that it recognizes the impossibility of states being able to maintain constant vigilance in relation to any and all possible new norms. It therefore has a degree of appeal, both conceptually and pragmatically.

However, the 'unaware subsequent objector rule' comes with its own problems (even beyond the problems already considered in section III in relation to subsequent objection in general). Firstly, there is the question of how 'immediate' the objection needs to be following the state gaining awareness, especially given that effective objections are, of course, supposed to be persistent. Must the state issue 'rapid fire' objections as soon as it becomes aware of a new binding custom, to ensure both persistence and immediacy? Such an approach to persistent objection seems unlikely, and is not found in state practice.

Secondly, the point at which a state becomes 'aware' is going to be just as difficult to pin down as the point at which the custom has crystallized. Identifying this point in time—the point of 'awareness'—would be extremely problematic. Other than perhaps inferring this from the actions of a state, which may be possible in some instances, the most probable source that one could consult to ascertain whether a state was or was not aware of a developing norm would be the state itself, which is hardly likely to act as a reliable barometer of its own level of awareness. If this version of subsequent objection were accepted, then one could expect states to constantly claim that they were unaware of a new custom until that custom appeared to be contrary to their immediate interests; at which point they would suddenly 'become aware' and then object.[199]

A slightly more nuanced version of this limited form of subsequent objection might therefore be to *presume* awareness based on a 'reasonable likelihood' test: when a rule becomes sufficiently 'visible', the state is presumptively aware of

[198] Fon and Parisi, n. 3, 5.

[199] For example, in *Fisheries*, the United Kingdom claimed that it was not aware of Norway's objections to the 10-mile rule, and thus that Norway's objections could not be opposable to it. See *Fisheries* (*United Kingdom v Norway*), reply submitted by the Government of the United Kingdom of Great Britain and Northern Ireland, 1950 ICJ Plead., vol. II, 291, particularly at paras 58 and 71. Of course, this was not a state arguing that it should be exempted as a subsequent objector because it was previously unaware that a new custom had formed but, rather, that it was unaware of another state's persistent objections (which, as was discussed in Chapter 3, section III, must be openly communicated to be effective). Nonetheless, it is telling that the ICJ did not believe the United Kingdom's assertion, holding that 'the United Kingdom could not have been ignorant'. *Fisheries*, merits, n. 19, 139.

it. However, it is telling that none of the writers who advocate the 'unaware subsequent objector rule' make this suggestion of a presumptive awareness approach.[200] Perhaps this is because it would again pose more questions than it would answer (for example, how 'visible' would the practice need to be to trigger the presumption?). Moreover, the operation of the timeliness criterion is already premised on just such a presumption: if a norm crystallizes—which requires widespread and consistent state practice, remember—then it is presumed that states will have previously become aware of the practice creating that norm. Of course, this presumption is arbitrary and will not always be correct. There is no doubt that a state could find itself bound by a custom of which it was not previously aware.

To illustrate the 'unaware state' problem with an example from practice, it was noted in section I.*ii* that the objections of various equatorial states in relation to the geostationary orbit of satellites around the equator were unsuccessful in the mid-1970s. This was on the basis that these objections occurred after the right to deploy geostationary equatorial satellites had crystallized into customary international law (meaning that the objecting states were 'subsequent objectors' and, thus, were bound).[201] The objecting states, however, argued that this position was manifestly unfair, on the basis that the

> terms of international law [on the geostationary orbit of satellites] were elaborated when the developing countries could not count on adequate scientific advice and were thus not able to observe and evaluate the omissions, contradictions and consequences of the proposals which were prepared with great ability by the industrialized powers for their own benefit.[202]

In other words, the equatorial states argued that, if a customary international law permitting satellite overflight had crystallized, it should not bind them, because they had not possessed the resources to extrapolate the legal implications of the practice, and were therefore not 'aware' enough to have been able to persistently object. Having become 'aware', they argued that they had a right to exemption via subsequent objection.

That the objections of these equatorial states to a norm allowing for satellite overflight were unavailing[203] highlights the fact that the previously 'unaware' subsequent objector will be given short shrift. This also demonstrates something else, however. The likelihood of a state being unaware of a forming custom may be especially acute in relation to developing states or other states with comparatively limited resources. More powerful states are likely to have more resources to monitor state practice, understand technological advancement and its implications, and so on: thus putting them in a better position to identify emerging custom

[200] Although, having said this, McClane does advocate something similar in relation to the period of the norm's emergence: that there is a presumption of acquiescence to the emerging norm once it has become sufficiently 'visible', at which point this presumptive acquiescence can itself be viewed as contributing to the norm's crystallization. See McClane, n. 6, 23.

[201] See n. 33–n. 42 and accompanying text.

[202] Bogota Declaration, n. 33, section 4.

[203] See n. 39–n. 42 and accompanying text.

in time to persistently object. Developing states, in contrast, may well have a less sophisticated information network, and less manpower to sift through and analyse the huge amounts of ongoing state practice around the world.[204] They also may not have the technical expertise to fully appreciate the implications of the practice.

Some writers have argued that the comparative lack of resources of developing states will also mean that they are *less able to object*, even if they are aware of their need to.[205] However, this is probably something of an overstatement. As was argued in Chapter 3, objection need not take the form of 'acts': statements will suffice.[206] Even the least developed states of the world have the resources, today, to issue official press releases so as to effectively persistently object. The more pertinent concern is whether they have the resources to realize that they need to.[207]

The fact that the timeliness criterion is likely to be more burdensome for developing states is not something that should be lightly dismissed, especially as such indirect discrimination can be viewed through the prism of post-colonialism and modern political imperialism.[208] However, to some extent, this simply reflects the extra-legal inequality of international relations. For example, as has already been noted, the objections of the equatorial states to the customary law right of satellite overflight were unsuccessful. Their subsequent objections were rejected by numerous other states, irrespective of their argument to have been unaware of the implications of the cumulative practice due to resource limitations.[209] Indeed, the objectors ultimately accepted this fact and abandoned their position.[210] We have already seen in Chapters 4 and 5 that the 'power' of the objector influences the acceptable degree of persistence or consistency for successful persistent objection.[211] In relation to the timeliness criterion, too, 'weaker' states may find objection more difficult.[212] This may not sit easily with the notion of the sovereign equality of states,[213] but it is the reality of the operation of the persistent objector rule.

[204] Trachtman, n. 146, 22.

[205] See Charney, n. 6, 539 (making this point implicitly); and Quince, n. 5, 41.

[206] See Chapter 3, section IV.*i*.

[207] Kelly, n. 189, 522.

[208] Making this point generally in relation to the implications of the timeliness criterion, see Bradley and Gulati, n. 52, 6–7; and Trachtman, n. 6, 233.

[209] See, for example, the position taken by states as set out in n. 40.

[210] St. John, n. 38.

[211] See, respectively, Chapter 4, section III, particularly text following n. 75; and Chapter 5, n. 141 and accompanying text.

[212] It is worth noting that, somewhat ironically, the problem of identifying the crystallization point for a customary international law norm, and the sheer amount of state practice that needs to be considered to keep track of developments in custom, has been exemplified by the significant increase in the number of states through the decolonization process. See D.F. Vagts, 'International Relations Looks at Customary International Law: A Traditionalist's Defence' (2004) 15 *European Journal of International Law* 1031, 1039. Thus, the states that gained independence during the decolonization process to some extent contributed to the difficulty in keeping track of state practice, an issue that seems to have had a disproportionately negative effect on them in relation to persistent objection.

[213] Koskenniemi, n. 3, 444–5.

Ultimately, it is evident from practice that a lack of awareness of a customary norm's emergence by an objecting state prior to crystallization—even if that lack of awareness was unavoidable because of the state's limited resources—does not enable it to gain exemption through subsequent objection: *ignorantia legis neminem excusat.* This problem is, in any event, somewhat mitigated in the twenty-first century. This is in part because the Internet and modern mass media mean that it has become increasingly possible for states—even the smallest states—to monitor huge amounts of information concerning the practice of others comparatively easily.[214] It is also worth remembering that an increased trend towards customary international law development in the context of international organizations (such as, for example, the UN General Assembly) means that states are more likely to be involved in, or at least aware of, this process.[215] The 'awareness issue' nonetheless remains a concern for the operation of the persistent objector rule; for good or ill, the dissenting state must be as vigilant as possible in relation to new customary practice if it wishes to avoid being later bound.

VI. States With No Interest in the Emerging Norm

Even if a state is aware of practice contributing to an emerging norm, it may well not object if it has no direct interest in the norm during the period of emergence. Given that protest is often a politically self-damaging act,[216] it is of no surprise that states will be particularly wary of objecting in instances where they feel that they will, in any event, remain entirely unaffected by a (still only potential) resultant norm of customary international law.[217] Yet if the state *later* develops an interest post-crystallization, then it will find itself bound.[218] To extrapolate true consent from the silence of a state that will remain entirely unaffected by an emerging norm if it emerges is obviously a stretch,[219] and to expect states to object where they have no interest in the norm in question can be viewed as being rather onerous. Some commentators have therefore seen the implications of the timeliness criterion for states that had no interest in the norm while it was developing as being unacceptable,[220] or at least highly problematic.[221]

Most notably, Guzman has argued that states that develop an interest in an existing customary norm should be able to gain exemption by virtue of subsequent objection, albeit only if their objections are 'clear and consistent *from the moment that they have significant interest in the issue*'.[222] This is a similar argument to that

[214] Trachtman, n. 146, 22. [215] Stein, n. 3, 466; and Villiger, n. 5, 40.

[216] See Chapter 3, n. 32–n. 34 and accompanying text; and Chapter 8, section II.

[217] D'Amato, n. 12, 100. [218] Kontorovich, n. 3, 875.

[219] Ibid.; I.M. Lobo de Souza, 'The Role of Consent in the Customary Process' (1995) 44 *International and Comparative Law Quarterly* 521, 534; and McClane, n. 6, 17.

[220] Bradley and Gulati, n. 12, 253; Bradley and Gulati, n. 52, 27–8; Guzman, n. 29, 169–71; and Quince, n. 5, 79–81.

[221] Byers, n. 55, 146. [222] Guzman, n. 29, 169–71, quoted at 171, emphasis added.

made by those who support subsequent objection for a state from the point at which it gains awareness of the norm, as discussed in the previous section. As noted, Guzman limits his particular 'subsequent objector rule for newly interested states' proposal by requiring that the dissenter begins to persistently object as soon as its interests are affected in a 'significant' way.[223] This is so as to guard against opportunistic withdrawals 'on the eve of an action that is in violation of' the customary rule in question.[224] However, as with identifying the point where a state becomes 'aware' of a norm, it will be extremely difficult to determine when a state has developed a 'significant interest' in a customary norm (as opposed, say, to a 'partial interest' or a 'minor interest').[225] The degree of a state's 'interest' in any particular norm will, again like its 'awareness', inevitably be a largely subjective matter.[226] And if we are to base any determination of the stage at which a state is significantly interested on when a state *says* that it has become so, then Guzman's claim that his proposal guards against opportunism appears rather hollow.

It is impossible to identify with certainty the points where a custom begins to emerge and crystallizes too, of course.[227] However, at least these points on a norm's timeline—chimera-like as they may be—seek to identify a common threshold for all states: after all, a norm of customary international law crystallizes at a single point. In contrast, the point at which a state becomes 'interested' will vary from state to state, inevitably leading to increased uncertainty. A 'subsequently interested' state would also gain the benefit of having witnessed the (in)efficacy and (in) effectiveness of the rule for other states, while reserving its position as to whether to join the custom or remain apart from it. Under such a system, a state would be best served by staying silent during a norm's formation, and then later claiming that it did so because it had no 'interest' in objecting (allowing it to object whenever suited it most). This would make the already rather bumpy playing field of customary international law formation yet more uneven.

Taking a similar view to Guzman, but moving beyond his *de lege ferenda* position, Quince has argued that it is *already* the case that subsequent objection is acceptable where the state has developed an interest in a customary norm after its crystallization.[228] There is nothing to support Quince's claim that states can, as the law stands, subsequently object if they develop an interest in the norm after its crystallization.[229] A survey of state practice suggests that states simply do not make this assertion. The only potential example of a state seeking to gain exemption to an established customary norm having 'acquired an interest' in it (at least, the only potential example from practice that this writer has been able to identify)

[223] This is in contrast to Bradley and Gulati, who argue that because states' interests are continually developing and changing, a state should be able to develop at any point where its interests are affected by the norm in question. See Bradley and Gulati, n. 12, 253.

[224] Guzman, n. 29, 170.

[225] Something Guzman himself notes: ibid., 170, footnote 245. See also Ingman, n. 72, 50.

[226] Ibid.

[227] See section IV.*ii*. Guzman makes this point in defence of his proposal: see Guzman, n. 29, 170, footnote 245.

[228] Quince, n. 5, 79–81.

[229] ILA Final Report, n. 3, 27 and 39.

relates to Ethiopia's acquisition of a coastline in 1950, following its controversial 'subsuming' of Eritrea.

In the context of what at that time was a notably fluctuating and transitional customary law of the sea, Ethiopia asserted in 1953 that the baseline for measuring its territorial sea would be taken from the high-water line rather than the usual low-water line.[230] It may therefore be arguable that Ethiopia sought exempt status having become an 'interested state' by virtue of gaining a coastline. Measuring the baseline from the low-water line had already become common practice at this time, but whether it was considered by states to be the starting point in customary international *law* in 1953 is not entirely clear.[231]

Yet even if it is accepted that Ethiopia had in fact been subsequently objecting to a binding customary rule (after having gained an interest in it post-crystallization), in the *Eritrea/Yemen* arbitration in 1999, the Tribunal rejected any suggestion that the high-water line was an acceptable baseline for measuring the Ethiopian (or, by 1999, of course, once again Eritrean) territorial sea.[232] The Tribunal considered that the low-water line was the correct approach where there was no particular equitable reason for deviating from it: indeed, it noted the Ethiopian assertions from 1953 and then ignored them.[233] This would suggest that even if Ethiopia had indeed subsequently objected because it had developed an interest, this did not result in it (or its successor state) gaining an exemption from the norm.

This one instance of state practice—which is of extremely dubious value—aside, there is nothing supporting Quince's *de lege lata* claim that states can acquire exempt status through subsequent objection simply because they have later gained an interest. It is notable that even Guzman—perhaps the most vocal critic of the timeliness criterion in relation to 'yet-to-be interested states'—has accepted that, *under the current law*, 'a state that fails to object during the formation of the rule remains bound by it regardless of its later attempts at protest ... even if the state had no interest in the rule at the time of its emergence but subsequently came to be affected by it'.[234]

Notwithstanding the lack of state practice on this question, there are also good policy reasons for rejecting Guzman's *de lege ferenda* proposal, just as is the case with subsequent objection generally. While states may well be averse to objecting to emerging norms where they cannot, at the time, envisage that it will matter to them whether or not the norm ultimately emerges, it is precisely this element of the persistent objection rule that guards against opportunism and abuse. The

[230] J.H. Spencer, *Ethiopia at Bay: A Personal Account of the Haile Selassie Years* (Los Angeles, Tsehai, 2006), 249.

[231] For example, the ICJ implied that this was the case two years earlier, in 1951, although it was not entirely explicit on the point. See *Fisheries*, merits, n. 19, 128. The rule that the 'normal baseline' constituted the low-water line was adopted in Convention on the Territorial Sea and the Contiguous Zone, 29 April 1958, 516 UNTS 205, Article 3 (and then later in United Nations Convention on the Law of the Sea (UNCLOS), 10 December 1982, 1833 UNTS 3).

[232] *Award of the Arbitral Tribunal in the second stage of the proceedings between Eritrea and Yemen (Maritime Delimitation)*, decision, 1999, Part IV, http://legal.un.org/riaa/cases/vol_XXII/335-410.pdf, para. 135.

[233] Ibid. [234] Guzman, n. 29, 165.

persistent objector rule requires that a state objects in the abstract: before things 'get real'. This is undoubtedly an onerous requirement, but it is a key function of the timeliness criterion: it minimizes the possibility for frivolous exemption. Moreover, there will actually be extremely few instances where a state will be entirely uninterested in an emerging customary norm and have *no realistic possibility of becoming so interested*, but then will later develop a significant interest of this kind. It does not seem entirely unreasonable to require states to consider emerging customary international law with one eye on the future. If a silent state later develops an interest in a norm of customary international law from which it wishes to be exempt, then being bound by that norm is simply the price that the state pays for its short-sightedness.

VII. 'Instant' or 'Accelerated' Customary International Law

The notion of 'instant' customary international law was famously promulgated by Cheng in 1965, in the context of space law.[235] Cheng's argument was that customary international law governing outer space had emerged 'instantly', because only two states—the United States and the Soviet Union—had any interest in the norms in question. The claim here is that custom can crystallize without any formative state practice at all. Despite a few more recent attempts to identify other examples of 'instant' custom,[236] however, the concept has not gained much support[237] and has been at least implicitly rejected by the ICJ.[238] Indeed, the present author does not accept the possibility of truly 'instant' custom in the sense presented by Cheng: at least some amount of state practice must have occurred.[239]

However, while it is argued here that genuinely *instant* custom does not occur, it is certainly true that, in particular circumstances of 'fundamental change', norms of customary international law can crystallize extremely quickly.[240] As the ICJ famously asserted in the *North Sea Continental Shelf* cases in 1969:

> [T]he passage of a short period of time is not necessarily ... a bar to the formation of a new rule of customary international law ... [However] an indispensable requirement [for such

[235] B. Cheng, 'United Nations Resolutions on Outer Space: "Instant" International Customary Law?' (1965) 5 *Indian Journal of International Law* 23.

[236] See, for example, B. Langille, 'It's "Instant Custom": How the Bush Doctrine became Law after the Terrorist Attacks of September 11, 2001' (2003) 26 *Boston College International and Comparative Law Review* 145.

[237] See Arajärvi, n. 164, 23; Boyle and Chinkin, n. 146, 21; and L. Condorelli, 'Custom' in M. Bedjaoui (ed.), *International Law: Achievements and Prospects* (Paris, UNESCO, 1991), 179, 201.

[238] *Nicaragua*, merits, n. 187, para. 184. As noted by Boas, n. 92, 79.

[239] J.A. Green, 'Book Review: M.P. Scharf, *Customary International Law in Times of Fundamental Change: Recognizing Grotian Moments*' (2014) 63 *International and Comparative Law Quarterly* 781, 781.

[240] See, for example, Scharf, n. 3.

a process to occur] would be that within the period in question, short though it might be, state practice, including that of states whose interests are specially affected, should have been both extensive and virtually uniform in the sense of the provision invoked;- and should moreover have occurred in such a way as to show a general recognition that a rule of law or legal obligation is involved.[241]

Thus, in restricted circumstances, customary international law can crystallize extremely quickly. Given that this is not exactly an instantaneous process, however, perhaps a better term to use than 'instant' custom for the phenomenon identified by the ICJ is 'accelerated' custom. There remain relatively few examples of custom forming over a notably short period of time in this way,[242] but it does happen on occasion.[243]

To the extent that accelerated customary international law does emerge, it can be seen as presenting a particular problem for the would-be persistent objector. Accelerated custom formation squeezes the gap between points *a* and *b* in *Figure 6.1* down to an especially narrow 'window' for objection.[244] One might argue that the chances of a state being unaware of the custom's formation—and thus of it having no genuine chance to object to it—may well be increased if the norm in question crystallizes in double-quick time.[245] It is also worth recalling that persistent objection must be just that: *persistent*.[246] If a norm of customary international law crystallizes over a short period of time, then even a sharp-eyed objector that has spotted its imminent emergence will find it difficult to object more than a handful of times, which may mean that it falls short of complying with the persistence requirement.[247]

Irrespective of such concerns, it again appears that a dissenting state simply has to accept that it is bound by the crystallized customary international law, irrespective of how quickly the process of crystallization occurred. The fact that the custom's formation was 'accelerated' does not lead to an exception for subsequent objectors. As an example, one might note the position taken by a handful of states[248] in relation to the International Criminal Tribunal for the former Yugoslavia's (ICTY) assertion, in its 1995 decision on the defence motion for interlocutory appeal on jurisdiction in the *Tadić* case, that the notion of war crimes was not limited to international armed conflict, but also extended to non-international armed conflict.[249] Despite the ICTY's suggestion that its position merely reflected existing customary international law on this point,[250] there is little question that individual criminal responsibility for war crimes was

[241] *North Sea Continental Shelf* cases, merits, n. 26, para. 74.

[242] Boyle and Chinkin, n. 146, 21.

[243] See the examples discussed in Scharf, n. 3.

[244] Bradley and Gulati, n. 12, 201 and 243; and Scharf, n. 3, 220.

[245] Byers, n. 55, 161.

[246] See, generally, Chapter 4, in relation to the persistence criterion.

[247] Elias, n. 16, 49.

[248] Specifically China, Russia, India, Indonesia, Pakistan, and Turkey.

[249] *Prosecutor v Dusko* Tadić *(a/k/a 'Dule')*, 1995, ICTY, decision on the defence motion for interlocutory appeal on jurisdiction, http://www.icty.org/x/cases/tadic/acdec/en/51002.htm, generally, but particularly at paras 87–137.

[250] Ibid., particularly at para. 117.

only accepted as existing in relation to international armed conflict in 1995.[251] However, within just a few years, the customary international law had almost certainly changed, stemming from the self-fulfilling prophecy of this assertion in *Tadić* and riding on the wave of political goodwill that briefly emerged in the immediate post-Cold War period.[252]

A handful of states objected to the claim that the notion of war crimes was applicable in non-international armed conflict,[253] but in the context of an accelerated process of customary legal change, these objections appear to have been insufficiently persistent during the (small) window of emergence, and then were too late once the door had slammed shut following the crystallization of the norm. Indeed, even those objectors that are not parties to the Rome Statute of the International Criminal Court (ICC),[254] and have therefore avoided adopting the conventional formalization of the applicability of war crimes to non-international armed conflict in Article 8.2(c) of that treaty, seemingly nonetheless accepted that this had become customary international law that was binding upon them.[255]

Therefore, it appears that objectors to 'accelerated' custom will be bound, unless they are able to persistently object during the short period of its emergence.[256] It is worth noting that the difficulties associated with this possibility can easily be overstated, however, for a number of reasons. Firstly, as has been noted, the accelerated crystallization of new customary international law remains an uncommon occurrence. In the vast majority of cases of customary international law formation, states will have a much longer period within which to object. Secondly, as stated by the ICJ in the above quoted passage from *North Sea Continental Shelf*, for custom to crystallize at an accelerated rate it requires a special degree of uniformity and general acquiescence: the near-universal acceptance of the custom is what allows it to form so quickly in the first place. Indeed, on the rare occasions where accelerated custom occurs, this will usually involve particularly 'visible' state practice (such as a near-universally accepted multilateral treaty, or the widespread acceptance of a particular position taken in UN

[251] See, for example, Final Report of the Commission of Experts Established Pursuant to Security Council Resolution 780 (1992), 27 May 1994, UN Doc. S/1994/674, para. 52.

[252] Scharf, n. 3, 150.

[253] See A.M. Danner, 'When Courts Make Law: How the International Criminal Tribunals Recast the Laws of War' (2006) 49 *Vanderbilt Law Review* 1, 35.

[254] Rome Statute of the International Criminal Court, 17 July 1998, 2187 UNTS 3.

[255] For example, China, India, Russia, and the United States all voted in the Security Council in February 2011 to refer the matter of war crimes and crimes against humanity in the context of the Libyan civil war to the ICC. See Security Council Resolution 1970, 26 February 2011, UN Doc. S/RES/1970; 'In Swift, Decisive Action, Security Council Imposes Tough Measures on Libyan Regime, Adopting Resolution 1970 in Wake of Crackdown on Protesters', Security Council Meetings Coverage, 6491st meeting, 26 February 2011, UN Doc. SC/10187/Rev.1; and Scharf, n. 3, 152.

[256] Although see the Second Report on Identification of Customary International Law (M. Wood, Special Rapporteur), International Law Commission, Sixty-sixth session, 22 May 2014, UN Doc. A/CN.4/672, 41; and Meijers, n. 57, 23–4, both seemingly taking a different view: that states must be afforded enough time to be able to resist a newly emerging rule before they can be considered to be bound by it.

documents or debates).[257] Therefore, contrary to the suggestion that accelerated custom will inevitably reduce the chances of a state being aware of a forming custom, in reality it may be that case that states are *more likely* to know that an accelerated custom is emerging: while the objector may admittedly not have much time to object, it is at least likely to be aware that it needs to.

Finally, while writers have at times argued that objections must occur 'over a long period'[258] for the persistent objector rule to be effective (presumably because of the need, under the persistence requirement, for a notable degree of repetition of the dissenter's position), this may not necessarily be the case. It was argued in Chapter Four that the exact degree of persistence required will depend on the context.[259] Of course, the longer an objector has to repeat and therefore cement its position, the more effective its objections are likely to be.[260] In the context of accelerated custom, however, a vocal dissenter that objects at least a few times in the short window of emergence may be seen as having done enough.[261] It is also worth keeping in mind that in the modern age of immediate communication, the amount of time that an objector requires to be able to convey multiple statements of objection is, itself, now much less than would have been the case in the past.[262]

One must therefore be careful not to exaggerate the problem that accelerated custom might pose for potential persistent objector states. Nonetheless, the faster a custom forms, the more vigilant the would-be persistent objector must be, so as to be able to object in time.[263] On the rare occasions where states would have wished to remain exempt from an accelerated customary international law norm, the dice are (once again) seemingly somewhat loaded against the dissenter.

VIII. New States

If it is accepted that a state can only gain exemption from customary international law if it objected prior to crystallization, then any state that came into being after that point will be bound irrespective of the fact that it had no opportunity to object whatsoever. In relation to states that have come into existence after the custom in question has crystallized, then, the timeliness criterion does not just mean that it is extremely difficult for the state to lodge an effective persistent objection: it means that it is necessarily *impossible* for it to do so. In 1950, in its pleadings in the *Fisheries* case, the United Kingdom asserted this position in no uncertain terms. Indeed, it likely overstated things by claiming that 'the right of

[257] Stein, n. 3, 467. [258] Charlesworth, n. 30, 195; and Quince, n. 5, 60.

[259] See Chapter 4, section III. [260] Loschin, n. 3, 164.

[261] For example, the ILA Final Report, n. 3, 60 and 64 took the view that an explicit dissenter state to a custom emerging from a near-universally agreed upon resolution of the UN General Assembly would not be bound by any customary international law norm that 'instantly' resulted from it. See also the position taken by arbiter Rene Dupay in *Texaco Overseas Petroleum Co. v Libyan Arab Republic* (1978) 17 *International Legal Materials* 1; Boyle and Chinkin, n. 146, 226; and Thirlway, n. 6, 88.

[262] Byers, n. 55, 160. [263] McClane, n. 6, 6.

a State to dissent from a customary rule cannot be regarded as absolute. There is *universal agreement* that a new State has no option but to adhere to generally accepted customary law'.[264]

This issue of new states and customary international law exemption has, more than any other, troubled commentators considering the persistent objector rule's timeliness criterion. It has been argued that, if the rule is truly about voluntarism, then the fact that new states have no opportunity to object fundamentally undermines the rule's purported *raison d'être* and its internal logic.[265] If, on the other hand, voluntarism is not considered to form the conceptual basis for the rule (at least in its absolute form), then there is seemingly an inherent injustice in extending a right of opt-out to existing states but denying new states the same possibility.[266]

As with the indirectly discriminatory effect that the timeliness criterion has on 'weaker' or developing states in terms of the increased possibility of them being unaware of emerging custom (as discussed in section V), the fact that newly constituted states are forced to accept the law as they find it can be viewed through the prism of post-colonial theory.[267] The imposition of the 'agreed' customary norms of the established order upon new states essentially provides for a never-ending succession of *faits accomplis* on the part of the existing powers.[268]

As such, some commentators have argued that there is a particular, limited right of subsequent objection reserved for new states, if they object to existing custom within a 'reasonable period of time' following their acquisition of statehood.[269] As Judge Ammoun asserted in his *North Sea Continental Shelf* separate opinion: 'The right [to gain exemption through objection] of countries becoming independent which have not participated in the formation of rules which they consider incompatible with the new state of affairs, is preserved.'[270]

Adopting a more *de lege ferenda* approach, others have argued that new states *should* be entitled to gain exemption through subsequent objection, even though they accept that such states currently are not so entitled.[271] Taking either version of this argument, as with similar assertions of a right of subsequent objection for the formerly 'unaware' or 'uninterested' state, such an approach would simply replace one set of problems with another. For example, how much time is a 'reasonable amount of time' following the acquisition of statehood? This is not to mention that in many instances an entity's statehood can long remain a contested issue, as can be seen most recently from the continuing uncertainty and disagreement over the status of Kosovo.[272]

[264] *Fisheries*, reply submitted by the United Kingdom, n. 199, 428, emphasis added.

[265] Kelly, n. 189, 513 and 524–5.

[266] Dumberry, n. 3, 797–8.

[267] Bradley and Gulati, n. 52, 7; Dixon, n. 6, 35; Stein, n. 3, 467; Kelly, n. 189, 524–5; and Trachtman, n. 6, 233.

[268] Kritsiotis, n. 17, 128.

[269] Fon and Parisi, n. 3, 6. See also Quince, n. 5, 62; and Villiger, n. 5, 34.

[270] *North Sea Continental Shelf* cases, merits, n. 26, separate opinion of Judge Ammoun, para. 31, footnote 2.

[271] See, for example, Guzman, n. 29, 173–4.

[272] See, generally, D.I. Efevwerhan, 'Kosovo's Chances of UN Membership: A Prognosis' (2012) 4 *Goettingen Journal of International Law* 93; J. d'Aspremont and T. Liefländer, 'Consolidating the Statehood of Kosovo: Leaving the International Law Narrative Behind' (2013) 1 *Journal of European*

The majority position in doctrine is overwhelmingly that new states cannot gain exemption to existing custom.[273] More importantly, once again, it seems clear from state practice that new states will indeed be bound by rules that have come into being prior to them having gained statehood, irrespective of the fact that such states cannot possibly have objected in time. Admittedly, it is true that during the 1950s and early 1960s (following the bulk of the decolonization process), a number of newly established post-colonial states formally objected to certain existing rules of customary international law.[274] A useful example in that context, which has at least been alluded to as being an instance of 'new state subsequent objection' by some writers,[275] is the customary international law on expropriation: in particular, the duty to pay full compensation for the nationalization of foreign-owned property (the so-called 'Hull formula').[276] For obvious reasons, post-colonial states were particularly against such a requirement, and objected to it vigorously at the time.[277] However, there is no evidence that

and International Affairs 8; and *Accordance with International Law of the Unilateral Declaration of Independence in Respect of Kosovo*, advisory opinion, 2010 ICJ Rep. 403.

[273] *Third Restatement*, n. 3, Section 102, Comment (d); ILA Final Report, n. 3, 24–5 and 27; Abasheikh, n. 6, 41; Akehurst, n. 6, 27–8; R.B. Baker, 'Customary International Law in the 21st Century: Old Challenges and New Debates' (2010) 21 *European Journal of International Law* 173, 177; Charney, n. 4, 2; Fitzmaurice, n. 3, 24–5; Guldahl, n. 5, 54; D. Harris, *Cases and Materials on International Law* (London, Sweet and Maxwell, 7th edn, 2010), 96 (analogizing new states to an individual born into a state and thus finding themselves subject to its laws from the outset); L. Henkin, 'International Law: Politics, Values and Functions' (1989-IV) 216 *Recueil des cours* 11, 56–8; Hillier, n. 76, 74; Kontorovich, n. 3, 874; Loschin, n. 3, 165; Mendelson, n. 6, 239 and 244; M. Mendelson, comments made at 'The Law of Armed Conflict: Problems and Prospects' conference to mark the publication of the ICRC Study on 'Customary International Humanitarian Law', Chatham House, 18 April 2005, http://www.blackstonechambers.com/news/publications/law_of_armed_conflic.html, 7–8; D. Murray, 'How International Humanitarian Law Treaties Bind Non-State Armed Groups' (2015) 20 *Journal of Conflict and Security Law* 101, 117; Schachter, n. 32, 34; Scharf, n. 3, 30 and 42; Steinfeld, n. 3, 1656; M. Sørensen, 'Principes de droit international public' (1960–I) 101 *Recueil des cours* 1, 45–6; J. Tasioulas, 'Customary International Law and the Quest for Global Justice' in A. Perreau-Saussine and J.B. Murphy (eds), *The Nature of Customary Law: Legal, Historical and Philosophical Perspectives* (Cambridge, Cambridge University Press, 2007), 307, 314 (noting that 'even positivists' take this stance); C. Tomuschat, 'Obligations Arising for States Without or Against Their Will' (1993) 241 *Recueil des cours* 195, 305–6; Trachtman, n. 6, 232; T. Treves, 'Customary International Law' in R. Wolfrum (ed.), *Max Planck Encyclopaedia of Public International Law, vol. II* (Oxford, Oxford University Press, 2012), 937, 945, para. 38; J.H.W. Verzijl, *International Law in Historical Perspective, vol. I: General Subjects* (Utrecht, A.W. Sijthoff, 1968), 38; and Virally, n. 3, 138 (arguing that the contention that new states are bound by customary international law predating their existence is 'beyond dispute').

[274] Akehurst, n. 6, 27; Bradley and Gulati, n. 12, 228 and 231; A.V. Lowe, 'Do General Rules of International Law Exist?' (1983) 9 *Review of International Studies* 207, 212 (generally, on newly independent states claiming that they should not be bound by international law norms that they have not consented); Stein, n. 3, 467; and Thirlway, n. 6, 54.

[275] See, for example, Dixon, n. 6, 35.

[276] In 1938, in relation to Mexico's nationalization of foreign-owned oil fields, the United States Secretary of State Cordell Hull argued that international law required Mexico to pay 'prompt, adequate, and effective' compensation. This has since become known as the 'Hull formula'. See G.H. Hackworth, *Digest of International Law, vol. III* (Washington, Government Printing Office, 1942), 652–66, quoted at 659 (reproducing the original correspondence).

[277] P.M. Norton, 'A Law of the Future or a Law of the Past? Modern Tribunals and the International Law of Expropriation' (1991) 85 *American Journal of International Law* 474, 478.

these post-colonial states gained an exemption to the existing customary rules on expropriation.[278]

Diverging somewhat from the Hull formula's requirement for 'full compensation', various resolutions of the General Assembly during the 1960s and 1970s—fuelled primarily by the votes of 'new' developing states—presented a shift towards a rather more flexible standard of what was termed 'appropriate compensation'.[279] However, there has been significant debate as to whether this was sufficient to alter the customary international law standard.[280] Subsequent case law would seem to indicate that the Hull formula remains the correct basis for the obligation in custom,[281] and since the 1990s many developing states have formally accepted the Hull formula (or something akin to it).[282]

For those who argue (probably correctly) that the Hull formula remains the customary standard,[283] there is evidence that the new states that objected to this were unable to avoid its pull, and today accept it explicitly.[284] Even if one takes the view that the obligation has been *modified* to a customary 'appropriate compensation' standard, this would necessarily be the result of the collective *opinio juris* on the part of the developing states in question, which has (arguably) led to a degree of alteration of the law.[285] Opposition to the customary law of expropriation is, therefore, clearly not an example of successful subsequent objection by a group of newly created states. It is either an example of existing rules being imposed on, and ultimately accepted by, new states, or—perhaps—an instance of the usual process of state practice and *opinio juris* contributing to normative change.

More generally in relation to new states' objections during the decolonization period to existing custom, the same pattern can be identified: the states in question were unable to gain specific exemptions from existing custom.[286] This not to say that the dissatisfaction of the post-colonial states as to the content of the law imposed upon them was left entirely unaddressed. There were significant normative changes implemented by treaty law, or by the development of custom (as was potentially the case with the expropriation example). In instances where change was not forthcoming through legal development, however, the states in question ultimately accepted that they were bound.[287]

[278] See, generally on expropriation, Harris, n. 273, 474–5.

[279] See General Assembly Resolution 1803 (XVII), 14 December 1962, UN Doc. A/5217, 15; General Assembly Resolution 3171 (XXVII), 13 December 1973 UN Doc. A/9030, 52; General Assembly Resolution 3201 (S-VI), 1 May 1974, UN Doc. A/9559, 3; and General Assembly Resolution 3281 (XXIX), 12 December 1974, UN Doc. A/9631, 50.

[280] *Cf.*, for example, M.H. Mendelson, 'Compensation for Expropriation: The Case Law' (1985) 79 *American Journal of International Law* 414; and Norton, n. 277.

[281] See Norton, n. 277, 479–88 (discussing various decisions in detail).

[282] Dumberry, n. 67, 396.

[283] *"Indirect Expropriation" and the "Right to Regulate" in International Investment Law*, Organisation for Economic Co-operation and Development Working Papers on International Investment (OECD Publishing, 2004), http://dx.doi.org/10.1787/780155872321, 2, footnote 1.

[284] Ibid., 936–7.

[285] D.P. Fidler, 'Revolt Against or From Within the West? TWAIL, the Developing World, and the Future Direction of International Law' (2003) 2 *Chinese Journal of International Law* 29, 41–2.

[286] Stein, n. 3, 467.

[287] Thirlway, n. 6, 54.

Beyond the decolonization process, which was inevitably rather *sui generis*, new states simply do not claim an inherent right of exemption from existing customary international law.[288] For example, following the dissolutions of the Soviet Union, Yugoslavia, and Czechoslovakia, *none* of the newly constituted European states expressed any indication that they saw themselves as being anything other than bound by the existing rules of customary international law. Many of these new states quickly confirmed in their constitutions that they were bound by the corpus of customary international law and, indeed, thereby incorporated it directly into their domestic law.[289] The approach of these new post-cold war states led Bankas to conclude in 2005 that 'in reality, new states ... follow norms of existing customary international law without question'.[290] Similarly, writing in 1993, Charney stated that 'few, if any, new states attempt to make objections to existing customary law norms and *none hold special exemptions*'.[291]

There is little question that the denial of a right of persistent objection to new states in relation to established norms has its roots, at least in part, in the political 'imperialism' of existing states.[292] As can be seen from the continued role of 'recognition' in the process of the establishment of statehood itself,[293] the international community remains something of a private 'gentlemen's club'. This is a club to which it is difficult to gain entry; to stand any chance of getting in, one is largely dependent on the goodwill of the current members, and must abide by the club's existing rules. This may be disconcerting in a system that is at least nominally premised upon the sovereign equality of states, but in the context of the persistent objector rule it does have an underpinning rationale of maximizing stability and consistency.

To ensure the continuity and certainty of the existing system, new states cannot simply select from the existing rules *à la carte*.[294] One might, of course, say the same of the possibility for exemption through prior persistent objection: i.e. that allowing for exemption *at all* causes instability and uncertainty.[295] That criticism is correct as far as it goes, but the difference is that the scope for persistent objection only applies—on a rolling basis—to a comparatively limited number

[288] See Tomuschat, n. 273, 305; and Virally, n. 3, 138–9.

[289] See ILA Final Report, n. 3, 25 (providing examples from the constitutions of various former Soviet states).

[290] E.K. Bankas, *The State Immunity Controversy in International Law: Private Suits against Sovereign States in Domestic Courts* (Berlin, Springer, 2005), 162.

[291] Charney, n. 6, 539, emphasis added.

[292] Bradley and Gulati, n. 12, 230; Bradley and Gulati, n. 52, 6; Kelly, n. 189, 524–5; and Quince, n. 5, 41.

[293] See, generally, J. Crawford, *The Creation of States in International Law* (Oxford, Oxford University Press, 2nd edn, 2006), 1–36; and T.D. Grant, *The Recognition of States: Law and Practice in Debate and Evolution* (Westport, Praeger, 1999).

[294] Malanczuk, n. 6, 47. See also G.M. Danilenko, *Law-Making in the International Community* (Dordrecht, Martinus Nijhoff, 1993), 115–16 (albeit that Danilenko ultimately takes a rather equivocal position on the possibility of new states objecting); Henkin, n. 273, 57; Kaczorowska, n. 3, 42; Kontorovich, n. 3, 913; H. Waldock, 'General Course on Public International Law' (1962) 106 *Recueil des cours* 1, 52–3.

[295] Dumberry, n. 3, 798. See also Guzman, n. 29, 173–4.

of emerging norms, upon which no states yet rely. To allow new states to exempt themselves from any or all existing rules of the system (a list containing some rules that necessarily stretch as far back as the existence of customary international law itself) is something very different. New states would be able to reject customary rules that have been used and accepted by all states for hundreds of years, something that would be spectacularly destabilizing for international law.

It is worth noting that this approach of prioritizing stability and certainty in relation to new states has parallels elsewhere in the system, such as in the largely uncontested principle of *uti possidetis*.[296] Indeed, in the same way as joining an international organization such as the UN or EU requires acceptance of the organization's rules, so too does entry into the international community of states.[297] This is not to say, as some have argued,[298] that one can therefore reconcile the imposition of existing custom on new states with voluntarism, on the basis that states have 'originally consented' to all of the norms of the system simply by virtue of joining it. New states may well not be aware of all of the existing rules of custom. In addition, they have little genuine 'choice' on the matter: given the various entitlements that states enjoy and the disadvantages of not attaining statehood for an aspiring state, any 'consent' that a new state may give in relation to the validity of the existing secondary rules of the system is given over a political barrel.[299] This 'original consent' argument is a fiction,[300] but the more practical fact that any institution or system requires a degree of stability and continuity holds true. Nonetheless, it is clear that voluntarism again insufficiently explains the workings of the persistent objector rule.[301]

For good or ill, as the law stands, new states cannot be persistent objectors to existing rules of customary international law. There are strong policy reasons for supporting this position, and it is borne out by reference to state practice. It is also worth keeping in mind that new states can (and do) contribute state practice and *opinio juris* towards altering rules of customary international law that they find objectionable.[302] Following decolonization, a significant proportion of the

[296] For example, the ICJ stated in *Case Concerning the Frontier Dispute* (*Burkina Faso/Republic of Mali*), merits, 1986 ICJ Rep. 554, para. 30, that '[i]nternational law—and consequently the principle of *uti possidetis*—applies to the new state ... immediately and from that moment onwards'. Dumberry, n. 3, 797 argues that this indicates that the Court would reject the notion of a new state gaining exemption to any existing rule of custom through subsequent objection. This is likely a correct assessment of what the Court would decide, although it perhaps reads too much into the *Frontier Dispute* decision in and of itself. See Danilenko, n. 294, 116–18.

[297] Abasheikh, n. 6, 41.

[298] Ibid. See also R. Jennings and A. Watts, *Oppenheim's International Law, vol. I: Peace* (New York, Longman, 9th edn, 1996), 14–15; and Kaczorowska, n. 3, 42 (taking this view implicitly).

[299] M. Craven, *The Decolonization of International Law: State Succession and the Law of Treaties* (Oxford, Oxford University Press, 2008), 14; and Tomuschat, n. 273, 305.

[300] Condorelli, n. 237, 203; Hall, n. 61, 289; E. Lauterpacht (ed.), *International Law, Being the Collected Papers of Hersch Lauterpacht, vol. I: The General Works* (Cambridge, Cambridge University Press, 1970), 57; Lobo de Souza, n. 219, 533–4; and Tomuschat, n. 273, 305.

[301] Abasheikh, n. 6, 41; and Charney, n. 4, 16.

[302] ILA Final Report, n. 3, 25; *Third Restatement*, n. 3, 'Reporter's Note', commentary to Section 102, Comment (d); Akehurst, n. 6, 28; Byers, n. 55, 145; and Virally, n. 3, 139.

international community comprised 'new states'. Collectively, they were able to notably direct and alter the future pattern of customary international law (albeit that power realities nonetheless limited the impact of their numerical advantage somewhat).[303]

IX. Restrictions on When States Can Object Even Within the 'Period of Emergence'?

It has been argued throughout this chapter that the timeliness criterion requires a state to have persistently and consistently objected during the nebulous grey zone of the 'period of emergence' (albeit that it is essentially impossible to determine the exact point of the start of a norm's emergence or the point of its crystallization into binding customary international law). Yet it may further be asked whether there are any limitations for the timing of objection even *within* this period.

i. Is objection from the very outset required?

Lim and Elias have asked whether 'dissent is supposed to be expressed from the earliest articulations of a nascent rule'.[304] This is because it has been occasionally suggested in doctrine that, to gain exemption, a state has to begin objecting immediately following the point at which the norm begins to emerge in practice (that is, from point *a* as it appears on *Figure 6.1*), and then must continue to object throughout the period of its emergence. Admittedly, this notion—that states must object from the very first sign of formative practice—has rarely been suggested unambiguously. For example, Judge Lachs asserted in his dissenting opinion to the majority decision in the *North Sea Continental Shelf* cases that a state can gain exemption under the persistent objector rule if it 'opposed the rule *from its inception*'.[305] The exact meaning of this articulation of the timeliness requirement is not entirely clear, but it certainly can be read as suggesting that objection must start at the beginning of the period of the norm's emergence. However, some have made this argument rather more clearly: for example, Abass holds that states should 'commence their objections *right from the start of the evolution of a custom*'.[306] A number of other writers seemingly share this view, albeit that most are less explicit in this regard.[307] Indeed, the present author himself has

[303] See Bankas, n. 290, 162 (giving examples); and Fidler, n. 285, 38.

[304] Lim and Elias, n. 70, 148.

[305] *North Sea Continental Shelf* cases, merits, n. 26, dissenting opinion of Judge Lachs, 229, emphasis added.

[306] Abass, n. 95, 47, emphasis added.

[307] See Abasheikh, n. 6, 44; A. Cassese, 'General Round Up' in A. Cassese and J.H.H. Weiler (eds), *Change and Stability in International Law-Making* (Berlin, de Gruyter, 1988), 165, 167; Chalecki, n. 6, 19; Fon and Parisi, n. 3, 5; Guzman, n. 93, 188 and 197; Lau, n. 155, 498; Lobo de Souza, n. 219, 533; Malanczuk, n. 6, 48; Quince, n. 5, 61; Ragazzi, n. 144, 63; M.N. Shaw, *International Law* (Cambridge, Cambridge University Press, 7th edn, 2014), 64–5; Thirlway, n. 6,

elsewhere said that states must 'object persistently and *throughout the development of the rule*',[308] which similarly suggests that a state that begins to object *part way though* the period of the rule's emergence would find itself bound by the norm in question on crystallization.

This writer should have chosen his words more carefully in his previous publication, because the implication that a state must object from the very outset of the 'period of emergence' is incorrect. This is, first, because the uncertainty inherent in identifying the point at which custom 'begins to emerge' would make complying with such a requirement almost impossible, and so open to interpretation as to lose all meaning.[309] Moreover, it has already been argued in previous sections that—for good, if contestable, policy reasons—states will be bound post-crystallization even if they were unaware of the emergence of the custom until it was too late or subsequently developed an interest in it. There is no good reason, however, to require states to suffer the further burden of having to spot the earliest signs of embryonic practice and begin objecting, or to deny states that develop an interest *during* the period of a norm's emergence from being able to gain exemption.

Practice seems to support this conclusion. As an example, one can consider the United States' position on the customary international law 'right to food', discussed in Chapter 4.[310] It will be recalled that the Special Rapporteur of the Commission on Human Rights on the Right to Food identified the United States as an exempt persistent objector to this norm in 2005,[311] and that this assertion was then tacitly accepted by other UN member states (strongly suggesting that the United States does indeed hold this status). The origins of the right to food can be traced to the 1943 'Hot Springs conference' which set up an Interim Commission leading to the establishment of the Food and Agriculture Organization (FAO) in 1945.[312] The Hot Springs conference was convened under the initiative of United States President Franklin D. Roosevelt.[313] Following on from this, the first explicit articulation of a right to food appeared in Article 25 of the non-binding 1948 Universal Declaration of Human Rights,[314] which, of course, the United States voted to adopt.[315] As such, the United States was arguably a leader in the early state practice concerning a right to food security, or, certainly, it can be said

13; Villiger, n. 5, 34; Virally, n. 3, 136; and D. Weissbrodt, 'Execution of Juvenile Offenders by the United States Violates International Human Rights Law' (1988) 3 *American University Journal of International Law and Policy* 339, 368.

[308] Green, n. 189, 144, emphasis added. [309] Guzman, n. 29, 170, footnote 245.

[310] See Chapter 4, n. 73–n. 75 and accompanying text.

[311] *The Right to Food*, note by the Secretary-General, transmitting the interim report of the Special Rapporteur of the Commission on Human Rights on the Right to Food in accordance with General Assembly Resolution 59/202, 12 September 2005, UN Doc. A/60/350, 23, footnote 44.

[312] R.W. Philips, *FAO: Its Origins, Formation and Evolution, 1945–1981* (Rome, Food and Agriculture Organization of the United Nations, 1981), 12–13.

[313] Ibid., 5–6.

[314] Universal Declaration of Human Rights, General Assembly Resolution 217 (III), 10 December 1948, UN Doc. A/RES/3/217 A.

[315] See *Yearbook of the United Nations*, 1948–9 (1950), I, II, 535.

that it did not explicitly oppose this from the outset. The United States did not begin objecting to a possible customary international law right to food until the 1970s (at least, not persistently and consistently).[316]

However, the customary right to food had a long gestation period, despite its early appearance in the 1948 Universal Declaration: the preponderance of evidence suggests that the right did not crystallize until somewhere in the 2000s.[317] The United States has been a persistent and consistent objector since the 1970s, and this has been enough to cement its position as an exempt state irrespective of the fact that the start of the norm's 'period of emergence' can be clearly traced back to at least the Second World War. The United States did not begin objecting until some 'mid-point' during the norm's 'period of emergence', but once the United States *did* begin objecting, its objections were sufficiently persistent and consistent for it to secure exempt persistent objector status.

Of course, states do on occasion object right from the earliest stirrings of normative change. In subsection IV.*ii*, the United States' opposition to the precautionary principle was used to demonstrate that states can, and in some instances do, object from the very outset of any discernible state practice. It was argued in that subsection that there is no need for the state to wait until practice becomes particularly 'notorious' if it has already identified potential shifts in practice at an earlier point.[318] However, saying that the United States was able to object from the very outset in relation to the precautionary principle is not the same as saying that it *had to*. States may at times object 'from the outset' but, for the most part, this does not reflect how dissenters behave.[319] Most states begin objecting at a point somewhere during the 'period of emergence'. States need not object from the very start but, '[r]ather, the rule develops over time and a state must object at some point during the period in which the rule is emerging'.[320]

ii. How late can a state object?

The conclusion that states need not object from the very earliest signs of normative change triggers a further question: how *late* in the process of customary international law formation may a dissenter begin objecting before it is considered not to have met the timeliness requirement and is, thus, forced to accept the new norm in question? Having considered this question in some detail, McClane found nothing in state practice or doctrine to identify a particular 'end date' for persistent objection, other than the point of crystallization itself: 'A state may properly assert an objection ... until usage has become a customary international law norm which would bar all states (including the would-be objector) from subsequently objecting.'[321]

316 See, generally, E. Messer and M.J. Cohen, 'US Approaches to Food and Nutrition Rights, 1976-2008' (2009) *Hunger Notes*, http://www.worldhunger.org/articles/08/hrf/messer.htm. Various specific examples of objection on the part of the United States are set out in Chapter 4, n. 74.

317 For evidence of the crystallization of the right, see ibid, n. 73.

318 See n. 171–n. 184 and accompanying text.

319 Lim and Elias, n. 70, 150.

320 Guzman, n. 29, 170, footnote 245.

321 McClane, n. 6, 26.

Elias too has concluded that '[t]here appears to be no specific requirement as to when the objection is expressed',[322] other than the requirement that this must occur before the point of crystallization.

While there is nothing to contradict this assertion as a technical understanding of the timeliness requirement, it is again worth keeping in mind that objection must also be *persistent*.[323] It was noted in section VII (in relation to the implications of 'accelerated custom' for persistent objection) that the less time a state has to object, the less likely it is that its objections will be viewed as being sufficiently persistent. Again, of course, one must remember that persistence is a context-specific requirement; in some instances, a relatively low degree of 'persistence' may suffice.[324] Nonetheless, while a state can object 'at the last minute' if it wishes, it will inevitably be more difficult in these circumstances for it to establish the persistence of its objections. The uncertainty as to when norms of customary international law crystallize makes such an approach a dangerous game: a state may think that it has time to object (persistently), but then find that the ship has in fact sailed. Would-be dissenters are therefore wise to object as soon as possible in the 'period of emergence'.[325] Indeed, more generally, the longer a state objects, the more credible and entrenched its position becomes, meaning that its exemption will be easier to protect post-crystallization.[326]

X. Continued Objection Post-Crystallization

Finally in this chapter, it is worth noting that for the persistent objector rule to provide a state with a legal exemption to a customary international law norm, that state must not only persistently and consistently object during the formation of a norm, but must also *continue* its persistent/consistent objection following the norm's crystallization. This view has been expressed by a number of academic commentators,[327] albeit at times in a rather vague manner.[328] The International Committee of the Red Cross (ICRC) Study on *Customary International Humanitarian Law* too has taken the view that 'the State concerned must have

[322] Elias, n. 3, 284, para. 15.

[323] See, generally, Chapter 4, in relation to the persistence criterion.

[324] See ibid., section III.

[325] Third Report on Identification of Customary International Law (M. Wood, Special Rapporteur), International Law Commission, Sixty-seventh session, 27 March 2015, UN Doc. A/CN.4/682, para. 91. See also Elias, n. 3, 284, para. 15; Kaczorowska, n. 3, 41; and Lim and Elias, n. 70, 150.

[326] Abass, n. 95, 47; and Loschin, n. 3, 166.

[327] See Byers, n. 55, 102–3; Cassese, n. 3, 178; Guzman, n. 29, 164–5; Hillier, n. 76, 74; Loschin, n. 3, 150; Meijers, n. 57, 23; Quince, n. 5, 61; Ragazzi, n. 144, 63; and Villiger, n. 5, 34.

[328] For example, D. Bölükbaşı, *Turkey and Greece: The Aegean Disputes—A Unique Case in International Law* (London, Cavendish, 2004), 206; and Charney, n. 6, 539 both hold that objection must occur up 'to the present', implicitly suggesting that they see continued objection beyond crystallization as being required.

objected to the emergence of a new norm during its formation *and continue to object afterwards*'.[329] Similarly, the ILC's Special Rapporteur on Customary International Law, Sir Michael Wood, noted in his third report in 2015 that a prior persistent/consistent objector that 'maintains its objection after the rule has crystallized, is not bound by it',[330] and the draft conclusions of the ILC's Drafting Committee, provisionally adopted in July 2015, also reflect this view: 'the rule [that has been objected to] is not opposable to the State concerned *for so long as it maintains its objection*.'[331] The same position was also expressed in 2015 by the Asian-African Legal Consultative Organization (AALCO).[332]

This is not the same argument as that made by those who support the subsequent objector rule. The claim here is essentially that while subsequent objection is in itself insufficient to gain exemption, a prior persistent objector must *maintain* its objection even after crystallization, otherwise its exempt status is revoked or lapses and, at that point, the previously exempt objector will find itself bound.[333] In other words, one might say that to stay exempt, a state must be both a persistent *and* a subsequent objector.

There is little question that this position is correct. There are a number of examples from practice of states failing to maintain their persistent or consistent objections post-crystallization, and thus being viewed as having abandoned their exempt position. This is sometimes explicit, as was the case with the objections of Mauritania with regard to the practice of female genital mutilation. As was discussed in Chapter 3, Mauritania had persistently and consistently objected to the prohibition of the practice in customary human rights law up until 2005.[334] However, due in part to increasing political pressure from human rights organizations and other states, it abandoned its position in 2005. That year, Mauritania reversed its stance by adopting Ordonnance n°2005-015,[335] Article 12 of which

329 J-M. Henckaerts and L. Doswald-Beck (eds), *Customary International Humanitarian Law, vol. I*, International Committee of the Red Cross (ICRC) Study (Cambridge, Cambridge University Press, 2005), xlv, emphasis added.

330 Third Report on Identification of Customary International Law, ILC, n. 325, para. 85.

331 ILC, Text of the Draft Conclusions, n. 2, 5, Draft Conclusion 15: Persistent Objector, emphasis added. See also 'Identification of Customary International Law', Statement of the Chairman of the Drafting Committee, Mr. Mathias Forteau, 29 July 2015, International Law Commission, Sixty-seventh session, Geneva, 4 May–5 June and 6 July–7 August 2015, 19 (reflecting the general agreement in the ILC Drafting Committee to this effect).

332 Comments on the ILC Project on Identification of Customary International Law, Asian-African Legal Consultative Organisation (AALCO), annexed to Report by S. Jusoh, Chairman of the AALCO's Informal Expert Group on Customary International Law, 24 March 2015, http://www.aalco.int/54thsession/AALCOIEG%20Chairman's%20Statement%20and%20Special%20Rapporteur's%20Report%2020150324.pdf, 5, *Comment K on the Persistent Objector Rule* (the state must have objected to the norm 'at the beginning of its formation *and persisted ever since*'; emphasis added).

333 Byers, n. 55, 103.

334 Mauritania long objected to the regulation of certain Islamic practices, including FGM. For examples, see Chapter 3, n. 196. See Lau, n. 155, 508, footnote 53.

335 Ordonnance n°2005-015 portant protection pénale de l'enfant, 2005, Présidence du Conseil Militaire pour la Justice et la Démocratie, Republique Islamique de Mauritanie, http://legislationmauritanienne.files.wordpress.com/2011/06/ordonnance-nc2b02005-015-portant-protection-pc3a9nale-de-l_enfant.pdf.

criminalized the practice of FGM. Prior to 2005 Mauritania was considered an exempt persistent objector (even to such a crucial human rights norm).[336] After 2005 it was no longer seen as a persistent objector, because it had not continued to maintain its position post-crystallization.[337]

Taking a rather more 'classic' example, Japan was considered by many to be a persistent objector to the expansion from the traditional 3-mile exclusive fisheries jurisdiction to a 12-mile zone from the Second World War until 1977.[338] Certainly, Japan continued to *act* as though it was exempt during this period, even in the face of widespread consensus as to a shift in the customary law of the sea during the mid-1960s.[339] By 1977 and the passing of The Law on the Territorial Sea (Law No. 30 of 1977) in Japan, however, it was clear that Japan was no longer consistently objecting to the 12-mile limit.[340] There is little question that, on this basis, Japan was viewed by other states as having abandoned its exempt status: 'while Japan was a persistent objector, it was not bound; it only became bound when it had ceased to object.'[341]

A state cannot simply persistently and consistently object *up until* the point where the customary norm in question crystallizes and then either go silent or act inconsistently. It must keep up its objections even beyond crystallization if it wishes to stay exempt. It is worth noting that this requirement is not strictly an aspect of the timeliness criterion, but rather an *extension* of it, as well as being a reflection of the importance of the persistence and, particularly, consistency criteria, in relation not just to gaining but also to *maintaining* exempt status.[342] Again, a requirement for continued persistent objection can be justified by the policy goal of treating exceptions narrowly: if a state is not willing to continue to voice its dissent consistently, then it would seem reasonable to assume that it has changed its policy to one of acceptance of the relevant norm (or, at least, one of grudging acquiescence).

XI. Conclusion

It has been argued throughout this chapter that the traditional understanding that persistent objectors must object prior to the crystallization of the norm being

[336] See Lau, n. 155, 507–8; and Quince, n. 5, 77.

[337] See 'Legislative Reform to Support the Abandonment of Female Genital Mutilation/Cutting', (2010) UNICEF Report, http://www.unicef.org/policyanalysis/files/UNICEF_-_LRI_Legislative_Reform_to_support_the_Abandonment_of_FGMC_August_2010.pdf, 7, 21, and 46.

[338] See, for example, I. Brownlie, *The Rule of Law in International Affairs: International Law at the Fiftieth Anniversary of the United Nations* (Dordrecht, Martinus Nijhoff, 1998), 25.

[339] See Charney, n. 4, 11–12.

[340] See ibid., 12 (particularly sources cited at footnote 52); and S. Oda and H. Owada (eds), 'Annual Review of Japanese Practice in International Law XV (1976-77)' (1985) 28 *Japanese Annual of International Law* 59, 94–6 (generally, but particularly in relation to The Law on the Territorial Sea (Law No. 30 of 1977)). Japan remained an (inconsistent) objector for a number of years after 1977, in that it still attempted to apply the 3-mile limit to certain specific areas; see ibid., 96.

[341] Elias, n. 16, 43.

[342] On the de facto difficulties in maintaining exempt status, see Chapter 8, section II.

objected to is correct. Doctrine does not generally support the notion of subsequent objection, and there are good policy reasons for this. Reference to state practice also indicates that states wishing to gain exemption from customary international law norms must object prior to the crystallization of the norm in question.[343] It is notable that supporters of the subsequent objector rule almost never reference instances of successful subsequent objection in state practice: indeed, the present author would contend that there are no such examples. The position of the subsequent objector is, quite simply, 'untenable'.[344] Having said this, states do, of course, subsequently object, and this can be relevant to the content and applicability of customary international law norms in that they are necessarily altered by states adopting an attitude apart. If a sufficient number of other states adopt the position of a subsequent objector then the custom will change. It is, however, important to distinguish such trendsetting contrary behaviour from the subsequent objector rule that is supported by some commentators.

The timeliness requirement for persistent objection is, in itself, relatively easy to identify. However, amid the inherent uncertainty surrounding the process of the formation of customary international law, the criterion is extremely difficult to apply in practice. States may find that they are bound by customary international law that they had only a limited opportunity to object to (or no genuine opportunity to object to at all), for a variety of reasons: because they were unaware of the emerging norm, because they had no interest in it prior to crystallization, because it formed at an accelerated rate, or because they did not acquire statehood until after it had crystallized. The implications of the timeliness criterion in such circumstances are, perhaps, somewhat overstated at times, but they nevertheless highlight the limitations of the persistent objector rule in protecting state autonomy and reflecting the voluntarist theory of international law. Indeed, the voluntarist understanding of the persistent objector rule does not adequately explain the requirement for states to object prior to crystallization.

The timeliness criterion is undoubtedly an onerous one. However, it can be identified in practice, and can be justified based on the policy goals of maximizing stability in the system and limiting exceptionalism. States know—and seemingly accept—that once the trap of custom has snapped shut, all are caught: this is simply one of the rules of the game. The timeliness requirement means that dissenting states have the difficult task of taking steps to ensure that they are as aware as possible of any emerging custom. Objectors must also be forward-thinking with regard to the possible later effects of emerging customs on them and ensure that they are ready to object quickly and loudly if a custom emerges at an accelerated rate. Quite simply, states must pay significant attention to the stage at which they object,[345] and, even then, this may not avail them.

[343] *Cf.* P.B. Stephan, 'Disaggregating Customary International Law' 21 *Duke Journal of Comparative and International Law* 191, 204 (incorrectly suggesting that the only support for the timeliness criterion is to be found in the writings of scholars).

[344] Villiger, n. 5, 36.

[345] Colson, n. 155, 958.

PART III

THE LIMITATIONS AND ROLE OF THE PERSISTENT OBJECTOR RULE

7

Peremptory Norms and Persistent Objection

Part III of this book now turns to the limitations and role of the persistent objector rule. This chapter begins this final part by examining the commonly advanced contention that the 'escape hatch'[1] provided by the persistent objector rule cannot be 'opened' in relation to *jus cogens* norms. A significant majority of scholars have expressed the view that a state cannot exempt itself from a peremptory norm through persistent objection, even when the usual criteria for the rule's operation (set out in Part II: i.e. objection, persistence, consistency, and timeliness) are met.[2]

[1] D.A. Colson, 'How Persistent Must the Persistent Objector Be?' (1986) 61 *Washington Law Review* 957, 957; and T.L. Stein, 'The Approach of the Different Drummer: The Principle of the Persistent Objector in International Law' (1985) 26 *Harvard International Law Journal* 457, 472.

[2] See, for example, O. Abasheikh, 'The Validity of the Persistent Offender Rule in International Law' (2004) 9 *Coventry Law Journal* 40, 44; A. Abass, *Complete International Law: Text, Cases, and Materials* (Oxford, Oxford University Press, 2nd edn, 2014), 48; C.A. Bradley and M. Gulati, 'Withdrawing from International Custom' (2010) 120 *Yale Law Journal* 202, 213; M. Byers, 'Conceptualising the Relationship Between *Jus Cogens* and *Erga Omnes* Rules' (1997) 66 *Nordic Journal of International Law* 211, 217, and 223; J.I. Charney, 'The Persistent Objector Rule and the Development of Customary International Law' (1985) 56 *British Yearbook of International Law* 1, 19; J.I. Charney, 'Universal International Law' (1993) 87 *American Journal of International Law* 529, 541; O. Corten, 'The Russian Intervention in the Ukrainian Crisis: Was *Jus Contra Bellum* "Confirmed Rather than Weakened"?' (2015) 2 *Journal on the Use of Force and International Law* 17, 21; J. Curci, *The Protection of Biodiversity and Traditional Knowledge in International Law of Intellectual Property* (Cambridge, Cambridge University Press, 2010), 161–3; P.G. Danchin, 'U.S. Unilateralism and the International Protection of Religious Freedom: The Multilateral Alternative' (2002–3) 41 *Columbia Journal of Transnational Law* 33, 76; E. David, 'L'objecteur persistent, une règle persistent?' in P. Tavernier and J-M. Henckaerts (eds), *Droit international humanitaire coutumier: enjeux et défis contemporains* (Brussels, Bruylant, 2008), 89, 93; P. de Visscher, 'Cours général de droit international public' (1972) 136 *Recueil des cours* 1, 75; D.P. Fidler, 'Challenging the Classical Concept of Custom: Perspectives on the Future of Customary International Law' (1996) 39 *German Yearbook of International Law* 198, 210; V. Fon and F. Parisi, 'Stability and Change in International Customary Law' (2004) 21 *American Law and Economics Association Annual Meetings* 1, 6; C.A. Ford, 'Adjudicating *Jus Cogens*' (1994–5) 13 *Wisconsin International Law Journal* 145, 146–7; J.D. Fry, 'Pluralism, Religion, and the Moral Fairness of International Law' (2014) 3 *Oxford Journal of Law and Religion* 393, 413; C.G. Guldahl, 'The Role of Persistent Objection in International Humanitarian Law' (2008) 77 *Nordic Journal of International Law* 51, 58, 61–2, and 84; M.A. Hansen, 'Preventing the Emasculation of Warfare: Halting the Expansion of Human Rights Law into Armed Conflict' (2007) 194 *Military Law Review* 1, 17; D. Harris, *Cases and Materials on International Law* (London, Sweet and Maxwell, 7th edn, 2010), 32–3 (noting that this is the view of 'some writers' but not necessarily subscribing to it); P. Hulsroj, '*Jus Cogens* and Disarmament' (2006) 46 *Indian Journal of International Law* 1, 8; R. Kolb, 'Selected Problems in the Theory of Customary International Law' (2003) 50 *Netherlands International Law Review* 119, 136; D. Kritsiotis, 'On the Possibilities Of and For Persistent Objection' (2010) 21 *Duke Journal of Comparative*

This view has also been endorsed in international[3] and domestic[4] case law. The most notable judicial expression of this position was Judge Lachs' assertion in his dissent in the *North Sea Continental Shelf* cases that 'a general rule which is not of the nature of *jus cogens* [cannot] … prevent some States from adopting an attitude apart [if they have fulfilled the criteria for persistent objection]'.[5] This undeniably represents the majority view; indeed, in 2007, the International Law Commission (ILC) set out this position in particularly vehement and unequivocal language: 'it is *inconceivable* that a persistent objector could thwart … a norm [of *jus cogens*].'[6] For the ILC at least, then, the possibility of maintaining an exemption gained

and International Law 121, 132–4; H. Lau, 'Rethinking the Persistent Objector Doctrine in International Human Rights Law' (2005–6) 6 *Chicago Journal of International Law* 496, 495–8, and 504–5; B.D. Lepard, *Customary International Law: A New Theory with Practical Applications* (Cambridge, Cambridge University Press, 2010), 7 and 38; L. Loschin, 'The Persistent Objector Rule and Customary Human Rights Law: A Proposed Analytical Framework' (1996) 2 *University of California Davis Journal of International Law and Policy* 147, particularly at 163; A.V. Lowe, *International Law* (Oxford, Oxford University Press, 2007), 58; F.F. Martin, *The Constitution as Treaty: The International Legal Constructionalist Approach to the U.S. Constitution* (Cambridge, Cambridge University Press, 2007), 73; M.E. O'Connell, 'Affirming the Ban on Harsh Interrogation' (2005) 66 *Ohio State Law Journal* 1231, 1243, footnote 47; V.M. Padmanabhan, 'The Human Rights Justification for Consent' (2013) 35 *University of Pennsylvania Journal of International Law* 1, 3 and 17–18; K. Parker and L.B. Neylon, '*Jus Cogens*: Compelling the Law of Human Rights' (1988–9) 12 *Hastings Journal of International and Comparative Law* 411, 418; C. Quince, *The Persistent Objector and Customary International Law* (Denver, Outskirts Press, 2010), 39, 61, and 74; D. Shelton, 'Normative Hierarchy in International Law' (2006) 100 *American Journal of International Law* 291, 292; A. Steinfeld, 'Nuclear Objections: The Persistent Objector and the Legality of the Use of Nuclear Weapons' (1996) 62 *Brooklyn Law Review* 1635, 1640, and 1677–80; J. Tasioulas, 'Customary International Law and the Quest for Global Justice' in A. Perreau-Saussine and J.B. Murphy (eds), *The Nature of Customary Law: Legal, Historical and Philosophical Perspectives* (Cambridge, Cambridge University Press, 2007), 307, 310, and 313; and H. Thirlway, *International Customary Law and Codification* (Leiden, A.W. Sijthoff, 1972), 110. See also Report of the International Law Commission, Sixty-seventh session, 4 May–5 June and 6 July–7 August 2015, UN Doc. A/70/10, advance unedited version, 24 August 2015, 40, para. 94 (noting that some members of the ILC took the view, during the consideration of the 'Identification of customary international law' topic at the Commission's Sixty-seventh session, that the persistent objector rule 'could not be applicable to … rules having a peremptory character (*jus cogens*)'); *Restatement of the Law, Third, Foreign Relations Law of the United States*, American Law Institute, 1987, Section 102, Comments (d) and (k) (implying, when the comments are taken together, that states cannot persistently object to *jus cogens* norms, although this is not explicit); and Comments on the ILC Project on Identification of Customary International Law, Asian-African Legal Consultative Organisation (AALCO), annexed to Report by S. Jusoh, Chairman of the AALCO's Informal Expert Group on Customary International Law, 24 March 2015, http://www.aalco.int/54thsession/AALCOIEG%20Chairman's%20Statement%20and%20Special%20Rapporteur's%20Report%2020150324.pdf, 5, *Comment K on the Persistent Objector Rule.*

[3] See, for example, *Furundžija*, trial judgment, 1998, ICTY, Case No. IT-95-17/1-T, particularly at paras 153–5 (while the Tribunal did not explicitly refer to the persistent objector rule, a strong implication of its judgment is that the peremptory status of the prohibition of torture precludes the possibility of any derogation through persistent objection).

[4] *Siderman de Blake v Republic of Argentina*, United States Court of Appeals for the Ninth Circuit 965 F.2d 699 (9th Cir. 1992), per Fletcher J., 715–16.

[5] *North Sea Continental Shelf* cases (*Federal Republic of Germany v Netherlands, Federal Republic of Germany v Denmark*), merits, 1969 ICJ Rep. 3, dissenting opinion of Judge Lachs, 229.

[6] Report of the International Law Commission, Fifty-ninth session, 7 May–5 June and 9 July–10 August 2007, UN Doc. A/62/10, 101, emphasis added.

through persistent objection to norms that have since become *jus cogens* is simply beyond question: peremptory norms trump the persistent objector rule.

This chapter assesses that majority view. Section I sets out what peremptory norms are and—at least in a broad sense—how they come into being. Section II then briefly clarifies that the question is not whether a state can gain exemption to a *jus cogens* norm but whether its pre-existing exempt status 'decays', or is superseded by the norm to which it had been a persistent objector becoming peremptory. The chapter then turns, in section III, to the rationale underpinning the majority claim—based on the moral imperative of peremptory norms—and notes that this rationale is not easily reconciled with the commonly asserted purpose of the persistent objector rule. Section IV considers the two regularly referenced examples from state practice relating to persistent objection and *jus cogens* norms: the policy of apartheid in South Africa and Rhodesia and the objections of the United States to the juvenile death penalty. Finally, section V briefly considers the possibility of persistent objection to the *very concept* of peremptory norms.

I. The Nature of Peremptory Norms

Peremptory or '*jus cogens*' norms are 'fundamental [international] legal norms from which no derogation is permitted'.[7] *Jus cogens* norms are therefore 'higher' norms of the international legal system from which states cannot deviate.[8] This chapter is not the place to provide a detailed discussion of the way in which peremptory norms of international law come into being.[9] Nonetheless, it is worth

[7] H. Charlesworth and C. Chinkin, 'The Gender of *Jus Cogens*' (1993) 15 *Human Rights Quarterly* 15, 15.

[8] Although there is significant support for the concept of *jus cogens* in doctrine, it is worth noting that there remains a good deal of general academic debate as to the scope, nature, and, indeed, very existence of *jus cogens* norms. This is not the place to discuss these debates in any detail. In brief, some writers have questioned the potentially negative impact of peremptory norms on the structure and functionality of the international legal system. See, for example, P. Weil, 'Towards Relative Normativity in International Law?' (1983) 77 *American Journal of International Law* 413. The political motivations that underpin the concept of *jus cogens* have also been brought into question. See, for example, R.P. Barnidge, Jr, 'Questioning the Legitimacy of *Jus Cogens* in the Global Legal Order' (2008) 38 *Israel Yearbook of Human Rights* 199, 203–10. A number of writers have taken such arguments further and questioned the very existence of *jus cogens* norms. See, for example, G.A. Christenson, '*Jus Cogens*: Guarding Interests Fundamental to International Society' (1987–8) 28 *Virginia Journal of International Law* 585; and M.J. Glennon, 'Peremptory Nonsense' in S. Breitenmoser, B. Ehrenzeller, and M. Sassòli (eds), *Human Rights, Democracy and the Rule of Law:* Liber Amicorum *Luzius Wildhaber* (Zürich, Nomos, 2007), 1265. Suffice it to say here that the present author accepts the existence of *jus cogens* norms, albeit that he has reservations about the tendency to uncritically ascribe such hallowed status to any given norm based purely on the preferences of the individual bestowing this eminent standing and without the genuine application of the criteria set out in Vienna Convention on the Law of Treaties (VCLT), 23 May 1969, 1155 UNTS 331, Article 53.

[9] For a more detailed analysis of the manner in which *jus cogens* norms are created, see A. Orakhelashvili, *Peremptory Norms in International Law* (Oxford, Oxford University Press, 2006), 36–130.

recalling here the positivist understanding of how such norms emerge. The most widely quoted definition of a *jus cogens* norm comes from Article 53 of the 1969 Vienna Convention on the Law of Treaties (VCLT):

> A treaty is void if, at the time of its conclusion, it conflicts with a peremptory norm of general international law. For the purposes of the present Convention, a peremptory norm of general international law is a norm accepted and recognized by the international community of States as a whole as a norm from which no derogation is permitted and which can be modified only by a subsequent norm of general international law having the same character.[10]

Using Article 53 as *the* definition of *jus cogens* is admittedly not entirely satisfactory. This is primarily because Article 53 relates to conflicts between peremptory norms and *treaties*, not to *jus cogens* norms in the context of other legal sources, such as customary international law. Article 53 is clear that the definition is given '[f]or the purposes of the present Convention'. It is therefore evident that Article 53 was not designed to act as a definition for the *jus cogens* concept per se.[11] Nonetheless, that provision offers a useful starting point for identifying a peremptory norm, and it is today largely accepted as the key touchstone for the creation and content of rules of *jus cogens*.[12] Thus, simply put, for a norm to be considered peremptory, it must be 'accepted and recognized by the international community of States as a whole' as qualifying as this special 'type' of norm from which no derogation is permitted.

Having said this, it is fairly clear that acceptance and recognition of peremptory status by the 'international community of States as a whole' does not necessitate *universal* acceptance by states as to the peremptory character of any given norm. As the chairman of the Drafting Committee of the VCLT made clear in 1968, it is enough for 'a large majority' of states to take such a position,[13] and this is clearly now the majority view on the formation of *jus cogens* obligations.[14] This

[10] VCLT, n. 8, Article 53. Complementing Article 53 is Article 64 of the VCLT, which states: '[i]f a new peremptory norm of general international law emerges, any existing treaty which is in conflict with that norm becomes void and terminates.' See also *Questions relating to the Obligation to Prosecute or Extradite* (*Belgium v Senegal*), judgment, 2012 ICJ Rep. 422, para. 99 (suggesting similar criteria to those that appear in Article 53 for the creation of peremptory norms).

[11] See E. de Wet, 'The Prohibition of Torture as an International Norm of *Jus Cogens* and Its Implications for National and Customary Law' (2004) 15 *European Journal of International Law* 97, 98–9. In addition, as of 16 August 2015, only 114 states are party to the VCLT, a little over half of all UN member states. See UN Treaty Collection: Status of the Vienna Convention on the Law of Treaties, 1969, https://treaties.un.org/pages/ViewDetailsIII.aspx?src=TREATY&mtdsg_no=XXIII-1&chapter=23&Temp=mtdsg3&lang=en. It is also noteworthy that six states—Belgium, Russia, Japan, The Netherlands, Sweden, and the United States—have made minor reservations of differing types with regard to Article 53, although none of these states exclude the Article's applicability per se. For discussion, see J.A. Green, 'Questioning the Peremptory Status of the Prohibition of the Use of Force' (2011) 32 *Michigan Journal of International Law* 215, 219–20.

[12] See L. Hannikainen, *Peremptory Norms (*Jus Cogens*) in International Law: Historical Development, Criteria, Present Status* (Helsinki, Lakimiesliiton Kusannus, 1988), 3.

[13] United Nations Conference on the Law of Treaties, 26 March–24 May 1968, 80th meeting of the committee of the whole, 21 May 1968, UN Doc. A/CONF.39/C.1/SR.80, 472.

[14] This view is not unanimous, however. For example, McClane argues that universal acceptance *is* required for the emergence of a new *jus cogens* norm, and therefore that single states can veto the

notion of a 'large majority' bestowing *jus cogens* status is rather at odds with a positivist, voluntarist conception of international law as being built on state consent.[15] Nonetheless, this is, for most, justified by the need to avoid a single state vetoing a peremptory norm (which will, almost necessarily, be a 'fundamental', value-based norm) accepted as such by all others.[16]

It is worth noting that if absolute universality is unnecessary for *jus cogens* norms to emerge, as most claim, this means that a single state that dissents from the emerging peremptory rule cannot preclude a norm from acquiring super-norm status. Indeed, if universality was required, then the question of the possibility of persistent objection to peremptory norms would be moot: persistent objection to a 'peremptory norm' would in itself preclude that norm from becoming peremptory in the first place.[17] Persistent objection inherently constitutes non-acceptance, and if universal acceptance were required for peremptory norms to emerge, as a strict reading of Article 53 might suggest, that would be the end of the matter: the persistent objector would not be bound by the 'ordinary' customary rule in the usual way, and its objection would also preclude that 'ordinary' rule becoming peremptory. Instead, it is generally agreed that the act of persistent objection will not halt the march of a norm towards peremptory status, if that status is accepted by the vast majority of other states.[18] The question, then, is whether the objector remains apart from the *jus cogens* norm once it has acquired such status.

II. Clarifying the Majority View: Peremptory Norms and the 'Decay' of Persistent Objector Status

As noted above, the assertion that states cannot exempt themselves from norms of *jus cogens*, once established, is ubiquitous in the literature.[19] It is important, however, to note that the commonly repeated assertions that states 'may not persistently object to *jus cogens* norms'[20] or that persistent objection requires that 'la

birth of new peremptory rules: in other words, he takes the view that persistent objection overrides peremptory status, not the other way around. See J.B. McClane, 'How Late in the Emergence of a Norm of Customary International Law May a Persistent Objector Object?' (1989) 13 *International Law Students Association Journal of International Law* 1, 25.

[15] See G.M. Danilenko, 'International *Jus Cogens*: Issues of Law-Making' (1991) 2 *European Journal of International Law* 42, in general, but particularly at 48–57; Glennon, n. 8, particularly at 1266 and 1268; and Hannikainen, n. 12, 49.

[16] See, for example, R. Nieto-Navia, 'International Peremptory Norms (*Jus Cogens*) and International Humanitarian Law' in L.C. Vohrah, F. Pocar, Y. Featherstone, O. Fourmy, C. Graham, J. Hocking, and N. Robson (eds), *Man's Inhumanity to Man: Essays on International Law in Honour of Antonio Cassese* (The Hague, Kluwer Law International, 2003), 595, 612.

[17] See H. Thirlway, *The Sources of International Law* (Oxford, Oxford University Press, 2014), 159–60 (questioning whether universality is indeed required, and—if it is—asking whether this means that a single persistent objector may be able to 'block' norms from acquiring peremptory status).

[18] Loschin, n. 2, 163–4, footnote 89.

[19] See sources cited in n. 2.

[20] Danchin, n. 2, 76.

norme coutumière nouvelle n'appartienne pas à la catégorie des normes du *jus cogens*'[21] are actually, in themselves, axiomatic. It is self-evident that a state cannot gain exemption to a *jus cogens* norm through persistent objection to it. Given the status of peremptory norms as 'higher level' norms of fundamental value sitting at the pinnacle of the international legal system, it is almost inconceivable that a norm will attain peremptory status at the point at which the norm itself comes into being. Established conventional and customary norms *acquire* peremptory status, usually over many years: they are not 'born' with it.[22] This is evident from the fact that the requirements for becoming a peremptory norm are significantly more onerous than those for the crystallization of an 'ordinary' customary international law norm.[23] Indeed, Article 53 VCLT explicitly defines peremptory norms by reference to 'general international law',[24] indicating that 'candidates for *jus cogens* would appear to be forthcoming from that pool of existing norms that can already claim the status of general international law, or of custom'.[25]

The timeliness criterion for persistent objection means that states cannot gain exemption through subsequent objection.[26] It follows that by the time a norm that has its basis in custom attains peremptory status it will, in essentially all cases, already be binding on the state in question (that is, unless that state has previously gained an exemption to the norm through its persistent objections).[27] Those that take the view that states cannot persistently object to *jus cogens* norms are, therefore, in fact arguing that the exempt status of *existing* persistent objectors will be *overridden* if the norm from which the dissenter had previously gained exemption takes on a peremptory character (i.e. persistent objector status can no longer be maintained, de jure).[28] As Curci phrases this, once a norm is considered

[21] de Visscher, n. 2, 75.

[22] See P. Dumberry, 'Incoherent and Ineffective: The Concept of Persistent Objector Revisited' (2010) 59 *International and Comparative Law Quarterly* 779, 799; McClane, n. 14, 25; D.D. Tladi, '*Jus Cogens*', Annex to Report of the International Law Commission, Sixty-sixth session, 2014, UN Doc. A/69/10, para. 9 ('a norm of general international law *rises to* the level of being peremptory'; emphasis added); and S. Yee, 'Report on the ILC Project on "Identification of Customary International Law"' (Report by the Special Rapporteur of the Asian-African Legal Consultative Organisation (AALCO) Informal Expert Group on Customary International Law) (2015) 14 *Chinese Journal of International Law* 375, 392, para. 60 (arguing that there is a strong presumption that *jus cogens* norms cannot 'come into being as an instant custom').

[23] See U. Linderfalk, 'The Effect of *Jus Cogens* Norms: Whoever Opened Pandora's Box, Did You Ever Think about the Consequences?' (2007) 18 *European Journal of International Law* 853, 862 (describing a 'two-tier' notion of *opinio juris*).

[24] VCLT, n. 8, Article 53. [25] Kritsiotis, n. 2, 133.

[26] See, generally, Chapter 6, in relation to the timeliness criterion.

[27] Dumberry, n. 22, 799.

[28] Dumberry sees this as a significant flaw in the theory of persistent objection, in that well established exempt objectors will 'sudden[ly]' find themselves bound by norms that have acquired peremptory status. See ibid., 799. It is questionable whether such a change in normative status is likely to be as sudden as Dumberry suggests: *jus cogens* status *evolves*. Moreover, simply because a state has a long-standing exemption does not in itself mean that it is, or should be, entitled to maintain it, unless one takes a strictly voluntarist approach to international law (which would, in any event, not allow for the possibility of *jus cogens* norms, except for those that had received universal state acceptance). On voluntarism in relation to the persistent objector rule, see Chapter 9, particularly at section I.

peremptory, 'the status of the persistent objector *decays*'.[29] This is, admittedly, a relatively minor clarification, and is not one that goes to the substance of the majority view itself (i.e. that exemption from *jus cogens* norms by virtue of persistent objection is impossible). Nonetheless, it is worth keeping in mind.

III. The Rationale for the Majority View on Persistent Objection and Peremptory Norms

For the majority of writers, the rationale underpinning the view that peremptory status precludes exemption through objection is based on a conceptualization of the *purpose* of peremptory norms, as being aimed at protecting the most crucial values of common interest and moral importance.[30] It is understandably seen as undesirable, once 'the international community as a whole' (meaning, as has been noted, *virtually* all states) has 'accepted and recognized' a given international law norm as being of such importance that it cannot be derogated from, to allow a single state to maintain an exemption from that norm. On this basis, Rozakis has argued that allowing a single state to extricate itself from the universal binding force of *jus cogens* norms would 'be absurd'.[31]

Indeed, the very concept of a norm that cannot be derogated from can be viewed as being intuitively at odds with the persistent objector rule, the primary *raison d'être* of which is to exempt the state from the application of the norm in question.[32] The persistent objector process, therefore, is seen by many as being inherently contrary to the concept of *jus cogens*.[33] Some scholars have taken this further, and argued that the entire rationale underpinning the *jus cogens* 'project' in international law was to override the will of persistent objectors in areas of

[29] Curci, n. 2, 161, emphasis added. See also Padmanabhan, n. 2, 8 (in relation to the example of the prohibition of apartheid, discussed in section IV); Thirlway, n. 17, 159 (asserting that the majority view is that 'if a rule of *jus cogens* develops, no one can claim *to have been* a persistent objector'; emphasis added); and Yee, n. 22, 392, para. 60 ('[a]s soon as the objected-to rule at issue becomes a *jus cogens* norm, the persistent objector loses its privilege').

[30] See, for example, R.B. Baker, 'Customary International Law in the 21st Century: Old Challenges and New Debates' (2010) 21 *European Journal of International Law* 173, 177; Dumberry, n. 22, 798 (noting this reasoning in the literature but—given that he ultimately rejects the persistent objector rule per se—not subscribing to it); Lepard, n. 2, 250–1; R. St. J. Macdonald, 'Fundamental Norms in Contemporary International Law' (1987) 25 *Canadian Yearbook of International Law* 115, 131; Quince, n. 2, 39; A. Roberts, 'Traditional and Modern Approaches to Customary International Law: A Reconciliation' (2001) 95 *American Journal of International Law* 757, 765, and 783; Steinfeld, n. 2, 1678; Tasioulas, n. 2, 313; and Thirlway, n. 2, 110.

[31] C.L. Rozakis, *The Concept of* Jus Cogens *in the Law of Treaties* (Amsterdam, North Holland Publishing Company, 1976), 78.

[32] M. Ragazzi, *The Concept of International Obligations* Erga Omnes (Oxford, Clarendon Press, 1997), 67.

[33] See M. Bos, 'The Identification of Custom in International Law' (1982) 25 *German Yearbook of International Law* 9, 43; Ford, n. 2, 146; Kritsiotis, n. 2, 133–4; Lowe, n. 2, 58; Shelton, n. 2, 301; and M. Szappanyos, 'Obligatory or Voluntary?—Participation in the UPR' (2012) 150 *Studia Iuridica Auctoritate Universitatis Pecs Publicata* 273, 276.

crucial importance.[34] This is something of an oversimplification, but certainly the goal of overriding contrary views of 'the minority' in areas of fundamental importance goes to the heart of the *jus cogens* concept. If one accepts that *jus cogens* norms can (and do) exist within international law,[35] it logically follows, as a matter of legal theory, that the inherent nature of *jus cogens* means that even objector states will be bound once a norm reaches this status. To conclude otherwise would be to contradict the nature of peremptory norms and their place within the international legal system.

The idea that persistent objection is unavailing in the context of peremptory norms is so entrenched in doctrine that it has been argued that the principle that the persistent objector rule is inapplicable in relation to *jus cogens* norms *is itself* a *jus cogens* norm.[36] In the view of the present author, this goes too far: there is nowhere near enough evidence from state practice to support a finding that the inapplicability of persistent objection to peremptory norms has been 'accepted and recognized by the international community as a whole' as a super-norm in its own right.[37] Nonetheless, if one focuses on the nature and function of *jus cogens* norms, it seems intuitively correct to hold that persistent objectors should be bound by such norms just like any other state.

The problem with this position, of course, becomes evident if one approaches the question from the opposite starting point, by focusing instead on the nature and function of the persistent objector rule, which—at least in theory—is supposed to allow states to exempt themselves from norms of international law to which they have not consented. Some writers have therefore criticized the majority view that persistent objectors will nonetheless be bound by peremptory norms on the basis that denying exemption from such norms would amount to an erosion of the sovereign right of states to consent (or not) to rules of international law.[38] This voluntarist critique is undeniably correct, as far as it goes. If a state is unable to maintain exempt persistent objector status in relation to *jus cogens* norms, then such norms run contrary to the notion that states must consent to all rules of international law that bind them: something that could be viewed as undermining the very purpose of the persistent objector rule. As Koskenniemi notes, the relationship between *jus cogens* and persistent objection is a point where an irresistible force and an immovable object of international legal theory collide.

[34] D. Shelton, 'International Law and "Relative Normativity"' in M. Evans (ed.), *International Law* (Oxford, Oxford University Press, 4th edn, 2014), 137, 151.

[35] Not all commentators do, of course: see, for example, Christenson, n. 8, 585; and Glennon, n. 8, 1265.

[36] Hulsroj, n. 2, 8.

[37] See section IV for a discussion of the limited amount of state practice in relation to attempts to maintain persistent objector status to *jus cogens* norms.

[38] See, for example, A. Cassese, *International Law in a Divided World* (Oxford, Clarendon Press, 1986), 178. See also P. Malanczuk, *Akehurst's Modern Introduction to International Law* (New York, Routledge, 7th edn, 1997), 48 (seemingly indicating that persistent objection to *jus cogens* norms is possible, but that this would require more onerous criteria to be met than is the case for persistent objection in relation to 'regular' norms of customary international law; whether Malanczuk subscribes to this position is far from clear, however).

If we allow for persistent objection to *jus cogens* this undermines the superior nature of those norms, turning them into ugly, 'regular' rules; if we say that *jus cogens* norms can steamroll even otherwise legitimate objections, then this undermines the idea that persistent objection acts to protect state consent.[39]

However, the absolute voluntarist conception of international law, and of the persistent objector rule in particular, must be rejected, at least in its more extreme forms.[40] Persistent objection does not protect sovereign autonomy absolutely. This means that there is an inherent policy choice underpinning any decision to prioritize either the function of persistent objection or that of peremptory norms. For the majority of commentators at least, this collision between the underlying functions of *jus cogens* norms and persistent objection is resolved by prioritizing the need for peremptory norms to be universal. This is perhaps unsurprising: *jus cogens* norms are inherently value-based and community-centric, whereas persistent objection is, at least in part, the champion of individual interests and exceptionalism. If the majority view is correct and peremptory norms trump persistent objection, then this of course further undermines the voluntarist understanding of the persistent objector rule.[41]

IV. Persistent Objection to Peremptory Norms in State Practice

Ultimately, of course, it is the practice of states that is the most important factor in determining the position of persistent objectors in relation to peremptory norms, irrespective of whether any given writer prioritizes the moral imperatives of the *jus cogens* project or the sanctity of state autonomy. If states are in fact able to maintain exemption from peremptory norms through persistent objection in practice, then the majority view that they cannot do so would be difficult to support.

i. The examples: apartheid and the juvenile death penalty

There are two commonly referenced examples that are said to support the majority view that the persistent objector status 'decays' in relation to *jus cogens* norms. The 'classic' example of unavailing objection in relation to a *jus cogens* norm is the continued objections of South Africa and Rhodesia to the customary international law norm prohibiting the policy of apartheid. As applicants in the *South West Africa* cases, Ethiopia and Liberia argued in their oral submissions that South Africa 'may not claim exemption from a legal norm which has been created

[39] M. Koskenniemi, *From Apology to Utopia: The Structure of International Legal Argument* (Cambridge, Cambridge University Press, reissue, 2005), 325. See also Thirlway, n. 17, 159.

[40] See Chapter 9, particularly at section I.

[41] See ibid., n. 38 and accompanying text.

by the overwhelming consensus of the international community, and consensus verging on unanimity'.[42] This argument has subsequently met with a great deal of support. The apartheid example—presented as demonstrative of the impossibility of retaining exemption in relation to *jus cogens* norms—was famously referenced by both Stein[43] and Charney[44] in their respective seminal articles on the persistent objector rule from 1985, and the practice of one or both of South Africa and Rhodesia has been regularly cited by other writers since then as evidence confirming the majority view.[45]

The customary international law prohibition on the policy of apartheid had emerged by the early 1970s, having its roots in various preceding human rights treaty obligations.[46] South Africa and Rhodesia had maintained a degree of persistent objection to this customary prohibition, both by way of 'deed' (through their continuance of the policy) and declarations that they were not bound by the customary norm.[47] This position was, of course, not accepted by the international community of states,[48] with huge pressure of various types being placed on South Africa and Rhodesia to conform to this international legal obligation while they continued to employ the policy in the 1970s and, in the case of South Africa, the 1980s and early 1990s. Various writers have ascribed peremptory status to the prohibition of apartheid, and see this as the reason that the objections of South Africa and Rhodesia were ultimately unavailing.[49]

[42] *South West Africa* cases (*Ethiopia v South Africa, Liberia v South Africa*), Reply of Mr Gross (Ethiopia and Liberia), 1966 ICJ Plead., vol. IX, 305.

[43] Stein, n.1, 463 and 473–4.

[44] Charney, 'The Persistent Objector Rule', n. 2, 15 (although Charney did not specifically identify the prohibition of apartheid as being *jus cogens*, but rather saw the South African and Rhodesian inability to maintain their objector status as examples of the broader phenomenon of political pressure ultimately undermining persistent objection: in relation to this phenomenon, see Chapter 8, section II).

[45] See, for example, Abasheikh, n. 2, 44; Charney, 'Universal International Law', n. 2, 539; Curci, n. 2, 163, footnote 83; Dumberry, n. 22, 791; O. Elias, 'Some Remarks on the Persistent Objector Rule in Customary International Law' (1991) 6 *Denning Law Journal* 37, 46–7; Guldahl, n. 2, 58; M.H. Mendelson, 'The Formation of Customary International Law' (1998) 272 *Recueil des cours* 155, 235–6; Roberts, n. 30, 784; Steinfeld, n. 2, 1655; and J. Tasioulas, 'Custom, *Jus Cogens*, and Human Rights' in C.A. Bradley (ed.), *Custom's Future: International Law in a Changing World* (Cambridge, Cambridge University Press, forthcoming), pre-publication version, *Social Science Research Network*, 20 March 2015, http://papers.ssrn.com/sol3/papers.cfm?abstract_id=2581763, 11.

[46] As evidenced, for example, by the International Convention on the Suppression and Punishment of the Crime of Apartheid 1973, entered into force 1976, 1015 UNTS 243, which has 109 states parties, as of 17 August 2015.

[47] For example, South Africa explicitly held that it was a 'persistent objector' to the prohibition on apartheid in *South West Africa* cases (*Ethiopia v South Africa, Liberia v South Africa*), Rejoinder of Dr VerLoren van Themaat (South Africa), 1966 ICJ Plead., vol. X, 9–10.

[48] C. Tomuschat, 'Obligations Arising for States Without or Against Their Will' (1993) 241 *Recueil des cours* 195, 289.

[49] See works cited in n. 45, and also J. Dugard, *International Law: A South African Perspective* (Cape Town, Juta & Co., 3rd edn, 2008), 32; L. Henkin, *International Law: Politics and Values* (Leiden, Brill, 1995), 39; and Mendelson, n. 45, 235–6. Indeed, the present author has himself previously expressed the same view: see J.A. Green, 'India and a Customary Comprehensive Nuclear Test-Ban: Persistent Objection, Peremptory Norms and the 123 Agreement' (2011) 51 *Indian Journal of International Law* 3, 25–6; and J.A. Green, 'Persistent Objector Teflon? Customary International Human Rights Law and the United States in International Adjudicative Proceedings'

The other example that is commonly identified as supporting the proposition that persistent objector status is unsustainable against peremptory norms relates to the policy of the United States with regard to the juvenile death penalty.[50] In particular, the issue of juvenile executions was considered in two decisions of the Inter-American Commission on Human Rights (IACmHR): *Roach and Pinkerton v United States*,[51] and *Domingues v United States*.[52] In both instances the United States argued that, if there existed a customary prohibition on the execution of persons who were less than eighteen years old at the time of the commission of the relevant offence, it was nonetheless exempt as a persistent objector.[53] It may be said that there was certainly a persistent pattern of objection on the part of the United States that would prima facie support this claim.[54]

In *Roach and Pinkerton*, in 1987, the IACmHR examined whether imposition of the death penalty on the petitioners by American courts for crimes committed before their eighteenth birthdays (the petitioners indeed having been executed before the end of the proceedings) violated various provisions of the (non-binding) American Declaration of the Rights and Duties of Man 1948[55] 'as informed by customary international law which prohibits the imposition of the death penalty for crimes committed by juveniles under eighteen'.[56]

The Commission determined, firstly, that *if there was* a customary international law prohibition on the juvenile death penalty, the United States would indeed not be bound by any such norm, on the basis of its persistent objection to the norm's emergence.[57] Secondly, however, the IACmHR held that there was not only an established customary norm prohibiting the execution of juvenile offenders, but that this norm was peremptory in nature.[58] One would assume that this

in J.A. Green and C.P.M. Waters (eds), *Adjudicating International Human Rights: Essays in Honour of Sandy Ghandhi* (Leiden, Brill Nijhoff, 2015), 167, 175 and 188.

[50] See, generally, D. Weissbrodt, 'Execution of Juvenile Offenders by the United States Violates International Human Rights Law' (1988) 3 *American University Journal of International Law and Policy* 339.

[51] *Roach and Pinkerton v United States*, 1987 IACmHR, Report No. 3/87, Case 9647.

[52] *Domingues v United States*, merits, 2002 IACmHR, Report No. 62/02, Case 12.285.

[53] See *Roach and Pinkerton v United States*, memorandum of the United States to the Inter-American Commission on Human Rights in Case 9647, IACmHR 147, OEA/ser.L/V./II.71, doc. 9 rev. 1, 15; and *Domingues v United States*, response of the government of the United States to May 1, 2000 Petition, Case No. 12.185 (Michael Domingues), http://www.state.gov/documents/organization/16525.pdf, 10–11.

[54] Bradley provides significant prima facie evidence of the United States' persistent objection to an emerging customary international law norm on juvenile executions, with its objections starting well before any possible norm could have crystallized. See C.A. Bradley, 'The Juvenile Death Penalty' (2002–3) 52 *Duke Law Journal* 485, particularly at 492–500. However, the present author ultimately takes the view that the United States' objections were not sufficiently *consistent*. See Chapter 5, n. 6–n. 23 and accompanying text.

[55] American Declaration of the Rights and Duties of Man, 2 May 1948, OEA/Ser.L./V.II.23, doc. 21, rev. 6. Specifically, the petitioners alleged violations of Article I (right to life), Article VII (special protection of children) and Article XXVI (cruel, infamous, or unusual punishment): see *Roach and Pinkerton*, merits, n. 51, para. 34.

[56] *Roach and Pinkerton*, merits, n. 51, para. 34.

[57] Ibid., para. 54.

[58] Ibid., para. 56.

then meant that the Commission saw American objections as being unavailing (given that, in the view of the IACmHR, the persistent objector rule is inapplicable in relation to *jus cogens*). Yet, in something of a *volte-face*, the IACmHR then determined that—while a peremptory prohibition on juvenile executions existed—it was not clear that the age limit for identifying a 'juvenile' for this purpose was necessarily set at *eighteen*.[59] The Commission felt that a new norm specifically prohibiting the executions of individuals aged less than eighteen years when their offence was committed was 'emerging' at the time, but that this had not yet emerged.[60] This meant that the policy of the United States in executing sixteen-year-old offenders did not violate the (peremptory) customary legal prohibition after all.[61]

Leaving aside the question of whether it is conceptually possible to identify a peremptory norm while simultaneously concluding that there is no agreement as to the parameters of that norm (in this case an age threshold), the IACmHR's report in *Roach and Pinkerton* clearly acts as authority for the claim that persistent objection is unavailing in relation to norms of *jus cogens*, even if only ultimately in the abstract.[62]

Following the Commission's report in *Roach and Pinkerton*, there were increasing suggestions that—from the early 1990s onwards—a norm prohibiting the execution of persons *under the age of eighteen* had crystallized as binding customary international law.[63] Certainly, there exists a good deal of evidence indicating that this was the case.[64] This development in the general acceptance of the customary prohibition meant that the IACmHR felt it was on firmer ground when next it was presented with the juvenile death penalty issue.

In the 2002 *Domingues* case, the IACmHR again had the opportunity to scrutinize the policy of the United States concerning juvenile executions: here in relation to the death sentence imposed by the state of Nevada on an individual who was sixteen years old at the time that he committed two homicides.[65] The United States once more argued that it was exempt from the prohibition on juvenile executions—or at least exempt from a rule that takes eighteen rather than sixteen

[59] Ibid., para. 60. [60] Ibid.

[61] Ibid. Although the Commission nonetheless saw the United States as being in violation of customary international law norms reflected in Articles I and II of the American Declaration of the Rights and Duties of Man: ibid., paras 61–5.

[62] Dumberry, n. 22, 788.

[63] See, for example, Amnesty International, 'United States of America: Open Letter to the President on the Death Penalty', 1994, https://www.amnesty.org/en/documents/amr51/001/1994/en/, particularly the state practice referenced at 8.

[64] The state practice supporting the establishment, in the early 1990s, of a customary norm prohibiting juvenile executions is set out in detail in E.F. Sherman, Jr., 'The U.S. Death Penalty Reservation to the International Covenant on Civil and Political Rights: Exposing the Limitations of the Flexible System Governing Treaty Formation' (1994) 29 *Texas International Law Journal* 69, 88–90. See also Loschin, n. 2, 154–8; and *Commonwealth of Pennsylvania v Hector Huertas*, motion to preclude the Commonwealth from seeking the death penalty against a juvenile and consolidated memorandum of law, 2002, CP 0009-0941, CTD, 19–25, both similarly providing detailed evidence for the customary status of the prohibition.

[65] *Domingues*, merits, n. 52, paras 1–2.

as the threshold for minority executions—on the basis that it was a persistent objector.[66]

Unlike in *Roach and Pinkerton*, by 2002 the IACmHR felt comfortable in asserting that there was indeed a customary prohibition on the execution of juveniles *aged less than eighteen* at the time of the commission of their offence.[67] It then rejected the United States' claim of exemption from that customary norm on the basis, inter alia, that the prohibition on the execution of juveniles had the status of a norm of *jus cogens*:

> [T]he Commission considers that the United States is bound by a norm of *jus cogens* not to impose capital punishment on individuals who committed their crimes when they had not yet reached 18 years of age. As a *jus cogens* norm, this proscription binds the community of States, including the United States. The norm cannot be validly derogated from, whether by treaty or by the objection of a state, persistent or otherwise.[68]

In other words, in 2002 the IACmHR was less equivocal than it had been in 1987: the juvenile death penalty was prohibited by a *jus cogens* norm, and the United States was therefore in violation of that prohibition irrespective of its persistent objection.[69]

The United States Supreme Court subsequently ruled, in *Roper v Simmons*[70] in 2005, that the juvenile death penalty constituted cruel and unusual punishment and was therefore unlawful under the American Constitution. This decision has been seen by some as likely being a result of the IACmHR's findings in its *Domingues* report,[71] and thus evidence that—in both law and fact—persistent objection no longer pays once a rule acquires *jus cogens* status.

The two examples discussed above—apartheid and the juvenile death penalty—certainly appear to support the majority view that persistent objection is unavailing in relation to peremptory norms. Indeed, in the case of the United States and juvenile executions, *Domingues* indicates that even the most powerful state in the world cannot maintain persistent objector status against rules of *jus cogens*.

ii. Does state practice actually support the proposition that peremptory norms trump persistent objection?

While they are commonly cited by writers as confirming the proposition that persistent objection is unavailing in relation to peremptory norms, the apartheid and the juvenile death penalty examples must actually be treated with a degree of caution: the 'state practice' that is argued to establish the impossibility

[66] See Response of the Government of the United States (Michael Domingues), n.53; and *Domingues*, merits, n. 52, para. 14.

[67] Ibid., para. 83. [68] Ibid., para. 85. [69] Shelton, n. 2, 313.

[70] *Roper v Simmons*, 2005, 543 U.S. 551.

[71] See, for example, S. Babcock, 'Human Rights Advocacy in United States Capital Cases' in C. Soohoo, C. Albisa, and M.F. Davis (eds), *Bringing Human Rights Home, vol. 3* (Westport, Praeger, 2008), 91, 105.

of persistent objection to *jus cogens* norms is far from conclusive with regard to that proposition.[72] This is, most notably, because there is very little practice from which to actually draw such a conclusion. South Africa/Rhodesia (apartheid) and the United States (juvenile death penalty) aside, one struggles to identify any instances where states have tried to maintain persistent objector status in relation to a peremptory norm.[73] This is perhaps unsurprising, given that the creation of *jus cogens* norms requires near-universal agreement on the part of the international community of states. Dissent is especially unlikely with regard to peremptory norms, because they inherently relate to fundamental values that are extremely widespread within the system, meaning that the rejection of such norms obviously entails significant political peril.[74]

It is also worth noting that the legal criteria for establishing any given norm as being peremptory are notably onerous: while universal acceptance is generally seen to be unnecessary, the test is nonetheless whether the vast majority of states of the world have accepted and recognized the norm as being peremptory.[75] The onerous nature of the test for peremptory status therefore also helps to explain the lack of state practice with regard to the rejection of *jus cogens* norms, in that it means that there are relatively few such norms in existence to which even the most contrary of states could try to continue to object.[76]

The burdensome nature of the test for a *jus cogens* norm to emerge, and indeed the uncertainty as to exactly how this occurs,[77] also means that peremptory status can be debated even in relation to fundamental rules of the international legal system that most would agree to be of a peremptory nature.[78] Thus, for example,

[72] Ragazzi, n. 32, 70 (noting that while in principle it is relatively clear that states cannot remain exempt from peremptory norms through persistent objection, '[i]n practice, things are somewhat more complicated').

[73] *Cf.* Green, 'India and a Customary Comprehensive Nuclear Test-Ban', n. 49, 25 (where the present author previously suggested, incorrectly, that there are '*a number* of examples where States have been unable to maintain persistent objector status in relation to peremptory (or, at least, arguably peremptory) norms'; emphasis added). This claim was based on the identification of the apartheid and juvenile death penalty examples. However, further investigation has shown that stating that there existed 'a number' of examples was undoubtedly an exaggeration.

[74] Shelton, n. 34, 156.

[75] Rozakis, n. 31, 15 (arguing that the tests for the formation (or alteration) of *jus cogens* norms as set out in Article 53 of the VCLT 'are quite severe').

[76] See Elias, n. 45, 40 ('the category of *ius cogens* is still largely an empty box, subject to a few possible exceptions'); and Quince, n. 2, 62.

[77] A. Boyle and C. Chinkin, *The Making of International Law* (Oxford, Oxford University Press, 2007), 17; Danilenko, n. 15, particularly at 43 and 45; Fidler, n. 2, 211; C. Ochoa, 'Disintegrating Customary International Law: Reactions to "Withdrawing from International Custom"' (2010) 21 *Duke Journal of Comparative and International Law* 157, 166, footnote 40; and Tladi, n. 22, paras 9 and 15.

[78] For example, when one begins to actually test the prohibition of the use of force or the prohibition of genocide against the Article 53 criteria, it is far from self-evident that even these fundamental norms meet the required standard. See Green, n. 11, 126; S.T. Helmersen, 'The Prohibition of the Use of Force as *Jus Cogens*: Explaining Apparent Derogations' (2014) 61 *Netherlands International Law Review* 167 (both regarding the prohibition of the use of force); and D. Lisson, 'Defining "National Group" in the Genocide Convention: A Case Study of Timor-Leste' (2007–8) 60 *Stanford Law Review* 1459, 1463 (regarding the prohibition of genocide).

while the prohibition of apartheid is commonly seen as a *jus cogens* norm,[79] it must be admitted that this has largely just been assumed as self-evident without the peremptory credentials of the prohibition having been properly tested.[80] More notably, there has been significant debate as to the veracity of the IACmHR's conclusion that the prohibition of juvenile execution has acquired *jus cogens* status.[81] It is difficult to dispute that the prohibition is now customary international law—and, indeed, that it has been so for some time—but whether it is *peremptory* is far less clear: '[w]hile most scholars would tend to agree that the [prohibition of the] juvenile death penalty is ... established, few would agree that it is peremptory.'[82]

As such, of the two examples that *can* be identified as examples of states failing to maintain objector status in the face of a peremptory norm, one—or perhaps even both—may not in fact have related to a 'true' *jus cogens* norm at all. This is not to say that, for example, the prohibition of the juvenile death penalty was definitely not a peremptory norm at the time of the *Domingues* decision, only that it is very difficult to conclude with certainty that it was. Such difficulty in ascertaining whether any given norm has attained peremptory status means that, at least to an extent, 'the statement that a State cannot exempt itself from such rules merely begs the question'.[83]

The respective categorization of both South Africa and the United States as 'proper' persistent objectors to the norms in question may also be disputed. Although it is sometimes assumed that South Africa met all of the criteria for persistent objection—persistence, consistency, and timeliness[84]—existing treaty obligations that were incumbent on South Africa further cloud the issue as to whether it was a *consistent* objector. It has been pointed out that, in acceding to binding conventional restrictions on apartheid, South Africa was in fact far from consistent in its objections.[85] If it failed to meet the key consistency criterion for persistent objection, then it would not have qualified as a persistent objector state prima facie, irrespective of the peremptory status (or not) of the prohibition of apartheid.

Similarly, as we saw in Chapter 5, the United States' objections to the customary prohibition of the juvenile death penalty were insufficiently consistent for it to

[79] M. Byers, *Custom, Power and the Power of Rules: International Relations and Customary International Law* (Cambridge, Cambridge University Press, 1999), 186 and 194–5; and Hannikainen, n. 12, 467–89.

[80] P. Eden, 'The Role of the Rome Statute in the Criminalization of Apartheid' (2014) *12 Journal of International Criminal Justice* 171, 182–3.

[81] See, for example, Bradley, n. 54, 537–9; and Weissbrodt, n. 50, 369–71. *Cf. Hector Huertas*, motion, n. 64, 11 and 26–9.

[82] Loschin, n. 2, 169.

[83] O. Elias, 'Persistent Objector' in R. Wolfrum (ed.), *Max Planck Encyclopaedia of Public International Law, vol. VIII* (Oxford, Oxford University Press, 2012), 280, 285, para. 18. See also Guldahl, n. 2, 62 (qualifying her acceptance of the proposition that persistent objection cannot be maintained in relation to *jus cogens* norms by then stating that '[t]here is ... no agreement on the exact content of this concept [*jus cogens*], nor is there a generally accepted list of such norms').

[84] See, for example, Dumberry, n. 22, 791 (South Africa 'had timely and consistently objected to the emergence of a customary rule prohibiting [apartheid]').

[85] O. Schachter, 'International Law in Theory and Practice' (1982) 178 *Recueil des cours* 9, 119.

be considered an exempt persistent objector. This was the view of the IACmHR,[86] and there is strong evidence to suggest that the Commission was correct on this point.[87] The two examples from practice supporting the immunity of peremptory norms to persistent objection therefore may have both involved uses of the rule that did not fulfil its necessary requirements: meaning that the *jus cogens* question was essentially moot.

Finally, one might point to the fact that, with regard to the policy of apartheid, South Africa in particular continued to apply the policy for many years in the face of significant international opposition. This would indicate that the peremptory status of the prohibition had little practical effect on South Africa's de facto persistent objector status for a notable period. To an extent, the same can be said of the approach taken by the United States concerning juvenile execution (where the United States maintained its policy for a full three years after the unequivocal *Domingues* report). Perhaps this can be contextualized by the fact that, in both cases, the actions of the states concerned were generally viewed by others as a *breach* of international law, rather than being accepted as an example of an exempt persistent objector legitimately ploughing its own furrow.[88] In particular, the lengthy continuation of apartheid by South Africa perhaps, therefore, speaks more to the *efficacy* or *enforceability* of any requirement that even persistent objectors are bound by peremptory norms, rather than having implications for the proposition itself. Nonetheless, even if it is accepted that states cannot remain exempt from peremptory norms through persistent objection as a matter of law, practice shows that it is possible to maintain such a position as a matter of fact, even if not indefinitely.

The above discussion indicates that practice in support of the view that *jus cogens* norms suffer no dissenters actually appears rather equivocal on close inspection. However, perhaps the most significant finding from state practice is not the limited support for the proposition that states cannot maintain exemption to peremptory norms provided by the apartheid and juvenile death penalty examples. It is, instead, the fact that the present author has been unable to identify a single instance of a state remaining exempt from a *jus cogens* norm: 'ultimately *no State* has been able to maintain persistent objection to a peremptory norm.'[89] The *absence* of practice in this context may therefore tell us rather more than the

[86] *Domingues*, merits, n. 52, para. 85.

[87] See Chapter 5, n. 6–n. 23 and accompanying text.

[88] In relation to the policy of apartheid, see, for example, Byers, n. 79, 195; and Dugard, n. 49, 32. In relation to the juvenile death penalty, see, for example, the view of the UN Sub-Commission on the Promotion and Protection of Human Rights, which explicitly affirmed in 2000 that 'the imposition of the death penalty on those aged under 18 at the time of the commission of the offence is contrary to customary international law' and '[*c*]*ondemn*[*ed*] *unequivocally* the imposition and execution of the death penalty on those aged under 18 at the time of the commission of the offence'. See UN High Commissioner for Human Rights, Sub-Commission on the Promotion and Protection of Human Rights Resolution 2000/17, 18 April 2000, http://www.unhchr.ch/huridocda/huridoca.nsf/6d123295325517b2c12569910034dc4c/09597876bb508210c125697300448a18, emphasis in original.

[89] Green, 'Persistent Objector Teflon?', n. 49, 175, emphasis in original.

paucity of actual examples that we have. It is difficult to conclude whether the lack of dissenters to peremptory norms is due to a *legal* distinction that formally insulates such norms from persistent objection, or whether the political pressure associated with *jus cogens* norms (or norms that are commonly said to be *jus cogens*) simply means it is practically untenable for states to maintain exemption. The rhetorical power of the concept of *jus cogens* is such that it imposes intransgressible obligations as a matter of fact, irrespective of matters of law: it is thus extremely unlikely that dissenters will be able to escape the pull of a peremptory norm, whether the persistent objector rule is 'technically' applicable to super-norms or not.[90]

V. Persistent Objection to the *Jus Cogens* Project

A final issue that needs to be briefly raised in this chapter is whether a state can be a persistent objector, not to a specific *jus cogens* norm, but to the secondary rules of international law establishing and delimitating the very concept of *jus cogens*.[91] In particular, France was famously an outspoken critic of the *jus cogens* project from the outset.[92] It was the only state that voted against the inclusion of Article 53 in the VCLT and it remains a non-party to that treaty. Up until quite recently France still—occasionally, but repeatedly[93]—voiced its discontent over the concept.[94] Whether France's objections in this regard were sufficiently persistent and/or consistent for it to meet the persistent objector rule's operational requirements is perhaps debatable, but one could at least make the argument that France had, even into the first decade of the twenty-first century, the hallmarks of a persistent objector to the notion of *jus cogens in abstracto*. Indeed, it is notable that as recently as 2012, in a brief solicited by the Conseil d'État, Guillaume argued that France remained a persistent objector to the entire doctrine of *jus cogens*.[95]

Having said this, in recent years France has begun to grudgingly accept the concept of peremptory norms to some extent: as Pellet has stated, 'Asterix has stopped its rearguard action against the notion'.[96] Objection must be maintained

[90] Charney, 'The Persistent Objector Rule', n. 2, 19–20.

[91] A question raised by Stein, n. 1, 480. See also Danilenko, n. 15, 56–7 (arguing that persistent objectors to the concept of *jus cogens* per se are exempt from its application to them).

[92] See O. Deleaux, 'Les positions françaises à la Conférence de Vienne sur le droit des traités' (1969) 15 *Annuaire français de droit international* 7, 14–20.

[93] A. Cassese, *Five Masters of International Law* (Hart, Oxford, 2011), 24 (interview with R-J. Dupuy).

[94] See, for example, Report of the Human Rights Committee, vol. I, General Assembly, Official Records, Fifty-first session, Supplement no. 40, 1997, UN Doc. A/51/40, 117.

[95] G. Guillaume, 'Avis d'*amicus curiae* (article R. 625-3 du Code de justice administrative)' (2012) 28 *Revue française de droit administratif* 19, 20, para. 11 ('une telle coutume [on the nature and effect of *jus cogens* norms] ne lierait d'ailleurs pas la France, demeurée "objecteur persistant"').

[96] A. Pellet, 'Comments in Response to Christine Chinkin and in Defense of *Jus Cogens* as the Best Bastion against the Excesses of Fragmentation' (2006) 11 *Finnish Yearbook of International Law* 83, 89.

even after crystallization, of course, and, if it is not, then any exempt status is lost.[97] Therefore, if France ever was a persistent objector to the concept of *jus cogens*, it is almost certainly not any longer. The question of whether it is possible for a state to object to the notion of peremptory norms per se has moved into the realm of the academic.

It is highly questionable whether it is possible for a state to gain exemption through persistent objection, not from a 'rule' as such, but from a description or concept that identifies characteristics that are associated with a set of rules, or, indeed, from the secondary rules of international law per se.[98] Even if such a thing were possible, the rationale underpinning the majority view that substantive *jus cogens* norms overcome the right to persistently object would equally apply to a situation where a state objected to the concept of *jus cogens* itself. It would just as effectively defeat the intransgressibility of *jus cogens* norms to allow for exemption from them on the norm-administering procedural level as it would at the substantive level.

Indeed, if one accepts that the value-based imperative for universal compliance with peremptory norms outweighs the voluntarist concept of state autonomy in relation to the binding force of international law, then persistent objection to the overall concept of *jus cogens* is even less palatable, as it would allow a state to gain exemption from all such norms 'at once', based on a single process of persistent objection. Lepard indicates on this basis that any such claim of persistent objection from the secondary 'meta-rules' underpinning *jus cogens* would be 'doomed in advance to failure'.[99] This is almost certainly correct as a practical matter. There is, after all, a good reason why France stopped vocally opposing *jus cogens*: it became clear that the ship in question had sailed. Again, however, it remains rather difficult to be certain whether it was *legally* impossible for France to maintain objection to the very concept of *jus cogens* or whether the impossibility in this regard flowed rather more from the political 'weight' that the *jus cogens* project has acquired. The question is now moot in any event, and so will not be explored further here.

VI. Conclusion

The conceptual impasse that plagues the peremptory norm/persistent objector intersection and the questionable degree of assistance provided by the commonly advanced examples of apartheid and the juvenile death penalty mean that the ILC's confident assertion that 'it is *inconceivable* that a persistent objector could thwart … a [*jus cogens*] norm'[100] is perhaps not quite as self-evidently correct

[97] See Chapter 6, section X. [98] Byers, n. 79, 195. [99] Lepard, n. 2, 252.

[100] UN Doc. A/62/10, n. 6, 101, emphasis added. See also Guide to Practice on Reservations to Treaties with commentaries, 2011, International Law Commission, UN Doc A/66/10/Add.1, commentary (19) to guideline 3.1.5.3, 375; and Formation and Evidence of Customary International Law: Elements of the Previous Work of the International Law Commission that Could be Particularly Relevant to the Topic, 2013, Memorandum by the Secretariat, UN A/CN.4/659, 28, footnote 97 (this document set out and reviewed the previous views of the ILC in relation to customary international law).

as one might initially assume. However, the fact is that no state has ultimately been able to maintain objection to a peremptory norm: whether this is legal or merely political reality may ultimately be something of a red herring, at least in a practical sense in the context of international relations. Indeed, the relationship between *jus cogens* and persistent objection will rarely have practical significance, not least because the use of the persistent objector rule is relatively uncommon per se; in relation to near-universally agreed value-based peremptory norms, its use has been—and is likely to continue to be—rarer still (especially bearing in mind that there are actually very few peremptory norms that have been established at present). If a norm is 'accepted and recognized' as being peremptory by the international community, the chances of individual states attempting to swim against the tide will be, in the vast majority of instances, rather slim. The question of persistent objection to peremptory norms is therefore likely to pose more theoretical problems for scholars than practical ones for states.[101] Nonetheless, the theoretical problems remain and cannot be easily resolved: nor should they be too lightly dismissed.[102]

Taken together, the conclusions of the IACmHR in relation to the juvenile death penalty (as well as the positions taken by other international judicial or arbitral bodies), the morally compelling arguments concerning the nature of peremptory norms as inherently all-encompassing, the substantial weight of majority academic opinion, and the crucial fact that no state has been able to maintain exempt status in relation to peremptory norms (at least not indefinitely) lead this writer to ultimately tend towards following the majority in concluding that, as a matter of *law* (and not just fact), persistent objection has no effect in relation to peremptory norms. If a norm acquires peremptory status, any previously exempt persistent objectors will find that their exempt status has legally 'decayed'. However, none of the evidence that may be advanced for this proposition is entirely conclusive, and so the present author reaches this conclusion rather more tentatively than many others have done.[103]

[101] See Helmersen, n. 78, 192 ('The preclusion of persistent objection [for *jus cogens* norms] would … be relatively unimportant [in practice].') *Contra* Thirlway, n. 17, 159, footnote 57 ('This [the question of whether states can maintain persistent objection in relation to rules that become peremptory norms] may be more than a *hypothèse d'école*').

[102] The present author may have himself been guilty of overly downplaying the conceptual problems that plague the relationship between persistent objection and *jus cogens*. See Green, 'Persistent Objector Teflon?', n. 49, 176 ('[o]verall, then, it is relatively uncontroversial to state that … norms that have been accepted and recognised as being peremptory—the prohibitions on torture, apartheid, genocide, slavery, et al.—are legally immunised from the possibility of State exemption through persistent objection'; footnotes omitted).

[103] The present author is perhaps therefore more closely aligned to the view expressed by Byers in this regard than that of the majority: '*Jus cogens* rules would also seem to preclude the establishment of legal exceptions through the creation of a rule of special customary international law and the conclusion of treaties, *as well as, perhaps, persistent objection*.' Byers, n. 79, 188, emphasis added. See also Helmersen, n. 78, 172 ('*Jus cogens may* also exclude the possibility of being exempt from a rule based on "persistent objection"'; emphasis added).

8

Maintaining Exemption

'Fundamental' Norms and Extra-Legal Factors

As has already been examined in previous chapters, a notable minority critique of the persistent objector rule is that—for all its ubiquity in doctrine—the rule is not supported by actual state practice. The 'hard' version of this argument is that states *never* invoke the persistent objector rule. Another variation of essentially the same claim is that any invocation of the rule is inevitably ignored by the wider community of states, and thus that the objector will necessarily find itself unable to act as an exempt state once the norm to which it has objected has crystallized. These critiques of the persistent objector rule were dismissed at the outset of this book, in Part I. State usage and invocation of the persistent objector rule is rare, but it does occur—and there are instances where states have been able to maintain exempt status from the binding force of a norm of customary international law to which they have previously persistently objected. Evidence of the rule's operation 'in action' has already been set out and examined in previous chapters.

However, there are similar, 'softer' versions of the critique of the persistent objector rule based on its usage in practice that require further investigation. The first of these, explored in section I of this chapter, is that persistent objection is not (or, perhaps, should not be) permissible in relation to particularly 'fundamental' customary international law norms, even those that have not attained *jus cogens* status. This claim has most commonly—although not exclusively—been made with regard to norms of customary international human rights law.

Section II then turns to a related claim made by critics of the persistent objector rule, which is that it is commonly unavailing, not just in the face of especially 'fundamental' norms, but in general. This is a more nuanced version of the incorrect assertion, already previously dismissed, that persistent objection *never* pays. The argument here is, instead, that the exempt status afforded by prior (and ongoing) persistent objection is often extremely difficult to maintain; indeed, it has been argued that that it is so difficult to maintain that in the *vast majority* of instances dissenting states will ultimately conform to the norm to which they have previously been objecting. Accepting that a tiny number of 'genuine' exempt objectors may exist, writers making this claim nonetheless take the view that the persistent objector rule is largely worthless in practice (at least, for most states most of the time).

I. The De Jure Applicability of the Persistent Objector Rule to (Non-Peremptory) 'Fundamental' Norms

i. Arguments for and against prohibiting persistent objection in relation to 'fundamental' norms

In 1950, in its pleadings in the *Fisheries* case, the United Kingdom asserted that:

> the right of a State to dissent from a customary rule cannot be regarded as absolute. There is universal agreement that a new State has no option but to adhere to generally accepted customary law. In addition, *where a fundamental principle is concerned, the international community does not recognize the right of any State to isolate itself from the impact of the principle.*[1]

Of course, it has already been argued in Chapter 7 that states are de jure unable to maintain exemption by virtue of persistent objection to norms that have acquired *jus cogens* status. Peremptory norms are by their very nature 'fundamental' norms, and the British claim made in the context of the *Fisheries* dispute might simply be seen as relating to *jus cogens* (albeit that the modern concept of *jus cogens* was still developing at that time,[2] and had not yet been rooted in positive law by the 1969 Vienna Convention on the Law of Treaties (VCLT)).[3] Thus, Thirlway, for example, endorses the United Kingdom's statement, but sees this as simply an affirmation of the view that persistent objection is unavailing in relation to peremptory norms.[4] However, it is far from clear whether the United Kingdom was referring to *jus cogens* when it spoke of 'a fundamental principle' in its *Fisheries* pleadings, and some commentators have interpreted this claim as relating not merely to peremptory norms, but also to other 'fundamental' rules of the international legal system.[5] It is notable that in its own pleadings Norway interpreted the United Kingdom's claim as a reference to the rules of maritime delimitation[6]—presumably correctly, given the context—and it is almost impossible to view such maritime norms as being peremptory.[7]

[1] *Fisheries* (*United Kingdom v Norway*), reply submitted by the Government of the United Kingdom of Great Britain and Northern Ireland, 1950 ICJ Plead., vol. II, 428–9, emphasis added.

[2] See, generally, M.M. Magallona, 'The Concept of *Jus Cogens* in the Vienna Convention on the Law of the Treaties' (1976) 51 *Philippine Law Journal* 521.

[3] See Vienna Convention on the Law of Treaties (VCLT), 23 May 1969, 1155 UNTS 331, particularly Articles 53 and 64.

[4] H. Thirlway, *International Customary Law and Codification* (Leiden, A.W. Sijthoff, 1972), 110.

[5] See, for example, P. Weil, 'Le droit international en quête de son identité—Cours général de droit international public' (1992-VI) 237 *Recueil des cours* 9, 200.

[6] *Fisheries* (*United Kingdom v Norway*), rejoinder submitted by the Government of the Kingdom of Norway, 1951 ICJ Plead., vol. III, 293.

[7] V-D. Degan, 'Consolidation of Legal Principles on Maritime Delimitation: Implications for the Dispute between Slovenia and Croatia in the North Adriatic' (2007) 6 *Chinese Journal of International Law* 601, 618.

In the years since the *Fisheries* decision, a number of writers have argued that persistent objection does not (or should not) allow a state to exempt itself from certain 'fundamental' norms of international law (especially what might be termed 'moral' or value-based norms), including when the 'fundamental' norm in question is *not* peremptory in nature.[8] Given the moral nature and oft-asserted universality underpinning human rights norms, they—more than any other breed of international legal rule—have been said to fall into this category of insulated non-peremptory customary international law norms.[9] International human rights law is therefore the prism through which much of the discussion in this section is filtered. However, it is important to note that it has also been asserted that non-peremptory rules of international environmental law, international humanitarian law (IHL), and, indeed, various international legal norms from other sub-fields are (or may be) exempt from persistent objection too, on the basis that they are also 'fundamental'. Thus, the analysis in this section relating to human rights is similarly relevant to other 'fundamental' international legal norms (actual or perceived), and reference will be periodically made to the sub-fields of IHL and international environmental law in particular.

Human rights are 'part of the concept of the international public order'[10] and the moral and societal 'weight' of such norms means that, for many, any kind of

[8] See, for example, B.D. Lepard, *Customary International Law: A New Theory with Practical Applications* (Cambridge, Cambridge University Press, 2010), 230–42; M. Bos, *A Methodology of International Law* (The Hague, T.M.C. Asser, 1984), particularly at 250; N. Petersen, 'The Role of Consent and Uncertainty in the Formation of Customary International Law' (2011) *Reprints of the Max Planck Institute for Research on Collective Goods*, http://www.coll.mpg.de/pdf_dat/2011_04online.pdf, 9; A. Roberts, 'Traditional and Modern Approaches to Customary International Law: A Reconciliation' (2001) 95 *American Journal of International Law* 757, 766; and O. Schachter, 'International Law in Theory and Practice' (1982) 178 *Recueil des cours* 9, 37–8. See also *South West Africa* cases (*Ethiopia v South Africa, Liberia v South Africa*), second phase, 1966 ICJ Rep. 6, separate opinion of Judge Nervo, 470 (perhaps obliquely endorsing this general understanding, although this is far from clear: '[t]here is no principle of general international law which could be validly invoked to contradict, or destroy, the essential purpose and the fundamental sources of the legal obligations rooted in the very existence of the Covenant, the mandates system and the Charter of the United Nations').

[9] See L.R. Helfer, 'Exiting Custom: Analogies to Treaty Withdrawals' (2010) 21 *Duke Journal of Comparative and International Law* 65, 73 (setting out but not clearly supporting this view); L. Henkin, 'Human Rights and State "Sovereignty"' (1996) 25 *Georgia Journal of International Law* 31, 38; H. Lau, 'Rethinking the Persistent Objector Doctrine in International Human Rights Law' (2005–6) 6 *Chicago Journal of International Law* 496, 496; Lepard, n. 8, 333–6; L. Loschin, 'The Persistent Objector Rule and Customary Human Rights Law: A Proposed Analytical Framework' (1996) 2 *University of California Davis Journal of International Law and Policy* 147, 147; J.J. Paust, 'The Complex Nature, Sources and Evidences of Customary Human Rights' (1995) 25 *Georgia Journal of International and Comparative Law* 147, 152; Petersen, n. 8, 13–14; and C. Quince, *The Persistent Objector and Customary International Law* (Denver, Outskirts Press, 2010), 62–3 and 76. See also F. Hampson and I. Salama, 'Working Paper on the Relationship between Human Rights Law and International Humanitarian Law', Commission on Human Rights, Sub-Commission on the Promotion and Protection of Human Rights, Fifty-seventh session, Item 3 of the provisional agenda, Administration of Justice, Rule of Law and Democracy, 21 June 2005, UN Doc. E/CN.4/Sub.2/2005/14, para. 70 ('[t]here is first the difficulty of determining whether the doctrine [of persistent objection] can be applied in the field of HRsL').

[10] I. Brownlie, 'The Decisions of Political Organs of the United Nations and the Rule of Law' in R. St. J. MacDonald (ed.), *Essays in Honour of Wang Tieya* (Dordrecht, Martinus Nijhoff Publishers, 1994), 91, 102.

deviation by an individual state should be precluded.[11] Indeed, it is commonly argued, if far from entirely agreed, that human rights are *intrinsically universal* in nature.[12] Against this conceptual background a significant amount of controversy has been generated in the literature (and among states) regarding reservations to human rights treaties,[13] and moral universalism and voluntarist sovereignty collide just as obviously in the context of persistent objection too.[14]

A number of the widely recognized peremptory norms of the international legal system have their basis in the field of international human rights law.[15] However, not all human rights norms are peremptory: indeed, ultimately, very few of them are. It will be recalled from Chapter 7 that the legal criteria for establishing any given norm as being peremptory are onerous.[16] Lau therefore correctly concludes that 'only a handful of human rights norms qualify as *jus cogens*, leaving the large majority of human rights laws susceptible to the persistent objector doctrine'.[17] The same may be said of both IHL[18] and international environmental law,[19] where even fewer norms—if *any*—can be uncontroversially identified as being peremptory. The insulation from exemption that the *jus cogens* project provides therefore ultimately only protects a relatively small number of what might be seen as 'fundamental' norms from the reach of the persistent objector rule.

[11] S. Hall, 'The Persistent Spectre: Natural Law, International Order and the Limits of Legal Positivism' (2001) 12 *European Journal of International Law* 269, 301–5.

[12] See, for example, J. Donnelly, 'Human Rights as Natural Rights' (1982) 4 *Human Rights Quarterly* 391, particularly at 397–8.

[13] See S. Ghandhi, 'The Human Rights Committee and Interim Measures of Relief' (2007) 13 *Canterbury Law Review* 203, 233; R. Goodman, 'Human Rights Treaties, Invalid Reservations, and State Consent' (2002) 96 *American Journal of International Law* 531; and C.J. Redgwell, 'Reservations to Treaties and Human Rights Committee General Comment No 24 (52)' (1997) 46 *International and Comparative Law Quarterly* 390.

[14] Loschin, n. 9, 161.

[15] See Report of the International Law Commission, Fifty-third session, 23 April–1 June and 2 July–10 August 2001, UN Doc. A/56/10, 85 (six of the seven norms listed by the ILC as being peremptory stem from international human rights law).

[16] See Chapter 7, section I; and Chapter 7, n. 75 and accompanying text.

[17] Lau, n. 9, 495 and 498. See also C.G. Guldahl, 'The Role of Persistent Objection in International Humanitarian Law' (2008) 77 *Nordic Journal of International Law* 51, 62; Loschin, n. 9, 163–4; Quince, n. 9, 62; and B. Simma and P. Alston, 'The Sources of Human Rights Law: Custom, *Jus Cogens*, and General Principles' (1988–9) 12 *Australian Yearbook of International Law* 82, 103. *Cf.*, *South West Africa* cases, second phase, n. 8, dissenting opinion of Judge Tanaka, 298.

[18] See S.C. Breau, 'The Constitutionalization of the International Legal Order' (2008) 21 *Leiden Journal of International Law* 545, 547–8; M. Mendelson, comments made at 'The Law of Armed Conflict: Problems and Prospects' conference to mark the publication of the ICRC Study on 'Customary International Humanitarian Law', Chatham House, 18 April 2005, http://www.blackstonechambers.com/news/publications/law_of_armed_conflic.html, 14; and R. Nieto-Navia, 'International Peremptory Norms (*Jus Cogens*) and International Humanitarian Law' *in* L.C. Vohrah, F. Pocar, Y. Featherstone, O. Fourmy, C. Graham, J. Hocking, and N. Robson (eds), *Man's Inhumanity to Man: Essays on International Law in Honour of Antonio Cassese* (The Hague, Kluwer Law International, 2003), 595.

[19] E.M. Kornicker Uhlmann, 'State Community Interests, *Jus Cogens* and Protection of the Global Environment: Developing Criteria for Peremptory Norms' (1998) 11 *Georgetown International Environmental Law Review* 101 (strongly supporting the emergence of various environmental protection norms as *jus cogens*, but nonetheless accepting that very few such norms have yet achieved that status).

The threat posed by the possibility of unilateral state exemption from the majority of human rights standards has led a number of commentators, taking a moral absolutist and universalist view of human rights, to argue that *all* human rights norms—be they peremptory or non-peremptory—are inherently immune from persistent objection.[20] Those taking this view argue that it is (or in some, rather more *lex ferenda* versions of this approach, should be) impossible to persistently object to any human rights norms. The most notable exponent of this position is Holning Lau, who argued in 2005 that '[t]he human rights regime's universality assumption is at odds with the effects of the persistent objector doctrine. By allowing individual states to exempt themselves from international human rights law, the human rights regime's universalist nature is necessarily compromised'.[21]

A decade earlier, that famous champion of universal human rights, Louis Henkin, took the same view, albeit rather more bluntly: 'the "persistent objector" principle does not apply [to human rights norms].'[22] Similar claims have been advanced with regard to norms of IHL[23] and international environmental law,[24] although admittedly less forcefully and often.

The main counter-argument to this position—that certain non-peremptory 'fundamental' norms are intrinsically exempt from persistent objection—is rooted in the idea that the persistent objector rule is supposed to preserve the voluntarist underpinnings of international law, and '[t]o abandon customary international law's strong positivist intellectual roots in favour of a new naturalism (whether expressed in the idiom of the "rationality" or "humanity" of favoured norms), would ... be folly'.[25] It has thus been asserted that moral or social imperatives should not (and, it is said by those taking this position, *do* not) override the sovereign autonomy of states: if they did this would be fundamentally destabilizing, as states would view the system as being illegitimate.

The theory that human rights are immune from persistent objection has been defended against this voluntarist argument through the assertion that there is an element of 'original consent' underpinning the international human rights law regime. In other words, it has been argued that by participating in the regime (for example, by signing and voting to adopt the Universal Declaration of Human

[20] See scholars listed in n. 9.

[21] Lau, n. 9, generally, but quoted at 501.

[22] Henkin, n. 9, 38.

[23] J.P. Paust, 'The Complex Nature, Sources and Evidences of Customary Human Rights' (1995–6) 25 *Georgia Journal of International and Comparative Law* 147, 152. See also D. Kritsiotis, 'On the Possibilities of and For Persistent Objection' (2010) 21 *Duke Journal of Comparative and International Law* 121, 137–40 (extrapolating this as a possible reading of the ICJ's determination that the IHL principles of distinction and the prohibition of unnecessary suffering are 'intransgressible' in *Legality of the Threat or Use of Nuclear Weapons*, advisory opinion, 1996 ICJ Rep. 226, para. 79).

[24] Petersen, n. 8, 7; and C. Tomuschat, 'Obligations Arising for States Without or Against Their Will' (1993) 241 *Recueil des cours* 195, 294–7. See also J.I. Charney, 'Universal International Law' (1993) 87 *American Journal of International Law* 529, 529 (making this claim rather more implicitly).

[25] D.J. Bederman, 'Acquiescence, Objection and the Death of Customary International Law' (2010) 21 *Duke Journal of Comparative and International Law* 31, 44. See also S. Estreicher, 'A Post-Formation Withdrawal from Customary International Law? Some Cautionary Notes' (2010) 21 *Duke Journal of Comparative and International Law* 57, 63.

Rights, or by ratifying the International Covenant on Civil and Political Rights (ICCPR)), a state consents to the universal and intransgressible nature of *all* human rights law: thus meaning that consent in relation to any particular human rights norm has already been established.[26]

Customary international law theory is plagued with fictitious or overstated notions of consent,[27] but—even in that milieu—the idea of ultimate original consent to all human rights norms now and forever (including consent to human rights not yet formed or even *conceived of*) seems really rather a stretch.[28] If the 'original consent' notion had any basis in truth, not only would reservations to human rights treaties be entirely and uncontroversially impermissible in all circumstances, but states also would be formally required to become party to any new human rights convention as soon as it became open for signature: states would already have given their consent to be bound by the treaty. Quite simply, the original consent theory is nonsense.[29]

Having said this, we know that universal consent is not required for the formation of *jus cogens* norms,[30] but that they nonetheless cannot be persistently objected to. The commonly advanced rationale for prohibiting persistent objection to *jus cogens* is based on the moral universalism of peremptory norms[31] and, given that the same trait is—many argue—inherent in all international human rights too (as well as in other 'fundamental' areas), 'ordinary' value-based norms should also be immune to persistent objection notwithstanding their non-peremptory character. In other words, if the 'consent issue' can be overcome regarding *jus cogens* norms because of the power of the moral imperative, why cannot the same be true for human rights *in toto* and for other non-peremptory 'universal' rules? The fiction of the original consent theory is actually unnecessary, because true consent is itself a fiction in the context of customary international law.[32] Why should there be a distinction here between *jus cogens* and other 'moral' norms: why would we, it might be asked, 'limit unilateral exit for matters of slavery and piracy (which are generally agreed to be *jus cogens* norms) but not for child labor…?'[33]

Normatively, a difference may perhaps be found in the onerous positivist test that a norm must meet to acquire *jus cogens* status. Peremptory norms may not

[26] Lau, n. 9, 503–5; and Quince, n. 9, 74 and 76.

[27] See Chapter 9, section I.*iii*, particularly at n. 64–n. 83 and accompanying text.

[28] It would be still more of a stretch to further extend this to areas such as international environmental law, where much of the substantive normative regime itself remains controversial and based on soft law provisions.

[29] J.A. Green, 'Persistent Objector Teflon? Customary International Human Rights Law and the United States in International Adjudicative Proceedings' in J.A. Green and C.P.M. Waters (eds), *Adjudicating International Human Rights: Essays in Honour of Sandy Ghandhi* (Leiden, Brill Nijhoff, 2015), 167, 184.

[30] See Chapter 7, section I.

[31] Ibid., section III.

[32] See Chapter 9, section I.*iii*.

[33] C. Ochoa, 'Disintegrating Customary International Law: Reactions to "Withdrawing from International Custom"' (2010) 21 *Duke Journal of Comparative and International Law* 157, 166 (a point made specifically in the context of discussing the proposal for allowing subsequent objection in C.A. Bradley and M. Gulati, 'Withdrawing from International Custom' (2010) 120 *Yale Law Journal* 202). See also Henkin, n. 9, 38; and Lepard, n. 8, 240–1.

require universal acceptance, but they do require *near*-universal acceptance.[34] That is why there are so few of them. Adhering to the positivist requirements of VCLT Article 53 (the acceptance and recognition of peremptory status 'by the international community of States as a whole') helps keep the concept of *jus cogens* in touch with reality, and thus actually *protects* and *validates* its value-based agenda.[35] *Jus cogens* norms are, or at least should be, natural law rules under careful positivist guard.[36] In contrast, 'ordinary' customary international human rights law norms, for example, do not require the same high level of state acceptance and recognition, but instead just the usual basic preponderance of practice and *opinio juris* as for any custom. *Jus cogens* and other 'fundamental' norms can be distinguished precisely because peremptory norms are inherently different: they are, after all, peremptory.[37]

There is likely to be significant difficulty in determining whether any given non-peremptory norm counts as being 'fundamental', and thus—for those taking this view—as being immune to the effects of persistent objection. Norms of human rights, IHL, and environmental protection have something of a unique ethical character, and one can therefore credibly argue that this means they should be exempt from exemption (as it were). Yet this claim is disputable. It is, of course, unclear where the 'boundaries' of these sub-fields begin and end.[38] One could also question whether it would indeed be beneficial, in practical terms, to insulate all norms within these sub-fields from the persistent objector rule, because limiting the possibility of a state opting out of a norm while the norm is still emerging could actually delay the crystallization of 'fundamental' norms rather than protecting them.[39]

Beyond this, though, it is evident that the claim that non-peremptory rules are immune from persistent objection on the basis of their 'fundamental' nature has also been made in relation to other norms, which do not have any notable ethical dimension. For example, while it is not entirely clear what norm or norms the United Kingdom was arguing to be 'fundamental' (and thus immune from exemption) in the *Fisheries* case,[40] it would be difficult to make a case that any of the rules on maritime delimitation at issue had acquired (or have since acquired) peremptory status,[41] or that they are of any special moral weight. It is notable that Norway agreed with the United Kingdom that

[34] See Chapter 7, section I.

[35] Green, n. 29, 185; and D. Shelton, 'Normative Hierarchy in International Law' (2006) 100 *American Journal of International Law* 291, 292.

[36] Green, n. 29, 185.

[37] F. Ingman, 'Persistent Objector—The Demise of a Hero?' (2008), unpublished Masters thesis, Lund University, http://lup.lub.lu.se/luur/download?func=downloadFile&recordOId=1558532&fileOId=1564685, 63.

[38] Charney, n. 24, 542 (arguing that the 'special classes' of norms in which a rule may or may not fall are irrelevant, because norms can be imposed on states irrespective of their objections per se).

[39] See C.A. Bradley, 'The Juvenile Death Penalty' (2002–3) 52 *Duke Law Journal* 485, 517; Ingman, n. 37, 61 and 63; and Loschin, n. 9, 168.

[40] *Fisheries*, reply of the United Kingdom, n. 1, 428–9.

[41] Degan, n. 7, 618.

'fundamental' rules were immune from persistent objection (again, without being clear as to whether this was restricted to peremptory norms),[42] but was *also* clear that the norms relating to maritime delimitation did not fall within this category.[43]

To take another example, Dumberry has argued that the rules (seemingly *all* of the rules) in the field of international investment law fall into the category of 'fundamental' norms that are immune from persistent objection, 'essentially because of the great importance of the few custom rules existing in that field and the fact that they represent universally recognized values'.[44] Leaving aside the fact that if all such norms are indeed 'universally recognized' then there *ipso facto* cannot exist any persistent objector states anyway, it is difficult—even without underrepresenting the 'importance' of the norms in question—to place investment law on anything like the same ethical plane as, say, human rights or environmental protection.

Identifying peremptory norms is already something of 'an "eye of the beholder" norm popularity contest',[45] but at least there exists the (comparative, if limited) objectivity of the test enshrined in VCLT Article 53. If 'other' fundamental norms are imbued with a distinctive normative character (in the sense that they cannot be persistently objected to), this is against the background of the fact that there is no way *whatsoever* of determining which norms would qualify: 'whether something is a fundamental concept can be acutely controversial, once one gets beyond those simply axiomatic to a system of international law, such as sovereignty and independence.'[46] If non-peremptory 'fundamental' norms indeed all possessed a Teflon coating with regard to state dissent, then claims regarding the *de jure* possibility of persistent objection would be an entirely subjective free-for-all.

[42] *Fisheries*, rejoinder submitted by Norway, n. 6, 292. [43] Ibid., 292–3.

[44] P. Dumberry, 'The Last Citadel! Can a State Claim the Status of Persistent Objector to Prevent the Application of a Rule of Customary International Law in Investor-State Arbitration?' (2010) 23 *Leiden Journal of International Law* 379, quoted at 379, but see in general and especially also 397–8. See also P. Dumberry, 'Can a State Claim the Status of "Persistent Objector" in Investor-State Arbitration?', 13 July 2009, *Kluwer Arbitration Blog*, http://kluwerarbitrationblog.com/blog/2009/07/13/can-a-state-claim-the-status-of-%E2%80%9Cpersistent-objector%E2%80%9D-in-investor-state-arbitration/.

[45] Green, n. 29, 183.

[46] M.H. Mendelson, 'The Formation of Customary International Law' (1998) 272 *Recueil des cours* 155, 242. See also *Committee on Formation of Customary (General) International Law*, Final Report of the Committee, 'Statement of Principles Applicable to the Formation of General Customary International Law', International Law Association, London Conference (2000), http://www.ila-hq.org/en/committees/index.cfm/cid/30, 29, footnote 73; O. Elias, 'Some Remarks on the Persistent Objector Rule in Customary International Law' (1991) 6 *Denning Law Journal* 37, 40 (arguing that the claim that persistent objection is impermissible in relation to norms of value is 'a question begging notion in itself'); and Weil, n. 5, 200. Further, it has been argued that all norms can be seen as having at least some 'moral' content, meaning that contrasting 'moral' and 'facilitative' norms is conceptually flawed: see L. Blutman, 'Conceptual Confusion and Methodological Deficiencies: Some Ways that Theories on Customary International Law Fail' (2014) 25 *European Journal of International Law* 529, 546.

ii. Dubious assertions of peremptory status

It is notable that rules that are almost certainly non-peremptory (based on any reasonable application of the VCLT Article 53 criteria) are regularly argued to have acquired a peremptory character, specifically so that state persistent objection to them can be validly overridden.[47] It is entirely understandable that some 'have strained to conclude that a norm is *jus cogens*'[48] in instances where the norm in question is of particular moral importance without the rigorous application of the positivist criteria for the creation of peremptory rules. However, whatever the merit or moral 'value' of any given legal rule, this does not in itself turn it into a peremptory norm; nor do pronouncements to this effect made by scholars, however numerous.[49]

The dubious finding of peremptory status for the prohibition of the juvenile death penalty by the Inter-American Commission on Human Rights (IACmHR)[50] in both *Roach and Pinkerton v United States*[51] and *Domingues v United States*[52] acts as an illustration. That the Commission was willing to stretch credulity in this regard indicates that there is no additional exemption from the effects of the persistent objector rule for 'fundamental' norms per se: the prohibition is indisputably a human rights norm, so if such norms truly are universally binding even on dissenters, the IACmHR would surely not have bothered trying to elevate its normative status any further.[53] Thus, in *Domingues*, the IACmHR 'agreed on the fact that a state can become a persistent objector towards a [non-peremptory] human right',[54] even if it did not explicitly state this. One might similarly point to the claimants' argument in *C* et al. *v Director of Immigration*[55] that the principle of *non-refoulement* had acquired the status of *jus cogens*.[56] It is fairly clear that the reason why the claimants made this assertion was because they were seeking to avoid a possible claim of persistent objection in response.[57] Yet, while not being

[47] See, generally, D. Shelton, 'International Law and "Relative Normativity"' in M. Evans (ed.), *International Law* (Oxford, Oxford University Press, 4th edn, 2014), 137, 152 (arguing that the 'literature is replete with claims that particular international norms form part of the *jus cogens* ... [including] all human rights, all humanitarian norms ... [and] the duty not to cause transboundary environmental harm'). In the environmental law context, such claims mirror the desire of some commentators to assert (with ethical, but without legal, justification) that clearly only 'emerging' customary environmental norms have already crystallized, because this acts to shift the burden of proof so that dissenters must establish that they are persistent objectors, rather than those states in favour of the norm having to establish that that norm has in fact formed. See D. French, 'Finding Autonomy in International Environmental Law and Governance' (2009) 21 *Journal of Environmental Law* 255, 269.

[48] Lepard, n. 8, 241. See also V.M. Padmanabhan, 'The Human Rights Justification for Consent' (2013) 35 *University of Pennsylvania Journal of International Law* 1, 3, and 18.

[49] R.P. Barnidge, Jr, 'Questioning the Legitimacy of *Jus Cogens* in the Global Legal Order' (2008) 38 *Israel Yearbook of Human Rights* 199, 205.

[50] See Chapter 7, n. 81–n. 82 and accompanying text.

[51] *Roach and Pinkerton v United States*, 1987 IACmHR, Resolution No. 3/87, Case 9647, para. 56.

[52] *Domingues v United States*, merits, 2002 IACmHR, Report No. 62/02, Case 12.285, para. 85.

[53] Green, n. 29, 188.

[54] Ingman, n. 37, 37.

[55] *C* et al. *v Director of Immigration*, 2008, 2 HKC 167.

[56] Ibid., para. 76.

[57] See ibid., para. 117; and O. Jones, 'Customary *Non-Refoulement* of Refugees and Automatic Incorporation into the Common Law: A Hong Kong Perspective' (2009) 58 *International and Comparative Law Quarterly* 443, 540.

peremptory,[58] *non-refoulement* would be difficult to see as anything but a 'fundamental' norm of the sort being discussed in this section.[59]

Similar examples—of dubious assertions of peremptory status so as to bypass the persistent objector rule—can be found in scholarship. Take Tabassi's argument that the alleged customary comprehensive nuclear test-ban is a *jus cogens* norm.[60] On this basis, Tabassi has asserted that prima facie persistent objector states (specifically India, Pakistan, and North Korea) would nonetheless be required to refrain from nuclear testing. Yet while a comprehensive prohibition on nuclear testing is certainly a rule of paramount importance to the international community generally (and so can be seen as being 'fundamental'),[61] it is impossible to argue that it has been 'accepted and recognized by the international community of states as a whole' as a norm from which no derogation is permitted.[62]

Likewise, in his 1996 article on persistent objection and nuclear weapons, Steinfeld determined, providing almost no evidence, that the *entire corpus* of IHL and—even less convincingly—international environmental law are peremptory in nature, so as to be able to conclude that these rules are not subject to persistent objection by nuclear weapon states.[63] Steinfeld's assertions as to the peremptory status of these entire sub-areas of international law are simply 'untenable'.[64]

These various claims as to the peremptory status of norms that are unquestionably non-peremptory indicate that those making them feel that however 'important' a norm may be, unless it is formally considered peremptory, an objecting state can gain exemption from it.

iii. Persistent objection to 'fundamental' norms in state practice

Irrespective of the arguments considered in the previous two subsections, the most persuasive evidence of the fact that non-peremptory rules—fundamental or otherwise—can be persistently objected to is, once again, to be found in state practice.[65] No state has successfully maintained persistent objection in relation to

[58] As was rightly concluded by Hartmann J, *C* et al., n. 55, paras 117–35. See also N. Coleman, '*Non-Refoulement* Revised Renewed Review of the Status of the Principle of *Non-Refoulement* as Customary International Law' (2003) 5 *European Journal of Migration and Law* 23, 46, footnote 114. *Contra* D. Moeckli, 'Of Minarets and Foreign Criminals: Swiss Direct Democracy and Human Rights' (2011) 11 *Human Rights Law Review* 774, 781.

[59] See, generally, Coleman, n. 58.

[60] L. Tabassi, 'The Nuclear Test Ban: *Lex Lata* or *de Lege Ferenda*?' (2009) 14 *Journal of Conflict and Security Law* 309, 347–50.

[61] K.M. Wable, 'The US–India Strategic Nuclear Partnership: A Debilitating Blow to the Non-Proliferation Regime' (2007–8) 33 *Brooklyn Journal of International Law* 719, 744.

[62] J.A. Green, 'India and a Customary Comprehensive Nuclear Test-Ban: Persistent Objection, Peremptory Norms and the 123 Agreement' (2011) 51 *Indian Journal of International Law* 3, particularly at 29.

[63] A. Steinfeld, 'Nuclear Objections: The Persistent Objector and the Legality of the Use of Nuclear Weapons' (1996) 62 *Brooklyn Law Review* 1635, 1640, and 1680–5.

[64] Guldahl, n. 17, 84.

[65] Shelton, n. 35, 294 (noting, generally, that '[t]he asserted primacy of all human rights law has not been reflected in state practice'.)

a peremptory norm,[66] whereas a number *have*—and continue to—in relation to non-peremptory human rights, IHL, and environmental norms.

One can, for example, point to the United States' position on the customary international law 'right to food', which has already been discussed in previous chapters.[67] It is fairly clear that the right to food crystallized as a binding rule of customary human rights law somewhere in the 2000s, if not before.[68] However, the United States remains an exempt persistent objector state to this human rights norm, as recognized by the Special Rapporteur of the Commission on Human Rights on the Right to Food in 2005,[69] and accepted by other states.[70]

In a similar vein, the so-called 'right to water' is illustrative. That right has been traditionally viewed as indirectly deriving from the 1966 International Covenant on Economic, Social and Cultural Rights (ICESCR),[71] Article 11 (right to an adequate standard of living),[72] but not as additionally being part of customary international law.[73] However, there is now a significant amount of *opinio juris* supporting the existence of the right in custom, as well as increasing amounts of uniform—if not yet comprehensive—state practice.[74] It is therefore apparent that the right is at least in the *process* of crystallizing,[75] and some commentators are now claiming that it has already crystallized.[76] Both the United States[77] and

[66] See Green, n. 29, 175; and Chapter 7, particularly at n. 89 and accompanying text.

[67] See, respectively, Chapter 4, n. 73–n. 75 and accompanying text; and Chapter 6, n. 310–n. 317 and accompanying text.

[68] See Chapter 4, n. 73 and accompanying text.

[69] *The Right to Food*, note by the Secretary-General, transmitting the interim report of the Special Rapporteur of the Commission on Human Rights on the Right to Food in accordance with General Assembly Resolution 59/202, 12 September 2005, UN Doc. A/60/350, 23, footnote 44.

[70] See Chapter 4, text following n. 75.

[71] International Covenant on Economic, Social and Cultural Rights, 16 December 1966, 993 UNTS 3.

[72] See, for example, T.S. Bulto, 'The Emergence of the Human Right to Water in International Human Rights Law: Invention or Discovery?' (2011) 12 *Melbourne Journal of International Law* 290, particularly at 314.

[73] See, for example, A.J. Kirschner, 'The Human Right to Water and Sanitation' (2011) 15 *Max Planck Yearbook of United Nations Law* 445, 464–5.

[74] See the detailed state practice and *opinio juris* in relation to the right to water set out in both P. Thielbörger, 'Re-Conceptualizing the Human Right to Water: A Pledge for a Hybrid Approach' (2015) 15 *Human Rights Law Review* 225, 238–43; and I.T. Winkler, *The Human Right to Water: Significance, Legal Status and Implications for Water Allocation* (Oxford, Hart, 2012), 65–97.

[75] See J. Scanlon, A. Cassar, and N. Nemes, *Water as a Human Right?* (Gland, IUCN, 2004), 9–10; and Winkler, n. 74, 96–7.

[76] Thielbörger, n. 74.

[77] See, for example, 'Views of the United States of America on Human Rights and Access to Water Submitted to the Office of the United Nations High Commissioner for Human Rights', June 2007, http://www2.ohchr.org/english/issues/water/contributions/UnitedStatesofAmerica.pdf; General Assembly, Official Records, Sixty-fourth session, 108th plenary meeting, 28 July 2010, UN Doc. A/64/PV.108, 8; and 'Explanation of Position: The Human Right to Safe Drinking Water and Sanitation Resolution, Statement of the Delegation of the United States of America', as delivered by Ambassador Keith Harper, US Representative to the UN Human Rights Council, Geneva, 27 September 2014, https://geneva.usmission.gov/2014/09/25/explanation-of-position-the-human-right-to-safe-drinking-water-and-sanitation/.

United Kingdom[78] have continued to persistently object to the right as being an aspect of customary international law, even while being broadly accepting in recent years of the right as a derivative of Article 11 ICESCR. In the case of the United States, then, its objection to a customary right to water is especially pertinent as it has not ratified the ICESCR. There has been essentially no criticism from other states in relation to this objector stance.[79] Despite some claims to the contrary,[80] it is clear that the United States and United Kingdom are exempt from any general customary international law right to water (or, at least, will be if/when it crystallizes).

Another useful example is the right to religious freedom, and specifically the right to *change* one's religion or belief.[81] In the view of the present author this human rights norm has crystallized as a binding rule of customary international law, prima facie applicable to all states.[82] However, a number of Islamic states have objected to this right, with a notable example being Saudi Arabia (which has lodged persistent and consistent objections since the 1940s).[83] The Human Rights

[78] See, for example, 'UK Position on Human Right to Water' (2006), https://www.gov.uk/government/uploads/system/uploads/attachment_data/file/36540/uk-position-human-right-water.pdf; UN Doc. A/64/PV.108, n. 77, 12–13; 'United Kingdom of Northern Ireland and Great Britain National Explanation of Vote on UN Human Rights Resolution 64/292 of 28 July 2010', Foreign and Commonwealth Office, https://www.gov.uk/government/uploads/system/uploads/attachment_data/file/35452/explanation-vote-un-july-2010.pdf; and 'United Kingdom of Northern Ireland and Great Britain National Explanation of Position on Human Rights Council Resolution 15/14 of 30 September 2010', Foreign and Commonwealth Office, https://www.gov.uk/government/uploads/system/uploads/attachment_data/file/35453/explanation-of-position-hrr15.pdf.

[79] See, for example, various statements made by states in the General Assembly (in relation to the adoption of General Assembly Resolution 64/292, 28 July 2010, UN Doc. A/RES/64/292), UN Doc. A/64/PV.108, n. 77.

[80] Thielbörger, n. 74, 242 and 245–6.

[81] This right is set out in various treaties and notable soft law documents, such as the Universal Declaration of Human Rights, General Assembly Resolution 217 (III), 10 December 1948, UN Doc. A/RES/3/217 A, Article 18; European Convention on Human Rights, 4 November 1950, ETS 5, Article 9(1); American Convention on Human Rights, 22 November 1969, 1144 UNTS 123, Article 12(1); General Assembly Resolution 60/166, 16 December 2005, UN Doc. A/RES/60/166, para. 4(a); and the International Covenant on Civil and Political Rights, 16 December 1966, 999 UNTS 171, Article 18(1) (albeit not entirely explicitly).

[82] See Lepard, n. 8, 347–64 (setting out, in detail, convincing evidence of state practice and *opinio juris* supporting the finding that the right is now binding in customary international law). *Contra* R.B. Lillich, 'Civil Rights' in T. Meron (ed.), *Human Rights in International Law: Legal Policy and Issues, vol. I* (Oxford, Clarendon Press, 1984), 115, 158–60.

[83] See, P.M. Taylor, *Freedom of Religion: UN and European Human Rights Law and Practice* (Cambridge, Cambridge University Press, 2005), 55–6 (listing a number of examples from 1948 to 1973). It should be noted that the other Islamic states that objected to the right to change one's religion or belief have not done so as persistently or consistently as Saudi Arabia. For example, while four Islamic states (including Saudi Arabia) initially abstained from the vote on the adoption of Article 18 (then 19) of the Universal Declaration of Human Rights in 1948 (see General Assembly, Official Records, Third session, 183rd plenary meeting, 10 December 1948, UN Doc. A/PV.183), ultimately only Saudi Arabia abstained from the final vote adopting the declaration as a whole. See M.A. Baderin, 'Islamic Law and the Implementation of International Human Rights Law: A Case Study of the International Covenant of Civil and Political Rights' in M.A. Baderin and M. Ssenyonjo (eds), *International Human Rights Law: Six Decades After the UDHR and Beyond* (Farnham, Ashgate, 2010), 337, 337. Therefore, it is difficult to view the other dissenting Islamic states as exempt persistent objectors.

Committee has asserted that the right to change one's religion or belief is, among other rights, 'protected unconditionally', and thus cannot be derogated from at all,[84] but it is unclear how the Committee reached this conclusion given that state practice would not seem to support it. Saudi Arabia has continued to object,[85] and other *states* have been generally accepting of this. It is fairly clear that Saudi Arabia is, therefore, a persistent objector to the human right to change one's religion or belief.[86]

The *Grand River v United States* arbitration, considered by a tribunal under NAFTA Chapter 11,[87] acts as an illustrative example of persistent objection to human rights in the more formalized arbitral context.[88] It will be recalled from Chapter 3[89] that the claimants in the case contended that the United States was in breach of a human rights law obligation 'to pro-actively consult with [indigenous persons] prior to taking legislative action that will have a substantial impact upon them',[90] and that the United States responded by asserting, inter alia, that it was a persistent objector to any such norm.[91] The 2011 final award in *Grand River* therefore amounted to the first opportunity in an adjudicative context to test the assertion that human rights norms are inherently insulated from persistent objection, even when they are non-peremptory. The Tribunal strongly implied that there was indeed a human right to indigenous consultation under customary international law,[92] but then failed to pronounce on the claim of the United States that it was a persistent objector. Indeed, it did not even *take note* of this claim.

Admittedly, the Tribunal concluded that, to the extent that there was a customary rule of indigenous consultation, this did not to apply to individual investors and so its scope did not extend to the claimants.[93] In other words, the United States' possible persistent objector status was not material to the decision. However, if human rights are as intrinsically and fundamentally immune from persistent objection as some would have us believe, one might expect that the

[84] Human Rights Committee, General Comment 22, Article 18, Forty-eighth session, 30 July 1993, Compilation of General Comments and General Recommendations Adopted by Human Rights Treaty Bodies, UN Doc. HRI/GEN/1/Rev.1, 35, para. 3.

[85] This is most obviously evident in its 'objection by deed': Saudi Arabia still outlaws conversion from Islam (apostasy), which remains punishable by death. See A. Saheed, 'Limitations on Religious Freedom in Islam' in S. Ferrari (ed.), *Routledge Handbook of Law and Religion* (Abingdon, Routledge, 2015), 369, in general, but particularly at 369–70.

[86] H. Thirlway, *The Sources of International Law* (Oxford, Oxford University Press, 2014), 159, footnote 57, and 183–4. *Contra* Lepard, n. 8, 364.

[87] *Grand River Enterprises Six Nations Ltd*, et al. *v Government of the United States of America*, final award, 2011, UNCITRAL/NAFTA, http://www.naftaclaims.com/disputes/usa/GrandRiver/GRE-USA-Award-Merits.pdf.

[88] For more detailed discussion of the proceedings in relation this point, see Green, n. 29, 185–8.

[89] See Chapter 3, n. 60–n. 65 and accompanying text.

[90] *Grand River*, claimants' memorial, merits phase, 2008, UNCITRAL/NAFTA, http://www.naftaclaims.com/disputes/usa/GrandRiver/GRE-USA-Merits-Memorial-R.pdf, particularly paras 184–92 and 213–17, quoted at para. 192.

[91] *Grand River*, counter-memorial of the respondent, merits phase, 2008, UNCITRAL/NAFTA, http://www.naftaclaims.com/disputes/usa/GrandRiver/GRE-USA-Merits-Counter-Memorial-R.pdf, 128–9, particularly at footnote 466.

[92] *Grand River*, final award, n. 87, particularly at para. 213.

[93] Ibid.

Tribunal would have at least *acknowledged* the United States' persistent objector claim, especially having seemingly indicated that the customary human right in question had indeed crystallized into law. It is telling that the Tribunal stayed silent on this point, and is perhaps even more telling that the United States felt entirely comfortable asserting persistent objector status to a non-peremptory human rights norm throughout the proceedings. *Grand River* therefore demonstrates that persistent objection to human rights norms is not only possible, but at times may be entirely *unremarkable* in the cut-and-thrust reality of international legal interaction.[94]

Another example, sitting at the intersection of international human rights law and international environmental law, is the so-called 'right to development'.[95] Given what has conservatively been called 'the fluidity of the definition'[96] of the right to development, and the ambivalence towards the right expressed by a number of western powers,[97] it is debatable whether it has crystallized into customary international law,[98] as least as a standalone right *in toto*.[99] However, there is a degree of state practice and *opinio juris* that one may see as supporting the view that it has.[100] Either way, more than any other state, the United States has maintained 'clear and consistent objection'[101] to the legally binding nature of the

[94] Green, n. 29, 188. Indeed, it is also notable there has been almost no *academic* commentary on the merits of the United States' persistent objector claim in the *Grand River* dispute. Having said this, see L.E. Peterson, 'Persistent Objector Argument also at Issue in NAFTA Case,' 14 July 2009, *Kluwer Arbitration Blog*, http://kluwerarbitrationblog.com/blog/2009/07/14/persistent-objector-argument-also-at-issue-in-nafta-case/ (providing a brief note on the claim).

[95] See, generally, Declaration on the Right to Development, annexed to General Assembly Resolution 41/128, 4 December 1986, UN Doc. A/RES/41/128; and A. Sengupta, 'On the Theory and Practice of the Right to Development' (2002) 24 *Human Rights Quarterly* 837.

[96] I.D. Bunn, 'The Right to Development: Implications for International Economic Law' (2000) 15 *American University International Law Review* 1425, 1434.

[97] See, for example, the position of Germany, set out in F. Kirchmeier, 'The Right to Development—Where Do We Stand? State of the Debate on the Right to Development' (2006) *Friedrich-Ebert-Stiftuung*, Dialogue on Globalisation, Occasional Papers No. 23, http://www.fes-globalization.org/publications/FESOccPapers23.pdf, 13–14.

[98] See L-H. Piron, 'The Right to Development: A Review of the Current State of the Debate for the Department for International Development' (2002), report commissioned by DFID's Social Development Department, http://www.odi.org/sites/odi.org.uk/files/odi-assets/publications-opinion-files/2317.pdf, particularly at 13–14.

[99] T. Kunanayakam, 'The Declaration on the Right to Development in the Context of United Nations Standard-Setting' in *Realizing the Right to Development: Essays in Commemoration of 25 Years of the United Nations Declaration on the Right to Development*, United Nations, Office of the High Commissioner for Human Rights (2013) HR/PUB/12/4, United Nations, Sales No. E.12.XIV.1, 17, 48 ('*certain aspects* of the right have become part of customary law'; emphasis added).

[100] See K. Iqbal, *The Right to Development in International Law: The Case of Pakistan* (Abingdon, Routledge, 2010), 115–40 (providing detailed evidence and analysis).

[101] P. Sands and J. Peel, *Principles of International Environmental Law* (Cambridge, Cambridge University Press, 3rd edn, 2012), 116. Examples of the United States' objections include: Report of the United Nations Conference on Environment and Development (Rio conference), 1992, UN Doc. A/CONF.151/26/Rev.1, vol. II, 17 ('[t]he United States does not, by joining consensus on the Rio Declaration, change its long-standing opposition to the so-called "right to development". Development is not a right'); 'Explanation of Vote on Right to Development, 61st Commission on Human Rights', statement delivered by Joel Danies, U.S. Delegation to the 61st Commission on Human Rights, 12 April 2005, http://2001-2009.state.gov/p/io/44595.htm; and 'US Explanation

right, and is thus seen as a persistent objector by a number of commentators.[102] Indeed, the United States is probably not the only one, but it has undoubtedly been the most vociferous objector. If it is *not* an exempt state, it is submitted that this is simply because the right has not yet crystallized, in which case the United States is almost certainly a persistent objector 'in waiting': there have been no notable challenges to the United States' oppositional position to the right from other states.

More firmly in the environmental context, one can point to the position taken by the United States from the earliest international discussions concerning the 'precautionary principle', as was examined in detail in Chapter 6.[103] There exists a debate as to whether a binding customary 'precautionary principle' has yet crystallized in international environmental law, but one can make a case that it has.[104] There is, at the very least, undoubtedly evidence of an emerging norm of environmental precaution apparent in state practice.[105] The United States has persistently and consistently rejected the existence of a precautionary principle under customary international environmental law.[106] It is relatively uncontentious that the United States continues to exist as an exempt persistent objector to the precautionary principle, or—for those who argue that the customary principle has still not yet crystallized—that it has effectively objected during the norm's formation and so will be able to gain exemption once it does crystallize.[107] This is so irrespective of the value-based imperative underpinning the norm as one of international environmental law.

To take a possible 'environmental' example that does not involve the United States, it has recently been argued that there now exists an outright prohibition

of Vote: Right to Development', 28 September 2012, Geneva, https://geneva.usmission.gov/2012/09/28/u-s-explanation-of-vote-right-to-development-resolution/.

[102] See Sands and Peel, n. 101, 116 and 216–17; and Iqbal, n. 100, 126–8 (albeit with some reservations about the consistency of the United States' practice).

[103] See Chapter 6, n. 173–n. 184 and accompanying text.

[104] W. Gullett, 'Environmental Protection and the "Precautionary Principle": A Response to Scientific Uncertainty in Environmental Management' (1997) 14 *Environmental and Planning Law Journal* 52, 57; and Sands and Peel, n. 101, 228. See also *Request for an Examination of the Situation in Accordance with Paragraph 63 of the Court's Judgment of 20 December 1974 in the Nuclear Tests* (*New Zealand v France*) case, order, 1995, ICJ Rep. 288, dissenting opinion of Judge Weeramantry, 342–4 (seemingly accepting the customary status of the principle, albeit not stating this explicitly).

[105] See R. Andorno, 'The Precautionary Principle: A New Legal Standard for a Technological Age' (2004) 1 *Journal of International Biotechnology Law* 11, generally, but particularly at 19; and A. Sirinskiene, 'The Status of Precautionary Principle: Moving towards a Rule of Customary Law' (2009) 4 *Jurisprudence* 349.

[106] See, for example, the practice detailed in J. Cameron and J. Abouchar, 'The Precautionary Principle: A Fundamental Principle of Law and Policy for the Protection of the Global Environment' (1991) 14 *Boston College International and Comparative Law Review* 1, 11–12 and 18, footnote 73.

[107] 'Precaution in International Sustainable Development Law', CISDL Legal Brief for the World Summit on Sustainable Development, Johannesburg, South Africa, 2002, http://cisdl.org/public/docs/news/brief_precaution2.pdf, 4; and A. Trouwborst, *Precautionary Rights and Duties of States* (Leiden, Martinus Nijhoff, 2006), 9, footnote 37. *Contra* R.B. Deloso, 'The Precautionary Principle: Relevance in International Law and Climate Change' (2005), unpublished Masters thesis, Lund University, http://www.lumes.lu.se/database/alumni/04.05/theses/rabbi_deloso.pdf, 38–9.

on all forms of whaling activity under customary international law.[108] However, the International Convention for the Regulation of Whaling (ICRW)[109] allows for exemption from amendments to its Schedule through formal 'objection',[110] thereby permitting exemption to the continuing moratorium on commercial whaling.[111] The Convention also allows for whaling for research purposes.[112] In the 2014 *Whaling in the Antarctic* case,[113] the ICJ concluded that Japan's whaling programme did not in fact constitute scientific research and was therefore unlawful, but in so doing implicitly rejected the notion that *all forms* of whaling are now contrary to international law. All of which suggests that a comprehensive whaling ban does not yet exist in custom. Having said this, there is mounting evidence that a large number of states oppose whaling per se, and this practice and *opinio juris* can at least be seen as underpinning a potential future general customary international law ban.[114]

As one of a handful of whaling states, Japan has taken great pains to try to justify its whaling activities within the terms of the ICRW,[115] even if unsuccessfully.[116] Yet it has resisted any wider customary international law restrictions,[117] and, indeed, has argued that there is a general customary international law *right* to whaling.[118] In any event, it is notable that even those commentators who argue that there is, or soon may be, a general customary prohibition accept that Japan, along with Iceland and Norway, are exempt persistent objector states.[119] At present, Norway has been able to maintain commercial whaling—legally, given its status under treaty law as an 'objector' to the moratorium on commercial whaling—and other states have largely accepted this legal exemption, even while placing political pressure on it to conform.[120] It is therefore highly unlikely that if a customary ban was to emerge (assuming that it has not already), other states would see Japan, Norway, and Iceland as anything other than exempt persistent objectors.

[108] D. Mence, 'The Cetacean Right to Life' (2015) 11 *International Journal of Law in Context* 17, in general, but particularly at 32–3.

[109] International Convention for the Regulation of Whaling (ICRW), 2 December 1946, 161 UNTS 2124.

[110] Ibid., Article V(3).

[111] The moratorium was put in place by the International Whaling Commission in 1982. It took effect from the 1985/1986 whaling season and remains in place. See International Convention for the Regulation of Whaling, 1946 Schedule (as revised by the International Whaling Commission), para. 10(e).

[112] ICRW, n.109, Article VIII.

[113] *Whaling in the Antarctic (Australia v Japan: New Zealand Intervening)*, merits, 2014, ICJ Rep., http://www.icj-cij.org/docket/files/148/18136.pdf.

[114] See A. D'Amato and S.K. Chopra, 'Whales: Their Emerging Right to Life' (1991) 85 *American Journal of International Law* 21; and H.S. Schiffman, 'The Protection of Whales in International Law: A Perspective for the Next Century' (1996–7) 22 *Brooklyn Journal of International Law* 303, 325–31.

[115] See Mence, n. 108, 32.

[116] See, generally, *Whaling in the Antarctic*, merits, n. 113.

[117] See, for example, *Whaling in the Antarctic (Australia v Japan)*, counter-memorial of Japan, vol. I, 2012, http://www.icj-cij.org/docket/files/148/17384.pdf, para. 101.

[118] See ibid., para. 2.4; and *Whaling in the Antarctic*, merits, n. 113, para. 57.

[119] See, for example, Mence, n. 108, 21 and 33; and Schiffman, n. 114, 331–3.

[120] See, for example, 'Norway-IWC Dispute on Whaling (NWHALE)', Case No. 53, *Trade and Environment database*, http://www1.american.edu/ted/NWHALE.htm.

Instances of state practice already examined in previous chapters tell the same story with regard to norms of IHL. We have seen, for example, that the United Kingdom is an exempt persistent objector to the purported customary international law prohibition on belligerent reprisals against civilians.[121] Similarly, the United States remains a persistent objector to the use of herbicides in armed conflict, as was, inter alia, reflected in the *Agent Orange* proceedings.[122] It will also be recalled that the International Committee of the Red Cross (ICRC) confirmed that France, the United Kingdom, and the United States are all exempt, as persistent objectors, from the application of the prohibition on the use of methods or means of warfare causing widespread, long-term, and severe damage to the natural environment (at least with respect to the use of nuclear weapons).[123] Interestingly, two of these examples—the use of herbicides during armed conflict and the prohibition of methods of warfare that may cause widespread, long-term, and severe damage to the natural environment—again sit at the intersection between two 'fundamental' areas: IHL and international environmental law. Yet states have been able to carve out exemptions nonetheless.

Ultimately, all the evidence—including state practice—indicates that, de jure, '*for all custom short of* jus cogens ... [states possess] the capacity for persistent objection.'[124] For good or ill, states can gain exemption through persistent objection however 'fundamental' the non-peremptory norm in question may be.[125]

[121] See Guldahl, n. 17, 76–7. See also J-M. Henckaerts and L. Doswald-Beck (eds), *Customary International Humanitarian Law, vol. I*, International Committee of the Red Cross (ICRC) Study (Cambridge, Cambridge University Press, 2005), 520–3 (appearing to identify this prohibition as being binding under customary international law). For an example of the United Kingdom's objections, see United Kingdom, *The Law of Armed Conflict*, D/DAT/13/35/66, Army Code 71130 (revised 1981), Ministry of Defence, prepared under the direction of the Chief of General Staff (1981), Section 4, 17. For more discussion of this usage of the persistent objector rule, see Chapter 3, n. 27–n. 29 and accompanying text.

[122] *In Re 'Agent Orange' Product Liability Litigation*, 2005, memorandum, order and judgment, United States District Court, Eastern District of New York, 373 F. Supp. 2d 7 (E.D.N.Y). For more discussion, see, respectively, Chapter 3, n. 117–n. 121 and accompanying text; and Chapter 5, n. 84–n. 98 and accompanying text.

[123] See ICRC IHL Study, *vol. I*, n. 121, 154. For more discussion see, respectively, Chapter 3, n. 27–n. 30 and accompanying text; and Chapter 5, n. 160–n. 166 and accompanying text.

[124] Jones, n. 57, 458–9, emphasis added.

[125] See ILA Final Report, n. 46, 29; D.R. Atkins, 'Customary International Humanitarian Law and Multinational Military Operations in Malaysia' (2007) 16 *Pacific Rim Law and Policy Journal* 79, 81 (specifically in the context of IHL); E. David, 'L'objecteur persistent, une règle persistent?' in P. Tavernier and J-M. Henckaerts (eds), *Droit international humanitaire coutumier: enjeux et défis contemporains* (Brussels, Bruylant, 2008), 89, 94–8 (specifically in the context of IHL); Green, n. 29, in general, but particularly at 183–8 (specifically in the context of human rights law); Guldahl, n. 17, particularly at 84–6 (specifically in the context of IHL); M.A. Hansen, 'Preventing the Emasculation of Warfare: Halting the Expansion of Human Rights Law into Armed Conflict' (2007) 194 *Military Law Review* 1, 17 ('[t]he persistent objector doctrine applies to the formation of customary human rights law, as well as customary humanitarian law'); Mendelson, n. 46, 242–4; T. Meron, 'International Law in the Age of Human Rights' (2013) 301 *Recueil des cours* 13, 396; and Padmanabhan, n. 48, 10 (specifically in the context of human rights law). This conclusion extends to non-peremptory *erga omnes* obligations, as noted by M. Byers, *Custom, Power and the Power of Rules: International Relations and Customary International Law* (Cambridge, Cambridge University Press, 1999), 198. *Contra* Report of the International Law Commission, Sixty-seventh session, 4 May–5 June and 6 July–7 August 2015, UN Doc. A/70/10, advance unedited version, 24 August

II. The Difficulty in Maintaining Exemption: Extra-Legal Factors

i. The claim that it is virtually impossible to maintain objection, de facto

It was argued in section I that, de jure, states can gain exemption through persistent objection to all non-peremptory norms, even 'fundamental' ones. However, some critics of the persistent objector rule have contended that the peremptory or non-peremptory status of the norm being objected to is largely irrelevant because, whatever the status of the norm in question and whatever the de jure effect of persistent objection, states are inevitably unsuccessful in trying to maintain exemption, de facto: 'In the early stages [of a norm's development] a number of States may object to the new behaviour, but over time social pressures and modern realities will cause those reluctant States to conform to the new norm.'[126]

In other words, even when the criteria for persistent objection are met, it has been said that states are in reality unable to maintain exempt status with regard to *all* norms (not just those of the 'fundamental' variety).[127] This argument is a

2015, 40, para. 94 (noting that some members of the ILC took the view, during the consideration of the 'Identification of customary international law' topic at the Commission's Sixty-seventh session, that the persistent objector rule 'could not be applicable to obligations *erga omnes*').

[126] J.I. Charney, 'The Persistent Objector Rule and the Development of Customary International Law' (1985) 56 *British Yearbook of International Law* 1, quoted at 21, but see generally. See also O. Abasheikh, 'The Validity of the Persistent Offender Rule in International Law' (2004) 9 *Coventry Law Journal* 40, 46; M. Akehurst, 'Custom as a Source of International Law' (1974–5) 47 *British Yearbook of International Law* 1, 27; O. Barsalou, 'La doctrine de l'objecteur persistant en droit international public' (2006) 19 *Revue québécoise de droit international* 1, 15; D.J. Bederman, *Custom as a Source of Law* (Cambridge, Cambridge University Press, 2010), 154–5; Byers, n. 125, 105, 158, 178, 181; A. Cassese, *International Law* (Oxford, Oxford University Press, 2nd edn, 2005), 163; B. Chigara, *Legitimacy Deficit in Custom: A Deconstructionist Critique* (Aldershot, Ashgate, 2001), 230–8; Charney, n. 24, particularly at 539; P. Dumberry, 'Incoherent and Ineffective: The Concept of Persistent Objector Revisited' (2010) 59 *International and Comparative Law Quarterly* 779, 793–4; D.W. Greig, 'Reflections on the Role of Consent' (1988–9) 12 *Australian Yearbook of International Law* 125, 173; Guldahl, n. 17, 57 (acknowledging this view but not necessarily sharing it); A.T. Guzman and J. Hsiang, 'Some Ways that Theories on Customary International Law Fail: A Reply to László Blutman' (2014) 25 *European Journal of International Law* 553, 558; W. Mansell and K. Openshaw, *International Law: A Critical Introduction* (Oxford, Hart Publishing, 2013), 23; H. Meijers, 'How is International Law Made?—The Stages of Growth of International Law and the Use of Customary Rules' (1978) 9 *Netherlands Yearbook of International Law* 3, 22; R. Müllerson, 'On the Nature and Scope of Customary International Law' (1997) 2 *Austrian Review of International and European Law* 341, 351, footnote 36; T.L. Stein, 'The Approach of the Different Drummer: The Principle of the Persistent Objector in International Law' (1985) 26 *Harvard International Law Journal* 457, 460–3; Steinfeld, n. 63, 1675; Thirlway, n. 86, 87–8; P-H. Verdier and E. Voeten, 'Precedent, Compliance, and Change in Customary International Law: An Explanatory Theory' (2014) 108 *American Journal of International Law* 389, 429; and M.E. Villiger, *Customary International Law and Treaties: A Manual on the Theory and Practice of the Interrelation of Sources* (The Hague, Kluwer, 2nd edn, 1997), 34.

[127] O. Elias and C.L. Lim, *The Paradox of Consensualism in International Law* (The Hague, Kluwer Law International, 1998), 74 (noting that, if this is true, it would 'negate[] the utility of the persistent objector rule; if dissent needs to be tolerated by other States, then it becomes practically useless as a means of allowing States to avoid unwanted obligations').

'softer' version of the claim, encountered previously in this book,[128] that the persistent objector rule is a fiction; this argument does not go as far as to deny the existence of the persistent objector rule, but instead critiques its *effectiveness*.

Abi-Saab thus takes the view that the difficulties in maintaining exemption mean that '[l]'objecteur tenace *ne peut être qu'un* phénomène transitoire'.[129] This goes too far, in that persistent objector status in not *inherently* transitory, but there is a degree of truth at the core of Abi-Saab's claim. It is extremely difficult for states to maintain objection indefinitely. This is for a range of extra-legal reasons. Swimming against the tide is a tiring business, and it is therefore perhaps not surprising that states will often give up and go with the flow: '[p]ersistent objectors may eventually yield under pressure from other states … [and] [p]ersistent objections thus tend not to be maintained for indefinite periods of time.'[130]

It is important not to overstate this issue, however. This is, firstly, because states have in fact maintained objections for long periods.[131] So this is demonstrably possible. Secondly, one must be clear that the extra-legal influences that will often limit the long-term effectiveness of the persistent objector rule do not affect its existence as a secondary rule of the international legal system: 'the possibility of effective preservation of the persistent objector status should not be confused with the legally recognized right not to agree with new customary rules.'[132] The objector may well decide that the advantages of maintaining its hard-won exempt status are outweighed by the costs (political or practical),[133] meaning that it stops objecting: states can, of course, abandon their objections at any time.[134] This certainly does not mean, however, that the state has to do so, de jure.[135] Nor does

[128] See, for example, Introduction, n. 27 and accompanying text.

[129] G. Abi-Saab, 'Cours général de droit international public' (1987-VII) 207 *Recueil des cours* 9, 181, emphasis added.

[130] Meron, n. 125, 394–5. See also G.M. Danilenko, *Law-Making in the International Community* (Dordrecht, Martinus Nijhoff, 1993), 112; M. Dixon, R. McCorquodale, and S. Williams, *Cases and Materials on International Law* (Oxford, Oxford University Press, 5th edn, 2011), 33; B.B. Jia, 'The Relations between Treaties and Custom' (2010) 9 *Chinese Journal of International Law* 81, 89–90; M. Ragazzi, *The Concept of International Obligations* Erga Omnes (Oxford, Clarendon Press, 1997), 65; and Weil, n. 5, 191–2 and 197–8.

[131] Take, for example, Turkey's objections to the extension of the limit on territorial waters to 12 nautical miles. Turkey had been objecting to the rule since the early twentieth century, but was particularly vociferous in objecting in the twenty-five years immediately prior to the adoption of the United Nations Convention on the Law of the Sea (UNCLOS), 10 December 1982, 1833 UNTS 3, and the crystallization of the norm as custom in the 1980s. Turkey remains a persistent objector. For further discussion, see, respectively, Chapter 2, n. 140–n. 144 and accompanying text; Chapter 3, n. 54–n. 59 and accompanying text; Chapter 5, n. 103–n. 113 and accompanying text; and Chapter 9, n. 196 and accompanying text.

[132] Danilenko, n. 130, 112. See also ILA Final Report, n. 46, 28; A. Abass, *Complete International Law: Text, Cases, and Materials* (Oxford, Oxford University Press, 2nd edn, 2014), 48; Dumberry, n. 126, 793–4; Elias, n. 46, 47; Guldahl, n. 17, 58; and K. Wolfke, *Custom in Present International Law* (Dordrecht, Martinus Nijhoff, 2nd edn, 1993), 66–7.

[133] Weil, n. 5, 191 and 199.

[134] Third Report on Identification of Customary International Law (M. Wood, Special Rapporteur), International Law Commission, Sixty-seventh session, 27 March 2015, UN Doc. A/CN.4/682, para. 93.

[135] Mendelson, n. 46, 237.

the difficulty in maintaining long-term exemption (in many cases) enervate the persistent objector rule: as will be discussed in Chapter 9, persistent objection has notable short-term benefits for states, even in instances where they might find it disadvantageous to maintain their exemption in the long term.[136]

ii. Extra-legal factors that may influence the objector's decision to keep objecting

Various factors may contribute to the cost/benefit calculation with respect to maintaining exemption for the objecting state, directly affecting its decision as to whether to continue objecting: 'Such factors have to be weighed in the balance when asking – as governments must – if persistent objection to the particular rule of international law is worthwhile ... Those who run States generally appreciate the quiet life as much as anyone else: the pressure to compromise is evident.'[137]

Extra-legal factors will, of course, inevitably influence the way in which all law is shaped and applied,[138] but this influence is especially evident in the context of persistent objection. This is because the objector is necessarily isolated from the rest of (or most of the rest of) the international community in relation to the norm in question, and thus is inevitably less well insulated from the influence of political pressure and other extra-legal factors. However, the relevance and implications of any particular extra-legal pressure or influence on a state's attempts to maintain exemption will, of course, vary from state to state and from one customary international law norm to another.[139] Some of the factors that may influence states' decision to maintain (or not maintain) persistent objection are discussed in this section, although it should be noted that the 'list' presented herein is not intended to be exhaustive.

One obvious relevant factor influencing the likelihood of a state maintaining persistent objector status will be familiar from section I of this chapter: that is, the 'fundamental' nature—the moral or value-based importance—of the norm being objected to. It was argued in section I that there exists no legal rule that formally insulates human rights norms and other 'fundamental' norms from persistent objection. However, the political pressure associated with the ideals of universalism that underpin many of the rules discussed in section I means that it is often practically untenable, or at least particularly undesirable, for states to maintain

[136] See Chapter 9, sections VI and VII, particularly at section VI.*iii*.

[137] A.V. Lowe, *International Law* (Oxford, Oxford University Press, 2007), 56–8, quoted at 57. See also Danilenko, n. 130, 112. Schachter, n. 8, 37–8 similarly argues that there are 'a variety of factors' that will affect the application of the persistent objector rule. However, Schachter appears to conclude that these factors contribute to the de jure applicability of the rule. Broadly speaking this should be dismissed, in that the influence of these factors will largely be in relation to maintaining objection de facto. See Mendelson, n. 46, 244. Having said this, it has been noted previously (see Chapter 4, section III; and Chapter 5, n. 139–n. 149 and accompanying text) that the 'acceptable degree' of both the 'persistence' and 'consistency' of objection—which are context-specific criteria—will depend at least in part on extra-legal factors.

[138] Greig, n. 126, 139.

[139] Jia, n. 130, 88.

exemption from them for long. There exists a special 'rhetorical power' not just to the concept of *jus cogens*, but to human rights, IHL, and environmental norms per se. Considerations of morality and universality make persistent objection to 'fundamental' norms harder in fact, even if not in law.[140] Irrespective of the de jure ability of states to persistently object to human rights obligations, for example, there is nothing to stop political pressure from being applied on persistent objectors to such standards (including after the norm in question has formed), to try to influence a renunciation of their isolationist position.[141] Indeed, it is the view of the present author that political pressure *should* be placed on such states to conform: it is, quite simply, morally desirable that they do so.[142]

It is not just the value-based nature of the norm being objected to that may cause de facto issues for persistent objectors, however. More pragmatically, the norm's 'reciprocal' nature may also have a notable influence on a state's decision as to whether to keep objecting. All norms of international law—being, as it is, an interactional system of networked obligations—have an element of 'reciprocity' to them, of course.[143] However, some norms involve rather more obvious correlative state obligations than others.[144] It has been said that where the 'relevant rule belongs to the group of contingent prescriptions that, in the same way as traffic rules on left-hand or right-hand driving, must be determined for the sake of legal clarity and avoiding disaster',[145] persistent objection will be extremely difficult,[146] or perhaps even entirely impossible,[147] to maintain.

One might assume that where a state holds an exemption to a norm of customary international law, other states will apply the previously existing law to that state as the lowest common legal denominator, and in recognition of the objector's de jure exempt status. This effectively would allow the objector to gain benefits to the direct detriment of the non-objecting (conformist) state: what has been described as a potential 'free rider' problem.[148] However, in practice the objecting state will suffer more from its position in such circumstances than the non-objecting state.[149] Where a dispute exists between states because the 'old' norm (applicable to the persistent objector) and the 'new' norm (applicable to everyone else) *directly contradict each other*, a choice will need to be made—which will necessarily impinge on the rights of one or other of the states concerned—as to

[140] Green, n. 62, 30–3; Green, n. 29, 190–1 (discussing international human rights law); Guldahl, n. 17, 85–6 (discussing IHL); Loschin, n. 9, generally, but particularly at 172; and Müllerson, n. 126, 354.

[141] Loschin, n. 9, 168. Similarly, see David, n. 125, 94–8 (arguing that while states can persistently object to IHL norms, they should not and—as a result—*do not* do so often).

[142] Green, n. 29, 191.

[143] A. D'Amato, 'Groundwork for International Law' (2014) 108 *American Journal of International Law* 650, 668–9.

[144] G. Norman and J.P. Trachtman, 'The Customary International Law Game' (2005) 99 *American Journal of International Law* 541, 563.

[145] Tomuschat, n. 24, 286.

[146] Byers, n. 125, 102–5 and 182; and Dumberry, 'The Last Citadel!', n. 44, 398–400.

[147] D'Amato, n. 143, 668–9.

[148] Dumberry, 'The Last Citadel!', n. 44, 399.

[149] Byers, n. 125, 103; and Mendelson, n. 46, 243–4.

which of the competing norms to apply. Irrespective of de jure persistent objector status, it should come as no surprise that the objector is likely to face significant difficulty in maintaining its position, given that the non-objecting state has the weight of majority opinion in its corner.[150] This is particularly evident when the dispute is one that is considered in a state agency or national court of a non-objecting state.[151]

Another relevant extra-legal factor is the 'power' of the state doing the objecting, which will underpin the extent to which it can withstand social pressure to conform to new customary norms.[152] For example, when one considers examples of the usage (or attempted usage) of the persistent objector rule by states, it is quite evident that the United States has attempted to employ the rule more often than any other state, and has also successfully maintained subsequent exempt status more often. This should come as no surprise: the United States is in a 'unique power position' in the world, and this inevitably affects its ability to resort to, and sustain, persistent objection.[153] It is hardly remarkable to note that the United States is 'comfortable with taking minority positions in international law'.[154]

On this basis, some have argued that the United States may be the *only state* today able to maintain persistent objector status,[155] while others have claimed that it is only 'powerful states' (if, perhaps, not only the United States) that can benefit from the rule de facto.[156] Either claim overstates the matter: 'weaker' states can, *and do*, gain and maintain persistent objector status. Similarly, there are times where even especially powerful states buckle under the pressure of politics and other extra-legal factors.[157] The same winds of social coercion buffet powerful persistent objectors just as much as less powerful ones: it is simply that more powerful states (and the United States in particular) are better able to weather the storm, and are thus going to come out the other side unscathed more often.

[150] Byers, n. 125, 104–5.

[151] Ibid., 103–4; and Dumberry, 'The Last Citadel!', n. 44, 398–400. See, for example, the objections by the Soviet Union and China to the emergence of the doctrine of restrictive immunity, discussed in section II.*iii*.

[152] W.W. Bishop, 'General Course on Public International Law' (1965-II) 115 *Recueil des cours* 151, 227; and Schachter, n. 8, 30.

[153] D.F. Vagts, 'International Relations Looks at Customary International Law: A Traditionalist's Defence' (2004) 15 *European Journal of International Law* 1031, 1039.

[154] Hansen, n. 125, 61.

[155] W. Wiltshire, 'Some Thoughts on UNCLOS and Customary International Law' (2009) *Information Dissemination: The Intersection of Maritime Strategy and Strategic Communications*, http://www.informationdissemination.net/2009/03/some-thoughts-on-unclos-and-customary.html.

[156] B. Kingsbury, 'Sovereignty and Inequality' (1998) 9 *European Journal of International Law* 599, 610; Ragazzi, n. 130, 65; and J. Tasioulas, 'Customary International Law and the Quest for Global Justice' in A. Perreau-Saussine and J.B. Murphy (eds), *The Nature of Customary Law: Legal, Historical and Philosophical Perspectives* (Cambridge, Cambridge University Press, 2007), 307, 312–13 (implying this conclusion rather than explicitly stating it). See also Tomuschat, n. 24, 289 ('as a persistent objector a big power which fears to be overwhelmed by an assault of Lilliputian forces can at least pretend that, by going it alone, it is simply making use of its rights rather than violating generally applicable rules of international law').

[157] Mendelson, n. 46, 237 ('[t]here is a diplomatic cost of being the "odd man out", and sometimes the price is deemed not worth paying, *even for superpowers*'; emphasis added).

Finally, as noted above, persistent objectors are inherently isolated state actors, at least in respect of the norm to which they are objecting. It is inevitable, however, that the *degree* of their isolation will influence their decision as to whether to try to maintain their exempt status.[158] If a notable number of states oppose an emerging rule of custom, then it is, of course, unlikely that the rule in question will crystallize at all.[159] Yet there is safety in numbers, even if those numbers are rather small, and it is not necessarily the case that a rule will have only one persistent objector state.[160] In instances where there is *more than one*, it will likely be politically easier for each member of the small group of objectors to maintain its objection.[161] Absolute isolation as a sole persistent objector, on the other hand, will mean that the pressure to conform is greater.[162]

The various factors that may influence the desirability for the objecting state of maintaining its objection—such as the moral or value-based nature of the norm, its 'reciprocal' nature, the power of the objector, and the degree of the objector's isolation—are, in practice, likely to be interrelated. Their respective effects are extremely difficult to quantify and, especially as we are in the extra-legal realm, it is almost impossible to try to predict how differing pressures may affect the de facto likelihood of maintaining objection. *Figure 8.1* visually illustrates the fact that there will often be an *interplay* of factors that will influence the objector. The figure should not necessarily be seen as a direct representation of that interrelationship: instead, it serves to demonstrate just how complex the cost/benefit calculation for objectors can be in determining whether or not to continue objecting (especially in the shaded area).

iii. State practice illustrating the influence of extra-legal factors on maintaining exemption

The previous subsection identified various extra-legal factors that may influence the de facto possibility of maintaining persistent objection, and it was argued that these factors will rarely operate in isolation. This subsection turns to some examples from practice to further illustrate the factors that have been identified.

158 A. Boyle and C. Chinkin, *The Making of International Law* (Oxford, Oxford University Press, 2007), 237; J-A. Carrillo-Salcedo, 'Droit international et souveraineté des États—Cours général de droit international public' (1996) 257 *Recueil des cours* 35, 94; P. Malanczuk, *Akehurst's Modern Introduction to International Law* (New York, Routledge, 7th edn, 1997), 48; and Villiger, n. 126, 192.

159 Guldahl, n. 17; A. Kaczorowska, *Public International Law* (Abingdon, Routledge, 4th edn, 2010), 41 Thirlway, n. 4, 116; and Villiger, n. 126, 36.

160 Jia, n. 130, 88 ('[t]here is no rule that prevents more than one state from becoming persistent objectors').

161 Danilenko, n. 130, 112; and O. Elias, 'Persistent Objector' in R. Wolfrum (ed.), *Max Planck Encyclopaedia of Public International Law, vol. VIII* (Oxford, Oxford University Press, 2012), 280, 281, para. 4.

162 D.A. Colson, 'How Persistent Must the Persistent Objector Be?' (1986) 61 *Washington Law Review* 957, 967; and Ragazzi, n. 130, 64–5.

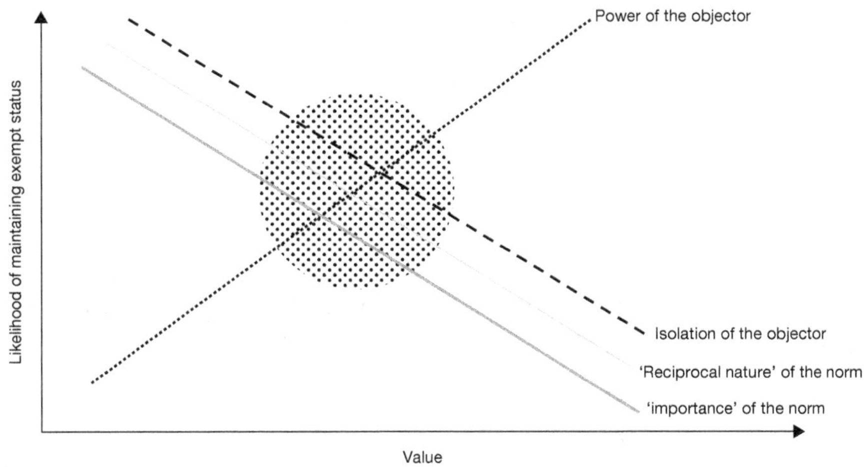

Figure 8.1 The effect of extra-legal factors on an objector's ability to maintain exemption

It was argued in section I.*iii* that there are examples of states acting as persistent objectors to 'fundamental' peremptory norms: but it will be recalled that most of the objector states in these examples were powerful western states, or—in the case of Saudi Arabia's objections to the freedom to change one's religion or belief—one of a group of states (meaning that Saudi Arabia is not an 'isolated' objector).[163] Such factors have helped the objectors resist the particularly intense political pressure to conform to especially 'fundamental' standards. It is no coincidence, for example, that the only state to have asserted persistent objector status with regard to human rights norms in international adjudicative proceedings is the United States.[164] More generally, however, maintaining objection to 'fundamental' norms is particularly difficult for most states.

For instance, consider the position of Mauritania with regard to the practice of female genital mutilation (FGM), which has been referenced in previous chapters.[165] The norm in question is one of customary international human rights law, assuming that it has in fact emerged.[166] Mauritania had persistently

[163] Having said this, as noted at n. 83, it is difficult to view the other Islamic states that objected to the right to change one's religion or belief as exempt persistent objectors, because their objections have not been sufficiently persistent or consistent. Nonetheless, their periodic objections provide significant political support to Saudi Arabia's exempt status.

[164] In *Roach and Pinkerton*, merits, n. 51; *Domingues*, merits, n. 52; and *Grand River*, final award, n. 87. See, generally, Green, n. 29.

[165] See, respectively, Chapter 3, n. 191–n. 198 and accompanying text; and Chapter 6, n. 334–n. 337 and accompanying text.

[166] It is arguable whether a prohibition on FGM has yet emerged in customary international law, but it can be said with a high degree of certainty that it is at least *emerging*, particularly given the unanimous adoption of General Assembly Resolution 67/146, 20 December 2012, UN Doc. A/RES/67/146.

objected to the prohibition of FGM.[167] It was—up until 2005—generally regarded as having met the criteria for persistent objection in relation to the emerging norm,[168] and was thus seen as being exempt from it (or, if one is of the view that the norm had not yet crystallized before this point, as being in a position that it *would have been* exempt from the norm once it crystallized).[169] However, the value-based imperative of the norm in question meant that Mauritania faced severe political pressure to conform. In 2005, Mauritania bowed to this pressure by reversing its stance in Ordonnance n°2005-015,[170] Article 12 of which criminalizes FGM. Article 12 almost certainly terminally undermines any possible persistent objector status,[171] highlighting the de facto difficulty in maintaining exemption to non-peremptory human rights norms, *especially* for less powerful states.

Power is not necessarily always a 'Teflon coating' in relation to maintaining persistent objection, however: as has been noted, a variety of extra-legal factors contribute to a state's decision to continue objecting or not. A number of what are often broadly referred to as 'indigenous rights' provide an interesting illustration of the complexity surrounding states' decisions to maintain exemption. There has been increasing agreement, particularly since the 1990s, that certain 'new' indigenous rights have attained the status of customary international law,[172] albeit that probably not all of the rights contained in the 2007 UN Declaration on the Rights of Indigenous Peoples[173] have crystallized in this way.[174] Four states can be identified as having been persistent objectors to the relevant customary international law norms: the United States, Canada, New Zealand, and Australia (all of which can, of course, be considered powerful, developed states). These states, for example, were the only states to vote against the UN Declaration (which 143

[167] Mauritania long objected to the regulation of certain Islamic practices, including FGM. For examples, see Chapter 3, n. 196.

[168] See Lau, n. 9, 507–8; and Quince, n. 9, 77.

[169] Lau, n. 9, 507–8.

[170] Ordonnance n°2005–015 portant protection pénale de l'enfant, 2005, Présidence du Conseil Militaire pour la Justice et la Démocratie, Republique Islamique de Mauritanie, http://legislationmauritanienne.files.wordpress.com/2011/06/ordonnance-nc2b02005-015-portant-protection-pc3a9nale-de-l_enfant.pdf.

[171] See 'Legislative Reform to Support the Abandonment of Female Genital Mutilation/Cutting', (2010) UNICEF Report, http://www.unicef.org/policyanalysis/files/UNICEF_-_LRI_Legislative_Reform_to_support_the_Abandonment_of_FGMC_August_2010.pdf, 7, 21 and 46.

[172] See *Committee on the Rights of Indigenous Peoples*, Interim Report of the Committee, International Law Association, The Hague Conference (2010), http://www.ila-hq.org/en/committees/index.cfm/cid/1024, 43–52 (endorsed by *Committee on the Rights of Indigenous Peoples*, Final Report of the Committee, International Law Association, Sofia Conference (2012), http://www.ila-hq.org/en/committees/index.cfm/cid/1024, 28–9); S.J. Anaya, *Indigenous Peoples in International Law* (Oxford, Oxford University Press, 2nd edn, 1996), 61–72; and B.L. Gunn, 'Overcoming Obstacles to Implementing the UN Declaration on the Rights of Indigenous Peoples in Canada' (2013) 31 *Windsor Yearbook of Access to Justice* 147. *Contra* A. Xanthaki, 'Indigenous Rights in International Law Over The Last 10 Years and Future Developments' (2009) 10 *Melbourne Journal of International Law* 27, 34–7.

[173] United Nations Declaration on the Rights of Indigenous Peoples, 2007, annexed to General Assembly Resolution 61/296, 13 September 2007, UN Doc. A/RES/61/296.

[174] ILA Interim Report, n. 172, 43.

states voted in favour of),[175] and all of them have objected repeatedly in various other ways.[176]

Given the 'fundamental' nature of the human rights norms in question, however, increasing political pressure has been placed on these states to conform. For its part, Australia explicitly endorsed the UN Declaration in 2009, and reversed its position on the customary status of a number of provisions contained within it.[177] It would therefore be difficult to still view it as an exempt persistent objector state.[178] Interestingly, a year later, in 2010, both Canada[179] and New Zealand[180] also endorsed the Declaration, which might suggest that the pressure to conform increased on them as they became more isolated following the Australian change of position (i.e. as the small group of objecting states diminished).

Having said this, while New Zealand was explicit about its reversal of position when endorsing the Declaration,[181] Canada has been notably more equivocal than Australia and New Zealand in endorsing the Declaration, arguing that it remains 'aspirational'.[182] Canada's position as a continuing persistent objector may therefore be debated, but its increasingly inconsistent practice since 2010 on indigenous rights has led to the claim being made that it too has now 'lost' its persistent objector status.[183] Even the United States, the last remaining state that was formally opposed to the Declaration, has now endorsed it.[184] However, the United States has done so very carefully so as to maintain its persistent objector

[175] See 'Indigenous Rights Outlined by UN' (2007) *BBC News*, http://news.bbc.co.uk/1/hi/in_depth/6993776.stm.

[176] For example, none of the four states is party to the International Labour Organisation Convention concerning Indigenous and Tribal Peoples in Independent Countries, No. 169, 27 June 1989. See also: New Zealand Ministry of Foreign Affairs and Trade, Human Rights: Indigenous Peoples, Declaration on the Rights of Indigenous Peoples, chronology of events since June 2006, http://www.mfat.govt.nz/Foreign-Relations/1-Global-Issues/Human-Rights/Indigenous-Peoples/draftdec-jun07.php (setting out a number of instances of objection by New Zealand); Report of the Special Rapporteur on the Rights of Indigenous Peoples: The Situation of Indigenous Peoples in the United States of America, 30 August 2012, UN. Doc. A/HRC/21/47/Add.1 (setting out much of the opposition of the United States in practice); L. Chappell, J. Chesterman, and L. Hill, *The Politics of Human Rights in Australia* (Cambridge, Cambridge University Press, 2009), 131–2 (listing seven policies under the Howard government in Australia that were directly opposed to indigenous rights); and Gunn, n. 172, 155–9 (setting out some of the various objections made by Canada).

[177] See, for example, 'Experts Hail Australia's Backing of UN Declaration of Indigenous Peoples' Rights' (2009) *United Nations News Centre*, http://www.un.org/apps/news/story.asp?NewsID=30382.

[178] Green, n. 29, 190–1.

[179] Canada's Statement of Support on the United Nations Declaration on the Rights of Ingenious Peoples' Government of Canada, 12 November 2010, https://www.aadnc-aandc.gc.ca/eng/1309374239861/1309374546142.

[180] 'Statement by Hon Dr Pita Sharples, Minister of Maori Affairs', New Zealand Ministry of Foreign Affairs and Trade, Ministry Statements and Speeches 2010, Ninth session of the United Nations Permanent Forum on Indigenous Issues, 19 April 2010, http://www.mfat.govt.nz/Media-and-publications/Media/MFAT-speeches/2010/0-19-April-2010.php.

[181] Ibid. [182] Canada's Statement of Support, n. 179.

[183] Gunn, n. 172, particularly at 165.

[184] 'Announcement of U.S. Support for the United Nations Declaration on the Rights of Indigenous Peoples: Initiatives to Promote the Government-to-Government Relationship & Improve the Lives of Indigenous Peoples', United States State Department, 15 December 2010, http://www.state.gov/documents/organization/184099.pdf.

status with regard to many of the Declaration's provisions and, more generally, has steadfastly refused to accept the obligations contained within it as being binding.[185] It seems clear that the United States remains a persistent objector to a number of indigenous rights,[186] which perhaps highlights the unique position of power for that state when it comes to shielding itself from political pressure to conform to 'fundamental' norms of customary international law.

An example that has been advanced in the literature on the persistent objector rule to highlight the difficulty (or, for some, impossibility) of maintaining objection—even for powerful states—concerns the Soviet Union's persistent objections to the shift in the customary international law position away from absolute sovereign immunity to a restricted immunity rule since the early changes in practice in the 1950s.[187] Despite almost certainly meeting the formal requirements of persistent objection,[188] the Soviet Union found that domestic courts in other jurisdictions began to apply restrictive immunity to its agencies and enterprises, irrespective of its de jure exempt status.[189] Writers have, further, made much of the fact that when this occurred, the Soviet Union did not then *invoke* the persistent objector rule in its defence.[190] Ultimately, although the Soviet Union maintained its objections for a while—something that should not be ignored[191]—it is true that in the end it gave up in the face of the fact that those objections were not availing it in other jurisdictions.[192]

China has also been a persistent objector to the restrictive immunity approach.[193] As with the Soviet Union, China has struggled to have its exempt position respected in foreign courts,[194] although its persistent objector position has, for example, been recognized by the judiciary in Hong Kong.[195] China has maintained its stance significantly longer—if perhaps not with much more in the way of tangible de facto benefit—than the Soviet Union did. Yet there are signs that China too is beginning to abandon its objections and reluctantly accept

185 See, generally, UN Doc. A/HRC/21/47/Add.1, n.176.

186 A good example evidencing this is the United States' claim in the *Grand River* dispute that it was an exempt persistent objector to the right of indigenous consultation (see *Grand River*, counter-memorial of the respondent, n. 91, 128–9), and the fact that the NAFTA Tribunal that heard the case did not even question this assertion (see, generally, *Grand River*, final award, n. 87). See n. 87–n. 94 and accompanying text for discussion.

187 See Byers, n. 125, 181; Stein, n. 126, 460–1; and Steinfeld, n. 63, 1654–5.

188 M.M. Boguslavsky, 'Foreign State Immunity: Soviet Doctrine and Practice' (1979) 10 *Netherlands Yearbook of International Law* 167, particularly at 170–4 (setting out the Soviet objections).

189 See Stein, n. 126, 461, footnote 13 (setting out a number of examples).

190 Ibid., 461; and Steinfeld, n. 63, 1655.

191 Norman and Trachtman, n. 144, 563.

192 Weil, n. 5, 191.

193 See, for example, *Democratic Republic of the Congo v FG Hemisphere Associates LLC (No 1)* 2011, 14 HKCFAR, Final Appeal Nos. 5, 6, and 7 of 2010 (civil), para. 44 (quoting a letter from the Office of the Commissioner of the Ministry of Foreign Affairs of China in Hong Kong: '[t]he consistent and principled position of China is that a state and its property shall, in foreign courts, enjoy absolute immunity, including absolute immunity from jurisdiction and from execution, and [China] has never applied the so-called principle or theory of "restrictive immunity"').

194 Verdier and Voeten, n. 126, 428.

195 *DRC v FG Hemisphere Associates*, final appeal, n. 193, para. 121, per Bokhary PJ.

restrictive immunity, as it has started acting somewhat inconsistently in relation to the doctrine.[196] The objections of China have therefore similarly been cited as an indication of the difficulty (or impossibility) of effectively maintaining persistent objector status.[197]

The move from absolute to restrictive immunity is perhaps the archetypal instance of a 'reciprocal' obligation to which states have persistently objected.[198] Indeed, it involves a differentiation of norm application that really only *matters* when immunity is being determined in the courts of non-objecting states: which means that the objector is at an inherent political disadvantage in terms of asserting its exempt position.

As Mendelson points out, there may be any number of (extra-legal) reasons why the Soviet Union did not invoke the persistent objector rule in relation to restrictive immunity in proceedings in foreign courts where the norm in question was at issue in the 1950s–1970s.[199] One of these reasons may well have been that the nature of the norm meant a 'double hit' for the Soviet Union, in that its stance led it to apply absolute immunity in its own courts while *also* facing hostility in trying to gain the same level of immunity elsewhere: persistent objection was, simply, hurting more than benefiting it.[200] However, the Soviet Union's motives in not invoking the rule can only be speculated on, and it is hardly surprising that the relevant foreign courts did not apply the persistent objector rule to the Soviet Union given that the rule was not advanced before them.[201] China, for its part, probably remains a persistent objector state: it continues not to recognize the doctrine of restrictive immunity per se, and consistently applies absolute immunity internally.[202] The fact that this position does not necessarily avail it in foreign courts does not undermine its legal right to reject the doctrine, only the practical *effectiveness* of that rejection.

The instances of persistent objection to restrictive immunity therefore do not undermine the de jure applicability of the persistent objector rule but, again, simply show that states may not wish to employ it in practice for a variety of extra-legal reasons, or may find in some circumstances that de jure and de facto exemption do not coincide: especially when it comes to obligations based on reciprocal recognition. It may well be correct to say that objection was essentially impossible to maintain de facto in relation to restrictive immunity, and that this, in practice, makes de jure exemption worthless: what use is an exemption if it is not recognized when it matters?[203] However, this finding—even if it holds true—cannot

[196] Consider the fact that China has signed (but not ratified) the United Nations Convention on Jurisdictional Immunities of States and Their Property, 2 December 2004, Doc. A/59/508 (adopted by General Assembly Resolution 59/38, 2 December 2004, UN Doc. A/RES/59/38, not in force).

[197] Verdier and Voeten, n. 126, 428–9.

[198] Meron, n. 125, 394–5; and Norman and Trachtman, n. 144, 563.

[199] Mendelson, n. 46, 235.

[200] Byers, n. 125, 104.

[201] Mendelson, n. 46, 235; and Guldahl, n. 17, 58.

[202] See, generally, O. Jones, 'Let the Mainland Speak: A Positivist Take on the Congo Case' (2011) 41 *Hong Kong Law Journal* 177.

[203] Verdier and Voeten, n. 126, 428–9.

be extrapolated to the persistent objector rule as a whole. Instead, it can at most be viewed as a consequence of the relatively unique nature of state immunity.

A similar example, also commonly referenced in the literature on the persistent objector rule,[204] relates to the states that sought to oppose the extension of the territorial sea from 3 to 12 nautical miles (from the 1930s at least up to the end of the 1970s). Crawford points out, for example, that not even the United States could prevent the establishment of a 12-mile territorial sea, or—ultimately—limit the effect upon it of the consensus among other states on the question. Its isolation meant that, politically, '[i]n the end that game was not worth the candle'.[205] Along with the United States, the United Kingdom and Japan were also persistent objectors.[206] All three states ultimately gave up on their objections,[207] under notable pressure to do so.[208] Again, the influence of increased political isolation was likely telling, as was the reciprocity that went to the heart of the norm being objected to: the very nature of a territorial sea means that its size will often impact upon the size of *other states'* territorial seas, making its determination another example of an especially 'reciprocal' norm. Yet it is worth noting that there may have been other influential factors. For example, for the United States, there were seemingly some notable diplomatic advantages in not pressing the territorial sea issue at the time, in terms of building sought-after relationships with other states.[209]

More importantly, it should be kept in mind that these three states successfully maintained their exempt status for a long period. For example, as Brownlie correctly notes, Japan actually applied the persistent objector rule 'with considerable success' in relation to various law of the sea norms from (roughly) 1945 to 1977.[210] Indeed, during this period, 'many States were prepared to sign bilateral agreements ... recognizing Japan's claim', even while supporting the general norm.[211] This hardly suggests that persistent objection cannot be maintained per se where the norm being objected to is particularly 'reciprocal', or that 'isolated' states necessarily cannot 'hold out'. Indeed, we have previously seen that Turkey continues

[204] See Abasheikh, n. 126, 46 (regarding Japan); Akehurst, n. 126, 27 (regarding the United Kingdom); Byers, n. 125, 104, 152, and 181; Chigara, n. 126, 232–3; Charney, n. 126, 12–13 (regarding Japan and the United States); M. Dixon, *Textbook on International Law* (Oxford, Oxford University Press, 7th edn, 2013), 34 (regarding the United Kingdom); Dumberry, n. 126, 791; and Elias, n. 46, 43.

[205] J. Crawford, 'Sovereignty as a Legal Value' in J. Crawford and M. Koskenniemi (eds), *The Cambridge Companion to International Law* (Cambridge, Cambridge University Press, 2012), 117, 124.

[206] Thirlway, n. 86, 87.

[207] See, for example, 'United States Ocean Policy', Statement of President Reagan, 10 March 1983, http://www.reagan.utexas.edu/archives/speeches/1983/31083c.htm (United States); the Territorial Sea Act 1987 (c. 49) (United Kingdom); and Law on the Territorial Sea and the Contiguous Zone (Law No. 30 of 1977, as amended by Law No. 73 of 1996), http://www.un.org/depts/los/LEGISLATIONANDTREATIES/PDFFILES/JPN_1996_Law.pdf (Japan).

[208] See, for example, Letter dated 22 August 1979 from the Vice-Chairman of the group of coastal States to the President of the Conference, UN Doc. A/CONF.62/90 (evidencing the pressure placed on the United States in particular).

[209] Mendelson, n. 46, 236.

[210] I. Brownlie, 'International Law at the Fiftieth Anniversary of the United Nations—General Course on Public International Law' (1995) 255 *Recueil des cours* 11, 42.

[211] Elias and Lim, n. 127, 23. See also Chigara, n. 126, 232–3.

to maintain its persistent objector status in relation to the extension of territorial waters—and has done so for decades—irrespective of the correlative implications of this in relation to Greece's corresponding claims, or the undoubted pressure that the adoption of the UN Convention on the Law of the Sea (UNCLOS)[212] placed upon it to conform.[213]

Finally, it is worth considering the objections of Bolivia to two decisions (the 'Cancun Agreements') adopted at the end of the 2010 UN Climate Change Conference.[214] Bolivia had persistently (and consistently) objected, formally and informally,[215] to the Agreements and refused to accept their adoption. Of course, the Cancun Agreements cannot be seen as creating any binding norms of customary international law in relation to climate change, even in spite of the overwhelming state support for them. Aside from the issue of whether custom can be 'instantly' created by decisions taken collectively by states in such fora,[216] the Cancun Agreements were specifically designed *not* to create legal obligations so as to foster consensus.[217] Bolivia could at most, then, be seen as a persistent objector 'in waiting'; it is probably more accurate to say that it was simply an 'objector' to an international agreement in a broader sense.[218]

The Bolivian position nonetheless tells us something about the difficulties of 'standing apart' in international legal interactions generally. Bolivia's objections were almost immediately overruled by other states, and it quickly gave up trying to pursue its position post-conference.[219] It might be said that Bolivia hit the 'perfect storm' of the extra-legal factors that have been discussed in this section. In the context of the political determination following the failures of the 2009 Copenhagen conference,[220] Bolivia—a 'less powerful' state—found itself entirely isolated as the sole objector to the development of 'fundamental' and notably 'reciprocal' universal standards concerning climate change. As a result, Bolivia was politically unable to maintain its persistent objector stance even before there

[212] UNCLOS, n. 131.

[213] See n. 131; Chapter 2, n. 140–n. 144 and accompanying text; Chapter 3, n. 54–n. 59 and accompanying text; Chapter 5, n. 103–n. 113 and accompanying text; and Chapter 9, n. 196 and accompanying text.

[214] Decision 1/CP.16, The Cancun Agreements: Outcome of the work of the Ad Hoc Working Group on Long-term Cooperative Action under the Convention, 2010, UN Doc. FCCC/CP/2010/7/Add.1; and Decision 1/CMP.6 The Cancun Agreements: Outcome of the work of the Ad Hoc Working Group on Further Commitments for Annex I Parties under the Kyoto Protocol at its fifteenth session, 2010, UN Doc. FCCC/KP/CMP/2010/12/Add.1.

[215] H.G. Schermers and N.M. Blokker, *International Institutional Law: Unity within Diversity* (Leiden, Martinus Nijhoff, 5th edn, 2011), 541.

[216] See Chapter 6, section VII, particularly at n. 235–n. 243 and accompanying text.

[217] See, for example, Decision 1/CP.16, n. 214, preamble.

[218] Bolivia has been identified as a 'persistent objector' state: see A. Collins, 'Agreeing to Disagree? (Or Bolivia and the Confusing Consensus Conundrum Part II)' (2011) tck, http://adoptanegotiator.org/agreeing-to-disagree-or-bolivia-and-the-confusing-consensus-conundrum-part-ii/; and Schermers and Blokker, n. 215, 542. However, this must be incorrect, at least in the sense of having gained formal exemption from a crystallized norm of customary international law.

[219] Collins, n. 218.

[220] See Schermers and Blokker, n. 215, 542; and S. Schiele, *Evolution of International Environmental Regimes: The Case of Climate Change* (Cambridge, Cambridge University Press, 2014), 75–82.

was any suggestion of the emergence of a customary international law norm to which it might later have become exempt.

III. Conclusion

Some commentators have understandably claimed that states cannot persistently object to non-peremptory emerging norms of customary international law where those norms are especially 'fundamental' (usually meaning moral or value-based in nature). It was argued in section I of this chapter that this is incorrect: persistent objection to such norms is perfectly possible as a matter of law. Significant uncertainty would be created by restricting persistent objection in this way, in that identifying which norms do or do not qualify as being 'fundamental' is essentially an impossible task. It is notable that courts, scholars, and claimants have repeatedly asserted peremptory status for norms that are almost certainly not peremptory in nature, so as to coat the norm in question with the persistent-objection Teflon that such status provides. This indicates that a norm's more nebulous 'fundamental' nature is not enough: only *jus cogens* norms are de jure immune. Most importantly, there are examples of states persistently objecting to norms that would presumably qualify as being 'fundamental'. There are not many such instances, but they do exist. This is the case in each of the fields of international human rights law, international humanitarian law, and international environmental law.

States can, therefore, de jure, gain exemption to any norms—other than peremptory norms—by way of persistent objection. However, as was examined in section II, *maintaining* the exemption gained by persistent objection is, for the most part, extremely difficult. While it is not the case, as some scholars have claimed, that maintaining objection is inherently impossible, a range of extra-legal factors commonly contribute to states ultimately deciding to give up their exempt status. A (non-exhaustive) list of some of these factors was considered in this chapter: the 'fundamental' nature of the norm being objected to (which, while not precluding de jure exemption, will likely make maintaining it much harder de facto: something which is generally desirable); the 'reciprocal' nature of the norm being objected to; the relative power of the objector; and the degree of isolation of the objector.

Ultimately, the examples from state practice discussed in subsection II.*iii* highlight, above all else, the extreme difficulty that states face in trying to maintain exemptions gained through persistent objection, at least indefinitely. It is true that in most cases the objector will eventually give up. More powerful states have a thicker skin when it comes to dealing with the pressure to conform, but even they may, at times, cave. However, states can and do maintain their exemptions, sometimes for many years. The difficulties associated with so doing are simply the political price that a state pays for standing apart. Lawyers are generally averse to considering the extra-legal influences on the content, application, or effectiveness of the law: but when it comes to the persistent objector rule, it would be naïve to ignore the political realities of going against the grain in international relations.

9

The Role and Value of the Persistent Objector Rule

This chapter examines the 'role' or 'value' of the persistent objector rule. The role of persistent objection has generally been considered from a theoretical perspective and, in particular, the commonly advanced theoretical rationale for the rule is based on a voluntarist understanding of the international legal system, coupled with the policy goal of preserving this structural basis for the system. However, as has been noted throughout this book, the voluntarist conception of international law is flawed, at least in its absolute form, and the 'voluntarist pedigree' of the persistent objector rule itself can also be questioned. Given that the usually presented rationale for the rule is somewhat dubious, then, it is fair to say that 'the role of the persistent objector exception is difficult to judge'.[1]

Section I of this chapter sets out and critiques the voluntarist conception of the persistent objector rule in more detail than has been done in previous chapters. Section II then considers competing theoretical approaches to international legal obligation, broadly grouped together as being 'communitarian' in nature. Such communitarian approaches have tended to dismiss the persistent objector rule along with their dismissal of voluntarism. It is argued in section III that holistic, absolutist theoretical accounts of customary international law fail to take into account its chaotic nature in reality. Section IV then argues that it is, therefore, problematic to appraise the value of the persistent objector rule from the perspective of either voluntarism or communitarianism. Drawing upon some insights from rational choice theory, it is argued in section V that the rule is inherently one of *balance*, and that its true value lies in its practical benefits both for individual objectors and the wider international community. From this starting point, section VI assesses the rule's various functional benefits as a 'safety valve'. Section VII then examines the contribution(s) that persistent objection can make to the development of customary international law. Finally, it is briefly noted in section VIII that many of the benefits of the persistent objector rule may, at least in part, stem from the *perception* of state autonomy that it creates.

[1] A.T. Guzman, *How International Law Works: A Rational Choice Theory* (Oxford, Oxford University Press, 2008), 197. See also M. Dixon, R. McCorquodale, and S. Williams, *Cases and Materials on International Law* (Oxford, Oxford University Press, 5th edn, 2011), 33 (arguing that the rule 'clearly has a role within the international legal system', but that it is difficult to conclude exactly what that role is).

I. Voluntarist Theory and the Persistent Objector Rule

i. The commonly advanced role for the rule: plugging the voluntarist 'gap'

As was noted in this book's Introduction, since the early nineteenth century, international law has been seen in predominant positivist understandings as being premised on state *consent*.[2] The international legal system's key positivist touchstones of state sovereignty and autonomy,[3] and, thus, the voluntarist thesis, stem from the theoretical roots of notions such as 'unity through diversity', egalitarianism, and Kantian individualism.[4]

Perhaps the most famous modern expression of the voluntarist theory remains the statement of the Permanent Court of International Justice (PCIJ), in the 1927 *Lotus* case, to the effect that:

> The rules of law binding upon States ... emanate from their own free will as expressed in conventions or by usages generally accepted as expressing principles of law and established order to regulate the relations between these co-existing independent communities or with a view to the achievement of common aims. Restrictions upon the independence of States cannot therefore be presumed.[5]

[2] The roots of this position can be traced back to earlier 'classic' writings on international law. See, for example, H. Grotius, *On the Law of War and Peace (De Juri Belli Ac Pacis Libri Tres)* (A.C. Campbell (trans.), Ontario, Batoche, 2001 (1625)), for example, at *vol. I* (13, 22, 55); and *vol. II* (98–9); E. de Vattel, *The Law of Nations, or Principles of the Law of Nature Applied to the Conduct and Affairs of Nations and Sovereigns* (J. Chitty (ed.), Philadelphia, T & J.W. Johnson, 6th American edn, 1844 (1758)), preface: particularly at v–vii, xiii, lvi, and lxv; F. de Vitoria, *Political Writings* (A. Pagden and J. Lawrence (eds), Cambridge, Cambridge University Press, 1991 (a collection of sixteenth-century writings)), for example, at 281; C. van Bynkershoek, *De Foro Legatorum Liber Singularis: A Monograph on the Jurisdiction over Ambassadors in both Civil and Criminal Cases* (G.J. Laing (trans.), Oxford, Clarendon Press, 1946 (1721/2nd edn, 1744)), for example, at chapter XIX, 106–7; and G.F. von Martens, *A Compendium of the Law of Nations, Founded on the Treaties and Customs of the Modern Nations of Europe* (W. Cobbett (trans.), London, Cobbett and Morgan, 1802 (1788)), for example, at 356. *Contra* C. Wolff, *Jus Gentium Methodo Scientifica Petractatum, vol. II* (J. Brown Scott (ed.), J.H. Drake (trans.), Oxford, Clarendon Press, 1934), 5–8 and 17–18 (seemingly endorsing voluntarism, but actually situating this within a wider, decidedly natural law, understanding of international law). For general discussion of the 'classic' approach to voluntarism, see R. Collins, 'Classical Legal Positivism in International Law Revisited' in J. Kammerhofer and J. d'Aspremont (eds), *International Legal Positivism in a Post-Modern World* (Cambridge, Cambridge University Press, 2014), 23.

[3] See D.P. Fidler, 'Challenging the Classical Concept of Custom: Perspectives on the Future of Customary International Law' (1996) 39 *German Yearbook of International Law* 198, 213; and M.E. Villiger, *Customary International Law and Treaties: A Manual on the Theory and Practice of the Interrelation of Sources* (The Hague, Kluwer, 2nd edn, 1997), 36.

[4] For discussion, see N. Petersen, 'The Role of Consent and Uncertainty in the Formation of Customary International Law' (2011) *Reprints of the Max Planck Institute for Research on Collective Goods*, http://www.coll.mpg.de/pdf_dat/2011_04online.pdf, 5.

[5] *Lotus* (*France v Turkey*) 1927 PCIJ Series A, No. 9, 18. The International Court of Justice (ICJ) has also expressed the same sentiment more recently. See *Barcelona Traction, Light and Power Company, Limited* (*Belgium v Spain*), judgment, 1970 ICJ Rep. 3, para. 89; and *Military and Paramilitary Activities in and Against Nicaragua* (*Nicaragua v United States of America*), merits, 1986 ICJ Rep. 14, para. 269.

It can be questioned, when one considers the *Lotus* proceedings as a whole, whether the PCIJ in fact endorsed voluntarism quite as unequivocally as this famous extract suggests.[6] This is somewhat beside the point, however, because this extract is what has entered into the general consciousness of international legal theory.

To an extent, an account of the binding force of international law that holds that the law applies to states because, and only when, they consent to it so doing remains the orthodoxy in modern doctrine. Voluntarism is still regularly advanced as explaining the basis of obligation in international law,[7] and is still commonly taught in law schools around the world.[8] Koskenniemi has thus stated that 'the metaprinciple of sovereign liberty ... remains valid'.[9] However, Dworkin somewhat overstated things when he said, in his posthumous 2013 publication on international law, that '[p]ositivism in that version [voluntarism] seems to be now generally accepted by practitioners and scholars of international law'.[10] Voluntarism certainly has its critics, as will be discussed throughout this section and in section II, but it is nonetheless true that international legal discourse is 'deeply impregnated with the voluntarist analysis of international law'.[11]

[6] See A. D'Amato, *The Concept of Custom in International Law* (New York, Cornell University Press, 1971), 189–90; and O. Elias and C.L. Lim, *The Paradox of Consensualism in International Law* (The Hague, Kluwer Law International, 1998), 41–4.

[7] See, for just some examples, J-A. Carrillo-Salcedo, 'Droit international et souveraineté des États—Cours général de droit international public' (1996) 257 *Recueil des cours* 35, 92; A.S. Chilton, 'A Reply to Dworkin's New Theory of International Law' (2013) 80 *The University of Chicago Law Review Dialogue* 105, 107; T. Christakis, 'Human Rights from a Neo-Voluntarist Perspective' in J. Kammerhofer and J. d'Aspremont (eds), *International Legal Positivism in a Post-Modern World* (Cambridge, Cambridge University Press, 2014), 421; G.M. Danilenko, 'International *Jus Cogens*: Issues of Law-Making' (1991) 2 *European Journal of International Law* 42, particularly at 47; L. Henkin, 'International Law: Politics, Values and Functions' (1989-IV) 216 *Recueil des cours* 11, 46; D. Lefkowitz, 'The Sources of International Law: Some Philosophical Reflections' in S. Besson and J. Tasioulas (eds), *The Philosophy of International Law* (Oxford, Oxford University Press, 2010), 187, particularly at 192–4; C.L. Lim and O. Elias, 'Withdrawing from Custom and the Paradox of Consensualism in International Law' (2010) 21 *Duke Journal of Comparative and International Law* 143, particularly at 147; I. MacGibbon, 'Customary International Law and Acquiescence' (1957) 33 *British Yearbook of International Law* 115; Petersen, n. 4, particularly at 2; O. Pomson and Y. Horowitz, 'Humanitarian Intervention and the Clean Hands Doctrine in International Law' (2015) 48 *Israel Law Review* 219, 244; O. Schachter, 'International Law in Theory and Practice' (1982) 178 *Recueil des cours* 9, 32–9; D. Shelton, 'Normative Hierarchy in International Law' (2006) 100 *American Journal of International Law* 291, particularly at 302; H. Thirlway, *The Sources of International Law* (Oxford, Oxford University Press, 2014), 10–13; and P. Weil, 'Towards Relative Normativity in International Law?' (1983) 77 *American Journal of International Law* 413, particularly at 420 and 433.

[8] Fidler, n. 3, 198.

[9] M. Koskenniemi, 'The Politics of International Law' (1990) 1 *European Journal of International Law* 4, 13.

[10] R. Dworkin, 'A New Philosophy for International Law' (2013) 41 *Philosophy and Public Affairs* 2, 5.

[11] A. Pellet, 'The Normative Dilemma: Will and Consent in International Law-Making' (1988-1989) 12 *Australian Yearbook of International Law* 22, 22. See also V.M. Padmanabhan, 'The Human Rights Justification for Consent' (2013) 35 *University of Pennsylvania Journal of International Law* 1, 2 and 5 (describing voluntarism as 'axiomatic').

In the 'contractual' context of treaties, identifying state consent to law-making is, to an extent,[12] relatively uncontentious: states are only bound by conventions to which they are a party.[13] In contrast, finding state 'consent' in relation to customary international law is far more problematic.[14] A true application of voluntarism to custom would require the unanimous explicit acceptance by states of any new rule.[15] Yet it is undeniable that customary international law can bind states that have not participated in the practice that contributed to its formation,[16] or have not explicitly consented to be bound by it.[17] Even the most ardent voluntarist would accept that the 'extremist view'[18] of voluntarism—that states must always *explicitly* consent to being bound by international law—is patently and demonstrably false in relation to customary international law.[19] There is no right of individual state veto to new norms of custom.[20] Any such notion is obviously contradicted by practice.[21] There are clear practical reasons for this, based on the

[12] Having said this, see section I.*iii*, n. 49–n. 56 and accompanying text.

[13] A. Aust, *Modern Treaty Law and Practice* (Cambridge, Cambridge University Press, 3rd edn, 2013), 87–113; and Thirlway, n. 7, 12.

[14] See H.C.M. Charlesworth, 'Customary International Law and the *Nicaragua* Case' (1984–5) 11 *Australian Yearbook of International Law* 1, 3 (comparing the relative ease of identifying state consent in treaty law with the problems inherent in so doing for custom).

[15] B. Stern, 'Custom at the Heart of International Law' (2001) 11 *Duke Journal of Comparative and International Law* 89 (M. Byers and A. Denise (trans.), originally published as 'La coutume au cœur du droit international: Quelques réflexions' *in Le droit international: unité et diversité: Mélanges offerts à Paul Reuter* (Paris, Pedone, 1981), 479), 98.

[16] M. Byers, *Custom, Power and the Power of Rules: International Relations and Customary International Law* (Cambridge, Cambridge University Press, 1999), 142; C. de Visscher, 'La codification du droit international' (1925) 6 *Recueil des cours* 328, 361–2; Fidler, n. 3, 201; E. Kontorovich, 'Inefficient Customs in International Law' (2006–7) 48 *William and Mary Law Review* 859, 874; Thirlway, n. 7, 54; and P. Weil, 'Le droit international en quête de son identité—Cours général de droit international public' (1992-VI) 237 *Recueil des cours* 9, 189.

[17] *Nicaragua*, merits, n. 5, para. 186; *Committee on Formation of Customary (General) International Law*, Final Report of the Committee, 'Statement of Principles Applicable to the Formation of General Customary International Law', International Law Association, London Conference (2000), http://www.ila-hq.org/en/committees/index.cfm/cid/30, 8, 23–4, and 31; M. Akehurst, 'Custom as a Source of International Law' (1974–5) 47 *British Yearbook of International Law* 1, 23; Byers, n. 16, 142; Dworkin, n. 10, 7; and J.P. Trachtman, 'The Obsolescence of Customary International Law' (21 November 2014), *Social Science Research Network*, http://papers.ssrn.com/sol3/papers.cfm?abstract_id=2512757, 18. See also *North Sea Continental Shelf* cases (*Federal Republic of Germany v Netherlands, Federal Republic of Germany v Denmark*), merits, 1969 ICJ Rep. 3, dissenting opinion of Judge Lachs, 229.

[18] Christakis, n. 7, 423.

[19] J. Tasioulas, 'Customary International Law and the Quest for Global Justice' in A. Perreau-Saussine and J.B. Murphy (eds), *The Nature of Customary Law: Legal, Historical and Philosophical Perspectives* (Cambridge, Cambridge University Press, 2007), 307, 313–14. Having said this, some Soviet theorists—a group that was famously voluntarist—did argue in the 1970s and early 1980s that, while custom required a tacit agreement to be bound, such agreement had to be manifested in the positive action or statement on the part of the state concerned. The classic example of this position (in the West, at least) is G.I. Tunkin, *Theory of International Law* (W.E. Butler (trans.), George Allen and Unwin, 1974), for example, at 123–33. However, even Tunkin accepted that it was difficult to reconcile this position with actual practice (see ibid., 128–9), and it was widely rejected outside of the Soviet Union even at the time: see W.M. Reisman, 'The Cult of Custom in the Late 20th Century' (1987) 17 *California Western International Law Journal* 133, 134–5.

[20] R. Higgins, *Problems and Process: International Law and How We Use It* (Oxford, Oxford University Press, 1994), 34.

[21] J.I. Charney, 'The Persistent Objector Rule and the Development of Customary International Law' (1985) 56 *British Yearbook of International Law* 1, 1, footnote 3.

realities of co-ordination and interaction: if all states were required to explicitly consent, customary international law would largely stagnate.[22] The voluntarist understanding of customary international law is, therefore, maintained through the notion that 'silence' in relation to emerging customary norms constitutes acquiescence. In other words, silence on the part of a state to an emerging norm of custom is generally presented as a form of tacit consent.[23]

It is here that the persistent objector rule is commonly seen as having a crucial function. The 'role' of the rule, as usually presented, is that it acts to facilitate the voluntarist explanation of international law. The rule is regularly seen as either a logical consequence of,[24] or affirmation of,[25] voluntarism. It has thus

[22] J.I. Charney, 'Universal International Law' (1993) 87 *American Journal of International Law* 529, 530; O. Elias, 'Persistent Objector' in R. Wolfrum (ed.), *Max Planck Encyclopaedia of Public International Law, vol. VIII* (Oxford, Oxford University Press, 2012), 280, 281, para. 3; Dworkin, n. 10, 7; J. Finnis, *Natural Law and Natural Rights* (Oxford, Clarendon Press, 2nd edn, 2011), 243; G. Gaja, 'The Protection of General Interests in the International Community—General Course on Public International Law' (2012) 364 *Recueil des cours* 13, 43; J.A. Green, 'India and a Customary Comprehensive Nuclear Test-Ban: Persistent Objection, Peremptory Norms and the 123 Agreement' (2011) 51 *Indian Journal of International Law* 3, 19; J.A. Green, 'India's Status as a Nuclear Weapons Power under Customary International Law' (2012) 24 *National Law School of India Review* 125, 139; A.T. Guzman and J. Hsiang, 'Some Ways that Theories on Customary International Law Fail: A Reply to László Blutman' (2014) 25 *European Journal of International Law* 553, 557; Stern, n. 15, 98; and Villiger, n. 3, 41.

[23] See, for example, J.L. Dunoff, S.R. Ratner, and D. Wippman, *International Law: Norms, Actors, Process: A Problem-Orientated Approach* (New York, Aspen, 2nd edn, 2006), 78–9; D.W. Greig, 'Reflections on the Role of Consent' (1988–9) 12 *Australian Yearbook of International Law* 125, 137; R. Kolb, 'Selected Problems in the Theory of Customary International Law' (2003) 50 *Netherlands International Law Review* 119, 141; MacGibbon, n. 7; J.O. McGinnis, 'The Comparative Disadvantage of Customary International Law' (2006) 30 *Harvard Journal of Law and Public Policy* 7, 9; H. Meijers, 'How is International Law Made?—The Stages of Growth of International Law and the Use of Customary Rules' (1978) 9 *Netherlands Yearbook of International Law* 3, 5, and 18; Stern, n. 15, 106; T. Treves, 'Customary International Law' in R. Wolfrum (ed.), *Max Planck Encyclopaedia of Public International Law, vol. II* (Oxford, Oxford University Press, 2012), 937, 945, para. 35; and Villiger, n. 3, 37–40.

[24] See *Restatement of the Law, Third, Foreign Relations Law of the United States*, American Law Institute, 1987, 'Reporter's Note' commentary to Section 102, Comment (d); O. Abasheikh, 'The Validity of the Persistent Offender Rule in International Law' (2004) 9 *Coventry Law Journal* 40, 43 and 46; O. Barsalou, 'La doctrine de l'objecteur persistant en droit international public' (2006) 19 *Revue québécoise de droit international* 1, 9; C.A. Bradley, 'The Juvenile Death Penalty' (2002–3) 52 *Duke Law Journal* 485, 516; D.A. Colson, 'How Persistent Must the Persistent Objector Be?' (1986) 61 *Washington Law Review* 957, 957–8; G.M. Danilenko, *Law-Making in the International Community* (Dordrecht, Martinus Nijhoff, 1993), 111; J. Klabbers, *International Law* (Cambridge, Cambridge University Press, 2013), 40; L. Loschin, 'The Persistent Objector Rule and Customary Human Rights Law: A Proposed Analytical Framework' (1996) 2 *University of California Davis Journal of International Law and Policy* 147, 150; A.V. Lowe, *International Law* (Oxford, Oxford University Press, 2007), 55 and 58; Padmanabhan, n. 11, 17; C. Quince, *The Persistent Objector and Customary International Law* (Denver, Outskirts Press, 2010), 69; C. Rousseau, *Droit international public, vol. I: introduction et sources* (Paris, Sirey, 1970), 320; T.L. Stein, 'The Approach of the Different Drummer: The Principle of the Persistent Objector in International Law' (1985) 26 *Harvard International Law Journal* 457, 459, 464, and 468; A. Steinfeld, 'Nuclear Objections: The Persistent Objector and the Legality of the Use of Nuclear Weapons' (1996) 62 *Brooklyn Law Review* 1635, 1646, and 1655–6; and Tunkin, n. 19, 130.

[25] Carrillo-Salcedo, n. 7, 92; H. Charlesworth, 'Law-Making and Sources' in J. Crawford and M. Koskenniemi (eds), *The Cambridge Companion to International Law* (Cambridge, Cambridge University Press, 2012), 187, 195; Charney, n. 21, 16; J. Crawford, *Brownlie's Principles of Public International Law* (Oxford, Oxford University Press, 8th edn, 2012), 28; Danilenko, n. 7, 47;

been described as 'the litmus test of positivism'[26] and 'the acid test of custom's voluntarist nature'.[27] A major theoretical obstacle to voluntarism is that states are clearly bound by custom to which they have not consented. The notion of silence as tacit consent can only have any meaning if there exists an option of *withholding* that consent, and this is said to be the mechanism of the persistent objector rule.[28] This is perhaps the primary reason for the ubiquity of the persistent objector rule in doctrine.[29] The rule plugs a bothersome gap in the prominent theoretical account of international law.[30] Indeed, it has been argued that the theoretical conundrum of voluntarism in the context of custom explains the very emergence of the rule.[31]

Ultimately, then, the persistent objector rule is seen as having 'value' based on a combination of theory and policy. The international legal system is commonly premised on state consent, but requiring explicit individual consent to custom is an impossibility. The persistent objector rule acts to bridge the voluntarist theory with the (seemingly incompatible) practical reality of custom.[32] It is therefore seen by many as being essential, in that it ensures the internal logic of the system.[33]

ii. The persistent objector rule is flawed as the guardian of voluntarism

The voluntarist theoretical basis for the persistent objector rule may be ubiquitous, but the persistent objector rule's credentials as the 'guardian of voluntarism' can be seriously questioned. From the voluntarist perspective, the persistent objector rule can be seen as theoretically incoherent, in that it only partially serves its apparent *raison d'être*: to preserve states' ability to consent to norms that bind them.

M.A. Hansen, 'Preventing the Emasculation of Warfare: Halting the Expansion of Human Rights Law into Armed Conflict' (2007) 194 *Military Law Review* 1, 17, 33–4; Henkin, n. 7, 50; A.V. Lowe, 'Do General Rules of International Law Exist?' (1983) 9 *Review of International Studies* 207, 207–8; Thirlway, n. 7, 13 and 87; Weil, n. 16, particularly at 189.

26 Tasioulas, n. 19, 316.

27 Weil, n. 7, 434.

28 M. Koskenniemi, *From Apology to Utopia: The Structure of International Legal Argument* (Cambridge, Cambridge University Press, reissue, 2005), 443.

29 See Introduction, section I, n. 16–n. 25 and accompanying text.

30 J.A. Green, 'Persistent Objector Teflon? Customary International Human Rights Law and the United States in International Adjudicative Proceedings' in J.A. Green and C.P.M. Waters (eds), *Adjudicating International Human Rights: Essays in Honour of Sandy Ghandhi* (Leiden, Brill Nijhoff, 2015), 167, 170.

31 C.A. Bradley and M. Gulati, 'Customary International Law and Withdrawal Rights in an Age of Treaties' (2010) 21 *Duke Journal of International and Comparative Law* 1, 2. See, generally, Chapter 1 in relation to the rule's historical emergence.

32 See Tasioulas, n. 19, 312 (identifying the persistent objector rule as 'a definitive component of the positivist doctrine of custom'); and P-H. Verdier and E. Voeten, 'Precedent, Compliance, and Change in Customary International Law: An Explanatory Theory' (2014) 108 *American Journal of International Law* 389, 427–8 (though ultimately suggesting that the rule has no value).

33 It is worth noting that this is a teleological argument in support of the rule based on its perceived *role*, rather than its formal legal basis (the latter being something that was examined in Part I of this book).

There are a number of aspects of the rule that belie its apparent consent-preserving function within the international legal system, which have already been examined in the previous chapters of this book. For example, voluntarism cannot explain the requirement of persistence.[34] A single objection—assuming that it is sufficiently clear—can surely act as an expression of a dissenting state's sovereign will not to be bound, and yet states that have only objected once (or a handful of times) are bound by the new norm nonetheless. Inconsistent objection is also generally an insufficient means of withholding consent, however many times the objecting state may have shown that it does not wish to be bound. Again, however, if the state has made it clear that it does not wish to be bound, then a number of contrary actions should not undermine that expression of sovereign will.[35] Objections lodged after the norm in question has crystallized are ineffective too, meaning that sovereign autonomy in international law apparently has a time limit.[36] The fact that subsequent objection does not lead to the objector gaining an exemption cannot be explained by voluntarism, because subsequent objection is just as much of a withdrawal of consent as objection prior to the norm's crystallization.[37] *Jus cogens* norms do not require unanimous acceptance to form, but nonetheless override the objections of a state however persistent, consistent and timely those objections might be.[38] Plus, of course, the persistent objector rule offers no protection to new states, which do not have any option whatsoever to withhold their consent to existing customary international law.[39]

[34] P. Dumberry, 'Incoherent and Ineffective: The Concept of Persistent Objector Revisited' (2010) 59 *International and Comparative Law Quarterly* 779, 795; C.G. Guldahl, 'The Role of Persistent Objection in International Humanitarian Law' (2008) 77 *Nordic Journal of International Law* 51, 59; A.T. Guzman, 'Saving Customary International Law' (2005–6) 27 *Michigan Journal of International Law* 115, 166; and M.H. Mendelson, 'The Formation of Customary International Law' (1998) 272 *Recueil des cours* 155, 239 (noting but not subscribing to this argument). See Chapter 4 (generally, in relation to the criterion of persistence; and at section II, particularly at n. 37–n. 40 and accompanying text, in relation to the criterion's relationship with voluntarism).

[35] Dumberry, n. 34, 795. See Chapter 5 (generally, in relation to the criterion of consistency; and at section II, particularly at n. 52 and accompanying text, in relation to the criterion's relationship with voluntarism).

[36] C.A. Bradley and M. Gulati, 'Withdrawing from International Custom' (2010) 120 *Yale Law Journal* 202, 205; Bradley and Gulati, n. 31, 5; Charney, n. 21, 16; Dumberry, n. 34, 795; Guldahl, n. 34, 59; Guzman, n. 34, 166; Guzman and Hsiang, n. 22, 556; and S. Hall, 'The Persistent Spectre: Natural Law, International Order and the Limits of Legal Positivism' (2001) 12 *European Journal of International Law* 269, 283. See, generally, Chapter 6 in relation to the criterion of timeliness.

[37] See ibid., section II, in relation to the timeliness criterion's relationship with voluntarism.

[38] L. Condorelli, 'Custom' in M. Bedjaoui (ed.), *International Law: Achievements and Prospects* (Paris, UNESCO, 1991), 179, 205; Charney, n. 21, 19–20, footnote 81; Dumberry, n. 34, 798–9; and J. Tasioulas, 'Custom, *Jus Cogens*, and Human Rights' in C.A. Bradley (ed.), *Custom's Future: International Law in a Changing World* (Cambridge, Cambridge University Press, forthcoming), pre-publication version, *Social Science Research Network*, 20 March 2015, http://papers.ssrn.com/sol3/papers.cfm?abstract_id=2581763, 8. See Chapter 7 (generally, regarding *jus cogens* and persistent objection; and at section III, particularly at n. 15–n. 18 and accompanying text, in relation to the relationship between *jus cogens* and voluntarism).

[39] Dumberry, n. 34, 797–8; Guldahl, n. 34, 59; Guzman and Hsiang, n. 22, 556; and Tasioulas, n. 38, 8. See Chapter 6, section VIII regarding new states and persistent objection.

All of the (onerous) requirements for persistent objection are illogical and arbitrary when viewed from a solely voluntarist perspective.[40] The limitations of the persistent objector rule in terms of preserving state consent are further compounded when it is recalled that even after all the formal legal 'i's are dotted and 't's are crossed for persistent objection, many objectors will still be unable to maintain their exempt status for long, de facto, because of various extra-legal pressures to conform.[41] Overall, it is clear that states can still be bound by customary international law norms to which they have explicitly withheld their consent through objection.

Critics of the persistent objector rule have, therefore, argued that if international law is truly based on the sovereign supremacy of states and state consent is a prerequisite for any binding legal norm, then states should be able to withdraw their consent however and whenever they wish, as well as being able to give it: '[a]ll that should matter should be the lack of consent.'[42] The hoops through which states must jump to become exempt persistent objectors are said to undermine the rule's value.[43] The persistent objector rule is seen as an inadequate means of protecting state consent, and should thus be discarded.[44]

iii. Voluntarism itself is flawed

The role or value of the persistent objector rule is thus potentially undermined by the fact that its various aspects limit its ability to ensure state autonomy with regard to the binding force of customary international law. Beyond this, however, and perhaps even more significant for the rule's purported *raison d'être*, is the fact that the voluntarist theory of international law is itself riddled with theoretical holes. It was noted in the Introduction to this book that the present author rejects the voluntarist understanding of international law, at least in its absolute form.[45] It is observable social fact that binding international law is not always derived from state will.[46] The 'tortured logical process'[47] of rooting the binding force of international law in the consent of states is both well known[48] and commonly glossed over.

[40] Fidler, n. 3, 213; and Guzman, n. 1, 188.

[41] See Chapter 8, section II.

[42] Dumberry, n. 34, 795.

[43] I.M. Lobo de Souza, 'The Role of Consent in the Customary Process' (1995) 44 *International and Comparative Law Quarterly* 521, 533.

[44] Bradley and Gulati, n. 31, 26; Dumberry, n. 34, 795–800; and J.P. Kelly, 'The Twilight of Customary International Law' (1999–2000) 40 *Virginia Journal of International Law* 449, particularly at 536.

[45] See Introduction, section IV.

[46] See B. Chigara, *Legitimacy Deficit in Custom: A Deconstructionist Critique* (Aldershot, Ashgate, 2001), 231–2; and Kelly, n. 44, generally, but particularly at 463.

[47] D.H. Joyner, '*Jus ad Bellum* in the Age of WMD Proliferation' (2008) 40 *George Washington International Law Review* 233, 265. See also R. Ago, 'Positive Law and International Law' (1957) 51 *American Journal of International Law* 691, 699–700.

[48] See, generally, J. Kammerhofer and J. d'Aspremont, 'Introduction' in J. Kammerhofer and J. d'Aspremont (eds), *International Legal Positivism in a Post-Modern World* (Cambridge, Cambridge University Press, 2014), 1.

Even with regard to treaties, so often presented as the archetypical consent-based source of international law,[49] one can question the extent to which they reflect the genuine consent of the states that they bind. While states must actively consent to be bound by treaties,[50] which do not impose obligations on third-party states,[51] they cannot have consented in a meaningful sense to the secondary rules about what a treaty *is*,[52] nor can they decide for themselves how to revoke their consent to be bound by a treaty.[53] States cannot enter into treaties that are contrary to *jus cogens* obligations.[54] The power imbalances underpinning the adoption of treaties, and general normalization of coercion in international relations, may also influence how genuine the consent of 'weaker' states really is in many instances.[55] On a more conceptual level, the 'democratic deficit' in international law means that state consent to the binding force of a treaty cannot be equated to the consent of the people that it then effectively binds.[56]

Rather more starkly, one might also note[57] the absence of state consent in relation to 'general principles of law recognised by civilised nations' (as another source of international law found in Article 38(1)(c) of the ICJ's Statute).[58] It is almost impossible to situate the application of such principles as law, binding on states, in a voluntarist account of the system;[59] that is, other than in the most abstract and indirect manner, on the basis that they are principles derived from domestic legal systems (and, thus, at a significant stretch, that such principles in some way represent the will of states).[60] Yet the idea that such principles have been derived from all—or even most—domestic systems would be an obvious fiction.[61] It has been suggested that states can perhaps at least control the extent to which a general principle, such as equity, is applied as law in relation to a particular dispute.[62] This claim also would be difficult to support, however: for example, it is notable that on the rare occasions when the ICJ has applied general principles, it has

[49] See, for example, Byers, n. 16, 142; R. Goodman, 'Human Rights Treaties, Invalid Reservations, and State Consent' (2002) 96 *American Journal of International Law* 531, 534; Padmanabhan, n. 11, 20; and B. Simma and A.L. Paulus, 'The Responsibility of Individuals for Human Rights Abuses in Internal Conflicts: A Positivist View' (1999) 93 *American Journal of International Law* 302, 305.

[50] Vienna Convention on the Law of Treaties (VCLT), 23 May 1969, 1155 UNTS 331, particularly Articles 9–15.

[51] Ibid., Articles 34–8.

[52] C. Brown, 'Ethics of Coexistence: The International Theory of Terry Nardin' (1988) 14 *Review of International Studies* 213, 215.

[53] Ibid.; A. Clapham, *Brierly's Law of Nations* (Oxford, Oxford University Press, 7th edn, 2012), 51; and Pellet, n. 11, 33.

[54] VCLT, n. 50, Articles 53, 64, and 71. See also Charney, n. 22, 534.

[55] T. Christiano, 'The Legitimacy of International Institutions' in A. Marmor (ed.), *The Routledge Companion to the Philosophy of Law* (Abingdon, Routledge, 2012), 380, 385–6 (referring to 'unfair advantage taking' generally in relation to the 'consent' of states in international law); and Pellet, n. 11, 42–5.

[56] Padmanabhan, n. 11, 8–9; and Tasioulas, n. 38, 9 (discussing voluntarism generally).

[57] See, generally, with regard to the relationship between voluntarism and 'general principles of law', Elias and Lim, n. 6, 208–29.

[58] Statute of the International Court of Justice, 26 June 1945, 59 Stat. 1055, 33 UNTS 93, Article 38(1)(c).

[59] Charney, n. 22, 535–6; Hall, n. 36, 292–3; and Pellet, n. 11, 38.

[60] Lobo de Souza, n. 43, 535.

[61] Charney, n. 22, 535.

[62] Greig, n. 23, 140–1.

not considered whether the principle in question has been accepted by the state concerned.[63]

The voluntarist understanding of customary international law, which is of course where the persistent objector rule is of relevance, is similarly strained (indeed, far more so than it is in the case of treaties). The notion of state *silence* as constituting consent for the formation of custom is difficult to reconcile with conceptions of genuine consent.[64] This is not least because 'consent' and 'absence of dissent' are, quite simply, different things.[65] It is also again the case that power discrepancies between states, and the inevitable coercion that follows, may well mean any concept of choice is illusory in the first instance.[66]

Further, consent through silence must be *informed* consent for it to constitute a meaningful expression of autonomy.[67] Given the flexible and at times rather opaque nature of customary international law formation, states may find that they are bound by a crystallized legal norm—because of their silence in relation to its emergence—before they were even aware that it was emerging.[68] Even if silence is accepted as 'consent' and it is assumed that all states are aware of current state practice that is contributing to a potential new norm, one might argue that consent to custom can never be truly 'informed'. This is on the basis that the process of customary international law formation means that a state's 'silent consent' is only relevant when, and therefore only *given in relation to*, the pre-legal practice that cumulatively contributes to the emergence of the norm in question.[69] Affirmation, silence, and objection are all equally irrelevant to the binding force of a customary norm once that norm has crystallized. This means that states can never be entirely sure what their silence is actually contenting *to*, as that silence only matters before the norm has crystallized and, thus, 'there is no common defined object to which consent could be expressed'.[70]

[63] See ibid., 536.

[64] ILA Final Report, n. 17, 39; Byers, n. 16, 142–6; Clapham, n. 53, 49–53; Charney, n. 21, particularly at 16–17; Charney, n. 22, 536–8; Fidler, n. 3, 208; Hall, n. 36, 288; Kelly, n. 44, 510 and 522; H. Kelsen, *Principles of International Law* (R.W. Tucker (ed. and revisions), New York, Holt, Rinehart and Winston, 2nd edn, 1966), 447–8; Lim and Elias, n. 7, 149; and Padmanabhan, n. 11, 8.

[65] Bradley and Gulati, n. 36, 214; Elias and Lim, n. 6, 57 and 72; Guzman, n. 1, 188; Guzman and Hsiang, n. 22, 556; J. Kammerhofer, 'Uncertainty in the Formal Sources of International Law: Customary International Law and Some of Its Problems' (2004) 15 *European Journal of International Law* 523, 533; P. Malanczuk, *Akehurst's Modern Introduction to International Law* (New York Routledge, 7th edn, 1997), 47–8; and J.B. McClane, 'How Late in the Emergence of a Norm of Customary International Law May a Persistent Objector Object?' (1989) 13 *International Law Students Association Journal of International Law* 1, 17.

[66] A. Buchanan, 'The Legitimacy of International Law' in S. Besson and J. Tasioulas (eds), *The Philosophy of International Law* (Oxford, Oxford University Press, 2010), 79, 90–2; Pellet, n. 11, 42–5; Quince, n. 24, 41; and Tasioulas, n. 19, 314 (arguing that this leads to 'an anaemic notion of consent'). *Contra* Elias and Lim, n. 6, 15 (arguing that there is a 'threshold of permissible coercion', and that just because coercion occurs does not undermine the voluntarist basis of customary international law).

[67] Buchanan, n. 66, 90–2; Byers, n. 16, 145–6; and Kelly, n. 44, 522.

[68] See Chapter 6, section V.

[69] Lobo de Souza, n. 43, 527–8.

[70] Ibid. *Contra* Elias and Lim, n. 6, 20 (arguing that this critique 'seems to be creating problems which do not exist').

Other critiques of voluntarism in relation to customary international law mirror those made in relation to the persistent objector rule more specifically,[71] which were discussed in the previous subsection. If custom was truly based on state consent, then newly emerging states would be entitled to opt out of existing custom: the fact that they cannot has been said to reduce 'the notion of consent to an absurd fiction'.[72] Similarly, if consent was the basis of legal obligation, then *jus cogens* rules would require universal acceptance before they could bind universally (or, at least, states would be able to maintain exemptions gained through persistent objection in relation to them).[73]

Scrambling to try to fit the round peg of voluntarism in the square hole of social reality, some scholars have argued that while states do not necessarily consent to every individual rule of international law that binds them, they do consent to 'the rules of the game'. In other words, it is argued that states consent to the secondary rules of international law that underpin the creation of the primary rules that bind them.[74] We have already encountered this argument in Chapter Six, specifically in relation to new states.[75] In that context, it is said that new states consent to existing rules of international law simply by 'joining the club' of the states of the world.[76]

This 'original consent'—or what Byers terms a 'system consent'[77]—argument fails to convince.[78] Firstly, this is because whether such 'consent once removed' can be viewed as meaningful, informed consent to any particular primary rule is questionable.[79] Secondly, and more importantly, however, states have clearly not explicitly consented to the secondary rules of the international legal system.[80]

[71] Something noted by Guldahl, n. 34, 60.

[72] Guzman, n. 34, 172. See also ILA Final Report, n. 17, 39; S. Besson, 'Theorizing the Sources of International Law' in S. Besson and J. Tasioulas (eds), *The Philosophy of International Law* (Oxford, Oxford University Press, 2010), 164, 175; Bradley and Gulati, n. 36, 214; Byers, n. 16, 145; Charney, n. 21, 16; Clapham, n. 53, 50; Hall, n. 36, 288–9; Lobo de Souza, n. 43, 533–4; Malanczuk, n. 65, 47; Quince, n. 24, 41; C. Tomuschat, 'Obligations Arising for States Without or Against Their Will' (1993) 241 *Recueil des cours* 195, 305–6; and M. Virally, 'The Sources of International Law' in M. Sørensen (ed.), *Manual of Public International Law* (London, Macmillan, 1968), 116, 138.

[73] Bradley and Gulati, n. 36, 214; Chigara, n. 46, 231–2; Christiano, n. 55, 387–8; D'Amato, n. 6, 191–3; Dworkin, n. 10, 7; Fidler, n. 3, 210; Padmanabhan, n. 11, 8; Pellet, n. 11, 38–9; A. Roberts, 'Traditional and Modern Approaches to Customary International Law: A Reconciliation' (2001) 95 *American Journal of International Law* 757, 784; and Tomuschat, n. 72, 306–7.

[74] See, for example, Byers, n. 16, 7–8 and 143–5; Lowe, n. 25, 208 (noting this as a possible way of viewing consent as the root of international law, but not necessarily subscribing to it); A. Roberts, 'Who Killed Article 38(1)(b)? A Reply to Bradley & Gulati' (2010) 21 *Duke Journal of Comparative and International Law* 173, 178–9; Steinfeld, n. 24, 1656; Thirlway, n. 7, 11; and Tomuschat, n. 72, 283 (noting, but not subscribing to this argument).

[75] See Chapter 6, section VIII, particularly at n. 298–n. 301 and accompanying text. Indeed, another version of the same broad 'original consent' argument was also discussed in Chapter 8, section I.*i*, particularly at n. 26–n. 29 and accompanying text, in relation to human rights norms. It has been claimed that states cannot persistently object to such norms because they have already consented to the human rights law regime as a whole. This claim was dismissed as a fiction in Chapter 8, on the grounds that it would, for example, oblige states to sign and ratify any and all new human rights treaties.

[76] See, for example, Byers, n. 16, 145.

[77] Ibid.

[78] Koskenniemi, n. 9, 22.

[79] Guzman and Hsiang, n. 22, 556.

[80] Ibid.

Even identifying implicit state consent (or, at least, the implicit consent of *all* states) to the secondary rules that govern the creation and binding force of the system's primary rules is impossible. The idea that secondary norms such as *pacta sunt servanda*, or the role of *opinio juris* in customary norm creation, were created through the consent of all members of the international community is difficult to reconcile with the fact that most of the system's secondary rules emerged because of their usage and acceptance by a relatively small number of European states.[81] In the case of new states, any 'consent' they may give to existing legal standards by virtue of agreeing to join the 'club of states' is illusory, as they have no other viable option but to do so.[82]

Ultimately, voluntarism is 'plagued by contradictions'[83] in relation to international law in general and customary international law in particular.

II. The Communitarian Alternative to Voluntarism and Its Perception of the Persistent Objector Rule

The various theoretical and practical holes in the voluntarist account of international legal obligation have, of course, led to a plethora of alternative explanations for the binding force of international law. This is certainly not the place to explore these alternative approaches in any detail.[84] Extremely crudely, however, one can identify a broadly 'communitarian' understanding of international law,[85] which increasingly serves as a mainstream competing theory to voluntarism. In simple terms, this communitarian approach prioritizes the 'will of the international community' above the will of individual states.[86]

Such an understanding is at times firmly linked to natural law ideas of inherent value.[87] As a famous example, one can point to Judge Cançado Trindade's assertion in his separate opinion in the *Pulp Mills on the River Uruguay* case that 'human conscience, the universal juridical conscience ... is ... the ultimate material "source" of all

[81] Ibid. For more discussion of the emergence of secondary rules of international law, see Introduction, section IV, particularly at n. 77–n. 89 and accompanying text.

[82] See Chapter 6, n. 299 and accompanying text.

[83] J. d'Aspremont, *Formalism and the Sources of International Law: A Theory of the Ascertainment of Legal Rules* (Oxford, Oxford University Press, 2011, paperback edn, 2013), 22.

[84] For an introduction to the key theoretical approaches to international law that will be right up-to-date, see the chapters in Part III of this forthcoming volume: A. Orford and F. Hoffman (eds), *The Oxford Handbook of the Theory of International Law* (Oxford, Oxford University Press, forthcoming 2016).

[85] See, generally, J. Rauber, 'On Communitarian and Constitutional Approaches to International Law' (2013) 26 *Leiden Journal of International Law* 201.

[86] See L. Oppenheim, *International Law: A Treatise, vol. I* (R.F. Roxburgh, ed., New Jersey, The Lawbook Exchange, 3rd edn, 2005, originally published 1920), 14–15 (identifying the notion of 'common consent', being 'the express or tacit consent of such an overwhelming majority of the members that those who dissent are of no importance whatever, and disappear totally from the view of one who looks for the will of the community as an entity in contradistinction to the wills of its single members').

[87] See, for example, Dworkin, n. 10; and Hall, n. 36.

law, and of the new *jus gentium* of our times'.[88] Other 'communitarian' accounts—while often still linked to notions of universal value—are grounded rather more in the pragmatic, co-ordination benefits of majority law-making (and the claim that majority law-making is an accurate description of the way in which international law works in practice). In other words, a positivist starting point is taken, but it is one that is premised on *consensus* rather than *consent*.[89] As described by Tomuschat:

> The fact is that the cohesive legal bonds tying States to one another have considerably strengthened since the coming into force of the United Nations Charter. The international legal order is not the same as it was 66 years ago when the PCIJ handed down its judgment in the *Lotus* case ... Given the developments triggered by the UN Charter, today a community model of international society would seem to come closer to reality than any time before in history. According to this interpretation, States live, as from their birth, within a legal framework of a limited number of basic rules which determines their basic rights and obligations with or without their will.[90]

In contrast to most theoretical understandings of the persistent objector rule, it has been argued by some commentators—adopting various versions of the broadly communitarian perspective—that the rule in fact confirms that the international legal system is *not* premised on state consent.[91] Somewhat ironically, given the rule's commonly asserted role, its existence is said to contribute to the fiction that silence is equated to acquiescence for the purposes of customary international law, thus confirming that 'genuine' consent is not actually required.[92] As noted in subsection I.*ii*, many features of the rule make no sense from a voluntarist perspective, and thus—it is claimed—indicate that the binding force of international law is not derived from consent at all. This argument has been disputed on the grounds that it is difficult to see the rule as corroborating a communitarian position that its nature as a voluntarist mechanism denies,[93] but this counter-argument assumes the very thing that communitarians reject: that the rule (or, indeed, the international legal system) is voluntarist in nature in the first place.

In any event, other than perhaps referencing the persistent objector rule to argue that its ubiquity in doctrine evidences the incoherence of voluntarism, the rule has been largely dismissed by those who take naturalist, communitarian positions (of whatever variation). This is quite understandable: if one rejects the notion that international law, and customary international law in particular, requires any individual state to consent to it before that state can be bound, then based on the commonly presented rationale for persistent objection, the rule seemingly has no

[88] *Pulp Mills on the River Uruguay* (*Argentina v Uruguay*), judgment, 2010 ICJ Rep.14, separate opinion of Judge Cançado Trindade, para. 68.

[89] See, for example, A. Cassese, *International Law* (Oxford, Oxford University Press, 2nd edn, 2005), 153–69; Charney, n. 21, 16–19; Higgins, n. 20, 17–38; D.P. O'Connell, *International Law, vol. I* (London, Stevens & Sons, 2nd edn, 1970), 15–16 (discussing this, as a species of the 'natural law' approach to international law); and J.P. Paust, 'Customary International Law: Its Nature, Sources and Status as Law of the United Nations' (1990) 12 *Michigan Journal of International Law* 59, generally, but particularly at 64–7, footnote 14.

[90] Tomuschat, n. 72, generally, but quoted at 210–11.

[91] See, for example, Kolb, n. 23, 144.

[92] Ibid.

[93] Elias and Lim, n. 6, 77.

role in the international legal system. If consent is irrelevant, then surely so too is a rule that acts to preserve it: '[w]ithout state consent as a theoretical foundation, the persistent objector rule loses coherency.'[94]

Indeed, the persistent objector rule has not just been rejected by the communitarian camp; it has also been the subject of a notable amount of hostility from those adopting this understanding. The rule is seen as representing an undesirable pandering to exceptionalism, state self-interest, and the power of the few over the goals of the many. It is unquestionable that 'persistent objectors frustrate the objective of universal participation in legal regimes',[95] and for those who (understandably) hold the universalization of key values dear—especially in the context of, say, the environment or human rights—the rule is a direct threat. Thus, Paust, for example, has vehemently argued that the persistent objector rule is 'illogical, false, *and threatening to the nature of customary international law*'.[96]

III. The Chaotic Reality of Customary International Law

International law, and customary international law in particular, is a chaotic business; it does not submit easily to neat theoretical conceptualization.[97] The oversimplification that many theoretical accounts of international law tend

[94] Fidler, n. 3, 209. See also Bradley and Gulati, n. 31, 4–5; Cassese, n. 89, 163 (although not necessarily rejecting the persistent objector rule); Charney, n. 21, 18–19; Charney, n. 22, generally, but particularly at 531–2; D'Amato, n. 6, 252–62 (in the context of making a distinction between particular custom and general custom); Elias and Lim, n. 6, 78; Guzman, n. 34, 166 (although not necessarily rejecting the persistent objector rule); Kelly, n. 44, 511–512; McClane, n. 65, 11 (although not necessarily rejecting the persistent objector rule); and Paust, n. 89, 64–7, footnote 14.

[95] E.J. Molenaar, *Coastal State Jurisdiction over Vessel-Source Pollution* (The Hague, Kluwer, 1998), 163.

[96] J.P. Paust, 'The Complex Nature, Sources and Evidences of Customary Human Rights' (1995–6) 25 *Georgia Journal of International and Comparative Law* 147, 152, emphasis added. See also B. Conforti, 'Cours général de droit international public' (1988-V) 212 *Recueil des cours* 13, 76 ('[l]a notion du persistent objector est enfin contraire à l'idée même d'un droit international général et commun à tous les Etats, idée qui … nous semble désormais ressentie dans le cadre de la communauté internationale'); P. Dumberry, 'The Last Citadel! Can a State Claim the Status of Persistent Objector to Prevent the Application of a Rule of Customary International Law in Investor-State Arbitration?' (2010) 23 *Leiden Journal of International Law* 379, 400; and Report of the International Law Commission, Sixty-seventh session, 4 May–5 June and 6 July–7 August 2015, UN Doc. A/70/10, advance unedited version, 24 August 2015, 40, para. 93 (noting that some members of the ILC took the view, during the consideration of the 'Identification of customary international law' topic at the Commission's Sixty-seventh session, that the persistent objector rule 'could lead to the fragmentation of international law').

[97] Koskenniemi, n. 9, in general, but particularly at 14 (arguing that this had led to international lawyers abandoning the search for theoretical coherence in relation to customary international law); Guzman, n. 1, 184 and 201 (arguing that much of the scholarship on customary international law has actually been 'atheoretical'); Lim and Elias, n. 7, 154–5; A. Somek, 'Beyond Kelsen and Hart' in J. Kammerhofer and J. d'Aspremont (eds), *International Legal Positivism in a Post-Modern World* (Cambridge, Cambridge University Press, 2014), 151, 173 (arguing that customary international law is a 'formally irrational form of law'; emphasis removed); and P.B. Stephan, 'Disaggregating Customary International Law' 21 *Duke Journal of Comparative and International Law* 191, particularly at 191.

to adopt in the interests of 'coherence' creates irreconcilable dichotomies.[98] Theoretical discourse on international law often presents a 'false choice ... between a strict legal positivism and a natural law approach',[99] and one might well note the presence of 'ideologues on either side in the debate'.[100] Thus, while the natural law/communitarian camp is prone to viewing the voluntarist account of international law as being 'flawed beyond redemption',[101] voluntarist/positivists counter that 'transempirical natural lawyers ... have no grasp of reality'.[102]

Customary international law has long been attacked from both sides of this debate: either on the basis that its processes do not sufficiently protect individual state autonomy (as states are bound without their express consent), or on the basis that it panders too much to what states do and not enough to what they *should* do.[103] A different version of this voluntarism/communitarianism divide can be seen in Koskenniemi's famous exploration of competing 'apologist' and 'utopian' approaches to international law,[104] but one can also recast broadly the same polarization in terms of '"positivism/naturalism", "consent/justice", "autonomy/community", "process/rule", etc.'[105]

A common sin of the legal theorist—if rarely of the legal practitioner—is to throw the baby out with the theoretical bathwater.[106] If a theoretical account of international legal obligation cannot explain *in absolute and irrefutable terms* all instances where international law is considered to be binding, there is a tendency for this to be seen as entirely undermining the theory in question. Not all binding international law is based on state consent, say the communitarians, so voluntarism is nonsense. States clearly view their will as being fundamental to law-making in practice—and will not feel obliged to follow law that they perceive as illegitimately imposed upon them—say the voluntarists, and so the idea that 'higher values' are the source of international law, or the notion that there is an accepted 'majority rules' system, are devoid of real-world credibility.

98 L. Blutman, 'Conceptual Confusion and Methodological Deficiencies: Some Ways that Theories on Customary International Law Fail' (2014) 25 *European Journal of International Law* 529, 545–6 and 551–2.

99 R.P. Barnidge, Jr, 'Between Legal Positivism and Natural Law: Idolising Law and Obfuscating Politics in International Law and the Chilcot Iraq Inquiry' (2011), work in progress, http://www.eisa-net.org/be-bruga/eisa/files/events/stockholm/Between%20Legal%20Positivism%20and%20Natural%20Law%20for%20SGIR%202010.pdf (cited with the permission of the author). See also Stern, n. 15, 102–3.

100 R.P. Barnidge, Jr, 'Submission to Iraq Inquiry in Response to Solicitation from International Lawyers', 31 August 2010, https://www.academia.edu/430208/Submission_to_Iraq_Inquiry_in_Response_to_Solicitation_from_International_Lawyers.

101 Dworkin, n. 10, 13.

102 Reisman, n. 19, 136.

103 D.J. Bederman, 'Acquiescence, Objection and the Death of Customary International Law' (2010) 21 *Duke Journal of Comparative and International Law* 31, 43.

104 See, generally, Koskenniemi, n. 28.

105 Koskenniemi, n. 9, 8.

106 Pellet, n. 11, 25 (using this phrase, perhaps somewhat ironically, to refer *only* to the voluntarist side of the debate). See also R. Müllerson, 'On the Nature and Scope of Customary International Law' (1997) 2 *Austrian Review of International and European Law* 341, particularly at 356 and 358.

In the view of the present author, there is no single satisfactory theoretical explanation for customary international law's binding force.[107] The system represents an uneasy balance between various (at times) competing imperatives of state autonomy, communitarianism, moral value, practicality, and certainty.[108] This is not to say that theoretical investigation should be abandoned: it is crucial to the development and *improvement* of international law, as well to strengthening its legitimacy.[109] Nor is it to say that the only alternative is naked, unchecked realism. State power is patently curtailed by international law in many instances.[110] Rather, it is this author's view that one must eschew the extremes of the prominent theoretical approaches to customary international law: 'we must abandon formalism and generalisation out of respect for social reality more clearly perceived and courageously accepted.'[111] There exist inherent (and largely unconscious) compromises between various competing theories and practical realities.[112]

Rejecting voluntarism as a 'perfect' account of international law's binding force does not mean that the will of individual states should no longer be seen as a crucial element of international law-making.[113] Indeed, it *has to be prominent* for states to be willing to accept the obligations that international law imposes on them: the international legal system would collapse without state will underpinning it to at least some extent.[114] There are, equally, and quite obviously, some instances where states are bound without their consent.[115] Ultimately,

[107] Blutman, n. 98, 551–2; Bradley and Gulati, n. 36, 215; Guzman, n. 34, 17; Kammerhofer, n. 65, 535–7 and 550; and Meijers, n. 23, 11.

[108] R.A. Falk, 'The Interplay of Westphalia and Charter Conceptions of the International Legal Order' in R.A. Falk and C.E. Black (eds), *The Future of the International Legal Order, vol. I: Trends and Patterns* (Princeton, Princeton University Press, 1969), 32, 33–41; and V. Fon and F. Parisi, 'Stability and Change in International Customary Law' (2004) 21 *American Law and Economics Association Annual Meetings* 1, 1.

[109] Blutman, n. 98, 538; Guzman, n. 1, 183 and 201; and Tasioulas, n. 38, 1.

[110] See Bederman, n. 103, 39–40; and G. Norman and J.P. Trachtman, 'The Customary International Law Game' (2005) 99 *American Journal of International Law* 541, 569–72. On the 'compliance pull' of international law generally, see T.M. Franck, *The Power of Legitimacy among Nations* (Oxford, Oxford University Press, 1990).

[111] C. de Visscher, *Theory and Reality in Public International Law* (P.E. Corbett (trans.), Princeton, Princeton University Press, revised edn, 1968), 163. See also Simma and Paulus, n. 49, 306 ('[t]here is neither complete determinacy nor complete indeterminacy').

[112] F. Ingman, 'Persistent Objector—The Demise of a Hero?' (2008), unpublished Masters thesis, Lund University, http://lup.lub.lu.se/luur/download?func=downloadFile&recordOId=1558532&fileOId=1564685, 50; Lowe, n. 25, particularly at 207; and Simma and Paulus, n. 49.

[113] ILA Final Report, n. 17, 38–40; Christiano, n. 55, particularly at 381 and 392; Condorelli, n. 38, 204; P. de Visscher, 'Cours général de droit international public' (1972) 136 *Recueil des cours* 1, 74 ('[L]e facteur volonté qui n'est nullement indispensable à la naissance de la coutume, conserve son importance en la matière'); Guldahl, n. 34, 61; Guzman and Hsiang, n. 22, 554–5; Pellet, n. 11, 39; G.J. Postema, 'Custom in International Law: A Normative Practice Account' in A. Perreau-Saussine and J.B. Murphy (eds), *The Nature of Customary Law: Legal, Historical and Philosophical Perspectives* (Cambridge, Cambridge University Press, 2007), 279, 296; M.N. Shaw, *International Law* (Cambridge, Cambridge University Press, 7th edn, 2014), 7–8; and Tomuschat, n. 72, 291.

[114] A. Boyle and C. Chinkin, *The Making of International Law* (Oxford, Oxford University Press, 2007), 25; and Simma and Paulus, n. 49, 303.

[115] See section I.*iii*.

'rejection of consent cannot be equated with an absolute elimination of voluntarism; neither does it involve an absolute attribution of universal status to majority rule'.[116]

Customary international law endures precisely because of its contradictions. Its strength is not to be found in theoretical coherence but in the advantages that its inherent flexibility provides to not just states, but also courts, scholars, and *anyone else* engaged with the international legal system.[117] The absence of a theoretical 'trump card' means that custom can be credibly invoked in the name of state autonomy *or* community values. This involves a 'happy confusion' of arguments and internal contradictions.[118] Such an explanation, if it can even be called that, 'might well violate lawyers' sense of aesthetics',[119] but it reflects the messy reality of customary international law in practice.

IV. The Limits of a Theoretical Approach to Assessing the Role of the Persistent Objector Rule

Where does all of this leave the persistent objector rule and its role in the international legal system? This author, like so many others, rejects voluntarism as a holistic account of legal authority. To an extent, that act of rejection means that the rationale of the persistent objector rule must itself be rejected, at least as it is most commonly presented. Indeed, just like customary international law itself, the persistent objector rule faces attacks from both sides of the voluntarism/communitarianism theoretical divide: from one perspective the rule does not do enough to protect state autonomy; from the other it does too much to protect state autonomy.[120] The requirements for persistent objection are notably onerous, as we have seen in previous chapters,[121] and even if a state meets these requirements, it is difficult for it then to maintain its acquired exemption de facto.[122] States do use the rule, of course, but only rarely.[123] One might therefore question what 'role' or 'value' the rule ultimately has.

To attempt to answer this question it is necessary to 'untether' the persistent objector rule from absolute theoretical accounts of international law. Both supporters and critics of the rule tend to assess its value in relation to

[116] Elias, n. 120, 48. See also E. Lauterpacht (ed.), *International Law, Being the Collected Papers of Hersch Lauterpacht, vol. I: The General Works* (Cambridge, Cambridge University Press, 1970), 56–66; and Müllerson, n. 106, 358.

[117] S. Estreicher, 'A Post-Formation Withdrawal from Customary International Law?: Some Cautionary Notes' (2010) 21 *Duke Journal of Comparative and International Law* 57, 58.

[118] Koskenniemi, n. 9, 12.

[119] Kammerhofer, n. 65, 536.

[120] O. Elias, 'Some Remarks on the Persistent Objector Rule in Customary International Law' (1991) 6 *Denning Law Journal* 37, 47.

[121] See Chapters 4, 5, and 6 for discussion of the problems associated with the application of the requirements of persistence, consistency and timeliness. See also Conclusion, n. 44–n. 49 and accompanying text, for a more general discussion of the onerousness of being a persistent objector.

[122] See Chapter 8, section II.

[123] See Chapter 2, section II.

state consent.[124] Indeed, it has been argued that '[*a*]*ll* arguments supporting the persistent objector rule are based on the view that international law is the product of the consent of states'.[125] This is incorrect: other arguments have been advanced, as will be discussed in sections VI and VII. The flawed assumption made by many critics of the rule (from whatever theoretical starting point) that it can only have value in relation to voluntarism should be rejected.

A second flawed assumption made by the persistent objector rule's critics, building upon the first, is to conclude that—even if one accepts that the role of the rule is necessarily related to voluntarism—the rule can *only* be of value if it protects a state's ability to consent *in all circumstances*. Just because the rule's voluntarist pedigree is undermined in some instances, however, does not mean that it is fundamentally valueless in relation to protecting the will of states. Again, to argue this is to throw the baby out with the bathwater.

Attempting to identify the 'value' of persistent objection by way of grand theoretical inquiry only gets us so far. Fidler has argued that, because the purported voluntarist basis for the rule is flawed, '[t]he remaining line of defence [against claims that the rule has no value] is that State practice recognizes the persistent objector rule'.[126] This is presented by Fidler as an indication that the rule may *have no meaningful value*, because he questions whether it is in fact practised.[127] We have already seen in this book that it is.[128] It is worth keeping in mind, therefore, that '[w]hatever the theoretical underpinnings of the persistent objector principle, it is recognised by international tribunals and in the practice of states'.[129]

It was argued in Chapter 2 that the use of the rule by states (and its 'social acceptance' by courts, tribunals, and scholars) confirms its existence as a secondary rule of the international legal system. Indeed, contrary to claims that the persistent objector rule is losing its relevance in international law,[130] based on the (debatable) contention that so-called 'modern' custom is of an inherently more communitarian nature,[131] in recent years the usage of the rule in practice has increased.[132] Yet usage itself does not provide insight into the *desirability* of the rule. The very fact that states use the persistent objector rule does, of course, suggest that it has value. However, to identify what that value *is*, the question is *why* states use it: therefore, it is necessary 'to consider the persistent objector rule in a more systematic way, to identify its potential benefits, and to judge its desirability'.[133]

[124] Bradley and Gulati, n. 36, 234.
[125] Charney, n. 22, 541.
[126] Fidler, n. 3, 209.
[127] Ibid.
[128] See, particularly, Chapter 2, section II.
[129] Crawford, n. 25, 28.
[130] Quince, n. 24, 69; and H. Lau, 'Rethinking the Persistent Objector Doctrine in International Human Rights Law' (2005–6) 6 *Chicago Journal of International Law* 496, 503–4, and 506.
[131] See Roberts, n. 73, in general, but particularly at 759 and 766.
[132] See Chapter 2, n. 149–n. 153 and accompanying text.
[133] Guzman, n. 34, 166.

V. A Focus on the Practical Benefits of the Rule

i. Rational choice theory

A number of writers—most notably Guzman,[134] but also Fon and Parisi,[135] Kontorovich,[136] Norman and Trachtman,[137] and Petersen,[138] among others—have taken a different approach to assessing the persistent objector rule's value, which is rooted not so much in grand theory but in the assessment of functional value.[139] These scholars have employed rational choice theory (or, in some cases, an approach based more generally on game theory, of which rational choice theory is a component) as a way of examining customary international law in general, and the persistent objector rule in particular.

Rational choice theorists have considered the role and value of the persistent objector rule by looking at its practical *benefits* (to both the objecting state and other states/the wider legal system), rather than its internal logic. This is not an entirely atheoretical investigation (rational choice *theory* is, after all, as its name would suggest, a theoretical approach), but it is a non-holistic theoretical approach that more accurately, in the view of the present author, reflects the reality of the rule's value.

Having said this, one must tread extremely carefully when applying rational choice theory to international law. This is, firstly, because its underlying assumption that states are inherently and necessarily 'rational' individual actors[140] is certainly not always borne out in practice.[141] Secondly, and more disconcertingly, some rational choice theorists have combined the approach with 'a hyperactively realist perspective of international relations',[142] and the consequent denial of international law's binding force. The realist approach of identifying power as the only relevant factor in states making choices (be they rational or irrational) is highly undesirable from a moral perspective, in that it denies international law's (undeniable) ability to promote human good.[143] From a more empirical perspective, it can also be said that such an approach does not correspond to practice: states

[134] Ibid., 166–71; and Guzman, n. 1, 187–8 and 197–9.

[135] Fon and Parisi, n. 108, 7–11.

[136] Kontorovich, n. 16, 874–5 and 910–11.

[137] Norman and Trachtman, n. 110, 569.

[138] Petersen, n. 4, 5–10.

[139] Guzman, n. 1, 190.

[140] See, for example, Kontorovich, n. 16, 869 (explicitly making this assumption when adopting a rational choice approach).

[141] Norman and Trachtman, n. 110, 571; and Petersen, n. 4, 8.

[142] Bederman, n. 103, 40 (referencing the work of Goldsmith and Posner, and particularly their famous book: J.L. Goldsmith and E.A. Posner, *The Limits of International Law* (Oxford, Oxford University Press, 2006), which provides a realist/rational choice account of international law). See also Guzman, n. 1, 188–90.

[143] A-M. Slaughter, 'International Law in a World of Liberal States' (1995) 6 *European Journal of International Law* 503, 503.

undoubtedly respond to the 'compliance pull' of international law even when it is against their direct interests to do so.[144]

The present author does not adopt the rational choice methodology per se in this chapter, and self-consciously divorces any use of it herein from *realist* theory.[145] However, when approached with suitable caution, rational choice theory's appraisal of the persistent objector rule provides some helpful insights into the rule's value. Indeed, this author is of the view that the core claim that rational choice theorists have made about the persistent objector rule is correct: that its value should be assessed based on, and *can be seen in*, its functional benefits. This is the starting point for the subsequent analysis in this chapter.

ii. The balancing act at the heart of the persistent objector rule

Rational choice theorists have argued that the persistent objector rule represents a recognition of the inevitable occasions where states will oppose emerging norms of customary international law, and reduces the costs of such instances for both the international legal system and the individual dissenting state.[146] In so doing, the rule *spreads* the costs of situations of minority opposition to emerging norms between the objector and the wider community: 'if the persistent objector rule is desirable from a systematic perspective, it is because giving states the ability to object offers benefits that outweigh the costs.'[147]

The persistent objector rule cannot be understood as being inherently linked to voluntarism, nor should it be dismissed along with it.[148] In fact, the rule is not the guardian of state consent at all, but instead—reflecting the nature of customary international law itself—is a 'great compromise'[149] between different theoretical (and practical) concerns: the rule is inherently one of *balance*.[150] The element of compromise inherent in the rule is neatly illustrated when one recalls the manner

[144] See n. 110 and accompanying text.

[145] As does Guzman, n. 1, particularly at 189 (in relation to the application of rational choice theory to customary international law).

[146] Guldahl, n. 34, 61 (setting out the core claim of the rational choice theory work that has been done on the persistent objector rule without necessarily subscribing to it herself).

[147] Guzman, n. 34, 173.

[148] Koskenniemi, n. 28, 443, footnote 203 ('[i]t is not enough ... to show that the persistent objector rule cannot be held because consensualism is no longer in fashion').

[149] Ingman, n. 112, 67.

[150] Comments on the ILC Project on Identification of Customary International Law, Asian-African Legal Consultative Organisation (AALCO), annexed to Report by S. Jusoh, Chairman of the AALCO's Informal Expert Group on Customary International Law, 24 March 2015, http://www.aalco.int/54thsession/AALCOIEG%20Chairman's%20Statement%20and%20Special%20Rapporteur's%20Report%2020150324.pdf, 5, *Comment K on the Persistent Objector Rule*; Guldahl, n. 34, 52; B.B. Jia, 'The Relations between Treaties and Custom' (2010) 9 *Chinese Journal of International Law* 81, 89; Stein, n. 24, 475–6; Steinfeld, n. 24, 1646 and 1658; Weil, n. 7, 433; and Weil, n. 16, 193–6. *Contra* Elias and Lim, n. 6, 75–6 (arguing that the rule cannot be seen as a compromise because it does not adequately protect either majority law-making or state autonomy: in the view of the present author, this should be dismissed because the *nature of compromise* is that neither party will be entirely satisfied with the results).

in which the burden of proof operates in relation to persistent objection. While the rule allows for individual state exemption from norms of customary international law, it does so 'only by reversing the burden of proof in favour of a communitarian presumption of obligation'.[151]

One must be clear that the rule undertakes an *attempted* and not necessarily always *realized* balancing act. Nonetheless, the key claim made by the rational choice theorists—that the value of the rule is that it seeks to spread the costs of the implications of opposing state perspectives in relation to norms of customary international law—is correct. The rule is, but is not merely, a means of protecting against the 'tyranny of the majority'[152] (in that it allows states to gain exemptions to norms by which they do not wish to be bound). It also protects against the 'tyranny of the *minority*'[153] (in that it does not allows states to gain exemptions in all cases and places onerous requirements on the non-conformist state for it to secure and maintain its exemption).

Recognition of the delicate cost/benefit balancing act at the heart of the persistent objector rule helps to explain its onerous requirements. The criteria for the rule's operation raise the costs of exemption for the objector[154] to discourage deviation and promote universalism,[155] which has a greater overall utility. The costs to the objector offset the benefit of becoming or staying exempt. The costs to the objector also counterbalance the costs that other states, and the system as a whole, sustain by accommodating its position as an individual dissenter.[156]

The notion of balance also explains why exemption cannot, de jure, be maintained in relation to *jus cogens* norms (because of the moral and systematic costs of allowing this would be too high),[157] and why new states cannot persistently object (because of the destabilization that this would entail).[158] In such circumstances the costs to the system outweigh the benefits to the individual state. In many other circumstances, however, use of the persistent objector rule can have various systematic, practical benefits. Depending on the circumstances, the costs to the community of allowing exemption may be minimal when weighed against the benefit to the objector. Benefits for the objecting state will often *also* dovetail into benefits to the system (or, perhaps more accurately, into *a reduction in cost* to the system, in that the cost to the system would be greater if persistent objection were not permitted than they would be if it was). Overall, there are notable benefits in providing dissenting states with exemption (for both the objector and the community), just as there are benefits in ensuring that this provision is not

[151] R. Price, 'Emerging Customary Norms and Anti-Personnel Landmines' in C. Reus-Smit (ed.), *The Politics of International Law* (Cambridge, Cambridge University Press, 2004), 106, 123, emphasis removed.

[152] Fon and Parisi, n. 108, 25; and S. Yee, 'Report on the ILC Project on "Identification of Customary International Law"' (Report by the Special Rapporteur of the Asian-African Legal Consultative Organisation (AALCO) Informal Expert Group on Customary International Law) (2015) 14 *Chinese Journal of International Law* 375, 391, para. 58.

[153] Trachtman, n. 17, 19, emphasis added.

[154] Guzman, n. 1, 197.

[155] Fon and Parisi, n. 108, 28.

[156] Ibid., 2.

[157] See Chapter 7, section III.

[158] See Chapter 6, section VIII.

all-conquering.[159] Affording states an 'opt-out' from emerging customary norms ultimately promotes the effective functioning of customary international law in various respects,[160] and, thus, 'social welfare' in international relations.[161] The next two sections examine some of these benefits.

VI. The Persistent Objector Rule as a Safety Valve

i. Fear of majority rule

While 'absolute' voluntarism must be rejected, states remain the primary actors in international law, and they are unsurprisingly reticent to accept obligations as binding upon them without their consent.[162] States rarely accept the binding force of norms that they have not consented to,[163] albeit that they also grudgingly accept (in practice if not explicitly) that international law is non-voluntarist at times.[164] If customary international law is something that can be imposed on states in the face of their expressed dissent, then it would likely be perceived by them as an illegitimate attack on sovereign autonomy. It is important to note that to the extent that states themselves reference the role of the persistent objector rule, they very much cast it in terms of their sovereign autonomy and the legitimacy of customary international law's binding force.[165] For example, the United States recently endorsed the rule, in its 2015 *Department of Defense Law of War Manual*, in explicitly voluntarist terms:

> Even if a rule otherwise reflects customary international law, the rule is not binding upon a State that has persistently objected to that rule during its development. *This principle is an accepted application of the traditional principle that international law essentially depends on the consent of States.*[166]

[159] B.D. Lepard, *Customary International Law: A New Theory with Practical Applications* (Cambridge, Cambridge University Press, 2010), 229.

[160] Guldahl, n. 34, 86.

[161] Kontorovich, n. 16, 911.

[162] Charney, n. 22, 550; Danilenko, n. 7, 64 (providing examples of states taking this view during the debates over the UN Convention on the Law of the Sea); I. MacGibbon, 'Some Observations on the Part of Protest in International Law' (1953) 30 *British Yearbook of International Law* 293, 302 (giving the stark example of a statement made by Sir Edward Grey on behalf of the British government in 1912); and Schachter, n. 7, 32–3.

[163] Guzman and Hsiang, n. 22, 554.

[164] See Byers, n. 16, 149 (arguing that states acquiesce to the way in which customary international law develops); Elias and Lim, n. 6, 95–113 (concluding, at 112, 'that States are themselves not entirely consistent in the way they see the requirement of consent'); and Roberts, n. 74, 189.

[165] See Elias and Lim, n. 6, 33, footnote 10 (making this point, albeit perhaps going too far, by asserting that 'when States have referred to the principle [of persistent objection], they have *always* tied it to the idea(s) of state will/consent'; emphasis added).

[166] United States, *Department of Defense Law of War Manual*, 12 June 2015, http://www.dod.mil/dodgc/images/law_war_manual15.pdf, 34, emphasis added, references omitted. As another example, one might also consider the pleadings of the United States in the *Grand River* arbitration, where it asserted that '*States* and scholars regard [the persistent objector rule] *as central to the legitimacy of an international legal order* governed by rules of customary international law'. See *Grand River*, counter-memorial of the respondent, merits phase, 2008, UNCITRAL/NAFTA, http://www.naftaclaims.com/disputes/usa/GrandRiver/GRE-USA-Merits-Counter-Memorial-R.pdf, 129, footnote 466, emphasis added.

It has been said that the reason for the persistent objector rule's emergence in the mid-twentieth century was as a response to the decolonization process and the resulting increase in the number of states (with a corresponding plurality of perspectives and goals).[167] This assertion is correct, at least in part. The rule's conceptual roots are to be found in classic voluntarist theory, as was discussed in Chapter 1,[168] but the catalyst that truly birthed it was more practical. The process of customary international law formation became more complex and chaotic in the mid-twentieth century, and the need for a means of spreading the costs of this more plural, fast-paced, and interactional system increased. The rule's origins may be predominantly scholarly, but a key reason why the rule emerged in state practice was because of state fear of majority law-making in the new international legal landscape.[169]

This fear has only increased in recent years, with the rise of communitarian approaches to international law[170] and the emergence of the notion of so-called 'modern custom',[171] which at least purports to minimize the importance of state practice in customary international law-making.[172] In this context, it is perhaps not surprising that the usage of the persistent objector rule has increased in the twenty-first century.[173] The fact that states are aware of the option of persistent objection mitigates the fear of majority rule, and thus acts to mollify dissenters.[174] The rule 'permits the objecting state to feel secure that it is not directly threatened, in an overt legal way, by changes in the law which it opposes'.[175]

ii. Reducing the risks of violation, disengagement, or escalation

If the option of becoming a persistent objector were not available, some states—predictably, powerful states—may well simply violate a new norm to which they are strongly opposed once it has emerged.[176] States are obviously far more likely to comply with international legal norms that they have consented to or see as legitimate.[177] It is worth remembering that states would much prefer not to seek persistent objector status, given the significant difficulty and political costs of so doing: thus they only persistently object when they feel that the emerging norm

[167] Dumberry, n. 34, 782; Kelly, n. 44, 514; and E.T. Swaine, 'Bespoke Custom' (2010) 21 *Duke Journal of Comparative and International Law* 207, 213.

[168] See, particularly, Chapter 1, section I.

[169] McClane, n. 65, 3.

[170] Crawford, n. 25, 28; Steinfeld, n. 24, 1657; and Weil, n. 16, 198.

[171] See, generally, Roberts, n. 73.

[172] See Bradley, n. 24, 517; and T. Meron, 'International Law in the Age of Human Rights' (2013) 301 *Recueil des cours* 13, 395 (arguing that because of increased attempts to 'legislate' through custom in recent years, states have greater incentive to oppose new norms and that '[a]n entombment of persistent objections is thus premature').

[173] Crawford, n. 25, 28. See Chapter 2, n. 149–n. 153 and accompanying text.

[174] Byers, n. 16, 149; and Estreicher, n. 117, 61.

[175] Charney, n. 21, 22.

[176] Third Report on Identification of Customary International Law (M. Wood, Special Rapporteur), International Law Commission, Sixty-seventh session, 27 March 2015, UN Doc. A/CN.4/682, para. 90; Lau, n.130, 499; and Tomuschat, n. 72, 289.

[177] Ibid., 290.

poses a significant threat to their interests.[178] That being so, one can envisage that on some occasions a dissenting state would violate the new norm, were it not for the compromise of the persistent objector rule.

Making this point from the rational choice perspective, Kontorovich has noted that a customary international law norm would not 'be efficient as applied to [an] objector'.[179] In other words, forcing states to comply with norms against their express objections may well result in the violation of the norm in question. When the 'prisoner's dilemma' (from game theory) is applied to international law, the state actor is usually presented as having a binary choice in relation to legal norms that are contrary to its interests: (a) defection (violation of the norm), or (b) compliance.[180] In the simplest version of this dilemma, defection is considered to enrich the state, whereas compliance is seen as enriching the system.[181] Based on this model alone, one might well expect violation in all instances.

Violation of legal norms involves notable systematic costs. The norm in question loses credibility if violated, but—more importantly—so too does the legal system itself,[182] in that its wider credibility and the reciprocal premise at the heart of international legal obligation is strained.[183] This is particularly the case if violations occur repeatedly and/or over time.[184] Yet, the violation of a legal norm is not just harmful to the system or to other states, but to the violator itself, because violation entails significant reputational costs, which can lead to co-ordination problems for that state in the future.[185] This helps to explain state compliance with international law even when this appears to be against its short-term interests. However, when the costs of compliance are perceived by the state as outweighing the cost of violation, the state may breach international law.

The persistent objector rule therefore acts as a third option—a middle path—for the state: it is a 'safety valve' in this regard.[186] By persistently objecting, the state mitigates the costs to it of compliance *and* the costs of defection (both to the system and, by proxy, itself). The rule therefore lessens the likelihood of norm violation to the benefit of the system,[187] and also reduces the reputational harm that the objector might suffer by legitimizing its deviant behaviour.[188] Of course, objection will not eradicate this cost for the objector—persistent objectors certainly still suffer reputational harm—but this harm will be significantly less than the objector would suffer if it violated the norm in question.[189] The risk of various associated costs of norm violation (substantive, reputational, and systematic) is reduced by the rule.[190]

Beyond just violating an individual norm of customary international law, states—again, particularly powerful states—are more likely to engage with

[178] Byers, n. 16, 180. See also Stein, n. 24, 468 (describing the rule as a 'fallback' option); and Weil, n. 16, 195 (describing the rule as 'le dernier refuge du minoritaire').
[179] Kontorovich, n. 16, 911.
[180] See Norman and Trachtman, n. 110, 548–53.
[181] Ibid., 548.
[182] Ibid., 543.
[183] Guzman, n. 1, 191.
[184] Ibid., 191.
[185] Ibid., 192.
[186] Stein, n. 24, 479.
[187] Guzman, n. 34, 170.
[188] Guzman, n. 1, 198.
[189] Guzman, n. 34, 168.
[190] Guzman, n. 1, 198.

customary norm development per se because of the existence of the persistent objector rule.[191] *Legitimized* isolation in relation to a particular norm helps to keep powerful objectors 'in the game' rather more generally. Again, this is of benefit not just to the objector but also to the other players, and to the game itself. Without the persistent objector rule, one could envisage dissenting states withdrawing from the process of customary international law formation entirely, or denying its legitimacy per se.[192] This would have reputational costs for the state concerned, but, far more damagingly, systematic costs for the international community.

A related point is that the rule can 'provide a means whereby a State may protect its legal interests without using confrontational actions'.[193] It was argued in Chapter 3 that objection need not take the form of physical actions, and that many instances of persistent objection occur through statements alone.[194] Violation, on the other hand, involves actually acting in a contrary manner to the new or emerging norm, increasing the possibility of retaliatory responses and escalating tensions.[195] The compromise of the persistent objector rule reduces friction between states with deeply held opposing positions, particularly in relation to bilateral disputes. Take, for example, the dispute between Turkey and Greece over the size of Turkey's territorial waters in the Aegean Sea.[196] If Turkey had not been able to acquire persistent objector status to the 12-nautical-mile rule, one can easily envisage that the already tense relationship between the two states over their respective jurisdictions in the Aegean may have dangerously escalated.

The escalation of legal punch/counter-punch does not necessarily have negative diplomatic (or even aggressive, retaliatory) consequences, of course. However, more prosaically, it can also be time-consuming and expensive for a state to actually exercise a right that it wants to protect when—under the persistent objector rule—statements of objection will suffice. Colson provides a useful example involving the United States and Canada, where the persistent objector rule was not used:

> when the United States found out that Canada had taken steps to promote oil and gas development in continental shelf areas disputed by the United States, the United States believed it to be legally necessary to take its own steps toward leasing outer continental shelf areas disputed by Canada – to balance the ledger so to speak. This was an expensive and time-consuming way to show national resolve and to make a legal point.[197]

[191] Bradley, n. 24, 517; and Steinfeld, n. 24, 1674. [192] Ibid., 1639.

[193] Colson, n. 24, 964. See also Third Report on Identification of Customary International Law, ILC, n. 176, para. 90; Barsalou, n. 24, 9; and Guldahl, n. 34, 60.

[194] See Chapter 3, IV.*i*. [195] Colson, n. 24, 964; Guzman, n. 1, 192.

[196] See, generally, Y. Acer, *The Aegean Maritime Disputes and International Law* (Aldershot, Ashgate, 2003); D. Anderson, *Modern Law of the Sea: Selected Essays* (Leiden, Martinus Nijhoff, 2008), 91, particularly at footnote 14; and D. Bölükbaşı, *Turkey and Greece: The Aegean Disputes—A Unique Case in International Law* (London, Cavendish, 2004). See also, respectively, Chapter 2, n. 140–n. 144 and accompanying text; Chapter 3, n. 54–n. 59 and accompanying text; Chapter 5, n. 103–n. 113 and accompanying text; and Chapter 8, n. 131 and accompanying text, and n. 213.

[197] Colson, n. 24, 964.

Persistent objection can increase the predictability of the application of customary international law, as will be discussed in section VII.*ii* of this chapter. The formalization of states' legal positions, and the ability (or, at least, the increased ability) for them to predict what the obligations of various states will be once a customary norm has crystallized, reduces the risks of confrontation. Persistent objection means that everyone will already have a fairly good idea of where they will stand. As Mendelson notes, then, 'if [the rule] is a way of reducing friction and unnecessary quarrels about rights, that is no bad thing'.[198]

iii. Allowance for short-term adjustment

As the extra-legal costs of objecting mean that states rarely maintain their persistent objector status indefinitely,[199] much of the 'payoff' for the objector is likely to be in the short term. The rule is therefore often used, briefly, as a strategic tool.[200] Even a short period of exemption, however, allows the objector the opportunity to adjust to the emerging rule, giving it time to explore alternative ways of maintaining its interests or at least to take steps to minimize the impact of the emerging norm on those interests.[201] As Byers notes, 'a persistent objector, even if it is unsuccessful, may end up buying itself time by postponing the application of the new, generally applicable rule to itself and thus what it perceives to be the deleterious effects thereof'.[202]

Allowing time for such adjustments, through a formal process that reduces the reputational impact of deviation for the objector and legitimizes its position, not only lessens the likelihood of the state violating the norm in the short term, but significantly increases the likelihood of it *accepting* the new norm in the longer term. De facto, persistent objection often provides only a grace period for the objector, but this temporary period for adjustment should not be dismissed, because it too acts as a safety valve and may actually facilitate universal acceptance later in the norm's lifespan.[203]

VII. The Persistent Objector Rule and the Development of Customary International Law

In the previous section, it was argued that the persistent objector rule can produce a number of beneficial consequences by acting as a 'safety valve', for both objectors

198 Mendelson, n. 34, 240. 199 See Chapter 8, section II.

200 Charney, n. 21, 22–4; Dumberry, n. 34, 801–2; Kontorovich, n. 16, 910; and Tomuschat, n. 72, 289.

201 Third Report on Identification of Customary International Law, ILC, n.176, para. 90; Elias, n. 22, 282, para. 6; Barsalou, n. 24, 9; Mendelson, n. 34, 240; M.P. Scharf, *Customary International Law in Times of Fundamental Change: Recognizing Grotian Moments* (Cambridge, Cambridge University Press, reissue, 2013), 42; Tomuschat, n. 72, 289; and Weil, n.16, 197–8.

202 Byers, n. 16, 183.

203 Lowe, n. 25, 210 (arguing that persistent objection is 'merely [a] stage[] on the continuous road towards universal recognition of the new customary rule').

and other states alike. Beyond this it is important to consider the various ways in which the rule can facilitate customary international law development.[204] It is notable that even Charney, famously a persistent objector-rule sceptic, has said that 'the persistent objector rule, if it really exists, focuses more on the process of law development than on the status of a [single] State'.[205]

i. The emergence of new norms

If there were no available opt-out through persistent objection, states that were opposed to an emerging norm would likely fight far harder against its emergence, and this may slow down or—especially if the objector is a powerful state—even stop new norms from forming (irrespective of the fact that the objector has no de jure veto).[206] As the International Law Association's *Committee on Formation of Customary (General) International Law* phrased this, the rule means that 'the convoy of the law's progressive development can move forward without having to wait for the slowest vessel'.[207] It is worth noting—from a natural law/communitarian perspective—that the persistent objector rule may therefore facilitate the (speedy) creation of more progressive 'value-based' norms that would otherwise not emerge (or, at least, would emerge more slowly).[208]

Indeed, persistent objection may hasten the crystallization of an emerging norm in a number of ways. The dissenter's objections might draw attention to practice that is occurring. This may encourage other states—in disagreement with the objector but made aware of the embryonic practice because of its objections—to contribute their own practice/*opinio juris* to the developing norm, adding to the normative snowball rolling towards crystallization.[209] Or it may be that, by objecting, the dissenter casts some doubt as to the emergence of the rule, which then leads to a strengthening of the resolve of the states engaged in the relevant practice to assert the norm's emergence and encourage others to do so.[210]

Speeding up the emergence of a norm that is viewed by the objecting state as undesirable can hardly be considered a benefit for that state, of course, which

[204] Macgibbon, n. 162, 293 (arguing that 'protest' in international law generally is 'apt to influence the development of customary rules').

[205] Charney, n. 21, 22.

[206] AALCO Comments on the ILC Project, n. 150, 5, *Comment K on the Persistent Objector Rule*; Bradley, n. 24, 516; Byers, n. 16, 183; Elias, n. 22, 281, para. 3; Estreicher, n. 117, 61; Fon and Parisi, n. 108, 2; Mendelson, n. 34, 239–40; and Scharf, n. 201, 42.

[207] ILA Final Report, n. 17, 28. *Contra* Guzman, n. 34, 165–6 (doubting whether the rule does in fact facilitate norm development in this way, although actually only supporting this view by providing critiques of the rule's voluntarist credentials).

[208] Estreicher, n. 117, 61; and Loschin, n. 24, 168.

[209] Barsalou, n. 24, 15–16; D'Amato, n. 6, 70; R-J. Dupuy, 'Coutume sage et coutume sauvage' in C. Rousseau and S. Bastid (eds), *Mélanges offerts à Charles Rousseau: la communauté international* (Paris, Pedone, 1974), 75, 85; and M. Ragazzi, *The Concept of International Obligations* Erga Omnes (Oxford, Clarendon Press, 1997), 65.

[210] Jia, n. 150, 90.

would obviously prefer that no norm emerged at all. However, faster norm development may well be of benefit to the wider community. Standing apart from the majority comes with associated risks and, if the objector does inadvertently speed up the norm's emergence, it will still have its exempt status to fall back on.

Entirely conversely, persistent objection may slow down, or even stop, a norm's development.[211] The rule provides a formal opportunity for the dissenting state to persuade others to adopt its position, pre-crystallization, which might mean—if enough states are persuaded—that no new norm is formed at all.[212] Or, if the norm does crystallize, the exempt status held by the objecting state can continue to act as a platform from which it can try to change the perceptions and actions of other states and thus create a 'different equilibrium rule'[213] of customary international law:

> In some cases ... the persistent objector rule may serve to allow the persistent objector to spearhead a better rule of customary international law on the very same subject matter. Yesterday's persistent objection may well be today's standard embodiment. Yesterday's persistent objector may well be today's standard carrier.[214]

The persistent objector rule is, therefore, in part a lobbying or negotiation tool.[215] A strategic, often short-term, role for the rule is that it is a means by which the objector can place pressure on the majority of states to change their practice.[216] The process of persistent objection can act to pressure other states to accommodate the objector's interests (or some of its interests), by encouraging the adoption of a position of compromise in relation to the nature of the emerging rule.[217]

A good example in this regard is the fact that the United States was—for a period in the late 1980s and early 1990s[218]—almost undeniably a persistent objector state[219] in relation to certain customary norms reflected in provisions of

[211] Higgins, n. 20, 34.

[212] Byers, n. 16, 105; Elias, n. 22, 285, para. 19; and Trachtman, n. 17, 10.

[213] L.R. Helfer, 'Exiting Custom: Analogies to Treaty Withdrawals' (2010) 21 *Duke Journal of Comparative and International Law* 65, 70.

[214] Yee, n. 152, 391, para. 58. See also Elias, n. 120, 49; Hansen, n. 25, 33; and Jia, n. 150, 88.

[215] Dumberry, n. 34, 801–2. See also Charney, n. 21, 22.

[216] See ibid., 23 (referring to the possibility of the rule being used as 'leverage').

[217] Elias, n. 120, 49; and Ragazzi, n. 209, 65. See also Swaine, n. 167, 212 (noting that, in such circumstances, the 'threat' of persistent objection may be as valuable to the objector as persistent objection itself: a state saying—in the very early stages of a norm's emergence—that it *will* persistently object if other states do not take notice of its views could itself act 'a bargaining chip ... behind the scenes').

[218] See, as an example of the United States' persistent objection during this period, 'United States Ocean Policy', Statement of President Reagan, 10 March 1983, http://www.reagan.utexas.edu/archives/speeches/1983/31083c.htm.

[219] See C.E. Biblowit, 'Deep Seabed Mining: The United States and the United Nations Convention on the Law of the Sea' (1984) 58 *St. John's Law Review* 267, 299; Colson, n. 24, 965–6; Elias, n. 22, 282, para. 6; C.E. Remy, 'U.S. Territorial Sea Extension: Jurisdiction and International Environmental Protection' (1992) 16 *Fordham International Law Journal* 1208, particularly at 1216–17; and Weil, n. 16, 190. It is worth noting that the United States never explicitly *invoked* persistent objector status in relation to deep seabed mining during this period. See T. Stein, during the discussion appearing in A. Cassese and J H.H. Weiler (eds), *Change and Stability in International Law-Making* (Berlin, de Gruyter, 1988), 13. This certainly does not mean that the United States was not a persistent objector, however: see Mendelson, n. 34, 236; and, more generally, Chapter 3, section II.

the 1982 UN Convention on the Law of the Sea (UNCLOS)[220] concerning deep seabed mining.[221] The United States is probably no longer an exempt persistent objector state today, however.[222] It was receptive to the provisions on deep seabed mining in the 1994 UNCLOS Part XI Implementation Agreement, and, in the early 2000s, the Bush administration was broadly accepting of that Agreement.[223] The United States is also now an observer at the International Seabed Authority (ISA).[224] Tellingly, in 2013, the American company Lockheed Martin obtained a licence from the ISA (through its British arm, UK Seabed Resources) to prospect for polymetallic nodules in a certain area of the seabed,[225] and there are indications that licences may be directly granted to American companies from 2016.[226]

The United States has therefore (slowly, quietly) stopped objecting, having previously been an exempt persistent objector. At first glance, this may appear like an example (of the sort discussed in Chapter 8) of extra-legal factors—here, the isolation of the United States and the associated political pressure to conform—meaning that a state struggles to maintain its exempt status.[227] However, the United States was actually able to maintain exempt status for some years before changing its stance. It ultimately did so because the regime to which it was objecting softened to accommodate it. The 1994 Implementation Agreement, for example, specifically addressed many of the United States' concerns in relation to the deep seabed mining provisions of UNCLOS: indeed, that can be seen as its purpose.[228] Thus, objection was no longer considered by the United States as being imperative.[229] The United States gained obvious benefits from its persistent objector status: it was able to integrate itself within the international legal framework, in a way that suited it, without even joining UNCLOS. Persistent objection, for a period, provided it with this opportunity. As Elias has put it, specifically in

[220] United Nations Convention on the Law of the Sea (UNCLOS), 10 December 1982, 1833 UNTS 3.

[221] General restrictions on deep seabed mining have arguably been customary international law since the 1970s. See Letter dated 24 April 1979 from the Chairman of the Group of 77 to the President of the Conference, UN Doc. A/CONF.62/77 (asserting, in 1979, that 119 states took this view). See also L.F.E. Goldie, 'Customary International Law and Deep Seabed Mining' (1978–9) 6 *Syracuse Journal of International Law and Commerce* 173, particularly at 179–82.

[222] Villiger, n. 3, 35. See, generally, B.H. Oxman, 'The Third United Nations Conference on the Law of the Sea: The Tenth Session (1981)' (1982) 76 *American Journal of International Law* 1, 2–13.

[223] See J.E. Noyes, 'U.S. Policy and the United Nations Convention on the Law of the Sea' (2007) 39 *George Washington International Law Review* 621, 621, particularly at footnote 3.

[224] International Seabed Authority, Observers, https://www.isa.org.jm/observers.

[225] 'Lockheed to Use Soviet Submarine Hunt Data in Sea Mine Plan', *BloombergBusinessweek*, 14 March 2013, http://www.bloomberg.com/news/articles/2013-03-14/lockheed-to-use-soviet-submarine-hunt-data-in-seabed-mining-plan.

[226] D. Shukman, 'Deep Sea Mining "Gold Rush" Moves Closer', *BBC News*, 18 May 2013, http://www.bbc.co.uk/news/science-environment-22546875.

[227] See Chapter 8, Section II.

[228] See Letter from President Clinton, 'Presidential Letter to Transmittal of the Law of the Sea Convention', 6 October 1994, reproduced in J.A. Roach and R.W. Smith, *Excessive Maritime Claims* (Leiden, Martinus Nijhoff, 3rd edn, 2012), 658–60. See also Jia, n. 150, 107–8; and D. Harris, *Cases and Materials on International Law* (London, Sweet and Maxwell, 7th edn, 2010), 411–12.

[229] Guldahl, n. 34, 58.

relation to the United States' practice regarding deep seabed mining: '[a]gain, persistent objection does seem to pay.'[230]

Such strategic uses of the persistent objector rule should not be negatively viewed as a 'tyranny of the minority' result of persistent objection, however. After all, the majority of states may well ignore the protestations of the objector, meaning that (at least as regards the formation or content of the norm) the objector's lobbying has no effect. If the objector convinces other states to change their practice, then it is, in fact, the position of the *majority* that wins out (it is just that this position will have been changed in light of the dissenter's objections). It is worth noting, for example, that a number of *other* states are now taking advantage of the customary shift post-1994 concerning deep seabed mining that the United States was able to influence while acting as a persistent objector.[231] Equally, if the objector is not able to convince other states to follow it, then, again, it can retreat to the (relative) safety of the exemption that it has acquired.

ii. Predictability

Another systematic value that the persistent objector rule has in the process of customary international law formation relates to the effect that it has on the *expectations* of states, and the increased ability for them to rely on those expectations.[232] Given the difficulty in determining when a customary international law has, or will, crystallize, persistent objection can provide the system with a much needed degree of predictability.[233] This, in turn, promotes stability[234] and the 'smooth operation of international community'.[235]

Indeed, the effect of the rule on the predictability of customary international law development and application has a number of aspects. Firstly, the dissenting state acquires a degree of certainty in relation to the future (in)applicability of the norm to it. So long as it complies with the various criteria for the rule's operation, a dissenter can be relatively sure that—at least for a while—it will not be bound. Secondly, other states are given advance warning of the likelihood that the objector will not be accepting or complying with the norm in question post-crystallization, so that they too can shape their expectations accordingly.[236] Thirdly, persistent objection sheds light on, and thus puts *other states* on notice of, the (otherwise relatively opaque) emergence of a potential new customary international law norm.[237] This has value because other states may not have been aware

230 Elias, n. 120, 45. 231 See Shukman, n. 226.

232 Guzman, n. 34, 167; Guzman, n. 1, 197; and Petersen, n. 4, 10.

233 See Barsalou, n. 24, 9; Dumberry, n. 34, 801 (not necessarily subscribing to this argument); Guldahl, n. 34, 60; and Lau, n. 130, 499 and 505–6. Interestingly, while Barsalou uses the term 'prévisibilité' (i.e. 'predictability') to refer to this phenomenon, Guldahl and Lau both use the word 'foreseeability'. In the view of the present author, the former term is preferable because use of the rule does not mean that a state can foresee how or when a customary norm will form, only that persistent objection makes it is more likely that the effects of that emergence can be predicted.

234 Fon and Parisi, n. 108, 26. 235 Steinfeld, n. 24, 1674.

236 Guzman, n. 1, 198; and Petersen, n. 4, 10. 237 Byers, n. 16, 183.

that the custom was forming at all, allowing them to object themselves (potentially, if there are enough of them, to stop the norm forming), or to contribute to the practice/*opinio juris* if they so wish. Either way, the act of putting states on notice has positive implications for wider participation in, and thus the legitimacy of, the system.

iii. The dialectical value of persistent objection: improving the scrutiny and quality of norms

The persistent objector can also have a *dialectical* function in customary international law development. More than just putting states on notice as to the possible emergence of a new norm, persistent objection—which inherently involves the presentation of a contrary viewpoint—acts to inform other states of potential issues with the emerging norm that they had not previously considered, thus 'encouraging [them] to consider their actions carefully'.[238] In other words, it places front-and-centre the concerns that the objecting state has regarding the emerging (or emerged, in the case of ongoing objection post-crystallization) norm in question. The majority of states may or may not take heed of the objector's concerns, but, either way, the rule facilitates interstate discourse. It provides a means for the objector to present formal alternative viewpoints without the fear of being viewed as an unlawful recalcitrant. Indeed, the rule's requirements of unequivocal, persistent, and consistent objection means that dissenting states must—if they wish to have any chance of later avoiding an emerging norm's binding force—try to articulate a clear, rational counter-position.

The fact that other states will be faced with alternative perspectives on an emerging norm, advanced in the context of a process of persistent objection, increases the potential for compromise in relation to norm development: 'objection by some States may lead to modification of the new rule in order to achieve an accommodation between the views of the States that subscribe to the new rule and those of the objecting State or States.'[239] We have already seen this in section VII.*i*, in relation to the United States' objections to norms governing deep seabed mining.[240]

Indeed, the increased scrutiny that the very act of objection will bring in relation to accumulating practice and *opinio juris* is, in many cases, likely to improve the substantive 'quality' of the norm that ultimately emerges as part of customary international law. In most instances, as we know, it is very difficult for states to maintain their exemptions for long, de facto.[241] Persistent objector states are well aware of this reality. It is undoubtedly in their interests (and they *know* it is in their interests) to engage with the development of the emerging norm in question to 'improve' it (from their perspective, at least). The persistent objector rule provides a formal mechanism, and the social 'space', to facilitate dialectic exchange

[238] Ibid.

[239] Elias, n. 22, 282, para. 6. See also Third Report on Identification of Customary International Law, ILC, n.176, para. 90; Elias, n. 120, 49; and Jia, n. 150, 90.

[240] See n. 218–n. 231 and accompanying text.

[241] See Chapter 8, section II.

in instances where otherwise such exchange may not occur. This acts to improve the 'quality' of any emergent norm.

Having said this, the possible implications of the rule in terms of it increasing the likelihood of a compromise being reached between the objector and other states as to the content of the emerging norm might be viewed negatively. There is a tendency to see persistent objection as a conservative rule, which leads to anti-progressive 'results' in terms of norm development.[242] The perception is that valuable developing social norms will be 'dialled down', or even abandoned, to accommodate the self-interested objector.[243] Yet, states on the whole are quite a conservative bunch; it is a mistake to assume that the development of 'fundamental' norms with high value-pedigree will always be best served by supporting the view of the majority of the international community. For example, it has been argued—from a liberal political theory perspective—that the persistent objector rule can have an important role in protecting liberal principles, 'in that it allows a liberal State to keep itself free of majoritarian norms generated by non-liberal States'.[244] This may be somewhat optimistic, but it is true that even if one is to adopt a value-based (rather than positivistic) approach to international law, the optimum value for international society is not necessarily inherently embodied in the practice/*opinio juris* of the majority.

It has also been contended—from a rational choice perspective—that norms of customary international law that emerge where there exists a persistent objector will, in fact, be 'suboptimal' in terms of either quality or utility. This is on the basis that the option of persistent objection means that dissenters do not need to engage with the relevant norm's development (as they know that they will be exempt from it), whereas, if there was no option of persistent objection, the dissenting state would have to reach a compromise with the majority, leading to a 'better' resulting norm.[245] This argument is difficult to support, because it ignores the fact that, if denied the option of persistent objection, dissenters (at least, powerful states that are dissenters) would be more likely to reject or violate the new norm than take a seat at the negotiation table. This is to say nothing of the fact that, because of the deformalized manner in which custom emerges, there is—in relation to the majority of new customary norms—no 'negotiating table' at which states can sit. It is nonetheless true that compromising over emerging norms may mean, on some occasions, that the resulting norm is more anodyne and less effective than it would otherwise have been. Persistent objection, however, increases the possibility of compromise; it does not *require it.*

It is also worth noting that increased scrutiny of an emerging norm is valuable even if the objector's concerns are ultimately dismissed by the majority, which then continue to contribute to the emergence of the norm in question just as before, because it helps to ensure that the majority do truly support the rule that is emerging. The potential for compromise also has systematic value, because the

242 Weil, n. 16, 196 (describing but not subscribing to this critique of the rule).

243 See, generally, Charney, n. 22.

244 Fidler, n. 3, 242.

245 Fon and Parisi, n. 108, 26.

more states that support any given norm of customary international law, the more practical utility that norm is likely to have.

Of course, the dialectic function of the persistent objector rule should not be overstated, because persistent objection itself is rare: the vast majority of customary international law norms will crystallize without persistent objection occurring. It is certainly not the case that the persistent objector rule is *necessary* for new norms of customary international law to emerge, or for them to emerge effectively.[246] It would be a stretch to argue, as a strict voluntarist might, that the system of customary international law would collapse without the persistent objector rule. However, this does not mean that the rule does not add value to the process. It is again worth recalling that the significant political costs of being a persistent objector mean that states only persistently object when they are strongly opposed to the emerging norm in question,[247] and these are precisely the circumstances where debate and scrutiny of *why* the objector has such strong opposition are of real value. Overall, '[p]ersistent objectors play a dialectical role in the development, maintenance and change of customary rule, similar to an opposition party in a national legislature'.[248]

VIII. The Role of State Perception

A key benefit of (hard-won) persistent objector status for the objecting state, of course, is that it gains 'a shield against norms that impose harmful externalities' upon it.[249] As we have seen throughout this book, states can, and do, gain de jure exemptions to customary international law norms by way of their persistent objections. However, it is worth briefly noting that many of the wider benefits that the rule provides to both the dissenting state and the international legal system discussed in this chapter derive not just from situations of actual, de jure exemption, but also from (rather less tangible) state *perception*.

We know that the rule only acts as a shield in certain circumstances,[250] and states are aware that any exempt status that they gain is unlikely to be maintained indefinitely. As such, some of the benefits that derive from granting objecting states exempt status—for example, those relating to the state's engagement with norm development and its acceptance of new norms in the longer term—will, in some instances, have as much to do with the objector's perception that its sovereignty has been respected than with any actual maintainable exemption that it gains. If a state feels that its 'voice has been heard', this in itself has systematic value.

Indeed, in this author's view, the persistent objector rule would be valuable even if it were *never used*, simply as a face-saving device. A state can reluctantly accept

[246] Elias and Lim, n. 6, 76. [247] Byers, n. 16, 180. [248] Ibid., 183.

[249] Kontorovich, n. 16, 911.

[250] Elias and Lim, n. 6, 31 (arguing that the rule provides 'a *limited* role to consent'; emphasis added).

a new norm that it does not like, knowing that it ultimately would have found it very difficult to remain exempt from it anyway (de facto, at least), and yet present itself as sovereign and autonomous: i.e. 'if we had really wanted to, we could have persistently objected—therefore accepting this new norm is our choice'.

Overall, perception is crucial, because the perceptions of states affect how they act, and those actions have direct implications for customary international law (its effectiveness, binding force, and development).[251] This is certainly not to say that the persistent objector rule is merely a means of creating *false* state perceptions that may have beneficial consequences. Rather, it is simply to say that one must recognize the fact that the rule has value not just in terms of what it actually does, but also in terms of the perception of autonomy that it engenders.

IX. Conclusion

The traditional voluntarist rationale for the persistent objector rule as a mechanism to protect the role of state consent in relation to customary international law cannot be supported, at least not entirely. This is because the voluntarist account of international law cannot explain its binding force (or, more accurately, cannot explain all of the instances where international law is binding on states). Similarly, various aspects of the persistent objector rule mean that it does not always provide states with an opportunity to withhold their consent to customary international law norms.

The persistent objector rule is, therefore, theoretically incoherent, at least if approached from the perspective of either voluntarism or communitarianism. Interestingly, in his famous article on the persistent objector rule from 1985, Stein mused that '[l]ogical consistency … may not be the most important value at stake here'.[252] Stein's suggestion was critiqued in 2010 by Dumberry, who essentially argued that the most important value of the rule was *precisely* its logical, theoretical coherence.[253] Dumberry's suggestion must be rejected: the claim that a legal rule only has value if it fits a particular conception of the system in which it operates, and, even then, only if it is always effective, is simply impossible to support. To argue that the rule has no value because its voluntarist pedigree is not absolute goes too far, as does a rejection of the rule from alternative communitarian positions. After all, states use the rule, and they must do so for a reason.

It has been argued in this chapter—partially drawing on insights from rational choice theory—that the value of the persistent objector rule must be assessed, not in relation to sweeping theoretical claims, but in relation to its functional benefits, both to the objector and to the international legal system. One of these benefits,

[251] Roberts, n. 73, 762 (arguing that '[l]egal rules are more likely to engender respect in a decentralised system … if they result from a process *perceived* as legitimate'; emphasis added).

[252] Stein, n. 24, 476.

[253] Dumberry, n. 96, generally, but in reference to Stein's position at 391. See also Dumberry, n. 34.

of course, is the actual legal exemption that the rule can provide a dissenting state. However, beyond this direct benefit to the objector, which is hard-won, the rule actually plays, or can play, 'a number of important roles in the system of customary international law'.[254] These roles have been explored in this chapter, and include mollifying states' fears of majority rule; reducing the risks of violating customary international law or disengaging from the customary process; reducing the risk of confrontation between states; allowing short-term adjustments to be made by the objector before it accepts the norm in question; increasing the predictability of the process of customary international law development; and facilitating dialectical exchange, which encourages the scrutiny of emerging customary norms (with the potential for valuable compromise, and the emergence of 'better', and better recognized, norms as a result).

At the heart of the persistent objector rule is an act of balance, in that it seeks to minimize, and *spread*, the costs—to both the objector state and the international community—of situations where a norm is strongly opposed by an individual state (or a small group of states). It is far from perfect in undertaking this task, but it is clear that the rule can, and does, provide, in rational choice speak, various 'efficiency gains' for the international legal system.[255] As such, the persistent objector rule can 'reasonably claim a permanent place [in the system] ... even when the positive emphasis in the law-creating process is shifted from consent to the less ridged notion of consensus'.[256]

It is, however, important not to overstate the persistent objector rule's value. After all, the rule is only used exceptionally, and the system of customary international law would—almost certainly—carry on without it in a form not too dissimilar from how it currently operates, were the rule to be abandoned. Not that it is necessarily always easy to maintain such a degree of perspective when one is writing a nine-chapter book on the rule, of course. The present author can mollify himself in this regard, though, by noting that just because it is difficult to see the rule as being entirely fundamental to the operation of customary international law, this does not mean that it is not an important and beneficial secondary rule of the international legal system: 'Même si elle ne peut recevoir qu'une application peu fréquente et presque toujours provisoire, sa sauvegarde [of the persistent objector rule] est précieuse'.[257]

Quite simply, the persistent objector rule 'is justified because it adds value',[258] and it does so in various ways.

[254] Elias, n. 22, 282, para. 6. [255] Guzman, n. 1, 198.

[256] M. Sørensen, 'Theory and Reality in International Law' (1981) 75 *American Society of International Law Proceedings* 140, 147.

[257] Weil, n. 16, 200–1. [258] Guzman, n. 34, 171.

Conclusion

It is worth recalling the International Law Commission (ILC)'s current working text on the persistent objector rule, which was set out in this book's Introduction. At the time of writing, the ILC has recently (in August 2015) taken note of a set of draft conclusions provisionally adopted by its Drafting Committee as part of the Commission's ongoing work on the topic 'Identification of customary international law'. Draft conclusion 15, on the persistent objector rule, provides:

1. Where a State has objected to a rule of customary international law while that rule was in the process of formation, the rule is not opposable to the State concerned for so long as it maintains its objection.
2. The objection must be clearly expressed, made known to other States, and maintained persistently.[1]

This definition is representative of the general understanding of the rule. The ILC has neatly set out the commonly accepted elements, and criteria for the operation, of the persistent objector rule (although, sadly, it has failed to identify a separate criterion of consistency, as have so many other commentators who have considered the rule, at least explicitly).[2]

The commonly agreed elements of persistent objection, as presented in the ILC's definition, will be well known to all international lawyers. The ubiquity of the rule in doctrine[3] has meant that its basic aspects are extremely familiar. However, it is worth noting that, were we to go back only one generation of international lawyers, this easy familiarity with the rule would not be present. The persistent objector rule is a new rule. Admittedly, its conceptual and theoretical roots stretch back at least to the eighteenth century.[4] Yet the rule's critics have been nonetheless broadly correct in asserting that there is comparatively little evidence that the persistent objector rule, as commonly presented today, existed prior to 1945.[5]

[1] 'Identification of Customary International Law: Text of the Draft Conclusions Provisionally Adopted by the Drafting Committee', International Law Commission, Sixty-seventh session, Geneva, 4 May–5 June and 6 July–7 August 2015, UN Doc. A/CN.4/L.869, 5, Draft Conclusion 15: Persistent Objector.

[2] See, generally, Chapter 5 in relation to the consistency criterion, and particularly at n. 48–n. 50 and accompanying text, in relation to the fact that this criterion is often not properly acknowledged in the literature.

[3] See Introduction, section I.

[4] See Chapter 1, particularly at n. 24–n. 33 and accompanying text.

[5] See writers cited in ibid., n. 9.

In fact, the modern persistent objector rule emerged in the mid-twentieth century. This emergence was initially driven by the rule's appearance in international law scholarship,[6] as well as by the (less than unequivocal) endorsement of it by the International Court of Justice in the *Asylum*[7] and *Fisheries*[8] cases. Since the 1950s, however, the rule has been accepted by the wider international community, not only in scholarship, but also in case law[9] and, pertinently, in state practice.[10] The rule certainly is used by states, in spite of some claims to the contrary,[11] and states do gain exemptions from new norms of customary international law as result. Yet while the rule is used, it is not used often: most norms of customary international law form without any persistent objection occurring at all.

It is important to note that, for all of its ubiquity in doctrine and our familiarity with its main elements, one can still come across significant misunderstandings in the literature of what the rule is, even in the most basic sense. For example, in 2011, Martin argued that the International Centre for the Settlement of Investment Disputes' arbitral practice concerning the definition of investment is, *in itself*, 'a persistent objector' to the previously accepted '*Salini* Tests'.[12] In fact, Martin's argument does not relate to the persistent objector rule at all, but instead concerns differences of approach in adjudicative decision-making.

Similar misunderstandings can also be identified outside of academic scholarship. For example, the Report of the Independent International Fact-Finding Mission on the Conflict in Georgia (IIFFMCG),[13] which was set up by the Council of the European Union[14] following the August 2008 conflict between Russia and Georgia,[15] incorrectly identified two instances of what the Mission considered to be persistent objection. The IIFFMCG report took the view that the Russian Federation had objected to a possible precedent on the acquisition of statehood created by Kosovo's declaration of independence, and thus was barred from invoking this precedent in relation to South Ossetia or Abkhazia, as a 'persistent objector'.[16] The Mission also concluded that Russia had previously persistently opposed the controversial notion of humanitarian intervention as a justification for the use of military force, and thus could not invoke this in relation to its intervention in Georgia.[17] It is doubtful whether new customary international law norms were created by Kosovo's declaration of independence

[6] See Chapter 1, section I.

[7] *Asylum* (*Columbia v Peru*), merits, 1950 ICJ Rep. 266, 277–278.

[8] *Fisheries* (*United Kingdom v Norway*), merits, 1951 ICJ Rep. 116, 131.

[9] See Chapter 2, section I.

[10] See ibid., section II.

[11] See Chapter 2, writers cited at n. 117.

[12] A. Martin, 'Definition of "Investment": Could a Persistent Objector to the Salini Tests be found in ICSID Arbitral Practice?' (2011) 11 *Global Jurist* 1.

[13] Report of the Independent International Fact-Finding Mission on the Conflict in Georgia (IIFFMCG), 30 September 2009, in three volumes.

[14] European Union Council Decision 2008/901/CFSP of 2 December 2008 concerning an independent international fact-finding mission on the conflict in Georgia, Official Journal of the European Union 323/66.

[15] See, generally, J.A. Green and C.P.M. Waters (eds), *Conflict in the Caucasus: Implications for International Legal Order* (Basingstoke, Palgrave Macmillan, 2010).

[16] IIFFMCG report, n. 13, vol. II, 141.

[17] Ibid., 284.

in 2008[18] or the 1999 NATO bombings.[19] Irrespective of their status in law, however, the purported norms in question would be of a *facilitating* nature: a right of secession, a right of humanitarian intervention. It is clear that neither instance represents an example of persistent objection even prima facie. What the IIFFMCG report actually identified were, at best, dubious instances of *estoppel*,[20] not persistent objection at all.

Such fundamental misunderstandings of the persistent objector rule are concerning, but are also fairly unusual. As reflected in the ILC text, there is (at least broad) agreement that for the rule to take effect the objector must *object, persistently* and *consistently*, to an *emerging* norm of custom *before that norm crystallizes* into binding customary international law. However, these oft-referenced criteria are not actually all that well understood. A key aim of this book has been to try to shed some light on these requirements, particularly by focusing on their operation in state practice. It is therefore worth summarizing here the book's main findings concerning the criteria for persistent objection.

It is relatively straightforward to say that only states can be persistent objectors.[21] In terms of what state objection *entails*, this can take a variety of forms. It is important to note that states can, and commonly do, object to the *existence* of the norm in question, rather than to its specific applicability to them, and—as such—may not explicitly invoke the persistent objector rule at all, even while acting as a persistent objector state.[22] This fact is often overlooked by the commentators who have examined the rule, and helps to explain exaggerated claims about the lack of state usage of it.

Objection by way of statement alone will be sufficient for a persistent objector to gain exemption, as will objecting through a combination of both words and deeds.[23] However, it is unlikely that deeds *alone* will be sufficient.[24] Objection must also be openly expressed, so that it is effectively communicated to other states,[25] but, other than that, it can take any one of a number of forms.[26]

If a state wishes to rely on the persistent objector rule, as the rule's name would suggest, it must have objected *persistently*. State practice demonstrates that single or isolated objections will not suffice.[27] While voluntarist theory cannot explain

[18] For discussion, see A. Peters, 'Has the Advisory Opinion's Finding that Kosovo's Declaration of Independence was not Contrary to International Law Set an Unfortunate Precedent?' in M. Milanović and M. Wood (eds), *The Law and Politics of the Kosovo Advisory Opinion* (Oxford, Oxford University Press, 2015), 291. See, generally, *Accordance with International Law of the Unilateral Declaration of Independence in Respect of Kosovo*, advisory opinion, 2010 ICJ Rep 403.

[19] For critical discussion, see, for example, N.S. Rodley and B. Çali, 'Kosovo Revisited: Humanitarian Intervention on the Fault Lines of International Law' (2007) 7 *Human Rights Law Review* 275.

[20] See, generally, D. Bowett, 'Estoppel before International Courts and Tribunals and its Relation to Acquiescence' (1957) 33 *British Yearbook of International Law* 176; and A. D'Amato, *The Concept of Custom in International Law* (New York, Cornell University Press, 1971), 199–215 (focusing on estoppel in relation to customary international law formation and applicability).

[21] See Chapter 3, section I. [22] See ibid., section II. [23] See ibid., section IV.*i*.

[24] See ibid. [25] See ibid., section III. [26] See ibid., section IV.*ii*.

[27] See Chapter 4, particularly at section I.

this requirement of persistence, the criterion is justified by more pragmatic, practical concerns. The need for persistence tests the will of the objector to ensure that the rule is not used frivolously and, at least to an extent, promotes clarity and certainty.[28] Having said this, it is difficult to predict precisely *how* persistent the objector must be. The necessary degree of persistence is context-specific, and various factors (including extra-legal factors) will influence how often any given objector will have to object in relation to any given norm.[29] Dissenting states are thus best served by objecting as often as possible.

As well as objecting persistently, a dissenting state must object *consistently*: indeed, the 'persistent objector rule' should actually be called the 'persistent and consistent objector rule'. Consistency is not the same thing as persistence, in spite of the two criteria often being unhelpfully amalgamated in doctrine.[30] The consistency criterion requires that a state objects with 'absolute consistency', meaning that it at no point explicitly contradicts its dissenting position.[31] An objecting state is also generally expected to object at appropriate instances where the norm being objected to is 'at issue', or where its interests in relation to that norm come into question.[32] If it does not, its silence may well be interpreted as being inconsistent with its stance of objection. Yet a degree of failure to object when one might reasonably have expected such an objection may be acceptable, so long as the dissenter has for the most part objected where the norm has been at issue.[33] States are not expected to object when the norm that they are objecting to is not at issue, apropos of nothing, either.[34] Nor does the consistency criterion require states to also object to other norms that are substantively 'similar' to the norm to which they are objecting.[35]

Dissenting states must object prior to the crystallization of the norm to which they are objecting. There is no subsequent objector rule, despite a small minority of writers advocating this.[36] There are good policy reasons for this timeliness criterion, related to the maximization of stability in the system and limiting exceptionalism,[37] and—unlike the subsequent objector rule—the criterion can be identified in state practice.[38] However, applying the timeliness criterion may sometimes be difficult, given the uncertainties surrounding the point of crystallization, which acts as the 'end date' for effective persistent objection.[39] The criterion also may seem overly demanding for states that were unaware of the emerging norm,[40] or had no interest in it prior to crystallization.[41] Instances of 'accelerated' customary international law formation might also cause difficulties, as there will obviously not be much time for states to object.[42] For new states, the timeliness criterion is not just burdensome, of course: it means that persistent

[28] See ibid., section II, particularly at n. 41–n. 45 and accompanying text.
[29] See ibid., section III. [30] See Chapter 5, n. 48–n. 50 and accompanying text.
[31] See ibid., section III. [32] See ibid., section IV. [33] See ibid.
[34] See ibid. [35] See ibid., section V.
[36] See Chapter 6, particularly writers cited at n. 29. [37] See ibid., section III.
[38] See ibid., section I.*ii*.
[39] See ibid., section IV.*ii*, particularly at n. 146–n. 168 and accompanying text.
[40] See ibid., section V. [41] See ibid., section VI. [42] See ibid., section VII.

objection is entirely impossible (other than in relation to as yet uncrystallized norms).[43] Overall, it is clear that states must pay significant attention as to when they may need to begin objecting, and even the most vigilant state may still find that its objections come too late.

These various requirements for the successful operation of the persistent objector rule are, especially when it is considered that they are *cumulative* requirements, extremely onerous.[44] It is putting it rather mildly to say that 'the standards for the persistent objector doctrine are difficult to meet'.[45] One should keep in mind that much of this difficulty relates to the *uncertainty* of the application of the rule's requirements in practice. For the most part, their operation is context-specific, and their parameters are hazy. However, this is largely a reflection of the uncertain nature of customary international per se rather than a critique that is specific to the persistent objector rule.

Even leaving aside the uncertainty of the rule's criteria, there is no question that they are 'stringent requirements'.[46] It has been noted throughout this book that persistent objection is an exception, and exceptions should be treated narrowly.[47] Providing states with an 'opt-out' from emerging norms of customary international law has its systematic benefits,[48] but there is no reason to make it easy for the objector: the dice are, and *should be*, loaded in favour of the majority. However, states are, at least to an extent, aware of the rules of the game. The criteria for the persistent objector rule's operation may be somewhat uncertain, but states know that their silence will lead to them being bound by norms of customary international law once they crystallize, and that they need to object repeatedly, vociferously, and early to be able to gain exemption.[49] The key question, then, is how much does the state really want to be exempt?

[43] See ibid., section VIII.

[44] See D. Bölükbaşı, *Turkey and Greece: The Aegean Disputes—A Unique Case in International Law* (London, Cavendish, 2004), 217; A.T. Guzman and J. Hsiang, 'Some Ways that Theories on Customary International Law Fail: A Reply to *László* Blutman' (2014) 25 *European Journal of International Law* 553, 557–8; E. Kontorovich, 'Inefficient Customs in International Law' (2006–7) 48 *William and Mary Law Review* 859, 910; D. Murray, 'How International Humanitarian Law Treaties Bind Non-State Armed Groups' (2015) 20 *Journal of Conflict and Security Law* 101, 117; and M. Ragazzi, *The Concept of International Obligations* Erga Omnes (Oxford, Clarendon Press, 1997), 64.

[45] C.A. Bradley and M. Gulati, 'Withdrawing from International Custom' (2010) 120 *Yale Law Journal* 202, 240.

[46] 'Identification of Customary International Law', Statement of the Chairman of the Drafting Committee, Mr Mathias Forteau, 29 July 2015, International Law Commission, Sixty-seventh session, Geneva, 4 May–5 June and 6 July–7 August 2015, 18 (reflecting the discussions in the ILC Drafting Committee); and Report of the International Law Commission, Sixty-seventh session, 4 May–5 June and 6 July–7 August 2015, UN Doc. A/70/10, advance unedited version, 24 August 2015, 36, para. 73 (noting that the Special Rapporteur for the ILC's ongoing work on the 'Identification of customary international law', Sir Michael Wood, stressed during the consideration of the topic at the ILC's Sixty-seventh session that the rule has 'stringent requirements').

[47] See, generally, G. Boas, *Public International Law: Contemporary Principles and Perspectives* (Cheltenham, Edward Elgar, 2012), 94–5.

[48] See Chapter 9, sections V–VIII.

[49] D.W. Greig, 'Reflections on the Role of Consent' (1988–9) 12 *Australian Yearbook of International Law* 125, 136–7.

Not only are the criteria for persistent objection severe, but even if they are complied with, the objecting state may at times find itself bound. For example, it is commonly argued that persistent objection is unavailing in relation to peremptory norms (or, more accurately, that an exemption gained through persistent objection will be overruled by the norm in question acquiring peremptory status).[50] This proposition is actually not as self-evident as many claim, partly because there is so little state practice against which it can be tested: states almost never try to remain exempt from peremptory norms.[51] However, the positions taken by various judicial or arbitral bodies and writers, and the morally compelling arguments concerning the nature of peremptory norms as being inherently all-encompassing, certainly strongly suggest that the majority view is correct.[52] Crucially, no state has been able to maintain exempt status in relation to peremptory norms (at least not indefinitely).[53] It is relatively clear, therefore, that *jus cogens* status trumps persistent objection. However, it is not the case—as some commentators have argued[54]—that states are precluded from persistently objecting to any and all norms that might be considered as being 'fundamental', where such norms are non-peremptory in nature. Practice indicates that states can, for example, persistently object to human rights norms, norms of international humanitarian law, and environmental law norms.[55]

Gaining de jure exemption through persistent objection is a difficult business, given the onerousness of the criteria for the rule's operation. *Maintaining* that exemption, de facto, is also extremely difficult for states, at least in the long term.[56] A range of extra-legal factors commonly contribute to objectors ultimately deciding to give up their exempt status. Such factors include the 'fundamental' nature of the norm being objected to; the 'reciprocal' nature of the norm being objected to; the relative power of the objector; and the degree of isolation of the objector.[57] The persistent objector rule is therefore usually—although not necessarily—a temporary mechanism.

Taking all of these elements of the persistent objector rule together, *Figure 10.1* summarizes its operation.

The difficulties in both gaining and maintaining exemption through persistent objection help to explain why the rule is not often used. States will only employ it as a last resort.[58] Given that its effectiveness as a shield for the dissenter is comparatively

[50] See Chapter 7, particularly sections I and II.

[51] See ibid., n. 73 and accompanying text.

[52] See ibid., section VI.

[53] See J.A. Green, 'Persistent Objector Teflon? Customary International Human Rights Law and the United States in International Adjudicative Proceedings' in J.A. Green and C.P.M. Waters (eds), *Adjudicating International Human Rights: Essays in Honour of Sandy Ghandhi* (Leiden, Brill Nijhoff, 2015), 167, 175.

[54] See Chapter 8, particularly writers cited at n. 8.

[55] See ibid., section I.*ii*.

[56] See ibid., section II.

[57] See ibid., sections II.*ii* and II.*iii*.

[58] See M. Byers, *Custom, Power and the Power of Rules: International Relations and Customary International Law* (Cambridge, Cambridge University Press, 1999), 180; T.L. Stein, 'The Approach of the Different Drummer: The Principle of the Persistent Objector in International Law' (1985) 26 *Harvard International Law Journal* 457, 468; and P. Weil, 'Le droit international en quête de son identité—Cours général de droit international public' (1992-VI) 237 *Recueil des cours* 9, 195.

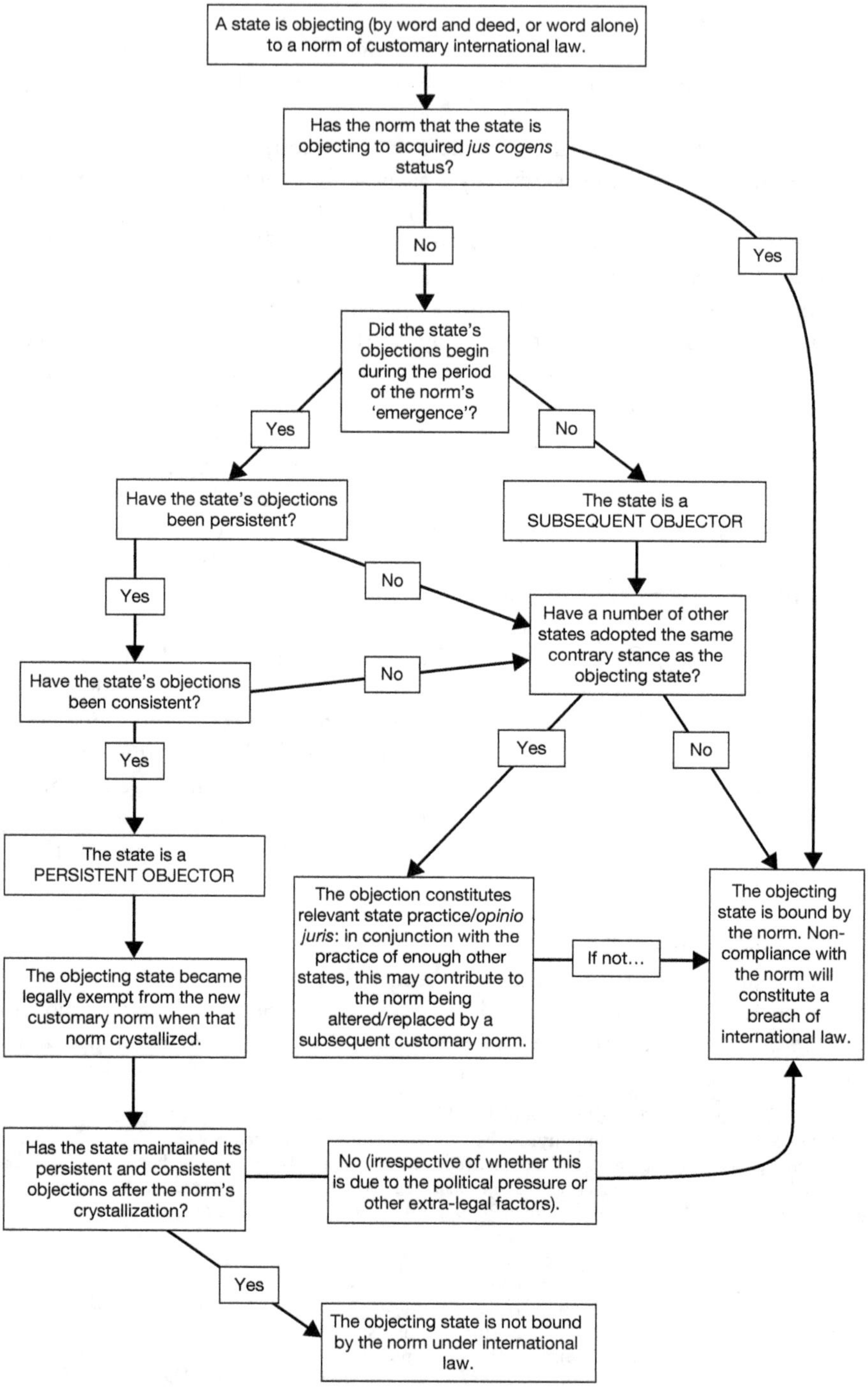

Figure 10.1 An overview of the process of persistent objection

limited, one might question whether the rule has any real value in the international legal system. The traditional rationale for the persistent objector rule is, of course, a voluntarist one: the rule is usually said to protect state autonomy in relation to the binding force of customary international law.[59] However, the voluntarist account of international law cannot explain the binding force of custom, at least not *in toto*.[60] If voluntarism is not the basis of international legal obligation and the rule is limited in its ability to protect states from the binding force of customary international law, then perhaps it does not have any value as a secondary rule of international law.

To an extent, it is true that the persistent objector rule can be seen as being theoretically incoherent. However, its theoretical coherence is nowhere near as important as its practical effects. It has been argued in this book that the rule certainly has value.[61] This value can be found, not in terms of the rule's ability to underpin sweeping theoretical claims, but in its functional benefits. The rule can be of benefit to the objecting state—certainly in the short term and, occasionally, beyond—but it can *also* reduce the costs that state opposition to an emerging norm would entail for the wider international legal system.

At times, of course, the role of the rule is precisely what voluntarists say it is: it provides a legal exemption for the dissenting state. However, beyond this, the rule can have a number of less obvious benefits.[62] These benefits all stem from the fact that, at its core, the persistent objector rule is about *balance*.[63] The rule seeks to minimize, and spread, the costs—to both the objector state and the international community—of situations where an emerging norm is strongly opposed by one (or a handful) of states. In so doing, the rule has value in facilitating the operation of customary international law in practice.

The persistent objector rule is rife with contradictions. The rule is ubiquitous in the literature, and yet is rarely used by states. It allows states to gain exemption from the binding force of new norms of customary international law (thus serving a voluntarist purpose), but it clearly does not provide such exemption in all circumstances (and has various criteria and elements that cannot be reconciled with its purported voluntarist rationale). The rule's criteria are generally considered to be well known, and yet actually what these criteria mean or how they work is not well known at all. There is a degree of disconnect between the de jure exemptions that states can gain and the de facto maintenance of those exemptions. The rule is seen in equal measure, depending on who one might ask, as utterly fundamental to the structural integrity of international law or as a largely worthless footnote to it. Indeed, while persistent objection is accepted by most scholars as a relatively benign secondary rule of the international legal system, a notable minority view it as an extremely dangerous concept. Overall, it is difficult to dispute D'Amato's contention that the persistent objector rule is a 'curious notion'.[64]

[59] See Chapter 9, particularly at section I.*i*.

[60] See ibid., section I.*iii*, particularly at n. 64–n. 83 and accompanying text.

[61] See, in particular, ibid.

[62] See ibid., sections VI and VII.

[63] See ibid., particularly at section V.*ii*.

[64] A. D'Amato, 'Human Rights as Part of Customary International Law: A Plea for Change of Paradigms' (1995–6) 25 *Georgia Journal of International and Comparative Law* 47, 63.

Although there already exists a significant amount of literature touching on, and academic discussion of, the persistent objector rule, this book is one of the first detailed examinations of it. The author has sought to assess the rule's existence, contours, limitations, and value in depth. Given the ubiquity of the rule in scholarship since the mid-twentieth century, such an examination was long overdue. Even the detailed investigation undertaken herein, however, only gets us so far. This is because, like customary international law itself, the persistent objector rule has inherent uncertainties at its core. One cannot provide precise answers to at least some of the key questions concerning how the rule functions—for example, exactly *how* persistent and consistent the objection needs to be—because, in relation to these sorts of questions, there *are no* precise answers to give.

It is hoped, however, that this book has helped to increase the general understanding of this often misunderstood rule. The discussions of the persistent objector rule in recent years have become notably polarized: the rule has been both cherished and vilified. Such polarization is unhelpful and inaccurate. It is notable that writers taking either a positive or a negative perspective of the rule have generally done so without significant study of it, particularly in relation to the actual usage of the rule by states. This book has therefore aimed, at least where possible, to go beyond the scholarly examinations of the rule and to focus on persistent objection 'in action' in state practice.

The importance of the persistent objector rule must not be overstated. It is hard to envisage the system of customary international law coming crashing down if the persistent objector rule were, tomorrow, entirely abandoned by states. The rule represents an exception to the usual operation of customary international law in more ways than one, and many of its benefits are transitory. Equally, claims that the rule should be dismissed should, themselves, be dismissed. The rule is used by states, and there are various valuable consequences of that usage for the international legal system. This means that, one way or another, '[i]t is ... impossible to ignore the "persistent objector" doctrine'.[65]

[65] A. Pellet, 'The Normative Dilemma: Will and Consent in International Law-Making' (1988–9) 12 *Australian Yearbook of International Law* 22, 37.

Bibliography

BOOKS

Abass, A., *Complete International Law: Text, Cases, and Materials* (Oxford, Oxford University Press, 2nd edn, 2014)

Acer, Y., *The Aegean Maritime Disputes and International Law* (Aldershot, Ashgate, 2003)

Anaya, S.J., *Indigenous Peoples in International Law* (Oxford, Oxford University Press, 2nd edn, 1996)

Anderson, D., *Modern Law of the Sea: Selected Essays* (Leiden, Martinus Nijhoff, 2008)

Arajärvi, N., *The Changing Nature of Customary International Law: Methods of Interpreting the Concept of Custom in International Criminal Tribunals* (Abingdon, Routledge, 2014)

Aust, A., *Modern Treaty Law and Practice* (Cambridge, Cambridge University Press, 3rd edn, 2013)

Baderin, M.A., and Ssenyonjo, M. (eds), *International Human Rights Law: Six Decades after the UDHR and Beyond* (Farnham, Ashgate, 2010)

Bankas, E.K., *The State Immunity Controversy in International Law: Private Suits against Sovereign States in Domestic Courts* (Berlin, Springer, 2005)

Bederman, D.J., *Custom as a Source of Law* (Cambridge, Cambridge University Press, 2010)

Bedjaoui, M. (ed.), *International Law: Achievements and Prospects* (Paris, UNESCO, 1991)

Besson, S., and Tasioulas, J. (eds), *The Philosophy of International Law* (Oxford, Oxford University Press, 2010)

Black-Branch, J.L., and Fleck, D. (eds), *Nuclear Non-Proliferation Law* (The Hague, T.M.C. Asser Press, 2014)

Boas, G., *Public International Law: Contemporary Principles and Perspectives* (Cheltenham, Edward Elgar, 2012)

Bölükbaşı, D., *Turkey and Greece: The Aegean Disputes—A Unique Case in International Law* (London, Cavendish, 2004)

Bos, M., *A Methodology of International Law* (Amsterdam, TMC Asser, 1984)

Boyle, A., and Chinkin, C., *The Making of International Law* (Oxford, Oxford University Press, 2007)

Bradley, C.A. (ed.), *Custom's Future: International Law in a Changing World* (Cambridge, Cambridge University Press, forthcoming)

Breitenmoser, S., Ehrenzeller, B., and Sassoli, M. (eds), *Human Rights, Democracy and the Rule of Law:* Liber Amicorum *Luzius Wildhaber* (Zürich, Nomos, 2007)

Brownlie, I., *Principles of Public International Law* (Oxford, Oxford University Press, 1st edn, 1966)

Brownlie, I., *The Rule of Law in International Affairs: International Law at the Fiftieth Anniversary of the United Nations* (Dordrecht, Martinus Nijhoff, 1998)

Brunnée, J., and Toope, S.J., *Legitimacy and Legality in International Law: An Interactional Account* (Cambridge, Cambridge University Press, 2010)

Byers, M., *Custom, Power and the Power of Rules: International Relations and Customary International Law* (Cambridge, Cambridge University Press, 1999)

Carranza, M.E., *South Asian Security and International Nuclear Order: Creating a Robust Indo-Pakistani Nuclear Arms Control Regime* (Farnham, Ashgate, 2009)

Cassese, A., *International Law in a Divided World* (Oxford, Clarendon Press, 1986)

Cassese, A., *International Law* (Oxford, Oxford University Press, 2nd edn, 2005)
Cassese, A., *Five Masters of International Law* (Hart, Oxford, 2011)
Cassese, A., and Weiler, J.H.H. (eds), *Change and Stability in International Law-Making* (Berlin, de Gruyter, 1988)
Chappell, L., Chesterman, J., and Hill, L., *The Politics of Human Rights in Australia* (Cambridge, Cambridge University Press, 2009)
Chigara, B., *Legitimacy Deficit in Custom: A Deconstructionist Critique* (Aldershot, Ashgate, 2001)
Clapham, A., *Brierly's Law of Nations* (Oxford, Oxford University Press, 7th edn, 2012)
Craven, M., *The Decolonization of International Law: State Succession and the Law of Treaties* (Oxford, Oxford University Press, 2008)
Crawford, J., *The Creation of States in International Law* (Oxford, Oxford University Press, 2nd edn, 2006)
Crawford, J., *Brownlie's Principles of Public International Law* (Oxford, Oxford University Press, 8th edn, 2012)
Crawford, J., and Koskenniemi, M. (eds), *The Cambridge Companion to International Law* (Cambridge, Cambridge University Press, 2012)
Cryer, R., *Prosecuting International Crimes: Selectivity and the International Criminal Law Regime* (Cambridge, Cambridge University Press, 2005)
Curci, J., *The Protection of Biodiversity and Traditional Knowledge in International Law of Intellectual Property* (Cambridge, Cambridge University Press, 2010)
D'Amato, A., *The Concept of Custom in International Law* (New York, Cornell University Press, 1971)
d'Aspremont, J., *Formalism and the Sources of International Law: A Theory of the Ascertainment of Legal Rules* (Oxford, Oxford University Press, 2011, paperback edn, 2013)
Danilenko, G.M., *Law-Making in the International Community* (Dordrecht, Martinus Nijhoff, 1993)
de Vattel, E., *The Law of Nations, or Principles of the Law of Nature Applied to the Conduct and Affairs of Nations and Sovereigns* (J. Chitty (ed.), Philadelphia, T & J.W. Johnson, 6th American edn, 1844 (1758))
de Visscher, C., *Theory and Reality in Public International Law* (P.E. Corbett (trans.), Princeton, Princeton University Press, revised edn, 1968)
de Vitoria, F., *Political Writings* (A. Pagden and J. Lawrence (eds), Cambridge, Cambridge University Press, 1991 (a collection of sixteenth century writings))
Dekker, I.F., and Post, H.H.G. (eds), *The Gulf War of 1980–1988: The Iran–Iraq War in International Perspective* (Dordrecht, Martinus Nijhoff, 1992)
Dixon, M., McCorquodale, R., and Williams, S., *Cases and Materials on International Law* (Oxford, Oxford University Press, 5th edn, 2011)
Dixon, M., *Textbook on International Law* (Oxford, Oxford University Press, 7th edn, 2013)
Dugard, J., *International Law: A South African Perspective* (Cape Town, Juta & Co., 3rd edn, 2008)
Dunoff, J.L., Ratner, S.R., and Wippman, D., *International Law: Norms, Actors, Process: A Problem-Orientated Approach* (New York, Aspen, 2nd edn, 2006)
Elias, O., and Lim, C.L., *The Paradox of Consensualism in International Law* (The Hague, Kluwer Law International, 1998)
Evans, M.D. (ed.), *International Law* (Oxford, Oxford University Press, 4th edn, 2014)
Falk, R.A., and Black, C.E. (eds), *The Future of the International Legal Order, vol. I: Trends and Patterns* (Princeton, Princeton University Press, 1969)

Fastenrath, U., Geiger, R., Khan, D-E., Paulus, A., von Schorlemer, S., and Vedder, C. (eds), *From Bilateralism to Community Interest: Essays in Honour of Judge Bruno Simma* (Oxford, Oxford University Press, 2011)

Ferrari, S. (ed.), *Routledge Handbook of Law and Religion* (Abingdon, Routledge, 2015)

Finnis, J., *Natural Law and Natural Rights* (Oxford, Clarendon Press, 2nd edn, 2011)

Franck, T.M., *The Power of Legitimacy among Nations* (Oxford, Oxford University Press, 1990)

Freestone, D., and Ijlstra, T. (eds), *The North Sea: Basic Legal Documents on Regional Environmental Cooperation* (Dordrecht, Martinus Nijhoff, 1991)

Frey, K., *India's Nuclear Bomb and National Security* (New York, Routledge, 2006)

Fuller, L.L., *The Morality of Law* (Fredericksburg, Yale University Press, revised edition, 1969)

Goldsmith, J.L., and Posner, E.A., *The Limits of International Law* (Oxford, Oxford University Press, 2006)

Grant, T.D., *The Recognition of States: Law and Practice in Debate and Evolution* (Westport, Praeger, 1999)

Green, J.A., and Waters, C.P.M. (eds), *Conflict in the Caucasus: Implications for International Legal Order* (Basingstoke, Palgrave Macmillan, 2010)

Green, J.A., and Waters, C.P.M. (eds), *Adjudicating International Human Rights: Essays in Honour of Sandy Ghandhi* (Leiden, Brill Nijhoff, 2015)

Grotius, H., *On the Law of War and Peace* (*De Juri Belli Ac Pacis Libri Tres*) (A.C. Campbell (trans.), Ontario, Batoche, 2001 (1625))

Guzman, A.T., *How International Law Works: A Rational Choice Theory* (Oxford, Oxford University Press, 2008)

Hackworth, G.H., *Digest of International Law* (Washington, Government Printing Office, 1942)

Hannikainen, L., *Peremptory Norms (*Jus Cogens*) in International Law: Historical Development, Criteria, Present Status* (Helsinki, Lakimiesliiton Kusannus, 1988)

Harris, D., *Cases and Materials on International Law* (London, Sweet and Maxwell, 7th edn, 2010)

Hart, H.L.A., *The Concept of Law* (Oxford, Oxford University Press, 2nd edn, 1994)

Henckaerts, J-M., and Doswald-Beck, L. (eds), *Customary International Humanitarian Law*, International Committee of the Red Cross (ICRC) Study (Cambridge, Cambridge University Press, 2005)

Henkin, L., *International Law: Politics and Values* (Leiden, Brill, 1995)

Higgins, R., *Problems and Process: International Law and How We Use It* (Oxford, Clarendon Press, 1994)

Hillier, T., *Sourcebook on Public International Law* (London, Cavendish Publishing, 1998)

Iqbal, K., *The Right to Development in International Law: The Case of Pakistan* (Abingdon, Routledge, 2010)

Jennings, R., and Watts, A., *Oppenheim's International Law* (New York, Longman, 9th edn, 1996)

Kaczorowska, A., *Public International Law* (Abingdon, Routledge, 4th edn, 2010)

Kammerhofer, J., and d'Aspremont, J. (eds), *International Legal Positivism in a Post-Modern World* (Cambridge, Cambridge University Press, 2014)

Kelsen, H., *General Theory of Law and State* (A. Wedberg (trans.), New York, Russell and Russell, 1945)

Kelsen, H., *Principles of International Law* (R.W. Tucker (ed. and revns.), New York, Holt, Rinehart and Winston, 2nd edn, 1966)

Klabbers, J., *International Law* (Cambridge, Cambridge University Press, 2013)

Koskenniemi, M., *From Apology to Utopia: The Structure of International Legal Argument* (Cambridge, Cambridge University Press, reissue, 2005)

Lauterpacht, E. (ed.), *International Law, Being the Collected Papers of Hersch Lauterpacht* (Cambridge, Cambridge University Press, 1970)

Lauterpacht, H., *The Function of Law in the International Community* (Oxford, Oxford University Press, 1933)

Lauterpacht, H., *The Development of International Law by the International Court* (London, Stevens & Sons, revised edn, 1958)

Le droit international au service de la paix, de la justice et du développement: Mélanges offerts à Michel Virally (Paris, Pédone, 1991)

Lepard, B.D., *Customary International Law: A New Theory with Practical Applications* (Cambridge, Cambridge University Press, 2010)

Lowe, A.V., *International Law* (Oxford, Oxford University Press, 2007)

McBeth, A., *International Economic Actors and Human Rights* (Abingdon, Routledge, 2010)

MacDonald, R. St. J. (ed.), *Essays in Honour of Wang Tieya* (Dordrecht, Martinus Nijhoff Publishers, 1994)

Malanczuk, P., *Akehurst's Modern Introduction to International Law* (New York, Routledge, 7th edn, 1997)

Mansell, W., and Openshaw, K., *International Law: A Critical Introduction* (Oxford, Hart Publishing, 2013)

Marmor, A. (ed.), *The Routledge Companion to the Philosophy of Law* (Abingdon, Routledge, 2012)

Martin, F.F., *The Constitution as Treaty: The International Legal Constructionalist Approach to the U.S. Constitution* (Cambridge, Cambridge University Press, 2007)

Martinez, L., *Communication Satellites: Power and Politics in Space* (Deadham, Artech House, 1985)

Meron, T. (ed.), *Human Rights in International Law: Legal Policy and Issues, vol. I* (Oxford, Clarendon Press, 1984)

Milanović, M., and Wood, M. (eds), *The Law and Politics of the Kosovo Advisory Opinion* (Oxford, Oxford University Press, 2015)

Miller, R.A., and Bratspies, R.M. (eds), *Progress in International Law* (Leiden, Martinus Nijhoff, 2008)

Mills, A., *The Confluence of Public and Private International Law: Justice, Pluralism, and Subsidiarity in the International Constitutional Ordering of Private Law* (Cambridge, Cambridge University Press, 2009)

Molenaar, E.J., *Coastal State Jurisdiction over Vessel-Source Pollution* (The Hague, Kluwer, 1998)

O'Connell, D.P., *International Law, vol. I* (London, Stevens & Sons, 2nd edn, 1970)

O'Connell, D.P., *The International Law of the Sea* (Oxford, Clarendon Press, 1982)

Oduntan, G., *Sovereignty and Jurisdiction in Airspace and Outer Space: Legal Criteria for Spatial Delimitation* (Abingdon, Routledge, 2012)

Oppenheim, L., *International Law: A Treatise, vol. I* (R.F. Roxburgh, ed., New Jersey, The Lawbook Exchange, 3rd edn, 2005, originally published 1920)

Orakhelashvili, A., *Peremptory Norms in International Law* (Oxford, Oxford University Press, 2006)

Ørebech, P., Bosselman, F., Bjarup, J., Callies, D., Chanock, M., and Petersen, H. (eds), *The Role of Customary Law in Sustainable Development* (Cambridge, Cambridge University Press, 2005)

Orford, A., and Hoffman, F. (eds), *The Oxford Handbook of the Theory of International Law* (Oxford, Oxford University Press, forthcoming 2016)

Parson, L.S., *Management of Marine Fisheries in Canada* (Ottawa, National Research Council of Canada, 1993)

Pauwelyn, J., Wessel, R.A., and Wouters, J. (eds), *Informal International Lawmaking* (Oxford, Oxford University Press, 2012)

Pentassuglia, G., *La rilevanza dell'obiezione persitente nel diritto internazionale* (Bari, Laterza, 1996)

Perreau-Saussine, A., and Murphy, J.B. (eds), *The Nature of Customary Law: Legal, Historical and Philosophical Perspectives* (Cambridge, Cambridge University Press, 2007)

Philips, R.W., *FAO: Its Origins, Formation and Evolution, 1945–1981* (Rome, Food and Agriculture Organization of the United Nations, 1981)

Quince, C., *The Persistent Objector and Customary International Law* (Denver, Outskirts Press, 2010)

Ragazzi, M., *The Concept of International Obligations* Erga Omnes (Oxford, Oxford University Press, 1997)

Rai, A.K., *India's Nuclear Policy after Pokhran II* (New Delhi, Dorling Kindersley, 2009)

Realizing the Right to Development: Essays in Commemoration of 25 Years of the United Nations Declaration on the Right to Development, United Nations, Office of the High Commissioner for Human Rights (2013) HR/PUB/12/4, United Nations, Sales No. E.12.XIV.1

Reus-Smit, C. (ed.), *The Politics of International Law* (Cambridge, Cambridge University Press, 2004)

Roach, J.A., and Smith, R.W., *Excessive Maritime Claims* (Leiden, Martinus Nijhoff, 3rd edn, 2012)

Rosenne, S., *Provisional Measures in International Law: The International Court of Justice and the International Tribunal for the Law of the Sea* (Oxford, Oxford University Press, 2004)

Rousseau, C., *Droit international public, vol. I: introduction et sources* (Paris, Sirey, 1970)

Rousseau, C., and Bastid, S. (eds), *Mélanges offerts à Charles Rousseau: la communauté international* (Paris, Pedone, 1974)

Rozakis, C.L., *The Concept of* Jus Cogens *in the Law of Treaties* (Amsterdam, North Holland Publishing Company, 1976)

Sage-Fuller, B., *The Precautionary Principle in Marine Environment Law: With Special Reference to High Risk Vessels* (Abingdon, Routledge, 2013)

Sands, P., and Peel, J., *Principles of International Environmental Law* (Cambridge, Cambridge University Press, 3rd edn, 2012)

Scanlon, J., Cassar, A., and Nemes, N., *Water as a Human Right?* (Gland, IUCN, 2004)

Scharf, M.P., *Customary International Law in Times of Fundamental Change: Recognizing Grotian Moments* (Cambridge, Cambridge University Press, reissue, 2013)

Schermers, H.G., and Blokker, N.M., *International Institutional Law: Unity within Diversity* (Leiden, Martinus Nijhoff, 5th edn, 2011)

Schiele, S., *Evolution of International Environmental Regimes: The Case of Climate Change* (Cambridge, Cambridge University Press, 2014)

Shaw, M.N., *International Law* (Cambridge, Cambridge University Press, 7th edn, 2014)

Shihata, I.F.I., *The Power of the International Court to Determine Its Own Jurisdiction* (The Hague, Martinus Nijhoff, 1965)

Soohoo, C., Albisa, C., and Davis, M.F. (eds), *Bringing Human Rights Home* (Westport, Praeger, 2008)

Sørensen, M. (ed.), *Manual of Public International Law* (London, Macmillan, 1968)

Spencer, J.H., *Ethiopia at Bay: A Personal Account of the Haile Selassie Years* (Los Angeles, Tsehai, 2006)

Stürchler, N., *The Threat of Force in International Law* (Cambridge, Cambridge University Press, 2007)

Tavernier, P., and Henckaerts, J-M. (eds), *Droit international humanitaire coutumier: enjeux et défis contemporains* (Brussels, Bruylant, 2008)

Taylor, P.M., *Freedom of Religion: UN and European Human Rights Law and Practice* (Cambridge, Cambridge University Press, 2005)

Thirlway, H., *International Customary Law and Codification* (Leiden, A.W. Sijthoff, 1972)

Thirlway, H., *The Sources of International Law* (Oxford, Oxford University Press, 2014)

Tremblay, L.B., *The Rule of Law, Justice and Interpretation* (Bakerville, McGill-Queen's University Press, 1997)

Trouwborst, A., *Precautionary Rights and Duties of States* (Leiden, Martinus Nijhoff, 2006)

Tucker, R.W., *The Law of War and Neutrality at Sea* (Washington, US Government Print Office, 1955)

Tunkin, G.I., *Theory of International Law* (W.E. Butler (trans.), George Allen and Unwin, 1974)

van Bynkershoek, C., *De Foro Legatorum Liber Singularis: A Monograph on the Jurisdiction over Ambassadors in both Civil and Criminal Cases* (G.J. Laing (trans.), Oxford, Clarendon Press, 1946 (1721/2nd edn, 1744))

Verzijl, J.H.W., *International Law in Historical Perspective* (Utrecht, A.W. Sijthoff, 1968)

Villiger, M.E., *Customary International Law and Treaties: A Manual on the Theory and Practice of the Interrelation of Sources* (The Hague, Kluwer, 2nd edn, 1997)

Vohrah, L.C., Pocar, F., Featherstone, Y., Fourmy, O., Graham, C., Hocking, J., and Robson, N. (eds), *Man's Inhumanity to Man: Essays on International Law in Honour of Antonio Cassese* (The Hague, Kluwer Law International, 2003)

von Martens, G.F., *A Compendium of the Law of Nations, Founded on the Treaties and Customs of the Modern Nations of Europe* (W. Cobbett (trans.), London, Cobbett and Morgan, 1802 (1788))

Wellens, K., *Negotiations in the Case Law of the International Court of Justice: A Functional Analysis* (Farnham, Ashgate, 2014)

Wilmshurst, E., and Breau, S. (eds), *Perspectives on the ICRC Study on Customary International Humanitarian Law* (Cambridge University Press, Cambridge, 2007)

Winkler, I.T., *The Human Right to Water: Significance, Legal Status and Implications for Water Allocation* (Oxford, Hart, 2012)

Wolfke, K., *Custom in Present International Law* (Dordrecht, Martinus Nijhoff, 2nd edn, 1993)

Wolff, C., *Jus Gentium Methodo Scientifica Petractatum* (J. Brown Scott (ed.), J.H. Drake (trans.), Oxford, Clarendon Press, 1934)

Wolfrum, R. (ed.), *Max Planck Encyclopaedia of Public International Law* (Oxford, Oxford University Press, 2012)

BOOK CHAPTERS

Babcock, S., 'Human Rights Advocacy in United States Capital Cases' in C. Soohoo, C. Albisa, and M.F. Davis (eds), *Bringing Human Rights Home, vol. 3* (Westport, Praeger, 2008), 91

Baderin, M.A., 'Islamic Law and the Implementation of International Human Rights Law: A Case Study of the International Covenant of Civil and Political Rights' in M.A. Baderin and M. Ssenyonjo (eds), *International Human Rights Law: Six Decades After the UDHR and Beyond* (Farnham, Ashgate, 2010), 337

Besson S., 'Theorizing the Sources of International Law' in S. Besson and J. Tasioulas (eds), *The Philosophy of International Law* (Oxford, Oxford University Press, 2010), 164

Bethlehem, D., 'The Methodological Framework of the Study' in E. Wilmshurst and S. Breau (eds), *Perspectives on the ICRC Study on Customary International Humanitarian Law* (Cambridge University Press, Cambridge, 2007), 3

Breau, S., 'Civilian Casualties and Nuclear Weapons: The Application of the Rule of Distinction' in J.L. Black-Branch and D. Fleck (eds), *Nuclear Non-Proliferation Law, vol. I* (The Hague, T.M.C. Asser Press, 2014), 105

Brownlie, I., 'The Decisions of Political Organs of the United Nations and the Rule of Law' in R. St. J. MacDonald (ed.), *Essays in Honour of Wang Tieya* (Dordrecht, Martinus Nijhoff Publishers, 1994), 91

Buchanan, A., 'The Legitimacy of International Law' in S. Besson and J. Tasioulas (eds), *The Philosophy of International Law* (Oxford, Oxford University Press, 2010), 79

Capps, P., 'International Legal Positivism and Modern Natural Law' in J. Kammerhofer and J. d'Aspremont (eds), *International Legal Positivism in a Post-Modern World* (Cambridge, Cambridge University Press, 2014), 213

Cassese, A., 'General Round Up' in A. Cassese and J.H.H. Weiler (eds), *Change and Stability in International Law-Making* (Berlin, de Gruyter, 1988), 165

Charlesworth, H., 'Law-Making and Sources' in J. Crawford and M. Koskenniemi (eds), *The Cambridge Companion to International Law* (Cambridge, Cambridge University Press, 2012), 187

Christakis, T., 'Human Rights from a Neo-Voluntarist Perspective' in J. Kammerhofer and J. d'Aspremont (eds), *International Legal Positivism in a Post-Modern World* (Cambridge, Cambridge University Press, 2014), 421

Christiano, T., 'The Legitimacy of International Institutions' in A. Marmor (ed.), *The Routledge Companion to the Philosophy of Law* (Abingdon, Routledge, 2012), 380

Collins, R., 'Classical Legal Positivism in International Law Revisited' in J. Kammerhofer and J. d'Aspremont (eds), *International Legal Positivism in a Post-Modern World* (Cambridge, Cambridge University Press, 2014), 23

Condorelli, L., 'Custom' in M. Bedjaoui (ed.), *International Law: Achievements and Prospects* (Paris, UNESCO, 1991), 179

Crawford, J., 'Sovereignty as a Legal Value' in J. Crawford and M. Koskenniemi (eds), *The Cambridge Companion to International Law* (Cambridge, Cambridge University Press, 2012), 117

David, E., 'L'objecteur persistent, une règle persistent?' in P. Tavernier and J-M. Henckaerts (eds), *Droit international humanitaire coutumier: enjeux et défis contemporains* (Brussels, Bruylant, 2008), 89

Dupuy, P-M., 'A propos de l'opposabilité de la coutume générale: enquête brève sur "l'objecteur persistant"' in *Le droit international au service de la paix, de la justice et du développement: Mélanges offerts à Michel Virally* (Paris, Pédone, 1991), 257

Dupuy, R-J., 'Coutume sage et coutume sauvage' in C. Rousseau and S. Bastid (eds), *Mélanges offerts à Charles Rousseau: la communauté international* (Paris, Pedone, 1974), 75

Elias, O., 'Persistent Objector' in R. Wolfrum (ed.), *Max Planck Encyclopaedia of Public International Law, vol. VIII* (Oxford, Oxford University Press, 2012), 280

Falk, R.A., 'The Interplay of Westphalia and Charter Conceptions of the International Legal Order' in R.A. Falk and C.E. Black (eds), *The Future of the International Legal Order, vol. I: Trends and Patterns* (Princeton, Princeton University Press, 1969), 32

Gioia, A., and Ronzitti, N., 'The Law of Neutrality: Third States' Commercial Rights and Duties' in I.F. Dekker and H.H.G. Post (eds), *The Gulf War of 1980–1988: The Iran–Iraq War in International Perspective* (Dordrecht, Martinus Nijhoff, 1992), 221

Glennon, M.J., 'Peremptory Nonsense' in S. Breitenmoser, B. Ehrenzeller, and M. Sassòli (eds), *Human Rights, Democracy and the Rule of Law: Liber Amicorum Luzius Wildhaber* (Zürich, Nomos, 2007), 1265

Green, J.A., 'Persistent Objector Teflon? Customary International Human Rights Law and the United States in International Adjudicative Proceedings' in J.A. Green and C.P.M. Waters (eds), *Adjudicating International Human Rights: Essays in Honour of Sandy Ghandhi* (Leiden, Brill Nijhoff, 2015), 167

Guzman, A.T., and Meyer, T.L., 'Customary International Law in the 21st Century' in R.A. Miller and R.M. Bratspies (eds), *Progress in International Law* (Leiden, Martinus Nijhoff, 2008), 197

Kammerhofer, J., and d'Aspremont, J., 'Introduction' in J. Kammerhofer and J. d'Aspremont (eds), *International Legal Positivism in a Post-Modern World* (Cambridge, Cambridge University Press, 2014), 1

Kunanayakam, T., 'The Declaration on the Right to Development in the Context of United Nations Standard-Setting' in *Realizing the Right to Development: Essays in Commemoration of 25 Years of the United Nations Declaration on the Right to Development*, United Nations, Office of the High Commissioner for Human Rights (2013) HR/PUB/12/4, United Nations, Sales No. E.12.XIV.1, 1

Lefkowitz, D., 'The Sources of International Law: Some Philosophical Reflections' in S. Besson and J. Tasioulas (eds), *The Philosophy of International Law* (Oxford, Oxford University Press, 2010), 187

Lillich, R.B., 'Civil Rights' in T. Meron (ed.), *Human Rights in International Law: Legal Policy and Issues, vol. I* (Oxford, Clarendon Press, 1984), 115

Nieto-Navia, R., 'International Peremptory Norms (*Jus Cogens*) and International Humanitarian Law' in L.C. Vohrah, F. Pocar, Y. Featherstone, O. Fourmy, C. Graham, J. Hocking, and N. Robson (eds), *Man's Inhumanity to Man: Essays on International Law in Honour of Antonio Cassese* (The Hague, Kluwer Law International, 2003), 595

Ørebech, P., and Chanock, M., 'Towards Sustainability: The Basis in International Law' in P. Ørebech, F. Bosselman, J. Bjarup, D. Callies, M. Chanock, and H. Petersen (eds), *The Role of Customary Law in Sustainable Development* (Cambridge, Cambridge University Press, 2005), 384

Pauwelyn, J., 'Fragmentation of International Law' in R. Wolfrum (ed.), *Max Planck Encyclopaedia of Public International Law, vol. IV* (Oxford, Oxford University Press, 2012), 211

Pauwelyn, J., 'Is It International Law or Not, and Does It Even Matter?' in J. Pauwelyn, R.A. Wessel and J. Wouters (eds), *Informal International Lawmaking* (Oxford, Oxford University Press, 2012), 125

Peters, A., 'Has the Advisory Opinion's Finding that Kosovo's Declaration of Independence was not Contrary to International Law Set an Unfortunate Precedent?' in M. Milanović and M. Wood (eds), *The Law and Politics of the Kosovo Advisory Opinion* (Oxford, Oxford University Press, 2015), 291

Postema, G.J., 'Custom in International Law: A Normative Practice Account' in A. Perreau-Saussine and J.B. Murphy (eds), *The Nature of Customary Law: Legal, Historical and Philosophical Perspectives* (Cambridge, Cambridge University Press, 2007), 279

Price, R., 'Emerging Customary Norms and Anti-Personnel Landmines' in C. Reus-Smit (ed.), *The Politics of International Law* (Cambridge, Cambridge University Press, 2004), 106

Saheed, A., 'Limitations on Religious Freedom in Islam' in S. Ferrari (ed.), *Routledge Handbook of Law and Religion* (Abingdon, Routledge, 2015), 369

Shelton, D., 'International Law and "Relative Normativity"' in M. Evans (ed.), *International Law* (Oxford, Oxford University Press, 4th edn, 2014), 137

Somek, A., 'Beyond Kelsen and Hart' in J. Kammerhofer and J. d'Aspremont (eds), *International Legal Positivism in a Post-Modern World* (Cambridge, Cambridge University Press, 2014), 151

Stein, T., during the discussion appearing in A. Cassese and J H.H. Weiler (eds), *Change and Stability in International Law-Making* (Berlin, de Gruyter, 1988), 13

Tasioulas, J., 'Customary International Law and the Quest for Global Justice' in A. Perreau-Saussine and J.B. Murphy (eds), *The Nature of Customary Law: Legal, Historical and Philosophical Perspectives* (Cambridge, Cambridge University Press, 2007), 307

Tasioulas, J., 'Custom, *Jus Cogens*, and Human Rights' in C.A. Bradley (ed.), *Custom's Future: International Law in a Changing World* (Cambridge, Cambridge University Press, forthcoming), pre-publication version, *Social Science Research Network*, 20 March 2015, http://papers.ssrn.com/sol3/papers.cfm?abstract_id=2581763

Thirlway, H., 'The Sources of International Law' in M.D. Evans (ed.), *International Law* (Oxford, Oxford University Press, 4th edn, 2014), 91

Tomuschat, C., 'Universal Periodic Review: a New System of International Law with Specific Ground Rules?' in U. Fastenrath, R. Geiger, D-E. Khan, A. Paulus, S. von Schorlemer, and C. Vedder (eds), *From Bilateralism to Community Interest: Essays in Honour of Judge Bruno Simma* (Oxford, Oxford University Press, 2011), 609

Treves, T., 'Customary International Law' in R. Wolfrum (ed.), *Max Planck Encyclopaedia of Public International Law, vol. II* (Oxford, Oxford University Press, 2012), 937

Virally, M., 'The Sources of International Law' in M. Sørensen (ed.), *Manual of Public International Law* (London, Macmillan, 1968), 116

Wood, M., 'Teachings of the Most Highly Qualified Publicists (Art. 38(1) ICJ Statute)' in R. Wolfrum (ed.), *Max Planck Encyclopaedia of Public International Law, vol. IX* (Oxford, Oxford University Press, 2012), 783

Wood, M., and Sender, O., 'State Practice' in R. Wolfrum (ed.), *Max Planck Encyclopaedia of Public International Law*, online edition (Oxford University Press), 2014 update, http://opil.ouplaw.com/view/10.1093/law:epil/9780199231690/law-9780199231690-e1107?rskey=N2neCH&result=3&prd=EPIL

JOURNAL ARTICLES

Abasheikh, O., 'The Validity of the Persistent Offender Rule in International Law' (2004) 9 *Coventry Law Journal* 40

Abbott, K.W., and Snidal, D., 'Hard and Soft Law in International Governance' (2000) 54 *International Organization* 421

Abi-Saab, G., 'Cours général de droit international public' (1987-VII) 207 *Recueil des cours* 9

Ago, R., 'Positive Law and International Law' (1957) 51 *American Journal of International Law* 691

Akehurst, M., 'Custom as a Source of International Law' (1974–1975) 47 *British Yearbook of International Law* 1

Andorno, R., 'The Precautionary Principle: A New Legal Standard for a Technological Age' (2004) 1 *Journal of International Biotechnology Law* 11

Atkins, D.R., 'Customary International Humanitarian Law and Multinational Military Operations in Malaysia' (2007) 16 *Pacific Rim Law and Policy Journal* 79

Baker, R.B., 'Customary International Law in the 21st Century: Old Challenges and New Debates' (2010) 21 *European Journal of International Law* 173

Barnidge, Jr, R.P., 'Questioning the Legitimacy of *Jus Cogens* in the Global Legal Order' (2008) 38 *Israel Yearbook of Human Rights* 199

Barsalou, O., 'La doctrine de l'objecteur persistant en droit international public' (2006) 19 *Revue québécoise de droit international* 1

Basdevant, J., 'Règles générales du droit de la paix' (1936-IV) 58 *Recueil des cours* 471

Bederman, D.J., 'Acquiescence, Objection and the Death of Customary International Law' (2010) 21 *Duke Journal of Comparative and International Law* 31

Beier, J.M., 'Siting Indiscriminacy: India and the Global Movement to Ban Landmines' (2002) 8 *Global Governance* 305

Biblowit, C.E., 'Deep Seabed Mining: The United States and the United Nations Convention on the Law of the Sea' (1984) 58 *St. John's Law Review* 267

Bishop, W.W., 'General Course on Public International Law' (1965-II) 115 *Recueil des cours* 151

Blutman, L., 'Conceptual Confusion and Methodological Deficiencies: Some Ways that Theories on Customary International Law Fail' (2014) 25 *European Journal of International Law* 529

Boguslavsky, M.M., 'Foreign State Immunity: Soviet Doctrine and Practice' (1979) 10 *Netherlands Yearbook of International Law* 167

Bos, M., 'The Identification of Custom in International Law' (1982) 25 *German Yearbook of International Law* 9

Bowett, D., 'Estoppel before International Courts and Tribunals and Its Relation to Acquiescence' (1957) 33 *British Yearbook of International Law* 176

Bradley, C.A., 'The Juvenile Death Penalty' (2002–2003) 52 *Duke Law Journal* 485

Bradley, C.A., and Gulati, M., 'Withdrawing from International Custom' (2010) 120 *Yale Law Journal* 202

Bradley, C.A., and Gulati, M., 'Customary International Law and Withdrawal Rights in an Age of Treaties' (2010) 21 *Duke Journal of International and Comparative Law* 1

Breau, S.C., 'The Constitutionalization of the International Legal Order' (2008) 21 *Leiden Journal of International Law* 545

Breau, S., 'State Practice, Customary Humanitarian Law and Civilian Casualties of Armed Conflict' (2014) 1 *State Practice and International Law Journal* 45

Brewster, R. 'Withdrawing from Custom: Choosing between Default Rules' (2010) 21 *Duke Journal of Comparative and International Law* 47

Brown, C., 'Ethics of Coexistence: The International Theory of Terry Nardin' (1988) 14 *Review of International Studies* 213

Brownlie, I., 'International Law at the Fiftieth Anniversary of the United Nations—General Course on Public International Law' (1995) 255 *Recueil des cours* 11

Bulto, T.S., 'The Emergence of the Human Right to Water in International Human Rights Law: Invention or Discovery?' (2011) 12 *Melbourne Journal of International Law* 290

Bunn, I.D., 'The Right to Development: Implications for International Economic Law' (2000) 15 *American University International Law Review* 1425

Byers, M., 'Conceptualising the Relationship Between *Jus Cogens* and *Erga Omnes* Rules' (1997) 66 *Nordic Journal of International Law* 211

Cameron, J., and Abouchar, J., 'The Precautionary Principle: A Fundamental Principle of Law and Policy for the Protection of the Global Environment' (1991) 14 *Boston College International and Comparative Law Review* 1

Cannizarro, E., 'Il mutamento dei paradigmi della scienza giuridica internazionalista e la dottrina Italiana' (2014) 1/14 *Annuario di diritto comparator e di studi legislative* 77

Carrillo-Salcedo, J-A., 'Droit international et souveraineté des États—Cours général de droit international public' (1996) 257 *Recueil des cours* 35

Charlesworth, H.C.M., 'Customary International Law and the *Nicaragua* Case' (1984–1985) 11 *Australian Yearbook of International Law* 1

Charlesworth, H., and Chinkin, C., 'The Gender of *Jus Cogens*' (1993) 15 *Human Rights Quarterly* 15

Charney, J.I., 'The Persistent Objector Rule and the Development of Customary International Law' (1985) 56 *British Yearbook of International Law* 1

Charney, J.I., 'Universal International Law' (1993) 87 *American Journal of International Law* 529

Cheng, B., 'United Nations Resolutions on Outer Space: "Instant" International Customary Law?' (1965) 5 *Indian Journal of International Law* 23

Chigara, B., 'European/Southern African Development Community (SADC) States' Bilateral Investment Agreements (BITS) for the Promotion of Foreign Investments vs Post-Apartheid SADC Economic and Social Reconstruction Policy' (2011) 10 *Journal of International Trade Law and Policy* 213

Chilton, A.S., 'A Reply to Dworkin's New Theory of International Law' (2013) 80 *The University of Chicago Law Review Dialogue* 105

Christenson, G.A., '*Jus Cogens*: Guarding Interests Fundamental to International Society' (1987–1988) 28 *Virginia Journal of International Law* 585

Coleman, N., '*Non-Refoulement* Revised Renewed Review of the Status of the Principle of *Non-Refoulement* as Customary International Law' (2003) 5 *European Journal of Migration and Law* 23

Colson, D.A., 'How Persistent Must the Persistent Objector Be?' (1986) 61 *Washington Law Review* 957

Conforti, B., 'Cours général de droit international public' (1988-V) 212 *Recueil des cours* 13

Corten, O., 'The Russian Intervention in the Ukrainian Crisis: Was *Jus Contra Bellum* "Confirmed Rather than Weakened"?' (2015) 2 *Journal on the Use of Force and International Law* 17

Crawford, J., 'Chance, Order, Change: The Course of International Law—General Course on Public International Law' (2013) 365 *Recueil des cours* 9

Czapliński, W., 'Sources of International Law in the *Nicaragua* Case' (1989) 38 *International and Comparative Law Quarterly* 151

D'Amato, A., 'The Concept of Special Custom in International Law' (1969) 63 *American Journal of International Law* 211

D'Amato, A., and Chopra, S.K., 'Whales: Their Emerging Right to Life' (1991) 85 *American Journal of International Law* 21

D'Amato, A., 'Human Rights as Part of Customary International Law: A Plea for Change of Paradigms' (1995–1996) 25 *Georgia Journal of International and Comparative Law* 47

D'Amato, A., 'Groundwork for International Law' (2014) 108 *American Journal of International Law* 650

d'Aspremont, J., and Lieflānder, T., 'Consolidating the Statehood of Kosovo: Leaving the International Law Narrative Behind' (2013) 1 *Journal of European and International Affairs* 8

Danchin, P.G., 'U.S. Unilateralism and the International Protection of Religious Freedom: The Multilateral Alternative' (2002–2003) 41 *Columbia Journal of Transnational Law* 33

Danilenko, G.M., 'International *Jus Cogens*: Issues of Law-Making' (1991) 2 *European Journal of International Law* 42

Danner, A.M., 'When Courts Make Law: How the International Criminal Tribunals Recast the Laws of War' (2006) 49 *Vanderbilt Law Review* 1

de Visscher, C., 'La codification du droit international' (1925) 6 *Recueil des cours* 328

de Visscher, P., 'Cours général de droit international public' (1972) 136 *Recueil des cours* 1

de Wet, E., 'The Prohibition of Torture as an International Norm of *Jus Cogens* and Its Implications for National and Customary Law' (2004) 15 *European Journal of International Law* 97

Degan, V-D., 'Consolidation of Legal Principles on Maritime Delimitation: Implications for the Dispute between Slovenia and Croatia in the North Adriatic' (2007) 6 *Chinese Journal of International Law* 601

Deleaux, O., 'Les positions françaises à la Conférence de Vienne sur le droit des traités' (1969) 15 *Annuaire français de droit international* 7

Dominguez-Redondo, E., 'The Universal Periodic Review—Is There Life beyond Naming and Shaming in Human Rights Implementation?' (2012) 24 *New Zealand Law Review* 673

Donnelly, J., 'Human Rights as Natural Rights' (1982) 4 *Human Rights Quarterly* 391

Dumberry, P., 'The Last Citadel! Can a State Claim the Status of Persistent Objector to Prevent the Application of a Rule of Customary International Law in Investor-State Arbitration?' (2010) 23 *Leiden Journal of International Law* 379

Dumberry, P., 'Incoherent and Ineffective: The Concept of Persistent Objector Revisited' (2010) 59 *International and Comparative Law Quarterly* 779

Dworkin, R., 'A New Philosophy for International Law' (2013) 41 *Philosophy and Public Affairs* 2

Eden, P., 'The Role of the Rome Statute in the Criminalization of Apartheid' (2014) *12 Journal of International Criminal Justice* 171

Efevwerhan, D.I., 'Kosovo's Chances of UN Membership: A Prognosis' (2012) 4 *Goettingen Journal of International Law* 93

Elias, O., 'Some Remarks on the Persistent Objector Rule in Customary International Law' (1991) 6 *Denning Law Journal* 37

Elias, O., 'The Nature of the Subjective Element in Customary International Law' (1995) 44 *International and Comparative Law Quarterly* 501

Estreicher, S., 'A Post-Formation Withdrawal from Customary International Law? Some Cautionary Notes' (2010) 21 *Duke Journal of Comparative and International Law* 57

Fastenrath, U., 'Relative Normativity in International Law' (1993) 4 *European Journal of International Law* 305

Fidler, D.P., 'Challenging the Classical Concept of Custom: Perspectives on the Future of Customary International Law' (1996) 39 *German Yearbook of International Law* 198

Fidler, D.P., 'Revolt Against or From Within the West? TWAIL, the Developing World, and the Future Direction of International Law' (2003) 2 *Chinese Journal of International Law* 29

Fitzmaurice, G., 'The Law and Procedure of the International Court of Justice, 1951–54: General Principles and Sources of Law' (1953) 30 *British Yearbook of International Law* 1

Fon, V., and Parisi, F., 'Stability and Change in International Customary Law' (2004) 21 *American Law and Economics Association Annual Meetings* 1

Ford, C.A., 'Adjudicating *Jus Cogens*' (1994–1995) 13 *Wisconsin International Law Journal* 145

François, J-P-A., 'Règles générales du droit de la paix' (1938) 66 *Recueil des cours* 1

French, D., 'Finding Autonomy in International Environmental Law and Governance' (2009) 21 *Journal of Environmental Law* 255

Fry, J.D., 'Pluralism, Religion, and the Moral Fairness of International Law' (2014) 3 *Oxford Journal of Law and Religion* 393

Gaja, G., 'Positivism and Dualism in Dionisio Anzilotti' (1992) 2 *European Journal of International Law* 123

Gaja, G., 'The Protection of General Interests in the International Community—General Course on Public International Law' (2012) 364 *Recueil des cours* 13

Georgiades, E.A., 'The Imia Islets: A Beginning to the Maritime Delimitation of the Aegean Sea Dispute' (2011) 17 *Ocean and Coastal Law Journal* 103

Ghandhi, S., 'The Human Rights Committee and Interim Measures of Relief' (2007) 13 *Canterbury Law Review* 203

Ghose, A., 'Negotiating the CTBT: India's Security Concerns and Nuclear Disarmament' (1997) 51 *Journal of International Affairs* 239

Gillia, B.A., 'Female Genital Mutilation: A Form of Persecution' (1997) 27 *New Mexico Law Review* 579

Glennon, M.J., 'Raising *The Paquete Habana*: Is Violation of Customary International Law by the Executive Unconstitutional?' (1985–1986) 80 *Northwestern University Law Review* 321

Goldie, L.F.E., 'Customary International Law and Deep Seabed Mining' (1978–1979) 6 *Syracuse Journal of International Law and Commerce* 173

Goodman, R., 'Human Rights Treaties, Invalid Reservations, and State Consent' (2002) 96 *American Journal of International Law* 531

Green, J.A., 'Docking the *Caroline*: Understanding the Relevance of the Formula in Contemporary Customary International Law Concerning Self-Defence' (2006) 14 *Cardozo Journal of International and Comparative Law* 429

Green, J.A., 'India and a Customary Comprehensive Nuclear Test-Ban: Persistent Objection, Peremptory Norms and the 123 Agreement' (2011) 51 *Indian Journal of International Law* 3

Green, J.A., 'Questioning the Peremptory Status of the Prohibition of the Use of Force' (2011) 32 *Michigan Journal of International Law* 215

Green, J.A., 'India's Status as a Nuclear Weapons Power under Customary International Law' (2012) 24 *National Law School of India Review* 125

Green, J.A., 'Book Review: M.P. Scharf, *Customary International Law in Times of Fundamental Change: Recognizing Grotian Moments*' (2014) 63 *International and Comparative Law Quarterly* 781

Greig, D.W., 'Reflections on the Role of Consent' (1988–1989) 12 *Australian Yearbook of International Law* 125

Guldahl, C.G., 'The Role of Persistent Objection in International Humanitarian Law' (2008) 77 *Nordic Journal of international Law* 51

Gullett, W., 'Environmental Protection and the "Precautionary Principle": A Response to Scientific Uncertainty in Environmental Management' (1997) 14 *Environmental and Planning Law Journal* 52

Gunn, B.L., 'Overcoming Obstacles to Implementing the UN Declaration on the Rights of Indigenous Peoples in Canada' (2013) 31 *Windsor Yearbook of Access to Justice* 147

Guzman, A.T., 'Saving Customary International Law' (2005–2006) 27 *Michigan Journal of International Law* 115

Guzman, A.T., and Hsiang, J., 'Some Ways that Theories on Customary International Law Fail: A Reply to László Blutman' (2014) 25 *European Journal of International Law* 553

Hall, S., 'The Persistent Spectre: Natural Law, International Order and the Limits of Legal Positivism' (2001) 12 *European Journal of International Law* 269

Hampson, F.J., 'The Relationship between International Humanitarian Law and Human Rights Law from the Perspective of a Human Rights Treaty Body' (2008) 90 *International Review of the Red Cross* 549

Hansen, M.A., 'Preventing the Emasculation of Warfare: Halting the Expansion of Human Rights Law into Armed Conflict' (2007) 194 *Military Law Review* 1

Hart, H.L.A., 'Positivism and the Separation of Law and Morals' (1958) 71 *Harvard Law Review* 593

Hartmann, J.F., '"Unusual" Punishment: The Domestic Effect of International Norms Restricting the Application of the Death Penalty' (1983) 52 *University of Cincinnati Law Review* 655

Helfer, L.R., 'Exiting Treaties' (2005) 91 *Virginia Law Review* 1579

Helfer, L.R., 'Exiting Custom: Analogies to Treaty Withdrawals' (2010) 21 *Duke Journal of Comparative and International Law* 65

Helmersen, S.T., 'The Prohibition of the Use of Force as *Jus Cogens*: Explaining Apparent Derogations' (2014) 61 *Netherlands International Law Review* 167

Henkin, L., 'International Law: Politics, Values and Functions' (1989-IV) 216 *Recueil des cours* 11

Henkin, L., 'Human Rights and State "Sovereignty"' (1996) 25 *Georgia Journal of International Law* 31

Hill, S.F., 'Necessity Defense and the Emerging Arbitral Conflict in Its Application to the US-Argentina Bilateral Investment Treaty' (2007) 13 *Law and Business Review of the Americas* 547

Hoelck Thjoernelund, M.C., 'State of Necessity as an Exemption from State Responsibility for Investments' (2009) 13 *Max Planck Yearbook of United Nations Law* 423

Hulsroj, P., '*Jus Cogens* and Disarmament' (2006) 46 *Indian Journal of International Law* 1

Jia, B.B., 'The Relations between Treaties and Custom' (2010) 9 *Chinese Journal of International Law* 81

Johnson, D.H.N., 'Acquisitive Prescription in International Law' (1950) 22 *British Yearbook of International Law* 332

Jones, O., 'Customary *Non-Refoulement* of Refugees and Automatic Incorporation into the Common Law: A Hong Kong Perspective' (2009) 58 *International and Comparative Law Quarterly* 443

Jones, O., 'Let the Mainland Speak: A Positivist Take on the Congo Case' (2011) 41 *Hong Kong Law Journal* 177

Joyner, D.H., '*Jus ad Bellum* in the Age of WMD Proliferation' (2008) 40 *George Washington International Law Review* 233

Kammerhofer, J., 'Uncertainty in the Formal Sources of International Law: Customary International Law and Some of Its Problems' (2004) 15 *European Journal of International Law* 523

Kelly, C.R., 'Law of the Sea: The Jurisdictional Dispute over Highly Migratory Species of Tuna' (1987–1988) 26 *Columbia Journal of Transnational Law* 475

Kelly, J.P., 'The Twilight of Customary International Law' (1999–2000) 40 *Virginia Journal of International Law* 449

Kingsbury, B., 'Sovereignty and Inequality' (1998) 9 *European Journal of International Law* 599

Kingsbury, B., 'The Concept of "Law" in Global Administrative Law' (2009) 20 *European Journal of International Law* 23

Kirschner, A.J., 'The Human Right to Water and Sanitation' (2011) 15 *Max Planck Yearbook of United Nations Law* 445

Kolb, R., 'Selected Problems in the Theory of Customary International Law' (2003) 50 *Netherlands International Law Review* 119

Kontorovich, E., 'Inefficient Customs in International Law' (2006–2007) 48 *William and Mary Law Review* 859

Koplow, D.A., 'ASAT-isfaction: Customary International Law and the Regulation of Anti-Satellite Weapons' (2008–2009) 30 *Michigan Journal of International Law* 1187

Kornicker Uhlmann, E.M., 'State Community Interests, *Jus Cogens* and Protection of the Global Environment: Developing Criteria for Peremptory Norms' (1998) 11 *Georgetown International Environmental Law Review* 101

Koskenniemi, M., 'The Politics of International Law' (1990) 1 *European Journal of International Law* 4

Kritsiotis, D., 'On the Possibilities Of and For Persistent Objection' (2010) 21 *Duke Journal of Comparative and International Law* 121

Kwakwa, E., 'Belligerent Reprisals in the Law of Armed Conflict' (1990–1991) 27 *Stanford Journal of International Law* 49

Langille, B., 'It's "Instant Custom": How the Bush Doctrine became Law after the Terrorist Attacks of September 11, 2001' (2003) 26 *Boston College International and Comparative Law Review* 145

Lau, H., 'Rethinking the Persistent Objector Doctrine in International Human Rights Law' (2005-2006) 6 *Chicago Journal of International Law* 496

Lauterpacht, H., 'Sovereignty over Submarine Areas' (1950) 27 *British Yearbook of International Law* 377

Lim, C.L., and Elias, O., 'Withdrawing from Custom and the Paradox of Consensualism in International Law' (2010) 21 *Duke Journal of Comparative and International Law* 143

Linderfalk, U., 'The Effect of *Jus Cogens* Norms: Whoever Opened Pandora's Box, Did You Ever Think about the Consequences?' (2007) 18 *European Journal of International Law* 853

Lisson, D., 'Defining "National Group" in the Genocide Convention: A Case Study of Timor-Leste' (2007–2008) 60 *Stanford Law Review* 1459

Lobo de Souza, I.M., 'The Role of Consent in the Customary Process' (1995) 44 *International and Comparative Law Quarterly* 521

Loschin, L., 'The Persistent Objector Rule and Customary Human Rights Law: A Proposed Analytical Framework' (1996) 2 *University of California Davis Journal of International Law and Policy* 147

Lowe, A.V., 'Do General Rules of International Law Exist?' (1983) 9 *Review of International Studies* 207

McClane, J.B., 'How Late in the Emergence of a Norm of Customary International Law May a Persistent Objector Object?' (1989) 13 *International Law Students Association Journal of International Law* 1

Macdonald, R. St. J., 'Fundamental Norms in Contemporary International Law' (1987) 25 *Canadian Yearbook of International Law* 115

MacGibbon, I., 'Some Observations on the Part of Protest in International Law' (1953) 30 *British Yearbook of International Law* 293

MacGibbon, I., 'Customary International Law and Acquiescence' (1957) 33 *British Yearbook of International Law* 115

McGinnis, J.O., 'The Comparative Disadvantage of Customary International Law' (2006) 30 *Harvard Journal of Law and Public Policy* 7

Magallona, M.M., 'The Concept of *Jus Cogens* in the Vienna Convention on the Law of the Treaties' (1976) 51 *Philippine Law Journal* 521

Martin, A., 'Definition of "Investment": Could a Persistent Objector to the Salini Tests Be Found in ICSID Arbitral Practice?' (2011) 11 *Global Jurist* 1

Meijers, H., 'How is International Law Made? The Stages of Growth of International Law and the Use of Customary Rules' (1978) 9 *Netherlands Yearbook of International Law* 3

Mence, D., 'The Cetacean Right to Life' (2015) 11 *International Journal of Law in Context* 17

Mendelson, M.H., 'Compensation for Expropriation: The Case Law' (1985) 79 *American Journal of International Law* 414

Mendelson, M.H., 'The Formation of Customary International Law' (1998) 272 *Recueil des cours* 155

Meron, T., 'International Law in the Age of Human Rights' (2013) 301 *Recueil des cours* 13

Moeckli, D., 'Of Minarets and Foreign Criminals: Swiss Direct Democracy and Human Rights' (2011) 11 *Human Rights Law Review* 774

Müllerson, R., 'On the Nature and Scope of Customary International Law' (1997) 2 *Austrian Review of International and European Law* 341

Murray, D., 'How International Humanitarian Law Treaties Bind Non-State Armed Groups' (2015) 20 *Journal of Conflict and Security Law* 101

Narula, S., 'The Right to Food: Holding Global Actors Accountable under International Law' (2005–2006) 44 *Columbia Journal of Transnational Law* 691

Nollkaemper, A., 'Wither *Aut Dedere*? The Obligation to Extradite or Prosecute after the ICJ's Judgment in *Belgium v Senegal*' (2013) 4 *Journal of International Dispute Settlement* 501

Norman, G., and Trachtman, J.P., 'The Customary International Law Game' (2005) 99 *American Journal of International Law* 541

Norton, P.M., 'A Law of the Future or a Law of the Past? Modern Tribunals and the International Law of Expropriation' (1991) 85 *American Journal of International Law* 474

Noyes, J.E., 'U.S. Policy and the United Nations Convention on the Law of the Sea' (2007) 39 *George Washington International Law Review* 621

Ochoa, C., 'Disintegrating Customary International Law: Reactions to "Withdrawing from International Custom"' (2010) 21 *Duke Journal of Comparative and International Law* 157

O'Connell, M.E., 'Affirming the Ban on Harsh Interrogation' (2005) 66 *Ohio State Law Journal* 1231

Oda, S., and Owada, H. (eds), 'Annual Review of Japanese Practice in International Law XV (1976–77)' (1985) 28 *Japanese Annual of International Law* 59

Oduntan, G., 'The Never Ending Dispute: Legal Theories on the Spatial Demarcation Boundary Plane between Airspace and Outer Space' (2003) 1 *Hertfordshire Law Journal* 64

Oellers-Frahm, K., 'Buchrezension: Pentassuglia, Gaetano, *La rilevanza dell'obiezione persitente nel diritto internazionale*' (1997) 57 *Zeitschrift für ausländisches öffentliches Recht und Völkerrecht* 1180

Oxman, B.H., 'The Third United Nations Conference on the Law of the Sea: The Tenth Session (1981)' (1982) 76 *American Journal of International Law* 1

Padmanabhan, V.M., 'The Human Rights Justification for Consent' (2013) 35 *University of Pennsylvania Journal of International Law* 1

Parker, K., and Neylon, L.B., '*Jus Cogens*: Compelling the Law of Human Rights' (1988–1989) 12 *Hastings Journal of International and Comparative Law* 411

Parks, W.H., 'The ICRC Customary Law Study: A Preliminary Assessment' (2005) 99 *American Society of International Law Proceedings* 208

Paust, J.P., 'Customary International Law: Its Nature, Sources and Status as Law of the United Nations' (1990) 12 *Michigan Journal of International Law* 59

Paust, J.P., 'The Complex Nature, Sources and Evidences of Customary Human Rights' (1995–1996) 25 *Georgia Journal of International and Comparative Law* 147

Pellet, A., 'The Normative Dilemma: Will and Consent in International Law-Making' (1988–1989) 12 *Australian Yearbook of International Law* 22

Pellet, A., 'Comments in Response to Christine Chinkin and in Defense of *Jus Cogens* as the Best Bastion against the Excesses of Fragmentation' (2006) 11 *Finnish Yearbook of International Law* 83

Pomson, O., and Horowitz, Y., 'Humanitarian Intervention and the Clean Hands Doctrine in International Law' (2015) 48 *Israel Law Review* 219

Ramsden, M., 'Using International Law in Hong Kong Courts: An Examination of Non-Refoulement Litigation' (2013) 42 *Common Law World Review* 351

Rauber, J., 'On Communitarian and Constitutional Approaches to International Law' (2013) 26 *Leiden Journal of International Law* 201

Redgwell, C.J., 'Reservations to Treaties and Human Rights Committee General Comment No 24 (52)' (1997) 46 *International and Comparative Law Quarterly* 390

Reisman, W.M., 'The Cult of Custom in the Late 20th Century' (1987) 17 *California Western International Law Journal* 133

Remy, C.E., 'U.S. Territorial Sea Extension: Jurisdiction and International Environmental Protection' (1992) 16 *Fordham International Law Journal* 1208

Roberts, A., and Sivakumaran, S., 'Lawmaking by Nonstate Actors: Engaging Armed Groups in the Creation of International Humanitarian Law' (2012) 37 *Yale Journal of International Law* 107

Roberts, A., 'Traditional and Modern Approaches to Customary International Law: A Reconciliation' (2001) 95 *American Journal of International Law* 757

Roberts, A., 'Who Killed Article 38(1)(b)? A Reply to Bradley & Gulati' (2010) 21 *Duke Journal of Comparative and International Law* 173

Rodley, N.S., and Çali, B., 'Kosovo Revisited: Humanitarian Intervention on the Fault Lines of International Law' (2007) 7 *Human Rights Law Review* 275

Schachter, O., 'International Law in Theory and Practice' (1982) 178 *Recueil des cours* 9

Schiffman, H.S., 'The Protection of Whales in International Law: A Perspective for the Next Century' (1996–1997) 22 *Brooklyn Journal of International Law* 303

Sengupta, A., 'On the Theory and Practice of the Right to Development' (2002) 24 *Human Rights Quarterly* 837

Shelton, D., 'Application of Death Penalty on Juveniles in the US' (1987) 8 *Human Rights Law Journal* 355

Shelton, D., 'Normative Hierarchy in International Law' (2006) 100 *American Journal of International Law* 291

Sherman Jr , E.F., 'The U.S. Death Penalty Reservation to the International Covenant on Civil and Political Rights: Exposing the Limitations of the Flexible System Governing Treaty Formation' (1994) 29 *Texas International Law Journal* 69

Simma, B., and Alston, P., 'The Sources of Human Rights Law: Custom, *Jus Cogens*, and General Principles' (1988–1989) 12 *Australian Yearbook of International Law* 82

Simma, B., and Paulus, A.L., 'The Responsibility of Individuals for Human Rights Abuses in Internal Conflicts: A Positivist View' (1999) 93 *American Journal of International Law* 302

Sirinskiene, A., 'The Status of Precautionary Principle: Moving towards a Rule of Customary Law' (2009) 4 *Jurisprudence* 349

Slaughter, A-M., 'International Law in a World of Liberal States' (1995) 6 *European Journal of International Law* 503

Söllner, S., 'The "Breakthrough" of the Right to Food: The Meaning of General Comment No. 12 and the Voluntary Guidelines for the Interpretation of the Human Right to Food' (2007) 11 *Max Planck Yearbook of United Nations Law* 391

Sørensen, M., 'Principes de droit international public' (1960-I) 101 *Recueil des cours* 1

Sørensen, M., 'Theory and Reality in International Law' (1981) 75 *American Society of International Law Proceedings* 140

Stein, T.L., 'The Approach of the Different Drummer: The Principle of the Persistent Objector in International Law' (1985) 26 *Harvard International Law Journal* 457

Steinfeld, A., 'Nuclear Objections: The Persistent Objector and the Legality of the Use of Nuclear Weapons' (1996) 62 *Brooklyn Law Review* 1635

Stephan, P.B., 'Disaggregating Customary International Law' 21 *Duke Journal of Comparative and International Law* 191

Stern, B., 'Custom at the Heart of International Law' (2001) 11 *Duke Journal of Comparative and International Law* 89 (M. Byers and A. Denise (trans.), originally published as 'La coutume au cœur du droit international: Quelques réflexions' *in Le droit international: unité et diversité: Mélanges offerts à Paul Reuter* (Paris, Pedone, 1981), 479)

Strupp, K., 'Les règles générales du droit de la paix' (1934) 47 *Recueil des cours* 258

Swaine, E.T., 'Bespoke Custom' (2010) 21 *Duke Journal of Comparative and International Law* 207

Szappanyos, M., 'Obligatory or Voluntary?—Participation in the UPR' (2012) 150 *Studia Iuridica Auctoritate Universitatis Pecs Publicata* 273

Tabassi, L., 'The Nuclear Test Ban: *Lex Lata* or *de Lege Ferenda*?' (2009) 14 *Journal of Conflict and Security Law* 309

Tamanaha, B.Z., 'A Socio-Legal Methodology for the Internal/External Distinction: Jurisprudential Implications' (2006) 75 *Fordham Law Review* 1255

Thielbörger, P., 'Re-Conceptualizing the Human Right to Water: A Pledge for a Hybrid Approach' (2015) 15 *Human Rights Law Review* 225

Tomuschat, C., 'Obligations Arising for States Without or Against Their Will' (1993) 241 *Recueil des cours* 195

Trachtman, J.P., 'Persistent Objectors, Cooperation, and the Utility of Customary International Law' (2010) 21 *Duke Journal of Comparative and International Law* 221

Triggs, G., 'The Public International Lawyer and the Practice of International Law' (2005) 24 *Australian Yearbook of International Law* 201

Vagts, D.F., 'International Relations Looks at Customary International Law: A Traditionalist's Defence' (2004) 15 *European Journal of International Law* 1031

van Steenberghe, R., 'The Obligation to Extradite or Prosecute' (2011) 9 *Journal of International Criminal Justice* 1089

Verdier, P-H., and Voeten, E., 'Precedent, Compliance, and Change in Customary International Law: An Explanatory Theory' (2014) 108 *American Journal of International Law* 389

Wable, K.M., 'The US–India Strategic Nuclear Partnership: A Debilitating Blow to the Non-Proliferation Regime' (2007–2008) 33 *Brooklyn Journal of International Law* 719

Waldock, H., 'General Course on Public International Law' (1962) 106 *Recueil des cours* 1

Walker, G.K., 'Professionals' Definitions and States' Interpretative Declarations (Understandings, Statements, or Declarations) for the 1982 Law of the Sea Convention' (2007) 21 *Emory International Law Review* 461

Walker, W., 'International Nuclear Relations after the Indian and Pakistani Test Explosions' (1998) 74 *International Affairs* 505

Weil, P., 'Le droit international en quête de son identité—Cours général de droit international public' (1992-VI) 237 *Recueil des cours* 9

Weil, P., 'Towards Relative Normativity in International Law?' (1983) 77 *American Journal of International Law* 413

Weiler, J.H.H., 'Editorial' (2013) 24 *European Journal of International Law* 1

Weissbrodt, D., 'Execution of Juvenile Offenders by the United States Violates International Human Rights Law' (1988) 3 *American University Journal of International Law and Policy* 339

Yee, S., 'Report on the ILC Project on "Identification of Customary International Law"' (Report by the Special Rapporteur of the Asian-African Legal Consultative Organisation (AALCO) Informal Expert Group on Customary International Law) (2015) 14 *Chinese Journal of International Law* 375

Xanthaki, A., 'Indigenous Rights in International Law Over The Last 10 Years and Future Developments' (2009) 10 *Melbourne Journal of International Law* 27

ONLINE PUBLICATIONS

Barnidge, Jr, R.P., 'Submission to Iraq Inquiry in Response to Solicitation from International Lawyers', 31 August 2010, https://www.academia.edu/430208/Submission_to_Iraq_Inquiry_in_Response_to_Solicitation_from_International_Lawyers

Barnidge, Jr, R.P., 'Between Legal Positivism and Natural Law: Idolising Law and Obfuscating Politics in International Law and the Chilcot Iraq Inquiry' (2011), work in progress, http://www.eisa-net.org/be-bruga/eisa/files/events/stockholm/Between%20Legal%20Positivism%20and%20Natural%20Law%20for%20SGIR%202010.pdf (referenced with the permission of the author)

Benesch, S., McGrory, G., Rodriguez, C., and Sloane, R., 'International Customary Law and Antipersonnel Landmines: Emergence of a New Customary Norm' (1999), Allard K. Lowenstein International Human Rights Clinic, Yale Law School, Landmine Monitor, http://lm.icbl.org/index.php/publications/display?url=lm/1999/appendices/custom_law.html

Chalecki, E.L., 'Science before the Law: American Exceptionalism in the Kyoto Protocol and the Development of a Global Norm of Environmental Compliance' (2007) *Selected Works*, http://works.bepress.com/cgi/viewcontent.cgi?article=1000&context=elizabeth_chalecki

Collins, A., 'Agreeing to Disagree? (Or Bolivia and the Confusing Consensus Conundrum Part II)' (2011) tck, http://adoptanegotiator.org/agreeing-to-disagree-or-bolivia-and-the-confusing-consensus-conundrum-part-ii/

D'Amato, A., 'International Soft Law, Hard Law, and Coherence' Northwestern Public Law and Legal Theory Series, No. 08-01, 1 March 2008, available on the *Social Science Research Network*, http://papers.ssrn.com/sol3/papers.cfm?abstract_id=1103915

Deloso, R.B., 'The Precautionary Principle: Relevance in International Law and Climate Change' (2005), unpublished Masters thesis, Lund University, http://www.lumes.lu.se/database/alumni/04.05/theses/rabbi_deloso.pdf

Dumberry, P., 'Can a State Claim the Status of "Persistent Objector" in Investor-State Arbitration?' 13 July 2009, *Kluwer Arbitration Blog*, http://kluwerarbitrationblog.com/blog/2009/07/13/can-a-state-claim-the-status-of-%E2%80%9Cpersistent-objector%E2%80%9D-in-investor-state-arbitration/

Ingman, F., 'Persistent Objector—The Demise of a Hero?' (2008), unpublished Masters thesis, Lund University, http://lup.lub.lu.se/luur/download?func=downloadFile&recordOId=1558532&fileOId=1564685

Kirchmeier, F., 'The Right to Development—Where Do We Stand? State of the Debate on the Right to Development' (2006) *Friedrich-Ebert-Stiftuung*, Dialogue on Globalisation, Occasional Papers No. 23, http://www.fes-globalization.org/publications/FESOccPapers23.pdf

Mendelson, M., comments made at 'The Law of Armed Conflict: Problems and Prospects' conference to mark the publication of the ICRC Study on 'Customary International Humanitarian Law', Chatham House, 18 April 2005, http://www.blackstonechambers.com/news/publications/law_of_armed_conflic.html

Messer, E., and Cohen, M.J., 'US Approaches to Food and Nutrition Rights, 1976–2008', (2009) *Hunger Notes*, http://www.worldhunger.org/articles/08/hrf/messer.htm

Papanicolopulu, I., '*Mauritius v. United Kingdom*: Submission of the Dispute on the Marine Protected Area around the Chagos Archipelago to Arbitration', *EJIL:Talk!*, 11 February 2011, http://www.ejiltalk.org/mauritius-v-united-kingdom-submission-of-the-dispute-on-the-marine-protected-area-around-the-chagos-archipelago-to-arbitration/

Petersen, N., 'The Role of Consent and Uncertainty in the Formation of Customary International Law' (2011) *Reprints of the Max Planck Institute for Research on Collective Goods*, http://www.coll.mpg.de/pdf_dat/2011_04online.pdf

Peterson, L.E., 'Persistent Objector Argument also at Issue in NAFTA Case,' 14 July 2009, *Kluwer Arbitration Blog*, http://kluwerarbitrationblog.com/blog/2009/07/14/persistent-objector-argument-also-at-issue-in-nafta-case

Piron, L-H., 'The Right to Development: A Review of the Current State of the Debate for the Department for International Development' (2002), report commissioned by DFID's Social Development Department, http://www.odi.org/sites/odi.org.uk/files/odi-assets/publications-opinion-files/2317.pdf

St. John, D., 'The Bogotá Declaration and the Curious Case of Geostationary Orbit', *Denver Journal of International Law and Policy*, 'The View From Above' Blog, 31 January 2013, http://djilp.org/3494/the-bogota-declaration-and-the-curious-case-of-geostationary-orbit/

Thiratangsathira, U., 'The Precautionary Principle in International Environmental Law (with a Special Focus on the Marine Environment of Thailand)' (2010), unpublished PhD thesis, Queen Mary, University of London, 2010, https://qmro.qmul.ac.uk/jspui/handle/123456789/405

Trachtman, J.P., 'The Obsolescence of Customary International Law' (21 November 2014), *Social Science Research Network*, http://papers.ssrn.com/sol3/papers.cfm?abstract_id=2512757

Waibel, M., '*Mauritius v. UK*: Chagos Marine Protected Area Unlawful', *EJIL:Talk!*, 17 April 2015, http://www.ejiltalk.org/mauritius-v-uk-chagos-marine-protected-area-unlawful/

Wiltshire, W., 'Some Thoughts on UNCLOS and Customary International Law' (2009) *Information Dissemination: The Intersection of Maritime Strategy and Strategic Communications*, http://www.informationdissemination.net/2009/03/some-thoughts-on-unclos-and-customary.html

Zgonec-Rožej, M., and Foakes, J., 'International Criminals: Extradite or Prosecute?' (2013) *Chatham House*, Briefing Paper, IL BP 2013/01

UNITED NATIONS DOCUMENTS

1948 General Assembly, Official Records, Third session, 183rd plenary meeting, 10 December 1948, UN Doc. A/PV.183

1948 Universal Declaration of Human Rights, General Assembly Resolution 217 (III), 10 December 1948, UN Doc. A/RES/3/217 A

1950 *Yearbook of the United Nations*, 1948-1949 (1950), I, II

1962 General Assembly Resolution 1803 (XVII), 14 December 1962, UN Doc. A/5217

1968 United Nations Conference on the Law of Treaties, 26 March–24 May 1968, 80th meeting of the committee of the whole, 21 May 1968, UN Doc. A/CONF.39/C.1/SR.80

1973 General Assembly Resolution 3171 (XXVII), 13 December 1973 UN Doc. A/9030

1974 General Assembly Resolution 3201 (S-VI), 1 May 1974, UN Doc. A/9559

1974 General Assembly Resolution 3281 (XXIX), 12 December 1974, UN Doc. A/9631

1978 General Assembly, Committee on the Peaceful Uses of Outer Space, Legal Sub-Committee, Seventeenth session, summary records, 5 April 1978, UN Doc. A/AC.105/C.2/SR.297

1979 General Assembly, Committee on the Peaceful Uses of Outer Space, Scientific and Technical Sub-Committee, Sixteenth session, summary records, 26 February, 1979, UN Doc. A/AC.105/C.1/SR.219

1979 General Assembly, Committee on the Peaceful Uses of Outer Space, Legal Sub-Committee, Eighteenth session, summary records, 9 April, 1979, UN Doc. A/AC.105/C.2/SR.314

1979 Letter dated 22 August 1979 from the Vice-Chairman of the group of coastal States to the President of the Conference, UN Doc. A/CONF.62/90

1979 Letter dated 24 April 1979 from the Chairman of the Group of 77 to the President of the Conference, UN Doc. A/CONF.62/77

1982 Official Records of the Third United Nations Conference on the Law of the Sea, Volume XVII (Plenary Meetings, Summary Records and Verbatim Records, as well as Documents of the Conference, Resumed Eleventh Session and Final Part Eleventh Session and Conclusion), 1982, UN Doc. A/CONF.62/SR.189

1986 Declaration on the Right to Development, annexed to General Assembly Resolution 41/128, 4 December 1986, UN Doc. A/RES/41/128

1987 Second International Conference on the Protection of the North Sea, London, 24-25 November 1987, Ministerial Declaration, http://www.ospar.org/html_documents/ospar/html/2nsc-1987_london_declaration.pdf

1990 Ministerial Declaration on Sustainable Development in the ECE Region, 1990, Bergen, UN Doc. A/CONF.151/PC/10

1992 Rio Declaration on Environment and Development, 1992, annexed to the Report of the United Nations Conference on Environment and Development, UN Doc. A/CONF.151/26

1992 Report of the United Nations Conference on Environment and Development (Rio conference), 1992, UN Doc. A/CONF.151/26/Rev.1

1993 Human Rights Committee, General Comment 22, Article 18, Forty-eighth session, 30 July 1993, Compilation of General Comments and General Recommendations Adopted by Human Rights Treaty Bodies, UN Doc. HRI/GEN/1/Rev.1

1994 Final Report of the Commission of Experts Established Pursuant to Security Council Resolution 780 (1992), 27 May 1994, UN Doc. S/1994/674

1995 Letter dated 21 June 1995 from the Permanent Representative of Turkey to the United Nations addressed to the Secretary-General, 23 June 1995, UN Doc. A/50/256 – S/1995/505

1995 General Assembly, Official Records, Fiftieth session, 29th plenary meeting, 11 October 1995, UN Doc. A/50/PV.29

1996 General Assembly, Official Records, Fiftieth session, 125th plenary meeting, 10 September 1996, UN Doc. A/50/PV.125

1996 Declaration on World Food Security, 1996, Rome, World Food Summit, 13-17 November 1996

1996 General Assembly Resolution 51/54, 10 December 1996, UN Doc. A/RES/51/45

1996 General Assembly Resolution 50/245, 10 September 1996, UN Doc. A/RES/50/245

1996 'Interpretative Statements for the Record by the Government of the United States of America', reproduced in *Report of the World Food Summit*, Food and Agriculture Organization of the United Nations, 1996, Annex II, http://www.fao.org/docrep/003/w3548e/w3548e00.htm#Annexii

1997 General Assembly Resolution 52/38, 9 December 1997, UN Doc. A/RES/52/38

1997 Report of the Human Rights Committee, vol. I, General Assembly, Official Records, Fifty-first session, Supplement no. 40, 1997, UN Doc. A/51/40

1999 General Assembly Resolution 53/77 [N], 12 January 1999, UN Doc. A/RES/53/77

1999 Security Council, Official Records, Fifty-fourth year, 3988th plenary meeting, 24 March 1999, UN Doc. S/PV.3988

1999 UN Department for Disarmament Affairs, *The United Nations Disarmament Yearbook* (1999) 24

2000 UN High Commissioner for Human Rights, Sub-Commission on the Promotion and Protection of Human Rights Resolution 2000/17, 18 April 2000, http://www.unhchr.ch/huridocda/huridoca.nsf/6d123295325517b2c12569910034dc4c/09597876bb508210c125697300448a18

2001 Draft Articles on the *Responsibility of States for Internationally Wrongful Acts, with commentaries*, adopted by the International Law Commission at its fifty-third session, November 2001, http://legal.un.org/ilc/texts/instruments/english/commentaries/9_6_2001.pdf

2001 'State Responsibility: Comments and observations received from Governments', International Law Commission, Fifty-third session Geneva, 23 April–1 June and 2 July–10 August 2001, 19 March 2001, UN Doc. A/CN.4/515

2001 Report of the International Law Commission, Fifty-third session, 23 April–1 June and 2 July–10 August 2001, UN Doc. A/56/10

2001 Consideration of reports submitted by states parties under article 40 of the covenant, Second Periodic Report, Israel, Human Rights Committee, 4 December 2001, UN Doc. CCPR/C/ISR/2001/2

2002 'International Alliance against Hunger', Declaration of the World Food Summit: *five years later*, 2002, Rome, 10-13 June 2002

2003 Letter dated 2 April 2003 from the Permanent Mission of the United States of America to the United Nations Office at Geneva addressed to the secretariat of the Commission on Human Rights, UN Doc. E/CN.4/2003/G/73

2004 Report of the International Law Commission, Fifty-sixth session, 3 May–4 June and 5 July–6 August 2004, UN Doc. A/59/10

2004 General Assembly Resolution 59/38, 2 December 2004, UN Doc. A/RES/59/38

2004 UN Human Rights Committee, General Comment No. 31 [80], UN Doc. CCPR/C/21/Rev.1/Add.13, 2004

2005 Hampson, F., and Salama, I., 'Working Paper on the Relationship between Human Rights Law and International Humanitarian Law', Commission on Human Rights, Sub-Commission on the Promotion and Protection of Human Rights, Fifty-seventh session, Item 3 of the provisional agenda, Administration of Justice, Rule of Law and Democracy, 21 June 2005, UN Doc. E/CN.4/Sub.2/2005/14

2005 Report of the Sessional Working Group on the Administration of Justice, Commission on Human Rights, Sub-Commission on the Promotion and Protection of Human Rights, Fifty-seventh session, Item 3 of the provisional agenda, Administration of Justice, Rule of Law and Democracy (Antoanella-Iulia Motoc, Chairperson-Rapporteur), 10 August 2005, UN Doc. E/CN.4/Sub.2/2005/11

2005 *The Right to Food*, note by the Secretary-General, transmitting the interim report of the Special Rapporteur of the Commission on Human Rights on the Right to Food in accordance with General Assembly Resolution 59/202, 12 September 2005, UN Doc. A/60/350

2005 *Voluntary Guidelines to Support the Progressive Realization of the Right to Adequate Food in the Context of National Food Security*, adopted by the hundred and twenty-seventh session of the FAO Council, November 2004, Food and Agriculture Organization of the United Nations, Rome, 2005, http://www.fao.org/docrep/009/y7937e/y7937e00.htm

2005 General Assembly Resolution 60/166, 16 December 2005, UN Doc. A/RES/60/166

2006 General Assembly, Official Records, Sixtieth session, 72nd plenary meeting, 15 March 2006, UN Doc. A/60/PV.72

2006 General Assembly Resolution 60/251, 3 April 2006, UN Doc. A/RES/60/251

2006 *Study Group of the International Law Commission*, Report finalised by M. Koskenniemi, 'Fragmentation of International Law: Difficulties Arising from the Diversification and Expansion of International Law' (2006), UN Doc. A/CN.4/L.682

2006 Report of the International Law Commission, Fifty-eighth session, 1 May–9 June and 3 July–11 August 2006, UN Doc. A/61/10

2007 Report of the International Law Commission, Fifty-ninth session, 7 May–5 June and 9 July–10 August 2007, UN Doc. A/62/10

2007 United Nations Declaration on the Rights of Indigenous Peoples, 2007, annexed to General Assembly Resolution 61/296, 13 September 2007, UN Doc. A/RES/61/296

2007 General Assembly, Official Records, Sixty-second session, Sixth committee, Summary record of the 22nd meeting, 1 November 2007, UN Doc. A/C.6/62/SR.22

2007 General Assembly, Official Records, Sixty-second session, Sixth committee, Summary record of the 23rd meeting, 2 November 2007, UN Doc. A/C.6/62/SR.23

2007 General Assembly, Official Records, Sixty-second session, Sixth committee, Summary record of the 24th meeting, 2 November 2007, UN Doc. A/C.6/62/SR.24

2007 'The Obligation to Extradite or Prosecute (*Aut Dedere Aut Judicare*) [Agenda item 6]': comments and observations received from governments, International Law Commission, 2007, UN Doc. A/CN.4/579 and Add. 1–4

2008 General Assembly, Official Records, Sixty-third session, 70th plenary meeting, 18 December 2008, UN Doc. A/63/PV.70

2008 General Assembly Resolution 63/187, 18 December 2008, UN Doc. A/RES/63/187

2008 General Assembly Resolution 63/235, 22 December 2008, UN Doc. A/RES/63/235

2010 General Assembly, Official Records, Sixty-fourth session, 108th plenary meeting, 28 July 2010, UN Doc. A/64/PV.108

2010 General Assembly Resolution 64/292, 28 July 2010, UN Doc. A/RES/64/292

2010 Survey of Multilateral Conventions which may be of Relevance for the Work of the International Law Commission on the Topic 'The Obligation to Extradite or Prosecute (*Aut Dedere Aut Judicare*)', International Law Commission, Study by the Secretariat, 2010, UN Doc. A/CN.4/630

2010 'The Right to Adequate Food', Office of the United Nations High Commissioner for Human Rights, 2010, Fact Sheet No. 34, http://www.ohchr.org/Documents/Publications/FactSheet34en.pdf

2010 Decision 1/CP.16, The Cancun Agreements: Outcome of the work of the *Ad Hoc* Working Group on Long-term Cooperative Action under the Convention, 2010, UN Doc. FCCC/CP/2010/7/Add.1

2010 Decision 1/CMP.6 The Cancun Agreements: Outcome of the work of the *Ad Hoc* Working Group on Further Commitments for Annex I Parties under the Kyoto Protocol at its fifteenth session, 2010, UN Doc. FCCC/KP/CMP/2010/12/Add.1

2011 Security Council Resolution 1970, 26 February 2011, UN Doc. S/RES/1970

2011 'In Swift, Decisive Action, Security Council Imposes Tough Measures on Libyan Regime, Adopting Resolution 1970 in Wake of Crackdown on Protesters', Security Council Meetings Coverage, 6491st meeting, 26 February 2011, UN Doc. SC/10187/Rev.1

2011 Guide to Practice on Reservations to Treaties with commentaries, 2011, International Law Commission, UN Doc A/66/10/Add.1

2012 Consideration of reports submitted by states parties under article 40 of the covenant, Fourth Periodic Report, United States of America, Human Rights Committee, 22 May 2012, UN Doc. CCPR/C/USA/4

2012 Report of the Special Rapporteur on the Rights of Indigenous Peoples: The Situation of Indigenous Peoples in the United States of America, 30 August 2012, UN. Doc. A/HRC/21/47/Add.1

2012 General Assembly, Official Records, Sixty-seventh session, First committee 20th meeting, 5 November 2012, UN Doc. A/C.1/67/PV.20

2012 General Assembly Resolution 67/146, 20 December 2012, UN Doc. A/RES/67/146

2013 General Assembly, Sixty-eighth session, Third committee agenda item 69(b), revised draft resolution: The right to food, 20 November 2013, UN Doc. A/C.3/68/L.60/Rev.1

2013 Formation and Evidence of Customary International Law: Elements of the Previous Work of the International Law Commission that Could be Particularly Relevant to the Topic, 2013, Memorandum by the Secretariat, UN A/CN.4/659

2014 Second Report on Identification of Customary International Law (M. Wood, Special Rapporteur), International Law Commission, Sixty-sixth session, 22 May 2014, UN Doc. A/CN.4/672

2014 Tladi, D.D., '*Jus Cogens*', Annex to Report of the International Law Commission, Sixty-sixth session, 2014, UN Doc. A/69/10

2014 'The Obligation to Extradite or Prosecute (*Aut Dedere Aut Judicare*)', Final Report of the International Law Commission, 2014, adopted by the ILC at its sixty-sixth session, in 2014, and submitted to the General Assembly, http://legal.un.org/ilc/texts/instruments/english/reports/7_6_2014.pdf

2015 Interim Report: Draft Conclusions on the 'Identification of Customary International Law', Statement of the Chairmen of the Drafting Committee, Mr Gilberto Saboia, 7 August 2014, International Law Commission, Sixty-sixth session, Geneva, 5 May–6 June and 7 July–8 August 2014

2015 Third Report on Identification of Customary International Law (M. Wood, Special Rapporteur), International Law Commission, Sixty-seventh session, 27 March 2015, UN Doc. A/CN.4/682

2015 'Identification of Customary International Law', Statement of the Chairman of the Drafting Committee, Mr Mathias Forteau, 29 July 2015, International Law Commission, Sixty-seventh session, Geneva, 4 May–5 June and 6 July–7 August 2015

2015 'Identification of Customary International Law: Text of the Draft Conclusions Provisionally Adopted by the Drafting Committee', International Law Commission, Sixty-seventh session, Geneva, 4 May–5 June and 6 July–7 August 2015, UN Doc. A/CN.4/L.869

2015 Report of the International Law Commission, Sixty-seventh session, 4 May–5 June and 6 July–7 August 2015, UN Doc. A/70/10, advance unedited version, 24 August 2015

OTHER DOCUMENTS, WEB RESOURCES AND MEDIA

1918 United Kingdom: Letter of 25 April 1918 by the Secretary of State for Foreign Affairs, cited by Lord Beresford, HL Deb 16 July 1918, vol. 30, cc898-915

1948 American Declaration of the Rights and Duties of Man, 2 May 1948, OEA/Ser.L./V.II.23, doc. 21, rev. 6

1975 United States: Executive Order 11850 of Apr. 8, 1975, 40 FR 16187, 3 CFR, 1971-1975 Comp., 980, http://www.archives.gov/federal-register/codification/executive-order/11850.html

1976 Declaration of the First Meeting of Equatorial Countries, 3 December 1976 (Bogota Declaration), http://www.jaxa.jp/library/space_law/chapter_2/2-2-1-2_e.html

1977 Japan: Law on the Territorial Sea and the Contiguous Zone (Law No. 30 of 1977, as amended by Law No. 73 of 1996), http://www.un.org/depts/los/LEGISLATIONANDTREATIES/PDFFILES/JPN_1996_Law.pdf

1980 United States: *Air Force Commander's Handbook* (1980)

1981 United Kingdom: *The Law of Armed Conflict*, D/DAT/13/35/66. Army Code 71130 (revised 1981), Ministry of Defence, prepared under the direction of the Chief of General Staff (1981)

1983 United States: 'United States Ocean Policy', Statement of President Reagan, 10 March 1983, http://www.reagan.utexas.edu/archives/speeches/1983/31083c.htm

1987 *Restatement of the Law, Third, Foreign Relations Law of the United States*, American Law Institute, 1987

1987 United Kingdom: Territorial Sea Act 1987 (c. 49)

1988 Greece: Letter from the Permanent Representative of Greece, dated 5 September 1988, registered at the Secretariat General on 6 September 1988–Or Fr

1989 International Labour Organisation Convention concerning Indigenous and Tribal Peoples in Independent Countries, No. 169, 27 June 1989

1993 United States: *Operational Law Handbook* (1993)

1994 Amnesty International, 'United States of America: Open Letter to the President on the Death Penalty,' 1994, https://www.amnesty.org/en/documents/amr51/001/1994/en/

1996 Goozner, M., 'Holdouts Endanger Nuclear Treaty', *Chicago Tribune*, 11 September 1996, http://articles.chicagotribune.com/1996-09-11/news/9609110214_1_test-ban-treaty-five-declared-nuclear-powers-nuclear-weapons

1997 Declaration agreed at the Conference for a Global Ban on Anti-Personnel Mines, Brussels, 24-27 June 1997, transmitted to the Conference on Disarmament by a letter dated 9 July 1997 by the Office of the Permanent Representative of Belgium to the Conference on Disarmament, CD/1467

1997 'Turkey: Citing Security Concerns, Ankara Opposes the Ban', *Turkish Daily News*, 4 December 1997

1998 'Official Explains Why Turkey Won't Sign Landmines Agreement', *Anatolia News Agency*, 16 October 1998

1999 Landmine and Cluster Munitions Monitor, International Campaign to Ban Landmines, 'Turkey', http://www.the-monitor.org/index.php/publications/display?url=lm/1999/turkey.html

1999 Joint Statement of the Minister of Foreign Affairs of the Republic of Turkey, H.E. Ismail Cem and the Minister of Foreign Affairs of the Republic of Bulgaria, H.E. Ms Nadezhda Mihhailova, on the 'Agreement between the Republic of Turkey and the Republic of Bulgaria on Non-Use of Anti-Personnel Mines and their Removal from or Destruction in the Areas Adjacent to their Common Borders', Sofia, 22 March 1999

1999 International Law Commission: The Obligation to Extradite or Prosecute (*Aut Dedere Aut Judicare*), Amnesty International Report (London, Amnesty International Publications, 2009)

2000 *Committee on Formation of Customary (General) International Law*, Final Report of the Committee, 'Statement of Principles Applicable to the Formation of General Customary International Law', International Law Association, London Conference (2000), http://www.ila-hq.org/en/committees/index.cfm/cid/30

2000 'Egypt, Others Urged to Sign Mine Ban Treaty' (2000) International Campaign to Ban Landmines, Africa Policy Information Center, https://www.essex.ac.uk/armedcon/story_id/Egypt%20and%20others%20urged%20to%20sign%20Mine%20Ban%20treaty.pdf

2002 'Precaution in International Sustainable Development Law', CISDL Legal Brief for the World Summit on Sustainable Development, Johannesburg, South Africa, 2002, http://cisdl.org/public/docs/news/brief_precaution2.pdf

2002 Tzilivakis, K., 'Greece Ratifies Ottawa Treaty', *Athens News*, 30 March 2002

2002 United States: 'U.S. Mission to the UN Agencies for Food and Agriculture, Rome, Reservation', 2002, http://www.fao.org/docrep/MEETING/005/Y7106e/y7106e03.htm#P192_62571

2002 Precaution in International Sustainable Development Law', CISDL Legal Brief for the World Summit on Sustainable Development, Johannesburg, South Africa, 2002, http://cisdl.org/public/docs/news/brief_precaution2.pdf

2004 *"Indirect Expropriation" and the "Right to Regulate" in International Investment Law*, Organisation for Economic Co-operation and Development Working Papers on International Investment (OECD Publishing, 2004), http://dx.doi.org/10.1787/780155872321

2005 United States: 'Explanation of Vote on Right to Development, 61st Commission on Human Rights', statement delivered by Joel Danies, U.S. Delegation to the 61st Commission on Human Rights, 12 April 2005, http://2001-2009.state.gov/p/io/44595.htm

2005 Mauritania: Ordonnance n°2005-015 portant protection pénale de l'enfant, 2005, Présidence du Conseil Militaire pour la Justice et la Démocratie, Republique Islamique de Mauritanie, http://legislationmauritanienne.files.wordpress.com/2011/06/ordonnance-nc2b02005-015-portant-protection-pc3a9nale-de-l_enfant.pdf

2006 United Kingdom: 'UK Position on Human Right to Water' (2006), https://www.gov.uk/government/uploads/system/uploads/attachment_data/file/36540/uk-position-human-right-water.pdf

2007 United States: Bellinger III, J.B., and Haynes II, W.J., 'A US Government Response to the International Committee of the Red Cross Study on Customary International

Humanitarian Law', reproduced in 'Reports and Documents' (2007) 89 *International Review of the Red Cross* 433

2007 United States: 'Views of the United States of America on Human Rights and Access to Water Submitted to the Office of the United Nations High Commissioner for Human Rights', June 2007, http://www2.ohchr.org/english/issues/water/contributions/UnitedStatesofAmerica.pdf

2007 'Indigenous Rights Outlined by UN' (2007) *BBC News*, http://news.bbc.co.uk/1/hi/in_depth/6993776.stm

2008 European Union Council Decision 2008/901/CFSP of 2 December 2008 concerning an independent international fact-finding mission on the conflict in Georgia, Official Journal of the European Union 323/66

2008 Turkey: 'The Outstanding Aegean Issues', policy document of the Republic of Turkey Ministry of Foreign Affairs (2008), http://www.mfa.gov.tr/maritime-issues---aegean-sea---the-outstanding-aegean-issues.en.mfa

2009 United States: 'Explanation of Position by Craig Kuehl, United States Advisor, on Resolution L.30, Rev. 1—The Right to Food, in the Third Committee of the Sixty-fourth Session of the United Nations General Assembly', 19 November 2009, http://usun.state.gov/briefing/statements/2009/132187.htm

2009 'Experts Hail Australia's Backing of UN Declaration of Indigenous Peoples' Rights' (2009) *United Nations News Centre*, http://www.un.org/apps/news/story.asp?NewsID=30382

2009 Report of the Independent International Fact-Finding Mission on the Conflict in Georgia (IIFFMCG), 30 September 2009, in three volumes

2010 *Committee on the Rights of Indigenous Peoples*, Interim Report of the Committee, International Law Association, The Hague Conference (2010), http://www.ila-hq.org/en/committees/index.cfm/cid/1024

2010 New Zealand: 'Statement by Hon Dr Pita Sharples, Minister of Maori Affairs', New Zealand Ministry of Foreign Affairs and Trade, Ministry Statements and Speeches 2010, Ninth session of the United Nations Permanent Forum on Indigenous Issues, 19 April 2010, http://www.mfat.govt.nz/Media-and-publications/Media/MFAT-speeches/2010/0-19-April-2010.php

2010 United Kingdom: 'United Kingdom of Northern Ireland and Great Britain National Explanation of Vote on UN Human Rights Resolution 64/292 of 28 July 2010', Foreign and Commonwealth Office, https://www.gov.uk/government/uploads/system/uploads/attachment_data/file/35452/explanation-vote-un-july-2010.pdf

2010 'Legislative Reform to Support the Abandonment of Female Genital Mutilation/Cutting', (2010) UNICEF Report, http://www.unicef.org/policyanalysis/files/UNICEF_-_LRI_Legislative_Reform_to_support_the_Abandonment_of_FGMC_August_2010.pdf

2010 United Kingdom: 'United Kingdom of Northern Ireland and Great Britain National Explanation of Position on Human Rights Council Resolution 15/14 of 30 September 2010', Foreign and Commonwealth Office, https://www.gov.uk/government/uploads/system/uploads/attachment_data/file/35453/explanation-of-position-hrr15.pdf

2010 'Planning for a Sustainable Future: A Federal Sustainable Development Strategy for Canada', Government of Canada, Sustainable Development Office, 'Environment Canada', October 2010, https://www.ec.gc.ca/dd-sd/default.asp?lang=En&n=06E31414-1

2010 Canada: Statement of Support on the United Nations Declaration on the Rights of Ingenious Peoples' Government of Canada, 12 November 2010, https://www.aadnc-aandc.gc.ca/eng/1309374239861/1309374546142

2010 United States: 'Announcement of U.S. Support for the United Nations Declaration on the Rights of Indigenous Peoples: Initiatives to Promote the Government-to-Government Relationship & Improve the Lives of Indigenous Peoples', United States State Department, 15 December 2010, http://www.state.gov/documents/organization/184099.pdf

2010 New Zealand: New Zealand Ministry of Foreign Affairs and Trade, Human Rights: Indigenous Peoples, Declaration on the Rights of Indigenous Peoples, chronology of events since June 2006, http://www.mfat.govt.nz/Foreign-Relations/1-Global-Issues/Human-Rights/Indigenous-Peoples/draftdec-jun07.php

2011 'Universal Periodic Review of Venezuela', Human Right's Watch's Submission to the Human Rights Council, 21 March 2011, http://www.hrw.org/news/2011/03/21/universal-periodic-review-venezuela

2012 United States: 'US Explanation of Vote: Right to Development', 28 September 2012, Geneva, https://geneva.usmission.gov/2012/09/28/u-s-explanation-of-vote-right-to-development-resolution/

2012 Guillaume, G., 'Avis d'*amicus curiae* (article R. 625-3 du Code de justice administrative)' (2012) 28 *Revue française de droit administratif* 19

2012 *Committee on the Rights of Indigenous Peoples*, Final Report of the Committee, International Law Association, Sofia Conference (2012), http://www.ila-hq.org/en/committees/index.cfm/cid/1024

2013 'Lockheed to Use Soviet Submarine Hunt Data in Sea Mine Plan', *Bloomberg-Businessweek*, 14 March 2013, http://www.bloomberg.com/news/articles/2013-03-14/lockheed-to-use-soviet-submarine-hunt-data-in-seabed-mining-plan

2013 'Extension Report: Turkey', Permanent Mission of Turkey to the United Nations, Geneva', 29 March 2013, 2013/62441669/73841, http://www.apminebanconvention.org/fileadmin/APMBC/clearing-mined-areas/art5_extensions/countries/Turkey-ExtRequest-Received-29Mar2013.pdf

2013 Shukman, D., 'Deep Sea Mining "Gold Rush" Moves Closer', *BBC News*, 18 May 2013, http://www.bbc.co.uk/news/science-environment-22546875

2013 'One Million Landmines "Still Buried in Turkey" ', *Global Post*, 29 November 2013, http://www.globalpost.com/dispatch/news/afp/131129/one-million-landmines-still-buried-turkey

2014 Ottawa Convention, Third Review Conference of states parties in Maputo in June 2014, http://www.maputoreviewconference.org/

2014 United States: 'Explanation of Position: The Human Right to Safe Drinking Water and Sanitation Resolution, Statement of the Delegation of the United States of America', as delivered by Ambassador Keith Harper, US Representative to the UN Human Rights Council, Geneva, 27 September 2014, https://geneva.usmission.gov/2014/09/25/explanation-of-position-the-human-right-to-safe-drinking-water-and-sanitation/

2015 United States: *Department of Defense Law of War Manual*, 12 June 2015, http://www.dod.mil/dodgc/images/law_war_manual15.pdf

2015 Comments on the ILC Project on Identification of Customary International Law, Asian-African Legal Consultative Organisation (AALCO), annexed to Report by S. Jusoh, Chairman of the AALCO's Informal Expert Group on Customary International Law, 24 March 2015, http://www.aalco.int/54thsession/AALCOIEG%20Chairman's%20Statement%20and%20Special%20Rapporteur's%20Report%2020150324.pdf

International Campaign to Ban Landmines, http://www.icbl.org/index.php/icbl/Universal/MBT/Making-the-MBT-Universal

ICRC, 'Rule 76: Herbicides', http://www.icrc.org/customary-ihl/eng/docs/v1_rul_rule76
ICRC, 'United States of America: Practice Relating to Rule 76: Herbicides', http://www.icrc.org/customary-ihl/eng/docs/v2_cou_us_rule76
International Seabed Authority, Observers, https://www.isa.org.jm/observers
'Norway-IWC Dispute on Whaling (NWHALE)', Case No. 53, *Trade and Environment database*, http://www1.american.edu/ted/NWHALE.htm
Outer Space Treaty, information on status, http://www.fas.org/nuke/control/ost/text/space5.htm
UN Treaty Collection: Status of the Vienna Convention on the Law of Treaties, 1969, https://treaties.un.org/pages/ViewDetailsIII.aspx?src=TREATY&mtdsg_no=XXIII-1&chapter=23&Temp=mtdsg3&lang=en

Index

The manufacturer's authorised representative in the EU for product safety is Oxford University Press España S.A. of el Parque Empresarial San Fernando de Henares, Avenida de Castilla, 2 – 28830 Madrid (www.oup.es/en or product.safety@oup.com). OUP España S.A. also acts as importer into Spain of products made by the manufacturer.

www.ingramcontent.com/pod-product-compliance
Lightning Source LLC
LaVergne TN
LVHW020057220926
848484LV00002BB/604
* 9 7 8 0 1 9 8 7 0 4 2 1 8 *